Screened Out

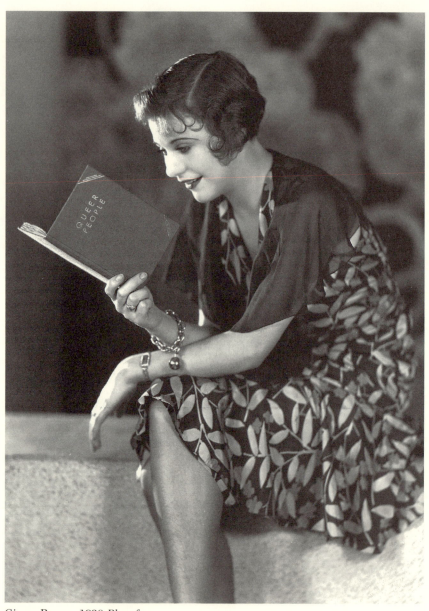

Ginger Rogers, 1930 *Photofest*

Screened Out

PLAYING GAY
IN HOLLYWOOD
FROM EDISON
TO STONEWALL

．．．

RICHARD BARRIOS

Routledge
Taylor & Francis Group

NEW YORK AND LONDON

Published in 2003 by
Routledge
29 West 35th Street
New York, NY 10001
www.routledge-ny.com

Published in Great Britain by
Routledge
11 New Fetter Lane
London EC4P 4EE
www.routledge.co.uk

Routledge is an imprint of the Taylor & Francis Group
Printed in the United States of America on acid free paper.

10 9 8 7 6 5 4 3 2 1

Library of Congress Cataloging-in-Publication Data

Barrios, Richard.
    Screened out : playing gay in Hollywood from Edison to Stonewall /
Richard John Barrios.
        p.   cm.
Includes bibliographical references and index.
    ISBN 0–415–92328–X (hb : alk. paper)
    1. Homosexuality in motion pictures.   I. Title.
    PN1995.9.H55 B37 2002
    791.43'653—dc21

                                                    2002004760

For

MILDRED MATHERNE

"Tante"

CONTENTS

Acknowledgments   ix

INTRODUCTION
Something about a Well   1

ONE
Silent Existences   15

TWO
Speaking Plainly   37

THREE
Codes of Behavior   55

FOUR
The Naked Moon   81

FIVE
Pansies and Lesbos of 1933   95

SIX
Legions and Decency   123

SEVEN
Turnabout: Life in a Coded World   145

EIGHT
Reluctant Flamboyance: Forties Escapism   167

NINE
Dark Passages: Forties Drama   183

TEN
Tempests and Teapots   213

ELEVEN
Something Evil   247

TWELVE
That Touch of Mink: Sex and the Sixties   275

THIRTEEN
The Wild Side   293

FOURTEEN
'I'm No Queer,' He Lied   317

FIFTEEN
Open Season   339

An Epilogue   363
Notes on Sources   367
Selected Bibliography   377
Index   381

ACKNOWLEDGMENTS

．．

It is perhaps fitting that this book, which examines a rather strange course of history, had its own peculiar evolution. Delays and digressions of all manner came with unsettling frequency, and the elements of writer's block became, ultimately, all too apparent and familiar. Perhaps, at some point, the odd odyssey of *Screened Out* may in fact warrant its own book, no doubt in a genre poised somewhere between slapstick comedy and existential horror. In any case it was, somehow, eventually completed, albeit far behind schedule. When I was finally able to take a breather and look back, I was stunned by the number of people who had helped me and supported the creation of this work. I can only extend my heartfelt thanks to all of them.

First off, I would like to give both gratitude and homage to all the women and men who gave me something to write about, those whose work made mine possible. The directors, writers, actors, technicians, and various others were often brave, frequently audacious, sometimes remarkably talented, and always, *always* interesting. Even the purported villains of this piece—the bluenoses and obstructionists and bigots—deserve thanks, for without them there would have been no struggle, no conflict, no sense of ultimate endurance. So to the Pangborns and Mineos, the Mackaills and Emersons, the Cukors and Premingers, and, yes, to all those cranky Breens: you made the history—I only wrote about it.

I must pay special tribute to those custodians of the history I've written about. To the film companies who have taken sufficient care of often forgotten old films, to the archives that preserve them, and to the various companies that have made them available on television and on home video, my gratitude, plus the hope that you are compensated so abundantly that you can make more of these films accessible. My warmest thanks as well to Turner Entertainment, especially to Richard May, who has done so much to let us see our past as reflected in our movies. Bravo Turner Classic Movies! I am grateful as well to the George Eastman House and the Museum of Modern Art for their ongoing efforts in preserving and exhibiting forgotten film. And special applause to the UCLA Film and Television Archive and its valiant, masterful preservation officer Robert Gitt: they have fought long and hard to bring film back from abysses of obscurity and disintegration, and without them we would be staring, all too often, at blank screens.

To anyone reading this book it will be clear that my work was made possible by the preservation of some fascinating documents from the movie past— scripts, studio correspondence, and especially that comedy-horror show, the Hays Office, more formally the Production Code Administration or Motion Picture Association of America. Two archives in particular were indispensable in this regard. The Cinema-Television Library at the University of Southern California is a combination of warehouse and treasure trove for the film historian. Among its collections are huge groups of scripts and correspondence related to films produced by MGM, Fox and 20th Century–Fox, Universal, and Warner Bros. For me, as for countless other writers and historians, Ned Comstock has been a tireless guide to many of the wonders of that collection. My thanks also to Noelle Carter and the rest of the staff. The Margaret Herrick Library of the Academy of Motion Picture Arts and Sciences contains an equally vast array of material. So vast, in fact, that it would probably take a book just to begin to detail its amazing holdings. For this book the prime source at the Herrick Library was the lovingly preserved papers of the Production Code Administration/Motion Picture Association of American, more familiarly the Hays Office. For anyone interested in the history of morality in the mid-twentieth century, the PCA files might be a good place to start. That ace research archivist Barbara Hall worked tirelessly to help me on my journey through the mazes of Breen and Hays-related correspondence. She also gave some inspired suggestions and was instrumental in helping me to find some crucial script pieces for the 1959 *Ben-Hur*. Thanks to the rest of the Herrick's able staff as well, particularly Jennifer Peterson, and to researcher Irene Liberatore for her first-rate assistance.

The Bobst Library at New York University has a remarkable microfilm collection as well as other exceptional holdings. I would also like to thank the New York Public Library at Lincoln Center, although most of its Performing Arts collection was unavailable during the time this book was being researched and written; all to a good cause, however, for the newly renovated library is now an even better resource. Thanks also to the Museum of Modern Art Film Library, the Library of Congress, the UCLA Library, the George Eastman House, the Society for Cinephiles, and the American Museum of the Moving Image (Astoria, Queens). Another invaluable resource that needs to be mentioned is the Internet Movie Database (www.imdb.com), a marvelously cross-referenced collection of screen credits and much else.

It was a conscious choice, in writing this history, to rely far more on histor-ical documents than on the memories and reminiscences of participants. Some of those have been recorded elsewhere (and have been employed here); in many cases, the "secretive" nature of the subject, and the long-ago time involved, meant that there were few resources left, few living memories left to plumb. Therefore, I decided that I would let the prime sources be the films themselves and the recorded vestiges of their creation and reception that remain to us. I did, however, interview a large number of men and women for their impressions and memories surrounding encounters, especially long-ago ones, with gays and lesbians on film. To all of them, a heartfelt thank-you.

The photo collection at Photofest is one of the world's finest, at least as regards images related to the performing arts. Most of the images in this book— the wonderful and the weird, the jaw-dropping and the annoying—are part of that collection. My thanks, as always, to Howard and Ron Mandelbaum and the wonderful Photofest staff. Thanks also to John Cocchi, for his bountiful gifts and vast knowledge of film, as well as for a number of other photographs.

At this point I must recognize a number of artists whose work has been particularly inspiring to me. Some of them are personal acquaintances, others I have known only through their work and reputation. All of them, however, have produced writing (often but not always about film) that so moved and delighted me that I found myself feeling that I must try to do the same. With his book *The Celluloid Closet*, the late Vito Russo is the preeminent pioneer in the exam-ination of homosexuality on film. I have paid tribute to his work in the body of this book, and I do so again here. Other literary voices that have been a major influence are David Chierichetti, the late Stephen Harvey, Clive Hirschhorn, the late Pauline Kael, Ethan Mordden, Miles Kreuger, and Ned Rorem, whose writing is as elegantly well wrought as his music (a major statement, that!). The creators of *Mystery Science Theater 3000* have shown me repeatedly how far barbed wit can penetrate to the essence of a film's quality (or lack of it). *MST3K* has also been one of my prime morale-raisers, something I could consistently rely on to cheer me in dark times. A special acknowledgment must go to the late William K. Everson. Not only was Bill the greatest of film historians, he was a writer of wit, grace, and remarkable clarity. He was also my dear friend and mentor. Knowing him was a privilege, and attempting in a small way to carry on his work is an honor.

With patience and generosity, a large number of people gave me help and advice. Dr. David Lugowski, colleague as well as dear friend, has done his own work in this same area, work of remarkable depth and scope. Thank you, David, for all your guidance and counsel, and thank you for (among innumerable other things) sharing with me the joys of deconstructing Joan Crawford. My thanks also to the encyclopedic and chivalrous Romano Tozzi, and to Henry Fera, whose copious talents include a limitless knowledge of tough cinematic women. Tom Toth is a wizard of an archivist, and many of his discoveries were crucial to my work here. I also joyfully acknowledge the contributions of Ed Maguire and Mary Atwood, Marc Miller, Anthony Slide, Robert Gitt (once again), Christopher Connelly, Gregory Maldonado, Michael Portantiere, Eric Spilker, John Coyle, Kevin Lewis, Peter Feliz, and David Mulkins. Edward Willinger has been a close friend, a trusted ally, and an unlimited source of encouragement, as has Alan Boyd. Professionally, Karen Latham Everson was instrumental (along with Sandra Sabathy Everson) in getting this book to the right publisher. Personally, my joy in and gratitude for her friendship is tempered only with the regret that she no longer lives in New York City. (Come back, Karen!) Two professionals who have helped me vastly are also treasured friends. Because of Ann Lang, hand therapist par excellence, I was able to regain the use of my right hand following a serious injury. Jacob Gershoni, who has given me counsel and support without cease, was instrumental in helping guide me past the gnarls of writer's block caused in part by that same injury.

I am immensely grateful to all those who responded favorably to my first book, *A Song in the Dark*. Without those wonderful and encouraging comments, and (all modesty aside) those reviews and the award from the Theatre Library Association, I seriously doubt that I would have embarked on a second project as blissfully esoteric as the first. To answer a question I've gotten over and over: no, this book is not a sequel to that first one. Obviously. But who knows what sequels the future might bring?

By definition, help comes from many different sources, and in ways too numerous to count. At some points, of course, it consists primarily of the presence of those who nurture and support us. It also consists, alas, of the absence of such people; in the course of this book's creation my world was dimmed by the loss of a number of those I respected and loved. In one way or another they all gave me care and sustenance, and the inspiration they gave me remains. There is, again, William K. Everson. There is also Jonathan Katz, the dear friend who encouraged me (and then some) to write about film. He was instrumental in the conception of this book when he called me one day to let me know about a film he'd just seen called *Our Betters*, featuring an *unbelievable* queen. Two remarkable women, Etta Shepherd and Sylvia Goldstein, encouraged me in unique ways, and in my own family my equally remarkable aunt, Mildred Matherne, was always there for me. And she still is. A salute, also, to my uncle, Larry Thibodeaux, Sr., and to my father, Manny Barrios. Daddy, the world is a different place since you've left it, and it was an especially poignant honor to be with you at the end of such a long, worthy life.

My agent, Robert Cornfield, has been warm, helpful and supportive; people like him go far to eliminate the memories of a writer's less happy encounters in the literary business. Speaking of which, my editor, William Germano, has given me advice and encouragement such as I have seldom known. His patience, his willingness to extend deadlines (many times), and his enthusiasm for this project have meant more to me than any number of words can convey. I would also like to thank the fine team at Routledge, especially Gilad Foss, Patty Garcia, Lisa Vecchione, and Donald J. Davidson, whose copy editing has been an absolute marvel.

Thomas Pickering, who has a working intelligence comparable to a large computer, worked tirelessly with me on getting this book into shape. Again and again, he helped me bear in mind the larger historical context into which these films must be placed. Over and over, he offered priceless advice and suggestions concerning history, philosophy, psychology, syntax, camp, and just about everything else. Tom, this book exists largely because of you.

When it comes time to define the words "strength" and "grace," I need look no further than to my mother, Tootsie. (Go ahead, call her that—everyone does!) We're talking major role models here, although I can't imagine anyone else equaling her triumphs over adversity. All I can do is add, in loving amazement, "What a woman!" I am also blessed, in my immediate family, with two (count 'em) ministers: my sister, the Rev. Peggy Foreman, and my brother-in-law, the Rev. Andy Foreman. Along with my terrific nephew, Jared Foreman, they have shown me, ceaselessly, exactly how a supportive and truly loving family functions. Among many other family members, all of whom deserve recognition (and nearly all of whom live in South Louisiana), I must mention in particular Anita Barrios, Mack Barrios, Keith Matherne, Spencer Gauthreaux, Miriam Sampey, and Dr. Tommy Ferguson. There is also, of course, my New York family. In addition to those already mentioned earlier, I would like to give loving thanks to my spiritual mentor, the wonderful Patricia Rothrock, and to the help, friendship, and prayers of the Revs. Amy Gregory, Dorcas Demasio, and K Karpen. Also, dear friends John and Roseann Forde, Diane Allen and Francesca Rhys, Rev. Bud Carroll and Millie Carroll, Bill Phillips, Sue Klein, Connie Coddington, Norma Justice, Ida Mottley, and, en masse, the congregation of the Church of St. Paul and St. Andrew. Darren Guin isn't a New Yorker, but this is a good place to thank him for his friendship. Karen Hartman *is* a New Yorker and, far more than that, she is one of the never-ending joys of my life.

At the first and at the last, my thanks must go to Jerry Bryant. For two decades he has been a close friend, movie buddy, confidant, and advisor, and without him I would not have considered a career as a film historian or writer. His contributions to this book are without number: there's no way I could count the phone calls from Houston that began with "I found another one!" after which he'd go on to tell me about *Voodoo Island, Johnny One-Eye,* and so many others. His friendship is an anchor in my life, his presence one of the beacons of my personal and professional existence. He is, in short, a blessing to me. There have been innumerable blessings attending this book, in fact, and they have enabled me to start it and stay the whole rocky course until it was done. I can only hope that in some way the final effort is worthy of the care and support given to me by so many in such abundance.

New York City
June 2002

Something about a Well

very now and again history is generous enough to give its narratives convenient entrance points. This present journey, then, begins with an obscure film from 1931. Its title, *The Secret Witness*, has nothing to do with the surreptitious lives of gays and lesbians for most of the twentieth century. It is not about a search for an identity or a sexuality, nor is it about the peculiar phenomenon of being visible while at the same time unseen. It is a murder mystery, and not a very good one, set in a hotel. Its featured players are Una Merkel and William Collier, Jr., and it was released by Columbia Pictures when that studio was still a lower-grade production company. No one remembers it, and justifiably so; even in 1931 the only thing anyone would have recalled about it was the plot's one gimmick, as clued by the title—the murder witness was a dog. What, then, does this expendable piece have to do with history? Go straight back, more than seven decades, to one of its early scenes: ZaSu Pitts, who specialized in fluttery-helpless shtick, plays the hotel's switchboard operator. While connecting calls for the hotel guests, she vacantly chats on the phone with her boyfriend. She is, she mentions, currently reading a book. "It's something about a well . . . I don't really understand it." As she says the word *well,* there is a cut to an insert shot of the book's cover: *The Well of Loneliness*, by Radclyffe Hall.

It is an incidental gag in an ordinary movie, but suddenly this negligible shard of popular culture becomes important by referencing a groundbreaking novel about lesbianism. For just a few seconds some forgotten history is retrieved. *The Well of Loneliness*, we can see, wasn't just known to a few dozen women who lived in Greenwich Village. It was famous enough, and scandalous and topical enough, to rate a funny gag in a production not geared to elite audiences. This was not an inside joke; Columbia movies weren't sophisticated enough to have those. A farm family outside Topeka going to see *The Secret Witness* may not have understood it, but quite obviously many thousands of other spectators did. They would have known of the book and its sensational reputation, and they would have laughed at the look of comic consternation on ZaSu's face as she talked about it.

What's being implied here? Received knowledge tells us that gays and lesbians were as hidden away onscreen as they seemed to be in real life and that the handful of films before the 1960s that portrayed them did so in coded and condemnatory ways. This vignette from *The Secret Witness* doesn't seem to fit this scheme, and it's not a unique case. Dozens, perhaps hundreds, of Hollywood films made around the same time contain gay and lesbian characters, allusions, and situations. This was mainstream pop culture, open and available to millions, and homosexuality was an accepted part of it. Nearly four decades before Stonewall, filmmakers were portraying it. Audiences saw and understood it. So much for the authenticity and objectivity of received knowledge.

Secret Witnesses

Film and its audience—which has the greater influence on the other? Of course, it's an unanswerable question, one that keeps returning as we ponder the history of gays and lesbians as portrayed on film. Has the audience determined film's course throughout the cataclysm of the past century, or have the movies led us? The concept of mass culture existed before the birth of film, but the pervasiveness of popular culture, the phenomenal extent of its effect on the population, was inconceivable until the those first crowds started going to the nickelodeons and discovering odd glimpses of unknown worlds and refracted versions of their own lives. Far more than print media, the movies were the first modern style setters: what to wear, what to eat, how to sit and stand, what kind of furnishings to buy, how to fix one's face and hair . . . how to behave, how to speak, how to relate to others, how to love and hate, how to know *oneself*. Film, in exchange, cannot invent what doesn't already exist. It reflects, reproduces, copies, caricatures. It learns from its audiences and imparts to them, sharing with its viewers a peculiar and intense collusion. We end up experiencing much of our lives and our relationships in terms of what we've seen on the screen. Who hasn't thrown (or hasn't wanted to throw) a fit in the manner of Bette or Brando, show vulnerability like Garland or Monroe, be witty like Mae or Woody, or tough like Bogie or Sigourney. We've lived much of our lives in terms of these people and how they act and what we can crib from them. They, in turn, have learned and taken much from us. The movies are us; we are the movies.

Given such a complicated relationship, is it just a coincidence that the wild ride we've shared with the movies has been paralleled by the various sexual revolutions of our time? Just think of the power of eroticism up there on the screen, so much more blatant than life. Who could not feel such a powerful tug? From Theda Bara onward the manifestation of sex on film has had an incalculable bearing upon sexuality as it translates into all our lives. The movies' influence on fashion, custom, even things as fundamental as language, have been profound, deservedly observed and analyzed over and over, but it's that troublesome thing sex which, as always, takes the forefront of the debate and the literature. Naturally, it's as strange and singular in its correlation to movies as it is to anything and everyone else. Just how reciprocal the relationship is between film and sex is the subject of a debate that will continue to the end of time. The bluntness of sexuality in its most obvious cinematic forms usually gains most of the attention, yet it is cinema's more allusive approaches to sex that carry some of its most potent weight. Here is where comes into play film's uncanny ability to spur identification and senses of self while simultaneously reflecting them. It is here, projected from the movies to deep inside us, where some of us have found ourselves.

The modern concept of homosexuality, essentially the way in which gay men and lesbians are comprehended, is generally felt to date to the mid-late nineteenth century. That makes homosexuality, as we now more or less know it, approximately the same age as the movies. Lord knows that the concepts of gayness are continually and still and ever being changed and reevaluated, and the history of the struggle for identification has finally, in the last decade or so, started to receive its deserved attention. But lesbians and gay men and the movies: *there* we have something unique, something with little or no comparison in any other aspects of our culture. For film has depicted homosexuality for a century in all manner of ways—implicit or blunt, tender or damning, with the greatest insight or with the crudest denigration. There has never been one clear course; for eight decades the images and portrayals have been consistently present and—regardless of what some historians or politicians or theologians say—they've run the almighty gamut. The love that dared not speak its name didn't, as far as the movies were concerned, need to—it was up on the screen, larger and sometimes clearer than life. It was there conveying messages to any spectator able to understand or identify with what was being said. It was, for a large part of that time, sneaked past censors and moral watchdogs, straight into the consciousness of its audiences. Since film is (theoretically) permanent, it presents us with historical documents of how gays were looked upon, by others and by themselves, all those decades ago. And these images were present in American film, as in American life, long before that damnable received (that is, mainstream heterosexual) wisdom tells us that it became accustomed, if not accepted. It was even up there for quite a while before ZaSu opened her copy of *The Well of Loneliness.*

That "conventional wisdom" notion elides peculiarly with gays on film. In some ways it's as if the entire history and recollection of gays on film, particularly as manifested in the late 1920s and early 1930s, have been shoved into the closet. Just as acceptance of homosexuality per se seems to occur in waves, so has even the willingness to recall its presence on film (never mind in society) come and gone. Especially when the films were unseen, it was most convenient for many to believe that the portrayals had never existed. Even many gays who saw them at the time forgot that they ever had. They had to wait decades for the reclamation to begin.[1]

Out of *The Closet*

In 1981, when Vito Russo's *Celluloid Closet* was published, there had been precious little thought, let alone examination, of film's portrayals of homosexuality. In fact, the overall literature, nonfiction variety, on same-sex love was still dismally sparse. One decade after the Stonewall riots, any thought that studies of gay culture might be viable or necessary was still a loopy concept. Russo's exposure of fairies in Hollywood's onscreen garden came, then, as a bracing surprise—things that had been known and pointedly ignored were suddenly being talked about, and with as much ferocity as intelligence. The timing of Russo's book was, in fact, more dramatic than anyone could have planned. On the one hand, it made eminent sense, coming at a time when the gay and straight communities alike were beginning to understand a tiny bit more about the gay past as well as the gay present. Yet the book also came at the dawn of the Reagan administration—not the most shining hour for the gay rights movement—and at the very beginning of the appalling health crisis that completely transformed the notion of gay life in America. Russo's angry tone reflected the tenor of the Gay Liberation era, and it was prophetic as well. The intolerance he decried, especially when applied to what was manifested in films of the 1960s and '70s, was only the prelude to some of the horrors of the mid-'80s. The violent feelings shown onscreen in tawdry films translated into widespread prejudice against AIDS victims, indeed against all gays and lesbians. Russo essentially did for film what ACT UP did for AIDS awareness, and in much the same fashion. He opened up a world and a culture that had almost never been discussed before under any circumstances, exposing prejudices and hurts that previously were allowed to pass unnoticed. For this writer, for thousands of others interested in film or gay culture or in the social and sexual

---

[1] This kind of forgetting was made vividly clear and rather poignant during interviews conducted for this book. One older person, for example, intimately connected with show business, insisted that there had been no such thing in early thirties cinema, and was quite skeptical when informed just how many there had been.

history of the century, Russo performed an immense service. He illuminated trends and films and whole schools of thought; he also—as he came to realize when he worked on the revised edition of *The Celluloid Closet* six years later—opened the doors for other types of approach to this rich and provocative mine.

The Celluloid Closet is invaluable—and now here is the "however." As worthy and vital as *The Celluloid Closet* was and is as polemic—eye-opening, chilling, and funny filled with righteous and justifiable annoyance, even rage—it isn't the whole story. Russo never intended it to be. He had opinions and points, and he wrote about the films that best illustrated them, and which were available to him. His view of gays on films is perhaps best summed up when he discusses that watershed of gay movies, *The Boys in the Band*, and illuminates a quote from its director, William Friedkind: "This film is not about homosexuality, it's about human problems. I hope there are happy homosexuals. They just don't happen to be in my film." Russo comments, "Nor have they been in any other major American release before or since."

Russo's view seems acutely, painfully pertinent to the late 1970s. It seems less so today, given the enormous upwelling of gay characters and themes in mainstream and independent films and television. Russo, who died in 1990, would doubtless be pleased at most of these developments; his work helped foster them. However, he ignored a sizable chunk of the history that preceded *The Boys in the Band*. Even his book's wonderful title is more representative of the time of its writing than of film history as a whole. The concept of closets cannot always be applied fairly to films or actors or audiences in earlier years. In that pre-Stonewall age, pre-Mattachine even, the dynamics were completely different. In hindsight, perhaps "hotel" might seem a more accurate metaphor: some guests checking in under assumed names or in disguise, others sneaking in undetected, an ostentatious few sweeping in and moving directly into the penthouse. That, in summary, is what can be seen in gayness on film in earlier years.

To judge by *The Celluloid Closet*, there was only an insignificant number of films from the 1920s to the 1950s to depict characters disposed to same-sex relationships. It tells us of *Call Her Savage*, with its trip to a Greenwich Village gay bar, and *The Warrior's Husband*, and a few others. There are discussions of several actors who made their names playing "sissies," and a few pertinent others for those who cared to read between the lines. Not to invoke any tired *Titanic* metaphors here, but, folks, there's a giant iceberg out there. Dozens, even hundreds, of films were not mentioned, and a whole spectrum of homosexuals—including some quite happy ones—didn't make the cut. Some of this may have had to do with the nature of the arguments being made, and accessibility was obviously a great part of the problem as well. Russo was writing before many of these films were being circulated on videotape, and unless there's a key name in the cast list (such as Franklin Pangborn), there would be no reason to sift through or even stumble upon a lot of these movies. Who except the most diehard buffs or Late Show addicts would have known about something like *Manhattan Parade* (1931), for example, which crystallizes the (often truth-based!) myth of the Broadway stage as a haven for the most over-the-top male prima donnas? How could someone know, unless privy to some obscure insider knowledge, that *The Uninvited* (1944) became a cult film for lesbians during World War II? And who on earth would ever think of looking for an explicit (and not particularly judgmental) lesbian portrayal in a crummy horror movie like *Voodoo Island* (1957)? The written history on the gay and lesbian aspects of these films is quite sparse, and some crucial sections of it were simply not obtainable by Russo at the time: studio records and the papers of the Motion Pictures Producers and Distributors of America—the Hays Office—which regulated Hollywood's films for forty years and which frequently had a great deal to say about sexual deviance on the screen. At some points Russo's omissions are startling. Nowhere does he mention George Cukor's *Our Betters*, for example, with its arch Somerset Maugham atmosphere and wildly queer, and in 1933 controversial, dance instructor. For Cecil B. DeMille's Roman holiday *The Sign of the Cross* (1932), Russo confines his reference to a photo of Charles Laughton's Nero accompanied by his undressed slave boy. Well and good—but there's no reference to the central set piece of the movie, the apocalyptic dance of lesbian seduction "The Naked Moon," which contributed immensely to the censorship clampdown of the mid-thirties. Even a well-known later film like *Compulsion* (1959), a fictional version of the sensational Loeb and Leopold case, gets no mention.

Without *The Celluloid Closet* there would be nothing of what has followed, which naturally includes this book. We might be aware of a number of the films it discusses, even some of those it neglects, but we would have lacked Vito Russo's passion and focus. Those qualities, plus his scholarship, were what made that book essential. Essential, but not the final word. The infinity of history and the richness of film preclude such limits. There is much more to regale us, horrify us, intrigue us, and inspire us. A heartfelt salute, then, to Russo and his great achievement. Now on to more of the history.

Through a Lens Darkly

How do we approach these movies? What do they mean? What kind of histories and inferences can we derive from them? There are even more answers than there are spectators, and the possibilities and implications are limitless. Theoretical, psychological, sociological, or political, these films give us enough material to settle and start countless arguments, to make or disprove infinite assumptions or theories, and to serve as material for hundreds of anecdotes. Some retrospective overlay is unavoidable, of course, but this is a relatively straightforward history, and mainly a previously untold one. To give these films too much a sense of a Darwinian teleology—treating them as components in an inevitable evolution—would be preposterous. The light of hindsight does enable us to see things more clearly, certainly—actors who were gay in real life, for example, seem more evidently so to our heightened sense of such things. Otherwise these works are best viewed in terms of what they gave their audiences, how they gave it, and how they were received—all verifiable components. Through them many of the larger considerations become clearer, particularly those related to the changing face of homosexuality in the twentieth century.

Note the use of the word *verifiable*. There's been quite a cottage industry in the past decade or so adding film history to the controversial concept of "outing." And what a quagmire this rapidly becomes! Let's face it: the private life of a performer or director does matter, particularly when it has bearing on his or her work. Would Franklin Pangborn's body of work have had such resonance if, as seems staggeringly unlikely, all the gay vibes he gave were fabricated? Could a film as gay as *Lady in the Dark* have possibly been directed by a more heterosexual director than Mitchell Leisen? When Barbara Stanwyck became the first major Hollywood star to play an out lesbian (in *Walk on the Wild Side*, 1962), did the (numerous and unproved) rumors about her private life have no bearing whatsoever? The proposition must extend to writers and designers as well and other personnel too; William Mann's book *Behind the Screen* (2001) makes a convincing case for the prevalence of such people and their influence upon the cinematic product. It is, in fact, unthinkable that there would have been the number and range of lesbian and gay moments on film in the thirties, forties, and fifties without the involvement of a large number of in-the-life participants. It's so interesting a subject, both as history and as gossip, that's it's tempting to let it spin along without any brakes. Nevertheless: don't let the subject get too confused. The twenty-first century, after all, is hardly the first time that a huge number of performers were striving mightily to avoid any intersection between their private lives and public personas. Some stars did and do live parts of their lives on film—Marlene Dietrich's on- and offscreen gender-bending is a good example, as is the air of effete superiority affected by Clifton Webb in his performances and in his life. But you can look pretty much in vain through the films of Ramon Novarro for real homoerotic implications. No matter how much Novarro may read to us as gay (which he was), his gayness was kept separate from his stardom, at least until his incongruity as a "virile" romantic lead became obvious. Certainly, the offscreen lives of certain performers can be an issue when dealing with their films. With Rock Hudson, who engaged in gay role-play in several films, there is layer upon layer of artifice—during an era of profound hypocrisy and denial, here was a gay actor playing straight offscreen, and onscreen playing straight playing gay. Don't ever let it be denied, either that it can make for a great deal of sport to try to score outing points by rooting around in old closets for gay skeletons. Just remember, in doing so, that it's best to stick to the history, and to the facts.

One of the most illuminating aspects of these movies—in fact, a crucial reason to see and study them—is the museum-quality glimpse we get into how gays and lesbians were seen by others, and in some ways how they saw themselves. The movies of the time, especially those made prior to 1940, were reflective of the two basic stereotypes that had existed and evolved for several decades. One stemmed from medical literature beginning with Krafft-Ebbing, and was borne out in *The Well of Loneliness*. Male and female homosexuals, it held, were essentially creatures of inverted gender, men trapped in women's bodies and vice versa. The second stereotype involved the repercussions from the Oscar Wilde trial. Wilde became the image, the focal point even, for all male homosexuality. No matter that Wilde himself was of vigorous and hulking build; he was the paradigm of the gay "aesthete"—delicate, supercilious, rarefied. In short, effeminate—the source of that time-honored "pansy" stereotype.[2] These, then, were not concepts invented by the movies, simply propagated by them. The world of the "third sex" shown by the movies was an evocation of the popular image: a place of large women trundling about smoking cigars, sometimes being mistaken for men, and of fragile little men who tend (or, rather, waft) toward the fluffy and in some cases go so far as to sport makeup. Also, because of the concept of gender inversion, cross-dressing could be looked upon with asperity, especially when done by a man. The line between gender switching and queerness can be troublesome, and remains so today. With all the wobbly variance, the two are frequently easy to confuse and even conflate. All these variations are, to be sure, measured against that implicit and enforced paradigm that forever attempts to hit us over the head, white male heterosexuality. The deviations from that course became viewed, with increasing suspicion, as the alien. The targets of derision, scorn, ridicule, violence. That view informed much of American culture for most of the twentieth century, and in far too many places and situations it continues to this day. Hate, we learn all the time, dies a hard and slow death.

---

[2]These two crucial "types" have been discussed at length in (among other places) two outstanding books: *An American Obsession: Science, Medicine, and Homosexuality in Modern Society* by Jennifer Terry (University of California, 1999), and Alan Sinfield's *The Wilde Century: Effeminacy, Oscar Wilde, and the Queer Moment* (Columbia University, 1994). They show the roots of the stereotypes that persist, despite all evidence to the contrary, into the twenty-first century. For anyone innocent enough to think these notions now blessedly obsolete, tune in to talk radio sometime.

Sissies and tough women, pansies and dykes—these are words and stereotypes and images that will confront us again and again here. How monumental their offense seems, often as odious as the racial and ethnic pigeonholing that looms so large and vile in cinema history. Many detest the gay stereotypes. Often the first reaction is to cringe and then, with a nervous laugh, move on to open hostility. It's easier to do that than to confront the images in their context or to find that the actualities of these shorthand references, as insensitive as they seem after many decades, were not completely bigoted. Ignorant and lazy and frequently false . . . but how often in those days did film depict *any* groups of people with candor, subtlety, and honesty? This is Hollywood we're talking about here, home of the lowest-common-denominator ethic. Raising too vehement an objection to some of the early lavender images, or associating them solely with condemnatory intentions, is to wrench them out of their time and milieu and assign to them much heavy anachronistic baggage. Seldom, until the 1940s and beyond, were gay characters presented with overt malice. Ghettoized yes, marginalized often—but as seen in comparison with some of the racial stereotypes of the same early years (Stepin Fetchit and his fellows), gays and lesbians were often given positive treatment. Sometimes they were granted some dignity and self-awareness (as the isolated actor of color would be). Many who disagree with these statements see the effeminacy and mincing of the men, the cartoony bullishness of the women, and cry foul. Sometimes it's difficult not to. Yet the visible presence onscreen of these characters certainly counted as a positive factor for many thousands, and there isn't always the ridicule or condemnation that one expects. They weren't, one way or another, put down with any greater force than overstuffed dowagers, skinny spinsters, or cranky codgers. Not to mention Irish cops, Jewish merchants, or Italian gangsters. The filmmakers who put gay images up for all to see had more personal knowledge of them than they did of most of the racial or ethnic minorities they depicted; by the 1920s, after all, Hollywood had an established underground same-sex community. To cast too harsh a retrospective eye on these images misjudges their context and value. A chaotic century's worth of hindsight, of memories and ridicule and gay-bashing and hate crimes, can play some funny tricks on the spectator and on the historian. Don't be too put off by these movies—there's enough there that's authentic to tell us something about who we were and where we've been.

Queer Flashes

In their century of shared existence, film and homosexuality have charted a striking course. Sometimes film reflects precisely how gays were viewed in the American experience, and at other times the distortion is epic. In the films of the teens to twenties, the occasional references start popping up on the screen in mostly wide-eyed ways, as if observed by a hick suddenly arriving in a wicked big city. They echo the American consciousness at the time, when homosexuality was something spectators had heard whispers about, as in the trials of Oscar Wilde or, later, Loeb and Leopold. It was an exotic world of the "other," with lesbians as part of a decadent and quite foreign realm and gay men (pansies) as sources of nervous laughter. By the late 1920s, film became audible and more frank, partly in Hollywood's acknowledgment of the fact that many Americans did indeed know what sex was. In the early sound era, particularly in the raw and gutsy cinema of the early Depression, the gloves were off: it seemed that every fifth or sixth Hollywood movie contained a character or a reference to the gay and lesbian experience. There were, in fact, more visibly gay and lesbian characters onscreen at this time than at any other point in American cinema until the late 1980s. Even casual random screenings of titles will bear out this fact. With some exceptions the onscreen time of these characters was brief (as it would be for other minorities), but a major impression was being made by what the trade paper *Variety* called "queer flashes."

In 1934 it all seemed to stop. Only in recent years have historians realized just how much the Legion of Decency and the newly enforced Motion Picture Production Code changed the movies. However ludicrous it seems now, this crusade to save America from the supposed filth-mongers was a cultural war, and the repercussions were staggering. Such was the power of the movement that America's life changed along with its movies. The year began with *Flying Down to Rio*, featuring a flock of undressed women cavorting on the wings of planes; it ended on a vastly dissimilar plane (both air- and moral) with *Bright Eyes*, featuring Shirley Temple singing "On the Good Ship Lollipop" to a horde of adoring flyboys. So many things vanished from film after the middle of 1934: women's navels, occupied double beds, getting away with murder without being punished, any sense of a bedroom as something other than a sleep chamber, drug use, the attractiveness of lawlessness, and, essentially, being an out gay man or lesbian. The women gave up their short haircuts and tailored suits and cigars, and the men toned down the effusive gestures and the goo-goo eyes. The buzz words, too, were gone: *pansy* needed to have a botanical connotation, and fairies existed only in children's stories. Lavender, the great gay granddad of code words, became a far less mentioned color. The once flamboyant gay men and women became, basically, dowdy spinsters and nervous bachelors—presences onscreen that reflected the way they lived in many places, especially outside New York and Hollywood. The signals or words or sheer "gaydar" that might work for gay men or women in the real world were up on the screen as well. In a way the movies were functioning as an extension of the gay subculture, broadcasting the messages to those in the know and in the life. Occasionally there would be, onscreen as in reality, the coded term or the telltale gesture; and there would be the presence of someone like the divine Franklin Pangborn to clue in knowing viewers. Gayness onscreen was still present, then, if far less conspicuous. In these shadowy and guarded times, some gallant and intrepid men and women kept the gayness in the movies, often at great professional risk. If you knew what to look for, you saw it.

In the immediate prewar years these messages were fairly congruent with the closeted, special nature of much of "the life." Occasionally, as in the 1940s world of film noir, there was something more forward, and usually tinged with negativity. After World War II, as more men and women moved away from home and started to claim their identities, Hollywood's insistently "don't tell" attitude remained stubbornly in tune with the general repression of the Eisenhower years, and especially with the blatant hypocrisy of the McCarthy era. The Roy Cohns of the 1950s found equivalents in such movies as *Cat on a Hot Tin Roof* and *Tea and Sympathy*, which twisted every which way to avoid dealing with the gay issue head-on. Yet that quiet procession of gay images in films continued, usually under the radar. That the Eisenhower decade began with *Caged* and ended with *Suddenly, Last Summer* indicates that the movies were starting to grow up, just a little. As the fifties became the sixties, there finally began something more open, as the Production Code was eventually stretched to the breaking point. Freedom in those years immediate before and after the Stonewall riots, did not necessarily mean liberation, at least in a positive sense. With films free to portray all types of sexuality frankly, rampant homophobia seemed to be the price for increased visibility. At the point when Vito Russo wrote *The Celluloid Closet*, gayness in commercial American film was an ocean of adversity. The painfully slow advances being made in society were mocked in most movies. Gays and lesbians were demonized, villified, ridiculed. Not that anyone noticed at the time, but the early thirties, with their sympathetic fairies and powerful dykes, had been far more positive. One had to turn to television and foreign films to get anything with a positive or realistic tone. Finally, as a seemingly homo-allergic ex-movie star president prepared to depart, mainstream film opened a few more doors. *Torch Song Trilogy*, *Longtime Companion*, *Basic Instinct* (the doors weren't always favorable ones!), *Philadelphia*: the profile was being raised. By century's end, the upturn had steadily progressed, and the old-style virulent attacks continued to blast as loud as ever. The messages of the Christian Right sometimes made the Catholic Legion of Decency seem enlightened by comparison, and some politicians, entertainers, and commentators attempted a macho posture by assuming the attitude of "no homos allowed." The contradictions are as strange today as they have ever been, and even in a more permissive age there are the stereotypes, the insults, the crimes against decency and humanity, the staggering misinterpretations on all sides.

And through it all, film has continued to hold up its strange mirror—alternately reflecting, repressing, ridiculing, suggesting, condemning, questioning . . . and even, on occasion, accepting. Screening in, as well as screening out.

Walk on the Wild Side

The writing of this history, like any history, required that choices be made—consciously. One choice was to confine the book to American film and the mass audience that viewed it. For the most part, experimental or underground film doesn't factor in, despite the audacious innovations of Kenneth Anger, Jack Smith, and others. The rise of the new queer cinema in the 1990s made for a vastly different art. It brought many independent works into the cinema mainstream. That, again, is another history; the primary focus here is on film that affected the largest audiences, mainly before the age of Stonewall. Having Stonewall as the cutoff point may seem eccentric to many; isn't that, after all, where it was supposed to have started? No . . . that's where it all changed. In the nine months between the Stonewall riots and the premiere of the film of *The Boys in the Band*, gayness was transformed on the streets and on the screen. This is definitely a history with a first and second act, and it is that underdog, unfamiliar first act that this book chronicles. Given the number of films involved, it would be impossible (and repetitive) to discuss all of them in detail. Some are referred to in passing; others, particularly marginal or questionable titles, are not mentioned; and hundreds of instances from silent and early sound cinema still await discovery. On the whole, tracking the spectrum of films is more important here than digging up every last title. The decision to limit the book's scope to American film is admittedly a tad ambiguous, simply because several foreign films—*Maedchen in Uniform*, *Victim*, the Fassbinder films, *La Cage aux Folles*—had great American success and influence. That impact is undoubtedly part of this story, but the social differences between Europe (in particular) and the United States are vast, and the developments of their cinemas are, in this case, separate. *The Celluloid Closet* gave us a fine introduction to gay and lesbian European cinema and its repercussions in the United States; beyond that, as with queer cinema, it rates coverage in depth. Any takers? Though the main emphasis is on feature films, short subjects get a brief look in as well. Considering the riotous procession of fairies, pansies, and other exotic species that flamed across the animated screen during the 1930s, it would be a major loss not to include cartoons, apart from which is the fact that they're a lot of fun. Television, on the other hand, deserves a whole shelf of books devoted to its reflection of and impact upon gayness. In the early 1970s it began to outstrip film in a forward-looking view of gayness and has continued that course without cease over three decades. Even in the early 1990s, who would have envisioned *Will and Grace* and *Queer as Folk?*

A quick word on terminology is in order: it's impossible to find just the right words to please everybody. For some, terms like *queer* and *dyke* are joyous badges; for others, they are poisonous. Some other early terms like *fairy* and *pansy* can sting as well. And despite Ellen DeGeneres's epochal admission "Yep, I'm gay," not everyone will approve of using the word *gay* to refer to women as well as men. All those terms are used here at various times, and are employed with care and with the greatest respect. Labels are the necessity of the historian; fortunately, they can also be our friends.

As far as the research materials needed to recount this era, primacy is obviously given to the films themselves, in this case many, many films that have never been written about with reference to their gay elements and a few that are entirely unfamiliar under all circumstances. Written evidence on them—what caused them to happen and how they were received—can vary wildly. Much of it simply wasn't written about at the time, and the censors were so notoriously unsophisticated that they missed a lot of what was going on. Still, the papers of the Motion Picture Producers and Distributors of America, known generally as the Hays Office, tell us much about what was included, what was too gamy to let pass, and, most crucially, how America looked at its movies. If it seems that a good deal of emphasis is given to what the Production Code officials thought of a movie, it is because they were the people controlling what America saw on the screen. Their vigilance over gay and lesbian contact continued unabated, if somewhat selectively, for over thirty years. As will be seen, sometimes the gay content was too subtle for them, and sometimes they just seemed to be looking the other way. The script files for many of these films survive as well, and they can be very illuminating: if you think that what was included in the films can be jarring or eye-opening, you might look up some of the screenwriters' wilder ideas that never saw the light of day. Gay and lesbian press during the twilight years was fairly sporadic, although occasionally things did surface; just as interesting is the occasional take that surfaces in the mainstream press on some of the homoerotic aspects of these movies. And there are the spectators, those going to see these movies when they were new, who occasionally would see surprising references to their own lives in what was going on up there on the screen. More than occasionally these movies—even with their trivial and silly little characters and fleeting moments—would give a struggling or closeted person in the audience a sense of a whole world out there, a clue to an identity, a feeling that he or she wasn't entirely alone. One would like to believe that someone like Franklin Pangborn actually knew, on some level, that he was serving as an eccentric, flustered beacon over a dark and intimidating sea.

Film, as subjective and selective as it is, gives us the ability to catch privileged glimpses of who and where we've been. Not everyone, of course, cares to look back. Some are mistaken enough to find the looking back irrelevant. That dog don't hunt, however: how better can we learn where we're headed than by seeing how we've gotten to where we are? These strange, brave pioneers, making their timorous statements that gayness did indeed exist, must be remembered. Even when they were only granted fleeting seconds of images, they were making statements that fly joyously in the face of the conception that, in years past, no one knew what homosexuality was. Of course they knew, most of them, and the movies were and are there to tell about it. The glimpses that survive for our perusal may not always be of documentary quality, perhaps, but they have their own particular authenticity. They illuminate the mockery of homophobic naysayers, they demonstrate the cheap pandering of those who didn't care, and they point up the brave, sometimes covert messages of those for whom it all truly did matter. These films are unique records of a century and a culture, documents telling us how some people set about to form a way of life. Later in the twenty-first century, when the same-sex experience will stop being an issue for most people, these old films will remain to remind us of the joyful and terrible struggle of the years when being out on the screen carried a special charge, when lavender was more than a color and the pansy was not a flower.

ONE

Silent Existences

T he movies and gayness have had oddly parallel lives these past hundred years. Both of them have grown, mutated, regressed sometimes, ever taken unexpected turns. By the end of that shared century of existence, both were generally accepted yet fiercely argued over, mainstreamed while being frequently decried, discussed and argued over, praised and banned, legislated and regimented. Both remained without a standard clear-cut form. Neither, any longer, was merely a shadow on the wall.

At the outset of the twenty-first century the pervasiveness of the discussions and arguments over gayness and cinema (as well as gayness *in* cinema) contrasts powerfully with their origins. In the early years both were fleeting, nebulous, almost intangible. Movies were momentary flickers in machines or on tacked-up sheets; people who were bold enough to consider themselves gay and lesbian existed either behind locked doors or in the most ghettoized subareas of the population. Therefore, and not surprisingly, trying to find traces of gay or lesbian characters in American films before the 1920s is like sending Diogenes to Washington, D.C., to search for an honest man. So many of the pre-1920 films themselves are completely lost, and in those that aren't there seem to be precious few gay whiffs. Moreover, there is next to nothing in the way of paper trails—censor notes, studio correspondence, and such. Not even reviews. And, of course, the audiences to whom such moments might have spoken are now gone. This all changed with the advent of the studio system, and then with the coming of sound, where there is more tangible history (and more extant films) to deal with. Until then it's all up for grabs. Lurking through this chapter, then, is a subtext: the scattershot methodology by which we undertake a search for gay cinema prehistory. Future film scholars and detectives take note that archives and museums, perhaps attics and basements, likely contain some totally forgotten titles, some unknowable fragments of celluloid, with fleeting moments of an emerging sexual presence. The sissies and the tough women, and the more subtle portrayals as well, are awaiting their retrieval from dusty film cans.

While that search goes on, and we begin to see gay and lesbian images from the earliest years of film, we can sometimes be jolted by the bluntness of the stereotypes. It's at that point where it's probably best to take a deep breath, step back, and remember historical context: what passed for formalized gay/lesbian life in those early years did, in fact, frequently follow specific patterns of role-playing. There were, in a real sense, inherent stereotypes in place even before the movies began. "The Third Sex" was not a descriptive, not a pejorative, term. Radclyffe Hall's novel *The Well of Loneliness*, for all its importance, reflected the psychiatric tenor of the time in propagating the myth that gay women were men trapped in female bodies. The Oscar Wilde scandal set forth the whole concept of the dandified pansy. Drag balls were the rage in the early decades of the century, and many men bold or hip enough to consider themselves homosexual most often referred to their peers as "she." The more heterosexualized participants in same-sex relationships simply regarded fairies as the alien other.[1] Therefore, their presences in early films are, for all the affront, fairly representative of how they were treated when they ventured out into the real world.

The first couple of decades of American film were not a time, all in all, when gray areas, let alone those having to do with sex, were generally a factor. In the days of Theda Bara, how much was there in the movies of erotic nuance? If historical accuracy is to be the goal instead of psychological analysis, we must constantly be on our guard to maintain perspective. From the dawn of movie time, for example, there is that lovely little lyrical male-male waltz that makes such an appropriate close to the documentary film *The Celluloid Closet*. It's an experimental Edison sound film from the mid-1890s, and among other things it serves to remind us of a theme that will recur again and again: the face of gay images is a changing one. What seems gay now was seen as nothing out of the ordinary a hundred years ago, and men or women engaged in same-sex dancing was not necessarily a cause for raised eyebrows. Throughout these pages, the conflict between intention and effect is always at hand, and will ever need to be confronted. The search for *deliberate* gay images in the early years of cinema in particular is quite a tough proposition. Unless there's a really outlandish characterization at work, it's safe to assume equivocal intentions

---

[1]Millions of people participated in same-sex acts and relationships while completely eschewing any notion that they were of that dreaded "Third Sex." If they were cast in the role that suited their given gender, they were exempted from guilt by association. Their direct descendants haunt the Internet today, growing hostile at the notion of being labeled one of *them*, yet seeking furtive encounters as a respite from spouse-and-kids domesticity. Denial, thou art fresh and ever with us.

Pioneer Spirit: Billy Quirk strikes an attitude, and vice versa, in *Algie, the Miner.*

on the part of the filmmakers, with cinematic loopholes present for those who require them.

Two early characters, however, have emerged from the rubble of nitrate powder and deterioration that forms the first decades of American cinema. Both are in comedy shorts, where everyone was a target. What is less expected, perhaps, is that the first of them came from the legendary first woman director in film history. *Algie, the Miner* (1912) was produced and supervised by Alice Guy-Blaché, who often seemed to zero in on provocative subject matter, even in trivial short comedies. (Leave it to the French, albeit a transplanted French-woman working in New York.) Algie (Billy Quirk) is heterosexual only in that he has a girlfriend. Otherwise, he's a card-carrying flamer. Even this early, all the mannerisms are there for the filmmakers to heighten and caricature: the dandi-fied air, fluttering hands, pursed and apparently rouged lips, sly smile, and eyes that he bats while fondling the barrel of a pistol which he examines as if it were cloisonné (or something less elegant). He is sent west for a year by his fiancée's disapproving father to prove his manhood. Even before he gets to the mining camp, his nelliness gets him in all manner of trouble, as when he asks two men for directions and they pull a gun. When they decide not to shoot him, he shows his gratitude by kissing them. Eventually he bonds with a butch character named Big Jim, strikes it rich, and returns home a tougher man without makeup to claim his bride. Algie's queerness (or, if you like, effeminacy) shows through in everything he says, does, and is. One visual detail in particular stands out: a pair of outsized tapering starched Joan Crawfordish cuffs that give him the look of a debauched pilgrim. Costume and accessory cues would be the norm for such characters for many years to come, setting up an easy shorthand that something is in the air. The flower in the lapel, the little mustache, the waving handkerchief were all ways to code a gay man's presence onscreen. (If the films had been in color, there would also have been red neckties and green carnations.) For lesbians, a jacket and tie, slicked-back hair, and an occasional cigar or monocle would do the trick. The code words were important too: *dearie, whoops!, lavender, fairy,* and the double-edged *pansy.* In movies, quick communication carries a far higher premium than subtlety or even accuracy. Yet Guy-Blaché and her crew give Algie and audiences an escape clause. Despite everything we see, he is capable of a quick overhaul to conventional he(te)roism, something not unlike the transformations espoused today by certain right-wing moralists. Algie thus has the distinction of being cinema's first queer tease, and possibly one of the rare examples of successful conversion therapy.

Our Algie predated Charlie Chaplin's entrance into film by one year. By 1918 Chaplin was the biggest star in movies, and no one flattered him more sincerely than Billy West, who starred in a series of films that were Chaplin in all but name. The mustache, the costume, the whole persona—such was West's plagiaristic shtick. *His Day Out* (1918) is typical (even the title recalls Chaplin's *A Night Out*); West/Chaplin as an incompetent barber wreaks havoc on customers and bystanders. Two future stars are present in support of West (silent leading woman Leatrice Joy and Oliver Hardy, both of whom will be encountered again in these pages), but our attention zooms in on another, unidentified actor playing one of Billy's put-upon customers. Looking like the well-fed love child of Colette and Quentin Crisp, he is a shade more flowery than Algie—a stocky and heavily made-up dandy with an unruly head of hair and a snappish attitude. Instead of cutting his hair, West ties it up in ribbons and quickly throws a hat on it—and when he later accidentally knocks if off, the dandy is ridiculed by bystanders. West, however, mollifies him with a quick kiss and all is well. Notice that while the pansy may indeed be a butt of gags for the audience, in the context of the film he's only ridiculed when people see his absurd hairdo; any kind of character, man or woman, could have functioned in such a role. Film, it seems, was starting to speak to those who were already in on the joke.

The *real* Chaplin was one of the first cinematic practitioners of the time-honored queer-panic shtick, wherein someone would be heard or seen out of context and mistaken for gay. It will crop up again and again here, just as it is still with us in pop entertainment: witness Jerry Seinfeld's "I've been outed, and I was never inned!" In *Behind the Screen* (1916), Chaplin plays a put-upon sceneshifter at a movie studio, with Edna Purviance as a gate-crashing aspiring actor disguised as a boy. Their flirtation is interpreted by Chaplin's burly fore-man, who thinks he has stumbled into a genuine garden of pansies. To signal that he knows what's going on, he immediately begins to mince and flit, the out-raged Chaplin retaliates, and the conflict grows until finally a pie fight ensues. Even this early, the foreman's mocking imitation contains a lexicon of identi-fiable mannerisms. Most important, audiences—which for a Chaplin movie would be vast—knew what was going on.

Edna Purviance's male disguise in *Behind the Screen* raises another issue that will recur, and rankle, frequently: that strange, ambiguous relationship between gayness and gender switching. Cross-dressing, especially on film, has never traveled one direct course. The double standard between a woman dressed as a man and vice versa is well known—one is essentially accepted, as in Purviance above, and the other is ridiculed. In the early years of film there would be a great deal of confusion about what, exactly, cross-dressing might connote. It was very popular in film at this time, a continuation of time-honored traditions of theatrical comedy long before people knew exactly what camp was. As practiced by such masters as Chaplin and Fatty Arbuckle, it had far more to do with masquerade and buffo than it did with sexuality. Even the burly and butch Wallace Beery did a series of films (*Sweedie*) in which he played a Swedish housemaid. It was all in fun, an extension of what audiences had seen in vaudeville houses, and most hints of sexual suggestiveness come only retroactively. Nevertheless, putting drag in front of a close-up camera made for a different dimension, heightening the ambiguity as it weakened the illusion. In the very early 1900s, a skinny comedian named Gilbert Saroni appeared in a series of short *Old Maid* films that now seem like utter low campfests. *The Old Maid in the Drawing Room* (1901) is a good example: Saroni (with perhaps three teeth in his head) carries on in prissy affront, and the spectacle seems less suited to a drawing room than it does a Greenwich Village bar minutes before closing time.

Was it the sexual duplicity underlying drag that caused it to be so popular at this time? Or had the "white heterosexual male" paradigm not yet been so firmly established? One thing is certain: Julian Eltinge was a major star in the teens and twenties, the most famous female impersonator in the business and the most popular drag act in movies before Lassie. He was the centerpiece of a series of vehicles made between 1914 and 1925 bearing titles such as *The Clever Mrs. Carfax*, *The Countess Charming*, and *Madame Behave*. They were mostly comedies where, in order to trap a fiend of some kind or other, a red-blooded

American male masqueraded as a woman with astonishing verisimilitude. They served as an extension of Eltinge's carefully nurtured image—that he was indeed a virile heterosexual who just happened to be a whiz at acting like an utterly believable woman.[2] His movies set him up as sort of a Douglas Fairbanks with brassieres, a gambit which occasionally could throw audiences for a loop. The critic for *Motion Picture News*, for example, begged viewer indulgence for the uncertain tone of *The Clever Mrs. Carfax:* "It is marred at the very start by a 'College Reunion' scene which represents college men as 'loving' to assume feminine attire." However, lest audiences begin to assume the worse, this same critic assured them: "As the young [male] lover, Mr. Eltinge makes many of our juvenile leading stars appear effeminate beside him." A companion piece to the Eltinge films was Mack Sennett's *Yankee Doodle in Berlin* (1919), wherein drag star Bothwell Browne played an aviator who poses as a cooch dancer to seduce and defeat the Kaiser and his minions, and rescues the heroine (Marie Prevost) by disguising *her* in soldier drag.[3]

Picking through the fossilized remains of early American film occasionally yields some other finds. In D. W. Griffith's first feature, *Judith of Bethulia* (1913), something close to a gay character pops up in the form of a eunuch, played by J. Jiquel Lanoe, who forms the film's only comedy relief. Since no one knew exactly how a biblical (or apocryphal) eunuch would act, Griffith and Lanoe were able to denote "eunuchness" through expectedly effeminate means, with Lanoe's hands waving in disdain for the women around him. Once again the lines between gayness and gender confusion—and here, castration—are being wildly blurred. One year later *A Florida Enchantment* blurred them far more. Historians frequently turn to it as an example of a bona fide comedy of sexual confusion, and, startlingly enough, it holds up under scrutiny. An adaptation of an 1891 novel and a subsequent play, it's the first example of the wolf-in-sheep's-drag sex farces that later included *Turnabout*, *Goodbye Charlie*, and Blake Edwards's *Switch*—even, Lord help us, *Myra Breckinridge*. Somehow, through reincarnation or some type of voodoo, the souls of men or women are magically implanted into bodies of someone of the opposite sex. This naturally

---

[2]So well fostered was Eltinge's straight-man-in-a-dress persona that it was the subject of a silent-movie gag. In *Seven Chances* (1925) Buster Keaton becomes infatuated with a picture of Eltinge outside a theater and goes backstage to pay "her" court. He soon emerges battered and defeated. Eltinge's heterosexual veneer, of course, was a phenomenon of its time. Naturally it would today be absolutely unthinkable that a probably gay performer would *ever* feel any need to hide behind such an elaborate false front. Wouldn't it?

[3]Browne, a real trouper, made a series of personal appearances at openings of *Yankee Doodle in Berlin*. Audiences were mesmerized as, backed by six Mack Sennett bathing beauties, he reprised the harem dance that brought the Kaiser down. Certainly it was less of a stretch for him than playing a he-man flyboy.

gives a built-in framework for comedy-of-errors confusion, which of course (and even in 1914) includes a healthy portion of titillation. What makes this early film so fresh (in both senses of the word) is the fashion in which the premise is followed through: the magical sex-change seeds taken by the heroine (Edith Storey), her maid (Ethel Lloyd), and her fiancé (Sidney Drew) change the gender of the soul while retaining the old body—thus becoming fantasy versions of what gays and lesbians were considered at the time, a man trapped in a woman's body and vice versa. And though the three of them eventually find the comfort of cross-dressing, they each first spend time in what appears to us (and the other characters) as same-sex flirtation. With Edith Storey, in particular, a fair amount of footage is devoted to her dalliances with several women, which are handled with some skill. Her scenes both in and out of drag have an unexpected delicacy that was, quite possibly, never intended. Interestingly, her flirtatious behavior as a woman is permitted (though it raises eyebrows), and when she dresses as a man, she is accepted as one. When Drew ogles one man, while still in male attire, the police are called. His subsequent drag routine, which involves his carrying on in a manner that makes Divine seem like Audrey Hepburn, fools nobody.[4] The message being broadcast is, again, of the double standard: female gender-bending is more to be tolerated than male. With maleness as the standard-bearer, a man in drag is a transgressor, but a woman dressed as a man can be exciting; certainly, in subsequent films heroines would be disguised as boys far more often than the reverse. In the case of *A Florida Enchantment*, the film itself was felt to be the chief transgressor; apparently its subversion of "normality" was too outré for many to countenance. When he gave the film a monumental pan, *Variety* critic Sime Silverman was apparently reflecting a consensus:

> The most silly "comedy" ever put on the sheet [screen]. . . . There is as much fun in it as a Continental battle. . . . The picture should never have been put out, for there's no one with any sense of humor whatsoever, or intelligence either, who can force a smile while watching this sad "comedy."

He also reported numerous walkouts at the screening he attended. Were audiences outraged by *A Florida Enchantment*? Bored? Confused? Uncomfortable? Certainly the film was far outside the mainstream of its time, and what seems cryptic even today must have been flabbergasting in 1915. Even its "it was only a dream" cop-out ending doesn't completely clear things up, for when Storey

---

[4]Ethel Lloyd, as the maid, has it worse. Her character is said to be mulatto, but the makeup is pure blackface, and as soon as she swallows the enchanted seed, she starts boozing and behaving as violently as the ugly caricatures in *The Birth of a Nation*.

wakes up, she still appears to have the box of seeds, along with the letter explaining their power. Or does she? This curious and engaging tease of a movie doesn't fully explain. Like equally provocative and more important films, it raises its questions without providing answers.

Putting outrageous behavior into the context of a dream became a venerable film staple. Despite its title, *The Dream Lady* (1918) was not given over to that device, although it did have a subplot of some interest: Sydney Brown (Kathleen Emerson) prefers men's clothes to women's and finally meets a man who admires her qualities and proposes to her—sort of a cross-dressed forebear of *Sylvia Scarlett*, and with enough equivocation to create a tingle. While the sexual aspects of such films as *A Florida Enchantment* and *The Dream Lady* were not much remarked on at the time, they were sufficiently self-evident to be comprehended. Cinema in the teens is so often thought of as the zenith of quaint, with Chaplin twirling his cane and Mary Pickford bouncing her curls and Pollyanna-ing her way through movie after saccharine movie. Actually, there was some pretty strong meat for the time. Director Lois Weber, for example, had an uncanny knack for zeroing in on all sorts of issues, up to and including abortion. For sexual ambiguity, it was still a bit early for anything other than comic allusiveness or fantasy. Some historians have looked to King Vidor's *The Other Half* (1919), a melodrama of male bonding and social reform, for intimations of secret things, but contrast this with what was going on in Germany at the same time: the breakthrough gay drama *Anders an die Anderen* (Different from the Others) for which, despite the growing American vogue for German cinema, a U.S. release would have been most unlikely. For Americans who could barely accept a fantasy-comedy about gender reversal, a serious look at contemporary gayness would have provided too many jolts.

The 1920s, with all its jazz and roar, has come to signify the era when many people first discovered worldly pleasures, particularly booze and sex. Between the postwar boom and Prohibition and new types of music and dance, the decade, rightly or wrongly, is synonymous with high living. A great portion of this impression comes from the movies, and these years saw American cinema come forth as a dominant cultural force. The "classical" studio/production system emerged in all its beveled efficiency, Hollywood became established definitively as the hub of world cinema, and the morality of film people was first monitored on a large scale on and off the screen. The early twenties was the time of the most notorious accumulation of scandals in cinema history: the Fatty Arbuckle rape case, the William Desmond Taylor murder, Wallace Reid's death from drug addiction. With the heightened attention to offscreen Hollywood morality, it was decided to keep a close eye on onscreen doings. This led to the rise of one Will H. Hays, postmaster general under President Warren Harding (whose administration had its own stockpile of scandals) and one of the certifiable oddballs of film history. Under Hays's prissy and crafty and ferretlike gaze, the studios united in a self-policing system called the Motion Picture Producers and Distributors of America, presently the Hays Office. The policing made the studios more wary of the offscreen behavior of its personnel, and no doubt put increased reserves in the payoff coffers of the Los Angeles Police Department. The effect of this vigilance on the onscreen Hollywood product was interesting, for although some of the lurid themes of teens cinema were no longer acceptable, the studios pretty much did what they wanted without an inordinate amount of interference. State and city censorship boards (the worst were in Pennsylvania, Ohio, and Chicago) still had the power to cut or ban films, but apart from them carefully packaged sex sold extremely well.

No one packaged sex better than Cecil B. DeMille, who is in fact responsible for one of the first overt (if fleeting) views of same-sex love in American film. DeMille had started out in 1913 as a serious filmmaker, but by 1922 he had discovered that sex, decadence, and opulence made for longer box-office lines than did dramas in the style of James Fenimore Cooper. His gambit was as hypocritical as it was irresistible: you can't condemn anything sinful without demonstrating it. Accordingly, he decided to graphically condemn the revels of the emergent Jazz Age not only by showing them but by equating them with the orgies that (in the DeMille version of history) led to the downfall of the Roman Empire. His melodrama *Manslaughter*, about a thrill-mad socialite (Leatrice Joy) who commits a hit-and-run, digressed abruptly to a lurid flashback of just what exactly caused Rome to fall. Said sins included a pair of women embracing with both lust and affection, placed by DeMille in a prominent spot just inside the entrance to the hall where the orgy is in progress. Did the throngs who saw *Manslaughter* catch the reference or know what it was about? Hard to say, but the director's sapphic garnish qualifies as one of the first, if not the first, in American cinema. When DeMille revisited pagan revels a year later in the first *Ten Commandments*, he kept the licentious Israelites in mixed pairs.

Other ancient world decadence came from a more candid quarter than Cecil B. DeMille. The film version of Oscar Wilde's *Salome* shot in 1922 by Alla Nazimova is an almost unparalleled curio. Would that it were a masterpiece as well, but its particular artifice and calculated degeneracy are far more of the stage than the cinema. Nazimova was one of the rare stage stars of the time who translated well to film, but the films she produced herself (usually with her common-law husband, Charles Bryant, credited as director) tended to be theatrical in a way that doesn't come across. *Salome*, with its Aubrey Beardsley-inspired décor by Natacha Rambova (Rudolph Valentino's wife and Nazimova's presumed lover), looks like a masterpiece and moves like a snail when it moves at all. Nor is it specifically gay in any tangible detail. If, as has been alleged, the cast of *Salome* was exclusively gay and lesbian, this fact doesn't seem to impart any particular weight to what's on the screen. (The *Variety* critic smelled a rat here: "The heroic figures were given a decided appearance of femininity.") What does seem evident, under any circumstances, is a gay aesthetic: the film smells like lavender and incense, courtesy of the synthesized efforts of Wilde, Nazimova, Bryant, Rambova, and Beardsley. As with some later Hollywood productions having a heavily gay creative team (*Our Betters*, *Lady in the Dark*, *Yolanda and the Thief*), the choices made in staging and design seem just too—well, choose the words: hothouse, precious, outré, camp, rarefied—for what might wryly be called "conventional heterosexual filmmaking." In the case of *Salome*, the costumes alone would have been enough. Some movies don't appear to have a straight bone in their bodies.

Nazimova's garden of biblical delights is an extreme demonstration of the effect creative personnel can have on a production. Independently produced (and critically and commercially reviled) *Salome* would be an anomaly in any era, yet even in mainstream Hollywood cinema at this time increasing attention was paid to "that kind of life." The studio system was now in place, writers, directors, and designers were under contract, and social life in the film colony became progressively more wide-open and accepting. This is not to say that film suddenly took on alternative sexuality, but starting in the mid-1920s more references and characters started appearing, not necessarily in a condemnatory fashion. Stan Laurel's short comedy *The Soilers* was an especially striking early entry, playing on the *Algie, the Miner* technique of placing gay attitudes in a rough ambience. As with Algie, the setting is Out West, and the attitude comes from a flouncing cowboy who moons and flirts as he nurses a crush on Laurel. There are calf eyes and calls of "my hero," and finally a flowerpot for Laurel's head when this Algie's love is spurned. In 1923, as now, some guys don't take rejection gracefully.

Around the time of *The Soilers*'s release, several major practitioners of the art of cinematic sissyism were beginning to ply their trade. The very names of Edward Everett Horton and Franklin Pangborn will cause some (straight and gay alike) to wince and others to smile and chuckle. Again, the issue of "Effeminate = Gay" in cinema is not one easily settled. The sissies who began to proliferate in films of the twenties and thirties were no one's idea of virility . . . but, when viewed as objectively as possible, how offensive or invalid does that necessarily make them? The most visible gay men then were the Quentin Crisps, who wore makeup, dressed as they pleased, and did interesting things with the color and style of their hair. Next to them, a Franklin Pangborn seems like General Patton. And if it is true that some of these characters get ridiculed onscreen, many do not; nor are all of them solely sideline fixtures. As with so many facets of both private and public sexuality, it's an uncomfortable issue and a wildly subjective one. Harvey Fierstein, interviewed in the *Celluloid Closet* documentary, praises the sissies on the grounds that visibility, any visibility, is of prime importance. Vito Russo and others have seemed to react with hostility and, occasionally, odd rationalizations, admiring the actors but decrying the uses to which they were put by the forces of heterosexism. There are no easy answers, and at some point a historian can but present the images and open up the discussion, knowing that for different people they will have wildly dissimilar impacts. Some people will praise the artistry of a Pangborn as they bemoan its misuse, while others will prefer to revel in both the subversiveness of it all and the actor's skill. Still others will just shut the whole matter out and deny that there were any gay characters in films prior to the late 1960s.

Edward Everett Horton, who entered films in 1922, spent the first years of his cinema career as a generic, that is, non-sissy, character actor, including the lead in an early version of *Ruggles of Red Gap*—prim, but not yet prissy. Franklin Pangborn did not arrive until 1926, so the sobriquet of First Professional Sissy in Films goes to a less easily remembered but still worthy recipient, Johnny Arthur. Fittingly enough, Arthur made his film debut in 1923 in something called *The Unknown Purple*. One of his biggest early roles came in the 1925 opus *The Monster*. Even with Lon Chaney as the star, this was not so much a horror film in the *Phantom of the Opera* tradition as a comic melodrama, with Chaney as the proprietor of an extremely questionable sanatorium and Arthur as the Milquetoast who proves himself. He is entirely convincing as a general-store clerk with a detective-school diploma who bunglingly foils Chaney's nasty schemes, though a less persuasive facet of his role is as the Guy Who Wins the Girl. Even the heroine he silently adores (Gertrude Olmstead) seems to sense what Arthur is really about. In an early scene she comes to the store, and our Johnny moons silently. She tells him what she's come for: a bag of pansy seeds. That he is flustered has less to do with her request than her presence . . . but the message to the audience is unmistakable. This, in fact, is one of the earliest examples of one of the most popular of gay-oriented code words; the word *pansy* was at the time not necessarily pejorative, but from this time until its use was banned from movies in 1934 it had one meaning only. Even as the film tells us that pantywaists, given a fair opportunity, are real men too, it undercuts the premise by the casting of Arthur and the insertion of the pansy line. The romantic aspects of *The Monster* are left in as much of a shambles as Lon Chaney's laboratory.

Even as the script of *The Monster* hedges and dodges its way around perceptions of Johnny Arthur's sexuality (or at least that of his character), he is given a love interest, however ill-fitting. Far more often, characters of indeterminate sexuality were sidelined into situations where romantic relationships

JOHNNY ARTHUR

Real name: John Williams. Born Scottsdale, Pa., May 10, 1883; died Woodland Hills, Calif., December 31, 1951

Some cinematic sissies dither, others get all haughty, and still others suffer in affronted silence (as in some of Mr. Pangborn's priceless facial expressions). Johnny Arthur existed onscreen in a constant state of anxiety, balancing precariously at midpoint between dread and displeasure. His established image was not so much effeminate as it was, more subversively, a drastic departure from any kind of conventional masculinity. Small of frame and beady of eye, Arthur often seemed less a person than a prissy rabbit nearing a breakdown, and his exhaustive repertoire of high-strung tics formed the basis of his career. By the time he made his screen debut he had been acting on the stage for upward of two decades. Silent film deprived him of one of his prime assets, a voice so whiny that it probably caused early speaker systems to hum and buzz incessantly. Yet his skill was such that he was able to transfer his act to the silents relatively intact, in comedy shorts and in features like *The Monster.* With the coming of sound he featured prominently in several of the earliest all-talking films, including an indelible appearance in the operetta *The Desert Song* (1929). In Warner Bros.' all-star revue *The Show of Shows* (1929), he was spotted prominently as a sissy pirate. This least leading-mannish of character actors starred in a feature film only once, playing a young bridegroom (despite all evidence to the contrary) in *Personality* (1930). After the early 1930s he toned down the contra-machismo and played up the anxiety; thus tamed, he segued into appearances as an ever-worried father in the *Our Gang* shorts—first as Spanky's dad, later as Darla's. By the time he costarred as the Japanese caricature Suki Yaki (read Hirohito) in *The Nazty Nuisance* in 1943, his early pioneer work as a cinematic flamethrower was long forgotten. Much of Arthur's early work is apparently lost, but for those familiar with his work only in his *Our Gang* period his earlier, lavender-and-fraying-lace persona will deliver a major jolt.

were not a factor. For the most part, American film was far too frightened to consider the depiction of a same-sex couple, yet not so addled as to wedge these characters into ludicrously inapt heterosexuality. To some, this seems like desexualization, emasculation (or defeminization) of the characters to keep them safely and unthreateningly on the outside. Yet, at very least, the point arises: is seeing someone like Johnny Arthur ludicrously teamed with a leading lady any less objectionable than seeing a Franklin Pangborn with no visible partners? The scripts don't generally aver that these sideline characters lack personal lives; like characters of color in early films, such considerations become, forcibly, a nonissue.

Even when not beset by ghoulies, as here in *The Monster*, Johnny Arthur always managed to look spooked. Lon Chaney admires his cranium while Walter James and Knute Erickson menace from the side.

Twenties cinema, in its gamier incarnation, pushed to turn up the heat whenever possible, in the teasing promise of advertising if not in the tamer delivery onscreen. The antics of such sex stars as Rudolph Valentino and Clara Bow were expertly packaged to seem more daring than they actually were, as anyone seeing *The Sheik* or *It* today will testify.[5] So it was also with some of the portrayals of gay/effeminate/sissified insert-adjective-here characters who started appearing onscreen in the mid-twenties. They, too, can deliver less than expected—too timorous to be explicit, stereotypes without the courage of their caricatural convictions. One of the more celebrated of Jazz Age movie pansies is a good example: George K. Arthur's turn as couturier Madame Lucy in *Irene* (1926). The role had been prominent in the original stage musical, and at first it seems that the filmmakers heightened the character to make Lucy the brightest

---

[5]Not that films of the time shunned genuine eroticism. Greta Garbo's love scenes with John Gilbert in *Flesh and the Devil* and *A Woman of Affairs* look like the real thing, which is pretty much what they were.

flower in the Hollywood garden. "As I live and hemstitch, she's impossible!" Lucy burbles at one point, decrying Irene's inability to wear high fashion. Lucy (who has inherited his aunt's dress shop; we never learn his original name), supercilious and snippy as he is, still remains more flighty than femmy. Even with a foil of an assistant, a severe woman with close-cropped hair, and a scene in which he jumps onto a chair when he sees a mouse, Arthur pulls back from the further implications of the character and often seems reserved. Small and delicate-featured, the British-born Arthur was cast in several similar assignments, but there was something reticent, almost tasteful, about his portrayals that gave them, inadvertently, a dose of realism. Perhaps if *Irene* had come a few years later as an early movie musical, Madame Lucy's potential (such as it was) might have been better realized.[6] With this role, as with many subsequent ones, there was a tabula rasa quality, which is obviously what one critic had in mind when he commented that "[there is] nothing fresh, vulgar or objectionable about the way Arthur plays it, just 'sissified' and funny, so even the average lay mind will absorb it as desired."

Hollywood's writers and directors, who were constantly aiming their product toward the average lay mind, knew full well that the world of haute couture (à la Madame Lucy's salon) was, like the theatre, a safe haven for homosexual behavior. Consequently, they would return there often. The sissy dress designer is, of course, a time-honored stereotype not entirely unrooted in actuality. By 1926 the major studios all had designers in their employ, a majority of whom were men, a majority of whom were gay. If men like Howard Greer (who worked at Paramount) and Mitchell Leisen (under contract to Cecil B. DeMille) were not real-life equivalents of silly Madame Lucy, their preferences were well known. (As a designer and later as a director, Leisen was often thought to be particularly flagrant, although in actuality he had numerous affairs with women.) Lucy's emotional excesses had their equivalents in the studios as well: MGM designer Gilbert Clark, according to Howard Greer, was "more temperamental than the stars he was called upon to dress," and after a run-in with Greta Garbo he was out. A few more whiffs of the design world turned up in 1926 in the sex comedy *Fig Leaves*, which, like *Irene*, featured a fashion show photographed in early two-color Technicolor (with gowns by the soon-to-be-legendary Adrian), as well as a temperamental designer (André, played by

---

[6]By the time *Irene* was remade in 1940, the likes of a flaming Lucy were impossible. The plot was restructured to consolidate the Lucy character with that of the romantic lead, thus eliminating any excessive flouncing or question of preference. One seditious touch remained, however: the film's opening credits are accompanied by marionettes of the stars, Anna Neagle and Ray Milland. When the credits for set and costume design flash onscreen, the Milland puppet's wrists suddenly go alarmingly limp.

André de Beranger). In this case André's interest in the heroine is as more than a mannequin, and despite his froufrou manner he makes his lustful intentions clear. Eve (Olive Borden) is not attracted, yet she stays on at his salon because she loves wearing his clothes. *Fig Leaves* was only the second film directed by Howard Hawks, an unequivocally heterosexual man who somehow revisited gay subthemes in his films again and again. At one point in *Fig Leaves* the hero's sidekick mimics runway technique by posing with hand on swinging hip, looking for all the world like a battered refugee from Madame Lucy's. Again, with the camera close up, it looks as much like a parody of nelliness as it does of fashion models. A few months after *Fig Leaves* came a fuller-strength portrayal than either de Beranger or Arthur. *Exit Smiling*, produced by MGM, featured two screen debuts: its star, Beatrice Lillie, and, in a major supporting role, Franklin Pangborn. The silent film's fascination with the theatre was again apparent, as Lillie played a slavey doing menial work for a low-grade itinerant troupe. Pangborn played—no, not a costume designer—the troupe's leading man/ham, given the revealingly ornate name Cecil Lovelace. Cecil is a one-man hissy fit, and naturally Lillie bears the brunt of much of his tantruming. Even this early, Pangborn's looks and manner caused him to be typecast; his appearance was not of leading-man caliber, a virile demeanor was nowhere in evidence, and he seemed far better suited to comedy than anything else. So he began to specialize in nervous characters with a certain frazzled dignity and an equivocal sexuality. If the roles he played most often skirted issues of sex, the message was delivered with sufficient impact to anyone willing to listen. Cecil Lovelace, while demonstrating some of the Pangborn persona, is actually nastier than the characters the actor usually portrayed. It would take the coming of sound for Pangborn's inherent likability to emerge. Not that many had the chance to experience his advent onscreen: *Exit Smiling* was a monumental flop, listed in exhibitor polls as the film that audiences liked least in late 1926.

Pangborn's Lovelace was one of the templates for a similar performance in a late silent, *The Matinee Idol* (1928). As with *Fig Leaves*, it's an early work of an esteemed director—one of Frank Capra's freshman efforts for fledgling Columbia Pictures, and until recently thought lost. Bessie Love stars as the leading lady of a twelfth-rate Podunk theatrical troupe suddenly imported to Broadway for the sole purpose of making the sophisticates laugh condescendingly (some of Capra's Heartland themes were already coming into play). One major member of the troupe is, as a title card tells us, "Eric Barrymaine, who played deep-dyed villains with a soprano voice." He is portrayed, silently yet eloquently, by David Mir, a Russian-born actor and costume designer with a willowy figure, big eyes, and pencil-line mustache—all traits that would serve as shorthand for cinema sissies for years to come. Whatever his personal life or

A masquerade party to remember in *The Matinee Idol*. From left, Lionel Belmore, Sidney D'Albrook, Johnny Walker, Bessie Love, and David Mir as the dashing Eric Barrymaine. *Photofest*

theatrical gifts (his bows look more like curtsies), Barrymaine is a valued part of the company, and is only put down by the big-city outsiders. When the hero (Johnny Walker), a Broadway actor working incognito with the troupe, first sees Eric, he asks one of the other actors, "Who is that, Helen of Troy?" But note that Eric is stoutly and immediately defended as being "a great actor!" Later, when he first sets foot in a Broadway theater, a burly stagehand immediately gets the message, suddenly mincing, batting his eyes, waving one hand flittingly, and calling out "Whoops, dearie!" Eric, who doesn't understand this mockery, seems hurt and confused—Capra seems to imply that the man is still a stranger to his own sexuality, or at least to the stereotypes he seems to evoke. Later, he recovers sufficiently to attend a masquerade party, for which he dons a short dress, pantalettes, and Mary Pickford curls—again in all innocence despite the Bo Peep-on-drugs couture. As before, no one in the troupe bats an eye, and at the end of the film, after the company's Broadway adventure, he's back to menacing Bessie Love in tent-show melodramas. His integration into his own theatrical family is complete, accepted, and happy. He may be as deficient in self-awareness as he is in acting ability, but as Mir's performance clearly shows, he thrives in his milieu. Unlike the many cinema sissies who were tossed in as quick seasoning in short scenes, this one is a prominent part of the texture of the film, and since there were scores of backstage comedies produced in the 1920s it's tempting to ponder what other lost low-budget films out there might feature characters similar to the obliging Mr. Barrymaine.

The worlds of fashion and theatre depicted in the films discussed so far were expected places for gay (or at least excessively aesthetic) men. Placing such characters in ill-fitting settings, however, was a different and less beneficent proposition. Incongruity has eternally been a comedy staple, and on occasion it would be supplied by gay characters used to provide some fairly unkind laughs. A staggeringly obscure western from 1927, *Wanderer of the West*, is so second-hand that its star is the lesser-known sibling of a popular cowboy actor—Kermit Maynard (here called Tex), brother of Ken. For whatever inconceivable reason, *Wanderer* drags in a store clerk named Clarence (a name frequently serving as the signal for a gay character), played by Al Rogers, who is announced by a title card as "One of Nature's mistakes in a country where men were men." There are reminiscences here of *Algie, the Miner* as well as *The Soilers* and Johnny Arthur in *The Monster*, but here more than in other films the character is regarded as unwelcome, alien, an expendable aberration. The "Nature's mistake" line sounds like something from Dr. Laura Schlesinger, while the insistent tone of "where men were men" reminds us again of gay men as the horrible threat to straight masculinity. This lavender-fish-out-of-water gambit would come back again and again, with pretty much the same distasteful effect, into the twenty-first century. The joke in *Wanderer of the West* is supposed to be on Clarence, although ultimately it's on filmmakers trying to score a couple of paltry yuks in their $1.98 western.

So—where are the women? In twenties cinema (as later on), the onscreen portrayals of gay or disputable sexuality tend to be dominated by men. But a fascinating film from 1925 decidedly tilts the balance. *My Lady of Whims* is one of dozens of low-budget efforts in which Clara Bow appeared prior to becoming a top star. With her "It" Girl identity yet to be established, Bow played everyone in everything, up to and including a misbegotten adaptation of, no fooling, *The Rime of the Ancient Mariner*. *Whims*, adapted from a magazine serial called "Protecting Prue," was a wan harbinger of her ultimate identity as the hottest of all jazz babies. It heralded a few other things as well, being an early cinematic look at that bohemian Sodom, Greenwich Village. Bow starred as Prudence Severn, an heiress and budding novelist who deserts upper-class stuffiness and moves to the Village "for atmosphere." She sets up housekeeping with Wayne Leigh (Carmelita Geraghty), a slightly older and visibly protective sculptor. ("I express myself in clay," Wayne announces.) Smelling trouble, Prudence's father

As *My Lady of Whims*, Clara Bow is chatted up by Donald Keith, while her roommate, sculptor Wayne Leigh (Carmelita Geraghty), tries to contain her jealousy.

sends adventurous young Bart Greer (Donald Keith) to the Village to bring her back home "before it's too late." The expected complications are piled on until the equally predictable fade-out of Prue and Bart embracing.

Its elegant title and potentially racy plot imply that *My Lady of Whims* might be quite a romp. But as produced by unimaginative trolls at a penny-ante studio (Arrow Pictures), it's a dead duck, so ineptly assembled that Clara Bow's costume in her first scene changes completely from one shot to the next. Its evocation of Village atmosphere consists of a small street set that could be Sioux Falls, and the script is more intent on delivering would-be zingers than it is in developing characters or plot. All this ineptitude is probably responsible for the portrayal of Wayne as implicitly something more than a roommate. Had this film been produced at a respectable large studio, the character would have been eliminated altogether or had her name feminized or been made into a man-crazy flapper. Here, as portrayed by the tall and slender Geraghty, she is reserved, composed, and clearly in charge. When Bart first barges in and introduces himself to Prue, there are two close-ups of Wayne glowering, and later, when Prue impulsively decides to run off with a roué, she tenderly caresses Prue's face and asks her if she really wants to elope. At one point Bart's sidekick warns him, "This district is fulla wise-crackin' dames and you ain't safe alone!" Yet—and typically, even with all the implications—Wayne is wedged into an absurd romance with the imbecilic sidekick, who apparently has forgotten his aversion to wisecrackin' dames. Despite this, the underlying message seeps through clearly, from the character's name all the way down the line. One critic quite properly noted of the film's confused characterizations that "the motives or intent of the characters . . . are not properly emphasized. The result is that you are left guessing in several places as to the why or wherefore of the proceedings." For certain women in the audience taking note of Wayne's severity versus Prudence's frilliness, the real why and wherefore required little guessing.

Wayne is an early and comparatively softened example of a particular stereotype in twenties and thirties films: the severely tailored, mannish woman unawakened by the love of the right man. This character stands at an opposite end from other paradigms of the twenties—the jazz baby (Bow, Colleen Moore), the madonna (Lillian Gish, Dolores Costello), and the mature, sexually aware woman (Norma Talmadge, Greta Garbo). The object seems to be that of a tease: flirt with the notions of lesbianism or at least equal rights with men, but ultimately pull back from any dangerous implications. The Repressed Mannish Spinster (RMS) turns up often in the late silent and early sound eras. And there's no mistaking the shorthand intentions behind her existence: her closely clipped hair, tailored tweeds, a monocle sometimes, and a general disdain for all things male spell out a simplified distillation of *Well of Loneliness* Lite.

Most typically, the RMS would appear in supporting roles or even bits, mostly as a foil for the leading woman. Several times she got to headline in a film. *The Clinging Vine* (1926) featured Leatrice Joy as a severe and successful businesswoman, A[ntoinette]. B. Allen, who, when overhearing someone decry her lack of feminine charm, decides she would prefer the love of a good man and undergoes a makeover. Her close-fitting suits are replaced by frilly organdies, and she learns to flirt and bat her eyes. In this case, the character's supposedly deficient femininity was synonymous with her hard-driving business ethic—and neither, the movie ultimately says, are what women should be. Antoinette was the grandmother of the Rosalind Russell–style comic businesswomen in 1940s comedies, but with a harder, more sexually ambivalent edge.

A PICTURE OF THE STARTLINGLY DIFFERENT WOMAN OF TOMORROW.
IT'S FOR EVERY WOMAN WHO'S EVER SAID—"GOD, I WISH I WERE A MAN!"
FOR EVERY MAN WHO'S EVERY SAID—"WHAT'S THE MATTER WITH THESE
MODERN WOMEN?"

Thus ran print ads for *The Crystal Cup* (1927), the champion RMS film of its day. For genuine ambiguity, the plot of this one, adapted from a 1925 novel by Gertrude Franklin Atherton, wins the palm:

> After she sees her father mistreat her mother, heiress Gita Carteret (Dorothy Mackaill) becomes emotionally scarred and develops an intense hatred of all men. Dressing in the most masculine of clothes, she abandons all feminine mannerisms and pursuits. Under duress, she attends a fancy ball, where her tuxedo draws gasps as well as the admiration of two men, John Blake and Dr. Geoffrey Pelham. After being warned that her behavior is spawning potentially harmful gossip, she coerces Blake into an in-name-only marriage. While Blake works on a novel, she becomes close friends with Pelham, developing an attraction to him that frightens her. Blake eventually becomes frustrated at the platonic nature of his relationship with Gita, and bursts into her room one night. Terrified, Gita shoots him, and as he dies he realizes that she and Pelham belong together. Now cured of her hostilities, Gita dons feminine attire and embraces Geoffrey.

Alas, *The Crystal Cup* seems to be a lost film, so it's impossible to know just how strangely its trash-compacted mix of dimestore Freud and *True Confessions* came off. Reviewers (as opposed to critics) in 1927 generally liked it, with special praise reserved for Dorothy Mackaill's adept characterization, natty manner with men's fashions, and the tough-guy way she lit matches by striking them on her thumbnail.[7] In such a factory-crafted entertainment, it's safe to assume that most of the plot's psychosexual underpinnings went untouched, as the critic for *Motion Picture News* observed: "Had it been treated honestly it might have stirred up some agitation. But the idea was developed with half an eye on the box-office, consequently its pathological suggestions are but faintly indicated." Spectators, then, could enjoy the spectacle of the luscious Mackaill butching it up as a man-hater, and those so disposed would be turned on by seeing her in trousers—all with the full knowledge that she'd be a frock-donning butterfly by the time it was over. In both this and *The Clinging Vine* were admonishments to women's independence, plus warnings on the perils of straying too far from conventional femininity. Unlike the Madame Lucys and Eric Barrymaines of twenties cinema, who were at least allowed to flourish in their own milieu, there was no room for women who aspired to something more, or different, than tradition.

At least one twenties film gave an unapologetic glimpse (and that's the word) of lesbianism. It's in a later Clara Bow film, the Academy Award–winning blockbuster *Wings* (1927). In the big Folies-Bergères scene midway through the movie, the camera tracks forward past tables of various habitués—some loving,

---

[7]She had borrowed (and perhaps even learned) the one-handed trick from western star William S. Hart, and reprised the routine in 1931 when she played a tough hooker in *Safe in Hell*.

While her grandmother (Edythe Chapman) cautions her to lighten up, man-hating Gita Carteret (Dorothy Mackaill) remains tweedily insouciant in *The Crystal Cup. Photofest*

some fighting. In the former category is a pair of young women in suits (skirts, not trousers), their eyes locked on each other. One reaches over and delicately caresses the other's cheek. Perhaps this was director William Wellman's way of condemning French liberality, but most likely it was meant simply as a bit of spicy scene-setting. "Oooh, la la, ze French are zo naughty" and all that. Unlike the embracing couple in *Manslaughter*, there are no judgments, condemnations, or punishments—just a Parisian couple in love, and seen by tens of millions of people in a smash hit. Few if any of these millions of viewers, by the way, saw fit to write Paramount or Congress in protest of this bit of lesbian love.

Wings is also notable for the all-but-palpably homoerotic behavior of its leading men, Richard Arlen and Buddy Rogers. Throughout the movie they seem far more bonded to each other than to female leads Bow and Jobyna Ralston, and under the circumstances, the characters' names, David and John(/Jack), are particularly significant. "Surpassing the love of women" indeed. Likely the director's own memories of First World War flyer-buddyship factored in but, perhaps inadvertently, the two actors are so dreamy-looking, and genuinely beautiful, that it's hard not to read subtext into it. For later and somewhat wised-up audiences who made jokes about Paul Newman–Robert Redford buddy pics, this one would really have been an eye-opener. In 1927 the majority of viewers were content to see two movie stars playing good friends—and, just as surely, some men in the audience could let their minds stray to what could be going on. The kinship/romance reaches its peak during Arlen's prolonged death scene, cradled in Rogers's arms, the two of them stroking each other's hair as Buddy murmurs, "Nothing means more to me than your friendship!" At this point in the scene, audiences at latter-day *Wings* screenings have been known to grow impatient for the implication to come to the surface. They begin to shout, nearly en masse, "Kiss him! Kiss him!" Which Rogers finally does, and on the lips.

With its enormous flight and combat scenes, *Wings* was state of the art in 1927, one of the outsized spectacles Hollywood produced just prior to the hysterical rush to sound. One of the last lavish silent productions caught in the transitional shuffle was D. W. Griffith's *Lady of the Pavements*, which was shot in 1928 and released in 1929 with a few tacked-on talking and singing scenes. Appearing only in the silent portion was the redoubtable Franklin Pangborn, cast as a dancing teacher cowed into submission by the volatile Lupe Velez. In the two-plus years since *Exit Smiling* he had stayed busy as a supporting actor, in *Getting Gertie's Garter* (1927) even playing a character named Algy. There had been one big opportunity for him as well: the lead in a *Charlie's Aunt*-style farce called *My Friend from India*. Though it afforded him the opportunity for exotic disguises, Pangborn as a playboy who finally gets the girl was not something calculated to bring in the customers. *My Friend from India* flopped, and Pangborn moved back to supporting roles. By the time he made *Lady of the Pavements*, in fact, he had already made the transition to sound in one of the first all-talkies, Warner Bros.' *On Trial* (1928). Alongside him in the supporting cast of *On Trial:* Johnny Arthur. The coming of sound film—one of the most rapid and chaotic cultural revolutions in history—would be giving cinematic gayness a voice in more ways than one.

TWO

Speaking Plainly

SCENE: *Women's chorus dressing room in a Broadway theater*

The chorus, in costume, begins to rush out the door to go onstage. They are intercepted at the doorway by an agitated costume designer.

COSTUME DESIGNER: Girls! Girls! Be careful of my hats!

A tall wardrobe woman lumbers over to confront him

WARDROBE WOMAN: I *told* you they were too high and too wide!

COSTUME DESIGNER (*putting one hand on hip and fixing a withering gaze on her*): Well, Big Woman, I design the costumes, not the doors for the theater!

WARDROBE WOMAN: I know that. If you had, they'd have been done in *lavender!*

COSTUME DESIGNER (*in disdain*): Hmmmph!!

It was the first movie musical, the template for everything that has come afterward. *The Broadway Melody*, which opened early in 1929, was the first all-talking film made by Hollywood's biggest studio, MGM, and the first sound film to win an Academy Award as Best Picture. It loomed as large as *The Jazz Singer* in introducing the public to the new talkies—and movie audiences to the sound as well as the sight of an unequivocally gay character.

History books and documentaries do not exaggerate when they speak of a "talkie revolution": at few times in modern history has so much changed with such speed and chaos. Audiences' perceptions were refitted, viewing habits were upended, methods of production and exhibition were completely over-hauled, careers were ended and begun, fortunes were made and lost—all in a matter of months, with the world watching and a microphone picking it up. In some ways it was bonanza time, for the astronomical film grosses in 1929 seemed to justify the technical glitches, halting technique, and chronic ineptitude. Artistically, the "All Talking! All Singing!! All Dancing!!!" era was a noisy mixed bag, and so it would be for gay characters onscreen. The dialogue exchange quoted above would have seemed innocuous written out on silent-film titles; for audiences to *hear* the wardrobe woman's steely tones juxtaposed with the breathy outrage and harrumphing of the costume designer was a whole different and audible proposition. For better and worse the microphone made all the difference.

Fueled by gab and noise, early sound films took easy advantage of the new dimension. There was talk without cease, naturally, and jangly sound effects, plus music whenever possible. Musicals burst onto the talkie scene as a full-blown new genre, dominated by the studios' singular, even relentless penchant for backstage stories. *The Broadway Melody*, smash that it was, paved the way for dozens of imitators. Besides their musical numbers, often splashed in early Technicolor, these backstage movies offered a regimented lexicon of Xeroxed characters and stock situations. There was all the slangy dialogue that theatre folk allegedly throw around, which was a great way to show off the microphones, and there were all the prototypes: the sister act or song-and-dance man trying for a big break, the beautiful unknown being discovered, the harried producer, the lecherous stage-door johnny. Plus the gay designer or other functionary. Because of musicals, gay male characters—to use perhaps a more appropriate name, sissies—were more evident than they had ever been. The designer in *The Broadway Melody*, Del Turpe, is portrayed by Drew Demarest, a fortyish actor of medium height, thin of hair and frame, with unmemorable features and a voice that seems to drawl and whine simultaneously.[1] Regardless of the size of his hats, Turpe is a movie pioneer, the first of his audible breed and also something of a summation of everything gay in American cinema up to 1929. Madame Lucy's influence is obvious, Turpe shares with Cecil Lovelace a peevish temperament, and like Eric Barrymaine (though obviously far more talented and accomplished) he's accepted in his own milieu. Like Eric also, and like Algie, the miner, he is a sitting duck for harassment, and the movie intends to present the ridicule as at least partly justifiable. Turpe gushes and simpers over the beauty of one of his costumes, finally erupting in manic schoolgirlish gig-

---

[1]Although the name Del Turpe is not spoken on the screen, it appears in the movie's credit sheet. During his twenty-year film career, Demarest sometimes used the spelling Demorest. Not that the need arose very often onscreen: he most commonly played bit roles and received no billing. The wardrobe woman is, alas, unidentified, although as a possibly gay character, she also rates a mention; she does seem fond of touching the showgirls, and her physical appearance is, well, big.

Dress rehearsal jitters pit costume designer (Drew Demarest) against wardrobe woman in *The Broadway Melody.*

gles. His voice annoys his boss, Zanfield [*sic*], who threatens him with "You'll giggle yourself right out of a job one of these days!" Evidently he's meant to annoy the audience as well, not least in the way that his voice joins with his mannerisms to reinforce the stereotypes. Not only does his gayness cause him to run afoul of his boss and the Big Woman who complains about his hats, but he's also harassed by a bystander. One of the yes-men who shadow the show's backer, hearing Turpe go on about a costume, minces, "It's the most gorgeouseth thing I've ever seen, you sweet little cutie!" He isn't particularly trying to imitate Turpe's voice, not even his giggle; instead, he goes for a generic fag imitation, complete with a lisp that Turpe lacks. This hanger-on receives no reprimand, and as Turpe leaves the scene and the film, he has clearly felt himself used as the butt of jokes. This is likely not his first contact with such rudeness, and presumably he will follow this hit show with similar revues, similar gowns, similar battles with wardrobe women, and more ridicule. Perhaps here *The Broadway Melody* is giving its audience more realism than it intended. Brief as it is, this moment seems to strike at the taunts and torments gays and lesbians have endured for eons, from schoolyard teasing all the way to Matthew Shepard. Not that Turpe is alone, for there is in fact a whole crowded assortment of backstage archetypes on display in *The Broadway Melody*, drawn with cynical relish: the temperamental tenor, the spiteful chorus girl, the budget-minded producer, and the smarmy stage-door lech waiting to land the next willing victim. The sissy designer actually gets off lighter than most of the others, especially the tenor, who is so obnoxious that one of the stagehands tries to drop a spotlight on him. Amidst all this, Turpe still seems to stand out. Perhaps it has something to do with the novelty of seeing someone so clearly gay in such a conspicuous position, and also hearing that word *lavender* directed at him with such force. By 1929 the word *lavender*, like *fairy* or *pansy*, had one principal connotation. (*Gay* was also in use at that time, but not as widespread as these.) The wardrobe woman is clearly not on good terms with Turpe; obviously they've clashed before, and if he can razz her for her size, she can use that buzzword to zero in on his swishiness. The sight and sound of that wardrobe woman barking out that word was a sure sign to millions of viewers that moviegoing had changed radically in just a few months' time. A preliminary script of *The Broadway Melody* had in fact gone even further with Turpe by extending his scene in the dressing room and having him run on to greater heights of irritation. After he leaves in a huff, the nasty chorine turns to the others and laughs, "Don't mind him. She's just one of us!" Whoever "she" was, the role and the performance set the pattern for backstage films for the next few years.

Before *The Broadway Melody* had even started filming, a far different musical was in progress at Warner Bros., although various complications delayed its release until spring 1929. It's stretching things a little to call *The Desert Song* a movie musical, for while it has a full quota of songs, it's basically a movie only in the sense that microphones and cameras loaded with film were used to record it.[2] On Broadway it had been one of the most popular operettas of the twenties. On film, despite the music and hammy skullduggery, it's early-talkiedom at its most stringent, and only the music and some of the performances keep it from being a sedative as a movie.

Nothing else in this *Desert Song* can compare, at any rate, with Johnny Arthur, who is far more vivid in sound than he had been in silents. As Benny Kidd, a society reporter supposedly in Morocco for his health, he is first seen as a pair of loud plaid knickers billowing over a skinny backside. Natty in his beret and sweater, he's captured and dragged into the desert camp of the dissident Riffs, and then starts to talk:

---

[2]For more on *The Desert Song* and all the other pioneer movie musicals, the reader is directed, with due modesty, to my book *A Song in the Dark: The Birth of the Musical Film* (1995).

FIRST RIFF: Ahhhh . . . a spy!

SECOND RIFF: Speak!

BENNY (*to Second Riff as he dusts himself off*): How's everything, big boy?

FIRST RIFF: He's a spy—let's kill him!

BENNY: Stop! Don't do that! Do you want everybody to hate you? Don't be so effeminate! Where do you think you are, in Chicago? You can't do this to me, I'm an American—United States.

SECOND RIFF: What are you doing in Morocco?

BENNY: Nothing. Make me an offer.

SECOND RIFF: Search him.

(*First Riff starts feeling in Benny's back pocket. Benny flinches and jumps.*)

BENNY: Ohhhh, don't do that—I'm funny that way!

And so it continues, Arthur's wrists waving and his eyes popping all the while. On Broadway the role had been played by Eddie Buzzell, a breezy wisecracker of a musical comic. His Benny was a standard comic second lead, a smart-aleck hypochondriac whose yellow streak compels him to flee from both desert bandits and his flirty secretary Susan. In casting Arthur in the role, Warner Bros. obviously assumed that one comic was as good as another, no matter how non-breezy. The result is a constant subversion of the author's intent. In Arthur's gesticulating hands, Benny's hypochondriasis is transformed into a neurosis flaming enough to illuminate the desert sky. As Susan, Louise Fazenda pursues Arthur so tirelessly that a viewer can only construct an alternative script having to do with repression, denial, and plain stupidity. On Broadway the highlight of this secondary romance had been the song and dance "It" (as in Sex Appeal). The dialogue lead-in to the number remains in the film, but the song was either never filmed (it's hard to picture Arthur carrying a tune) or cut before the premiere. Without "It," and with the casting of Arthur, the whole relationship becomes inconsonant beyond reckoning. In an equivalent silent version it all might have worked, albeit strangely. But Arthur's distinctive way with his mock-ambivalent lines seems to indicate only one thing.

By statement or inference, plan or accident, *The Broadway Melody* and *The Desert Song* instituted a tradition of gayness in musical cinema. The trend continued promptly in the second backstage musical made in that 1929 torrent of hoofers, chorines, and big Broadway breaks. *Syncopation* is a forgotten film, little seen for seven decades, with some historical significance as one of the first sound features shot in New York and as the first release of a newly inaugurated studio, Radio Pictures, presently RKO. Early talkies made in New York had a way of looking drab and cramped; this one, shot at the Pathé Studio in Harlem, is Exhibit A. The mythic grandeur (as it were) of *The Broadway Melody* is nowhere found in this stale and cheaply done story of a vaudeville dance team that breaks up after making the big time. Nevertheless, one character stands out in this dreary procession: Sylvester Cunningham, a terminally snooty interior decorator who makes the temperamental Del Turpe look like Father Flanagan. As personified by British actor Mackenzie Ward, Sylvester is as thin and affected as the cigarette holder he grandly lofts, as unnecessary as the French phrases that glaze his conversation. He serves one plot function only: to demonstrate what happens when Flo (Barbara Bennett), the ambitious half of the dance team, loses touch with her roots and tries to go highbrow without her earthy husband Benny (Bobby Watson). All it takes is a limp-wristed handshake and one utterance of "Tout ensemble!" for Benny to get Sylvester's number: "Better not open the window," he cracks, "he's liable to fly away!" And later: "Good luck with your next batch of fudge!"[3] In Sylvester's every scene, his haughty air and cigarette holder make him a walking symbol of the false values Flo covets until she flops on her own and returns to Benny and vaudeville. *Syncopation*'s production schedule overlapped with that of *Melody*, and it was based on a novel to boot, so it's unlikely that Sylvester's superficial resemblance to the Turpe character was intended. That coincidence was a harbinger of what musicals could contain. Mackenzie Ward made a sufficient Sylvesterish impression to rate reviewer comments—one of the few times in those days that a gay character was singled out as such. *Variety*'s "Bige" praised Ward's contribution and, using one of the less venerable gay euphemisms, termed Sylvester "a nance interior decorator."

In these first three movie musicals the power of sound film gave the portrayal of gay characters yet another basis—the vocal—in which to ground the roles and the stereotypes. Two trends for the talkies are already noticeable. One has the character and characterization all there in the writing, as with Turpe in *Broadway Melody*. It had been predetermined that the costume designer would follow tradition and be an effeminate gay man, after which the casting was consistent with that and the actor took it from there. With *The Desert Song*, even when the role had originally skirted such contours, the force of the actor outweighed the initial intent; casting could confer on sound cinema a stronger and stranger impact than anyone realized. The result would be sufficiently lavender to be apparent to most viewers even without being signaled by another character's observations. Sound heightened those observations as well, for hearing that yes-man mimic Turpe and equate a lisp with his nonmasculinity was more vivid than the mockery in silent films. Nevertheless, and despite Sylvester's hauteur

---

[3]The joke, actually, was more on Benny, or at least Bobby Watson, than on Sylvester. After this one brief brush with leading-manhood, Watson himself became, in effect, the biggest fag in movies. As one of the most frequent and visible portrayers of gay characters in pre-1935 films, he will be heard from again in these pages. Loudly.

and potential for fudge-making, the portrayals of gay characters in these early musicals, and gays and lesbians in early (before the enforced Production Code) sound cinema in general, was fairly matter-of-fact. Certainly they were used for occasional laughs, but as often as not they were in on the joke as well. When there was mockery, it most often came from yahoos (*Broadway Melody*) or the military (*Sailor's Luck*). Surely this did not imply widespread acceptance . . . but the generally positive nature of the characters needs to be emphasized, especially when compared with the horrors in store when gays became visible in cinemas once again three and more decades later.

After *The Broadway Melody* and *Syncopation*, with their vivid gay men, the remaining 1929 musicals were diligent, if seldom emphatic, with their gay characters. Sometimes a gay character or reference was more necessary to the general ambiance than to the drama. In *Why Bring That Up*, for example, a panning camera picks up various details of backstage activity, including a pair of chorus boys. One of them enthuses to the other, "And my new drapes are the most lovely shade of lavender." It's barely audible, almost subliminal, as if director George Abbott felt he had to do it but didn't want it to provide too much of a distraction from the main plot.[4] Similarly, in *Gold Diggers of Broadway*, a running gag has comedian Winnie Lightner forever rehearsing a line ("I am the Spirit of the Ages, and the progress of civilization") and always getting it wrong. At one point she comes out with "I am a fai . . . a fai . . . No, I'm not a fairy!"

Madame Lucy him/herself, George K. Arthur, also turned up in a backstage yarn, MGM's *Chasing Rainbows* (shot in 1929, released in 1930). Designed as a touring-company clone of *Broadway Melody*, it had the same stars (Charles King and Bessie Love) and some of the same situations. Obviously it was felt that the Del Turpe/Drew Demarest "magic" required replication as well, for preliminary scripts clearly tag the Arthur character as the leading man's glaringly effeminate valet. By the time it was on the screen the role had been toned down, at least in part through Arthur's performance, which pulled away from the gay implications even more strongly than in *Irene*. That other Arthur, Johnny, figured prominently in *She Couldn't Say No*, also a 1929–30 production and now evidently a lost film. It was a change-of-pace vehicle for the boisterous Winnie Lightner, going dramatic as a cabaret singer in love with a gangster, and for Arthur it was also more serious than usual. Playing her pianist, he supplied both sympathy and support—a 1929 equivalent of Roddy MacDowell in *Funny Lady* or, perhaps, Thelma Ritter in *All About Eve*.

No costume designers or other frilly types are in evidence in the behind-the-footlights epic *Glorifying the American Girl*, produced by Paramount at its

---

[4] In a movie starring a cork-faced vaudeville team known as the Two Black Crows, a casual gay stereotype is hardly the chief problem.

Long Island studio. The more subtle gay presence in it is offscreen, in the person of choreographer Ted Shawn. Though married for years to modern-dance pioneer Ruth St. Denis, Shawn was at very least bisexual, and his dances did not lack for homoerotic insinuation. Although the rather clumsy *Follies* ensembles of *Glorifying the American Girl* gave no scope to his abilities as a creator, they did allow him to flaunt his predilection for beefcake. Alone among early musicals, this one glorifies (or fetishizes) the American boy's form along with the girl's: several tableaux feature, along with the expected Ziegfeld beauties, an assortment of well-muscled hunks wearing very, very little. Their presence reflects Shawn's interest in the male body, both those of others and his own (into old age, he would send friends nude pictures of himself). Instead of the standard scrawny chorus-boy types, Shawn cast genuine athletes, among them Olympic champion Johnny Weissmuller in his first film appearance. Though publicity played up his presence, he received no billing, and his Adonis in the Technicolor "Loveland" finale never gets very close to the camera.[5]

The musical boom burned out in the spring of 1930, but even as it was tapering off, a couple of the later films were significantly gay. *Just Imagine* was, of all things, a science-fiction musical comedy set in the future (of 1980), with the expected gags arising when a Rip van Winkle from 1930 wakes up in the strange new world. As the awakened sleeper, Swedish-dialect comic El Brendel was, as was his wont, painfully unfunny—with the exception of one good line during *Just Imagine*'s climactic trip to Mars. Brendel and his cohorts are ushered in to meet the Queen of Mars, Looloo (Joyzelle), and her attendant Boko (Ivan Linow), who has the physique of a wrestler, the face of a thug, and the manner of a manicured French poodle. As Boko makes eyes at Brendel & Co. and smiles coyly, Brendel makes an obvious and funny observation: "She's not the queen—*he* is!" Even so, Boko is not treated with undue condescension or malice by either the Martians or the visitors. Like the theatrical types seen so far, he fits comfortably into his chosen environment. *Kiss Me Again* was a light operetta from Warner Bros. that showed how far technique and style had advanced in the two years since *The Desert Song*. Unfortunately, it was shot in mid-1930 and released in the no-musicals-wanted dog days of 1931, so few audiences availed themselves of a prime early piece of camp from the unexpected person of Frank McHugh. The amiably boobish character actor who seemed to head the supporting cast of every other Warner Bros. film of the 1930s costarred in *Kiss Me Again* as the henpecked manager of a chichi fashion salon. Compelled to look at but not touch all the gorgeous models, he sings "(I'll Always Be Just) a Make-Believe Ladies Man" to bemoan his frustration, to

---

[5]Three years later, when he signed with MGM, the studio pretended that *Tarzan the Ape Man* was his debut, and few were the wiser.

which the chorus of models responds by pulling him about and sticking various items of their apparel on him. Glitteringly done up in haute-garage-sale drag, he assumes poses and prances around the salon—an early version of voguing— until his wife catches him. Strutting along that wobbly borderline between gender inversion and gayness, McHugh displays a conspicuous relish at being so decked out. Given the hilarious juxtaposition of his dumpy frame with a model's runway attitude, the ultimate impression is that he's really enjoying it just a little too much. It possibly seemed like a straight (give or take a bit) comedy turn in 1931, but now it carries unavoidable and irresistible overtones.

With its comic drag and gay-friendly attitude, "Make-Believe Ladies Man" was typical of what comedians could get away with. So was one bit by the archetypal second-rate comedy team Bert Wheeler and Robert Woolsey in one of the biggest hits of 1929, *Rio Rita*. They sit together on the rail of a ship, each with a girlfriend perched on the other side. As the women chirp "Sweetheart, We Need Each Other," Wheeler and Woolsey pull at each other's ties, pinch one another's cheeks lovingly and then violently, and finally erupt into a slapping match. They sing the last line of the song to each other, kiss on the lips, and fall overboard. The musical theatre of the time was full of such comic traditions, giving wide latitude to jokes and behavior that today might seem too gay for many contexts. In some cases it was just a matter of being fey and whimsical in ways that burlesque and television comics rendered obsolete. In other instances, any sane viewer today will look at them and sputter a slack-jawed "What were they thinking?" Eddie Cantor, one of the most unequivocal of heterosexuals offstage, could on occasion seem just too precious, with his manically clapping hands and popping eyes. In *Whoopee!* (1930), the successful film version of his defining stage hit, he plays a scene with romantic lead Paul Gregory while almost constantly feeling and commenting admiringly on the bare-chested hunk's muscles. It's only a wee sliver of shtick, but nevertheless would hardly have been acceptable by a "regular" leading man instead of a comic. Nor, in all likelihood, would the scene in which Cantor and another actor compare surgical scars and look inside each other's pants. Some of Laurel and Hardy's bits involve similar comedy with clear gay undertones, as in their silent comedy *Liberty* (1929). As prison escapees trying to swap their uniforms for civilian attire, they are forever being interrupted by observers who, catching them literally with their pants down, can draw one conclusion only. It's the old gay-confusion gag as practiced by Chaplin and many others, but in *Liberty* it has significantly more of an edge. Instead of being mistaken for courtship, their actions are thought to be actual sexual activity—and *Liberty*'s audiences, like the onscreen bystanders, clearly were meant to get the message.

Of all the gays in early musicals, one stands apart, if not !out! Drew Demarest, who ushered them all in with snitty Del Turpe, reappeared in another of MGM's periodic attempts to recreate the *Broadway Melody* magic. *Lord Byron of Broadway* (1930) was an oddly downbeat story of an out-and-out heel of a songwriter, Roy (Charles Kaley), who makes fresh hay by sleeping his way to the top. Everything in his life, including a long string of women, is used as the basis for the songs he writes and performs. Hitching his wagon to a diva (Broadway singer Ethelind Terry, giving the most misconceived performance in movie-musical history), he gets the fame, the fancy duds, the swell apartment, and a butler-valet named Edwards, played by Demarest at his most restrained. Such stardom, ill-earned as it is, cannot last in stories like this, and Roy loses fame, money, diva, best friend, and true love . . . until, contrite, he finds forgiveness and redemption. At one point in Roy's slide gutterward, Edwards offers him money to help with the bills. The scene is blocked out so that Demarest is standing very close to Kaley, keeping his eyes fixed on him with a loving urgency that transcends that of even a devoted employee. Roy is too proud to accept the money, but the point has been made. It's highly unlikely that more than a handful of people who saw *Lord Byron of Broadway* had not already seen *The Broadway Melody*, and so they knew Demarest, who here receives prominent billing, as a flaming fruit with a thing for gorgeous garments. Edwards and Turpe are vastly different characters, of course, but Demarest bridges a great deal of the gap, and the quiet intensity of his gaze at Kaley bespeaks such a degree of unrequited between-the-lines love that it gives this peculiar film one of its best scenes.

The leitmotiv of this era, sound film's transformative power, had much of its longest lasting effect on the careers of silent stars. Some of these wordless icons were nearing a logical career finish anyway—Douglas Fairbanks was getting too old to continue his silent-screen calisthenics, and Mae Murray was {*choose any three*} (*a*) growing way overripe for her teasing-temptress roles, (*b*) the victim of blackballing by Louis B. Mayer, and (*c*) hands down, the most affected and deluded star who ever lived. Others were ready and rich enough to move on, such as Colleen Moore and Corinne Griffith, and presently Richard Barthelmess and Harold Lloyd. Some of the biggest of them—Mary Pickford, Gloria Swanson, Lillian Gish—were unable to reconfigure their silver-nitrated images and began to seem like another era's relics. Emil Jannings, Pola Negri, and Vilma Banky had difficulty with the language. Clara Bow and Buster Keaton had personal problems. Harry Langdon made bad career choices. Lon Chaney and Milton Sills died prematurely (as had Valentino, who didn't even make it to the talkies). Only a few had genuinely inappropriate voices, especially Norma Talmadge, who may have been the prototype for Lina Lamont in *Singin' in the Rain*. Conversely, others thrived: Wallace Beery, William Powell, and Marie Dressler all had career renaissances, Greta Garbo, Ronald Colman, Laurel and Hardy, and Norma Shearer all moved ahead undeterred, as did Lionel and (for a time) John Barrymore. Charlie Chaplin, meanwhile, danced unaffected above all the turmoil.

At the biggest of all the studios, three stars—MGM's A-list leading men— were put into tailspins. John Gilbert's fate has become legendary: an okay, ordinary voice, lousy roles, a drinking problem, and possibly some vindictiveness from the front office. With Ramon Novarro and William Haines it was different. Neither made any particular secret of being gay, much to Louis B. Mayer's chagrin, and though Novarro was extremely private, Haines was, for the time, quite proudly out in Hollywood society. In neither case was it felt that the actor couldn't or didn't make a successful transition to talkies. Novarro, in fact, attracted a great deal of attention with a trim tenor singing voice, and Haines's breezy silent-film wisecracking could translate onto sound film without too much fuss.[6] Yet both stars were hobbled by some of the factors that brought down their peers. Haines's Jazz-Age weisenheimers and Novarro's Ben-Hur heroes both seemed out of place in a new decade where the public was straining under the Depression crunch. Also, Haines had a modest weight problem, while Novarro's face grew puffy as he neared forty. More to the point, possibly, was the strange way in which sound film seemed to make them, especially Novarro, less romantically viable. Although neither was a so-called obvious (read: stereotypical) gay man, their voices, as paired with their slightly fading looks, did not necessarily contribute to the aura of conventional heterosexuality so relentlessly propagated by Hollywood then and Hollywood now. Would the same actors, if heterosexual, have fared the same way? Hard to say. In both cases there were extenuating circumstances. By the time Haines was involved in a scandal involving an alleged molestation, he had abandoned movies and was on his way to a successful career as an interior decorator. Novarro's decline was aggravated by alcoholism, which set up a vicious circle that affected both his career and his looks. Haines's third talkie, *Way Out West* (1930), is the only one in which his gayness truly seems to be a factor. As the title would lead us to expect, he plays an Eastern dude who finds himself, somewhat Algie-like, on a ranch—and naturally wisecracks and bungles his way to victory, winning the girl and getting the cowboys' respect. Less expected is the full compliment of gay affectations and jokes. Polly Moran plays a character named Pansy, and Haines jokes about her name with an untoward amount of relish. "I'm the freshest pansy you ever saw!" he chirps.[7] For

---

[6]At one point in 1929 he was announced for the lead in *Lord Byron of Broadway*, which would have been quite a change of pace.

[7]Perhaps not *the* freshest. An observation here that will, with luck, skirt snideness: by the time he made *Way Out West*, Haines had lost his trim (OK, boyish) figure. He spends a great deal of time in this movie in jeans, and turns his posterior to the camera quite a bit, and . . . Well, anyhow, a couple of years later he did slim down again.

anyone seeking gay text or subtext in any of Haines's movies, this is the one to study. Even without the later scandal or career decline, chances are that Haines would have been one of those silent actors who just wouldn't have made it over the long term in sound.

A search for truly gay hints in Ramon Novarro's film scripts yields no such nuggets as Haines's pansy cracks, not even in the evocatively titled 1930 opus *In Gay Madrid*. Then again, they don't really need to. Novarro's initial fame in silent film had been as a semi-second-string Valentino clone—then, as Ben-Hur, he reached front-rank stardom. Even with the heroics, there was something a little light about him. His features were as pretty as Buddy Rogers's, and his trim frame seemed a bit asthenic for rowing a Roman warship for months or winning a chariot race.[8] Even as these qualities were not necessarily going unnoticed by some critics, his films were popular and he was personally well liked. With *The Pagan* (1929), he surprised everyone by singing the hit "Pagan Love Song" on the synchronized soundtrack. Accordingly, the MGM powers thought that for the talkies Novarro should go operetta. Throughout the musical boom of 1929–30, he appeared only in light musicals that would compliment his soft-grained, Mexican-inflected tenor, and always in the company of a complementary and airy costar, the shrill ingenue Dorothy Jordan. *Devil May Care*, *In Gay Madrid*, and *Call of the Flesh* all earned profits, yet something seemed wrong. "Frankly, Ramon is one of the disappointments of the talkies," noted the British film journal *Picturegoer*, and so it was. MGM, protecting its investment, sought to prop up his career with a series of attention-getting roles. Most visibly, he was cast opposite Garbo in *Mata Hari*, and came out of it ludicrously outmatched: the idea that he might be the aggressor—"the man"—in this particular romance was undercut by every single thing seen and heard by the huge crowds attending *Mata Hari*. Garbo's authority and pansexual aura pointed up what the casting of Dorothy Jordan had not: as a leading man, Novarro was sweet, cute, and engaging, but he had neither the voice nor the manner of a virile lover as it was defined onscreen at the time. Sound had, in effect, outed him.[9] Over the next few years, MGM tried repeatedly to salvage his stardom and his image. Audiences were thus treated to a constellation of Novarros: as a college football

---

[8]Gay men have long appreciated the silent *Ben-Hur* for its high quotient of male flesh. If the homoeroticism was not precisely deliberate, it does seem inherent. Plus, on many levels it's also more fun than the remake.

[9]Novarro's troubled simulation of heterolust has a late-century equivalent in *Mr. Wrong* (1997), in which a pre-coming-out Ellen DeGeneres labored to make audiences believe in a screwball romance with Bill Pullman. While critics chose their words carefully, audiences read through the lines in the reviews and on the screen. Novarro in the thirties and DeGeneres in the nineties are exceptional cases, of course: lots and lots of gay performers—we'll never know just how many—have no difficulty in playing it straight on the screen. And, in many cases, off it as well.

hero in *Huddle*, a Chinese American in *The Son-Daughter*, a Native American in *Laughing Boy*, a return to the Valentino clonedom in *The Barbarian*, and finally back to musicals. More desperately, the studio attempted to stave off any whispers by manufacturing a romance with fellow MGM contractee Myrna Loy. Fake tabloid romances were nothing new, but this one seemed just a bit more purposeful and desperate: "A Secret Wedding for Myrna and Ramon?" heavy-breathed one article in 1933. "Ramon has never been one to talk about his love-life. . . . Were Myrna and Ramon dared by each other to penetrate their supposedly case-hardened exteriors?" Loy, who knew full well that Novarro was gay, was surprised, if not particularly amused, at hearing of the purported penetration, and finally the matter was dropped. Meanwhile, as the grosses dwindled and the aging process accelerated, the makeup department attempted to compensate by ringing his eyes in heavy eyeliner—not the most robust way to attack the problem. Soon there were roles at lower-rank studios and then semi-retirement, with Novarro retaining his leading-man dignity until the horrible end: his brutal murder in 1967 by a pair of hustlers.

Just as gay men were far more in evidence onscreen in this era, so it was behind the scenes. For straight and gay women alike there were fewer venues than for male designers, writers, and directors, but one prominent director's chair bore the name of an unapologetic and extremely talented lesbian. Dorothy Arzner was for many years the only successful woman film director in America, and not for nothing has her work become fertile territory for a generation of film scholars and feminists. There is little in the way of gay or lesbian romance in her films, yet the theme of female bonding that is a constant in her work sometimes echoes the male friendship of *Wings* as an indication of an affection different and occasionally greater. Exhibit A: Arzner's first talkie, *The Wild Party* (1929). Arzner, who had worked well with Clara Bow in silents, was entrusted with the delicate job of shepherding Bow's first uneasy appearance before the microphones. Just as in her silent smashes, Bow was rushed into a trashy story that allowed for minimal glimpses of her acting talent and maximum displays of her flesh. With her genial Brooklyn accent in occasional check, she tried her best to play Stella, a college student with a crush on professor Fredric March and a propensity for getting into trouble. No one in the audience was surprised that Clara would face expulsion from her stuffy all-female school, or that she and her dormmates spend more screen time in their underwear than in their classes. (They also cause a ruckus at a women's masquerade dance when they show up barely clad in skimpy tights. Ejected, they head for the nearest road-house to stir up trouble.) Even though the mid-twenties rage for college pictures continued well into the talkie era, the young women in Arzner's dorm seem just a bit more familiar with each other than those in other pictures. There is frequent and affectionate touching and caressing, and (shades of *My Lady of*

Whims) Stella has a special friend. Helen (Shirley O'Hara), the standard virginal-student-who-goes-wrong, confides in Stella, often while sitting on her lap. "I love her too," Stella sobs to Helen's caddish seducer. On paper, this drivel would read like any dimestore college romance; Arzner's staging, particularly of its dormitory intimacies, gives it a Johnny Arthur-like transformation into something palpably different. The reviews of *The Wild Party* preferred to remain on the subjects of Clara Bow's voice (some liked it, others didn't) and the general silliness of the material. Only occasionally did they single out the unusually fluent direction, and never did they speak of the uncommonly tight and personal bonds linking the 1930 graduating class of Winston College.

The Wild Party was simply a continuation, with sound, of the same commercial claptrap that had raked in the bucks in the silent era. Other early talkies went farther afield in search of material, to the point where the medium became a catchall for the most bizarre notions jammed alongside (and sometimes in the same film as) the most pedantic clichés. It was, and has remained, the most wide-open cinematic era since the birth of feature films. There were unceasing quests, in those first experimental years of talkiedom, for performers and stories to enhance and capitalize and cash in on all facets of the newfound audibility. Accordingly, in late 1929, a fly-by-night producer decided that it was time for the original Victor/Victoria, Julian Eltinge, to return to (as was memorably put in the first *A Star Is Born*) "the hurly-burly of the silver screen." *Maid to Order* was the basic Eltinge routine: a two-fisted detective (creatively named Julian Eltinge) foils a smuggling ring by posing as a nightclub chanteuse. Talkies gave Eltinge's art an additional layer, since he could sound like women as well as look like them, and in the course of *Maid to Order* he performed several songs. At the height of his fame in the late teens, this kind of thing might have found an audience, but not during an economic depression. In most places *Maid* did not run until 1932, and movies this cheap seldom played in good theaters. Apart from this, Eltinge was clearly aging. Like the divas he so proudly emulated with such allegedly heterosexual delight, he was now seeming less a coquette than a weary dowager.

Like *Maid to Order*, *The Dude Wrangler* (1930) was filmed on the cheap, and although its production company, Sono-Art, was one of the better-known independent studios, it lacked even *Maid*'s dubious prestige. As soon as it was possible for microphones to go out of doors, studios big and small returned to one of film's staple genres, the western. Sound enabled westerns to move, on occasion, from the standardized to the strange: this was where singing cowboys got started, and early talkie westerns could even stop dead in their tracks for unrelated musical sequences by specialty performers. *Pardon My Gun* (1930) had what appeared to be an entire vaudeville show spliced into the middle of it. *The Dude Wrangler* needed no musical performers to earn its status as an unconventional western. In no way, in fact, was it not a peculiar and seedy enterprise, designed in part to cash in on the fact that its stars, George Duryea and Lina Basquette, were former big names who had clearly stumbled. Two years earlier they were the leads in Cecil B. DeMille's heavily promoted flop *The Godless Girl*, and Basquette had figured notoriously in a child-custody trial following the death of her husband, Sam Warner, the most visionary of the Warner brothers. As with a number of silent actors lost in the talkie transition, they were reduced, by 1930, to taking Poverty Row jobs to make ends meet.

If *The Dude Wrangler* had been another cheap western, in this case a western comedy, it likely would have drawn no attention. The plot, adapted from a novel of the same name, superficially recalled that of the concurrent *Way Out West:* An aunt-dominated tenderfoot learns the ways of rugged westerners through the help of the girl who loves him, defeats his rival, and makes a go of his dude ranch. Nothing more than that, except a few comic bits and the presence of early-silent heartthrob Francis X. Bushman as the villain. Somehow, Sono-Art's publicity department smelled something gay in the air and (to mix metaphors torturously) put a stool under it and milked it for everything it could. The release of *The Dude Wrangler* coincided with a peaking phenomenon: possibly the first time since Ancient Greece that homosexuality was truly trendy. The club life in New York City, and a few other places as well, was under the lilac-scented influence of what promptly became known as "the Pansy Craze." Gay performers in, partially in, and out of drag became the rage, with such entertainers as Jean Malin and Karyl Norman becoming bona fide celebrities. So pronounced was the rage in New York that late 1930 saw the opening of a new night spot (Forty-eighth and Broadway) called the Pansy Club. Like most fads (hula hoops, the macarena, compassionate conservatism), it lasted only a short while . . . but oh, how brightly it blazed for that while.[10] Its effects were felt in movies over the next three years, and how odd that *The Dude Wrangler* was one of the first films to take the concept and prance with it. Its hero, Wally McCann, was portrayed onscreen as mild-mannered, even old-maidish, fond of chatting with his aunt's friends and exchanging recipes. But the ads dreamed up for *The Dude Wrangler* (see illustration) promised nothing less than an epic of pansydom, as if Clarence from *Wanderer of the West* had teamed up with Eric Barrymaine to open a bed and breakfast and hired Sylvester Cunningham to do the décor. While there was no way the film could live up to such hype, what is most significant is that the studio somehow felt that taking this tone would draw in the eager crowds. Evidently it was thought that an ordinary film would gain more attention than it warranted by spicing up the ads with a heavy dose of

---

[10]In a perhaps skewed tribute to the craze, a Broadway revue called *Sweet and Low* (1930) featured George Jessel's low-if-not-sweet rendition of "When the Pansy Was a Flower."

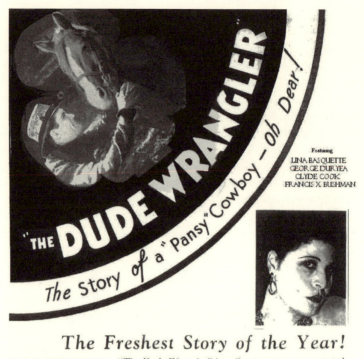

The Freshest Story of the Year!

"The Dude Wrangler" is a direct response to repeated requests by exhibitors for a relief from the sameness of the stories which have cluttered up our screens during the past year. Here is a comedy Western that tore the buttons off the vests of the critics at its preview. A wagon-load of laughs, sparkling dialog and swell trouping. Watch it set the industry talking!

Film Daily advertisement, May 1930. No comment necessary.

lavender. The precise target for these ads is a mystery. Were they supposed to appeal to sophisticated city folk? Uncertain, for while these were the people who went to pansy clubs, they rarely went to the movie houses that ran Sono's films. Rubes? They may or may not have known, or cared to find out, exactly what a pansy cowboy was. And since these ads ran in trade papers, was it thought that the pansy craze was so big that exhibitors would think a gay cowboy would create a box-office stampede? In any event there's no disputing that the ads were attention-grabbers; none of the major studios would ever have attempted so gamy a ploy. Contemporary reviews for *The Dude Wrangler* mentioned neither the ads nor anything about pansies, and after the standard lower-rung engagements, it disappeared without repercussion. Certainly it did nothing for Basquette or Duryea except help them to pay a few bills, and director

Richard Thorpe later moved to the opposite end of the Hollywood spectrum with a long tenure at MGM and such films as *Night Must Fall, Ivanhoe*, and *Jailhouse Rock*.[11] If a print of *The Dude Wrangler* exists today, it hasn't surfaced, but the advertising remains with us, and more than anything else, that's the heart of the matter. Without question, it's a weird demonstration of how prominent a place homosexuality, at least a certain stereotypical facet of it, could be presented in movies made at this time, and continue even as the pansy craze abated. Yet while the high profile remained, this kind of blatant "Oh, dear!" pitch to the public's curiosity about pansies would not surface again in mainstream cinema for another forty years, not until *The Boys in the Band* and *Staircase*. Besides demonstrating the far reach of the pansy craze, it seems to sum up the wide-open and bizarre nature of early sound films in general—anything to cause talk and be novel and make a buck. Pansies on the screen may not have been a major box-office draw, but they certainly could talk, and over the next four years they became increasingly less novel.

---

[11]He was also the initial director of *The Wizard of Oz;* his footage didn't work well and he was replaced. Never a distinguished talent, he fared better professionally than his stars. Basquette continued her colorful career and life with mixed success and immense verve, including a rendezvous with Hitler in the mid-1930s and a return to western terrain with the piquantly titled *Hard Hombre*. In her memoirs she mentions *The Dude Wrangler* only in passing. Duryea soon changed his name to Tom Keene, starred in King Vidor's *Our Daily Bread*, and then returned to low-budget westerns, dozens of them and not, oh dear, so much as one pansy cowboy. (One dingbat distributor did see fit to reissue *The Dude Wrangler* as a "straight" western, with the now-rechristened Keene listed as the sole star.) Near the end of his life Keene appeared in his most outré film since *The Dude Wrangler*, Ed Wood's *Plan Nine from Outer Space*.

THREE

Codes of Behavior

ostalgia is a temptation, high-gloss and rose-hued, and it can be a trap. It takes a clear head to be able to assess what parts of our pasts really do warrant the nostalgic longings that can sap our energies and preempt our desire to move ahead. One realm of nostalgia that does seem fully justifiable has to do with movies. Since the early 1980s, a great deal of affection and appreciation have been attached to a long-ago movie era that began roughly at the same time as the country was starting to feel the effects of the stock market crash, in mid-to-late 1930. It flourished for about four years, and came to a brusque end in mid-1934. It was a freewheeling age for movies, frank and fun, and it ended with a crackdown on cinematic morality by the Motion Picture Production Code and the Roman Catholic Legion of Decency. The shorthand for that era is "pre-Code," and as usual the term is inaccurate even as the nostalgia is comprehensible.

To call a film pre-Code is to evoke an age of movies at once grimy and glittery, when sin and crime could pay, murderers could walk away unpunished, couples could sleep in the same bed, and mothers could turn into hookers if there was a hungry mouth to feed. It was a time when film, while as prone as ever to make-believe, evoked more of a surface realism than was its wont. In a reflection of Depression anxieties, and to lure cash-poor spectators into movie houses, the movies became rawer and racier, sometimes more adult. Not necessarily of higher artistic quality, but with a certain validity that compensated for many shortcomings. Euphemisms took a holiday: characters who were not married were permitted to have sexual relations, sympathetic figures might have addiction problems, the government and other institutions would be heavily criticized, urban violence—both physical and emotional—was shown with unsettling immediacy, humor had a bitter edge, and it was clear that some people could be drawn romantically and sexually to others of their own sex. And yet this was not *prior* to the formulation of the Motion Picture Production Code. It was, rather, a nearly effortless, nose-thumbing defiance of it.

The Code began to lumber its way into existence late in 1929. The last silent films had seemed increasingly sex-driven and hedonistic to many—and then came sound, and suddenly more people were more uncomfortably aware of many things. With harsh clarity, sound erased illusion. Someone shot down on the silent screen was far less jarring absent the sound of gunfire. Innuendoes printed on silent title cards might be called spicy, yet when spoken aloud could suddenly sound uncomfortably intimate. Accordingly, and despite the enormous film grosses throughout 1929 and into 1930, some groups, many of them Roman Catholic, started to protest. Various organizations, mainly faith-based or women's groups, began letter-writing campaigns to the studios and to the Hays Office. These grass-roots movements were sufficiently well organized to hit on a common theme: they had had it with what the talkies were saying to American audiences.

The Roman Catholic Church, in particular, had by 1930 developed a fair amount of expertise in the area of film protest. Perhaps its proudest moment in this realm had come in 1927, when MGM released *The Callahans and the Murphys*, an "aren't-Irish-mothers-funny-when-they're-drunk?" roughhouse farce. The intersection of Irish and Catholic protest groups—lots of which, of course, were coexistent if not synonymous—made for a terrible racket. So loud were the objections that MGM went far beyond merely cutting or reshooting some scenes: it pulled the entire film from all distribution, literally never to be seen again. By the time some of the racier sound films were coming out two years later, the protesters had the routine down pat.

The Love Parade was a particularly large and glittery target for the protest groups. One of the biggest hits of late 1929, the Ernst Lubitsch operetta was both a critical and commercial smash, with Jeanette MacDonald sexually skirmishing with Maurice Chevalier amid a welter of sly remarks, visual puns, and risqué songs. That the entire erotic roundelay was done with consummate skill and taste was not enough to stave off the censoring hordes. Many areas of America were not prepared for a film that mocked sex, and for all its acclaim *The Love Parade* generated substantial hostility. Small towns in particular, which tended toward xenophobia, felt the whole thing to be a dirty joke made by foreigners at the expense of innocent Yankees. Soon the Hays Office was beset by a tide of neatly handwritten outrage. Other films drew fire as well, such as the raw service comedy-drama *The Cockeyed World* and the sophisticated *The Lady Lies*, with its tale of adultery told with dialogue containing a number of *damns* and *hells*. Censorship, which was usually executed by various state and city boards, was not doing its job with sufficient vigilance. For the moral guardians, appalled by the perceived excesses of the late silents, films such as these were portents of a national crisis.

Concurrent with the moralistic outrage was an unspoken undercurrent of mutual antipathy between Catholic moralists and Jewish movie moguls. Bigotry is always great fuel for moral outrage, and it was clear that peace had to be made in some way. Finally, a solution came in the form of a Motion Picture Production Code, a do's-and-don'ts group of rules and principles to govern American movies. It was written by a committee consisting almost entirely of Roman Catholic laymen and clergy, headed by Martin Quigley, the influential and conservative editor of the trade paper *Exhibitor's Herald.* His collaborators included his own parish priest, the editor of the Catholic magazine *America,* and Joseph I. Breen, a layman who worked for a number of Catholic organizations. Before its presentation to the film industry, the Code draft was edited and amplified by Fr. Daniel Lord, a movie-savvy Jesuit who had already served as a religious advisor to Cecil B. DeMille.

The Code, as it emerged from these men, was a moralistic laundry list of what would or wouldn't be right or *decent* for movies. There were principles both general (governing overall moral tone) and specific (prohibitions of vice, nudity, drugs, sexual perversion). Officials at the Hollywood office of the MPPDA would read all film scripts from major studios and would then comment on what was and wasn't permissible under the Code.[1] The producers would presumably employ their suggestions in the finished film, which would be viewed by Code people. Maintaining a watchful eye from the New York office was the legendary Will H. Hays, plus Martin Quigley with his widely read column. Having thus laid down the law, the reformers were pleased. So were the film moguls: dreading the moralists' interference and potential curtailment of profits, they retained a cunning perquisite. While agreeing to the Code and to having film scripts and productions governed by its strictures, they genially sabotaged the entire deal. Since the film industry was not specifically under the jurisdiction of the federal government, there was a question of authority if disputes arose between Code officers in the MPPDA and the studios. As it emerged, any disagreements would be taken to a board of arbitration . . . *made up entirely of studio executives.* The resulting rulings, not unexpectedly, did not tend to favor the Code. Were Quigley, Hays, and their fellows naïve? Did they have the blind faith to trust—of all people—movie producers? Actually, they were suspicious, but this deal was the only way that the code could be put into effect: the government was

---

[1]Over the four-decade history of the Production Code, both the official and informal names of its administering group changed frequently and sometimes confusingly. The overall group was the Motion Picture Producers and Distributors of America (MPPDA), which later became the Motion Picture Association of America (MPAA). In the pre-1934 days, the specific office dealing with Code affairs was the Studio Relations Committee. After the Code crackdown of '34, it became the Production Code Administration. Informally, the title varied: the Hays Office, the Breen Office, and later the Johnston Office. Such changes can play havoc with a historian's drive for trim consistency; even the letterhead on Code office correspondence seemed to change from week to week. The title, in fact, was pretty much the only flexible aspect of the Code.

not about to step in to handle this sort of dispute. To keep the peace, the studios would throw the Code people bones by acceding to changes in screenplays and permitting the occasional cut in a finished film.

The Code was ratified by the MPPDA on March 31, 1930, and Quigley's paper, among others, editorialized rhapsodically over the movies' new moral tone. With eerie precision, the Code took effect at the precise time that some massive changes were besetting the film industry. Audiences and studios alike were feeling the first effects of the Crash, and the first elated rush over the novelty of talking pictures was wearing off. Some highly touted films opened to disappointing returns, and by late summer film grosses were nosediving. The distress was heightened by a series of power struggles at several studios (particularly Fox), with receivership hovering just offscreen. The Jazz Age was over, the world suddenly seemed grim, and the Code would be used to govern an altered movie industry trying to appeal to changing tastes.

Homosexuality—termed "sex perversion" in the Production Code guidelines—was not the leading concern of Code officials or state censorship boards. Violence, excessive drinking, glorification of crime, and vulgar humor were all far more regular targets of the moralists, both under the national Code structure and with the still-empowered regional censors. Nudity and illicit sex, too, were far easier to regulate, insofar as regulation was possible. With free rein the unspoken rule of the day, both the baby and the bathwater were kept. The Code people fretted, made occasional cautionary suggestions, and did what they could to maintain smooth relations between the moralists and the studios. There was little, ultimately, that they could do to stop the studios from putting whatever content they wanted to in their films.

Movie history, as it has been handed down over seven decades, tells us about the famously daring pre-Code movies: *Scarface, The Story of Temple Drake, Baby Face, She Done Him Wrong*, and so on. What is seldom mentioned is the major onscreen presence during those years of gay and lesbian characters and allusions. Somehow, over the past few decades, some picturesque misapprehensions have arisen concerning the perception of homosexuality by the general public. These notions have even been given a title by some historians: "the gay exception." They posit that prior to the coming of the Stonewall riots and Gay Liberation, homosexuality, what little of it actually existed, was a matter of complete ghettoization, a thing completely alien to anyplace in America other than a few city blocks in Greenwich Village and San Francisco. Elsewhere in the country, it was unmentionable and all but unknowable. This went beyond "dare not speak its name" to somewhere near "nonexistent." The movies, this reasoning continues, were as shielded from gay forces as the rest of "normal" America; only a few slight hints of it crept in here and there to taint the respectability of clean pictures.[2] Not until somewhere in the mid-1990s was there any sort of public (or cinematic) acceptance of it. Or, if *acceptance* is too positive a word, perhaps *acknowledgment* will do. The elements of truth contained in this belief has more to do with the great American whitewashing of the 1950s—the Eisenhower and McCarthy years—which caused a great deal of history to go unattended and forgotten. The thriving gay and lesbian subcultures of the teens, twenties, and thirties get convincingly obliterated in a welter of licensed prejudice; such conspicuous things as the early-thirties pansy craze are naturally allowed to flame into oblivion. Fortunately, a large number of early 1930s films survive to serve as corrective. They were made to reflect the trends and views of their time, not create them. In so doing, they make some necessary revisionist history plainly obvious. This history can be stated as a three-point progression:

1. The millions of spectators going to movies in the early Depression years were frequently, even regularly, exposed to gay and lesbian characters on the screen.
2. A large number of those spectators in America as well as abroad knew plainly who these characters were and what they were about.
3. Those spectators, by and large, accepted the presence of these characters. Even when there was occasional ridicule or laughter, as existed with many cinema portrayals and archetypes, there was not *necessarily* judgment or condemnation.

In viewing these characters, we will see, surprise surprise, lots of caricature. A fair amount of condescension, too. Seldom will there be overt disapproval or even, as some gay historians have felt, the feeling that these people are too harmless to warrant the criticism or demonization. Hollywood, in those years, was just a bit more fair with its minorities, in some ways, than it later became. Silent film had already demonstrated that the portrayal of gays and lesbians would not follow one course only. Sometimes it reflected the prejudice or bogus psychology of the time, at times it was pejorative, and most commonly it reflected narrow stereotypical views—yet, very often, without malice. *The*

---

[2]Call it the "Don't ask, don't tell" theory, as inept and inappropriate as the policy applied to the U.S. military and perhaps emanating from some of the same forces. Fortunately, there is in this an entry in the Silver Lining Department: the purported unmentionablity of homosexuality during some of this time ensured that some boys and girls were able to grow up and come out with a comparative lack of inherent or applied guilt. Perhaps, some parents may have felt in retrospect, their kids *did* learn about being queer at the movies.

Matinee Idol may tell us that Eric Barrymaine is a hopeless simp, but it does not judge his character, his sexuality, or his place in his community. The films of the early 1930s offered a greater range than the silent years, and occasionally more ridicule. But, most conspicuously, the movies of the time tell us that homosexuality existed and was a part of (mostly urban) life in those years of national crisis. Lesbians and gay men were generally accepted, they would interact with others, and that pretty much was that.

The heightened portrayals of these characters came into film at a time when the industry was compelled to rethink its priorities, its material, and its audiences. The studio most responsible for bringing sound to movies, Warner Bros., was by late 1930 deeply awash in red ink. The huge profits of the first talkies had been squandered on inflated executive and star salaries and on an overstock of pricey escapism that no one went to see. Facing exorbitant losses, the studio changed its house style pronto: out with Technicolor operettas and overstuffed romances, and onward with rowdy comedies and urban dramas that cost little and had a chance to clear a profit. This grittier fare befitted the national mood, and other studios moved (through both imitation and instinct) in the same direction. These were not yet Depression tales, for Hollywood had not yet dealt with the Depression onscreen, but they were stories that seemed nonetheless to mirror the times and viewers' lives, regardless of what the Production Code might prescribe or prohibit. The films made in mid-1930 onward were stark, and frank, and even occasionally honest. They benefited from improved sound-film techniques, and in their efforts to attract audiences by reflecting the realities of the time, they systematically broke—or, more properly, disregarded—nearly every stricture of the new Code.

Four major films produced and released in mid-to-late 1930, *Little Caesar*, *Morocco*, *The Office Wife*, and *Just Imagine*, set the pattern for gay content in pre-Code American cinema. As in the silent days there would be the blatant cartoon stereotypes played for laughs or to establish a certain kind of exotic sophistication. At the same time, there would be the rarer depiction of sexuality through understatement and allusion, subtler undercurrents geared to and detectable by urban adult audiences, and generally invisible to the people at the Production Code office. The pansies and dykes, who far outnumbered their less obvious brothers and sisters, were occasionally targeted by Code officials. Yet even there, both the historian and the casual viewer can sometimes find a surprising range, regardless of the Code and the naysaying moralists. The Code people, in any case, were fairly helpless in the face of Hollywood's move toward the seamy side of the street. Code officials would shake their fingers at the studios sometimes, just as they did about violence and drinking and adultery, but seldom could they do anything. The only real power in clamping down on movies in those years lay in the hands of several of the state censorship boards.

Ohio and Pennsylvania were notorious for their prudishness, and movie audiences in those states grew wearily accustomed to mangled prints and abrupt jump cuts. Even so, the cuts were almost never of the gay allusions or characters: a stabbing or an exclaimed "Nuts!" drew far more fire than a man with a large carnation and a coy expression. The gay codes operated onscreen in much the same fashion as a red necktie would function on a metropolitan street, conveying gayness to those in the know, often past the eyes of outsiders.

At this time the film industry tended to view filmmaking as a series of cycles, like fashion trends, that would last a season or two, spawn imitators, then die. Two cycles that started up in 1930 gave special headaches to Code officials. One was the tear-jerking "confession" movie, in which some attractive young woman (played by the likes of Constance Bennett or Joan Crawford) would be put through the wringer: seduced, kept, abandoned, degraded, redeemed, etc. The other group of films comprised gangster pictures, enjoying a rebirth at Warner Bros. after a hiatus at the dawn of sound. These stories seemed more immediate than ever, none more so than their progenitor, *Little Caesar*. Code officials fretted over *Caesar*'s violence and glorification of evil but completely missed its homoerotic undertones: Caesar's unrequited crush on his golden-boy protégée (Douglas Fairbanks, Jr.). As Caesar, Edward G. Robinson emanated everything except sexual vibes, but through the dialogue and direction, particularly of Caesar's uninterest in women, the undercurrents came through clearly enough for intelligent audiences. Likewise the looks of loving admiration cast in Caesar's direction by his toadying henchman, played by George E. Stone. A few months later, Caesar's brother in crime, *The Public Enemy*, avoided the homoerotic implications in favor of more traditional stereotypes. Midway through Jimmy Cagney's rise to underworld fame, he is fitted for his first custom suit by a pair of tailors who are as solicitous as they are swishy. One tailor nods approvingly to the other as he measures Cagney's inseam, while Cagney reacts in a predictably feisty mix of confusion and hostility.

In the other hot film realm of that grim 1930–31 season, Warners had a hit de scandale with *The Office Wife*, a fairly flavorful and extremely compact (59 minutes) yarn about a secretary (Dorothy Mackaill, far less butch than in *The Crystal Cup*) and her married boss (Lewis Stone). It had already been a successful novel by Faith Baldwin, whose "adult" romances were most effective when read to the roar of a beauty parlor hair dryer. Baldwin's name was, in fact, such a draw that *The Office Wife* opened with a prologue featuring a Baldwinesque writer (here called Kate Halsey) setting up the main story by being assigned by publisher Stone to write about what really happens behind office doors. As enacted by Blanche Frederici, Kate/Faith is no frilly pop-purveyor or mousy scribe. Instead, this was the occasion for the return, now in sound, of the clipped, tweed-wearing, monocle-wielding Butchwoman, here sporting a man's fedora.

Whatever Baldwin's predispositions were in real life, in *The Office Wife* they were unquestionable, as Frederici engaged in jaunty masculine banter with Stone, disdained the intentions of the male animal, and puffed thoughtfully on her stogie. (Stone, offered one of her cigars, demurs: "Not one of yours, thanks.") Such characterizations would not be uncommon over the next few years, but this one remains singular and oddly inspiring: Kate Halsey (and Faith Baldwin, by implication) is strong, authoritative, talented, and good-humored. A woman in charge, in short, a paragon of the independent New Woman of the twenties that had been mocked in such films as *The Clinging Vine*. In *The Office Wife* she was portrayed as mildly eccentric, perhaps, certainly not heterosexual, and meriting her associates' affection and respect.

One of the first gay characters to run mildly afoul of the 1930 Production Code has already skittered through these pages. In *Just Imagine*, Ivan Linow played the Martian major domo Boko in such a fashion as to create a new sort of personal style: the burly mince. He, along with some of the movie's gamier gags, rated a chiding mention from a Code official, John V. Wilson, who wrote a tut-tutting letter to Fox studio executives several days after the premiere of *Just Imagine*. After complaining about some of the double entendres and racy comedy, Wilson regretfully noted that El Brendel's "Queen" line directed at Boko should be cut, and that some of Boko's gestures and business "seem[ed] to make it appear that he is 'queer.'" Such things, he warned, would fall prey to cuts at state censorship boards. Fox, adhering to the unspoken principle that the Code was to be endured and ignored, kept Boko in, loving gazes and all, and no state censors felt the need to chip away at any of his shtick.

At Paramount, filmmaking of a more mature sort was generating attention, and perhaps awe. Marlene Dietrich had arrived there in the spring of 1930, *The Blue Angel* already completed and a lucrative contract in hand. For her first American film, *Morocco*, she did everything right. Cushioned and coaxed (and also bullied) by her director and mentor and occasional lover Josef von Sternberg, Dietrich caused a sensation as Amy Jolly, the bruised fatalist of a cabaret singer who gives up everything to follow foreign legionnaire Gary Cooper into the desert. The exhaustively stylized goddess of the later films was not yet in evidence, so the audience was allowed to empathize with as well as admire Dietrich's portrait of a woman as human battlefield, passive yet perverse, conflicted but curiously hopeful. The perversity factored spectacularly in Amy's (and Dietrich's) choices for her Moroccan cabaret debut. To gasps and hoots from a rowdy audience, Amy saunters onstage in a tuxedo and top hat. Instantly, even before she began to growl out "Quand l'amour meurt," Dietrich had become legend. This wasn't a *Crystal Cup*–like character sketch; nor was it one of the umpteen times an actress would don boy's clothes and go for gamin appeal. It was an arresting statement about identity and self-presentation, above all about

With this kind of assurance, stage fright is a non-issue. Who else but Dietrich in *Morocco*, as supported by Paul Porcasi.

showmanship. Cross-dressing was a viable form of performance art in the Weimar Republic, and this foreign body was bringing it to a post-Eltinge American audience. As she showed just how forward Continental art and sexuality could be, the audience onscreen, and audiences all over America, capitulated even before she finished her song. The best was yet to come. As Amy accepts the applause, she passes a table of socialites. One pretty young woman has a flower in her hair, and Amy/Dietrich stares hard, asks for the flower, and after receiving it reaches down and kisses the girl on the lips. The audience roars. Amy slyly doffs her hat, and then tosses the flower to Gary Cooper. The scene still makes for breathtaking viewing. Has pansexuality ever been depicted with such economy and good cheer? Anything else bisexual in Amy's personality is kept under wraps for the remainder of *Morocco*, but the titillation was clear enough for those keyed in to Dietrich's sophisticated sense of humor.[3] It's hard to gauge just how

---

[3]It's fair to credit Dietrich with much of the humor, since von Sternberg, skilled as he was, was never what could be called a barrel of laughs, on or off the screen. Comic relief in his films tended to be either tiresomely bumptious, or so bone-dry that mainstream America didn't get it.

powerfully it went over with 1930 audiences, since not even the Production Code people uttered a peep about Amy's kiss, either in 1930 or for later reissue, when sexual standards in the movies were a great deal tougher. Perhaps some spectators saw it, and Dietrich, as being as exotic as von Sternberg's soundstage recreation of desert passion; what is indisputable is that *Morocco* made a large amount of money at a time when most films were dying, and that trousers, previously only seen on women as pajama-type outfits, soon became almost as conspicuous a sensation as Dietrich herself. For her next role, the Mata Hari-esque spy in *Dishonored* (1931), Dietrich wore aviator togs and a leather jacket (and in another scene, an oddly prophetic outfit of miniskirt and boots). Then, two films later, she returned to cabarets in von Sternberg's dauntingly outré take on the confession genre, *Blonde Venus* (1932). In this rococo cornucopia of attitudes and arabesques, Dietrich teases the audience with her takes on every conceivable variety of sex, up to and including bestiality and incest. Among the delights offered: the legendary "Hot Voodoo" number, with Dietrich as a jungle goddess donning and doffing an ape suit; the perverse humor of casting the exceedingly butch Cecil Cunningham in a fleeting bit as a loving mother; and Dietrich back in tuxedo for "I Couldn't Be Annoyed," matching *Morocco*'s ante by roguishly fondling a chorus girl's breast.

The pandrogyny of Marlene Dietrich is a fair demonstration of how wide-ranging and audacious a level early-thirties commercial cinema could attain. Few other filmmakers cared to take the chances von Sternberg did, either in terms of narrative presentation or in depictions of ambiguous sexuality. Yet even in the assembly-line studio system there were some artists of individuality and impudence. None have been more celebrated in retrospect than James Whale, who came into his own as a filmmaker in 1931. The fanciful story of his last days, *Gods and Monsters*, has made him better known than at any time since the heyday in which he reigned, not entirely willingly, as the king of the horror film. *Frankenstein* was his, of course, and *The Invisible Man*, and *Bride of Frankenstein*. The gayness of Whale's horror films is seldom on the surface, for his dry theatrical wit rarely permitted anything so overt. Instead, there are hints and symbols, coded references for viewers in the life who frequently had to communicate in code when in the outside world. Whale's misfit outsiders pitted against hostile mobs, his unholy same-sex friendships, and his amused skewing of hetero norms all form a base camp for queer film theory, which probes exhaustively and exhaustingly beyond the surface of these movies for the truths and intents revealed beneath. Fortunately, Whale was an aesthete and filmmaker, not a theorist, so his horror movies are imbued with a healthy portion of inside jokes and irreverent, very dark, comedy.

Comedy seldom gets darker or gayer than in *The Old Dark House* (1932), Whale's deadpan spoof of haunted-house chillers, in which a quintet of stranded outsiders stumbles into the decrepit digs of a family of loons. The Femms—yes, that's their surname—are a choice group: one sibling is an emaciated, neurotic priss (Ernest Thesiger), another is a fanatical gargoyle (Eva Moore), and another a gnomish arsonist kept behind locked doors (Brember Wills). There is also a desiccated mummy of a patriarch and, overseeing the whole lot, Boris Karloff as the mute and lecherous butler. Suspense and violence and death are all included, in deference to the genre, but Whale's intentions are less to scare than to poke fun at straight institutions—family, marriage, religion—and get in as many inside jokes as he possibly can, often with a gay slant. This was the first American film of Whale's fellow gay expatriate Charles Laughton, and at one point a character remarks of him, "He likes people to think he's ever so gay!"[4] Meanwhile, the hag-fanatic becomes so obsessed with young Gloria Stuart's body that she reaches toward her breasts twice. The pyromaniac, Saul Femm, scurries downstairs when released from his cell and, before attempting to murder Melvyn Douglas, exclaims, "My friend, I love you!" He also cites Scripture by exclaiming, "Saul loved David." One of the most private of Whale's jokes came with his casting the role of Sir Roderick, the ancient invalid pater-familias. The credits list the actor "John Dudgeon" in the role. Mr. Dudgeon's career was far shorter than that of his alter ego, character actress Elspeth Dudgeon, upon whose schoolmarm face were glued the whiskers of a 102-year-old man—cross-dressing as sneaky as Dietrich's, in a vastly different vein. Even as the undercurrents swirling through Whale's old dark house were subtle enough to withstand censor scrutiny, the Universal publicity department was hard-pressed to figure out quite the right way to market this offbeat movie. Finally, for some of the ads, they came up with a one-word blurb: "WEIRD!!"[5]

Even in more conventional movies around this time, sexuality was hardly cut and dried. The King of Hollywood's Old Guard, Douglas Fairbanks, Sr., employed an extended interlude of gay panic to enliven his 1931 *Reaching for*

---

[4]This is as good a place as any to ponder the use of the word *gay*, and when it came to mean something other than cheery and bright. According to George Chauncey's exhaustive *Gay New York*, its earliest uses cannot be determined; however, it seems that by the late 1920s it had become a well-known insider's code word in the pansy underground, only moving into wider usage forty or so years later. It will turn up a few more times unambiguously in 1930s films . . . and in any case it's pretty hard to imagine that Whale didn't know what it meant and who'd get the joke.

[5]Gay characters in Universal horror films were not confined to the James Whale pictures. *Dracula's Daughter* and *House of Horrors* will turn up later in this story, and even before Whale there was *Dracula* (1931) with its butch-femme pair of tweedy women riding in the coach with Renfield in the opening scene. Two 1932 horror-type films at other studios, *The Most Dangerous Game* (RKO) and *The Mask of Fu Manchu* (MGM), carried their gayness closer to the vest, with eroticized views of hunky leading men (Joel McCrea and Charles Starrett) and villains whose gayness seemed barely sublimated beneath a veneer of sadism.

the Moon, a film in dire need of enlivening. Conceived and shot as a musical with songs and story by Irving Berlin, it was, by release time, an unsatisfying jumble of comedy and romantic drama with all but one of its songs scissored out. One of its few memorable scenes came midway through, as Fairbanks, as a millionaire in pursuit of aviator Bebe Daniels, calls on his butler to provide lovemaking tips. The butler is played by Edward Everett Horton, heretofore an eccentric leading man and now moving into a position as one of film's most omnipresent character actors. Most of Horton's traditional onscreen persona came in the post-Code age, where his obvious gayness was filtered through layers of camouflage such as wives, girlfriends, and general eccentricity. In *Reaching for the Moon,* however, he is permitted, in effect, to seduce Douglas Fairbanks. After verifying that Daniels is willing to return male affection, he has Fairbanks climb into a patio swing with him, the better to teach him the moves as well as the words. As Horton puts his arms around Fairbanks, he starts with the love talk: "From the moment we met, I knew this had to happen." Naturally, someone (an electrical repairman) walks in on this tender scene and figures it for the real thing. The confusion continues as the electrician glares back and forth at the two men, until finally Horton offers to show him the problem he came to fix. "Come with me, my man, and I'll show you what's what." Right away the electrician snaps back: "I ain't your man . . . and I know what's what!" The dialogue, spoken and overheard, intensifies the old "mistaken for queer" ploy that silent films had used. Even working classes know what's what, i.e., same-sex affection, when they see it, and when they hear it too. So, presumably, did large numbers of spectators going to see *Reaching for the Moon.*

Throughout 1931, as film took on an ever-racier mien, the gay allusions continued to turn up. A few months after *The Public Enemy,* gay couture was once again the fashion at Warner Bros. in a ramshackle comedy titled *Manhattan Parade.* This forgotten little epic represented the tail end of the studio's early-sound obsession with musicals (though all its songs were cut), backstage stories, and fabulously unreal two-color Technicolor. Winnie Lightner starred as the head of a down-and-out theatrical costume company who connives her way to success with the help of some odd showbiz types. One of the oddest was Bobby Watson, coming full circle since *Syncopation* to play a gay designer similar to the one he mocked in that early musical. Here he is Paisley, the firm's talented and over-the-edge costume designer, and he gives the entire performance straight from a wildly waving pair of wrists. The voice is notably different from the one heard in *Syncopation,* tighter and higher, especially when Paisley starts to sputter through another hissy fit. He is first shown arguing with Lightner over the relative merits of maroon versus cerise—"Cerise is just so vulgar!" he insists—and is mollified only when Lightner bribes him with the offer of a new set of drapes. (Drapes were another code for onscreen pansies.)

BOBBY WATSON

Real name: Robert Watson Knucher. Born Springfield, Ill., November 28, 1888; died Hollywood Calif., May 22, 1965

With his slim frame, clipped tones, and relentlessly mobile wrists, he is the unsung pioneer of screen sissies. Indeed, his main fame lies elsewhere. During the 1940s, a distinctive haircut and mustache made him a dead ringer for the century's favorite villain, and he played Hitler in everything from low comedies to musicals to serious dramas. In 1952, older but still game, he was the elocution teacher in *Singin' in the Rain* ("Moses supposes his toeses are roses . . .") whose studio is trashed by Gene Kelly and Donald O'Connor. That this is his most widely seen role is fitting for the actor who helped start movie musicals back in 1929 with *Syncopation*. Like Johnny Arthur, he started in vaudeville and legit theater, and by the coming of sound had appeared in a few silent films, including D. W. Griffith's *That Royle Girl*. When his *Syncopation* hoofing drew few subsequent offers, he became the movies' preeminent pansy. While Franklin Pangborn was playing irate husbands in short comedies and Edward Everett Horton was moving from leads into supporting parts, Watson made a strong impression in comedies and musicals as various designers and gay functionaries. His shtick in these roles was far more a creation than the less fabricated efforts of Pangborn or Arthur: the Watson voice and mien were notably different in non-gay portrayals. After 1934, after his blatant pansy types were effectively banned from movies, he became a more generic character actor, often in unbilled appearances (such as one of the Emerald City repairmen restuffing the Scarecrow in *The Wizard of Oz*). Then came the war and steady employment as Hitler. In *That Nazty Nuisance* he appeared opposite the Hirohito of Johnny Arthur—an odd fate for two pre-Code sissies—and, billed soberly as Robert, he played the evil one in a leading role in *The Hitler Gang* (1944). Later on, with less call to play Hitler, he again became a more mainstream figure. Few of his gay roles are much seen these days—a post-Code turn in *Born to Dance* (1936) is the best known—but his portrayals merit remembrance and affection. They were witty and usually affectionate; in all truth, he played gay to far better effect than he played Hitler.

Unlike so many of the gay types in these years, Paisley is not confined to a couple of short scenes. He pops in and out through the whole movie, burbling, making pronouncements, stamping his foot in frustration. Silly sissy he undoubtedly is, yet his abilities earn him more respect than most of the other characters in the film—lunkhead producers, a pretentious lunatic of a director, and Lightner's conniving husband. *Manhattan Parade* survives only in black and white, but it's clear that the original Technicolor prints gave the opportunity

Bobby Watson in typical mode in *This Side of Heaven* (MGM, 1934). He's convinced that Mae Clarke will like the chintz, but she's less certain. Note the lapel flower. *Photofest*

for some color coding: Watson often is in lighter, apparently brighter colors than the other men in the cast, once in a loud smoking jacket and dark beret. "Couldn't you just die—tittering?" he says . . . and perhaps you could, but as long as you're a good designer you'll still get jobs.

As done to a crisp turn by Watson, Paisley was one of the most conspicuous of gay characters in sound films thus far, setting the tone for portrayals of that Uncle Tommy of onscreen gayness, the Pansy. Sissy. Fairy. Nance. Fruit. Queer. From early 1932 to mid-1934 and beyond, Hollywood reflected the (now-fading) pansy craze in earnest, steadily codifying gay men onscreen by dress, manner, voice, and gesture. The fedora hat, the gestures that alternately swept and minced, the little mustache, the flower in the lapel—the pansy was as immediately recognizable onscreen as he was on urban sidewalks (while millions of gay men and women without a codified look were allowed to pass undetected). For women, there would be less exposure, since the pansy craze had not been about male impersonation. Nor were there verbal labels. The portrayals, however, were numerous, and the look was even more distinctive than that of the men: jackets resembling men's waistcoats, starched shirts with neckties, close-cropped hair, monocles, cigars.

Paisley had the mannerisms to spare, but the defining look arrived onscreen in full-blown glory in another piece of late-1931 escapism, *Palmy Days*. An Eddie Cantor comedy with big musical numbers staged by Busby Berkeley, it was set mainly in an enormous bakery staffed entirely by chorus girls.[6] After some establishing shots of the Art Deco confection of a bakery, the film proper begins with a young clerk (Betty Grable, before stardom) at a counter taking orders. In rushes a foppish man with all the trademarks: white fedora, mustache, flower, and a walking stick tossed in.

> MAN (*Rapping impatiently on the counter with a gloved hand*): Young lady! I'd like to order a cake. I must have it in twenty-four hours. Here's my card.
> CLERK: What kind of cake would you prefer?
> MAN: A five-dollar one. A birthday cake. Chocolate. All chocolate. (*Stares into space mooningly*) I *love* chocolate!
> CLERK: Would you like a little rose on top?
> MAN: No . . . make it a pansy! (*He widens his eyes and bares his teeth in a "You know what I mean" smile, then hurries off*)

Grable takes the order to the kitchen and gives it to the head baker: "Very special order!" It's not really important that neither the man nor his cake is referred to again. Sure, it's a caricature—who isn't in a movie like this?—but once again it's clear that in many films of the time, gay characters (like those in *Office Wife, Just Imagine*, and *The Matinee Idol*), have a place, a milieu where they mingle with straights, are accepted at face value, and are neither punished nor censured.

"Banned from Bathroom by Hays Office, Pictures Hop into Pansy Stuff"

In its inimitably colloquial fashion *Variety* made this proclamation in its February 2, 1932, issue. In their search for easy off-color jokes, the article noted, movies could no longer use the men's room as a setting. Yet there waited another fertile source of blue humor. "No sooner has the local Hays office finished burying the

---

[6]Unlike *Reaching for the Moon* and *Manhattan Parade*, this one was permitted to keep its song and dances. That it was a major success owed much to Cantor's radio popularity and to the presence of a bodacious group of Goldwyn Girls—producer Samuel Goldwyn's house staff of chorines—who showed their cleavage to the camera while singing a song called "Bend Down, Sister."

lavatory as a locale than it is surrounded by pansies." It was not quite a full-fledged homosexual garden in movies, but industry observers were by this point noticing a trend. *Palmy Days* and *Manhattan Parade* had opened in late 1931, as did *The Secret Witness*, with ZaSu Pitts distractedly reading *The Well of Loneliness*. None of them, however, was judged responsible for the new lavender proliferation. According to *Variety* the source was, of all things, a newsreel. In early November 1931, cameramen from the Pathé, Fox, and Paramount newsreel units covered a large dog show held in Manhattan. Not exactly a top breaking story, this, but newsreels functioned exactly the way television news would later on, covering both the major events and the fluff pieces. Apparently the Paramount cameraman covering the dog show grew restless and decided to have some fun. With the Pathé and Fox cameras running, he pretended to be the mincing owner of a tiny dog given a medal for heroism, gushingly thanking all and sundry for the gorgeous honor bestowed on his little precious. Both Pathé and Fox decided to use the bit in their newsreel, Pathé with a whopping eighty seconds of footage devoted to the faux pansy.[7] The bit made an unexpected hit, the most attention- and laugh-grabbing newsreel item of the year. Pathé milked the applause by claiming (wink, wink) that the footage and the man were actually authentic. Paramount then proceeded to send the same cameraman to another show for a second on-camera display of canine-devoted effeminacy. Eddie Cantor, who occasionally purveyed lavender-scented jokes, then got into the act by arranging to run the clip as part of his vaudeville show at the Palace. Audiences were convulsed, the industry sat up and noticed, and suddenly a spur-of-the-moment joke had turned gays into the hottest thing in Hollywood humor.

Excepting that colorful aberration *The Dude Wrangler*, Hollywood had been slow to reflect the extent of the pansy craze. In reaction to that silly newsreel, however, the sheer volume would increase markedly. Almost immediately, there began a marked upturn in overt characters and references, ranging from momentary mentions to depictions of same-sex relationships, from nameless gay passersby to entertainers at gay bars. (The more covert references, the coded messages so dear to film theorists and such, are of course without number.) The occasional references and scenes in film since the late 1920s now increased astronomically. Both "pansy stuff"—the main thrust of the *Variety* article—and portrayals of lesbians became a part of the texture of Depression

---

[7]Sound bites were not quite as brief in newsreels then as they are now on television, but close enough. Eighty seconds was more time than newsreels usually gave to something as frivolous as anonymous gay men with pooches. It was more frequently given to items such as the one on the same newsreel program that showed massive quantities of confiscated cocaine being incinerated by the New York Police Department. Almost wistfully, *Variety* observed that "Broadway cokies have a hard time suppressing sighs" at the sight of so much good stuff going up in smoke.

cinema. Among the many films, the following table can serve as a representative buffet:

Selected Gay Scenes and Characters in Hollywood Films, 1930–1934

Film	Studio/Year	Genre	Scene/Character
Bed of Roses	RKO, 1933	Romantic drama	Franklin Pangborn as a nervous department store floorwalker.
Crooner	Warners, 1932	Satire	Effeminate man sits at table with masculine monocled woman listening to a nightclub singer. Man, dreamily: "I think he's superb." Woman (in deeper voice): "He's *lousy!*"
Dancing Lady	MGM, 1933	Backstage musical	In a "Then and Now" gag in the "Rhythm of the Day" sequence, a knight in armor turns into a flaming pansy.
The Death Kiss	World Wide, 1932	Murder mystery	Harold Minjir as Howell, a high-strung assistant at a movie studio.
Fast Workers	MGM, 1933	Farce	Tough-guy Robert Armstrong sees a female couple in a speakeasy and sneers, "They're making it tougher for us every day!" Later cut by orders of the Hays Office.
Fifty Million Frenchmen	Warners, 1931	Farce	Pansy confusion gags with lowbrow comics Olsen and Johnson.
Going Hollywood	MGM, 1933	Musical comedy	In a Tijuana bar a female couple dances very closely while Bing Crosby sings "Temptation."
Grand Hotel	MGM, 1932	Romantic drama	A tweedy lesbian couple dances cheek to cheek at the hotel bar; Ferdinand Gottschalk as Garbo's flitty assistant, Pimenov.

(Continued)

Selected Gay Scenes and Characters in Hollywood Films, 1930–1934 *(cont.)*

Film	Studio/Year	Genre	Scene/Character
Hell's Highway	RKO, 1932	Melodrama/ prison exposé	Burgess, a.k.a. "Cookie," cook at a brutal chain-gang camp, enjoys the favors of Blacksnake Skinner (C. Henry Gordon), the head guard.
Hips Hips Hooray	RKO, 1934	Musical comedy	Bobby Watson as a dance director.
Housewife	Warners, 1934	Romantic drama	Yahoo businessman Hobart Cavanaugh refers to crepes suzettes as "Pansy pancakes."
I'm No Angel	Paramount, 1933	Sex comedy	Mae West, spelling the name "Pinkowitz" to a telephone operator: "P, like in Pansy . . ."
International House	Paramount, 1934	Musical farce	Franklin Pangborn as the hotel manager in Wu Hu, China, telling his city's name to W. C. Fields. Fields, aghast: "Don't let the posy fool ya!" Also, a leering tuxedo-clad Chinese lesbian in the "She Was a China Teacup" production number.
Lady for a Day	Columbia, 1933	Comedy	Bag lady May Robson starts to get her makeover, and all men are banned from the room . . . but it's OK to let Pierre remain.
Lawyer Man	Warners, 1932	Drama	Attorney William Powell decides to leave his ideals behind and go for fast money. His shady client roster includes a masculine woman with monocle.
Life of the Party, The	Warners, 1930	Farce (formerly musical)	Winnie Lightner signaling to her coworker that the boss is coming: "Shhhh . . . the pansy!"
Little Giant	Warners, 1933	Comedy	Reforming gangster Edward G. Robinson makes a "pansy" wisecrack, later refers to a group of cronies as "fags."

(Continued)

Film	Studio/Year	Genre	Scene/Character
Moonlight and Pretzels	Universal, 1933	Backstage musical	Bobby Watson as "Bertie," a Broadway costume designer.
Movie Crazy	Paramount, 1932	Comedy	A mouse runs loose in a ballroom, and women scream and jump up on chairs . . . including sissy Grady Sutton.
Night after Night	Paramount, 1932	Comedy-drama	George Raft tells a rival mobster what kind of flowers he wants at his funeral: "Anything at all . . . except pansies!"
Night World	Universal, 1932	Multi-story drama	Paisley Noon as Clarence, who tarries insinuatingly in a nightclub men's room.
Oh, for a Man!	Fox, 1930	Comedy	Diva Jeanette MacDonald has a close encounter with masseuse Bodil Rosing.
One Hour with You	Paramount, 1932	Musical comedy	Charlie Ruggles discovers that his valet, Marcel (Charles Coleman) did so want to see him wearing tights.
One-Way Passage	Warners, 1932	Romantic drama	A barbershop trio singing in the first scene turns out to be two men and a very butch woman.
Only Yesterday	Universal, 1933	Romantic drama	Franklin Pangborn and Barry Norton as lovers; a lesbian tete-à-tete cut by orders of the Hays Office. (See chapter 5.)
The Phantom President	Paramount, 1932	Musical satire	A presidential candidate's most competent advisor is a severely tailored woman. Jimmy Durante, smelling Sidney Toler's cologne, cries, "Swish, sister, swish!"
Rebound	RKO, 1931	Sophisticated comedy	Ina Claire tells old flame Robert Williams that her husband has gone for the mail. Williams: "I've gone for male, that's all right!"

(Continued)

Selected Gay Scenes and Characters in Hollywood Films, 1930–1934 *(cont.)*

Film	Studio/Year	Genre	Scene/Character
Red Dust	MGM, 1932	Sex melodrama	Houseboy Willie Fung has fun playing with Jean Harlow's panties. Harlow: "You even find them in the jungle!"
Red Headed Woman	MGM, 1932	Sex comedy	Una Merkel fears Jean Harlow is going highbrow when Harlow uses the word *charming.* "Say, you're getting to sound like a pansy!"
Seventh Commandment, The	Hollywood Producers & Distributors	Exploitation melodrama	An innocent country bumpkin comes to the wicked big city and finds out (the hard way) about strip poker, venereal disease, and drag queens.
She Done Him Wrong	Paramount, 1933	Sex comedy/ melodrama	Mae West, visiting Sing Sing, runs into some old friends: a pair of burly lovers she calls "the Cherry Sisters."
The Tenderfoot	Warners, 1932	Comedy	Texan Joe E. Brown, just arrived in New York, thinks he's found a bunch of home-grown cowboys. They turn out to be a flock of chorus boys in western drag and makeup; they greet him with a big pansy "Wooooo!"
When Ladies Meet	MGM, 1933	Comedy-drama	Martin Burton as Walter, constant attendant to social butterfly Alice Brady.
Wine, Women, and Song	Chadwick, 1933	Backstage drama	Bobby Watson again, as Lawrence.
Winner Take All	Warners, 1932	Comedy	Jimmy Cagney has tailor trouble once more. This time, a Mr. Pettigrew lingers fondly on Cagney's backside while taking measurements.
Young as You Feel	Fox, 1931	Comedy	At a high society party, several young men flirt with each other, instead of their dates.

Big woooo: Fresh off the train from Texas, Joe E. Brown gets the standard pansy greeting from a flock of Broadway cowboys in *The Tenderfoot* (1932). *Photofest*

Many of these films are brief glimpses, but some are more extensive. The presence of a sissy in the tough prison melodrama *Hell's Highway* was a surprising touch, made more so by the fact that Cookie is obviously carrying on an affair with the head guard. Cookie's protector was even shown patting his favorite's posterior at one point—a scene which helped discourage RKO from attempting to rerelease *Hell's Highway* after the Production Code was toughened in 1934. Other 1932 films merit special mention because they venture far from the concept of a nance role or scene. *Tom Brown of Culver* (Universal) was one of the many apprentice works directed by William Wyler in the early, pre-prestige phase of his career. A tale of military-school rivalries and bondings, it offered several unexpected features. Chief among them is the homoerotically charged enmity between Tom Brown (played by a young actor named Tom Brown) and Bob Randolph (Richard Cromwell). The special edge of their relationship became most noticeable in a scene in which the two young men, rehearsing before the school dance, find themselves dancing together, edgily holding each other and staring eye to eye as they work out the steps. After this scene, they

Richard Cromwell (looking very Leonardo di Caprio-esque) and Tom Brown (playing Tom Brown) set off both alarms and undercurrents in William Wyler's *Tom Brown of Culver*. *Photofest*

become far more friendly. Part of the charge came from the casting of Cromwell, the movies' male ingenue of choice for the entire decade; like Dorian Gray, his dewy beauty seemed constant, and like Dorian and his creator, he was gay. For what was ostensibly a wholesome rite-of-passage movie set in an American Legion–sponsored school, *Tom Brown* offered another surprise: a shower scene with a couple of bare-bottomed teenaged cadets—one of several examples of off-hand nudity that the Hays Office allowed to pass without comment.

Late in his life, actor William Gargan described his 1932 film *The Sport Parade* as ". . . high camp. Boy meets boy; boy loses boy, boy gets boy." Is it really that? Well, for a B movie off the RKO assembly line it carries a fair amount of baggage. One of thirties cinema's seminal hunks, Joel McCrea, starred with Gargan in what seems on the surface to be a routine romantic triangle: two college friends go down separate paths and love the same girl (Marian Marsh). The contours, stated thus, were similar to something like three out of five movies produced by Hollywood that year. This triangle, though, operates every which way, and hardly covertly: *The Sport Parade* is a barely disguised tribute to bisexual

Torn Between Two Lovers? Marian Marsh is both axis and fifth wheel with Joel McCrea and William Gargan in *The Sport Parade.*

male bonding, garnished with abundant, lovingly shot displays of McCrea's physique as viewed in almost every configuration. McCrea's Sandy and Gargan's Johnny are the joint pride of their football team, constantly joshing and, yes, playing around in the shower. (Gargan snaps his towel lovingly at McCrea's rear.) Come graduation, Johnny gets a job writing a sports column, while Sandy sells out to a nasty promoter and becomes the 1932 equivalent of a World Wrestling Federation pinup boy. There are the expected complications over Irene (Marsh), an illustrator, but all ends happily after McCrea refuses to take a dive in a match and ends up with Irene (and with Johnny). And no, the bonding isn't only something that can be sensed covertly, lurking just beneath the surface. That became clear in recent years when *The Sport Parade* formed a large portion of the basis for a doctoral dissertation on gays in early thirties film. As it turned out, the film's head writer, Corey Ford, was implacably masculine yet sexually ambiguous, the kind of man's man who would disdain the Bobby Watson sissy types and yet, under the cover of camaraderie and machismo, lust after (and perhaps go after) his fellow man's men. That he intended this script as a paean to his passions becomes clear in a preliminary draft, which featured Sandy raffishly singing a ditty about "a bisexual built for two." That line predictably bit the dust before shooting started, but what stayed in (and was amplified by the director, Dudley Murphy), was that this was a film about two love affairs, neither of them Marsh's Irene, who is basically around for decorative camouflage.[8] One is between the McCrea and Gargan characters, the other involves the camera's love for Joel McCrea's physique—the final wrestling sequence becomes, through the eye of Murphy's camera, a virtual Buttfest.

An earlier wrestling match in *The Sport Parade* is equally illuminating. The audience members include a conventionally stereotypical pair of pansies who can't take the man-on-man violence. One waves a disdainful hand and says to the other, "Oh God, this is just brutal. Let's go!" Both are slender, youngish, with wavy hair and pale skin, physically the antithesis of the McCrea and Gargan characters. The message is startlingly clear: male love is not only for the effeminate cartoons shown to the public on movie screens and on the streets of Greenwich Village. It's also, and more preferably, for the guys who don't give themselves away, and who might arrange their lives to pursue women at the same time. At that, even this lavender duo is a shade unconventional for films: unlike Bobby Watson and some of the others, the look and manner of this unidentified pair really feels like the unfeigned real thing. And just before the camera cuts away from them, one takes the other's hand in his—a rare public display of affection that establishes that the pair, whatever the writer and director want the audience to think about them, really is a romantic duo.

A film like *The Sport Parade*, even with its flesh and frankness, was not the kind to draw the attention of the Production Code's Studio Relations Committee. The Committee had more visible fish to fry—a whole school of them—in a concurrently shot opus, *Call Her Savage*. Seen today, *Call Her Savage* is almost endearing in its overt drive to be as gamy a piece of sensationalism as it can possibly be. In 1932 it was actually viewed as having tastefully toned down its hot source material, a book of the same name by (male) novelist and sometime actor Tiffany Thayer. But heat is still written all over it, and it needed to be so. It was designed to grab as much attention as possible as the comeback movie for Clara Bow, whose white-hot career had gone cold two years earlier. As with *The Wild Party* and eight out of nine of her films, Bow's sexuality, not her acting

---

[8]This is a queer movie in every sense, and it reaches a suitably peculiar conclusion by cutting away before McCrea and Marsh have their final embrace. Instead, the last shot in the movie is sportscaster Robert Benchley announcing to his radio audience: "It *is* a girl! She's kissing Sandy! I can't watch this . . . Good night, folks!" As a gay footnote to a footnote, the burly opponent whom the willowy McCrea improbably subdues in the final match is played by *Just Imagine*'s own Boko, Ivan Linow.

ability, was to be keynoted, although *Savage* gave her the opportunity for heavy emoting. As Nasa, an untamed heiress who doesn't know she's a half-breed, Bow ran the gamut and kept going: whipping true love Gilbert Roland, marrying a syphilitic heel, turning tricks to raise milk money for her baby, cat-fighting with Thelma Todd, setting New York on its ear. At one point in her Manhattan sojourn, her escort (a socialite who's naturally working incognito as a gigolo) decides to take her slumming. "I've picked out a place to dine on the East Side," he tells her. "Only wild poets and anarchists eat there. Pretty tough . . ." The script then sets the scene:

> A gloomy, sordid cellar eating place on the east side—such a place as "Nuts" describe as artistic and normal people view with a nausea. Wild-eyed poets, long-haired anarchists—not a few pansies and a scattering of lesbians—workmen. They are all here. Jay escorts Nasa to a table much to the angry astonishment of the other patrons.

So ran the script. By the time it was up on the screen the locale had changed to "the Village"—no qualifier necessary—and instead of a mere establishing shot with bohemians at tables, the scene opened with a musical performance. Two young men (who bear a suspiciously strong resemblance to the gay couple in *The Sport Parade*), wearing aprons and lace caps and holding feather dusters as they skip between the tables, are finishing their number:

> Chambermaids, and we're dashing up and down the halls.
> Tra-la la la la la da da, Tra-la la la Tra-la la la
> Ohhh, tra la la
> [MAID ONE:] If a sailor in pajamas I should see, I know he'll scare the life out of me.
> [MAID TWO:] And on a great big battleship you'd like to be . . .
> [BOTH:] Working as chambermaids! (*Posing prettily*) Ta *da!*
> (*They wave their feather dusters and skip out.*)

In other words, this Greenwich Village cellar is a Hollywood re-creation of a third-sex nightspot. In comparison with the floor show, the melee that ensues when Bow and her escort confront the hostile downtowners is almost anticlimactic. Most of the customers are same-sex couples, ordinary-looking men and tailored but not mannish women: not a fedora or a monocle in sight. The wide-open nature of this club, and this life, is established by the presence of the wild-eyed radicals, led by Mischa Auer, who are responsible for driving out the newcomers. The gay and lesbian couples don't welcome the outsiders, but they aren't the ones who throw plates at them. (One woman holds her girlfriend close as the fight starts.) If the remaining minutes of *Call Her Savage* contain no more gays, there is still time for more excess. Give it credit: this movie is true to its own sleaziness, which makes it impossible to dislike. Like *Blonde Venus*, *Call Her Savage* is a Cook's Tour of human sexuality, so much so that its brief but striking sojourn in a gay club was one of the few scenes that didn't cause censor trouble.

From the formation of the Code, through the Pathé newsreel, onward to late-1932 depiction of gay couples and gay bars, it had been quite a trip. The frankness of film in general seemed constant, and the "pansy flashes" predicted by *Variety* early in 1932 were becoming more expansive and varied than most observers would have predicted. These flashes even extended to the Hollywood premiere of *Grand Hotel* at Grauman's Chinese Theatre on April 29, 1932. In the immense crowd of stars and industry folk, the police department managed to look past the Jean Harlows and Clark Gables to zero in on one couple in particular. A strikingly gowned woman and her tuxedoed escort were detained as they left the theater and then arrested; the woman was no woman, and public drag was illegal when not connected with onstage performance. Whether the pair had crashed the premiere illegally was not established; what mattered was that a public display of gayness had shaken up the industry's highest-profile event of 1932. Soon afterward, and with even more chutzpah than that gay couple, Cecil B. DeMille was preparing to have the last word on cinematic homosexuality.

FOUR

The Naked Moon

> It is an alluring dance. Dramatically, it had to be, to bring out by contrast the greater strength and purity of Mercia's faith. But some thought it too alluring.
>
> **The Autobiography of Cecil B. DeMille**

S omeone with just a little less egotism than Cecil B. DeMille would have been completely deflated at the outset of 1932. Seven years earlier, America's highest-profile director had left his home base, Paramount, in favor of independent production; apart from *King of Kings* (1927), this course was artistically dubious and financially disastrous. Then he went to MGM, only to discover that philistine autocracy played badly in the Dream Factory. In the course of three films (including a loonytoon musical called *Madam Satan*) he watched audience interest skid further. Deeply in debt, owing over a million and a half in back taxes, feeling as close to contrite as he was capable, he decided to go back to Paramount. Filmmakers who rebel against studios are not usually welcomed upon their return, particularly in the bleakest days of a depression. DeMille wangled a one-film deal which he knew was probationary, and a mogul warned him, "You are on trial with this picture." His only option was to risk everything he had.

To call DeMille the most ostentatious hypocrite in the history of film is to miss the point, although it's not inaccurate. He was, first and foremost, a person of supreme hubris, on the face of it a bit less complex than more genuinely talented filmmakers who operate in a mode of titanic self-directedness. Yet he was as skewed and contradictory as his films, and as unreal. Just as his oeuvre coerced carnality and self-righteousness into a bizarrely codependent relationship, so did the man himself. While his sins were as vast as those of any Hollywood narcissist, he retained a sense of his own piety as sincere as it was childlike. Fueled by the force of his contradictions, he barreled on with his career and his life, never giving up or giving in even as many around him despised everything he stood for. As he grew older and the artistry of his early films turned into blunt commercialism, his work increasingly began to mirror both his ego and his absurdity. On the surface, most of his movies seem a hopeless mix of reverence, sin, violent spectacle, and nineteenth-century theatre. Yet, with all their bombast, there's something compelling about the way these movies believe in themselves—everything is so completely of a piece that a parallel world is somehow created. Much of this conviction is grounded in the fact that DeMille possessed an almost eerie sense of how to give the public what it wanted while keeping the extremes firmly defined, ladling stern moralizing atop the sex and brutality. The logic behind it all was simple: in order to make audiences understand what evil is, you must show it. And damned if the old bastard didn't contort this lopsided equation into an ironclad proposition. The critics shook their heads in amazement, and the public thronged in.[1]

As the wheels in his head spun feverishly, DeMille bought the rights to *The Sign of the Cross*, a transcendently creaky play from 1895 by the British actor-producer Wilson Barrett. This fictional story of Christian martyrs in Nero's Rome would, he decided, be his bite-the-bullet return to Paramount. Unlike *Quo Vadis?* from which it stole heavily (with a few helpings of *Ben-Hur* tossed in), it ends on a note of ecstatic martyrdom, the curtain falling as the newly converted prefect and his Christian amour ascend the dungeon stairs to greet a pack of hungry lions. The Romans win the match, Barrett avers, and the Christians win the game. There had already been multiple stage productions of *The Sign of the Cross*, plus two silent film versions and a hilariously Victorian novelization. To recreate ancient Rome, DeMille had a budget of under $700,000—less than a third of what he spent on *The King of Kings*. Some of that money was his, and he pinched every penny.

The result, which premiered in December 1932, was everything DeMille wanted, a huge hit that went well beyond the usual Hollywood sin-and-redemption schlock with some indelible images: Christians trudging forward to the lions, gladiatorial action, Charles Laughton's Nero fiddling with his lyre, and Claudette Colbert's epochal bath in asses' milk.[2] Many years later, Pauline

---

[1]In later years, the trajectory became odder still: DeMille's style calcified, and the films became stagier and more regressive cinematically, yet their popularity only increased. Look at the 1956 *Ten Commandments* alongside other blockbusters of the time—*Giant, The Searchers, The Bridge on the River Kwai*. There's almost no point of contact with which to make a comparison; DeMille is still operating, blissfully and successfully, in the nineteenth century.

[2]Before her performance as the wicked empress Poppaea, Colbert had been slotted as a pleasantly generic leading woman. This performance was her breakthrough, although after playing another DeMille queen, Cleopatra, she took her career in a vastly different direction. When she died in 1996, the lacto-sensualist of *The Sign of the Cross* was one of her most often recalled performances.

Kael's retrospective *New Yorker* notice nailed it definitively: "DeMille's bang-'em-on-the-head-with-wild-orgies-and-imperiled-virginity style is at its ripest . . . just about irresistible." Not only irresistible for its kitsch, either, for it was visually stunning, in fact, one of the earliest of sound films to recapture the shimmering opulence of silent film. That it survived so well in the collective memory was quite an achievement, considering that for nearly sixty years it was seen only in mutilated form. Therein lies a tale as lurid and moralistic as any DeMille deigned to film.

The *Sign of the Cross*, as originally released, was one of the most extreme, even outrageous of Hollywood films made prior to the movie cleanup of 1934. The desperate circumstances under which DeMille made it drove him to reach further and deeper for his effects than he ever had, and in more contradictory directions. With the purse strings so tight, there could be no question of halfway measures: more sex than in *Baby Face,* more savagery than in *Scarface,* and with moralizing and preaching that attained vertiginous heights. *The Sign of the Cross* was a house deliberately, spectacularly divided against itself, a story of faith and martyrdom filled with carnal pagan zest. DeMille had renounced the concepts of subtlety and nuance in about 1917, and here those black-and-white extremes reached their pinnacle. Ultimately—and this was something he never acknowledged publicly—there was a high cost to his envelope pushing. *The Sign of the Cross* was one of the prime causes for the film cleanup of 1934, and along with other films it suffered the consequences of its audacity. It was twice reissued after the strengthening of the Production Code (in 1938 and again, with a ludicrous "modern" prologue, in 1944) with most of its excesses removed. As with other films suffering this indignity (ranging from *King Kong* to *Mata Hari*), the negatives were cut and the offending footage destroyed and eventually forgotten.[3] Only DeMille remembered, and only he retained a complete print of the film. Finally, in 1989, *The Sign of the Cross* was restored by the UCLA Film and Television Archive, with all DeMille's 1932 outrages back in place. Film preservation often reopens forgotten windows, and the new light shed on *The Sign of the Cross,* coupled with greater availability of the Production Code papers, made a few forgotten facts vividly apparent. DeMille's take on sex and violence was perhaps predictable; less so was the fact that *The Sign of the Cross* was the first major American film to create significant controversy over its homoerotic content, starting ripples that eventually affected the entire movie industry.

---

[3]Some of those cut films have been restored, thanks in part to private collectors with access to forbidden footage. Others, like *Love Me Tonight, Animal Crackers,* and *Cavalcade,* will probably never be seen again in their original form. With film considered a disposable commodity, the censor's shears cut deep.

DeMille's chief thrust with this "story of . . . magnificent faith and hero-ism," as he called it, was that it was insufficient to show merely the purity of Christianity in and of itself. It had to be heightened, and made commercial, by its juxtaposition with the decadence and evil of Rome. He began by establish-ing the counterpoint visually, in a way that has become a cliché in historical films: The Christians are a solemn bunch in homespun garments, with modest women and patriarchal old men straight out of Genesis. The Romans, naturally, are livelier, with clean-shaven men and painted women with spit curls, both sexes in body-baring outfits. Using this visual shorthand as an embarking point, DeMille set out to create a Roman holiday, an event that would turn empty Depression movie theaters into SRO coliseums. The last quarter of the film, the arena sequence, emerged as the most stomach-turning exhibition of violence yet seen in American cinemas. Gladiators and the Christian-hungry lions were the least of it, for there was a full menu of scandalous divertissements. Most notorious of them was a little number involving a naked blonde chained to a post, being visited by an amorous gorilla. There were also fistfights with spiked gloves, bearbaiting, and warring factions of pygmies and Amazon women tear-ing each other to bits.[4] DeMille had achieved the most epic hypocrisy of his life: as a devout Christian who relished violence and voyeurism, he gave his tale of a pure faith more gore than a horror film or gangster picture. Somehow, he felt, he needed to go further. Casting about for some type of contemporary gimmick by which pagan Rome could simultaneously repel and intrigue and arouse his audiences, he combined a little ancient history with a slug of Krafft-Ebbing. For the first time since *Manslaughter* in 1921, DeMille turned to homosexuality.

The common folk in DeMille's Rome, jawing slang, shooting dice, and bickering about their seats at the arena, were recognizable types from just about any street corner in America. The nobility, as presided over by Laughton's Nero, was more rarefied, suggesting some previously unknown intersection of Park Avenue and Christopher Street. Nobility and wealth can only spell perver-sity, and the union of Laughton's Nero and Colbert's Poppaea was hardly a love match. She was in eternal and randy pursuit of Fredric March, while he took time out from burning Rome to have a pedicure or a dalliance with a nearly naked slave boy. This hunky attendant (played by the well-muscled Georges

---

[4]One shot of an Amazon decapitating a pygmy still causes audiences to scream. The real "money shots," i.e., the lions chomping on the Christians, are actually little in evidence in the finished film—only two brief flashes. The reason was fiscal, not aesthetic or moral: one day in September 1932, as DeMille was shooting arena sequences, an assistant ran in and told him that the budget had just been used up. DeMille immediately yelled, "Cut!" and the picture was wrapped before more lion shots could be made. The original script had also specified a chariot race . . . but DeMille decided to substitute naked virgins for chariots, thus one-upping *Ben-Hur* and saving a great deal of money to boot.

Bruggeman) is the only apparent clue that DeMille intended Nero to be gay, yet Laughton's mannerisms are sufficiently outré to lend themselves to any manner of exotic conjecture. Costume dramas were rare in Depression cinema, and it was rarer still to have a famous figure portrayed with such unconventional élan. Laughton was credited with stealing the movie and, to DeMille's great satisfaction, the performance cemented his American fame. *Photoplay* ran an article about the phenomenon, tipping off Laughton's impact with the arch title, "Such a Naughty Nero": "The audience . . . howled with laughter. Rolled right out in to the aisles [and] wailed hysterically. . . . Charles Laughton, our popular English acquisition, has done a refreshingly original job in characterizing the witless emperor. . . . And how he loved doing it!" The *Times* of London reached back to comparisons with Oscar Wilde—the lavender archetype, of course—to assert that Laughton's "tittering [and] lady-like" Nero contained "suggestions of the decadent aesthete of the nineties."

Except for Marcus (March), the other male Roman aristocrats were divided between the corpulently straight (one horny old guy in particular makes a spectacle of himself at Marcus's orgy) and the ascetically effete. Ferdinand Gottschalk was a sixtyish character actor who specialized in playing spinsterish or prissy-mouthed old men. Like Laughton, he was not so much effeminate as just, apparently, completely free of hetero mannerisms. As the assistant to Garbo's neurotic ballerina in *Grand Hotel*, he was one of cinema's first evidently gay courtiers to a showbiz diva. In *The Sign of the Cross*, looking like a decrepit and depleted Bacchus, he dishes gossip and bon mots to anyone in earshot. Cautioning March about romancing the devout Mercia (Elissa Landi), he burbles, "I hear Christians aren't digestible!" And like Nero, he has a boytoy frequently in attendance.

DeMille saved his trump card for the orgy sequence that opened the second half of the film.[5] While the other Christians have been arrested, March has spirited Landi to his house, where he throws an orgy in time-tested Hollywood fashion: wine on tap, plush cushions, courtesans in shiny brassieres, and a nonstop harp-oboe-percussion musical combo. Though Landi is secluded from the revels, she has her hands full fending off March's advances, at which point the party guests barge in. Most conspicuously present is Ancaria (Joyzelle), whom March presents as "The wickedest and, uh, most *talented* woman in Rome." As the guests mock Landi, March decides that one of Ancaria's performances would be just the thing to thaw her. ("If that doesn't do it, she's dead!" offers one guest.) In Barrett's play, Ancaria sings to Mercia of the joys of hedonism in a song called

---

[5]In its opening engagements *The Sign of the Cross* ran in a reserved-seat roadshow format, a rarity during the Depression (because of higher ticket prices). As soon as viewers took their seats after the intermission, they were plunged into the orgy chez March.

Thus spake Cecil B. DeMille: Verily, Fredric March shall host an orgy, and Joyzelle will strive mightily to seduce Elissa Landi. Ferdinand Gottschalk shall watch in bemusement, and the audiences will come in droves. "The Naked Moon," *The Sign of the Cross. Photofest*

"Today the Roses Bloom," with the scene's kicker being that her performance is drowned out by a group of hymn-singing Christians being marched to their execution. Even in Barrett's archaic dramaturgy, the scene is effective in a pre-DeMillean way: the decadence is shown in order to be condemned, and virtue is invincible. DeMille was naturally loath to discard such a scene, though the ode to the good life sung by Barrett's Ancaria was far too anemic for this post–Jazz Age Rome. The first draft screenplay of *The Sign of the Cross* penciled in "Today the Roses Bloom" with a caveat that new lyrics were being written. What finally emerged was "The Naked Moon"—not quite a song, not quite a dance, and very definitely a piece of same-sex seduction. An epiphany and a train wreck, it's unquestionably the most outlandish set piece of DeMille's career.

    Reprinting the lyrics alone (some of which are not particularly discernible in Joyzelle's verbal lunges) does not begin to encapsulate these three-plus minutes of cinema. DeMille working at such full strength requires a diagram:

"The Naked Moon"

Ancaria (Joyzelle) chants:	Shot	Action
Under the naked moon, I've found you. We meet. I've seen you in my dreams	Medium long shot, Mercia and Ancaria center, Marcus far right, others around them	Ancaria throws off her cape, begins to circle Mercia. Caresses Mercia's shoulders and thrusts her pelvis toward her.
(Music plays)	Close-up	Male guest watches, aroused.
In dreams, indiscreet.	Medium shot	Ancaria runs hands down Mercia's body.
With tortures so sweet.	Close-up	Marcus watching approvingly.
(Music)	Medium shot	Ancaria gestures, then runs to Marcus.
	Close-up	Marcus grabs Ancaria's breasts, pushes her toward Mercia.
	Medium shot	Ancaria kneels, runs hands up Mercia's body.
	Close-up	Young woman fondles fat, inebriated old man.
	Close-up	Ancaria nuzzles Mercia, fondles her shoulders.
I've loved you in dreams	Medium long shot through torch flame	Ancaria thrusts her pelvis toward Mercia, then dances around her.
	Long shot	Ancaria dances and spins.
Breathe upon me	Close-up	Couple watching; man fondles woman's breast while she breathes heavily.
Draw me.	Close-up	Ancaria grabs Mercia's hair and kisses her neck.
Gently.	Medium close-up	Marcus watches approvingly.
Touch my heart.	Medium long shot	Ancaria wriggles her hips and puts Mercia's hand on her breast.
[Interruption by hymn]	[. . .]	[. . .]
Love will be warm	Long shot	Marcus pushes Ancaria to Mercia. Ancaria kneels and runs hands up Mercia's legs.

(Continued)

"The Naked Moon" *(cont.)*

Ancaria (Joyzelle) chants:	Shot	Action
In the gold of your hair. Feed from your lips,	Medium shot	Ancaria runs hands up Mercia's torso into her hair, dances around her, and fondles her while trying to shut out the hymn.
A-tremble with mysteries old,	Medium close-up	Marcus watches.
Persuasive,	Medium shot	Ancaria dances, grabs Mercia's shoulders.
Then bold.	Extreme close-up	Man and woman kissing, he grabs her hair and dance becomes visible through the strands.
Until he, madness, outstrips,	Medium shot	Ancaria dances and gestures, covers her ears.
I breathe upon you, Draw unto you, And let love spread his wings.	Medium long shot	Ancaria throws herself at Mercia's feet, moves upward caressing her, then dances around her.
We have been two, We shall be one.	Medium close-up	Marcus gestures anxiously to spur Ancaria on.
Both throb.	Close-up	Ancaria tries to kiss Mercia, who smiles as she hears the hymn.
[*Interruption by hymn*]	[. . .]	[. . .]
Oh! We have been two, We shall be one![6]	Long shot	Ancaria dances around Mercia, then slaps her.
[*Yells*] What are you smiling at?		

Never before, and very seldom since. Between Joyzelle's rhythmic mutterings and whore-of-Babylon hip swings, LeRoy Prinz's lurid choreography, the moaning oboe and sax music, and cinematographer Karl Struss's erotically glowing images, "The Naked Moon" leaps like a lightning bolt across seven decades. Its

---

[6]The screenplay credits coauthor Sidney Buchman with the lyrics. To understate the matter, "The Naked Moon" is a far cry from Buchman's later work on such films as *Mr. Smith Goes to Washington*. Originally, the lyrics ran "With writhings so sweet"; the Code Office cautioned DeMille's people that this line gave pause, so DeMille pretended to tone it down, substituted "tortures" . . . a clear case of six thrills of one, a half dozen of the other.

impact has changed, perhaps, since 1932, but not lessened.[7] When the restored version premiered at the American Museum of the Moving Image (Astoria, Queens) in 1989, the audience gasped and then tittered, as much at its eye-glazing eccentricity as at DeMille's intent. ("It's like performance art!" cheered one spectator.) The director's motives, of course, are as palpable as if the film were in 3-D. Repel the audience? Sure. Arouse them at the same time? No question. And Paramount was happy to contribute to the furor. Just prior to the premiere, a studio publicist gave the scene some lip-smacking advance notice when he observed to a reporter that "the sets are marvelous [and] the costumes spell sex. There's Claudette Colbert in a milk bath. And Fredric March using the sensuous Joyzelle to break down the resistance of Landi—mentally, and how!"

Canny prevaricator that he was, DeMille knew that, no matter how much Landi's Mercia resisted Ancaria's advances, lots of audience members, especially men, would be aroused as much as they would be repelled. He wanted the scene to appeal as much as to shock, a point he made clear to his niece Agnes when he hired her, in 1934, to create and perform an erotic dance for the barge sequence of *Cleopatra*. After she showed him what she planned to do, he gave her hell:

> Cecil said, "Oh, no, no! This won't do. There's no sex, there's nothing, there's no excitement. This wouldn't seduce anybody." And he said "This wouldn't seduce me." . . . I lost my temper [when] Cecil said, " I want the kind of dance we had in *Sign of the Cross*, a lesbian dance." I said, "I thought that was one of the funniest things I ever saw." And he said, "Well *baby*, that's the kind of humor we're looking for!"

Agnes de Mille, possibly to her relief, was fired from *Cleopatra*, and the new Production Code of 1934 ensured that DeMille would never again have a lesbian dance.

In this, the most homoerotically forward scene in the first seven decades of American cinema, DeMille had ingeniously opted for an insidious and non-stereotyped approach. Ancaria is a lithe, attractive woman, not a cigar-waving caricature. Additionally, she is shown working on Marcus as well as on Mercia, making her a Dietrichesque icon of all-embracing eroticism. (Appropriately enough, Dietrich herself created a sensation when she showed up at *Cross*'s Hollywood premiere in a tux and soft fedora.) As outlandish as the scene now appears, for a mainstream public seven decades ago its effect was mostly one of subtlety and cunning. The influential trade paper *Harrison's Reports* claimed that

---

[7]The trick shots with the burning torch and stroking hair, in particular, are among the most sexually heated visuals in a film crammed with them. And yes, in the "How Many Shots Can DeMille Include of Shoes and Feet?" sweepstakes, *The Sign of the Cross* ranks high.

most audiences wouldn't know what it was about: "A representation of Roman orgies . . . is quite real and bold, but it has been handled delicately; the average adult will not understand that it is a lesbian dance, and hardly any of the adolescents will know what is happening. This scene is an important part in the story." It soon became clear that more people knew what it was about than Harrison had estimated. As with so many of the gay and lesbian references in films of the time, it was there for those who knew, average adult or no. Unlike scenes in previous films, however, it was there for far longer, with far greater erotic impact, and with the clear implication that even though Marcus, with all his appeal, was unable to seduce Mercia, Ancaria would be more irresistible. And alongside its appeal there was also fear and dread: in depicting the wicked "them" attacking the pure "us," it made gayness something it had not seemed before—a threat.

Even in this era before the Legion of Decency and the enforced Production Code, it was clear that with "The Naked Moon" DeMille had gotten away with far more than the law normally allowed. Part of it had to do with that unshakable argument he had been making for so many years: you will never know what sin is unless you see it and see how virtue can triumph over it. A large portion, too, came from sheer clout. DeMille was the best-known director in the business, and his fame bought leeway with the Code people unavailable to lesser figures. And his own powers of persuasion were considerable. During the first week of shooting he had invited Col. Jason Joy, the head Production Code official on the West Coast, to visit the set. Colonel Joy was both impressed and completely snowed, telling DeMille that he had no objections to anything in the script and that "what I saw on the set . . . goes beyond my fondest expectations."[8]

The piety card turned up again when Paramount, hoping for a bit of divine recognition, sent a copy of the script to one of the most prominent members of New York's faith community, the Methodist Episcopal minister and theologian Christian F. Reisner. Evidently the thinking was that Dr. Reisner would advise his sizable flock to see a film that proved that Hollywood was, after all, a spiritual place. No doubt about it, the script made an enormous impression upon Reisner, whose reply to the Paramount advertising department ran, in part:

> The script sent to me is repellant and nauseating to every thinking Christian. It endeavors to get a lot of lewd scenes and sex appeal exhibitions on the screen and then dresses the whole with a cheap and unhistorical hodge-podge of hymns and incidents from sacred Christian martyrdom. Only an ignoramus concerning Christian history, feelings and facts would compose such a script. It is a cheap and disgusting attempt to present lewd performances under a sacred name and shielded by an ignorant notion of religion. . . . The whole picture is suggestive, unclean and unworthy of a great company like [Paramount]. . . .
>
> I feel chagrined to think that you had such a cheap notion of me as to think I would in any way commend it.

Gently underscoring his point, Reisner signed the letter "Yours in disgust."

Undeterred, DeMille continued to tout the upcoming film as a work of sanctity and shepherded it past the tough New York censor prior to its opening on Broadway and in Hollywood early in December. In New York it was noted that women were becoming ill during the arena sequence; consequently, the nastiest of those scenes—a naked girl set upon by crocodiles—was scissored out, not to be seen again until 1989. The reviews were quintessentially DeMillean:

---

[8]Later that fall, Colonel Joy was succeeded at the Code office by Dr. James Wingate. Viewing the completed print of *The Sign of the Cross*, Wingate filed objections to some of the arena scenes and portions of "The Naked Moon." DeMille ignored him.

respectful of showmanship and craft, less enthusiastic over the moralizing, condescending about the melodrama. *Variety* gave the devil his due:

> It has a double action scenario [which] is going to stir up some two-sided sen-
> timent wherever shown. It's going to make the church element dizzy trying to figure
> out which way to turn. The plot takes longshot chances with meddlers, much of it
> being some of the boldest censor-bait ever attempted in a picture. . . .
>
> Neat, deft and probably beyond reproach is the manner in which the scarlet
> punches are inserted. Every sequence in which religion wins out is built upon lurid
> details. The censors may object to the method, but they can't oppose the motive,
> and in the way "Cross" was produced one can't be in without the other. . . .
>
> Besides Ancaria, who sounds like "Aunt Carrie" as the dialog is read but who
> looks and acts like [a] stripper, there is Charles Laughton's expert Nero, who dou-
> bles as the degenerate emperor and musical pyromaniac as Rome burns.
>
> It's likely more trouble will come from the women than the censors. Some
> attempts herein to horrify for theatrical effects and dramatic results are unprece-
> dented on the screen. . . . Most of it will be nearly nauseating to those with sen-
> sitive stomachs. But all of it is holding . . . and although the first thought may be to
> turn away, there is something in the brutal slaughter that nails fascinated attention.

Ancaria's dance nailed just as much attention as the arena scenes, and
even more than Colbert's bath. Except in isolated and usually notorious
examples like the Loeb-Leopold trial, mainstream publications rarely brought
up homosexuality. Yet twice in late 1932 the press was compelled to cover
onscreen lesbianism. Just prior to *The Sign of the Cross*, Leontine Sagan's
Maedchen in Uniform had made a huge splash on the burgeoning circuit of
American art houses. Part of its appeal lay in the sensitivity and skill with
which Sagan told her story of life in a German girl's school, and part had to do
with the "Are they or aren't they?" nature of the tale. Some critics argued that
Sagan's schoolgirl heroine had a simple hero-worship crush on her austerely
beautiful teacher; others felt that Sagan was filling her cup from *The Well of
Loneliness*. In either case, *Maedchen in Uniform* was, unlike *The Sign of the
Cross*, an exercise in delicacy and taste. It made "The Naked Moon" seem that
much more lurid in comparison. *Commonweal*, reviewing the two films side by
side, praised Sagan's work while declaring *The Sign of the Cross* "nauseating"
and "the last straw in [Hollywood's] hypocrisy." Critic Richard Dana Skinner
singled out Ancaria's dance for special censure and exhorted right-minded people to complain "loudly and unceasingly until this particular stench is removed
from the American scene. Downright filth should take its chance honestly with
the public mind, but hypocritical filth and sadism are infamies to be wiped
out." Pioneer film historian Terry Ramsaye, writing in *The Motion Picture
Herald*, also complained at length:

We are required to see Marcia [*sic*] . . . made to stand the immobile focus of a bombardment of Lesbian wiles offered by a dancing wanton through some three or four minutes of screen time. This amazing interlude is dragged into the plot by its tail being the while entirely out of key with every element of such plausibility as the picture contains, and in addition a fertile source of objection in official quarters as well as an offense to the taste of the commonality. . . .

But as to the picture—they [DeMille's audiences] will shudder, they will gasp, they will cry, and they will love it, provided their sensibilities survive the odors of Lesbos and de Sade. It's that kind of picture and they are that kind of people.[9]

Such spectators as could afford $1.50 or $2 for a movie ticket flocked to *The Sign of the Cross* in its opening weeks, drawn as much by the scandalized reviews as by the return of lush silent-era spectacle. By Christmas week, however, the naysayers began to speak out, led by the religious community whose favor DeMille had sought to cultivate. *America*, the national Roman Catholic weekly newspaper, wondered how "The Naked Moon" had escaped the censors, and in a number of cities priests requested that their parishioners boycott DeMille's Christian epic. Cleveland's Bishop Joseph Schrembs tore into it during his New Year's sermon, calling it a "damnable hypocrisy" which "spilled out upon us all of the nastiness, all of the filth, all of the dirt the human mind and heart conceive."

DeMille had hoped for a sensation, but this much of a scandal had not figured in his plans. About the time that the priests and bishops issued their condemnation, he heard from Will H. Hays, who made it a point to step in when major film-related scandals were brewing. The encounter, as recalled by DeMille, became a key moment in his self-deification. Hays asked him what he was going to do about "The Naked Moon," and DeMille, that sturdy icon of free expression, recounted that his reply was an emphatic "Not a damn thing." The dance, he went on, stayed in the picture, and free speech had again triumphed over censorship and bigotry. The MPAA files reveal nothing of this particular conversation, and the dance did remain in the film throughout its American release (although a few shots were snipped out by the notorious Ohio censorship board). There were mixed reports on how much the Catholic backlash had dented the film's grosses. The returns on the initial reserved-seat engagements were indeed disappointing, which likely had far more to do with the fact that early 1933 was one of the lowest points of the Depression, and few could afford

---

[9]Ramsaye's objections were at least equal opportunity. He also complained about the crocodiles (though noting that they'd been removed subsequent to the premiere) and sniped that the gorilla scene "has its roots rather more closely in 'Ingagi' than in early Christian history." *Ingagi* (1930) was the original African-girl-meets-gorilla exploitation shocumentary, and by comparing such a sleazy piece to DeMille's work he was striking as low a blow as he could.

the tickets. When *The Sign of the Cross* moved onto low-price general release, however, the story changed. Along with a concurrent succèse de scandale, Mae West's *She Done Him Wrong*, it was credited with rescuing Paramount from receivership.

The calls to boycott, ultimately, had not worked. But DeMille's victory over the prudes was less heroic than he portrayed it. His insistence on having such a clear-cut and threatening gay element in his movie focused an enormous amount of attention on what movie producers could, when they had the where-withal and the chutzpah, put up there on the screen. Now, along with the violence of the gangster and horror films and the blatant sex of the Jean Harlow and Constance Bennett films, sexual irregularity was added to the moralizers' roster of Hollywood evils being fed to innocent filmgoers. Had "The Naked Moon"—clothed as it was in DeMille's lascivious sanctimony—tried less hard to both entice and repel, the cause célèbre might have been avoided. Instead, it made the situation markedly worse, prodding the Roman Catholic Church to come out more strongly than ever against Hollywood. The two most influential Catholic men in the film industry were Martin Quigley and Joe Breen, two of the forces behind the 1930 Production Code. Both were appalled that "that lesbian dance," as Quigley called it, had stayed in. Not until 1935 would Breen have the power to command that the scene be excised (which he did, posthaste). Yet, throughout 1933 and into 1934, as complaints of Hollywood licentiousness mounted, Breen, Quigley, and many others held tenaciously to their grudge. A year or so later, long after "The Naked Moon" had ceased running in theaters, their angered memory of Joyzelle's gyrations around Elissa Landi would bear bitter fruit.

FIVE

Pansies and Lesbos of 1933

An educated foreigner, strange to the land, might well conclude from the general moral precepts of ordinary movies that the country at large was engaging in a final orgiastic, razzle-dazzle dash to the devil. He might convince himself if he looked over the record and discovered that only five years ago hundreds of legal and official censors, under the watchful eye of chief wowser, Will Hays, made it almost impossible for a director to handle a manuscript dealing with any of the everyday facts of life.

Currently, our foreigner would find . . . pictures especially created for ladies who admittedly prefer pants to petticoats and he would find in almost every movie comedy some allusion to homosexuality.

Oddly enough, he would also find that even though the censors allow such things, the public cares so little about these antics it consistently stays away from the theatres.

Pare Lorentz, "The Cinema in Review,"
Vanity Fair, June 1933

America and American cinema were both reborn in 1933. Has any president taken office on a wave of expectations so great as that aimed at Roosevelt? If the economy took years to assume normalcy, the film industry made a massive upturn in very short order. Depressed economically and in some quarters artistically, the movie business began the restoration process in the four months between Roosevelt's election and his inauguration. While it would continue to reflect the Depression mood, film would also assume a more conscious role as the nation's favorite means of escaping tough realities. *The Sign of the Cross* had been one of the harbingers of the comeback of "big" movies—big less in budget than in must-seeability—and in the succeeding months it was joined by a select group of others: *Cavalcade, State Fair, She*

Done Him Wrong, 42nd Street, Gold Diggers of 1933, King Kong, Tugboat Annie, Dinner at Eight. In the midst of this upturn, the esteemed Pare Lorentz filed his objection in *Vanity Fair.* He was not alone in his views, but neither was he reflecting genuine public opinion. He was, in fact, quite wrong to think that the low film grosses of the previous few years had had more to do with content than with national indigence. Far more accurate than this was his irritated assertion that 1933 had seen a marked upturn in gay and lesbian images on film.

As far as gay cinema was concerned, 1932 had ended with an immensely conspicuous double dose of lesbianism. As forward as the Bobby Watsons of the screen had been, something in both *Maedchen in Uniform* and *The Sign of the Cross* seemed to portend even more in the way of cinematic candor and daring as well as in potential difficulty with censorship and religious groups. Without question, 1933 saw the greatest number and variety of overt gay portrayals thus far . . . and set a record that would endure for almost six decades. Over a year after the Pathé newsreel with the faux-fairy dog lover, lavender humor was still on the menu. The flavor-of-the-month pansy craze had already begun to fade in large cities, fueled by police crackdowns and righteous outrage. The movies, meanwhile, were a few steps behind the trend, as they sometimes can be. The year 1933 would be the peak of the movies' version of the pansy craze: the gay and lesbian characters in 1933 films were made increasingly more conspicuous, more titillating, more forward.

The upturn in volume and frankness naturally meant that the outrage increased incrementally as well. Moral objections to movies, in fact, were on the upswing in 1933, though not chiefly centered on Hollywood's growing fascination with alternative sexuality. Many of the protests coalesced around one curvaceous figure. Even back then, drag queens knew Mae West as a kindred life force; they both were able to make the roughest, funniest, and most accurate jokes about sex in general and sex with men in particular. Less open-minded observers trembled in horror, even as West's first starring films, *She Done Him Wrong* and *I'm No Angel,* finished the job, begun by *The Sign of the Cross,* of saving Paramount from receivership. Paramount was responsible for one of the other major taboo-breakers as well, *The Story of Temple Drake*—William Faulkner's rape-and-degradation shocker *Sanctuary* in all but name. Warner Bros. created a furor with Barbara Stanwyck sleeping her way up the corporate ladder in the infamous *Baby Face,* and late in the year did everything it could to dismantle Code strictures with the rowdy boys'-night-out comedy *Convention City.* The brouhaha over "The Naked Moon" was repeated several times during the year in varying contexts, and most often the producers would again win the battles. As far as homosexuality was concerned, Lorentz was not the only person that year to be shaking his head in wonderment that something so taboo heretofore could suddenly be dealt with so overtly. Many moralists shared his displeasure, while evidently the public was far less outraged.

Hot on the heels of *The Sign of the Cross* came another noisy censorship controversy, albeit over a far less important film. The tale of *So This Is Africa* is an instructive fable about what could happen when producers lacking Cecil B. DeMille's clout attempted to go too far. Instead of an ostensibly elevating prestige project, *Africa* was an openly cheesy comedy, a vehicle for the cheerfully lowbrow team of Bert Wheeler and Robert Woolsey. Until late 1932, Wheeler (the baby-faced ninny) and Woolsey (the smart aleck with glasses and cigar) had been the prime comic stars at RKO, making one daft and corny vehicle after another. A salary dispute caused their decampment to Columbia Pictures, at that time a minor studio with one ace director, Frank Capra. Columbia's Harry Cohn welcomed W&W to the lot with promises of packed theaters and profit percentage, and to clinch the deal it was decided that the duo, whose work had never been particularly tasteful, would go many steps further in a blue direction. *So This Is Africa* was a spoof of the jungle-film craze then in effect, Tarzan and documentaries and all the rest, with W&W as a pair of boobs who join a filmmaking expedition and bumble into a lost tribe of Amazons. There was ample opportunity for all kinds of incorrect jokes, puns, slapstick adventure, and mistaken-gorilla gags, as well as slots for songs and dances. The raciness stepped up in the last reel when the boys became embroiled in a marriage ceremony (to each other) and then, in drag, were lusted after by a pair of native men.[1] At the fadeout they are shown as native housewives with babies on their backs—again straddling, for comedic purposes, that peculiar line between queerness and inverted gender.

This hardly constituted comedy filmmaking for the ages à la Chaplin. *So This Is Africa* was cheap, fast, sometimes funny, and above all vulgar: lowdown lowbrow fare for audiences who needed a quarter's worth of laughs to help get through a rough season. As such, it was passed by James Wingate of the Hays Office's Studio Relations Committee. Wingate had approved *The Sign of the Cross* after DeMille refused to make cuts, and he felt *Africa* to be acceptable, if rowdy. It opened in some regional areas early in January 1933, after which Columbia prepared for its New York premiere by running it for the state censorship board and the eminent, influential National Board of Review. Both groups flatly refused to give the film a passing certificate, and Will Hays and the Code's New York office stepped in. Hays, his associate Joseph Breen, and publisher Martin Quigley had been aghast at Wingate's handling of *The Sign of the Cross*. Fearing more fallout from state censorship boards and religious groups, they decided that *So This Is Africa* was a battle they could win; unlike DeMille

---

[1]The men, like the Amazons, are white actors in very light brownface. Strange sex was a target for quick laughs in 1933, but not racial crossover.

and Paramount, Columbia had neither the prestige nor the pull to refuse the cuts or fight the bureaucrats. After waging an improbable war over this trashy piece of fluff, the studio acceded to a series of cuts that effectively savaged the movie. With Wheeler and Woolsey back at RKO and not available for retakes, *So This Is Africa* went out as it was, riddled with disfiguring gouges (some of which have since been restored, quite a few of which remain to this day). The Italian-American stereotyping of character actor Henry Armetta, the bottoms-up jokes and crude puns—all settled into the cutting-room dust; the marginally more subtle material having overt drag and gay subtext was allowed to remain some-what intact, even though *Variety* had said this was the most objectionable part of the movie. By the time *So This Is Africa* hit theaters, its reputation as a dirty movie had preceded it, and that made for sizable grosses. This did not mean that Wheeler and Woolsey came out ahead: Harry Cohn's creative bookkeeping ensured that their profit deal did not reach the low two figures.

Cavalcade, which had opened a few weeks prior to this to-do, was to *So This Is Africa* as a Bentley is to a Pinto. Its premiere was granted all the publicity of *The Sign of the Cross*, plus a large portion of something seldom given DeMille movies: respect. Even as early as 1933, Noël Coward's name signified class far above Hollywood norms, and his intimate epic, using one English family as a canvas for the changes of the twentieth century, had immense built-in prestige. Fox filmed it using British actors in almost every role, and the prizes at the end were ecstatic reviews, huge grosses, and an Academy Award as Best Picture. There were a few censorious reservations over the use of a few "damns" and "hells," and another scene drew sizable attention if little criticism. In the segment depicting post–World War disenchantment, a montage of headlines screaming of scandal, murder, divorce, suicide, and finally (gasp) "vice orgies" dissolves to a chic party in a private club. As the camera pans across various dancers and lounge lizards, a pair of women (one austere in black, the other frilly in white) sit dreamily, one taking the other's hand. The camera then picks up one young man clasping a slave bracelet onto the wrist of his young male partner. The point, evidently, is that postwar ennui (the scene also contains Coward's song "Twentieth Century Blues") leads to moral lassitude—a some-what hypocritical crowd-pleasing point to make.[2] In a film of this importance

---

[2]The idea for the gay couples came from Fox, not from Coward. According to *Cavalcade*'s costume designer, Earl Luick, the pairs were the brainchild of Fox production chief Winfield Sheehan. "Sheehan thought the picture was going to be a dud," Luick said. "And then after seeing the rushes he decided they had a knockout. So he wanted to put his finger in the pie, and his idea was to have two boys there, gay boys, and two lesbians." Luick obliged with a nattily tuxedoish gown for actress Betsey Beaton. The scene, unfortunately, suffered the same fate as "The Naked Moon," and without the eventual restoration. When *Cavalcade* was reissued in 1935, most of the shot with the lesbians was removed, although the slave-bracelet boys were allowed to remain.

and respectability, the scene was viewed as something of a milestone. Gay relationships could, it seemed, now be shown in prestigious projects as well as the run-of-the-mill fare. Some weeks after the premiere of *Cavalcade*, *Variety* noted a clear trend in an article preciously entitled "Tsk, Tsk, Such Goings On":

> Producers are going heavy on the pansy stuff in current pix, despite the watchful eyes of the Hays office, which is attempting to keep the dual-sex boys and lesbos out of films.
>
> With a "queer" flash in *Cavalcade*, [the filmmakers'] attitude is that if [a] picture of that type can get away with it, why not in the programmers.

Bearing out the thesis of *Variety*'s article was a film reviewed in that same issue of February 28, 1933. Like *Cavalcade*, *Our Betters* was awash in literary prestige: another esteemed (and gay) British writer, Somerset Maugham, and another look at life in the upper English classes. But unlike *Cavalcade*'s Marryot family nobly weathering the years, *Our Betters* looked witheringly at the intrusion of expatriates into the British nobility. The heroine, Lady Pearl Grayston (Constance Bennett), was a Yankee heiress rising (and social climbing) above her loveless marriage to a useless aristocrat. Her love-hate rival is an aging wreck of a duchess (Violet Kemble Cooper) obsessed with a continental gigolo (Gilbert Roland). During a few hours chez Pearl, sexual and social allegiances are strained and coddled, until finally Pearl's younger sister catches Pearl *in flagrante gigolo* and decides to return to America in disgust.[3] In Maugham's play, the ultimate cause of the rift between Pearl and Bessie (Anita Louise) is the arrival of Ernest, an affected dancing master whom Pearl has summoned to mollify the Duchess. Ernest's total absorption in triviality was carried forward into the film by director George Cukor and notably expanded. In the play Maugham had noted that Ernest is "a little dark man, with large eyes, and long hair neatly plastered down . . . dressed like a tailor's dummy [and] overwhelmingly gentlemanly. He speaks in mincing tones." Such was the designation carried in the screenplay for *Our Betters* approved by the Studio Relations Committee. However, the key for Cukor became the single word "mincing": for Ernest (Tyrell Davis) is portrayed less as a silly fop than as a rouged, twitty, fairy-winged pansy, the most extreme portrayal of this sort yet, and perhaps ever, seen in film. Ernest is onscreen for only a few minutes, but seldom, at least until Godot, would a character be given such a buildup.

---

[3]Given that Maugham's savage dissection is as tough on nouveau-riche Americans as on the Brits, it's worth noting that *Our Betters*, the play, premiered not in the United Kingdom but in the United States, in 1917, in Atlantic City(!). The British would wait six years to see the nasty fun Maugham was having partly at their expense.

As Duchess Minnie, Violet Kemble Cooper can but surrender to the rouged charms of Ernest (Tyrell Davis) in *Our Betters*. *Photofest*

Mentioned and discussed during much of the film, he clearly is meant to serve as *Our Betters'* deus ex machina. As well as providing the terminus for everything the film intends to resolve, he is heightened in importance by being given, literally, the last word. The play's curtain line had been spoken by the offended sister: "They're not worth making a fuss about. I'm sailing for America next Saturday!" The movie closes the proceedings with Ernest's fawning (perhaps leering) observation of the reconciliation of Pearl and the Duchess: "What an *exquisite* spectacle—two ladies of title kissing one another!"

Tyrell Davis (sometimes billed as Tyrrell) was a British character actor whose time in 1930s Hollywood was spent exclusively in silly-ass roles. His naturally effete appearance, much like that of a too-precious scarecrow, ensured that he would never reach leading-man status. Never, though, had he (or would he afterward) get a role such as Ernest, with his painted lips and tantrumettes and hyperaffected air. Cukor and associates were clearly going after some heavy (and heavy-handed) satire with this garish caricature, as critics were quick to notice. *Variety* punned that "At the finish they ring in a pansy dancing teacher . . . with rouged lips and all. It's the most broadly painted character of the kind yet attempted." In New York, where *Our Betters* preceded (and outgrossed) *King Kong* at Radio City Music Hall, Thornton Delehanty of the *Evening Post* complained that Davis's Ernest struck "the only false note in the picture. . . . [His] effeminacy is needlessly emphasized. Surely one can be effeminate without underscoring it with lipstick."

Delehanty's objections were not unsupportable either in 1933 or today. Even without Ernest, *Our Betters* seems an overwhelmingly gay movie, one of those films where it's easy to recast most of the female roles with men. Maugham's ear catches every human frailty and delusion, and Cukor's eye for detail assures an air of total artifice. In the diamond gleam and hardness of its machinations and the wry meanness of its repartee, it now seems a warmup for Cukor's *The Women* six years later.[4] Nor does Ernest's intrusion into the brittle and bitchy goings-on provide a letdown. He's somewhat of a shock, actually, and not a welcome one for many viewers. His appearance splits today's audiences: some cringe at his lip rouge and preposterous irrelevance, seeing him as the gay equivalent of Stepin Fetchit, the racist caricature who became for many the embodiment of bigotry. Others will laugh at the sheer outrageousness of it, in the way that some viewers of color look at Fetchit as an inside joke on the white system. For the first group, and in spite of the gay artists who created him, Ernest can seem a demeaning symbol of condescension and marginalization, the equation of gayness with totally affected effeminacy, a being at once sexually motivated yet completely desexed. For "men's men," the revulsion is astronomically heightened—Ernest is the nightmare that haunts those threatened by effeminacy. Yet there are also those who relish the subversive mantle he wears with such beauty-queen grandeur; he is, ultimately, the force through which all the conflicts are resolved. The arguments can volley back and forth for this most extreme of all Hollywood pansies, and none that see him will either forget him or go away noncommittal.

Will Hays and his underlings, reading both the reviews of *Our Betters* and the *Variety* article on the pansy trend, decided that once again graphic vice had made it to the screen while the West Coast office napped. In Hollywood, Code administrator James Wingate concurred helplessly, admitting that the Ernest he had approved in the script was far milder than the one in the completed film. When he did demand cuts, it was too late: sneaky RKO had already shipped out the prints. Hays, testing the waters for audience response to pansies, sent a spy to the Music Hall, where it was found that Ernest was greeted with appreciative (as opposed to derisive) laughter. Once again, Hays and Joe Breen and others felt outfoxed, and frustrated by the way the Code's weak strictures seemed to

---

[4]A few months after *Our Betters*, Cukor directed another RKO literary adaptation about women and their loves. However, it would be hard to think of two properties as dissimilar as *Our Betters* and *Little Women*.

encourage typical Hollywood duplicity. As with Ancaria and her dance, a system that allowed an Ernest to flourish was obviously not running according to plan, and if audiences were not going to reject such things, then there had to be another way to pull the plug. The immediate response was greater vigilance over Ernest-type characters: after *Our Betters* there was a marked pulling-back, not from homosexuality per se but from the cartoonish extremes. Ernest was, and would remain, the acme of the pansy craze, Hollywood chapter.

One of the reasons the *Variety* "Tsk, Tsk" piece caused the Hays Office distress was that it discussed several upcoming projects that ensured that Ernest's brothers and sisters would be sticking around for a while. Just the fact that famed gay comedian (and occasional drag artist) Jean Malin was being mentioned for several upcoming projects was an indication that barriers were falling down. And over at Fox, a uniquely gay production was actually on the soundstages. *The Warrior's Husband* had been a 1932 Broadway play by Julian Thompson, very loosely "borrowed" from Greek mythology and *Lysistrata*, and an early success for Katharine Hepburn. Fox bought the rights for its own prestige star, Elissa Landi, who starred as Antiope, an Amazon warrior princess.[5] Both the play and the film were essentially single-joke skits on the topic of role reversal: the Amazons are the "men" in their country, their husbands are sissy homebodies, and only when the macho Greeks defeat the women is the sexual balance set aright. The broadest jokes came not from the butchness of the women in power but from the silken delicacy of their consorts. Most conspicuous of them is Sapiens (Ernest Truex), the coy consort of Hippolyta (Marjorie Rambeau), queen of the Amazons. Both Sapiens and his father (Ferdinand Gottschalk) are depicted more as womanish men than as overt fairies—but the point is clear enough, and more than enough when Sapiens calls one of the intruding Greeks a hussy. It was equally clear when Fox let it be known that a number of real-life drag artists had been hired to portray the "men" of the country of Pontus. The troupe had been the chorus of the BBB Cellar Revue, a gay nightclub show billed with the slogan "Boys will be girls!" *Variety* reported that the temperamental queens would not accept the standard men's dressing room facilities and had to be mollified with a new deluxe changing room with lacy appointments.

---

[5]It also turned up, in 1942, as the basis for Rodgers and Hart's final musical show, *By Jupiter.*

Except for *The Sign of the Cross*, Landi's Hollywood career had not thus far embraced much in the way of "class." However, she herself was considered the goods, having written several novels and starred on Broadway in *A Farewell to Arms*. Besides which, she was a child of bona fide nobility, which unfortunately gave someone at Fox the idea of billing her as "the Empress of Emotion."

Marjorie Rambeau and Ernest Truex as an Amazonian couple in *The Warrior's Husband*. She has armor and artillery, he has peignoirs and pedicures. *Photofest*

Seen today, *The Warrior's Husband* is not quite the jaw-dropping fairyland its reputation would portend. For Truex, who specialized in mousy character roles, the flowing-gowned Sapiens often seems a shade reticent, certainly less so than a Bobby Watson would have been. His characterization shows much of what's wrong with the film itself, for it's really a concatenation of conflicted intent. There's a glossy prestige-picture production, neoclassical allusions, language striving to be witty and archaic and sophisticated all at once, and occasional clumsy gropes toward pseudoburlesque humor. In short, it's a curiosity—funny in spots, good to look at, but neither intelligent nor racy enough to make any kind of provocative statement on gender roles. As with *The Dude Wrangler,* it promised more of a pansy garden than it delivered. Part of the dilution came with the filmmakers, and the Hays Office did the rest. While this is one of the films for which the Production Code Administration file has not turned up, it was reported in *Variety* that "the panze scenes" had been trimmed. This may account for the evident absence in the film of the boys-will-be-girls BBB chorines, who seem far less in evidence than some rather large spear-carrying women. While the gayness and gender chaos are still readily detectable, there's obviously been denaturing beyond Fox's original intent. The reviews were neither good nor bad nor especially enlightening on the gay themes, and after the cuts there were no special outcries. Nor was it particularly a financial success. In the end, this odd movie was a blind alley as far as Hollywood gays were concerned, and perhaps its most intriguing aspect is the speculation it raises: If it had been a better or bolder or more important film, would similar or more daring enterprises have been attempted?

Fox Films, at that time, was a far cry from the Twentieth Century–Fox it later became, with Darryl F. Zanuck maintaining a firm hold over its Shirley Temple and brash musicals. In the early 1930s, Fox was in bad corporate shape, tottering on the brink of receivership and without a strong guiding management. Perhaps it was this flirtation with disaster that enabled the studio, on occasion, to try some of the most adventurous subject matter in Hollywood. Not that its films were always particularly good, but they did cast a wider net than usual for subject matter and often went further than other studios in raciness.[6] *The Warrior's Husband*, like *Just Imagine*, is a fair example of something that likely wouldn't have been made at another studio. Not even *Cavalcade* would have turned up elsewhere with the fidelity or authenticity it received at Fox. Accordingly, it was at this studio where, sometime in 1932, someone made the decision that as long as Fox was trifling with homosexuality, it should do so with something resembling verisimilitude. The studio proceeded to hire openly gay entertainers for several films. The two "chambermaids" in Fox's *Call Her Savage*, unbilled as they are, were very likely insiders in the gay cabaret field, and the studio actually publicized its hiring of a drag chorus line for *The Warrior's Husband.*

Fox also obtained the services of the best-known gay comedian in the business. In and out of drag, Jean (originally Gene) Malin had cashed in on the pansy craze with a vengeance, becoming a headliner in gay club revues in the early thirties and one of the first gay performers to break out into at least the fringe of the mainstream, all the while maintaining the gay identity: the anti-Eltinge, as it were. By early 1933 Hollywood's desire for pansies was such that Malin got the calls from the studios. In between appearances at Hollywood clubs and parties, he tested for a role in Paramount's *I Love That Man*, MGM announced him for *Dancing Lady*, and Fox hired him for an odd and unimportant hodgepodge of a comedy-drama called *Arizona to Broadway*. Malin was cast as "Ray Best," a female impersonator enlisted by gangster J. Carroll Naish

---

[6]A 1930 comedy, *Oh, For a Man!*, is a good example of Fox's risqué product, especially in a scene that teases the audience with the thought of Jeanette MacDonald getting just too close to a butch masseuse.

to imitate Mae West in a stage production.[7] Unfortunately, Malin and movies did not mix well. In and out of drag, his on-camera presence seemed recessive, restrained, and unhappy. Nor was a Mae West imitation a praiseworthy part of his arsenal of tricks: the Best/West/Malin performance of "Frankie and Johnny" managed to fall well short of an amateur night turn in a fourth-rate drag bar in Boise. Possibly, then, it was only an enhancement to his reputation that, as part of the anti-"panze" cleanup that spring, his name was deleted from the credits of *Arizona to Broadway*. With or without Malin, this time-filling tripe received no special attention.

Like *Arizona to Broadway*, *Sailor's Luck* (1933) was processed cheese off the Fox assembly line starring the studio's all-purpose urban wisecracker, James Dunn. A rowdy sailors-on-leave comedy directed by Raoul Walsh, *Luck* has drawn some latter-day attention for the presence of a gay swimming pool attendant. Played by Frank Atkinson, he waves coyly at Dunn and pals ("Hi, sailors!"), and earns from Dunn a pig-Latin putdown: "Hey, fellas, et-gay the ansy-pay." Atkinson's appearance doesn't go much further than that in the film, but the surviving script files of *Sailor's Luck* make it clear that a higher-profile gay presence had originally been planned. From the very beginning, it had been decided that the swimming pool sequence of *Sailor's Luck* would feature a gay character, and there had even been some casting planned: a performer named A. Martinez was penciled in to play Violetta, tagged by the script as "A Spanish Nance." Originally, Violetta was to appear only when heroine Sally Eilers hands him a woman's swimsuit by mistake, and he delightedly puts it on. Then, in a later script, Violetta is the brother-in-law of the pool manager, figuring quite tempestuously in a great deal of the action around the pool. When the idea of using Martinez was dropped, Violetta became Cyril, with whom the sailors engage in a mock flirtation. Finally, the part was trimmed some more until Cyril became the nameless non-Spanish nance of the final print.

The *Variety* piece on pansies had included a passing mention of the *Sailor's Luck* character, and as if to show what a gay time Hollywood was having in late February–early March 1933, that same issue of *Variety* ran reviews of *Our Betters* and two new Warner Bros. films. *Grand Slam* was a lighthearted yarn about the cutthroat world of professional contract bridge—early thirties movies could reach wide for subject matter—and featured Warren William, Loretta Young, and (among others) a butch woman with a monocle whom Frank

---

[7]Note that even as early as spring 1933 West was being treated as a drag queen. Malin apparently did not make it into *I Love That Man* or another Paramount film for which he was announced, *Girl Without a Room*. Nor is he in evidence in *Dancing Lady*. The one pansy in the completed film is not Malin, although he may have originally been featured in one of the many musical sequences shot for that film and later deleted.

McHugh mistakes for a man. The Barbara Stanwyck vehicle *Ladies They Talk About* seemed, on the surface, to be in the vein of tough Warner exposés and crime dramas, with Stanwyck as a bank robber doing time at the women's wing of San Quentin. However, after an opening sequence so realistically recreating a robbery that censors feared it could be a how-to primer, the movie lapsed into *Midnight Romance* fantasy. Instead of grim prison conditions, Stanwyck's jail time resembled a stay at a health spa, with glamorous inmates, beauty treatments on demand, and a laid-back air. The only grittier touches (besides Stanwyck's ingrained Brooklyn moxie) were incidental, such as the inmates yelling "New fish!" when Stanwyck first arrives, and a black inmate (Madame Sul-te-wan) talking back ferociously to an imperious white prisoner (Cecil Cunningham). Another jailbird in this glossy clink is a muscular woman with close-cropped hair and a cigar clamped in her mouth. "Watch out for her," Stanwyck's pal Lillian Roth cautions. "She likes to wrestle!" Like the other inmates, this one (actress unidentified) is spared the dreariness of prison grooming, being permitted instead to wear the standard Hollywood Dyke getup of a tailored outfit and little bowtie. "Mmmmm . . . hmmmm!" Stanwyck comments upon first seeing her, with a "Boy, have I sunk low!" air. Later, less expectedly, we see this butch prisoner's femme other half. The camera pans across the cells to take in after-hours vignettes that never occurred in any real-life jail, including a slumber party in lingerie, Cunningham cuddling her Pekingese, and the butch woman doing an exhibition round of calisthenics. Wearing a pair of man's pajamas and with the cigar still in her mouth, she goes through her paces to the delight of a frilly girlfriend sitting in the bed next to her. "You're just always exercising!" the femme marvels. *Ladies They Talk About* received numerous complaints through the Studio Relations Committee about the robbery scene, about the violence and discussion of prostitution. Only in strict Ohio, however, did the lesbianism cause any problem; Roth's "wrestle" line was cut. So it remained over the succeeding decades, when women's prison movies were one of the few places onscreen where lesbians were allowed to exist openly. This one is one of the first.[8]

During that same springtime for flamboyant gay characters, the movie musical was experiencing a renaissance. The national feeling of rebirth and Rooseveltian optimism contributed to the desire for this type of escapism, and the studios obliged as if it were 1929 all over again. Given the climate of the time, plus the fact that most musicals were set backstage, it could be divined that the 1933 equivalents of Del Turpe (from *Broadway Melody*) would soon be arriving. They did, indeed, but—partly as a backlash over Ernest, partly as a

---

[8]Apparently one of the first, anyway, because at least one major silent film dealing with the subject, Clara Bow's *Ladies of the Mob*, is lost, and probably others are as well.

reflection of the fading of the pansy craze—the gay musical arrivistes were sometimes a surprisingly low-key lot. The first successful musical of the year was the epochal *42nd Street*, its smash success fueled by Busby Berkeley's kinetocinematic musical numbers, the starring debut of the adorably clunky Ruby Keeler, and a sharp-edged backstage atmosphere courtesy of the Warner Bros. house style. The fantasy folklore of the basic plot—leading lady breaks ankle, director (Warner Baxter) finds unknown chorine (Keeler) to replace her, chorine finds stardom and love with leading man Dick Powell—was amusingly juxtaposed with tough wisecracks and a feeling of authentically grimy theatricality. Some of the insider attitude came from the original book, in which novelist Bradford Ropes evened the score with everyone who crossed him during his years as a Broadway chorus boy. While there were scenes and characters closely based on real-life Broadway dish, some of Ropes's dirt couldn't be filmed: in the novel, Billy Lawler, the Powell character, has only professional interest in the chorine, in fact promotes her mainly in order to solidify his status as the kept boy of Julian Marsh (Baxter). Some of the novel's racy relationships were hinted at onscreen, but this one was not even attempted. Nevertheless, it's not difficult to read the Marsh of the finished film, tough and talented, as a gay man; his personal life generally remains offscreen, although in one scene he asks his assistant, Andy (George E. Stone), to accompany him home. "I'm lonely," he explains.

Warner's second musical smash of the year, *Gold Diggers of 1933*, veered well around any gay characters—again, one detects a bit of Hays-induced hesitancy—and in the studio's third blockbuster that year, *Footlight Parade*, both the Code office and Warners saw to it that the intended gay character was whitewashed both in writing and casting. While Frank McHugh had done a draggy turn years earlier in *Kiss Me Again*, here he retains his standard persona of goofy harassment. The character's name (Francis) and profession (dance director) would have been prime turf for a Bobby Watson, but with McHugh it blossoms only briefly, when Francis tries to foist his latest protégé onto boss Jimmy Cagney. "Bring him up some time," Cagney cracks. "Maybe the three of us could knit some doilies." Bobby Watson himself turned up, feyer than ever, in a number of 1933–34 musicals, invariably as a choreographer or designer: *Moonlight and Pretzels*, *Wine, Women, and Song* (as "Lawrence," a coded name that guaranteed a lispy delivery), and *Going Hollywood*. A one-scene bit in Wheeler and Woolsey's *Hips Hips Hooray* was typical. When W&W suggest a dance step for his chorus line, Bobby pwotests, "Oh, my giwls could nevah do that, they'd bwuise!"

Bradford Ropes's backstage successor to *42nd Street*, *Stage Mother*, was published two months after Warner's musical hit opened. MGM speedily snapped it up and proceeded to expand on what little gay content it had. In the book, the ingenue is coached by a teacher who lisps, "I never got further than the chorus myself . . . but I just love performers." After the first scripts completely denatured the teacher, MGM turned to Bradford Ropes himself to spice it up. The teacher, with another lispy name (Mr. Sterling), suddenly became much more conspicuous and much more gay. He was played by actor Jay Eaton, and his one short scene in *Stage Mother* manages to pack in all possible insider words and references, a Baedeker on how Hollywood chose to portray openly gay men in mid-1933. Sterling, hand on hip, leads his charges through their paces:

> 1, 2 and 3 and 4
> We are fairies, we are elves, 1, 2, 3, 4 . . .
> Then we dip and pluck the rose, 1, 2, 3, 4 . . .
> Alice, Mary, Jean, and Lizzie, pay attention, follow me. 1, 2, 3, 4.

Besides the references to fairies, flowers, and "Mary," Sterling advises his students with a singsong, "Practice, practice practice!"[9] He tells stage mother Alice Brady that her daughter's dancing is "Thimply divine, my dear, thhhimply divine!" All these are the accepted clichés, albeit more densely packed than usual, but then, as the work on the script progressed, Ropes added a kicker to the scene:

> KITTY [Brady]: When can she start making professional appearances?
> STERLING: Oh, in a few more months, she's got a lot to learn!
> KITTY: Well, you help her out and you won't be sorry. (*Gives him the most knowing look possible*) I can throw a lot of good things your way!
> STERLING: (*in modified shock*) Mrs. Lorraine!
> KITTY: Why, Mr. Thterling! [*Quick dissolve to next scene*]

The implication is clear: Kitty, who has lots of connections in the theater, will help Sterling in ways personal as well as professional, i.e., fix him up with new boyfriends. To erase any doubt of her intention and toughness, Brady later blackmails a producer with incriminating snapshots and even attempts to pimp for daughter Shirley (Maureen O'Sullivan): backstage musicals were indeed tough, perhaps even honest, before they became denatured. Ropes wasn't much of a writer, but his observations were acute, and gays were an accepted part of his theatrical milieu, as they were in Broadway and vaudeville in the 1920s and 1930s.

---

[9]The cliché seems to be that a certain rhythmic reiteration is a gay signal. Perhaps Gertrude Stein was the model. In any case, think about thirty-five years ahead to the unforgettably queeny Carmen Giya in *The Producers*, purring, "White, white, white is the color of our carpet!"

Movies, and novels such as those by Bradford Ropes, were not the only gay entrée into the American home at the time, for there was also a gay radio star. *Myrt and Marge* was the on-air equivalent of *Stage Mother,* an inordinately popular soap opera that set its labyrinth of travails behind the *Follies* footlights. The titular duo (chums on the radio, mother and daughter in real life) naturally got most of the attention, but a fair amount of airtime went to Clarence, a smart-mouthed costumer. Perhaps even more than Bobby Watson's characters or the various onscreen Mr. Sterlings, Clarence was many a home listener's introduction to overt, snappish, and occasionally quite funny male femininity. His last name, too, was an evocative mouthful: Tiffingtuffer. Years later, a gay man recalled his early exposure to the show and to Clarence:

> When I was a kid, I listened to a network radio soap opera called *Myrt and Marge,* sponsored by Wrigley-Spearmint gum. They were Follies Girls, . . . Myrtle Spear and Margery Minter. It was called the Hayfield Follies and the show was a lot of life-backstage episodes. The costume designer was Clarence. Clarence was a screaming queen. Clarence was always having snits. . . . This was my introduction to [gay men]. Screamers having snits.

In 1933, as other audio celebrities cashed in on their popularity with film appearances, Myrt (Myrtle Vail) and Marge (Donna Damerel) and Clarence (Ray Hedge) all made a trip to the big screen with assists from Universal Pictures, who distributed the film, and the Three Stooges, who headed the supporting cast. M&M and Clarence were all top-billed by their radio names only and, as expected, their film turned out a tiresome conglomeration of backstage business, lame wisecracks, Stooge violence, and tacky musical numbers. Clarence/Hedge onscreen turned out to be an attractively slender, thirtyish man, nattily turned out without sartorial pansy excess. His onscreen footage was considerable—he was seldom offscreen for more than a few minutes at a time—yet remained somewhat segregated from the various romantic and theatrical wranglings. (And, needless to say, with no romantic wranglings of his own.) Only in a couple of scenes was he allowed center stage, and in one of them he was (for lack of a better term) the straight man for some Gracie-like cluelessness from Stooge sidekick Bonny Bonnell. His snittiness, which caused distress in that young listener quoted above, was toned town somewhat, albeit with one smart moment when Myrt hands him her feather headdress and admonishes him not to try it on. "SELF-ish!" he snips. Of course, a Clarence—no matter how diluted—will not appeal to all tastes. On the one hand, he's a sashaying demonstration of the constant equation of homosexuality not only with effeminacy but with the peculiar swishiness attendant to the theater: a hothouse bitchiness that trades humanity for surface humor. Yet there are reasons to praise Clarence and his effect. One was his unwillingness to "pass." Like so many others onscreen and in large cities, he found an enclave where both his professional talents and personal qualities were accepted. He is a clear part of the ensemble, helping out and connecting with his peers while not losing his individuality. He was himself; and in the 1930s and seven decades later a man proudly embracing his effeminacy is in for a rough time from within the gay community as well as without. Would a Clarence care about all that? Perhaps, yet so many Clarences survived to recall their glory time to later generations. Whether or not they should or could be role models is a personal choice; what is clearly true is that Clarence/Hedge is a forgotten pioneer, and through his radio exposure was, for many years, the country's most prominent openly gay presence.

The Ernests and even the Clarences were essentially cartoons, so it was hardly a surprise that the animated shorts of the early 1930s had similar characters. Cartoons then, even the ones from Disney, were not geared toward children. Betty Boop, after all, was essentially a sex object, and most of her films contained a full quota of dirty jokes: that short skirt had a lecher's hand running up it on more than one occasion. As in most live action films, this kind of blue fun didn't give too many folks a problem, and the Studio Relations Committee, weak as it was, was notably toothless when it came to shorts. Betty, as a consequence, was able, in *Any Rags?* (1931), to sing "Stick out your can, here comes the garbage man"—not necessarily a lyric dealing with waste disposal. And, intrepid soul that she was, she had a number of gay encounters. In *Dizzy Red Riding Hood* (1931), she picks flowers on the way to Grandma's, and is pleased to come across a pansy because, as a limp-wristed tree stump observes, "The fairies like them too!" In *Betty Boop for President* (1932), she gives a fearsome con the electric chair—which turns out to be a beauty treatment from which he emerges lustrous and queeny. As she waters the plants on *Betty Boop's Penthouse*, she runs across another pansy, and later goes after a nasty intruder with a spray can that turns him into a flitting ballet dancer. There was even a reference in a Boop short to a "man with the red necktie," a real insider reference to a coded piece of gay apparel. The references turned up at other studios also. Warner Bros.' *Freddie the Freshman* featured a gay student in its college lineup, and in *The Organ Grinder*, a monkey scampering around a clothesline falls into a pair of frilly panties and becomes an instant fairy. *King Klunk*, Universal's genial spoof of *King Kong*, sported a sacrificial native dance that turned into a rouged-lipped, limp-wristed chorus boy strut. In Walt Disney's *Egyptian Melodies* a hieroglyph sprang to life with the limpest of Bobby Watson wrists. *The Soda Squirt* (1933), directed by ex-Disneyite Ub Iwerks, was perhaps the most extreme of them all: a florid young man who makes Ernest look like General Patton accidentally drinks a Mickey Finn and turns into Mr. Hyde. Fortunately, he reverts to type when Flip the Frog spritzes him with "Eau de

A florescent customer places an order in *The Soda Squirt*.

Pansy." Nor were cartoon jokes limited to animated drawings: in MGM's *Hollywood Party* (1933, released 1934), Jimmy Durante has a close encounter with a gorilla with loose wrists and a coy air. "A chimp-pansy!" Durante notes in exasperation. And in Fox's offbeat *I Am Suzanne!* (also 1933–34), the climactic number, mixing live actors and marionettes, is set partly in hell; one of the denizens is a butch woman on strings who confesses she ended up in the land of the damned because she preferred dressing as a man!

Along with the cartoons and the newsreels, the other item on the movie menu, comedy shorts, could also be exceptionally fertile territory. Laurel and Hardy's *Their First Mistake* (1932) is the standard-bearer here, for it goes beyond the conventional gay jokes to evoke its own batty male marriage. The relationship between Laurel and Hardy in many of there movies may be seen as a charming-screwball love affair—at least, such an interpretation can be read into it by those so disposed. (The next sound you hear will be that of stubbornly old-school literalists and hetero L & H buffs huffing in annoyance.) The wonder of *Their First Mistake* is that it truly ups the ante: Hardy's wife sues him for divorce, citing alienation of affection. Stan is named the corespondent, and the two set up housekeeping and adopt a baby. Sure it's innocent fun . . . but to pre-tend, as some critics have, that there is no conscious evocation of gayness here is as absurd as it is historically inaccurate—part of that "gay exception" men-tioned in an earlier chapter. It's there—Laurel and Hardy are shown affection-ately sleeping together, for crying out loud—and it wasn't the first time either comic encountered it in his movies.

While the stereotypes were the ruling forces in 1933, there occasionally were more subtle maneuvers going on. Ruth Chatterton starred in Warner Bros.' *Female* as a man-eating executive who seduced and discarded underlings. One of her attempts, played by willowy Philip Reed, is a young designer somewhat oblivious to her charms. When she realizes why he isn't getting her message—apparently he's too "aesthetic"—she gives up. Warner's *Son of a Sailor* was a rowdy vehicle for large-mouthed comic Joe E. Brown, who in the previous year had had a memorable run-in with a bevy of chorus boys in *The Tenderfoot*. *Sailor* received a great deal of flack from Code officials for one scene in which Frank McHugh tries to instruct Brown in some of the niceties of courtship. Naturally they are overheard: by all their shipmates, en masse, who respond with what rapidly was becoming the standard fairy greeting: roll eyes, extend arm and hand grandly, and go "Wooooo!" This kind of gay-confusion scene had already turned up in *Reaching for the Moon* and others, but in the fall of 1933, with protests heating up, the Code officials were starting to be less amused.[10]

The Woman I Stole was an adaptation of a Joseph Hergesheimer novel, *Tampico*. Its forthright plot dealt with a South American plantation owner (Donald Cook), his wife (Fay Wray), and the outsider who comes between them (Jack Holt). Standard fare from Columbia Pictures, relatively well done and, with its surprisingly unsympathetic heroine, just the least bit misogynist. Perhaps it was predictable that Holt would end up leaving without the woman he stole, although Wray's character remained unexpectedly nasty and unre-deemed. But nothing topped the final scene for dead-in-your-tracks shock: Holt and Cook sharing a toast on the ship leaving from Tampico, Cook musing on the irony of Holt's having come to steal a man's wife and leaving with her husband instead! Then, to punctuate the whole thing, a native temptress (Raquel Torres) who'd earlier pestered Holt turns up one more time and is kicked out of the stateroom. Considering that nothing in the previous seventy minutes of *The Woman I Stole* offered any sort of homoerotic tension, it seems that the final

---

[10]Despite the Code problems with the "Woooo" scene in *Son of a Sailor*, Frank McHugh did it again the following year in Warners' Oscar-nominated *Here Comes the Navy*. As Jimmy Cagney is preparing to go on leave, McHugh signals him on how he should be courting his girl by blowing a kiss. A fellow sailor promptly hits McHugh with "Woooo, swish! What are you two guys, a coupla violets?"

scene was put in as a flash, an O. Henry twist to leave viewers agape. It was there not because of dramatic validity or even because it made sense sexually: it was simply tossed in to give a standard romantic triangle a slightly different contour and because, in mid-1933, it was possible to do so.

When Paramount announced that it was filming Noël Coward's *Design for Living*, the naysayers and prudes were appalled. This, after all, was not the respectable, even inspirational Coward of *Cavalcade* or *Bitter Sweet*. No, the uplift of *Design for Living* was strictly below the belt: this elegantly disreputable meditation on art and sex featured, with two leading men and a leading woman, a genuine ménage à trois. Whether the arrangement was sexual or merely emotional was left up to the viewer, but with Coward, Alfred Lunt, and Lynn Fontanne in the leads, the play had scored a hit on Broadway in early 1933. So much so, in fact, that its very title became a catchphrase for sophisticated naughtiness—and, on occasion, wide-open sexuality. Paramount bought the film rights almost immediately, knowing full well that massive renovation would be needed to get it past the Code and the state censorship boards. As with *Sanctuary/The Story of Temple Drake*, some observers feared that filming this property under any circumstances would be proof definitive of the collapse of western civilization. Duly warned by the Hays Office, director Ernst Lubitsch and his screenwriter, Ben Hecht, proceeded to turn Coward's play from a sexy romp to a slightly more solemn romance about a companionable living arrangement between a commercial artist (Miriam Hopkins), a painter (Gary Cooper), and a playwright (Fredric March). So complete was Hecht's renovation that he boasted that only one of Coward's lines had been retained: "For the good of our immortal souls!" Dr. Wingate of the Studio Relations Committee chipped in by specifying that the trio's flat have more than one bedroom, and a key new plot point was the trio's pact that their union is indeed platonic. With all the tinkering, any inference that the Cooper and March characters might have loved each other as well as Hopkins drifted into the wishful-implication department. Even the casting seemed designed to undercut any bisexual notions; however dreamy-looking Cooper and March were, they were carefully directed to avoid any *Sport Parade*–type intimations of close bonding. Their leading-man masculinity was further emphasized by giving the only other roles of any consequence to Edward Everett Horton as Hopkins's ineffectual boss/beau and Franklin Pangborn as the producer who helps make March's play a success. The resulting contrast between two of film's most virile lead actors and two of its most nervous nellies slyly makes the point that the only sexual traction existing between Cooper and March would be as rivals for Hopkins. The Pangborn character, in fact, drew a caution from Wingate to avoid any appearance of "sex perversion" in a scene (not used in the final print) where he sends March orchids. Even so, Pangborn's preferences were never in doubt. He is first seen having breakfast with a male companion, and as Hopkins presses him to read March's play she parries, "I'm sure you'll adore it . . . it's a woman's play!"

The public and critical response to *Design for Living* was interestingly mixed. Most of the New York press decried Hecht's preemptory elimination of both Coward's epigrams and central premise, and many felt Gary Cooper unsuited to Coward-y fare. Some others critics, and many audiences, were willing to take Lubitsch's work at its own level, as a serious-tinged romantic comedy free from ostensible precedents. *Variety*, in fact, proclaimed it superior to the original, an act of "literary heresy" that nevertheless justified all the liberties. For others, mostly outside the critical community, the work's notoriety onstage was enough. Even with the laundering, people like Joseph Breen of the Hays Office could look on it as a blank page and read into it whatever scandalous (and usually hetero) behavior they chose. In Breen's case this had fearsome implications: so diligently had he served as a Hays lieutenant that in December 1933 he replaced James Wingate as head officer of the Hays Office's Studio Relations Committee. The beleagured Wingate was demoted to the ranks of script readers, and Breen began to inspect submissions with a baleful eye.

While Franklin Pangborn's presence in *Design for Living* was not a flashpoint for the brouhaha, his reemergence into feature films in 1933 was as important to gays on film as the return of backstage musicals and the final days of the pansy craze. Since his *Exit Smiling* days he had worked nearly exclusively in two-reel comedies, mainly at the Mack Sennett studio and at MGM. With the character shorthand required in such little films, he was usually reduced to one personality trait. No, not *that* one; rather, it was his unique penchant for expressing a rainbow spectrum of outrage and mortification. He was often cast in roles where his capacity for being flustered would take center stage: as a put-upon husband in MGM's 1933 Technicolor short *Menu* (1933), he suffered not so stoically the indignities of wife Una Merkel's inept attempts at cooking. While still appearing in shorts, he made forays into features in 1932, such as a stint as a hotel manager in RKO's sharp-edged *The Half Naked Truth*. Then, in early 1933, he made what turned out to be a seminal appearance in Paramount's deranged musical farce *International House*. As the manager of another hotel—this one in Wu Hu, China—he had an immortal exchange with W. C. Fields.

FIELDS (*alighting from a just-landed gyrocopter*): Hey, Charlie, where am I?
PANGBORN: Wu Hu!
FIELDS (*pulls a flower out of his lapel*): Don't let the posy fool ya!

For the first time since *Lady of the Pavements*, everything gay in Pangborn was brought to the fore. All that was needed was his non-macho air—he often appeared

FRANKLIN PANGBORN

Born Newark, N.J., January 23, 1892; died Santa Monica, Calif., July 20, 1958

Just the name was unforgettable—a sound like the striking of two small gongs. To call him the archetypal gay actor (or, if preferred, actor playing gay-type roles) is to limit him unfairly. Pangborn was a wonderful artist by any standards, with razor timing, infinite rapport with other actors, the best double takes in the business, and (surprise! for it was revealed only a few times) an excellent tenor singing voice. Small wonder that comic masters such as W. C. Fields and Preston Sturges treasured his gifts and used them wherever possible. As with so many others, he came to film after considerable stage work (including a stint as Ben-Hur's nemesis Messala) and also served with honor in the Great War. In a time of oppression and repression, he was a small, mildly flaming beacon. Like his bountiful and stereotyped contemporary Hattie McDaniel his artistry was the more endearing for the way it charged past both cartoonishness and bigotry. One minute of Pangborn could make the dreariest of movies (*All Over Town* and *Love on Toast,* both 1937) momentarily sublime, or add the tastiest flower-trimmed icing to the cake of really good films (*The Palm Beach Story, The Bank Dick*). He could swoon over drapes (*Only Yesterday*) or Johnny Weissmuller's muscles (*Stage Door Canteen*) with the best of the pansies, yet his appeal owed little to precedent or ingrained stereotype. Maintaining a frayed dignity, he somehow deflected condescension without resorting to pithy comebacks. His quicksilver intimations of impatience and outrage were unmatchable, and if the pejorative term "nervous Nellie" could ever be a compliment, let him be the recipient. (A personal note: my first encounter with Pangborn was at about age six, in Shirley Temple's *Rebecca of Sunnybrook Farm.* Clearly, he wasn't handsome like the leading man, Randolph Scott, but there was something in the way he lived his silly role—Hamilton Montmarcy, understudy organist at a radio station who passes out just as he gets his big break—that seemed, well, divine. Outside of a couple of my aunts, I had never before seen a case of nerves so eloquently expressed.) While Pangborn will reappear in these pages, it is to be hoped that one day he will be given his full due: a *That's Pangborn!*-style medley of his greatest moments. His artistry, intelligence, and the sheer accumulation of joy he gave all warrant such homage. They also deserve the pointed tribute given him in 1985 by writer Boyd MacDonald:

> It is not faintly surprising to anyone who knows the truth about the military, as opposed to the Pentagon version, that Pangborn was wounded in the Argonne in World War I, while such he-men as John Wayne and Ronnie Reagan performed their heroic military acts exclusively on camera.

Panborn knew from heroism, and from survival. Long may he wave.

Franklin Pangborn takes no guff from George Burns, let alone Gracie Allen, in *International House. Photofest*

to be a high-strung rodent trying to assume an air of debonair composure—and Fields's mistaking the name of the Chinese city for the gay boys' mating call. Small as it was, the role in *International House* (which did draw some objection from the Studio Relations Committee) firmly and almost instantaneously defined his career; later that year, *Motion Picture Herald* noted that it had caused Pangborn's "popularity as a comedian [to take] a noticeable leap upward."

Through fortuitous timing, 1933 became Franklin Pangborn's *annus mirabilis.* The greater prominence he began to get onscreen coincided with the retreat of flamboyant gays on and off the screen. The winding down of the pansy craze was ongoing and, in many places, forcible—New York mayor Fiorello LaGuardia issued an edict forbidding drag queens anywhere between Fourteenth and Seventy-second streets, and the Los Angeles Police Commission announced a crackdown on entertainment featuring "female impersonators and their ilk." By the summer there were clear threats of film censorship in the air, and when all the portents were assembled, it was clear that gayness onscreen was heading toward more circumspect portrayals. The flamers from *Palmy Days* and *Stage Mother* would soon be as passé as they were persona non grata, and in their place would be the marvelous Mr. Pangborn. Generally, his sexuality onscreen was felt to be somewhat of a moot point, although in *Design for Living* and *Only Yesterday* (1933) he was given a young male companion. Pangborn's manner was such that he could pass unthreateningly in the straight world and serve such necessary functionary roles as manager, floorwalker, reporter, or executive, yet even in the straightest of settings could still amplify an attitude of goodhearted (if harried) gayness to those who could see. Early on, the studios feared his aura cast him too close to the edge of acceptability. Just as he was coming into his own as a character actor in *Professional Sweetheart* (1933), fearful studio publicists tried to play up, yes indeed, his offscreen machismo by noting that his sissyism was an onscreen-only entity. "Call [him] a sissy offstage," RKO's Press Department averred, "and he'll plant five hard knuckles on your proboscis."[11]

Pangborn's appearance in *Only Yesterday* has drawn special retrospective attention. He was cast as an interior decorator, a stock gay role that would seem automatically and pointedly irrelevant in the movie's Depression setting. While the stock market crashes and lives shatter, he gushes to his boyfriend Thomas (Barry Norton) about "that heavenly blue against that mauve curtain. . . . That kind of blue just does something to me!" For Vito Russo in *The Celluloid Closet*, here is the most negative of Pangborns, his very presence a graphic indictment of the mindless indolence of decadent gays in the face of national catastrophe. Yes, it can be seen that way—gayness equated with mindless upper-class folly. It can also be seen as a less judgmental portrayal of a certain class (urban aesthete) at a certain place and time. Jerry and Thomas apparently have a positive and perhaps loving relationship, and their particular world is one of design and beauty. Madame Lucy, Eric Barrymaine, Paisley, and Mr. Sterling lived in similar worlds, and all of them were respected and accepted, not simply tolerated for their abilities. To some, such lives seem ghettoized and marginalized, implying judgment and criticism. Others may find them living life as openly on their own terms as it was possible to do at the time. Finding a milieu in which to thrive and be accepted is no small achievement, and film portrayed these characters and their world with some degree of probity and without extreme judgment. *Only Yesterday* did draw some moralistic fire for gay content that did not involve Pangborn and Norton. In an opening party sequence, a conversation

---

[11]For whatever reason, RKO did decline to provide any proof of Pangborn punching out anyone who dared to question his preferences. Perhaps it's fortunate that Pangborn worked, during his peak years, primarily as a freelancer. A long-term studio contract might have meant one of those cosmetic marriages that even now still turn up.

between two mannishly dressed women was felt to be too explicitly lesbian in tone, and was cut from the film prior to its premiere.[12]

When Pare Lorentz complained about the proliferation of gay images in 1933 films, he was responding, as we do now, to an accumulation that measured far more in impact than it did in actual screen time. So many of these portrayals were fleeting, yet their effect was there for all to see. Even the most buffoonish moments spoke loudly of things otherwise left unsaid. What gay man going to see *Myrt and Marge* would not have been affected, one way or another, by Clarence? Who could have missed the point—the one joke, really—of *The Warrior's Husband?* Lorentz felt these characters and scenes to be harbingers of artistic and possibly moral decadence. The views held on the issue by the Roman Catholic Church certainly became clear when there were calls to boycott *The Sign of the Cross.* Tsk, tsk, such goings on, indeed, and from the middle of 1933 forward there was a clear pulling back. Particularly on the male front, Pangborn and Edward Everett Horton reflected a trend away from Ernest toward something more subtly "mainstream." For the time being, there were comparatively few objections to gay characters. The Hays Office was far more concerned, late in 1933, with Mae West, the heterosexual implications of *Design for Living* and MGM's *Queen Christina*, and the rowdily straight doings of Warner's *Convention City*.

There were a number of gamy moments in *Blood Money*, produced by Darryl Zanuck's new Twentieth Century (pre-Fox) company and released in November. This was another of those High Early Thirties pieces, like *Call Her Savage* and *The Sign of the Cross*, that attempted to sound every lurid note it could. George Bancroft starred as Bill Bailey, a police officer turned slick-shady bail bondsman, with a glittering Judith Anderson as the tough woman who loves him. The sympathetic portrayal of a hero up to his neck in illegal activities was just the thing to fire up the Joe Breens of the world, and for a while *Blood Money* was banned in both Ohio and Maryland.[13] Besides the seeming glorification of crime, there was also concern about the amount of skin revealed in a hula number and, especially, Frances Dee's role as a deb constantly on the lookout for a man who'll beat her up. "I'd follow him around like a dog on a leash," she informs Bancroft. Dee's masochism was portrayed for laughs at the same time it was set up as the real thing, and in fact was the

---

[12]Curiously enough, the print of *Only Yesterday* most frequently in circulation today has had the Pangborn scenes surgically removed, perhaps by a greedy fan; some admirers, unfortunately, can be pretty selfish.

[13]When a Maryland judge overturned the censorship board's ban, he decided to play movie critic. He said, in effect, that *Blood Money* couldn't incite viewers to commit crimes since it had already put them to sleep.

centerpiece of the movie's final scene. Where lesbianism was concerned, *Blood Money* hedged its bets. Anderson's thrill-seeking brother (Chick Chandler) is obviously amoral, a fact underscored by having him date a woman (Kathlyn Williams) who smokes cigars and wears men's clothes. Bearing out Pare Lorentz's fears, the script notes Williams's "monocle and tuxedo [and] Dietrich makeup," the Marlene archetype casting a long shadow. Yet the characterization was intended more as a game of heterosexual dress-up, as Chandler informs Anderson that Williams's mannishness is not what it appears, she's merely out for kicks. Unlike Dee and Chandler, with their hard-edged quests for physical abuse and underworld thrills, the mannish woman (the character is not named) is a simple tease, existing to push the Code envelope (at one point she gazes with seeming interest at another woman) and probably titillate male viewers, yet with an escape clause.[14] The ploy worked: the Williams character, like Dee's S&M wannabe, sidestepped the shears of the state censorship boards, which concentrated on physical brutality and hula-girl flesh.

A more elegant and substantial lesbian tease from late 1933 also received a pass from the censors. "Greta Garbo as *Queen Christina*" was in itself a coded message for wishful-thinking viewers, one (rumored) gay legend playing another. With Garbo at the height of her erotic and dramatic powers in the early 1930s, her cross-gender appeal was well known, even when not entirely comprehended. Herbert Blumer's book *Movies and Conduct* quoted one of the actress's younger fans, a high school girl: "I imagined myself caressing the [movie] heroes with great passion and kissing them so they would stay osculated. . . . I practiced love scenes either with myself or with a girlfriend. We sometimes think we could beat Greta Garbo, but I doubt it."

Male and female alike, Garbo's admirers were especially eager to see *Queen Christina*. Over a year before, she had left MGM to return to Sweden, the anxious studio fearing she might not return. When she was persuaded to do so, *Christina* was the specified comeback project and the monarch's well-documented predispositions were central to the concept. Along with the expected fictional romance with a dashing male, production head Irving Thalberg determined to mine some of the *Maedchen in Uniform* gold. He discussed the matter with scenarist Salka Viertel, one of Garbo's closest friends. After asking if she'd seen the Sagan film, he proposed that "Christina's affection for her lady-in-waiting [should] indicate something like that." Keep it tasteful, Thalberg said, and apparently he gave the

---

[14]Evidently the character was always intended as more tease than bi, as earlier script drafts show the same "out for laughs" explanation. The preliminary scripts also give the Bancroft character a line that didn't make it to the final cut. "Listen, Fag," he threatens a nosy cab driver, "how would ya like to make bubbles in the river?" The F word did turn up that same year in Edward G. Robinson's *Little Giant*, loaded with some, not all, of the connotations it would later acquire.

same suggestion to the rest of the battery of writers assigned to *Queen Christina*. In the many script drafts the project endured before it found its final form, Christina's scene with her lady-in-waiting, Countess Ebba Sparre, was toyed with constantly. Viertel's script drafts, some of which were written prior to the U.S. release of *Maedchen*, show a reluctance to hint at the (historically documented) relationship between the two women. Other writers went a great deal further. One script, by Ernest Vajda and Claudine West, contained the following scene, not used, of Ebba serving Christina her breakfast:

> Christina makes Ebba kneel before her. She takes a long draught of her soup, then gazes admiringly over the bowl and her attractive lady-in-waiting. How beautiful she is—like a morning flower washed in dew. She sets down her soup and caresses Ebba's cheek. The two women look strangely into each other's eyes. Then Ebba grows embarrassed, and . . . kisses the instep of the Queen's bare foot.

A later script by H. M. Harwood (who shared final screenplay credit with Viertel) had Christina discussing her uninspiring marital prospects with Ebba:

EBBA: Don't you like men?
CHRISTINA: I like them—because they are not women. (*Ebba's face drops*) Oh, not you, my little Sparre—you are my weakness—soft pretty little cat—what a pity I was not born a man. (*Takes her by the chin*) I would have made you queen. There would have been no trouble then about the succession.

In script sections sent to producer Walter Wanger four weeks later, Harwood expanded on Christina's sentiments by having her kiss Ebba instead of merely touching her face. The kiss and the implications came and went as the script developed and the film moved toward production. The Hays Office, observing that the script was treading on delicate ground, cautioned MGM over the "tinge of lesbianism." What finally made it to the screen in the scene between Christina and Ebba (Elizabeth Young) was a good morning kiss, on the lips. There is no breakfast or talk of succession, but there is an invitation to a sleigh ride, plans to meet later in the day, and Christina's promise that soon they will go away together to the country. As Ebba leaves, Christina kisses her again, on the cheek.

When Christina later overhears Ebba conspiring duplicitously with her (male) lover, her anger over the betrayal fuels her flight from the palace to a country inn. There, she finds the great (fictitious) love of her life, played by Garbo's former lover John Gilbert. Ebba returns near the end of the film, bring-

Since *Queen Christina* was one of Garbo's best roles, small wonder that Elizabeth Young is paying fond tribute. Retainer C. Aubrey Smith looks on, not for the first time. *Photofest*

ing the relationship full circle as Christina prepares to leave Sweden forever. In a scene added to the film as an afterthought, weeks after the main shooting had concluded, the countess pleads to accompany the queen to Spain. As Thalberg implied to Viertel when he requested she play the *Maedchen* card, the relationship between Ebba and Christina is made "interesting" without being explicit. Of equal interest were Garbo's scenes at the inn while disguised as a boy. A serving maid flirts with him/her, and John Gilbert finds himself feeling attracted without quite being sure why. As in earlier films, the signals were broadcast to those viewers who could comprehend them, this time in a film as accomplished and poetic as it was prestigious.

Once again there were problems with the censors and the Code officials. As with the antithetical *So This Is Africa* it was over everything except the gay content, which was evidently subtle enough to escape the shears. Joseph Breen, just assuming his power as Code czar, took on *Queen Christina* as his first crusade against the Hollywood heathens. He was livid over the queen's ecstatic interlude at the inn with her Spanish grandee and demanded numerous cuts and changes in this unsanctioned love affair.[15] Like DeMille and unlike puny Columbia, MGM resisted the tampering. The studio filed an appeal to the arbitrators; since they were all industry people, they ruled in favor of MGM. *Queen Christina* was released without cuts, and Breen and the cleanup groups fumed. This, at the very end of 1933, demonstrated once again the powerlessness of the Code and Hollywood's determination not to play by the rules. That this had happened in a film of genuine excellence was beside the point. To people like Breen and the members of church and civic groups, the prurient were inheriting the earth. Mae West was taking over, and sex in all its incarnations had become the calling card of American cinema. Earlier that year *Variety* had reflected the moralists' concerns by noting that the Production Code had all the effectiveness of a sieve. Chief proof of this was the fact that "over 80% of the world's chief picture output was partly, partially or completely flavored with the bedroom essence [including], especially during the past year, the stream of perversion." That stream, the article averred, would soon need to be "diked."

Unintentional double entendres aside, the observations were accurate. The Code was having the exact opposite effect of its original intent, sex was being portrayed onscreen with some degree of explicitness, and alternative sexuality had become commonplace and accepted by audiences. All this in a year when film grosses finally turned a corner after the previous Depression lows. Conservative zeal, in this case, was building, and over the following few months it proved to be a greater force than sexuality, greater even than money. Practitioners of onscreen sexuality—be they Mae West, Jean Harlow, Queen Christina, Ancaria, Ernest, Mr. Thterling, the drag queens in *The Warrior's Husband* or the butch teasers of *The Woman I Stole*—were about to be handed their own new deal.

---

[15]Some of the most vociferous objection was to an exquisite scene nearly unparalleled in American cinema: Garbo's "ballet," as choreographed by director Rouben Mamoulian, where she walks around the bedroom and feels all its furnishxings to better retain her glorious memories. When Breen and Co. saw Garbo stroking the bedpost, they suddenly developed a previously undetected Freudian bent. That this drew fire, and not the scenes with Ebba, says something fascinating about the eyes and minds of the beholders.

SIX

Legions and Decency

"Cockeyed philosophies of life, ugly sex situations, cheap jokes, and dirty dialogue aren't wanted. Decent people don't like this sort of stuff, and it is our job to see to it that they get none of it."
                                        Joseph Ignatius Breen, 1934

SCENE: *A popular Paris nightclub.*
The orchestra launches into a lively fox-trot and the dance floor fills up.
    A handsome young man makes his way over to one couple.
YOUNG MAN: May I cut in?
WOMAN: Why, certainly.
Without skipping a beat the man dances off with the woman's partner, an
    equally attractive young man. The club's owner (Al Jolson) observes the
    scene from the bandstand.
CLUB OWNER (*Pursing his lips, rolling his eyes, and making a mincing wave*
    with his arm): Boys will be boys—woooo!

he film is *Wonder Bar*, a musical melodrama produced by Warner Bros. in early 1934. In the intimate annals of early gay film history this scene holds a special place, and not simply because it was selected to lead off the documentary film *The Celluloid Closet*. Like a few other emblematic moments from little-known films, the *Wonder Bar* male-male dance resonates in a way that no one at the time could have realized. It sums up 1930s Hollywood's easy comfort with homosexuality. It evokes the end of the pansy craze, when films were moving away from cartoons toward more naturalistic images of gay men and women: these two are, in essence, a serious romantic couple. In its brevity and in the fact that we know nothing of these men and their lives besides this one dance, it conveys the fleeting quality of so many gay images on film. It

Out on the dance floor: Demetrius Alexis cuts in on John Marlowe in *Wonder Bar.* Dick Powell looks on, while Al Jolson prepares to make a mincing observation. *Photofest*

reminds us that homosexuality was often used in films of the time as a scene-spicing condiment. Al Jolson's leering comment forces our recollection that mockery and casual bigotry have always been with us. And in its timing—it was shot in January 1934, and the film was released two months later—we may note, ominously, that a precipice was awaiting gays in the movies. This was the year of the newly strengthened Production Code, and of the Roman Catholic Legion of Decency. Six months after these two young men danced off in *Wonder Bar,* their like was effectively banned from movies for the better part of four decades.[1]

It is well known that for many years a series of moral codes regulated what could and, more to the point, what could not be shown onscreen. The effects of

---

[1]*Wonder Bar* has another, less conspicuous gay character who manages to pack in two stereotypes for the price of one. In the notorious "Goin' to Heaven on a Mule" sequence—perhaps the black-face number to end 'em all—Al Jolson arrives in heaven and is measured for wings by a big sissy angel. Musical comedian Eddie Foy, Jr., who normally appeared high up on cast lists, picked up some quick money for this unbilled and unrecognizable bit.

these laws on the movies of the later thirties, forties, and fifties are equally familiar: married couples were forced to sleep in twin beds, navels were eternally hidden from sight, no immoral or illegal acts went unpunished, and on and on. For those who wonder about how the Code and the Legion were given the power to change the movies so radically, their saga runs, in its most concise form, something like this:

Grumblings over the content of film had existed ever since minute-long strips began to weave through boxes with eyepieces and cranks attached. Some public-minded people began to look upon such things as exotic dancers and kissing scenes as public menaces, and by the 1910s a number of states had instituted censorship boards to cushion the citizenry from whatever outrages this or that observer felt obliged to target. By 1923 a series of Hollywood scandals brought into question the morality of movies as well as moviemakers, and to stave off government regulation the industry selected former postmaster general Will H. Hays to serve as its spokesman and regulator. When protests grew, the 1930 Production Code came into being with high principles and ultimate unenforceability. In its wake, films trafficked in more adult and daring content with gangster films, unwed-mother tales, and the like. The arrival of Mae West as a full/overblown movie star in 1933 seemed to gather all the protests into one vociferous voice, and the Roman Catholic Church began to gear up for a crusade. While its earlier battle over *The Callahans and the Murphys* had been successful, later efforts, such as the attempted boycott of *The Sign of the Cross*, seemed as ineffective as the Production Code itself. By late 1933 there were calls in upper Church circles for drastic measures, and in April 1934 the Legion of Decency came into being. The Legion would name names: it decided which films were fit for Catholic consumption and which (the "Condemned" category) were not. Along with the regulations and boycotts, there were heightened threats of possible government intervention. Attempts to regulate the industry through the National Recovery Administration proved unsuccessful, and the ongoing pressure led the film industry's self-regulating body, the MPPDA, to make a crucial decision. Its 1930 Production Code would be strengthened, extended, and made more specific. Its enforcement would now be mandatory and strictly controlled. Hays associate Joseph I. Breen was appointed head of the new Production Code Administration, with the industry-given power to rule on the suitability of all film content. From July 1934 onward, all mainstream films would be given PCA seals to show their fitness for public exhibition. The Production Code's effectiveness was such that, with minor alterations and challenges, it survived until its replacement by the ratings system of the late 1960s.

So runs the nutshell history. Yet the Code's evolution hinges on forces vastly greater than a recitation of "a group of priests met on such-and-such date to discuss . . . ," and its influence and consequence are too vast to be easily contained. As with so many moralist and legalist causes, the move toward the Code is one of the most forthright demonstrations ever of an eternal truth of modern history: a relatively small minority, if sufficiently vocal, empowered, and well organized, can impose its will on a large majority. The public taste, even the public good, is in the opinionated hands of a few.

The Production Code became far more than a way to keep cleavage and vice out of movies. It was, literally, the American public's own imposed design for living. Its existence enabled the movies not only to reflect and influence the audience's culture, but to begin to dictate it. Two decades before the denial-feels-good Eisenhower era, five decades before the don't-worry-be-happy Reagan years, the Code forcibly eliminated life's franker ambiguities from movies and bade viewers do the same in their own lives. It was a document cast in black and white, limiting and simplifying the movies and those who saw them. It discouraged diversity, exalted conformity, and cast judgment ruthlessly. In 1936 there was a memorable line in the film *To Mary—With Love:* "They say the movies should be more like life. I say life should be more like the movies." But by the time Myrna Loy spoke those words, their sentiment was a tautology; two years earlier, the Code had already seen to it.

The Production Code, 1934 incarnation, did not emerge from nowhere. Nor was it an anomaly: in its genesis and ramifications lay the refractions of various currents of history, culture, and psychology. In the extremity of its effects upon creativity and candor in film, the Code tempts the historian toward polemic and righteous anger and ridicule. Even so, as someone was once wise enough to observe, "Both sides must be given, even if there is only one side." It might be difficult to deal dispassionately with the coming of the Code, yet to attach to it too slanted a reading is to perform a disservice. History, after all, is infinitely open, and has "many cunning passages, contrived corridors / And issues." (Thank you, T. S. Eliot.) Each person's path through those gnarly halls might best be served in this case by an examination of events and circumstances weighing on the Code's advent. The story of the Code is about far more than movies. It tells of colliding national trends, anti-Semitism, heterosexism, religious fervor, institutionalized spirituality, social crusades, corporate fear and miscalculation, and the force of an individual's will. Facts and trends and trivia, opinions and ideas, coincidences and paradoxes are all determinants here, along with the propulsive flow that ensures that history will ever and ever repeat itself. All these things form a buffet, a feast that enables us to draw our conclusions about the birth of the Production Code. Through this bounty, each of us may ultimately compose our own histories.

Noble Experiments

Paradoxes are as wondrous to the historian as they can be annoying to the spouse or pedant confronted with them. Prohibition and its repeal form, at least on the surface, one of history's great contradictory moments. In terms of moral behavior as well as alcohol consumption, "the Noble Experiment" had had precisely the reverse effect of what had been intended. Defying the law, as epitomized by the ban on alcohol, became a trendy national pastime. Through bootlegging and related activities crime became a far greater influence than ever before, also far better known and, sometimes, better appreciated. The morality of the Prohibition era, as reflected in the country's popular culture, was one of exuberance, daring, defiance, and general laissez-faire. This was the time of the first flourishing of jazz, which seemed impossible without high living and the enhancements of alchohol and drugs. Sex and sensuality became more visible in theater, film, music, dance, advertising. With all this, too, there was a public exploration of homosexuality in fiction, on the stage in plays such as *The Captive* and *The Green Bay Tree* and on film. In New York and a few other cities, the flourishing of the pansy craze was one of the most visible extensions of this go-to-hell enthusiasm.

As temperance people had done before Prohibition, there were the moralists who decried the sin of the movies and Hollywood's seeming insistence on presenting sex and crime as appealing and attractive. Accordingly, the film industry was given its equivalent of the Volstead Act, the 1930 Production Code, which had precisely the same effect as the ban on alcohol: it existed to be defied. Slowly at first, then with increasing boldness, the studios ignored the Code's directives. *Scarface* and *Red-Headed Woman* and *The Sign of the Cross* were clearly products of a time when film immorality, like drink, was supposedly banned, and yet rampant. The two were conjoined, of course, in the scores of movies in which drinking was shown to be the most appealing and desirable pastime imaginable.

Although the repeal of Prohibition was not a major item on President Roosevelt's agenda, it was ultimately part of the change sweeping the nation after his inauguration. For many, the return of sanctioned drinking was an indicator that better times were indeed part of the New Deal. It also carried a sizable price: it was as if the general sense of public good deemed itself a finite vessel, and when booze came back, other forms of permissiveness were expunged. There could, apparently, be room only for so much vice in the United States. It was at this time that drug laws began to come into effect. Early 1930s films had mentioned drugs frequently and even had songs about them; drugs were kinky, possibly, but not illegal. In 1935 this changed. So, even earlier, did policies concerning homosexuality: government officials and moralists bent on suppressing (or eradicating) homosexuality came out in force. With the hastened end of the pansy craze, there began the retreat of whatever meek advances homosexuality had made in the sphere of public acceptance. Police departments worked mightily to eradicate the public presence of homosexuality through a crackdown on otherwise unenforced loitering laws. Much of the remainder of the retreat came as a direct result of the new laws regulating drinking. In New York, all sales of alcohol were licensed through the State Liquor Authority, which monitored bars and other establishments to ensure that behavior therein would not be "disorderly." That one broad-based word became the authority's mandate to keep lesbians and gay men out of public establishments. Through their very existence homosexuals were presumed to be disorderly, and since they lacked the resources to combat the suppression, the SLA and similar organizations continued the arrests and harassments without cease. By the middle of the decade, it was clear that various forces had coalesced to put a big padlock on the closet door.

The great movie cleanup of 1934 was a continuation and extension of all these effects of repeal. The price the public paid for legal drinking was a further monitoring of "disorderly" behavior as done in actuality and as reflected onscreen. Through the proper spin-doctoring and propaganda, and through the righteous pronouncements of church leaders, film frankness was put on the same level as organized crime and poverty. It was, according to this party line, a national ill needing to be expunged, in fact, a major contribution to Depression misery, part of the "fear itself" that Roosevelt had stated. Just as drinking could be made to seem a good thing when properly monitored, so was filmgoing considered an evil because it was not being regulated appropriately. The New Improved Full-Strength Production Code, then, functioned as the film industry's Twenty-first Amendment, a symbol of supposed national well-being hailed by most as a needed boost to national morale. And just as the deliberately vague words *loitering* and *disorderly* became mandates to rid the public sphere of lesbians and gays, the simply worded (and slightly ungrammatical) phrase added to the 1934 version of the code in section II, no. 4, would be all the license required to kick the queers out of the movies for the next thirty-five years:

SEX PERVERSION or any inference to it is forbidden.

Movie-Made Children

On September 27, 2000, a congressional panel, chaired by Sen. John McCain (Rep., Arizona), convened a day of hearings in which the heads of major film studios were compelled to defend their marketing practices. A series of school shootings in the late 1990s, climaxing with the horrifying tragedy of thirteen dead students at Columbine High School in Littleton, Colorado, had compelled some members of Congress to shine an unforgiving glare on the industry. In the aftermath of Littleton, the American film industry served as an eye-catching and easily attackable target—the great corrupter of the young—and the themes continued to resound in Congress and in the concurrent presidential campaign. Specific and heavy criticism was directed toward the guidelines by which R-rated films could be advertised to children under seventeen. "I don't understand this language," McCain complained to the executives, referring to the studios' marketing policies. "I think it's filled with loopholes. . . . Why don't you just simply say that you will not market to children this kind of R rated material, that you will not market it to children under seventeen, period." As the attacks raged, some observers noted that, while the studios were certainly culpable, some of the attention might have been better focused on the easy accessibility of handguns. There was, however, no equivalent hearing involving an assembly of gun manufacturers or officers of the National Rifle Association.

The Motion Picture Research Council had taken five years to perform its research, and the results reflected poorly upon the American film industry. The findings were scathing: "A treacherous and costly enemy let loose at the public expense [and] subversive to the best interests of society," it said. The council was in no way connected with Senator McCain or his committee; it predated them, in fact, by more than seven decades. With funding by a Cleveland philanthropic group, the Payne Fund, the Research Council had conducted the study from 1928 to 1933, with its stated intention to examine the movies' corrupting effects on the young. The council's head, Rev. William H. Short, was a longtime advocate of government regulation of film content, and with the Payne grant he oversaw testing and interviews that in hindsight seem to have been geared to prove to everyone that the movies were contaminating America's youth. The study was conducted with commendable rigor, innumerable charts and figures, and some truly crackpot methodology, such as a device that measured the tremors of bedsprings to show the troubling dreams some movies gave the young. According to the council's all-but-preset findings, the new American generation was emotionally damaged, prone to emulation of movie violence, and overwhelmingly susceptible to lustful or aberrant behavior.[2] Gangster and crime films, of course, were the most decried culprits, with Jimmy Cagney's make-crime-seem-attractive appeal coming in for special attack. Eroticism in film was also a trouble spot, as were horror movies, although the Love That Dare Not Speak Its Name was all but absent from the findings.

---

[2]It belabors the point to find too many parallels between the Motion Picture Research Council and such later groups and advocates as the Family Research Council and Rev. Donald Wildmon. Nevertheless, some types of moral opportunism are eternal. In 1933, as many years later, the same techniques seem to work: pick your enemy, shade the findings in your favor, assume a righteous air, assume a higher ground than those who disagree with you, wave flag and Bible, and overlard with the phrase "for the good of our children." Works every time.

If the Council's findings lacked a certain objectivity, they were the acme of neutrality in comparison to the way in which they were presented to the public. An ambitious provocateur named Henry James Forman compressed the nine-volume results of the study into one tidy package of dynamite entitled *Our Movie-Made Children*. The relative caution of the council gave way to the ringing of a thousand alarms in the Forman book as he averred, in essence, that every movie ticket sold moved America's children one step closer to hell. Some critics did attempt to note that Forman made his points by wildly slanting findings that had often been quite debatable to begin with. Voices of reason generally tend to get lost in the frenzy surrounding "Save our children!" fervor, and such was the case here. In a cross-country book tour, Forman cried wolf, denounced the movies, preached to the converted, and exhorted the masses to press for government censorship of film. He also sold enough copies of *Our Movie-Made Children* to make it one of the best-selling books of 1933. With few in the media or academia willing to contradict him, Forman became an ad hoc moral spokesman for right-thinking (and Right-thinking) people. His words, and the council's more extreme findings, were fodder for newspaper editorials around the country. Hollywood was the corrupter of the young, the evil empire, the ultimate source for all the nation's ills.[3]

While Forman and the populace raged, Will Hays trembled. Although he had little to say publicly about *Our Movie-Made Children*, it was known that the Payne study was referred to around the Hays Office as the Payneful Study. It seemed a graphic and reproachful billboard for the failure of the Production Code, Hays, and his lieutenants. Nor was it a coincidence that the Motion Picture Research Council was headed by a clergyman, for while *Our Movie-Made Children* was a secular work, the fervor driving it was bona fide Old Testament wrath. And behold, in very short order the church would be taking on the argument over the movies.

Christian Soldiers

Despite Cecil B. DeMille's protestations to the contrary, the movies were a profoundly secular institution, and the pleasures they proffered were never going to sit upon the right hand of those making pronouncements from the pulpit. It was just Reverend Short's good fortune (or blessing) that the Motion Picture

---

[3]Everything Old Is New Again Department: Senator John McCain's words, all these years later, seem quite in tune with the days of the Payne study and *Our Movie-Made Children*: "I'd love to be the Super Censor," he told an interviewer following his committee's hearings. "I'd love to sit and watch movies every day and say which ones are suitable and which ones are not."

Research Council's findings were greeted by an America besotted, as it periodically is, with a renewed religious zeal. In the eighteenth century there had been the fervor of the Great Awakening, and the 1830s saw a flurry of evangelistic passion and revivalism in the American middle class. Such waves of interest are recurring, and many of them are long-lasting: the 1970s call to be Born Again started as a spiritual rebirth and over the course of two decades moved into the political arena with the rise of the Religious Right. In the 1920s and 1930s, the American soul was beset by fevers of similar intensity from two different factions declaiming piety and redemption. The Roman Catholic Church was one of them, here in one of its most powerful and public influential moments. The other contained, barely so, the evangelical enthusiasm bestowed by Aimee Semple MacPherson, Billy Sunday, and so many others. Both the Catholic Church and the evangelists had showbizzy aspects of their own, of course, and in their calls to repentance and devotion it frequently suited them to decry the movies.[4] For Protestants this tended to not carry a great deal of weight, despite Mr. Short and *Our Movie-Made Children;* the Mae West films, for example, racked up notably high grosses in the Bible Belt. The Catholic Church, however, preferred to lay its hands more firmly upon the pursuits of its parishioners, and not only in its pronouncements on such matters as marriage and birth control. The Church's officers regarded clean entertainment as a moral imperative and did not shy away from telling their flock about specifics. In sermons and editorials they constantly ripped into the licentiousness of popular entertainment, and the intensity of their fury frequently reaped benefits: witness MGM's humiliated withdrawal of *The Callahans and the Murphys*, which many Irish-Americans had regarded as personally slanderous. The 1930 Production Code, created largely by Catholics, was mainly an attempt to placate the Church, but as its ineffectiveness became clear to all, the hostilities resumed, and in a higher key.[5] *The Sign of the Cross*, with its torturous interlocking of spirituality and sex, was just the right kindling for Catholic flames. While the clergy's call for a boycott went mostly unheeded, the controversy instilled in some priests and bishops a sense of holy mission.

The mission began to find its destination in late 1933, following a discussion of cinematic corruption at the annual meeting of U.S. Catholic bishops. When they returned to their home dioceses, some of the bishops were sufficiently

---

[4]Billy Sunday did tend to give the movies more leeway than many of his fellow brimstoners. He even paid a good-humored and well-publicized visit to Mae West on the set of her seminal sinfest, *She Done Him Wrong.*

[5]This was not a time for hard feelings to go unmentioned, and the senior officers of the church were not afraid to lay the blame on the movie people. In Chicago, George Cardinal Mundelein wrote an open letter to his parishioners: "We believed we were dealing with moral gentlemen. We were mistaken."

inflamed to oversee the compilation of lists of objectionable films. Unlike the complaints lodged in *Our Movie-Made Children* the objections were nearly all made on grounds of sex. In Detroit, Msgr. John Hunt complained that 90 percent of Hollywood films were unfit for public viewing. Accordingly, the *Michigan Catholic* began to print lists of both commendable and—longer list!—undesirable movies. The first one it targeted was *Queen Christina*, noting that the queen's propensity for male attire made her a "perverted creature." Gradually the various movements coalesced into one major organization, the Legion of Decency, which formally came into existence in April 1934. Over 11 million good Catholics took the Legion's pledge:

> I wish to join the Legion of Decency, which condemns vile and unwholesome moving pictures. I unite with all who protest against them as a grave menace to youth, to home life, to country, and to religion. I condemn absolutely those salacious motion pictures which, with other degrading agencies, are corrupting public morals and promoting a sex mania in our land.
>
> I shall do all that I can to arouse public opinion against the portrayal of vice as a normal condition of affairs. . . .
>
> I unite with all who condemn the display of suggestive advertisements. . . .
>
> Considering these evils, I hereby promise to remain away from all motion pictures except those which do not offend decency and Christian morality. I promise further to secure as many members as possible for the Legion of Decency.
>
> I make this protest in a spirit of self-respect and with the conviction that the American public does not demand filthy pictures but clean entertainment and educational features.

It was promptly made clear that the strong wording of the pledge was not a mere gust of righteous hot air. Early in June Dennis Cardinal Dougherty of Philadelphia ordered a boycott of all films, and film receipts promptly plummeted to non-brotherly-love levels. In other areas, priests took to stationing themselves prominently outside movie houses running objectionable titles, casting a baleful eye on any parishioners coming in and out.

In a matter of a few weeks the forcefulness of the Catholic campaign had become a matter of national note. The outcries were given added urgency by the anger of certain influential Protestant and Jewish leaders, and the flames were further stoked by the ersatz irrefutable proof of *Our Movie-Made Children*. The pressure grew most intense, naturally, within the film industry, and was made more so by the fact that Joe Breen and publisher Martin Quigley were Roman Catholic in politics as well as faith: neither made a secret of his feelings about the state of the cinematic art and the character of those who created it. Here, in sum, was the faith community at its most vehement, assuming a moral high ground for the nation. In anger, righteousness, and pressure, this went far beyond anything seen before; next to this the furor over *The Callahans and the Murphys* was as a mild disagreement at a Knights of Columbus meeting. No, this holy crusade had all the fire of the original Religious Righter, Father Charles Coughlin, and a peremptory moralistic wrath unmatched until the abortion wars later in the century. An anger that was initially directed toward protecting Catholics from baser urges would, eventually, encompass film audiences all over the world.

Much of the take-no-prisoner zeal was directed toward Will Hays, whose terminally bland surface—folksy, phlegmatic, and conciliatory—masked the craft of the true player. His efforts to bridge the gap between the religious groups and the go-for-broke movie people left him in a lose-lose position. The 1930 Code had had the precise opposite effect of its original intent, and to the crusaders it seemed a Bastille-like symbol of all the country's ills, both moral and bureaucratic. The Legions of Decency set up in various cities operated on an independent basis, at least temporarily, to set aright the Code's weakness and irregularities.[6] Gradually they coalesced into a unified movement, with their activities closely supervised by Martin Quigley. Quigley's insider connections in the film industry were equaled, perhaps even overshadowed, by his close personal association with Father (soon to be Cardinal) Francis Spellman. Along with Quigley, the Legion operatives did their work with such rigor that a number of congressmen were sufficiently motivated to introduce bills calling for the regulation of film content. Seldom has the separation of church and state become so perilously and publicly blurred.

Successful boycotts, threats of government intervention, cacophonous public protests—alongside these, the film industry had little recourse. On June 22, 1934, the board of directors of the MPPDA met in New York. The purpose of the meeting was less discussion or negotiation than simple imposition. As the most powerful men in the business listened anxiously, Will Hays announced that the film industry now had "a police department." Then he introduced the department's new chief. As he accepted his appointment as Code administrator, Joseph I. Breen defined himself with characteristic élan: "I come from a race of people," he said, "who have a long history of committing suicide—on the other guy!" For the remainder of the meeting, and over the following two weeks, the scope of his suicidal power became manifestly clear as the Code was

---

[6]They operated in somewhat uncoordinated fashion, depending on the tastes of their administrators in each city. In Detroit *Murder at the Vanities* and *The Thin Man* were on the condemned list, while in Chicago they were given a B rating—neither approved nor forbidden for adults—and *Of Human Bondage* was passed in as many cities as it was condemned. The clearest directives, in fact, were issued in Philadelphia, courtesy of Cardinal Dougherty: if you were Catholic, you were forbidden to see any movies at all.

transformed from a suggested advisory to an ironclad proposition. Items vaguely mentioned in the 1930 Code, including sexual perversion, were made more specific; the new Code would be sufficiently detailed to offer its administrators nearly unlimited scope. The production and distribution of films would now be filtered through the moral and artistic vision of the Production Code Administration, and appeals filed against PCA decisions would no longer rest in the incestuous hands of the producers. In essence, all decisions related to Code matters would be administered by the ungloved iron hand of Joe Breen.

One of the Finest Women Who Ever Walked the Streets

Perhaps it's too easy, seven decades later, to bewail the changes/havoc/damage wrought by the coming of the 1934 Code. The litany of objections unfolds readily: anything that makes for less openness and honesty, that inhibits the integrity of a true artist (and some pre-Code filmmakers were that), that deigns to protect large groups of people from things to which they're entitled . . . the Code and the Breens who pushed for it seem, from a standard twenty-first-century liberal perspective, to merit stormy oceans of umbrage. And after decades without a Code, with sexual openness and excessive violence in films and all public media, the targets of the 1934 crusade seem staggeringly innocuous, far less coruscating a moral linchpin than, say, Robert Mapplethorpe. Outrages over something as sublime as *Queen Christina* seem as artistically indefensible as they are morally unnecessary. How dare anyone be offended?

Nevertheless, a bit of perspective-morphing makes it possible to see why the churches and others were getting so upset by 1933. While the frankness of most pre-Code films seems appealing to many of us now, there did arise, occasionally, the gratuitous rotten apple. Some things in some movies went unsettlingly far beyond the borders of good taste, and occasionally some low blows were struck. *Call Her Savage*, for example, is fun precisely because it strives, in depicting Clara Bow's odyssey, to leave no sexy or scorching stone uncovered. One scene, nevertheless, truly does go too far: an interlude that serves no other purpose than to show Bow wrestling playfully with her Great Dane. What seems tame to modern observers was far less so to some spectators in 1932, who knew of the scabrous tales (circulated in pornographic tattle-sheets) of Bow's purported romantic trysts with said canine. *The Sign of the Cross*, in certain senses the ultimate pre-Code movie, can still have a queasying effect on viewers with its arena brutality, and its effect on 1933 audiences was that much stronger; an exhibitor noted at the time, "I don't think anybody liked it because it is so very cruel and depressing." In certain 1933 films in particular, the gratuitous touches of sex or titillation seem akin to something on the Fox TV network in the 1990s. In some ways they were abusing their freedoms. Even in the most insubstantial trifles, the *So This Is Africa* type of seedy studio product, there is often a palpable sense that they're pushing to see just how much they can get away with. In the silly *Meet the Baron* (1933) there's a production number called "Clean as a Whistle" that exists for the sole purpose of allowing the MGM chorus line to shower onscreen and taunt viewers with the possibility of a nipple or two glimpsed through the spray. Harmless fun, sure, but in the face of growing religious and government ire it seemed a clear invitation for trouble. Then came a fleshy target around which all the anger could be draped.

In the history of movies, as everywhere else, there are occasionally dangled before us irresistible and somewhat lazy generalities: *The Jazz Singer* as the first sound film ("You ain't heard nothing yet!"); D. W. Griffith as the inventor of cinematic syntax and father of the closeup; 1939 as the greatest year in the history of Hollywood history; *Citizen Kane* (and later, perhaps, *Star Wars*) as the Event That Changed American Cinema. And . . . Mae West as the last straw responsible for bringing about the Production Code. How tempting it is to latch onto these icons, even while the truth is that they are seldom accurate, usually little more than the tip (if that) of their respective icebergs, concealing more than they reveal. Mae West, however, was nothing if not generous, and in her case there is more historical validity than is usual with history's shortcuts. A force as attention-grabbing as she would naturally take center stage in any controversy, and her name, effect, and outsized popularity turn up again and again in the articles and papers documenting the birth of the enforced Code. If she was not the moralists' ultimate nightmare, she was certainly the lush embodiment of most of their worst fears.

The reasons for West's notoriety are not necessarily imprinted on celluloid. As funny as she was, especially in her pre-Code vehicles *She Done Him Wrong* and *I'm No Angel*, and as suggestively sexual, her films do not appear, all these decades later, to be the most licentious of the Hollywood output. Rather, it was what she represented that posed the biggest threat. She was something the American public has always found troublesome: an independent, smashingly successful, sublimely egotistical, self-created woman. From Amelia Bloomer to Madonna, such people are moving targets, and West was more conspicuous, and self-assured, than most. Even after doing jail time for her frankness, and brazenly attempting to push the gay envelope with her play *The Drag*, she always managed to come out on top. That in itself would be enough to draw a fearful response from conservative quarters; still worse, atop the whole was the fact that her fortune and fame derived from her treating sex as a joke. Not a secret and sacred thing, nor a treasure saved for lawful wedlock—but something to be openly enjoyed, used, shared, and mocked. In so doing, she blithely appropriated the leading edge in the battle of the sexes. She could refer to herself as "one of the finest women who ever walked the streets," sing "A Guy What Takes His Time" to her panting admirers, and inform Cary Grant "You can be had." She could also, as demonstrated in her "Cherry Sisters" scene in *She Done Him Wrong*, be on easy terms with gays. Many millions of Americans were willing to share the joke, to the extent that *Wrong* and *Angel* exceeded even *The Sign of the Cross* in their grosses and rescued Paramount Pictures from receivership in 1933. Critics mostly raved, and as the clergy leaned toward descriptions such as "demoralizing, disgusting, suggestive, and indecent," West basked luxuriantly in the glare of worldwide awe.

In early 1934 West prepared for her third starring assault on American prudery, the provocatively titled *It Ain't No Sin*. After Joe Breen rejected the two submitted scripts, West and Paramount proceeded oblivious and undeterred. The advance ads for the film bore an unintentionally ominous air: a looming hourglass silhouette was captioned with the legend, "Coming events cast their shadows before." While production was still underway, the Legion of Decency was founded, its establishment due in no small part to the sensation West had created and to fearful anticipation of her next effort. Before *It Ain't No Sin* had run on any screen, the Legion denounced the movie and its star. It and she *were* sins, according to the Legion, and the new Production Code Administration concurred. For Joe Breen and his associates, *It Ain't No Sin* would be a test case to show how the rules had changed. The title was the first thing to go, followed by a good portion of West's cheerful amorality. Cut and partly reshot, the retitled *Belle of the Nineties* was an artistic letdown and a financial disappointment. The slow decline of West's career was now underway, and as her image grew more forcibly denatured, her scripts became ever more bland and she herself far less funny. Thus muzzled, she continued her battles against the Legion and the PCA for several years. The curves remained, but the impact was gone.

Of Bigotry and Breen

In one of her first radio broadcasts Eleanor Roosevelt hailed the ascendancy of Joe Breen, thus setting a certain imprimatur upon the whole Production Code process and crowning the new czar of the movies. Breen's entitlement to this crown was, in his and many minds, unquestionable. He knew how to deal with the studios, he knew film, and his stern tenacity got results. To his role as unofficial national arbiter of morals he brought the energized implacability of the true believer, a vitality readily apparent in a newsreel Breen appeared in shortly after assuming leadership of the PCA. As he intones the credo of the new Code, the forcefulness and terrible sincerity are as unquestionable as the self-

The changing face of movie morality: Production Code Administrator Joseph I. Breen.
Photofest

righteousness and the bad grammar: "The vulgar, the cheap, and the tawdry is out! There is no room on the screen at any time for pictures which offend against common decency—and these the industry will not allow."

One of the most powerful constituents of Breen's belief in both God and self was an enormous amount of bigotry. In the voluminous Breen correspondence, external as well as internal, there is a major paper trail describing precisely what he thought of the people in the film community. His extreme anti-Semitism was sadly common at the time, his homophobia was all but de rigueur, and these opinions would inform film content, and a large part of American culture, for many years. His feelings were only strengthened by the fact that the film people he reigned over were primarily Jewish and occasionally gay. Everything wrong with the movies was due to Them, as he wrote to an ally, Fr. Wilfred Parsons, in 1932:

> [The Jewish moguls] are simply a rotten bunch of vile people with no respect for anything but the making of money. . . . Sexual perversion is rampant [and] any number of our directors and stars are perverts. . . . These Jews seem to think of nothing but making money and sexual indulgence [and] are [also] the men and

women who decide what the film fare of the nation is to be. They and they alone make the decision. Ninety-five per cent of these folks are Jews of an Eastern European lineage. They are, probably, the scum of the earth.

Given his self-appointed status as the only moral person in the film industry, Breen made his personal beliefs—religious, moral, ethical, political, social—a major factor in his duties as chief Code administrator. Post-Code cinema, in the Breen's-eye view, had no truck with moral ambiguities or criticism of established institutions like government, law enforcement, and big business. Virtue would always find some compensation, sanctity could not be attacked, and any type of wrong was duly and visibly punished. Ethnicity had been a frequent subject of early thirties films, with stories about Jewish life (*The Heart of New York, The Symphony of Six Million*) and with black characters occasionally treated with something approaching respect (*Baby Face, This Day and Age*). Such things were now out (along with the vulgar, the cheap, and the tawdry). Post-Code cinema was a predominantly white and Gentile and heterosexual world, innocent wherever possible: the first big post-Code movie star was, after all, Shirley Temple. When the ethnic images couldn't be erased, they were made more subservient, and here was born the bleak golden age of Hollywood's racial insensitivity.

Breen's was the final word on what was included or omitted in films. He and his staff read and approved (or rejected) scripts before filming and then would give the necessary code certificate to the finished product. His opinions on acceptability naturally precluded any inclusion of a gay element; he had, after all, been an engineer of the revised Code that specified sex perversion as a no-no. In film after film after film he cautioned and warned against any inclusion of what he termed "a 'pansy' flavor," threatening that inclusion of such elements would render an entire film unacceptable. A finished film could and would be recut or reshot, as Breen's hated Jews and perverts trembled before his power and complete lack of self-doubt. Some years after his death one of his later associates in the Production Code Administration, Jack Vizzard, precisely encapsulated the essence of Joe Breen, and thus of the Code in general: "The mainspring of his vitality was the fact that he nurtured not the slightest seed of self-doubt regarding his mission or his rectitude. He was right, the moviemakers were wrong, and that was that."

100 Percent Pure

Even before the Legion of Decency turned up the heat, the movie industry had felt sufficient pressure to start an unofficial cleanup. Except for some startling moments here and there—*Wonder Bar* is a good example—most early-1934 movies seemed to pull back from the excesses and Ernests of the previous year. The Hollywood fascination with literary prestige (laundered as needed) had already begun in 1933 with Fox's *Cavalcade* and *Berkeley Square*, and then late in the year with a hit adaptation of *Little Women* and a flop version of *Alice in Wonderland*. Nevertheless, this drift was obviously deemed insufficient, for the fervor in 1934 was such that even the more denatured movies were put on the hit list. However mild Wheeler and Woolsey's *Hips Hips Hooray* seems, especially alongside the seedy *So This Is Africa*, it was one of the biggest targets early in the year. So were *Jimmy the Gent* and *He Was Her Man*, both with Jimmy Cagney, a presence almost as much of a flashpoint as Mae West. Most crucially, a trio of films in production in mid-1934 seemed to be positioned to bait the Code. Mae West's *It Ain't No Sin* (a.k.a. *Belle of the Nineties*) was joined by two other sensual-woman sagas: MGM's Jean Harlow vehicle *Born to Be Kissed* and Warners' *Madame DuBarry*, as embodied by the stunning and ahistorical figure of Dolores Del Rio. All three were excoriated while still in production, all added fuel to the censorship fires, and all were extensively reshot after July 1934, when the new Code was established. The Harlow film was retitled, in a burst of Breen-pleasing optimism, *100% Pure* . . . then ultimately given the noncommittal label *The Girl from Missouri*.[7] In all three cases the tampering was fairly evident, with plotlines that made hairpin turns in order to transform three sexually forward women into incomprehensibly nice girls. In the coming years, when suggestive scripts were run through the PCA maw, such alterations would be standard issue, albeit with the seams usually less visible.

Earlier films still in release after July 1934 suffered even greater indignities. Even as Breen maintained an aura of equability with the studios, a take-no-prisoners mentality was in the air. The other guy, or the industry's largest studio, would indeed be the one committing suicide. Remembering all too well the futile battles he had waged with studios over the previous months, Breen ordered the recall of dozens of titles for PCA-ordered cuts. Each print would be shipped back to the film exchange, the offending footage would be carefully excised, and the print returned to the theater. The censorious zeal of the time was nothing if not contagious. After MGM's *The Merry Widow* was given a Code seal and allowed to open, Martin Quigley and Will Hays took up the gauntlet. Mindful that MGM production head Irving Thalberg had won the appeal battle on *Queen Christina*, they professed outrage that Breen had passed such a dirty

---

[7]One relatively suggestive aspect of *The Girl from Missouri* that did escape the shears was the presence of a possibly gay character—a melancholy millionaire, played by the terminally dignified Lewis Stone, who makes friends with Harlow and then commits suicide. It's not there in the script, but there are hints for those wishing to read beneath the surface, thus setting the trend for gay and lesbian movie characters (and theorists) for decades.

picture as *The Merry Widow*. Following threats and recriminations on all fronts (including some dark hints from Quigley that the Catholic Church would enter the fray), Breen capitulated. The saucy, expensive, and essentially innocuous operetta was temporarily withdrawn, over Thalberg's heated objections, for twelve cuts.

In this age of Breen, particular micromanaging would be reserved for the recycling of previously filmed material. Stories remade after mid-1934 would be made to conform to the new rules of morality, regardless of whatever hash was made of plot sense or dramatic effectiveness. Thus, the otherwise accomplished 1940 version of *The Letter* forced Bette Davis to pay, through her murder, for shooting her lover, whereas the 1929 original (like the Maugham story and play) had cast its heroine (Jeanne Eagels) into a darker hell—living in a loveless marriage with the knowledge that she will always love the man she murdered.[8] In 1938, when James Whale remade his provocative 1933 *The Kiss before the Mirror* as *Wives under Suspicion*, the material was so denatured that one can sense Whale's dejection in every frame of the film.

One of the indisputably rotten aspects of the PCA agenda concerned the fate of pre-Code films given a theatrical reissue after 1934. In those pretelevision days it was fairly common practice for studios to recycle well-remembered titles to augment their new output, and with the Code now in effect old movies were subjected to the same strictures as new ones. The luckiest films were those Breen refused to reissue under any circumstances, such as *Design for Living*, *The Cat and the Fiddle* (Ramon Novarro living in sin with Jeanette MacDonald), and *She Done Him Wrong*. For many more, the reissues were permitted, after cuts were made of material deemed unsuitable for the post-Code world. *Mata Hari* lost most of Garbo's exotic dance and her postcoital love scene with Novarro; *Love Me Tonight* came out missing two songs and some dialogue; and varying degrees of indignity were inflicted on such important films as *A Farewell to Arms*, *Arrowsmith*, *Animal Crackers*, *The Public Enemy*, and *King Kong*. The PCA was only too happy to approve the prestige-laden *Cavalcade* for reissue two years after its release, but only after the removal of the shots of the lesbian couple. (Save for one quick flash, they remain missing from all surviving prints, an abrupt cut surviving to show where they once had been.) Not unexpectedly, Breen reserved a special portion of wrath for *The Sign of the Cross*. In 1935, notified that Paramount was considering a reissue, he immedi-

---

[8]*The Letter* (1940), fine film that it is, is a textbook case of the changes forced by the Code on filmmakers—who were able in this case to triumph over them. Not only did Davis's character pay for her crime, but it was then necessary to show her executioner, the murdered man's wife, being arrested. None of this was part of the original, in which the Eurasian wife of the remake was portrayed, as Maugham intended, as a Chinese mistress.

ately informed the studio that "The Naked Moon" (or, as he referred to it, "Anacaria's [sic] dance") had to go. It did go, finally, when *Cross* was rereleased in 1938 and (with a "modern" prologue) in 1944. For more than fifty years, all anyone saw of the sequence was the first line of the song, followed by the loud hymn-singing of the Christians.[9]

For nearly a year prior to the watershed cleanup, there had been somewhat of an unconscious prelude: the soft-pedaling of gay characters had begun in the middle of 1933 in reaction to the excesses of *Our Betters* and *The Warrior's Husband*. Rouge and lipstick on men were out, and so were obvious partners, as gay and lesbian characters continued onscreen in a notably more subdued, if still visible, light. The industry's most dependable purveyors of lavender, Bobby Watson and Franklin Pangborn, each turned up numerous times onscreen in 1934. Watson and his elaborately flailing wrists were conspicuous in two mid-level MGM films: in *The Gay Bride* he snipped his way through the role of a patronizing luxury car salesman, and in *This Side of Heaven* his interior decorator nattered about floral upholstery to Mae Clarke, who replied that the design in question struck her as "a bit too gay." Pangborn, back to solo-act status for 1934 (and thereafter), had one of his larger and more peculiar roles in *Tomorrow's Youth* (Monogram). In this micro-budgeted predecessor of *Kramer vs. Kramer*, Mr. P. costarred as the private tutor of young Dickie Moore, forever chasing after his "little man" and scrubbing him just a bit too hard in the bathtub. "I don't need any help to take a bath," Dickie protests. "What do you think I am, a sissy?"

Clean as a Whistle

By the autumn of 1934 the Code was in action, the Church officials were, if not satisfied, at least a great deal happier, and the profile of American movies had been vastly altered. There had not been such a chaotic time, or one fraught with such sweeping artistic change, since the beginning of sound. A short time prior to the coming of the enforced Code, the father of "The Naked Moon," Cecil B. DeMille, had made some pious utterances about the threatened cleanup. "All of Hollywood is under indictment for the sins of a few," he declaimed. "How can this be fair? . . . Do you chop down a tree because one of its branches is

---

[9]*The Sign of the Cross*, original version with lesbians, skewered pygmies, and hungry crocodiles, survived because DeMille retained a print. Other cut titles—some of them—were restored in later years because collectors or studios possessed the cut footage. Some, alas, will never be seen in their original forms; one of the most notorious of pre-Code titles, *Convention City*, seems to have disappeared completely.

decayed?" A few months later, as the tree was being made into kindling, DeMille had no choice but to hew to the same line as everyone else in the film community. And in its first few months, through interconnected layers of intimidation and relief and good public relations, the appearance was that the Code really had helped the movies. Grosses, always the bottom line, were clearly on the rise, aided in large part by the elimination of expenses incurred by the interference from state and local censorship boards, as well as the costly Philadelphia boycott. Code proponents such as Breen and the opportunistically adaptable Will Hays painted a glowing Technicolor picture, quickly citing the financial figures as proof that the new "wholesome" film wave was responsible for the crowds. In their proselytizing enthusiasm they neglected to report that the grosses had been on the rise ever since Roosevelt's election. Nor was it mentioned that the profits had been propelled in part by such no-no titles as *She Done Him Wrong*, *George White's Scandals*, and *The Sign of the Cross*.

Moviegoers had no choice but to go along with the Code: like medicine, it was supposed to be good for you. Even so, some fun-loving filmgoers vented their disapproval in movie houses. All PCA-approved films sported an onscreen Code seal and certificate number, and it was reported that in such cities as Chicago, Detroit, New York, Cleveland, and heavily Catholic Boston, the seal was loudly booed. Liberal members of the press and arts community likewise said no, and film critic Richard Watts of the *New York Herald Tribune* set forth an argument against the Legion of Decency that may seem, all these decades later, to best frame the whole situation:

> With the Western World showing more than an occasional sign of collapse, and everything from German terrorism to strikes and rumors of war darkening the horizon, you might think that the Legion of Decency could find some more serious matter to fight against than Mae West's terrible influence over the ten-year-old mind.

As 1934 ended, all in Hollywood seemed streamline-shiny, sterile and censor-proof. The year had begun, in this present account of, with a highly successful musical featuring gay characters out—truly and genuinely out—on a dance floor. It ended with an even more profitable musical featuring another gay character on another dance floor. The differences between the earlier and later characters, and between the dances, told the whole story. The character was now closeted to the point of sexlessness, and his dance partner was a woman. On the stage, the Cole Porter musical *Gay Divorce* had dealt mockingly with adultery and divorce. With such matters exceedingly unwelcome in a post-Code world, RKO and the Code people went back and forth with arguments and compromise until the script and the title were viably laundered. *The Gay Divorcée*, as it was now known, was scrutinized exhaustively by the PCA, still informally

EDWARD EVERETT HORTON

Born Brooklyn, N.Y., March 18, 1886; died Encino, Calif., September 29, 1970

A great character actor's prime asset is a unique voice. It's fitting, then, that millions of baby boomers first experienced Edward Everett Horton through his voice alone—as the mordantly decorous narrator of "Fractured Fairy Tales" on the *Rocky and Bullwinkle* TV series. Even without his elegantly gangling figure and spooked countenance, EEH had no trouble establishing his presence.

For years, Mr. Horton was Hollywood's highest-paid character actor, a dependable and welcome and unchanging presence. In leads and more frequently in scores of supporting roles, he embodied aristocratic befuddlement and bungled composure. He existed, it seemed, in order to be startled, a Sisyphus for the world's irregularities. It took almost nothing to rattle him, after which the skinny 6'2" frame would cringe and the rubber face would instantly assume its perennially contorted affect: even more than Pangborn or Johnny Arthur, EEH was most compelling when flustered.

He also embodied the complete inverse of sex appeal. Although he played some romantic roles early on and was frequently cast as husband or father, one could hardly think of him in terms of sex. Consequently, he was in many ways the ideal gay persona for a post-Code age, as duly demonstrated in late 1934 in *The Gay Divorcée*. In films such as *In Caliente* (1935) and *The Gang's All Here* (1943), he would find himself dancing with another man, and as he registered shock with his standard cry of "My word!," you could tell that this would indeed be his preference, were sexuality his lot. Like all great character actors, he had decades of stage experience, coming to film in 1923 as a quirky leading man and easily settling into the supporting niche he maintained for over forty years. His defining moment came with the play *Springtime for Henry*—even the title evokes him— in which he starred as a Milquetoast who learns about love. Oddly, he did not appear in the film version; if he had, the pantywaist portions would have been, as always, far more convincing than the romantic aspects. But then, Mr. Horton knew his audience well enough to know that it loved and remained faithful to him for one thing above all: his sheer, and eternally enduring, improbability.

known as the Hays Office, but one character managed to stir little attention. The second male lead, Egbert, spent the entire film fussing, fretting, and fending off women's advances. As played by Edward Everett Horton, Egbert was high-strung, persnickety, supercilious, and notably lacking in masculine airs. Egbert, in sum, was gay, but in Horton's hands, in a Code-mandated Hollywood, he was so desexed as to pass undetected under the Breen radar. One of his central moments was a musical sequence called "Let's K-nock K-nees," in which a

Pert in satin pajamas (worn previously by Dolores Del Rio in *Flying Down to Rio*), Betty Grable seems unaware that Edward Everett Horton (as "Aunt" Egbert) is completely uninterested. It's all part of *The Gay Divorcée*. *Photofest*

young Betty Grable exhorted Horton to prance on the dance floor and make some innocuous whoopee. Throughout the entire number, Horton reacts and dances with an abashed unwillingness so palpable as to form a closet without walls. Such, for some years, would be the fate of gays on film—present yet weirdly invisible, just as in life, and incapable of carnal feelings or, sometimes, simple human contact. With or without Al Jolson's condescending "Woooo" boys would still be boys, and girls would still like girls, in this post-Code world. Those insiders wishing or needing to locate them in the movies would, however, need to work quite a bit harder.

SEVEN

Turnabout

LIFE IN A CODED WORLD

In the fall of 1935 one final corporate event capped the changes that had so altered the film industry in the previous two years. The Fox Film Corporation, one of Hollywood's oldest and most financially precarious studios, was merged with Darryl F. Zanuck's new upstart Twentieth Century Pictures. With Zanuck at the helm, the company's profile was immediately and immensely transformed. Fox's old parade of quirky money-losers was succeeded by a brass-plated win-win series of musicals and comedies and mysteries. Everything was sunny and Shirley Temple, cheerful and Charlie Chan and Code-proof. The Fox merger covered all the bases: financial, artistic, philosophical, social, technological. With it, the so-called Golden Age of Hollywood was now firmly in place, and in the transition from Fox to Twentieth Century–Fox the precepts and ethos of this age are precisely demonstrated:

1. From start to finish, America's movies were its most complexly engineered, meticulously tooled manufactured product.
2. The American film industry was set up as a hierarchy of major and minor companies, each with its distinctive style and format.
3. With all the problems surrounding the transition to sound now erased, the studios' production machinery was being honed to an awe-inspiring level of expertise.
4. The most efficiently run studios were governed by one dominant personality, be it Zanuck at Fox, Jack L. Warner at Warner Bros., or Herbert J. Yates at Republic.
5. With Fox's golden child, Shirley Temple, leading the way, the star system had assumed its magically ruthless configuration of making, maintaining, and replacing the studios' prime assets.

6. The Production Code Administration was intimately involved with the writing and production of every Hollywood film. Both the script and the final cut of a movie were subject to approval by the Breen Office. After its release, a film could be subjected to further deletions ordered by state censorship boards or the Legion of Decency.

7. Audience attendance was on the increase, profits and film budgets were taking an upturn, and the corporations that owned the studios also owned theater chains—thus guaranteeing both supply and demand.

8. Seldom was a movie script the result of one dominant artistic force. For every writer credited on a film, there were generally ten to fifteen uncredited.

9. A few directors (John Ford, Fritz Lang, Cecil B. DeMille) were permitted a distinctive or idiosyncratic voice. Far more directors were gifted technicians whose work was tailored to reflect a "house" style.

10. The film industry was perhaps the country's biggest secret haven for gay men and lesbians, who were under contract to all studios as creative personnel, staff, and talent. Although an official code of silence protected their personal lives from public scrutiny, they were often able to impart glimmers of secret selves to the films they helped to create.

In the boom years between the coming of the Code and the beginning of World War II the studio system worked at peak strength, with an efficiency and productivity unmatched at any other time in cinema history. Artistic daring and emotional honesty were incidental components—the moguls and the Code generally saw to that—and the sheer homogeneity of Hollywood's product seems, in retrospect, vaguely alienating. It lacks the anything-goes character of sound film prior to Code enforcement, or the kinetic adventurousness of silent film, or the burgeoning neuroticism of film (especially film noir) in the mid and late forties. It also, on the surface, seems deficient in the more distinctive gay presence of those times in film. This lack is, nonetheless, deceptive.

The years 1935 to 1940 are not the most active time for gays and lesbians on film, but in some ways they are the most evocative, the time in the movies' first century of existence when America's favorite pop culture mirrored its gay life most precisely. Gays onscreen in that era were exactly like gays in real life: constantly present, fully integrated into the dominant hetero world, yet knowable only to those who would know them. They were simultaneously visible and hidden, to be perceived by others like them and by certain sharp and sympathetic others. Gayness was entering at this time a new, more secretive period, that nether time prior to the forties' wartime changes and absorption in Freud. The strictures surrounding the repeal of Prohibition were one of the leading factors here, and with the end of the pansy craze and the passing of Radclyffe

Hall–type candor, a flamboyantly visible gayness was far less acceptable. In the rules for film behavior, there were norms and policies clearly corresponding to this conspiracy of concealment. The Clarences who flourished so frenetically in the backstage world of *Myrt and Marge* were gone, and never would one find either the ostentatious same-sex affections of the couples in *Cavalcade* and *Wonder Bar* or the joking references to lavender or *The Well of Loneliness*. The code words and gestures and identifiable details of costume and grooming all were toned down in movies, as in life. The Ernest stereotypes so offensive to so many viewers at the time and later on were no more. To play gay on film took sneaky work on the part of the writers and directors. It also required the actors to be as gifted at subterfuge as they were at performing.

Franklin Pangborn, Edward Everett Horton, Cecil Cunningham, Patsy Kelly, Grady Sutton, Eric Blore, Barnett Parker, Rex O'Malley, and the pre-Hitler Bobby Watson were the dependable leading lights in the closeted constellation working at this time, all imparting subversive tinges to even the most innocuous of roles and plots. Regardless of their offscreen preferences, it seems clear that they knew exactly what they were doing, how they were coming across, and who would understand. Did they regard themselves as heroes, as intrepid, if subtle and surreptitious, pioneers? Likely not. They were survivors, these actors, and those who were gay offscreen were passing in a straight (if Hollywood-permissive) working world, like most gay people. And like many artists, they were still adept at letting aspects of their identity show through in their work in an unmistakable yet safe way.

In the 1937 comedy *It's Love I'm After*, Leslie Howard played a self-pitying Shakespearean ham. "Nobody loves me," he moans to his valet, Eric Blore. "*I* love you, sir!" offers Blore . . to which Howard retorts, "Don't confuse the issue!" It was by means of that very confusion that movies of this time, with their Blores and Pangborns, could get away with it. This elaborately cloaked, insider quality gives the gay portrayals in these movies a special charge; a viewer can sometimes sense the delicious glee the actors and filmmakers took getting these portrayals pass the literal-minded if watchful eyes of the Breen Office. They were preaching to the perverted, circumventing Code mandates with cleverness, subtlety, and a certain sly gallantry.

By 1935 the Production Code was square one for all film production, and not surprisingly it took Breen and his cohorts some time to get their bearings. Many of the no-nos involving violence, drugs, and nudity were easily enforceable, but as sexual ambiguity was by definition a less tractable trait, there were a few glaring infractions early on. An early example came in a late Fox Film production, *George White's 1935 Scandals*. Fox's first edition of the *Scandals*, a year earlier, had been one of the most reviled of all the censor-baiters, with a sight gag involving a toilet seat and a production number featuring a little girl strutting through a lewd fan dance while the sound track blared "Oh, You Nasty Man." The post-Code version was notably less *Scandal*-ous, so much so that the Production Code Administration commended Fox for its cleanup. The PCA's relief over the absence of bathroom jokes and kiddie porn blinded it to a dance involving a somewhat less nasty man. In the course of the anorexic plot, producer George White (played by producer George White) attends an amateur-night show in a small Georgia burg. A bearded and burly lumberjack type shambles onstage for his solo, which turns out to be the flittiest, flounciest mince of a pansy dance imaginable, with pursing lips, ethereally floating hands, and "Woooo"-type gestures. The incongruity is as complete as it is amusing: the rough façade versus the secret fruity inside, the gamy queer reference in a denatured dud of a movie. Around that same time (spring 1935) an Ub Iwerks cartoon called *Mary's Little Lamb* featured a similarly pungent dance. One of Mary's classmates, "Little Percy," a cute blonde Fauntleroy, gets up in front of the class to do a recitation. Instead of poetry, his turn is another flitty dance, complete with mincing and skips and precious gestures. The class reacts approvingly en masse with the standard gay salute: arm extended, hand turned out in a swirl, and a loud "Woooo!"[1]

Franklin Pangborn also checked in early in the new regime with several supporting roles, giving his most noteworthy performance in the least interesting film. A forgotten surf-and-turf Columbia programmer called *Eight Bells* featured Mr. P as Finch, the ever-helpful "captain's man" or valet. Looking dapper in his formal uniform, he bounces up the gangplank while jauntily singing "I Am a Gay Caballero," a ditty from 1928 which had already acquired a double entendre reputation. As used here (Pangborn sings it in two scenes), it is proof unarguable that the "G" word was in use this early on, within a community that obviously did not include the Breen watchdogs.[2] With his appearance in *Eight Bells*, Pangborn set the tone for his pattern of activity over the ensuing years: a blend of fussiness and, in this case, sunny diligence, that almost always enabled him to come in under the radar.

For the most talented gay directors in the business, the Code had notably little impact on two highly personal and clandestinely defiant 1935 projects. In

---

[1]By the following year, the salute was being removed for live-action films; a late appearance came in a musical number in Warner Bros.' *Cain and Mabel*, when Marion Davies greets a fey statue of Julius Caesar with the wave but not the "Woooo." Short subjects occasionally got away with more than features, and so in 1937 a Three Stooges short, *Slippery Silks*, featured one last (and very funny) bit featuring a wave and, courtesy of Curly and Larry, an epically loud "Woooo."

[2]For a concurrent 1935 use of *gay* in is-it-or-isn't it mode, try the hit MGM operetta *Naughty Marietta*. As Nelson Eddy shepherds Jeanette MacDonald through sinful 1700s New Orleans, they observe two drunken soldiers exiting a saloon, one slumped into the arms of the other. Nelson: "People are rather gay in this quarter of town!"

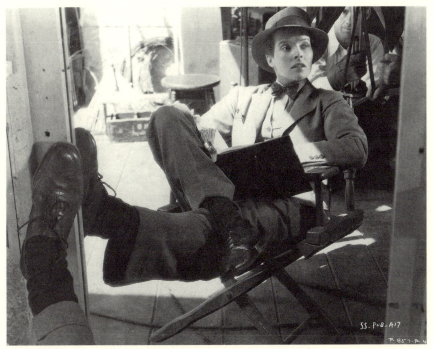

Katharine Hepburn shows what the well-crossed-dressed actor would wear on the set of *Sylvia Scarlett. Photofest*

spite of the fact that many male actors gave some of their best performances in his films, George Cukor was forever unable to escape the euphemistic and condescending label "woman's director." It can also be read "gay director," of course, though no comparable straight artist was called "man's director." Nor would directorial heteroism yield the disdain producer Samuel Goldwyn aimed toward the Cukor style when he commented that Cukor "tended to put lace panties on all his scenes." Except for Ernest in *Our Betters*, Cukor's films were exceedingly chary with gay characters and allusions, just as Cukor himself meticulously segregated the gay and straight portions of his personal life. Yet in 1935 he and Katharine Hepburn walked quirkily on the wild side in a somewhat mad project with the most pansexual allusions this side of Marlene Dietrich. *Sylvia Scarlett* was a bona fide cross-dressed movie curiosity, a cult film vastly ahead of its cultish time and a notorious box-office flop. As Sylvia, Hepburn spent a great deal of the time passing as a cute boy named Sylvester, drawing the admiration of women and the bemused attention of artist Brian Aherne, who notes that he has "a queer feeling when I look at you." Despite the provocative nature of the material, and Hepburn's androgynous charm, *Sylvia*

Scarlett was at best an endearing trifle, and the commercial chances of such an idiosyncratic project were zero. In a post-Code age, few observers cared to countenance such things as a central episode where Sylvia/Sylvester and company (including Cary Grant) form a group of strolling players called the Pink Pierrots. The Breen folk had raised a few objections over the material, especially one scene in which Hepburn-as-boy is unsure whether to go into the men's or ladies' room. The more subtle aspects of *Sylvia*'s sexual confusion were too covert to draw many objections, and it was that very intricacy, in this fey setting, that stamped *Sylvia Scarlett* as a covert statement of gay things—and, for the larger viewing public, an event to be avoided at all costs.

More insubordinate than Cukor, and more openly gay, James Whale directed his best, possibly *the* best, horror film, *Bride of Frankenstein*, early in the year. Whale was no fool where the Code was concerned, and his dealings with the PCA on *Bride* form a primer on how clever directors were able to get around the code to retain the adult material they really wished to keep. After sending Breen a suitably humble (and undoubtedly tongue-in-cheek) missive about how manfully he would strive to respect the Code, Whale clashed with the PCA over some predictably literal matters: violence, gruesomeness (doubtless in recollection of *Our Movie-Made Children*), and the cleavage displayed by Elsa Lanchester in the prologue, in which she played Mary Shelley.[3] Such concerns were precisely the sort of cosmetic objections that kept the Breen folk busy. Meanwhile, more subtle elements and allusions would waft past them, straight into the minds of discerning viewers. As a result, Whale's dark and gay sense of humor remained untouched, especially in Ernest Thesiger's macabre-queen portrayal of Dr. Pretorius and in *Bride*'s constant reiterations of countercultural bonding: Boris Karloff's monster finding happiness with the blind hermit, Frankenstein's unholy alliance with Pretorius, and the final courtship of the monster and his balky, hissing bride.

The first extended Code wranglings over gay matters occurred in the 1935–36 season. Both involved heated questions over lesbian content, but otherwise the situations and the films could not have been more different. At Universal, where *Bride of Frankenstein* and almost all of Hollywood's horror movies were produced, plans were afoot for a sequel to one of its major hits. The progenitor was *Dracula*, the new film would feature the bloodluster's daughter, and visions of sex-filled horror overtook Breen and company. A few months earlier, when Universal had proposed a film version of the English play *Love of Women*, the PCA rejected the material on grounds of lesbian content. It also said no to the early scripts of *Dracula's Daughter*, in which Dad himself figured

---

[3]For the film proper, in which she figured indelibly as the monster's consort, Lanchester sported a bound and bandaged torso that drew no censorious objections.

prominently. With a complete rewrite submitted to the PCA piecemeal as it came off the typewriter, the story's contour of sex and horror was made less blatant and more provocative. While the Countess's passion for a man who would save her remained, there were now added scenes with two female victims. In particular, there was a spellbinding encounter between the vampire (Gloria Holden) and a young street girl (Nan Grey) she picks up on the pretext of needing a model to sculpt. The PCA immediately picked up on the homoerotic undertones, cautioning the producers to treat the scene "in such a way as to avoid any suggestion of perverse sexual desire on the part of Marya or of an attempted sexual attack by her upon Lili." The studio seemed to comply, at least on the surface, yet the point of the scene was unmistakable, Grey's lush innocence counterpointed against Holden's saturnine urgency. Holden's intelligence, gothic beauty, and melancholy understatement carry the scene, and the entire film, well beyond horror-movie cartoonishness or parody to a place of unlimited subtext, where secret things can be made plain.

A more literal reading of a lesbian text posed some well-publicized difficulties around the same time for producer Samuel Goldwyn. While he was generally predisposed toward filming successful books and plays, he laughed in Lillian Hellman's face when she proposed that he film her Broadway success *The Children's Hour*. Set in a girls' school, it hinged upon a vicious brat's allegation of a lesbian relationship between the two headmistresses; one of them ends her life when she realizes that yes, she does indeed have those feelings. Such was viable fare for liberal Broadway, where it ran for nearly two years, but not 1935 Hollywood. Somehow Hellman convinced Goldwyn that the play was about the power, not the nature, of a lie, and that it could be rewritten to pass PCA muster.[4] Goldwyn, the legend goes, was sufficiently sold on the idea to hold his ground when an underling tried to talk him out of it.

> ASSISTANT: But, Sam, it's a play about lesbians!
> GOLDWYN: So? We'll make them Americans.

And so he did. He bought the rights with the full awareness—laid out in a letter from Will Hays—that he could not use the lesbian theme, nor the play's original title, nor any mention in advertising that this film was, indeed, *The Children's Hour*. (The onscreen credit, in fact, said "Original Story and Screen Play by Lillian Hellman.") His initial attempt to get around the lesbianism was

---

[4]The play was based on an incident in Scotland, and Hellman later said that she had used lesbianism as the subject of the lie because it was the most insidious falsehood one could spread. Obviously she was not conscious of a fact best viewed in retrospect: the play is also about the corrosive effects of homophobia.

From the first go-round for *The Children's Hour*, Bonita Granville bids Merle Oberon and Miriam Hopkins a fond farewell after wrecking their lives.

a rewrite having the two women, Martha and Karen, as transplanted English gentry who become involved in a scandal when one of their students dies, followed by accusations that Martha was involved with Karen's fiancé. As finally filmed under the title *These Three*, the women were again American, the suicide (and the child's death) was removed, and the lie was indeed about heterosexual passion. As Breen wrote to Will Hays, unwittingly imparting a hint of double meaning, "The suggestion of perversion [has] been removed and a straight love story substituted." Yet as directed by William Wyler—this was his breakthrough film—and acted by Miriam Hopkins and Merle Oberon, there existed enough ambiguity to hint at the possible subtexts of other relationships. For the climactic scene in which Martha (Hopkins) confesses that she does indeed love Dr. Cardin (Joel McCrea), Wyler kept the camera focused on her back: the effect is to give her feelings, whatever they are, a closetlike enclosure. Rapturously reviewed and financially successful, *These Three* was in its way a clear victory over the Code and even over the playwright. Hellman's play, powerful and well constructed as it was, was not a plea for sexual tolerance. Indeed, one underlying thesis of the play—that homosexuality could, if proven, warrant the destruction it causes—is what now seems the true perversion. Yet with Code prompting, Hellman's intensive restructuring job and, above all, the outstanding work of the director and cast, *These Three* retains possibilities of secret homoeroticism far less negative than those depicted in the play. A greater visibility of the original theme would, in this film at this time, have served only to demonize. As if in conscious demonstration of this, Wyler directed a remake of *These Three* a quarter-century later, now using Hellman's title and original theme. And lo, the "Americanized" 1936 rewrite remained the superior film. Who could have divined that Breen and Hays were capable, through their puritanical bungling, of effecting the right decision?

It would be four years until there was another major battle waged with Breen over a movie's gay-oriented content. Even so, the years 1936–38 in particular saw a surprising number of gay characters or gay moments. Some of them were "now you see them . . ." brief appearances, some were more extended, and some were strictly connect-the-dots for knowing viewers. All, in one way or another, escaped the PCA's vigilance, or at very least indicated its slowness on the uptake. By 1938 the Breen Office seemed finally to catch on, and decreased the portrayals for several years. Again the movies were following the national climate, phasing out the sore-thumb stereotypes just as "polite" society was being studiously and steadily heterosexualized. For thousands of gay men and lesbians going to the movies, some of these moments and actors would have to be viewed as tiny, friendly oases of validation or identification. Many of them were in musicals, possibly because the Breen office's attention was often diverted with the threat of too much skin showing in dance numbers. In MGM's *Born to Dance*, for example, Bobby Watson made a late appearance as a snitty stage manager, behaving for all the world as if the 1934 Code had never happened. An even bigger MGM musical of 1936, *The Great Ziegfeld*, featured an homage (probably unwitting) to *Myrt and Marge:* another fussy designer named Clarence, played by Broadway actor David Burns. Despite its seeming disinterest, the PCA did manage, in early 1936, to raise a fuss at Columbia over the operetta *The King Steps Out*. It featured a wildly over-the-top ballet master the script labeled "effeminate," and Joe Breen saw lavender: "We caution you against allowing any 'pansy' flavor to creep into the character," he warned Harry Cohn. After he viewed the finished film, with the role played by a pudgy Brit named Barnett Parker, he grew livid when he heard the master's admonition to his charges, "And please girls, remember that we are all ladies!" Even as he ordered the deletion of that line, far more than mere creeping remained in the final cut, for Parker and his flavor were as flaming as a Fire Island brushfire. As a result of such infractions, PCA vigilance began to increase, and with it greater studio compliance. By the time of Warner Bros.' *Talent Scout* in 1937, the insertion of gay characters in theatrical settings was so minimized as to be almost subliminal: a costume designer shows a fabric swatch to a studio mogul and he murmurs the surefire pansy signal, "Divine, simply divine!"—only so faintly as to sound like a mere rustle of tulle. The costumiers in *Broadway Melody* and *Manhattan Parade* would never have tolerated such reticence.

Several other Warner Bros. movies contained portrayals at once close to the pre-Code type and clearly denatured. In two low-budget comedies, gay-implied characters were seen as professional impediments to straight heroes. In *The Big Noise* (1936), hardworking businessman Guy Kibbee is forced out of his company when the stockholders prefer newer business methods. The character espousing these effete changes is Mr. Rosewater (André Berenger), the very name a clue to the audience about what to make of him. Warners' *The Tenderfoot* (1932) had memorably pitted yokel Joe E. Brown against a group of rouged chorus boys who slam-dunk him with a group "Wooooo!" Remade in a less permissive environment as *Dance Charlie Dance* (1937), it now implied alternative sexuality with the brusque, unwelcome presence of Jenny Wolfe, a coat-and-tie-wearing agent played by tall and homely Mary Treen. After a heated run-in with hero Stuart Erwin, she must then endure a parting riposte from wisecracker Glenda Farrell: "You forgot your cigar!" Farrell continued in this mode that same year in Warner's big-budget *Hollywood Hotel*, playing the factotum of a temperamental diva. Without visible effort, she short-circuits an eruption by a couturier (Curt Bois) who bears the more than oxymoronic name Butch:

> JONESIE [Farrell] (*indicating a pair of evening slippers*): You better dye these and send a pair of black ones too.
> BUTCH (*furiously*): You mean you want black ones too? Why don't you get her a pair of SKATES while you're at it? (*Points emphatically with his long cigarette holder*) *I* want a pair of *very* high-heeled-shoe sandals!
> JONESIE (*with terminal scorn*): What are ya gonna wear 'em with?

One of the best-remembered moments in this purportedly homo-free time came when, early in 1938, Cary Grant donned Katharine Hepburn's negligee in *Bringing Up Baby*. When he is questioned by her grandmother (May Robson), he leaps in the air to frenziedly proclaim, "I just went *gay* . . . all of a sudden!" Once again, the word was coded enough to make it through the Breen gauntlet; what makes its meaning indisputable is Grant's ensuing line: "I'm sitting in the middle of 42nd Street, waiting for a bus!" Here was the true subversive line, targeted directly to the insiders. For the majority of us who don't get it, George Chauncey explains in *Gay New York:*

CECIL CUNNINGHAM

Born St. Louis, Mo., August 2, 1888; died Los Angeles, Calif., April 7, 1959

A woman bearing a man's name was a potential icon for a secretive age, and this one delivered consistently. She had a look of grim austerity—tall (5'8"), somewhat gothic and gaunt, with close-cropped silver hair. More glorious yet was her voice. It was the sound of an extra-dry martini spilled onto a piece of parchment, a near-Wagnerian bass-baritone filled with blighted overtones of experience, reason, and cynicism. With no hint of tolerance for nonsense, she served as oracle and counselor for a generation of flighty lovers, most memorably as Irene Dunne's acidulous Aunt Patsy in *The Awful Truth*. Like most character performers, she came from the stage at the dawn of sound—those tones might have been devasting as Volumnia in *Coriolanus*—and settled in for the latter-life run in Hollywood. For twenty years she consistently stole scenes from younger, frequently less gifted leads. In pre-Code years her authority could function in seamy climes, as in her tough turns as a madam in *Safe in Hell* and *Susan Lennox*. Later on, she had a corner on no-nonsense spinster types and secretaries. Rarely did a Cunningham performance carry a sexual overtone, yet volumes were conveyed by her voice, look, manner, and even the names of her characters. As Carole Lombard's sidekick in Mitchell Leisen's *Swing High, Swing Low*, she operated under the single name Murphy, and in James Whale's *Wives under Suspicion* she was an executive assistant known, simply and appropriately, as Sharpy. In *King of Gamblers* (1937) she was a tough vice queen named Big Edna. Call it butchness or simply severity, with Cunningham you knew this was not merely someone's sweet old hetero aunt. In the 1940s she moved down the cast list in undistinguished dowager roles, and by the time she was sixty—an age she'd looked for many years—she was out of movies. While *The Awful Truth* serves well as her memorial, any Cunningham appearance is worthy of appreciation and some tinges of secret gay glee.

It seems likely that Grant used it precisely because those connotations amplified the homosexual meaning of his first line. In the late 1930s, when the film was made, Forty-second Street . . . was the primary cruising strip for the city's male prostitutes, including transvestite prostitutes, as Grant almost surely would have known. One of the reasons it acquired this status was that it was a heavily trafficked street and transportation hub, where men loitering would not draw particular notice—it was, in other words, the sort of place where a man who was cruising could quip that he was just waiting for a bus to anyone who inquired about his purpose.

For Cary Grant, whose sexuality was likely far more intricate than that of any of his onscreen roles, the moment was as anomalous as it was humorous.

Glamour takes many forms, and one of them is Cecil Cunningham in this mid-1930s portrait. *Photofest*

His offscreen life was otherwise completely, exhaustively separate from the effortless movie persona.[5] Such was (and is) the price paid by those of lofty position. Call it the maintaining of privacy or a deal with the devil, call it self-deception or compulsive role-playing, playing straight was the only game available for leading actors. No Pangborn perfidy or Cunningham craftiness was permissible. Directors, however, were in a far easier position than leading or even supporting actors. How often do directors' films serve as Rorschach guides to their psyches? A whole shelf of books might begin to answer it. For some gay directors working in this specific period, there were allusive possibilities—Dorothy Arzner's compulsive woman-bonding, Mitchell Leisen's bent toward the aesthetics of design—and for others, there were onscreen surrogates. Stage actor Rex O'Malley served in this capacity on two memorable occasions, for

---

[5]Pauline Kael, in her *New Yorker* analysis of Grant, noted the one time that the private and public Grants collided: the 1940 comedy *My Favorite Wife*. Observing the actor's unusually ineffective performance, she commented that the presence in the cast of "his close friend" Randolph Scott had evidently interfered with Grant's concentration.

Leisen and George Cukor. In Cukor's *Camille* (1936), O'Malley served, with elegant understatement, as the sounding board and support for Greta Garbo's dying courtesan. His Gaston belongs to the same half-world as her Marguerite, in all probability sharing her career. When the fair-weather demimonde gives way to poverty and tuberculosis, only Gaston remains to give moral and financial aid and help effect her reunion with Armand (Robert Taylor). The sexuality is not so much implied as felt, and O'Malley moves gracefully from acid barbs early on to moving and unsentimental sincerity in the final scenes; his is an exceptional, and truly *supporting*, performance. In its strength and discretion, O'Malley's role in *Camille* evokes much of Cukor's professional persona, for, like Gaston, the director thrived tactfully in an environment (Hollywood) filled with flash and parties and sex, and in his serious moments he would firmly guide many actors of both genders to their best performances.

For Mitchell Leisen, O'Malley functioned in a far less sympathetic capacity. Leisen, who began as a costume designer (for DeMille) and slowly moved to the director's chair, was perhaps more conspicuously gay than Cukor even as he married and had affairs with actresses. Both his flamboyance and his talent caused some rumblings from fellow artists on the Paramount lot. Preston Sturges allegedly became a director to prevent Leisen from "ruining" his scripts, and Billy Wilder, who had similar complaints, said some especially harsh things to writer Maurice Zolotow after Leisen's death: "Leisen spent more time with Edith Head worrying about the pleats on a skirt than he did with [me] on the script. . . . Leisen was too goddam fey. I don't knock fairies. Let him be a fairy. Leisen's problem was that he was a stupid fairy."[6]

The film on which Leisen and Wilder came to grief was *Midnight* (1939), one of the best comedies of the era. The demimonde of *Camille* was here a heartless Parisian high society where gay and straight men cater to the whims of wealthy women.[7] One of these women, Mary Astor, is having an affair with dashing Francis Lederer, while her other attendant, O'Malley, runs interference. Claudette Colbert, as a somewhat disreputable Cinderella, is dropped into this milieu by Astor's husband, John Barrymore, as a way to regain his straying wife. While Lederer and O'Malley both dress impeccably and serve as Astor's sounding-board appendages, the contrast is made clear: Astor loves Lederer, who makes a play for

---

[6]Zolotow continues in Wilder's vein by hacking away at Leisen's talent, sexuality, and even his physical appearance: "He was a tall, strikingly attired man. He was a very ugly man. . . . He flaunted his sexual proclivities [and] turned his home into a homosexual rendezvous." Wilder, at least, later qualified his comments.

[7]*Midnight* can be viewed as, among other things, an early look at women of privilege and the men who "walk" them. One of the women in *Midnight* is Hedda Hopper, and her walker is played by Leisen's lover, Billy Daniels.

Colbert, while O'Malley, who conspires with Astor to expose Colbert, has no evident affairs. His only romance is with high life and glittering subterfuge, as his Marcel notes: "I'm a telephone worshipper. Whenever a day comes without an invitation, I pray to my telephone as though it were a little black god. I beg of it to speak to me, to ask me out somewhere—anywhere where there's caviar and champagne." Late in life, Leisen protested that he had leaned on O'Malley to tone down his act: "I made Rex play his part in *Midnight* as straight as he could." Nothing in the final result betrays much of a suppressive effort, however, and the character's gayness seems as inherent in the script (by Wilder and Charles Brackett) as in the casting and direction; when Leisen remade *Midnight* in 1945 (as the indifferent *Masquerade in Mexico*), it took little more than a few altered pronouns to change the character to a woman, played by the queeny Natalie Schaefer.

Camille and *Midnight* were both products of the highest echelons of the Dream Factory's magic-makers. Let there now be examined, as a memento of a vastly different school of film production, a bona fide uncloseted gay movie, albeit one made by uncomprehending and talent-free straights: an exploitation melodrama called *Children of Loneliness*. This is such a fly-by-night piece that it can't even be given a definitive date of release. It was shot sometime in 1934 by something called Jewel Productions, and by 1937 the trade press was noting that it had been around "quite a bit"—like nudist camp and drug-scare movies, it ran in dingy dives specializing in adults-only films that would neither apply for nor be granted Production Code certificates. Jewel overreached sufficiently to claim that it was "inspired" by Radclyffe Hall's *Well of Loneliness*, although even ZaSu Pitts would have had trouble distinguishing Hall's original story in the queer-scare saga of Elinor, young, vulnerable, and afraid of men, and of Bobby, the butch roommate who preys upon her. For good measure, a secondary plot involved another young woman in love with an artist who turns out to be gay. In the course of sixty-eight minutes, there is a visit to a gay café complete with dining and dancing, Elinor finds true love with a fullback, Bobby is blinded by acid and run over by a truck, and the artist, Paul, commits suicide over his tortured love of men. Jewel Productions framed its epic in a prologue and epilogue on the dangers of homosexuality featuring one S. Dana Hubbard, M.D., allegedly of the New York Health Department. The cautionary tone taken by Dr. Hubbard was echoed in a statement Jewel included in the copyright submission, no doubt to ensure protection against arrests:

> *Children of Loneliness* is an educational and scientific presentation of an absorbing subject that deals with the manifestations, evil associations, and mental complexes that affect and misdirect normal adults into channels resulting in homo-sexuality. It points out in vivid form and manner the fact that it is an acquired anomaly requir-

ing only the influence of some exciting cause to become manifest. . . . In their effort to satisfy their desires these unfortunate people often stoop to the most loathsome practices.

However loathsome its denizens—or however much they practiced—it was clear from the beginning that *Children of Loneliness* was something short of a public service. Instead, it was another stop on that familiar route reaching from *The Sign of the Cross* to *Personal Best, Basic Instinct,* and, heaven help the world, *Showgirls*—all made with the conviction that lesbianism is a turn-on for many men, especially when it's framed in such a way as to make the male spectator feel he would have the ultimate edge. Male homosexuality, of course, would not be as attractive a proposition for this movie's target audience, so Paul's story is far subsidiary. His fate, at any rate, is just a shade nicer than Bobby's: after he's gone, his fiancée professes that if he had told her, she would've understood.

We may never see *Children of Loneliness* again; after some screenings in the mid-fifties, it vanished. Even so, enough of its companion pieces from the time survive—*Reefer Madness, Child Bride, Enlighten Thy Daughter,* and on and on—to indicate its quality and effect. To give adults-only spectators the feeling they'd been somewhere, it offered just enough titillation to get by: the overall theme, glimpses of couples at the café, and likely a shot or two showing a bit of (female) skin. Shot on the literal and figurative fringes of Hollywood without wit or ingenuity, it offered a muddy amalgam of melodrama, scare tactics, and meek sensationalism. The package naturally did not include production values: the sound recording was such that critics complained of echoes, and the only recognizable cast members were Luana Walters (Elinor) and Jean Carmen (Bobby), both fugitives from grade-C westerns. Dr. Hubbard, whoever he was, filled in whatever psychological or dramatic holes as remained after the plots wrapped and the homos died, just as early hard-core movies employed bogus sex therapists to put everything in a barely redeemable context, just in case.

One engagement of this terminally squalid gay epic was especially memorable. In November 1937 *Children of Loneliness* ran in downtown Los Angeles at the Tally's Criterion Theater, following a previous, similarly authentic Jewel production, *Love Life of a Gorilla.* As with numerous sex films, it was not only a screening but a full-blown multimedia presentation complete with lecture and promotional tie-ins. Fortunately for posterity, the *Motion Picture Herald* critic was present to record the event in some detail. After the film ended, a man came onstage, accompanied by three young women, and announced himself as a doctor. As the women stood patiently behind him, he proceeded to lecture awhile on the history and nature of sexual perversion, with mentions of Oscar Wilde and a few other noteworthy deviants. Then the distaff trio came forward, color-coded for easy identification. The woman in red was a nymphomaniac, the one in lavender was a normal girl looking forward to making babies, and the third, wearing white, symbolized purity. With their natures thus made manifest, the hypothetical physician hawked several pamphlets designed to explain, and likely cure, homosexuality, after which he and the women went into the audience selling them. At this point, at one early screening, the quartet was arrested by the Los Angeles Police Department on the charge of selling salacious literature and held for $500 bail apiece. The *Herald* critic ended his report by noting, for one of the first times in history, the reaction of gay audience members to a gay-themed movie:

> Your reporter inferred from the lisping comments of young men on his left and the throaty whispers of middle-aged women on his right that unless there are, as the lecturer declared, four million of these in the United States and even if there are, Mr. Sam Cumming of Jewel Pictures is going to have quite a time [getting them to attend his] picture.

Even in the closeted year of 1937, gays and lesbians apparently knew better. Presumably they knew in later years as well, for *Children of Loneliness* played the occasional fleabag engagement into the 1950s.

Other gay portrayals of the era in more mainstream venues were equally noteworthy, if less scandalous. Barnett Parker, momentarily stunning as the dance master in *The King Steps Out,* flitted in and out of a number of productions swathed in the blissful unawareness that the age of Wilde and Beardsley had reached its close. In *Live, Love, and Learn* (1937) Parker glistened as an interior decorator named Alfredo, about whom Joe Breen warned Louis B. Mayer: "There of course should be nothing suggestive of the 'pansy' about the characterization." Guess again: especially for the bland likes of a medium-budget MGM comedy, this performance really goes the limit. In one scene Alfredo enthuses, to the point of near-orgasm, over the boldness of his chosen fabrics. His client, Robert Montgomery, continues Alfredo's flouncing manner to respond that one design "would obviously bring out the *beast* in a man!" Parker reacts to Montgomery with pop-eyed amazement and a tinge of hopeful recognition. In Paramount's *Café Society* (1939) character actor Allyn Joslyn spat vitriol as Sonny DeWitt, a bitchy gossip columnist. For Joslyn, whose roles were usually supercilious or ineffectual, this was a rare foray into Rex O'Malley territory. An interview Joslyn gave near the end of his life bears out that these actors knew what they were doing: he recalled that he had played a homosexual in *Café Society* and that it had been one of his best roles. So nasty is Sonny that in one scene his mother (Jessie Ralph) is working on a needlepoint rug with his face at the center. "I can't wait to get it finished," Mom mutters, "so I can walk on it!" George Cukor's *The Women* (1939) is gay less in content than in ambient effect: this is as flagrantly gay as a big-studio movie can get, the camp embossed onto the filmstrip with every Adrian gown and Rosalind Russell outburst. One character, however, functions as a real gay presence, not just a drag-queen epiphany. The novelist Nancy (Florence Nash) refers to herself as "an old maid—a frozen asset," but in her dress and manner and intelligence she is less a spinster than a sane gay observer of a relentlessly trivial straight world.

Cukor also worked on two even bigger 1939 productions, in fact the very top contenders for the Ultimate Hollywood Classic award. His struggles on *Gone with the Wind*, and the reasons for his leaving the production, will forever be in dispute. Some historians go for the more gossipy reasons: that Cukor supposedly knew of Clark Gable's secret rough-trade-hustler past (allegedly, a tryst with William Haines), which eventually made Gable so uncomfortable that he screamed he wouldn't be directed by a fairy and had him discharged. Others cite Cukor's artistic conflicts with producer and control freak David O. Selznick. As with most history, the real story probably is in a tangled combination of these and other factors. Even before he started *Wind*, Cukor worked a couple of days on *The Wizard of Oz*, though he declined MGM's invitation to direct it. (His main contribution was to change Judy Garland's wig and makeup, making her less Shirley Temple and more Judy/Dorothy.) How Cukor would have dealt with Bert Lahr's Cowardly Lion is an interesting what-if; would the Lion have been even more fey, perhaps a feline cousin to Ernest in *Our Betters*? Likely not: Lahr's sublime clowning would probably have come out the same with Cukor as it did under Victor Fleming. The Lion is a self-proclaimed sissy, albeit an unwilling one; once again, there's that old tendency to equate cowardice with both unmanliness and gayness. Nevertheless, those gay-toned shticks beloved of such comics as Lahr and Eddie Cantor here find their ultimate, glorious, incarnation in this queeny King of Beasts, who makes his wrists go limp for effect and who protests, when denied an audience with the Wizard, "But I got a permanent just for the occasion!"

Columbia's *Too Many Husbands* (1940) was a typical bauble of the kind that will likely never be seen again—insignificant, devastatingly professional, an indifferent setting for stars to show off with nonchalant ease. Adapted from one of Somerset Maugham's least important works, it had a primeval plot unworthy of its creator: the one about the widow who has remarried and finds out that the husband she thought dead has been marooned on a desert island. Jean Arthur was the unwitting bigamist, and Fred MacMurray and Melvyn Douglas were spouses one and two. Amidst the expected "What am I going to do with two husbands?" bedroom-farce complications, there were contained some unmistakable gay allusions. The jealousy between the two husbands heightens when they are compelled to share a bedroom redecorated under Douglas's direction. As he takes in the room, MacMurray finds, in Douglas's ornate decorative tendencies, an easy way to lash his rival.

> MacMurray: I guess when you redecorated it you made it just what you wanted for your very own room.
> Douglas: Rave on, you wonderful thing!
> MacMurray (*looking at the draperies*) What's this stuff—mosquito netting?
> Douglas (*ruefully*) Dotted swiss.
> MacMurray (*with sibilant mockery*): "Dotted sswisss." You even look pretty when you say it! (*As Douglas continues to fume MacMurray walks over to the vanity table and picks up two large powder puffs.*) Hmmmm . . . which one is mine?

Male jealousy must naturally find every way to minimize the competition, and nothing spells putdown like "fag." The equation is "decorating ability = fussiness = unmasculine = gay." Overlard with appropriate lisps and code words like "wonderful thing," plus the male dread of looking "pretty." It helps also to have a smirkingly macho actor like Fred MacMurray, plus a Breen Office so worried about the script's bigamy that it doesn't comprehend the undercurrents.

For Marlene Dietrich the post-Code age was a time of retrenchment. Her association with Von Sternberg ended in 1935, and with it went most of the darker sexual edges of her persona. She abandoned the way of the androgyne completely until 1940, when she appeared again in male attire in the rowdy comedy *Seven Sinners*. By this time Dietrich had entered phase 2 of her American career, playing big-hearted dames who were whores in everything except onscreen title. As a café singer banned on every island in the South Pacific, Dietrich donned a navy uniform to sing "The Man's in the Navy" to an audience of cheering sailors. The echoes of *Morocco* were unavoidable, as was the difference between the earlier film's audacity and the more "nice" drag of a Breen-controlled era. Still, Dietrich's personality was so iridescent that when she doffed her sailor cap and assumed a roguish look, some sparks were unavoidable. She was a woman singing about the man in the navy, but she was also, clearly, the man himself.[8]

An era such as this, with its safe and cozily implied onscreen gayness, was fertile ground for the flustery nonmachismo of Franklin Pangborn. In 1937 alone he had roles (ranging from second leads to bit parts) in, count 'em, twenty-

---

[8]In *The Celluloid Closet* Vito Russo mentioned that a gay reference to "Bruce from Bombay" was sneaked into the scene in *Seven Sinners* in which Dietrich reads aloud from a sailor's little black book. Would that it were so: a close listen to the soundtrack reveals the name, as filtered through Dietrich's famed lisp, to be Ruth. And it's Twinidad.

six movies. Without discrimination he appeared in the classic (*My Man Godfrey, Mr. Deeds Goes to Town, A Star Is Born*) and the wondrously trivial (including the culinary trio *Doughnuts and Society, Love on Toast*, and *She Had to Eat*). Playing a tailor in *Mr. Deeds*, he effected a graceful rapport with Gary Cooper while measuring him for a suit (pants and innuendo included). In a lead role, that of a prima donna tenor, he managed to transcend the low-rent aspirations of the grade-D musical *High Hat* (1937). Perhaps it was his befuddled elegance as much as his lack of traditionally pansyesque tricks that kept the Breen people away even while they watched him closely. Some in-house correspondence makes it evident that the Code office was not unfamiliar with Pangborn's work and general effect, even as it generally tended to leave him alone . . . at least until 1940, which was in many ways Mr. P's most fateful year. It saw him collaborating happily with W. C. Fields in *The Bank Dick* as bank examiner J. Pinkerton Snoopington, embarking on a series of appearances for Preston Sturges, and running afoul of the Production Code Administration in the biggest controversy of his career.

The writings of Thorne Smith (1892–1934) centered on mildly risqué variations on a common theme: the intrusion of the supernatural into the everyday world, and the rattling effect it has on ordinary folks. Smith's enduring work is *Topper*, the one about chichi ghosts and the befuddled man they haunt. Among other less remembered titles—*The Night Life of the Gods, Dream's End, The Stray Lamb*—there is the 1931 novel *Turnabout*, which made coin with the same premise that, in film's ice age, had animated *A Florida Enchantment*. Call it sex change, role reversal, or trading places: a man and a woman find out how the other half makes out. In *Turnabout* the big switch is visited upon an upwardly mobile husband and wife who make the mistake of quarreling in front of a meddlesome graven image. As set off by Smith's archly artless prose, the turnabout produces mild laughs and some easy observations about the battle of the sexes. She, as he, is tossed into the macho maelstrom of Madison Avenue advertising, and he, now she, has to cope with all manner of femininity, including pregnancy. Sexuality wrenched out of context naturally makes for farcical confusion, with a host of risqué implications—many of them gay—to the fore. Such ribald novelty made *Turnabout* an obvious candidate for filming in the days prior to the enforced Production Code, and in 1932 it was announced as an upcoming MGM musical. By 1939 there had still been no film, and a *Turnabout* in the Breen era seemed unlikely. But producer Hal Roach determined to turn this situation about. Comedy—Laurel and Hardy and Our Gang and many more—was his business, and he was moving increasingly from two-reel shorts into feature films. His most successful feature had been made courtesy of Thorne Smith: *Topper*, in 1937, followed by two sequels. Except for its potential censorship problems, *Turnabout* seemed a logical successor in the *Topper* line,

Double-cross dressing: John Howard (feminine dismay) and Carole Landis (macho bravado) in a publicity shot for *Turnabout*. *Photofest*

and Roach began working on a script. The initial premise remained, pregnancy included, yet a crucial, even audacious change made for a gayer *Turnabout*. In the book, Sally-as-Tim is compelled to deal with the ad firm's most difficult client, an obnoxious hard-drinker named Tom Burdock. For the movie, the customer was made equally hard to please, albeit in different ways. He was made a prissy perfectionist whose evident gayness makes Tim (as Tim) uncomfortable, but who bonds with the new, more womanly Tim. There was no question about which actor was destined for the role. It amounted to a near-homage to Franklin Pangborn, for the new character's name was Mr. *Pingboom*. Right away, Breen reacted in characteristic mode:

Page 34: This characterization of Mr. Pingboom as a "pansy" is absolutely unacceptable, and must by omitted from the finished picture. If there is any such flavor, either in casting, direction, or dialogue, we will be unable to approve the picture

Page 36: In this connection, the following dialogue should be omitted: "the big petunia" . . . "The guy swishes, and I don't like swishers"

Page 37: The same applies to the following dialogue "Aw-w, why don't you say 'boo!' and stomp your foot. He'll run screaming our of the office"

Page 38: The same applies to the stage direction "He flutters out"

Breen was also hostile to the pregnancy angle, but this was the first time in years that a Code fight with a studio was dominated by a struggle against gay matters. Tim's homophobia—"I don't like swishers" was more than counterbalanced by Pingboom's rapport with Sally/Tim, which seemed to verge perilously and amusingly on gay bonding. "They've kept us apart too long," Pingboom gushes, as the bond between client and employee seems to spill into the personal arena.

The trouble was compounded by the tricky way Roach, who was both producing and directing, would depict the identity switch. The outer bodies remained the same, while the voices changed. Sally-into-Tim was thus portrayed by John Hubbard with feminine mannerisms and a woman's voice in male attire. As Tim in Sally's body, Carole Landis spoke with Hubbard's voice while smoking cigars and acting jauntily athletic. This was, in sum, the farthest-out queer material to reach the screen in seven years, and the scenes of Pangborn flirting with Hubbard were too vivid for the PCA to overlook. "We suggest omitting the action of [Tim] showing his legs to Pingboom, or *any action whatever* that might give a 'pansy' flavor to the scene," Breen fumed to Roach's people as he saw the scripts. "We must repeat that any 'pansy' flavor whatever, at any point in the story, will render the final picture unacceptable from the standpoint of the Production Code, and will make it necessary for us to reject it."

Roach forged ahead with *Turnabout,* as undeterred by the warnings from Breen as producers had been in the early thirties. In 1940, however, the power rested with the PCA, and when the completed print of *Turnabout* was submitted for a Code seal, it was rejected. After the deletion of a number of Pingboom's lines, the PCA granted the certificate, after which the Code-sanitized *Turnabout* proceeded to run afoul of the PCA's less secular alter ego, the Legion of Decency.[9] To escape the Legion's dreaded "C—Condemned" rating, Roach did some screenings to test audiences' acceptance of further cuts. They did, and

[9]It is most telling that in the PCA file on *Turnabout,* the use of the character's name, Pingboom, gradually gives way to the use of the actor's name, as in Breen's directive "You will edit out the possible bad inference of the Pangborn scene."

so more material with Pingboom was eliminated; the final scene, in which Tim remains pregnant even after the couples are put back in their accustomed bodies, was toned down but retained. Thus denatured, *Turnabout* went on to mild critical response and indifferent box-office returns. Despite and perhaps because of all the hard work, the combination of Smith satire and Roach slapstick had not blended as smoothly as it had in *Topper*. The script seemed less like a cohesive narrative than a strange revolving-door cocktail party, with loads of characters streaming in and out without reason, with the crude and the sophisticated colliding at will, and the whole of it garnished with some wholly extraneous slapstick. In short, *Turnabout* was far more a curiosity than an entertainment.[10] Too, the cuts demanded by the PCA and the Legion of Decency served only their traditional effect of adding to the confusion. In the surviving prints, Pangborn's role is truncated to the point of confusion, and his "courtship" of Hubbard goes for little; what now seems the most "daring" aspect is Hubbard's prissing and carrying on like Emery in some prehistoric road company of *The Boys in the Band*. Nevertheless, the mere existence of *Turnabout* makes it a key marker in the evolution of gays in the movies. Roach's audacity in making and releasing it is, under the circumstances, extraordinary. And for all its compromised unevenness you can still feel, as Roach puts Landis and Hubbard and the cast through their fey-frenetic paces, the cheerful whiff of sedition in the air.

For Franklin Pangborn, being disruptive was a fact of life; even as he suffered the indignity of brutal Production Code laundering, he remained intact, unapologetic, a peerless blend of gayness and graceful agitation. In the strange oppression of a Code-dominated Hollywood, he was somehow permitted to earn his paychecks and make his points. In the 1940s, through Preston Sturges classics and low-budget Universal dreck, his persona would remain the same, and after the *Turnabout* brouhaha there was a period when his very name seemed to strike terror in the Production Code offices; his roles in such films as *The Bank Dick* were given close scrutiny and due warning. The utter openness of his Pingboom characterization would and could not be repeated in a time when the watchdogs of decency had the power to withdraw a film and force its mutilation. Even so, and even as *Turnabout* was quickly being forgotten, movies and moral standards were beginning to chip away at Breenish decorum. The suppression continued, and the subversive triumphs over it multiplied.

---

[10]As with its Roach predecessor *Topper*, it went on to a later, short-lived incarnation as a sitcom (more than two decades after the original *Turnabout* was one of the most frequently run movies on early television). On TV, as on the big screen, the transsexuals found far less favor than the screwball ghosts. One queerly resonant piece of casting had the Landis role going to Sharon Gless, more than two decades before she portrayed the world's proudest mom-of-a-gay-son in the American version of *Queer as Folk*.

EIGHT

Reluctant Flamboyance

FORTIES ESCAPISM

I n 1941 Europe was at war, Depression misery was receding at home, and the movies were forged of lush brass. The possibility of war, for the United States, resembled that fabled elephant in the living room—not to be addressed, impossible to ignore. Speculation, that most useless of irresistible pursuits, enters the stage here. How much would the movies have changed if there had not been a World War II? How different would the lives of gays and lesbians be if that war had not happened? For all its obscene horror, the war gave them an opportunity to escape, to meet, to find themselves and be themselves. After the war, there was no turning back—instead, there was the exodus to such urban centers as New York and San Francisco. Film, in its garish audacity, charted this emergence, unwittingly reflecting gay life by evoking some of the closeted and open stirrings that so many servicemen and servicewomen effected through their time away from home.

In discussing the film of the 1940s, just prior to, during and after the war, one does not first turn to the word *restraint*. The archetypal forties film, after all, is *Casablanca*, a deliriously romantic mélange of intrigues and intensities. Think, then, how wild wartime movies got: the delusionary oeuvre of Maria Montez, the banana xylophonerie of *The Gang's All Here*, and the hyperneurotically expressionistic grit of film noir. Gay and lesbian allusions, which fit into such arenas with munificent nonchalance, seemed to split down the middle into two of the wildest movie extremes—giddiness and gloom. The airiest quarters of light entertainment, musicals and light comedy, were on the one hand, and dire melodrama and film noir lay on the other. In these two far sides of escapist passion, the steady presence of gay and lesbian characters continued and burgeoned. Sometimes the references were bolder than in the previous few years— films like *Turnabout* had been exceptions, if not aberrations—and even when they were sufficiently Breen-proof to get by, they were often startling. Along with the last vestiges of the pansy and the mannish spinster, there were some new types: stern women with a more gothic mien, willowy neurotic young men, and acerbic, sexually ambiguous sophisticates of both genders, all of them subtle yet still obvious. Breen and his hench-Coders were maintaining their vigilance, it is true, but film people, to pitch their films to more knowing audiences, were coming up with their own codes as well.

Forties cinema, at its best, had a surprisingly cultivated syntax, profoundly efficient and borderline audacious and sometimes visibly intelligent. Much of this was an unintended offshoot of the Production Code, which many filmmakers were learning to circumvent with some mastery.[1] Another contributing factor to the swank of forties cinema, particularly in its escapist mode, was the increasingly formalized gay and lesbian presence in the film colony, both in its work and in its society. At MGM, the voraciously heterosexual producer Arthur Freed supervised a team of artists turning out most of the decade's best musicals; his group was known, informally and affectionately and not inaccurately, as "the Fairy Unit," and comprised such talents as director Vincente Minnelli, choreographers (and later directors) Robert Alton and Charles Walters, designer Irene Sharaff, and musical stylists Roger Edens and Kay Thompson. Mitchell Leisen continued to put an equally palpable gay-toned stamp on a hugely successful series of Paramount films for most of the decade. His fame, though begrudged by some of his peers, was of sufficiently high profile that it could be said that his studio considered him an auteur: the directing credit on many of his forties films was a facsimile of his signature. George Cukor spanned both the artistic and social worlds with major films and popular parties, for both mixed and segregated gay and straight guest lists. Other studios had their artists as well, in direction, design, music, dance, and writing, and such influence extended beyond studio walls also. Talent agent Henry Willson, who worked independently as well as serving for a while under David O. Selznick, had a singular knack for discovering and renaming young actors whose visual appeal transcended any lack of ability. Under his tutelage, Robert Mosely became Guy Madison, Arthur Gelien was changed to Tab Hunter, and Roy Fitzgerald turned into Rock Hudson. So successful was the beefcake aspect of this enterprise, and so widely recognized was Willson's sexuality, that it was often, and often inaccurately, assumed that all of his clients were gay. Gays and straights mixed amiably after hours as well, as one actress later recalled: "It was kind of 'in' to go to gay clubs. A lot of us did that. It was considered sophisticated." Such

---

[1]There was actually a period of a few months, around 1941, when it was decided to relax the Code strictures on one of its most conspicuous no-nos, cleavage. Before too long, a few producers decided to push it too far, and so the barriers and necklines went back up.

nightspots as Café Gala offered chic Tinseltowners a taste of gay style at its most genially brittle, and such style would inevitably be echoed in many of the films, particularly in lighter fare.

In 1941 the shadowlands of noir had not yet become the more accustomed habitat for gays and lesbians on film, and there were strongly gay rumblings—squealing, actually—from a corner that was normally eons away from Café Gala–type gayness. When Walt Disney produced his fourth feature film it was, unlike *Snow White, Pinocchio,* and *Fantasia,* neither an all-out cartoon nor a spectacular achievement. *The Reluctant Dragon* was, in fact, an odd pastiche: part cartoon, part studio tour, part how-to primer on animation, and part wry commentary by Robert Benchley. After the studio's previous glories (and just prior to *Dumbo*) it was considered a potboiler and letdown, even something of a scam: shot during an animators' strike, its studio scenes substituted actors for the real artists. Unlike the animated perennials before and after it, it has received little play in the succeeding decades, up to the Disney ignominy of a humbly low-profile home-video release. It deserves more than that, if for no other reason than its title segment, a fully contained eighteen-minute version of Kenneth Grahame's tale of a medieval monster who favors socializing over warring. In 1939 Disney had made a predecessor of sorts in *Ferdinand the Bull,* and a certain gay subtext could be detected in Ferdinand's preference for flowers over violence.[2] In *Dragon,* a more boisterous piece, the typically inflated Disney style overtakes Grahame's amusing tribute to pacifism in ways both expected and unforeseen. The rowdy slapstick and overly ornate visuals might have been predicted; the true, unexpected kicker comes in the portrayal of the dragon. Grahame's dragon might be seen as a reptilian Rex O'Malley, rather cultivated and even suave. But in the Disney version, the characterization took its cue from the resplendent vocalizing—fruity in all senses of the word—of Barnett Parker. In a performance far more substantial than his bits in earlier comedies, Parker is, as Mae West would say, "a fascinatin' monstah," somehow intersecting Quentin Crisp with Divine. It's anything but subtle, of course, and anything but boring, with the outbursts of "Woooo!" and "OOOOhh!" sweeping all before it. Using Parker's vocal as the departure point, the animators did the rest, creating a wondrous creature of long fluttering lashes, swooping gestures, and bright red nail polish.

Perhaps the Disney people originally had something different in mind with their dragon, but Parker's characterization evidently gave them only one course. Pacifism in this case spelled softness, which spelled femininity, which spelled

---

[2] The word *flower,* in fact, was sometimes used as a Code-proof substitute for the banned *pansy.* In the MGM western *Gentle Annie* (1946) ranchhand James Craig is praised for his strength by having another character exclaim, "He ain't no flower!"

The man who made the dragon more than just reluctant: Even when Barnett Parker wasn't in costume, the effect was the same. Here he adds atmosphere to Louis XVI's court in *Marie Antoinette* (1938). *Photofest*

stereotypical homosexuality. That is not an uncommon pejorative equation, yet in this context such things are praised, or at least treated as far preferable to empty machismo. Tellingly, the *Variety* review twice referred to the dragon as a female, as "a pleasant old girl," in fact. But no, the Disney synopsis specifies that the dragon is male and given to composing effusive poetry about fleecy clouds and upside-down cakes. ("Your bottom is on your top, and your top is on your bottom!" Yep, that's what it says.) The hero called in to slay this supposedly fierce creature is also a benign sham: Sir Giles (St. George in the book; the voice by Claud Allister) is, beneath his armor, an ancient aesthete, given to his own versifying and a preference for not fighting. Beneath that armor, too, is a scrawny body shown in one odd scene when he has a bath in front of the spunky little boy who befriended the dragon. Considering that it was made at a time just prior to the outbreak of global war, *The Reluctant Dragon* sabotages traditional male roles in a pretty seditious fashion. While a James Whale might have made (sorry!) a whale of a piece out of it, the Disney treatment is all on the surface . . . yet quite a rich surface indeed, for this studio at this time.[3] The dragon and the boy and Sir Giles ultimately settle down to a civilized and quite ornate tea party, in effect telling the warmongering villagers to go to hell. Poetry and peace, niceness and nail polish, are infinitely preferable to battle. One critic mentioned that Parker's characterization added to "the fabulous amusement" of *The Reluctant Dragon*, and the nail could not have been hit on its lacquered head with more unintended eloquence.

Barnett Parker's death in 1942 helped speed the old-style pansy outrageousness to its close. The world and the face of homosexuality were changing, and in the fabric of forties cinema there was less room for this kind of giddiness. Franklin Pangborn and the corpulent Grady Sutton were working in a lower, toned-down key; Rex O'Malley was out of film completely; and only a few old-school sissies turned up. While Pangborn gave one of his most subdued performances in René Clair's *Flame of New Orleans* (1941), the unbilled character actor Gus Schilling pranced around to brief, spectacular effect as a New Orleans couturier. With Marlene Dietrich looking on, Schilling demonstrates *just* the right way to walk in a peignoir—a typically sly Clair touch that Breen singled out for disapproval. A more sour and transitional fashionista turned up in the 1942 comedy *Seven Days Leave:* Mr.Gifford (King Kennedy), the snooty proprietor of a bridal shoppe, who reacts with a haughty Jack Benny–esque "Well . . . !" to assorted outrages. The intent is obvious, but the character lacks the spirited impudence of the thirties pansies, even the flair of Curt Bois's designer in *Hollywood Hotel.* The portrayal, as obvious as it is, seems desultory, as if such things were wearing out their welcome in a world of wartime and Production Code–enforced morale boosting.

The final gasps of this sub-Wildean type of arch-pansyness occurred mostly at Paramount, which was the first of the film factories to produce an all-star wartime morale-rouser. The self-evidently titled *Star-Spangled Rhythm* (1942) featured a number of good and bad things, prominent among the latter being a peculiar gay tease of a sketch by George S. Kaufman called "If Men Played Cards as Women Do." Fred MacMurray, Ray Milland, Franchot Tone, and character actor Lynne Overman purported to show the inverse of wartime women at work: men at home assuming women's former roles of gossipy cardplayers. The

---

[3]While *The Reluctant Dragon* was not a musical, Disney did commission a title song (not sung in the movie) to promote it. A pity that Barnett Parker's dulcet tones could not have been lofted in the song's line, "Others fight, I run away. It's just because I'm built that way. I'm to be Queen of the May today!" (Copyright 1941 Broadcast Music, Inc. Music by Charles Wolcott, lyric by Ed Penner, T. Hee, and Charles Wolcott)

Also, in the Disney realm, there was in *Pinocchio* (1940) the nightmarish spectacle of Pleasure Island, the decadent all-boy paradise where bad living speeds the young players to a grisly end. It being Disney, we see nothing worse than loutishness and drinking and smoking . . . but you have to wonder.

unspoken point of the whole skit was that the actors were not playing men-as-women so much as they were doing gay-stereotype shtick, breaking down the wall between fake femininity and feigned effeminacy. In spite of the Kaufman wit, it all plays like a tatty predecessor of *The Boys in the Band*, with bitchy backbiting and a cheap ending with the sight of a mouse forcing them up onto their chairs. One wonders at the intention behind this twaddle. Was it an attempt to rouse the "real men" still out there into joining the war by branding them as queers? Was it intended to be demeaning? Hard to say; so insubstantial a piece it is that reading it as a warning against wartime indolence or perceived lack of masculinity attaches to it an undeserved gravitas. As in a number of these wartime variety shows, the actors don't seem particularly comfortable with their material, and ultimately the whole thing is not so much condescending, even, as it is spectacularly irrelevant, a vaudeville stunt without a purpose. Mince, it might be said, without the meat.[4]

Mitchell Leisen contributed his final thoughts on lavender in two wartime films at Paramount, each of which costarred one of the *Star-Spangled* cardplayers. In *No Time for Love* (1943) Fred MacMurray played a macho sandhog (tunnel digger) who rescues photographer Claudette Colbert from the hands of a effeminate weakling of a fiancé (Paul McGrath). Again, Breen was not amused: "This . . . must not be suggestive of a 'pansy,' " he warned the Paramount people. And perhaps it was not, as Breen understood pansies from the time of *Our Betters* or *Stage Mother*. Yet Leisen's whole point was to glorify the grimy masculinity of MacMurray and his breed at the expense of the arty "pantywaists" (the film's phrase) who surround Colbert. Besides McGrath, there is Richard Haydn, perennially arch in manner and voice, and Robert Herrick as, quite obviously, his lover. In one scene the two of them look over MacMurray, with Herrick grabbing Haydn's shoulder to murmur, "My dear, do you think we could harm this Viking?" Leisen portrays their effete uselessness with startling relish, and MacMurray's animosity toward such people is viewed as violent and probably justifiable—all in the name of romantic comedy of course, yet making for notably uncomfortable viewing when coming from this director.

The same archness Leisen decried in *No Time for Love* suffused every frame of his next project. *Lady in the Dark* is less a film than an overfertilized

---

[4]In the name of maintaining wartime morale, Paramount had attempted to insert several more gay jokes into *Star-Spangled Rhythm*, all of which ran afoul of the Production Code folks. One of Betty Hutton's songs, "He Loved Me till the All-Clear Came," ran into difficulty with its inclusion of the line, "I found out his name was Mame." Worse trouble was caused by Bob Hope's afterword to the card-playing skit. He had introduced the sequence by proclaiming its cast "four of our manliest men," but after it was done he returned to allege that he'd "never been too sure about those boys. They're always trying to borrow my bobby pins." After a heated dispute between Joe Breen and Paramount chief B. G. DeSylva, Hope's post-skit comments were scissored out of all prints.

hothouse flower with sprocket holes, possibly the most exorbitant piece of chichi kitsch to ever come from ostensibly sane filmmakers. On Broadway, in 1941, it had been revolutionary, a serious attempt to trace a woman's path through psychoanalysis with a Kurt Weill score and Ira Gershwin songs and huge dream sequences. At Paramount in 1943 (released 1944), the analysis was bluntly simplified, the score was largely dropped, and no visual surface was left undecorated. No matter that analysis was at this point rampant among the members of the film community: in this movie, Liza Elliott's job—fashion magazine editor—mattered far more than her emotional problems. Everything in this *Lady in the Dark* looks like a dream sequence, with bigger hair and brighter sequins than have ever existed before or since. Given the biggest Paramount budget up to that time, Leisen concentrated on the visuals and almost completely neglected sense or sensitivity. In this he was aided by glossy, miscast stars (Ginger Rogers and Ray Milland) and a design crew bent on confusing taste with Technicolor majesty. The result is insulated gay sensibility run riot, a shopping spree trying so hard to be chic that it forgets about providing cohesive entertainment. With its compulsive fashion fetish, it's Freudian only in ways the original authors never intended.[5]

Not quite buried under all the mink and dry ice is Hollywood's final statement on the traditional pansy. The role of Russell Paxton, an excitable and camp fashion photographer, had made a Broadway star of Danny Kaye, and as soon as work started on the movie script, Joe Breen cautioned Paramount about Russell. The character, he insisted, would have to be completely overhauled. Breen saw lavender in one Russell line in particular: "Oh, really—I'm so mad I could spit!" was argued over and tossed back and forth. Ultimately the line remained (twice actually), and Paramount attempted to undercut Russell's gayness through the casting of an actor not identified with such roles, who had a vaguely "alien" quality to imply that Russell might be a foreigner but wasn't necessarily a perv. Always vigilant where big-scale productions were concerned, Breen continued his mantra without cease:

> The dialogue given to the character Russell still suggests a "pansy" characterization to us. We understand that it is your plan to cast Mischa Auer in this character.

---

[5]Given that *Lady in the Dark* was directed by a former designer, perhaps its chic-on-steroids air should be expected, perhaps even tolerated. Such urges were, in fact, positively contagious. Ginger Rogers's dance partner in the dream sequences was Don Loper, then in the midst of changing careers from hoofing to fashion design. In 1945 he provided camp-auteurist double duty for the oddball Technicolor musical *Belle of the Yukon:* he staged the musical numbers *and* designed the costumes, in neither case providing an excessive amount of restraint or good taste. After this he hung up his dancing shoes and was content to be the public's idea of Couturier to the Stars. Remember him on *I Love Lucy?*

Mischa Auer, in one of his more restrained moments in *Lady in the Dark. Photofest*

> However, we feel that it will be necessary to rewrite a good deal of this dialogue, as, even with Auer playing the role, we feel that in its present form it would still contain a "pansy" flavor, and hence be unacceptable.

Nevertheless, and this would increasingly be the rule in subsequent years, the studio paid lip service to Breen and then went on its way. The only reason Auer's characterization doesn't seem more extreme is that, in a celluloid fashion victim like *Lady in the Dark,* a few more moments of outrageousness are mere coals to Newcastle. Auer was denied Kaye's big chance onstage—the patter song "Tchaikovsky" was filmed and then cut—but otherwise he misses no opportunity. Russell's temperamental outbursts to his models, his drooling over hunky Jon Hall, his bent for napping with a chic woman's sun hat over his face—it is almost as if this valedictory of the arch designing man was a calculated retrospective of the character. Bobby Watson, Curt Bois, Drew Demarest, Johnny Arthur are all hovering in the wings, just out of range of the Technicolor camera. "Mischa Auer carries the spot comedy load, hilarious as a somewhat swish photographer," was the approving comment from the *Hollywood Reporter.* That load was not simply that of comic relief for an elephantine movie; it was the accumulation of years of homosexuality as interpreted by cinema: condescending yet affectionate, effeminate yet strong, silly yet genuinely witty, simultaneously concealed and open.

While no other forties musical reached the gay-outré level of *Lady in the Dark*, several were comparably garish, and with gay hints lurking about. The top-grossing movie of 1943 defined the term *morale-rouser:* Warner Bros.' *This Is the Army* was the apotheosis of both flag-waving and (this is perhaps synonymous) of Irving Berlin Americana. An exhaustive pageant of stand-up-and-fight platitudes and production numbers, it included among its many servicemen-can-sing-and-dance delights a divertissement titled "Ladies of the Chorus," a number done all in fun and all in drag. As their fathers beam approvingly from the audience, a bunch of army guys prance merrily, doing their bit for the war effort all done up in blond wigs and ruffles. There's some crucial gay history here: the reminiscences, many years later, of some of the men who did routines like this one made it clear that USO touring companies featuring drag acts were safe havens for many gay draftees, allowing them to serve while being "themselves." As with *Star-Spangled Rhythm*, not even patriotic fervor was immune to the Breen Office smelling lavender. Berlin was compelled to rewrite portions of "Ladies of the Chorus," including the boys' admonishment to "Don't get any strange ideas." Those "strange ideas" not allowed to speak their name are the gay actuality of some of those guys in drag, and it now seems to be the truest inspiration of *This Is the Army*. The valiant campiness with which they served their country is far more compelling, ultimately, than the bland patriotism of the rest of the movie, especially the empty platitudes spoken onscreen (and forever afterward offscreen) by Ronald Reagan.

In the realm of home-front entertainment, a 1944 Fox musical called *Greenwich Village* had, despite the title, precious little in the way of gay or lesbian allusions. The script's original references to "short-haired women" and "free love" were deleted at the insistence of the PCA, and, despite its 1920s setting, there was little in the way of period flavor or (except for Carmen Miranda) diversion. What did remain was an odd scene at a Village *bal masqué* with burly mug William Bendix discovering his willowy dance partner to be a man in drag. Irate at first, then confused, ultimately nonplussed, Bendix just keeps dancing. MGM's *Broadway Rhythm* (1944) was the epitome of kitchen-sink-also-included extravagance, an unsifted mix of the gifted (Lena Horne), the insipid (tabula-rasa songbird Ginny Simms), and the baroque (a contortionist sister trio singing a song about potato salad while tying themselves into knots). Stuffed in with all the music and clashing color schemes was a scene evidently shot in a nonparallel cosmos: a young farmhand (Dean Murphy) suddenly launches, apropos of nothing, into nightclub impressions of President and Mrs. Roosevelt, Jimmy Stewart, and Ronald Colman. Then, as the *pièce de* résistance, he does possibly the most queenly Bette Davis takeoff to ever be conceived by man or woman, or indeed anything in between.

The postwar era saw a noticeable pulling back on even such meager moments of gayness. The supporting characters carried less implication, and the precious bad taste of design or overall texture was notably muted.[6] The pro- totypical gay of this buttoned-up escapist age was a persnickety fellow with beady eyes and a little moustache. Billy de Wolfe was an overtly queer presence who fancied himself covert. His movie roles tried awfully hard to make him "pass," so he was occasionally seen in his films as a lothario—a concept so at odds with his onscreen demeanor and offscreen manner as to challenge ratio- nality. In one Paramount musical after another, he fussed and fretted and gave qualified moral support to the likes of Bing Crosby, Betty Hutton, Veronica Lake, and lesser deities. Nastier than Pangborn, earthier than O'Malley, more incisive than Sutton, de Wolfe's unsubtle act seldom varied . . . even unto appearances on Doris Day's TV series in the 1970s. Like certain other film phenomena (Sonja Henie, Sandra Dee, Steven Seagal) he was of a time and atti- tude, and strictly nontranscendent. To behold his "Mrs. Mergatroyd" routine in *Blue Skies* (1946) is to court suicidal thoughts. Seeing him as a girl-hungry wolf in *Tea for Two* (1950) is tantamount to witnessing the birth of science fiction. Mister de Wolfe (so he liked to be called) now seems wearisome most of the time, funny on rare occasions, and likable only when he isn't trying too hard to be too funny or too straight.

Many musicals of this time offered nostalgia of one sort or another, and many of them did so by way of one of the more egregious trends of the time, and certainly the laziest possible excuse to present music: a bogus biography of a composer. From Rimsky-Korsakov to Richard Rodgers, music people got the Hollywood treatment. Lives with little drama (Jerome Kern) were jacked up, lives with darker sides (Robert Schumann) were flattened and romanticized, and as far as gay songwriters were concerned it was strictly "Don't ask, don't tell." Even more than other invisible gay presences on the screen or in American light, the musical bios were cinema's equivalent of a gay couple "straightening up" their home to conceal their relationship from visitors. One of the gayest of all composers, Cole Porter, was a natural for such treatment, espe- cially since he had already been hiding behind a marriage for many years. Nor was he about to refuse Warner Bros.' offer of $300,000 for the rights to his life

---

[6]After the immense flop of Vincente Minnelli's *Yolanda and the Thief* in 1945, musicals with a rarefied queer tone became less and less the norm. The postwar musicals that succeeded the likes of *Yolanda* tended to resemble the concurrent housing boom: the market became generic, flooded with blander and safer consumer items without distinctive (let alone rococo or Don Loper–esque) contours.

story and his songs—who would have? While Rex O'Malley would have been a more authentic choice, Porter's choice for his onscreen incarnation was Cary Grant, casting that did (given Grant's sexuality) have a tinge of internal logic, and also indicated that *Night and Day* (1946), would be a complete travesty biographically and even musically. Warners spent an enormous amount of time trying to come up with a viable story and engaged a battery of writers to transform Porter's life into a thing of heterosexuality and niceness, that is, something with as little resemblance as possible to the real thing. Among the writers assigned to tackle the daunting assignment was Jack Moffitt, whose memo to Warner honcho Hal Wallis revealed more than it intended.

> *The Life of Cole Porter* can be a "wholesome" story. It is the triumph of a hick [who] triumphs as a sophisticate. . . . Mr. Porter's life, though rich in incident, follows a simple, straight story line. . . . My talks with Mr. Porter convince me he will show a very cooperative attitude. He recognizes the plot needs of movie entertainment and agrees to interpretations that will assist the picture's box office. . . . He and his wife were drawn together by a mutual love of gayety.

A bit more "gayety," in the production if not in the script, would have worked wonders, for *Night and Day*, despite its considerable financial success, was a disgrace.[7] Another faux musical bio, MGM's *Words and Music* (1948), attempted to honor Richard Rodgers and his lyricist Lorenz Hart. A product of the Arthur Freed "fairy unit," it was a marginal improvement, musically speaking, over *Night and Day*, to which it bore some noteworthy similarities. Once again an actor of ambivalent sexuality played straight (Tom Drake as Rodgers), and, in the portrayal of his partner, a great deal of romantic whitewashing effected some major heterosexualization. With the help of a manic Mickey Rooney, Hart was transformed from a tortured gay to a nice guy who keeps falling in love with the wrong women. Except for giving audiences a chance to hear a few first-rate performers in songs like "Miss Otis Regrets" and "Thou Swell," *Night and Day* and *Words and Music* did as little for the cause of musical entertainment as they did in chronicling gay history.

If he did not receive quite the same Hollywood treatment as Hart or Porter, Danny Kaye certainly underwent a sea change in the journey from New York to California. Signed by Sam Goldwyn to occupy the niche of megabudget musical zaniness once occupied by Eddie Cantor, Kaye found himself altered in

---

[7]The only hint of the real Porter in *Night and Day* is the presence of Porter's gay buddy and cruising partner Monty Woolley, playing himself. There's no question, naturally, of Woolley being permitted to be any gayer on film than the cinematic Porter, but at least, five years earlier, he was able to get off one insider zinger to Bette Davis in *The Man Who Came to Dinner:* "Don't look at me with those cow eyes, you simpering Sappho!"

appearance as well as in affect. Blonder, WASP-ier, and with much of his fey-gay borscht belt humor expunged, he made his feature film debut in Goldwyn's 1944 extravaganza *Up in Arms*. While the queer shadings that had marked his stage role in *Lady in the Dark* were toned down for film, enough remained to account for a number of testy exchanges between Goldwyn and the Production Code administrators. One scene in *Up in Arms* that caused particular trouble brought back the venerable mistaken-for-gay gambit: on a crowded city bus, Kaye coaches fellow soldier Dana Andrews on how to romance his girl while eavesdropping bystanders think his sweet talk to Andrews is the real thing.[8] Even more Code-based whitewashing was necessary for a scene in which Kaye shares a bunk with a fellow soldier, whom he proceeds to caress while dreaming of Veronica Lake. As Breen patiently explained to Goldwyn, "Our experience indicates that any scenes in which one man is shown fondling another man are certain to give serious offense to motion picture audiences everywhere." Three years and three Kaye vehicles later, *The Secret Life of Walter Mitty* managed to bury James Thurber's whimsy in a garish onslaught of Goldwynist largesse and Kaye humor. As in the previous Kaye offerings, there was time out for one of the comic's specialties: a patter song with tongue-twisting lyrics by Sylvia Fine, Kaye's wife. The one in *Mitty* allowed Kaye, briefly and startlingly, to be gay, really gay: "Anatole of Paris" was the insanely camp tale of a put-upon hat designer, rendered by the star with oversautéed Gallic suavity and more flighty gestures than Bobby Watson in five movies. "I'm just like wine—I go to your head," Anatole boasts, and by the end of the song he has had it with difficult customers and wails directly into the camera: "I . . . *hate* . . . WOMEN!" For a few moments, Kaye has captured some of his old outrageousness, and the generic flattening of Hollywood is zealously and blessedly obliterated.

Romance on the High Seas (1948) was the definitive late-forties musical, with technical assurance shoring up a trivial script, and an air of genial mediocrity salted with just a few special things. History only recalls this movie because of a casting fluke—when scheduled lead Betty Hutton became pregnant, Warner Bros. gambled and won with a virtually unknown replacement, band singer Doris Day. One of the most iconic of stars, Day here starts her movie career as a raw and eager neophyte, as painted up and raring to go as a new sports car; in the course of her performance, the Dream Factory mechanism is at work almost audibly, willing this pleasant young woman into stardom. However much a joke Day became later on in her soft-focus squealing-virgin period, she's a charmer here, and there's some quite unwitting foreshadowing of the gay content that

---

[8]A similar scene informed the Three Stooges short *Brideless Groom* in 1947. Moe and Larry get so carried away with the thought of inheriting a fortune that they embrace and kiss. Naturally, someone sees it and Moe pushes Larry away in embarrassment—and, being a Stooge, does it violently.

GRADY SUTTON

Real name, Grady Harwell Sutton. Born Chattanooga, Tenn., April 5, 1906; died Woodland Hills, Calif., September 15, 1995

"Versatile" was not quite the way to describe him, for neither the act nor the look varied all that much in six decades. Nor did the Tennessee drawl ever go away. Tall and pudgy and staggeringly unthreatening, Sutton had the look of a giant squeeze toy and the affect of a moony eunuch with ambitions. The definitive Sutton role, one he played over and over, was that of the guy your sister could date without any fear. In *Hot Saturday* (1932) and *Stage Door* (1937) and *Anchors Aweigh* (1945) and countless others, he was the suitor every heroine was just dying to dump. His overt "sissy" parts were comparatively few—*Movie Crazy* (1932) and *Romance on the High Seas* are among the most prominent— but you always *knew*. Much of his initial fame was as one of the leads in a series of comedy shorts, "The Boy Friends," and with his crack timing and ease in getting laughs, he was never at a loss for work. In hundreds of movies and uncountable TV appearances, he was as genial as he was completely clueless, a hick in a big city or a doofus among the sharks. His air of blundering amiability made him, like Franklin Pangborn, a superb foil to W. C. Fields, who would occasionally have Sutton-esque roles specially created. When Fields insisted that Universal cast him in *The Bank Dick*, Universal retaliated by not putting Sutton in another film for three years. No matter—there were all the other studios, and he always worked. In his final years he grew notably belligerent at the prospect of being interviewed for having been a prototypical gay movie figure. Such considerations had not, to him, been part of his time or place; he had just been himself, done his job, and made people laugh a great deal.

would be so dominant a hallmark of her late-fifties and early-sixties style. For the first and only time in film, three of the gayest of character actors appear in the same movie: Franklin Pangborn, Grady Sutton, and Eric Blore. Pangborn, in the twilight of his film career, is permitted little of his old banked fire, though Blore, as a ship's doctor, flicks his lisps with endemic relish. With Sutton's brief scenes, we get a bona fide and very tiny gay subplot, sneaked past the PCA folk with conspiratorial glee. In the course of *Romance*'s amiably dumb plot, Doris Day takes a Caribbean cruise posing as wealthy Janis Paige, whose jealous husband (Don DeFore) hires private eye Jack Carson to tail her. Carson, believing Day to be Paige (it plays easier than it recounts), sends regular dispatches back to DeFore in New York, and when he finds himself attracted to Day, he lets DeFore know. Sutton, in one of the unbilled goods-and-services role he played millions of times, is the ship's radio operator. The first message Carson gives him

Grady Sutton, not giving John Wayne much to worry about in a 1942 Hal Roach comedy titled—seriously, folks—*Dudes are Pretty People.* The elaborately billowing kerchief is a lot more convincing than the hat. *Photofest*

to send to New York is "Start worrying. The other man has appeared." As Sutton reads the message, his face at first goes blank and then, as he takes the words literally, registers profound astonishment. Some minutes later, after Day's some-time beau Oscar Levant shows up, Carson comes with another report: "Prepare yourself for a shock. There are now two men in the picture." This time Sutton's face lights up like a dozen full moons. He looks at Carson with the joy of discovery and speaks his only line in the movie: "You'll let me know how it comes out, won't you?" And he bats his eyes at Carson with the bravado of a cotillion-load of coquettes: one secret gay believes he has discovered another, and there's queer bonding on the high seas. Fade to black. The role and the line are in the script without description or elaboration, and they were clearly intended as nonde-script episodes, with the radio operator as a generic busybody. Yet Sutton, possi-bly with the sanction of director Michael Curtiz, makes it a brief and unmistak-able evocation of a secret society whose members were permitted to connect only with the utmost caution.[9] Who would have thought that, in this pricey escapist bauble, there would be contained this secret compartment?

Grady Sutton's brief appearance in *Romance on the High Seas* marks the end of an age. His fluttering eyes and covert delight are accepted and even approved within the film's context, just as Mischa Auer and Anatole of Paris and the rest of them had been in their own worlds. The escapism of the forties had been delirious and mostly gay-friendly, and by decade's end such things were nearly gone. The froth was growing more drab and mechanical, and the gays and lesbians onscreen were changing as well. Forties dramas had already begun to look at them in a less friendly light, and, with growing intensity, such things would continue over the coming years.

---

[9]Curtiz pushed his luck in *Romance on the High Seas* with another gay moment. Oscar Levant boards the ship frantically searching for Day, and is approached by a steward.

STEWARD: May I help you, sir?

LEVANT: Well, you're not exactly my type, but you can take my bags.

Such exchanges were not all that uncommon in forties cinema, and into the fifties as well. They're so throwaway that they're typically overlooked, but they are indeed here in the movies and queer in meaning. Leave it to Groucho Marx to do it best when, in *Love Happy* (1949), a henchthug tries to wrest some hot diamonds from him. GROUCHO: We've only just met, and already he's asking me for things!

NINE

Dark Passages

FORTIES DRAMA

> Most moviegoers . . . will leave the theatre shaking their heads and wondering what it was all about, because [the] script has tried to picture without actually telling them of the love of the three principal men characters.
>
> *The Hollywood Reporter* review of
> *The Picture of Dorian Gray*

It's in the nature of our communication that over time words—labels—become coarsened. Their original meanings are disfigured and misinterpreted, cast pell-mell into the maw of commonspeak. Some excitingly specific terms have become homogenized and dulled, and it's hardly surprising that popular culture has been a lead culprit here, and a lead victim. Before the 1920s were far gone, for example, the term *jazz* had become prone to infinite distortion, and would remain so. *Diva* is a good one from more recent times, for by the end of the 1990s it had lost most of the excitement of its predominantly gay magic; forget connotations of opera, immortality, talent, or sublime outrageousness—it had been reduced to connoting any woman (and a few men) who wore makeup and had fans. Some other later ones are immediately apparent as well: *auteur*, *cult*, and, in fact, *popular culture*. So it is with the most overused of 1940s film terms: *film noir*. At this point, it seems that almost any movie made between 1939 and the 1960s that is not an overt comedy or musical can qualify. All that is required, it seems, are some shadows, a serious or menacing tone, and perhaps a sardonic or fatalistic air. Dubious characters are generally a part of it too, and here enter the gays and lesbians. In the realm of true film noir, where the darkness offers both menace and comfort, homosexuals wear distinctly detectable camouflage.[1]

As undefined a term as it has become, film noir is the leading currency of forties cinema, and as with horror film it lends itself to a wide range of implication and inference. Its negativism evokes the post-Depression and then postwar and nuclear ages, when cynicism seemed the most viable attitude. Its expressionistic look reminds us that American film often, and to its profit, borrows and reconfigures foreign (mostly Germanic) influences. In its inherent neuroticism are indicators of America's burgeoning interest in, and Hollywood's obsession with, psychoanalysis. Psychiatry was becoming, by the end of the 1930s, a familiar topic of conversation, a strange magic alternately derided and revered. With Southern California one of the main refuges for German-Jewish immigrants, many of them analysands of Freud himself, it was not long before the analysts and the movie people found each other. The actors and writers and directors turned out to be a eminently receptive audience, and it would be only a matter of time before the workings of the human mind, as explored by these artists with their shrinks, would be portrayed on film in a variety of ways.[2] Some of the more serious American films began to offer a minor primer on Freudianisms: the symbols and archetypes started becoming more prominent and more clichéd. The most direct results of this were the films that dealt with psychiatry itself: *Spellbound, The Snake Pit, High Wall*. In a larger sense, such interests were manifested in film's increasing obsession with the vagaries of human behavior, particularly in its darker manifestations. Film noir, immersed as it was in negative and fallible humanity, was the inevitable result. The connection between psychiatry and film noir becomes still more tightly focused when gays and lesbians are taken into consideration. With the rise of Freud and his disciples, the causes and treatment of homosexuality had changed entirely. The idea of the "woman trapped in the man's body" and such had been discredited, and more complex questions of cause and effect had been raised. Freud advocated the sympathetic treatment of homosexuals, but along with this heightened tolerance and timorous understanding of the issues there was also

---

[1]The film after which this chapter is named is a sort-of noir from Warner Bros. in 1947 starring Humphrey Bogart and Lauren Bacall. There aren't any overt (or perhaps even covert) gay references in it, but the title seems to evoke perfectly the gay and lesbian procession through the world of film noir. And, for those so inclined, it contains Agnes Moorehead's most over-the-top nasty performance.

[2]The most deranged bridge between psychiatry and the movies came late in the 1930s courtesy of the much-feared Hollywood columnist Louella Parsons. In a news item that was beyond even her standard level of crackpot misstatement, Parsons breathlessly reported that Warner Bros. would be engaging Sigmund Freud to serve as technical advisor for its dying-from-a-brain-tumor Bette Davis vehicle *Dark Victory*. Diligently, and with commendable restraint, Parsons explained to her readers that Freud was "probably the greatest psychoanalyst alive."

increased distrust, even demonization. What had earlier seemed tangential now was, in many minds, less marginalized and therefore less harmless. They were here among the "normal" folk—the Kinsey Report would verify that in short order—and as such were now a problem. Whether or not they could be "cured" was debatable—and this asinine debate continues, incredibly enough, into the twenty-first century—but what was certain was that they were different. Between the late 1930s and the postwar age, the United States underwent a sea change in how it looked at homosexuals, how they saw themselves, and how they would be handled by mainstream institutions and popular culture.

Film noir, in fact most of the "darker" forties cinema, reflected and sometimes charted these changes. As of the mid-forties, the Drew Demarests of another age were gone, and their cinematic sons and daughters could sometimes be dangerous. The nature of film noir is to obscure more than its reveals, and this concealment coupled with an urban setting offers numerous possibilities for gay inference. Who, after all, knew more about having to hide in the safe darkness of the big city? So they became, early on, part of the texture of these films . . . sometimes clearly defined, other times not. As with horror, noir thrives on ambiguity and multiple meanings, so sometimes it's impossible to tell sometimes exactly what's intended. This sense of wild-side possibility is what keeps the area of noir so ripe and enticing. Anything was possible—even, on occasion, when the specter of the Production Code was casting its own invasive shadow.

In some ways, the forties was a strict time for the Code, yet there were artists who searched for and found more adult ideas. Alcoholism and anti-Semitism, which had been avoided in earlier years, were two of the franker themes more available to filmmakers from mid-decade on. The pioneers in these two areas were *The Lost Weekend* (1945) and *Crossfire* (1947), both of them "serious" films that frequently acted like noir. More to the point, both were straightened-up versions of their original works. Had they been filmed as written, *Weekend* would have detailed a man's struggle with his gayness as well as his drinking, and *Crossfire* (from Richard Brooks's novel *The Brick Foxhole*) would have indicted homophobia, for its murder victim was originally gay, not Jewish. Movies obviously weren't ready to confront such things, so gay spectators had to settle for other portrayals.[3] As the giddiness of the Barnett Parker types subsided, there would sometimes be, in the portrayals of gay men and women onscreen, moments of truth filtered through the allusions and the negativity. Never, of course, were gays allowed to be the heroes, although they were sometimes the villains of noir, or the victims, or else occupied cans filled with red herring. Nor were all of the serious forties films in

---

[3]*The Lost Weekend* did, at least, offer some grim subsidiary gayness in the tough nurse (Frank Faylen) who attends the alcoholic Don Birnam (Ray Milland) and refers to him as "Mary Sunshine" and "Honeyboy." This guy's apparent gayness is as far from Pangborn as you can get.

which gay characters figured noir even in the term's vaguer sense. Yet there is a continuity to the mood and presentation of the men and women who played gay in these dark settings. The looming shadows of noir and its cousins enabled them, often enough, to be themselves, and in certain cases to present more rounded characters than they had previously. Too often the portrayals were weighted toward the disapproving, yet, as Dracula's daughter knew well, in the darkness there was life.

One of the most influential gay characters of the decade was its very first. *Rebecca*, Alfred Hitchcock's American debut, is a film most definitely on the cusp: part suspense, part romantic fiction, part proto-noir, part mystery. With producer David O. Selznick in charge and in full post–*Gone with the Wind* mode, *Rebecca* is filled to the brim with the trappings of sumptuous melodrama. Yet there is something more gloomy and intimate at its center: the dark and barely unspoken affection of Mrs. Danvers (Judith Anderson), the insanely competent housekeeper of Manderley, for her dead mistress, Rebecca de Winter. This love, manifested in a rigid preservation of everything Rebecca touched and represented, is the film's dark motivator, the force that threatens to destroy the second Mrs. de Winter (Joan Fontaine). The unforgettable scenes in *Rebecca* are not those of Fontaine with Laurence Olivier, but of Fontaine cowering before Anderson's gothic implacability. Hitchcock, in what was for him a rare foray into lesbian affection, depicts Danvers's adoration for the dead woman in an unforgettably fetishistic way—her fondling of Rebecca's clothes as if they are sacred sexual relics. Even Joe Breen spotted the implications there, and he sent Selznick letter after letter warning against either the allusions to Rebecca as a lesbian or to any hint that she and Danvers had had an affair. Nor is Danvers's love for Rebecca hidden: George Sanders, as Rebecca's slimy cousin and lover, refers to the housekeeper with jaunty familiarity as "Danny." The original script, in fact, had Danvers exclaiming to him, "She was not in love with you—or with Mr. de Winter—or anyone! She despised *all* men. She was above all that!" The other troublesome script point, that de Winter (Olivier) had murdered Rebecca and would remain unpunished, was deftly repaired—a murder turned into an accidental death—and so, perhaps as a compromise, the clothing scene was allowed to remain. With some wonderment, writer Susie Bright mused in the *Celluloid Closet* documentary, "She opens the *underwear* drawer! So sensuous!" Passion this deep and insidious will seldom go unpunished, so Danvers must perish in the burning Manderley to remove Rebecca's spell.[4]

---

[4]The following year, Judith Anderson returned in another melodrama with noir and gay elements: unfortunately, her austerely butch intensity was wasted in the title role of the RKO B film *Lady Scarface*. Shortly afterward she was back on Broadway, ideally cast as another obsessive and far greater lady, Lady Macbeth. Hitchcock, for his part, would touch upon lesbianism in 1941 in his Joan Fontaine-*Rebecca* follow-up, *Suspicion*, by including a pretty evident female couple as guests at a society dinner party.

With *The Maltese Falcon* (1941), more of the traditional noir qualities are present, although its unending lode of intrigue and appeal pushes a film like this beyond considerations of genre. A mystery, a private-eye story, a film noir, a dark look at thwarted dreams, it's also one of the few films of its decade in which the presence of a gay character is well established and unarguable. Even "outsiders," the people who react with disbelief when told that there were scores of gay characters in film before the 1970s, know about Joel Cairo. It helps that Dashiell Hammett's original novel presented Cairo's homosexuality as clearly as it did his deviousness and greed. John Huston, writing the script and directing for the first time, did everything he could to delineate Cairo as clearly onscreen as any of the other characters, and in so doing developed some of the subterfuge that would be used in the coming years to circumvent Joe Breen and the PCA. "This guy is queer," comments Sam Spade's secretary Effie in an early script treatment. Yes, quite, and in every sense, but be careful how it's portrayed. In Huston's original script (whose working title, *The Gent from Frisco*, was used until late in the day), when Effie brings Spade Cairo's scented calling card, the smell is "lavender." Not possible, said Breen to Jack Warner, and so gardenia was substituted, along with some flowery "exotic" music on the sound track to place Cairo. The casting placed him even better, for Peter Lorre's small frame and brittle neuroticism are subtle and perfect, so much so that Cairo's relationship with Wilmer the gunsel (Elisha Cook, Jr.), so widely discussed by later writers, was given a fairly free pass by the censors.[5] Huston's skill with the actors and the script puts everything across with meticulous tact; a world of corruption and greed—in fact, a world where almost everyone is a selfish bastard—is delineated with deceptive simplicity. Lorre, interestingly enough, had been under consideration for the role of Wilmer as well as Cairo, as was another small-framed German expatriate, Martin Kosleck, and also (oddly) Elia Kazan. Other Cairo candidates were Sam Jaffe, Curt Bois, Conrad Veidt, Turhan Bey, and Lee J. Cobb. None could have matched Lorre's effortless insinuation of corruption, presented without customary accoutrements of screen sissydom. "Make sure that he rounds out his words and enunciates as clearly as possible. . . . Also, don't try to get a nancy quality into him, because if you do we will have trouble with the picture." Such was production supervisor Hal Wallis's warning to Huston, who along with Lorre succeeded beyond measure. At least one critic praised the performance in terms as coded as that gardenia-scented card: "Peter Lorre brings a new delicacy to his typically slimy role of an artistic crook."

---

[5]The main worry was a scene in which Cairo seems to demonstrate physical affection for Wilmer by rubbing his temple. The word *gunsel*, which is at best sexually questionable, was never disputed, and—like so many other things in *The Maltese Falcon*—the relationship between the two men is defined by its haziness.

It would be hard to imagine Conrad Veidt, for all his skill, as a comparably effective Cairo, but the same year as *The Maltese Falcon* he portrayed a memorable decadent named Torsten Barring, in George Cukor's grim melodrama *A Woman's Face*. Once again, the evil is subtly limned, as in Veidt's sexual attraction to partner-in-crime Joan Crawford because of her disfigured face. And in his introductory scene, he is shown as taking intense voyeuristic pleasure in sexual variance: at a seamy roadhouse outside Stockholm, he beams raptly as two young women dance together. The women are not shown again, but they have contributed to the portrayal of Barring's nature. Once again, as in *Our Betters*, Cukor uses homosexuality to invoke the jaded and the sour, although Veidt so rejoices in conveying Barring's kinkiness that he provides needed uplift to a ponderous tale.

Onscreen lesbians also turned up in that domestic hotbed of (supposed) decadence, Greenwich Village. *The Seventh Victim* (1943) is part of that elite canon of Val Lewton horror movies in which subtlety and literacy were given primacy over monsters and scientists, and evil lay waiting in quiet places. There's no one greatest or most typical Lewton film; some would say *I Walked with a Zombie* and others *Curse of the Cat People*, but *The Seventh Victim* is up near the top of the list in many assessments. Its terrors are contained entirely within the plausible, as a young woman (Kim Hunter) comes to New York to search for her missing sister (Jean Brooks) and finds herself up against the insinuating evil of a satanic cult. The pace is measured, the terror muted, and perhaps the mantle of literacy is worn too self-consciously: how many movies open and close with a quote from John Donne? There is also, near the end, a scene rife with queasy sanctimony as the satanists receive their comeuppance by a psychiatrist reciting the Lord's Prayer. Ultimately, little of this detracts from the fascination of *The Seventh Victim*, much of which comes from the portrayal of the devil-worshiping Palladists. No Black Masses or robed rites for this bunch: they're a clique of sophisticated Greenwich Villagers whose gatherings resemble cocktail parties. They also resemble another secret society of worldly adults. As seen in *The Seventh Victim*, the Palladists are careful, composed, and well dressed, meeting in their Village apartment and conducting their business in measured civil tones. They could, in short, be a prototype for the Mattachine Society. The gay allusions do not end there, and do not seem unintended. Mrs. Redi (Mary Newton), one of the group's lieutenants, is strictly formula Hollywood lesbian—deep voice, severe dress, brusque take-charge air—and, in one startling scene, takes charge by barging into Hunter's apartment unannounced and walking into the bathroom where Hunter is showering. As we see her "mannish" hat silhouetted through the plastic curtain, she warns Hunter to stop looking for her sister and get out of town. Not until Mrs. Bates paid a visit to Marion Crane would movies offer a comparably creepy shower.

The Palladists pressure *The Seventh Victim* (Jean Brooks, left) to kill herself for betraying them. Mary Newton, as the domineering Mrs. Redi, stands center, with Ben Bard hovering over Brooks and Evelyn Brent at the piano. Brooks's pal Isabel Jewell is seated second right. *Photofest*

The seventh victim herself, Brooks, is said to be a "sensationalist" (i.e., hedonist) whose dabbling in satanism is part of her compulsive thrill seeking. With a bruised detachment that her mink coat and Cleopatra hairdo cannot hide, Brooks embodies sexual ambivalence. She has left her husband far behind, she has had an unsuccessful affair with her psychiatrist, and she is so fixated on suicide that she decorates her apartment with a noose. She has also, obviously, had an intense relationship with one of her coworkers (Isabel Jewell), a fellow cult member who becomes hysterical as the satanists attempt to spur Brooks toward suicide for betraying them. "I can't let you die! The only time I was ever happy was when I was with you!" It might be argued that this movie equates gayness with devil worship or witchcraft, thus serving as a harbinger of the right-wing hysteria of forty and fifty years later. Yes, Pat Buchanan did issue the pronouncement, in 1990, that "Promiscuous homosexuals appear literally hell-bent on Satanism and suicide." But really, *The Seventh Victim* is not about any of that. Like so many of Lewton's movies, it's about the destructive power of repression, the riskiness of conspiratorial secrecy, the high price paid by the world's misfits. Almost too overtly, it wears its subtlety and taste on its sleeve, and its secret world, be it devilish or gay or both, lingers far longer than more calculated movie frights.[6]

Paramount's *The Uninvited* (1944) borrowed some of the tone from the Lewton films without quite matching their erudite sensitivity. Skillful and entertaining, with echoes of *Rebecca* and subtly authentic chills, it won wide attention as the best American ghost story in years. Unfortunately, it expanded on some of the ideas of *Rebecca* to posit its chills on the premise that a lesbian relationship can give rise to a really nasty ghost. Its Mrs. Danvers, one possibly even more rigid and controlling, was Miss Holloway (Cornelia Otis Skinner), the proprietor of a mysterious "clinic" on the coast of Cornwall. She takes an excessive interest in Mary Meredith, one of her charges, and ultimately Mary becomes Miss Holloway's property in life in the same way that Mrs. Danvers owned Rebecca after her death. The power of that love, possessive and destructive, ultimately kills Mary and forces her spirit, malevolent and uninvited, to remain. Miss Holloway, as the keeper of the flame, must do all she can to keep the truth from being spoken and Mary's ghost from being exorcised. The sparks between the two women were clear enough, even in the script's postmortem de facto fashion, that even the sometimes-myopic Joe Breen caught them.[7] He cautioned Paramount against having the script hint too broadly of the nature of their relationship, and ostensibly the studio complied.

As the critics praised *The Uninvited*'s taste and intelligence, the forces of Catholicism weighed in on the negative side. The Legion of Decency bestowed its B rating, not for sexual undertones but for implying that such things as séances might have true "spiritistic" (the Legion's unique wording) value. The rating did little to deter audiences, and along with strong business there was a tie-in song hit, "Stella by Starlight." Then, as it continued to play to large audiences, *The Uninvited* began to draw a special group of spectators that had little interest in séances or ghosts. In April 1944 Will Hays, who was then in the oxymoronic position of being a powerful figurehead, received a letter from one

---

[6]Nor was it Lewton's last brush with homoeroticism. *The Ghost Ship* (1944) was filled with sailor beefcake, violence, phallic symbols, and repressed urges. It's both more inward and overt with its sexuality than *The Seventh Victim,* and despite those qualities not as interesting overall. (But for queer film theorists, its *Querelle Meets Billy Budd* undertones are a cornucopia.) In 1946 Lewton's *Bedlam* featured a nearly naked, literally golden boy, an asylum inmate painted gold for the delectation of jaded aristocrats. Like Shirley Eaton in *Goldfinger,* he dies of suffocation, and the gay/S&M undertones of the episode are too blatant to be ignored.

[7]A further hint of the relationship came in Miss Holloway's first scene, which is played out as the sound track blares the "Liebestod" from *Tristan und Isolde.* Love/death, indeed.

Implacable as well as gothic-chic, Cornelia Otis Skinner calmly dominates a tense Gail Russell in *The Uninvited. Photofest*

of the executives of the Legion of Decency. Its subject was *The Uninvited* and the unique reactions of some audiences going to see it:

> In certain theaters large audiences of questionable type attended this film at unusual hours. The impression created by their presence was that they had been previously informed of certain erotic and esoteric elements in this film.

The letter specified neither the predominant gender nor the precise nature of these spectators, but it did give a detailed rundown of scenes in *The Uninvited* that seemed to contain "erotic or esoteric implications." As it happened, the scenes in question all concerned Miss Holloway's relationship with Mary Meredith. Some of the specifics cited in the letter told the rest of the story:

> . . . The Commander [Mary's husband] telephones Miss Holloway [and] says, "You are the only one who can help," and refers to her power over Stella's mother

> . . . A scene . . . in which Miss Holloway gazes at Mary's portrait and apostrophizes her beauty thus, ". . . her radiant hair, milk white skin, charm . . ." and says something to the effect that it was in this room ". . . that the two of us dreamed and planned our lives. . . . what we would do together . . ."

> There is a distinct contrast in the masculinity of Miss Holloway's character and the dainty femininity of Mary's portrait.

What had happened was obvious: *The Uninvited* had become a lesbian cult movie, and as word of its content was passed along in the gay underground, large groups of queer spectators, predominantly women, went to see the movie at off-hours, free from an excessive or stifling straight presence. For several months the reproachful and protesting correspondence bounced around from Hays to Breen to Paramount and back to the Legion of Decency. No one claimed any awareness of how this happened, Paramount denied any intent to convey such messages, and everyone vowed to be more careful in the future. Indeed, for the next six years or so, there were few messages conveyed to the audience about women who loved women.[8] Nevertheless, as it played to packed houses for a number of months, *The Uninvited* had served a singular purpose. Under spooky and somewhat pejorative circumstances, it had given a sizable number of viewers a degree of support and sustenance. In some little covert moments tucked into a Hollywood ghost story, a number of gay castaways had found a safe haven.

Before the war, there had been something of an established Hollywood philosophy that bespoke delusions of class: when you film the great classics of literature with at least the illusion of faithfulness, you reap immense prestige laced with high grosses. MGM, that paragon studio of literary aspiration, was the industry leader in that tradition, with its adaptations of Shakespeare, Dickens, and Jane Austen.[9] Just as the war was winding down the studio returned to that tradition with a literary flashpoint, Oscar Wilde. Following a successful version of *The Canterville Ghost*, the studio permitted writer-director Albert Lewin to move into darker Wildean climes. No *Lady Windermere's Fan* or *An Ideal Husband* or even *The Importance of Being Earnest* for Lewin, but the far dicier *Picture of Dorian Gray*. Between Wilde's life and reputation, and *Dorian*'s own dark eroticism, there were potential hazards with fidelity on the

---

[8]One of these was in fact about anything but love. At the end of the fact-based *House on 92nd Street* (1945), the chief Nazi agent, Mr. Christopher, is revealed to be a woman (Signe Hasso) in drag: a fitting culmination to the "nasty Nazi dyke" type all too present in wartime propaganda films.

[9]Paramount checked in, in 1940, with an unexpected, valiant, and predictably unsuccessful entry: an adaptation of Joseph Conrad's *Victory*, featuring a somewhat obvious gay couple: the evil Mr. Jones (Cedric Hardwicke) and his "secretary" Ricardo (Jerome Cowan).

one hand and the Production Code on the other. Lewin, however, was not the typical cigar-chomping Hollywood type. He was, in fact, as esoteric as a movie producer could get, with his post-grad work in literature just a dissertation short of a Ph.D. After long stints assisting people like Erich von Stroheim and Irving Thalberg, he branched out on his own in 1942 with a successful film adaptation of Maugham's *Moon and Sixpence*—offbeat fare indeed for the war years. He decided to film *Dorian Gray* not through any inordinate love of the material, but because of its potentially heady combination of literary elegance, horror, and ornate décor. (There had already been, count 'em, six silent film versions.) The look of the piece, in fact, drew his greatest attention, between the portrait itself (seen mostly in Technicolor inserts spliced into the black-and-white film) and an almost stultifying sense of detail. It could be argued that Wilde suffered through the alignment of such priorities, yet one of *Dorian*'s main themes is, of course, the nature of appearances. Lewin's obsessions—which encompassed fetishes for ethnic dance and cats—caused the film to have one of the longest shooting schedules of any film up to that time. At a remarkable 127 days, it exceeded *The Wizard of Oz* and *The Good Earth* in the MGM annals, topped only by the massive *Ben-Hur* (1925). That Lewin was taking so much time—and $1.9 million—to shoot a horror movie (by Oscar Wilde, yet) sat ill with many at MGM, yet Louis B. Mayer defended Lewin and gave him the time and money to realize his conception of *Dorian*.

How well Lewin realized that vision has been a matter of dispute ever since the film opened in the spring of 1945. Some critics complained of artiness or overliteracy or plain obscurity, others of the casting of the cool, withdrawn Hurd Hatfield as Dorian. In some minds, Lewin's changes and digressions had ill-served both Wilde and cinema. Yet even at its high cost it turned a profit and went on to achieve the status of a minor classic, its peculiar flavor lingering after bigger films of its time were buried. For some, it is the apex of forties queer cinema, while others feel that it completely buried Wilde's insinuations under a layer of heterosexual MGM pomp. Perhaps, in fact, it's that very evanescence that makes this *Dorian* provocative. As with Dorian himself, not all the evil is visible, and some is barely hinted. Allusion, implication, even disengagement carry a great deal of weight here, yet there are always possibilities hinted and sometimes stated. Arguably, Lewin captured the precise cinema equivalent of Wilde so far as the evocation of sexuality is concerned. Just as Wilde was writing his novel under the ponderous strictures of Victorian morality, Lewin was producing his homage in a time when repression was the norm in American society and on the screen. Somehow, through writing and casting and the power of suggestion, more of the book's sexuality was retained than might have been predicted. It would have been easy to make *Dorian Gray* a straight (in both senses) horror film, brutal and blatant, and this is likely what would have happened at another studio or with another director. But Lewin, even with his massive affectations and largely because of them, did his best to honor Wilde. For those viewers familiar with *The Yellow Book*, the mention and presence in the film of that most scandalous and gay of Victorian periodicals was a major indicator of how Lewin would get away with it—with oblique taste and intelligence. "It's vile, evil, corrupt, decadent—I detest it!" says Basil Hallward (Lowell Gilmore), which is a great negative weight to be borne by a mere magazine. Hallward's daughter (Donna Reed) even looks at one of *The Yellow Book*'s Aubrey Beardsley drawings in one scene. There was also, direct from the book, the scene in which Dorian blackmails one of his old lovers (Douglas Walton) in order to dispose of Hallward's obtrusive body. Nothing is declared, everything is implied, and as with the Lewton movies the effect is all the more powerful for its understatement.

Lewin's casting of George Sanders as Lord Henry Wotton, Dorian's mentor, was acutely pertinent. Sanders was one of those actors whose offscreen heterosexuality (however well documented) did not necessarily translate to film, and Wotton's inherent superiority and bent for epigrams dovetailed into Sanders's salient quality as an actor, an effortlessly effected narcissism that evoked both Oscar Wilde and the haughtiest realms of queer snobbery. It would be expected that Lord Henry's corruption of Dorian is more a matter of viewer inference than anything else, yet just the sound of Sanders savoring the Wildeish barbs evokes worlds of jaded experience: "Most people die of a sort of creeping common sense and discover too late that the only things one never regrets are one's mistakes." "Women represent the triumph of matter over mind, just as men represent the triumph of mind over morals." "Faithfulness is merely laziness." This wearily acid tone was seldom far from many of Sanders's roles after 1945, which is why it's as difficult to envision him playing a "nice" person as it is to contemplate his playing a working-class dad. Irony and detachment were too inherent in Sanders's screen character for such things, which made him wrong for almost all conventional "hero" roles and right for *Dorian Gray* and *All About Eve*.[10]

Some of that superiority would always be present as well in Hurd Hatfield's screen roles, such as they were. He himself noted much later that Dorian had effectively killed his career:

> The film didn't make me popular in Hollywood. It was too odd, too avant-garde, too ahead of its time. After all, Albert Lewin always said he had made it for six friends. The decadence, the hints of bisexuality and so on, made me a

---

[10]In life, too, he ultimately lived up to that image without fail. Of all actors, he *would* be the one to commit suicide and leave a note explaining that he did it because he was plain bored.

Amidst the foliage of a Victorian conservatory, Lord Henry (George Sanders) and Dorian (Hurd Hatfield) commence their mutual admiration society in *The Picture of Dorian Gray. Photofest*

leper! Nobody knew I had a sense of humor, and people wouldn't even have lunch with me![11]

Hatfield was hardly a casting director's dream of a Dorian Gray. He was dark-haired and fine-boned, appealing (like the film itself) to a less vast audience than the novel's irresistible blond Adonis. And because he was a mere mortal, his complexion was found to lack the smoothness needed for Dorian-like perfection, which necessitated some buff-and-spackle help from the makeup and lighting people. But those factors make him, in fact, a memorable Dorian, wearing his youth like fine pottery wears its glaze, with an extra shimmer courtesy of

---

[11]This is the kind of role that stamps an actor's career, and so it was with Hatfield. Over the next four-plus decades of reasonably steady employment, he could never efface the image of the impassively ageless pretty boy with the nasty portrait upstairs. This was aided by the fact that Hatfield himself aged with startling grace over the years, and long before his death in 1998 had wearied of jocular inquiries about where the picture was hidden.

Harry Stradling's Oscar-winning cinematography. To some the characterization is too impassive, even blank, but Hatfield's interpretation, detached as it is, is quite valid, a Dorian too consumed by youth and self to have full contact with the mortal world. However polymorphous or decadent his sexuality, the film avers, it only becomes evil when carried to the self-absorbed extent that Dorian does. The real-life sexuality of this intensely private actor may have been a factor in the elusiveness of the performance as well—an updated version of the Johnny Arthur phenomenon of subtext overcoming text. Certainly, in subsequent years, this would be increasingly the case in leading roles as it had been earlier in supporting parts: an actor's projection of sexual ambivalence, on and possibly off the screen, could enable a director's subtle pursuit of a gay agenda.

The power of that subtext in *The Picture of Dorian Gray* is evident to any viewer with half a brain, a circumstance which may or may not have included the moral and critical observers at the time of its production and release. L'affaire *Dorian Gray* was one of the more singular incidents, in fact, in the history of the Production Code Administration, and a linchpin in the tortured, holier-than-thou relationship between the PCA and its less secular sibling, the Legion of Decency. Breen, or more likely his literate cohorts, had actually been pretty stringent with Lewin's script, dictating the deletion of a number of lines alluding to Dorian's behavior: "doing what was improbable," "pleasure which stops at nothing," and "searching for new sensations" were among the passages cut in order to steer the script away from that Breen bugaboo, "the inference of sex perversion." The finished film, having been toned down according to Code specifications, was granted a PCA seal. The Legion of Decency followed suit shortly afterward with an A-2 rating ("Morally Unobjectionable for Adults"). Then came the reviews, and for one of the first times in film history the critics dared to speak the name of a secret passion. Bosley Crowther of the *New York Times*—the so-called dean of U.S. film critics—didn't get it at all, complaining with emblematic obtuseness that *Dorian* was incomprehensible. It was the trade papers, normally the most literal-minded observers, who best knew what Lewin had done. Not since the coming of Breen had there been such outright talk of how a director could get gay content through the Code minefield.

> In the adaptation, Albert Lewin, who directed, has very subtly but unmistakably, pegged Gray for what he was, but it may go over the heads of a lot of people anyway.
> *Variety* (weekly)

> Mr. Lewin has accomplished as much as probably more than any other individual could in bringing as much of the story into pictures as possible, without shocking the audience completely out of the theatre and bringing the Legion of Decency to another boiling point. . . . In the removal of the things that Mr. Lewin had to remove from the Oscar Wilde piece, the picture becomes entirely too mental

for most moviegoers. . . . It's true that motion pictures, particularly during the past five years, have reached an adult stage, but we doubt that they have grown in stature sufficiently to handle the intelligence that was demanded of MGM in bringing this questionable subject to the screen. . . .

Hollywood Reporter

Those familiar with the tale will be completely satisfied with the fidelity of the Lewin screen treatment and the remarkable way in which he surmounted the obvious difficulties.

Variety (daily)

A finely, artistically and cunningly wrought study of the effects of the utter excesses of evil indulgence upon an individual . . . with no evidence to show that his dissipation follows any of the staple lanes of sinning (It's emphasized that he doesn't go for wine or women, although he does have a fondness for song) generally known about and recognized as acceptable for dramatic presentation. The corn belt and the deep South are areas, to name two that suggest themselves at once, where the customers could be expected to look up the theatre manger and ask him what, besides murder, the picture they'd just seen was all about—and to complain on behalf of their families if he told them.

Motion Picture Herald

A few weeks after the reviews ran, Joe Breen received, to his apparent shock, a letter from the Very Rev. Msgr. John T. McClafferty, the powerful head of the Legion of Decency. The Legion, along with people like trade-paper publisher Martin Quigley, frequently felt that Breen and his cohorts had sold out to the studios, deviating from the original intended hard moral line and caving in to the whims of the decadent evil moguls. Having read the *Dorian Gray* reviews, Fr. McClafferty clearly felt that his anti-Breen fire had new fuel.

There were portions in the picture which could be interpreted as conveying implications of homo-sexuality. In the light of the Code provision, "Sex perversion or an inference to it is forbidden," I know that you will wish that the greatest care be exercised lest story material or treatment of story material give even the remotest rounds for such reference or inference.

Breen immediately fired a wire back to the Legion, sputtering with shock, asking for an explanation of *exactly* what material had escaped all those watchful Catholic eyes, and finishing off with a bold if inaccurate denial: "This is first time in our experience with more than five thousand pictures that any such suggestion has come from a responsible source." McClafferty could only respond by sending him clips from the reviews, and without more material the matter was dropped. But the PCA, the Legion of Decency, and the studios all knew that the matter of *Dorian Gray*, coming as it did after the *Uninvited* controversy, showed the watchdogs to be less vigilant than usual. As a result, more liberal material might be increasingly possible. Three years earlier, Father McClafferty had spearheaded a triumph for the Legion when he forced MGM to reshoot and reedit portions of George Cukor's *Two-Faced Woman*. But a film with dark Wildean allusions is less tenable than a pop bedroom farce, and this time Lewin and MGM won the battle. "The rank and file will probably find it too difficult to understand . . . just what sort of sinful life the man was leading," one critic had complained. Yet a worldwide gross of nearly $3 million indicated that enough people had indeed understood.

The wranglings over *The Uninvited* and *Dorian Gray* coincided with some major industry changes, all of which served as the pivot of transition in the regulation of gay-themed material on the screen. In 1945 Will Hays retired from the Code's parent organization, now called the Motion Picture Association of America. The new head of the MPAA, an industrialist named Eric Johnston, gave a somewhat more forward-looking tone to the industry's self-regulating process. From this time onward, not coincidentally as the aging Breen participated less and less in the administration of his Code, there seems to have been a steadily growing, if unstated, leniency on the part of his associates. While the Code continued to crack down on cleavage, dance costumes, off-color language, and similar infractions, the subtle presentation of adult material would sometimes pass unscathed. Naturally there were some major flare-ups: the perceived blasphemy of the Italian import *The Miracle*, brouhahas over Jane Russell in *The Outlaw* and *The French Line*, extravagant wariness over *A Streetcar Named Desire*. Yet even as these continued, filmmakers developed more understated techniques to convey their points to audiences without Code interference. Breen's lieutenant, Geoffrey M. Shurlock, tended to be less rigid than his boss, and as his responsibilities increased, American film began taking a notably more mature tone. In the case of gay or lesbian content, Shurlock seems to have chosen his targets with some care, quite openly looking the other way to pass certain films without comment, while zeroing in on the more obvious mark of, to use a term that still popped up in Code correspondence, "pansy" content.

One result of this unofficial new approach to the Code strictures on gays can be seen in a cheap, blunt, and quite unsettling horror movie from 1946. *House of Horrors* is little better than its throwaway title—there's not even a house, though the working title was *Murder Mansion*. Coming at the tail end of the Universal horror film cycle, this was less a film than a piece of low-budget ($135,000) product, a Hollywood world away from *Dorian Gray*'s MGM class. In its tawdry way, however, it brandished some odd allusions.

Marcel DeLange (Martin Kosleck), an avant-garde sculptor, blames artistic snobbery for his lack of financial success, especially after critic F. Holmes Harmon (Alan Napier) thwarts his chance for a good sale. Just as the despondent Marcel is about to drown himself, he sees a figure in the water—a man of grotesque face and disfigured body, a serial killer known as the Creeper (Rondo Hatton). Fascinated by the man's face, Marcel rescues him, brings him home, and decides to use the Creeper as both a model and a tool of vengeance. After the Creeper murders a streetwalker, Marcel sends him to execute Harmon. Pinup artist Steven Morrow (Robert Lowery), whose work was also one of Harmon's targets, is soon suspected of killing Harmon. His girlfriend Joan (Virginia Grey), one of Harmon's colleagues, sets out to prove his innocence. The police attempt to trap Steven by having another art critic, Ormiston (Howard Freeman), run a scathing review of Steven's work. However, Ormiston also belittles Marcel's work in the article, and Marcel has another mission for the Creeper. Steven goes to Ormiston to harass him, but when Ormiston leaves the room to fix a drink, the Creeper snaps his spine. Beginning to suspect Marcel, Joan goes to visit him and steals a sketch of the Creeper. When he finds the sketch missing, Marcel sends the Creeper out to take care of Joan, but one of Steven's models is killed instead. Joan returns to Marcel to confront him, and the mad artist again calls on the Creeper. This time, however, it is Marcel himself who is murdered. The police shoot the Creeper, and Joan pledges to Steven that she will leave the art world behind and marry him.

Unlike nearly all the Universal output, there was no supernatural horror in this *House.* Instead of a Frankenstein monster or vampire or wolfman, it cruelly exploited the facial and bodily deformities of its real-life "creature," the acromegalic Rondo Hatton. "The Perfect Neanderthal Man," the admiring Marcel notes, and the viewing experience is made even queasier with the knowledge that Hatton would be dead from his illness in just a few months.[12]

Rondo Hatton's is not the only private self used by *House of Horrors.* Martin Kosleck, a member of the film community's sizable community of German emigrés, frequently served as a sort of second-string Peter Lorre and even, as noted earlier, was a runner-up for Lorre's prize role of Joel Cairo in *The Maltese Falcon.* With his compact frame and sensitive face he was not leading-man material, at least at the major studios, and so he found a ready niche during the forties as various Axis villains. Like Bobby Watson, he bore a sufficient resemblance to a top-echelon Nazi—Joseph Goebbels in this case—to guarantee employment during wartime, sometimes alongside Watson. He also found time for a respectable career as a painter, as well as a personal life that included a

---

[12]Hatton's Creeper character had also appeared in *The Pearl of Death, Jungle Captive,* and *The Spider Woman Strikes Back.* After *House of Horrors* Universal had him reprise the role in the bluntly titled *The Brute Man,* after which he promptly died. The studio, undergoing a rare spasm of good taste, decided not to risk accusations of pandering and postmortem exploitation. Instead of releasing *The Brute Man,* Universal sold the film outright to the bottom-rung studio PRC (Producers Releasing Corp., or more familiarly Pretty Rotten Crap). Hatton's swan song went out as a quintessential PRC effort—cheap, haphazard, and no credit to anyone involved.

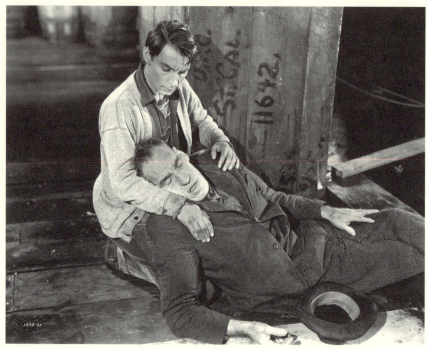

Not quite what Michelangelo envisioned. In *House of Horrors*, Martin Kosleck finds a kindred spirit in Rondo Hatton. *Photofest*

marriage to a wealthy woman of title and, concurrently, a lengthy relationship with actor Hans von Twardowski. His casting as Marcel DeLange in *House of Horrors* played on both his artistic bent and his gayness. As a self-proclaimed man of genius, Marcel is the perennial misfit; only his cat (with whom he has a lengthy chat in the first scene) understands him, at least until he discovers the Creeper. Throughout the movie, Marcel is the target of putdowns and condescension. He is, in fact, "the laughingstock of New York art critics," although Susan gives him a twisted compliment by saying he is "just a harmless little screwball." Marcel does seem to find some degree of happiness with his fellow outsider, the Creeper, at least until stirred to revenge by critical disapproval. The film goes into none of the details of their relationship, but there are hints: at one point there is a dissolve from a busty model being painted by the "normal" Steven to the misshapen Creeper as the subject of Marcel's masterpiece. When the Creeper starts to threaten Susan she lashes out to Marcel about "your ugly little pet," and when the Creeper kills Marcel, the artist's hands slowly slide down the killer's body, then reach out to caress his cat one last time.

If any aspects of gayness between Marcel and the Creeper are merely implicit, what is quite explicit is the film's portrayal of the art critic Ormiston. Joe Breen immediately pounced on the script's mention of Ormiston's "mincing walk": "You will have in mind that we cannot approve anything suggestive of a 'pansy' about his characterization here and elsewhere. This is important." Yet, as with Mischa Auer in *Lady in the Dark*, Howard Freeman was permitted to continue with his characterization, lofting his long cigarette holder and effulgently declaring that the police plot to use him as a decoy "sounds positively intriguing!" A film such as *House of Horrors* traditionally rates little in the way of attention, but its very oddness and bad taste are indeed positively intriguing. So is the fact that it marked the very end of Universal's fifteen-year run of horror films. Later, there would be the Abbott and Costello spoofs and the sci-fi pictures, but how odd that the cycle proper, which had attained a kind of greatness under James Whale, would wind down with one last example of aberrant male bonding: a tortured gay artist and a real-life Frankenstein creature.

While Joe Breen and his staff were yet locked into the notion of banning "anything suggestive of a 'pansy,' " homosexuality had changed on the screen as much as it had in American life. Through changing times, a depression and then a war, and the rise of psychoanalysis, the old fairy types were fast fading. The identifiable codes—the flower and fedora, the small mustache, the "whoops, dearie" catchphrases—were all dead by the middle of the Second World War, only to surface in nostalgic remembrances by some of the participants, perhaps, or in the minds of people like Joe Breen, who could think only in terms of specific signals and stereotypes. The new type of gay man onscreen, beginning in 1944, was not a subject for ridicule in most cases. In fact, he did much of the mocking himself, being acerbic, witty, and (to use a word of the time, not necessarily negatively) bitchy. These qualities were evident less because of how he looked or moved than how he tended to imply his superiority. Had *House of Horrors* been less clumsy, its art critics would qualify for the mantle of the new gay type: immersed in culture, intelligently sharp-tongued, not so much expendable to the main action as an interested observer of it. The prototype of this figure, who created a sensation in 1944, was a gay actor playing an ostensibly straight role.

When he appeared as the radio commentator Waldo Lydecker in *Laura*, Clifton Webb had been a Broadway star for thirty years. In 1944 he was in his mid-fifties, and the stage roles came less frequently, so he went to Hollywood. He had made several silents and an early talkie short, but *Laura* was treated as his debut. A murder mystery directed by Otto Preminger to emphasize both its adultness and chic, *Laura* was indeed sophisticated balm for the war years. It, and Webb-as-Waldo, were sensations. Waldo was a new kind of character. Fastidious and hypercritical, barbs ever at the ready, implacably convinced of

CLIFTON WEBB

Real name: Webb Parmalee Hollenbeck. Born Indianapolis, Ind., November 11, 1889; died Beverly Hills, Calif., October 13, 1966

Webb was as lucky as he was talented. How often is it that a middle-aged character actor is raised to (and maintains) star status? His first career had been marked by huge successes in musical revues, where his urbane manner fit in better than the more callow (at the time) talents of Fred Astaire; he got to introduce "Easter Parade" in *As Thousands Cheer* (1933). The gaunt, supercilious sophistication that tended to wear thin as he aged proved to be his making in movies: seldom were actor and role better matched than Webb and *Laura*'s Waldo Lydecker. Part of the ideal nature of it all, of course, was the fact that they were so similar: Webb was as snippy and superior as any of his characters. He did, however, have the gratitude and respect of Fox studio chief Darryl Zanuck, who saw to it that roles and income remained steady. His febrile devotion to his mother, Mabelle, was a legendary hoot in the Hollywood community; hosts knew that when Webb attended a party, his date would be not a boyfriend but his game if aging mom. Too soon, his roles became less quirky and more mainstream, including a series of improbable hetero amours (of which *Three Coins in the Fountain* is the most famous and strange) and a sticky (as opposed to subversive) stint as the title character in *Mister Scoutmaster*. Yet audiences knew, when they saw Webb, that whatever his surroundings he would be caustic, aloof, and unflappable. This was Webb, and his coworkers expected it and enjoyed him for it. When he had a smash with *Sitting Pretty*, he brushed off its producer's congratulations in characteristic form: "My dear boy," he snapped, "I have always been a success. One more hit will not unsettle me."

his immense value to humankind, he was also, as *Laura* played out, a new kind of villain. Waldo's homosexuality had been removed from the script early on, and if the rewritten character's bouts of hetero-jealousy sat oddly upon Webb's epicene deportment, his way with the dialogue and preternatural sophistication bore all before it. The voice alone would have carried the performance: the tone a courtly buzz saw, the razor diction dining on consonants as if they were truffled squab. Webb and *Laura* were nominated for Oscars, which went instead, and predictably, to the priests-are-people-too blarney of Barry Fitzgerald and *Going My Way*. Yet Webb scored the real victory, becoming one of the rare character actors who forever after received star roles and star billing.

Webb's first role after *Laura* was a Waldo retread, the jealous millionaire Hardy Cathcart in the noir *Dark Corner*. Then, in the studio's massive and Hollywoodized version of Maugham's *Razor's Edge*, he offered his own razorlike

A natural for both the tux and the look of snide detachment, Clifton Webb aims a baleful eye upon Gene Tierney, Vincent Price, and Judith Anderson in *Laura*. (All four of these actors played gay onscreen at one time or another; Tierney's turn came in the TV miniseries *Scruples*.)

glitter as Elliott Templeton, the greatest snob of all time. Unlike Waldo and Cathcart, Elliott evinced no interest in the opposite sex (or in the same sex, for that matter), no interest in anything other than being at the center of attention in the best circles and at the finest parties. *The Razor's Edge* was planned as Twentieth Century Fox's banner production of 1946, and indeed *Life* magazine celebrated it as the first great film of the postwar era. It was hardly that, although it was expensive and entertaining. Perhaps it would have more closely brushed greatness if, as originally planned, George Cukor had directed a screenplay by Maugham himself. Ultimately, Darryl F. Zanuck decided that the production bearing his name would also have his imprint and put both the script and the direction into other hands. (The final director, Edmund Goulding, often shared with Cukor that gay-euphemistic title "woman's director.") For Webb, however, there could be no substitute, and the wonder of his performance is that Elliott never becomes detestable. His insufferable snobbery becomes, in fact, curiously poignant, especially in the memorable death scene in which he dictates one final

RSVP to a hostess he loathes. Again, there were Oscar nominations for the film and for Webb, with *Variety* applauding the actor's "effete characterization."

Webb's next film, for which he received his only Best Actor Oscar nomination, was in some way his most audacious: as master aesthete cum babysitter Lynn Belvedere in the hit comedy *Sitting Pretty*. Retrospect alters few films as much as this one, for what seemed in 1948 a fun romp about a misanthrope seems now, in all unintentionality, a sly swipe at the heterosexual family unit. Could there be a gayer name than Lynn Belvedere? Could there be many things more subversive than having a child-loathing and obviously gay man as a babysitter *and* having him emerge victorious in all his supercilious superiority? In no way are overt sexual vibes implied about Webb's Belvedere, but decades of hindsight and a touch of gaydar give *Sitting Pretty* quite a charge. Belvedere came back for two more installments, neither up to the original, after which Fox channeled Webb's special personality into more clear-cut heterosexual territory. In father roles in *Cheaper by the Dozen* and *Titanic*, and as March King John Philip Sousa in *Stars and Stripes Forever*, Webb maintained his star status and snide air in a time when it was easier onscreen to play safe than play gay.

Children of Webb, they might be called, or Sons of *Laura*. They proliferated in film after 1945 and into the early fifties, very much in the Waldo/Webb mode, seldom as incisive as the original yet sometimes making a notable imprint all the same. A world away from the days of Del Turpe or Ernest the dance teacher, they were the essence of self-possession, forever in control of their situation, often serving as edgy Greek choruses. What little sympathy they could demonstrate was reserved for leading women; toward the leading men they were most often scathing. The cocktail party was the natural habitat for these men, who wore their neuroses and egotism as nattily as they did their dinner jackets, with their epigrams identifying them as surely as if they were sporting green carnations. More snide than O'Malley, more secure than Pangborn, and less silly than Sutton, they were too subtly drawn to attract Breen's Pansy Radar, but in the increasing sophistication of postwar cinema they were sufficiently obvious to the knowing spectator. They were present in film noir, in soap operas, musicals, and even comedies made after Webb became a star. The quintessential Webb Child turned up in the 1948 melodrama *The Velvet Touch*, in which Rosalind Russell played a Broadway diva mixed up in a murder case and, for a touch of real-life mystery (i.e., why did she do it?) essayed passages from *Hedda Gabler*. In its attempts at *Laura*-like atmosphere with a pre–*All About Eve* charge, the movie summoned forth its faux Webb in the character of Jeff Trent, a Broadway columnist. As played by Dan Tobin, Trent is the duplicitous lapdog of both Russell and her sullen rival, Claire Trevor, and obviously gay even as he squires a buxom starlet to a premiere. Tobin tries for the irresistible nastiness, his eyes sparkling at the hope of an exclusive, but seems too nice to fully take on Webb's lustrously jaded mantle. Even the name of Trent's newspaper column, "Broadway Chatter," seemed bland and cut-rate. The *Times*'s Bosley Crowther, ever a tin-eared oracle, was being notably Pollyannaish when he pronounced, "One only wonders why the theatre should be made so horrendous on the screen—a place of such strange and wild impulses." The problem with *The Velvet Touch*, and with Jeff Trent, is that they aren't strange and wild enough. Tobin, who was physically very much of the Bobby Watson/Jay Eaton school, was less effortfully snide and more amusing as a dum-dum heir in the retro-screwball comedy *Miss Tatlock's Millions* (1947), and later as an unctuous caterer dealing with Bette Davis in *The Catered Affair* (1956).

Paramount's late-1940s fascination with Billy de Wolfe was clearly intended as a nod in the direction of Webb, although prissy and fastidious did not a Waldo Lydecker make. More viably, *Winter Meeting* (1948) was saved from being Bette Davis's all-time dreariest vehicle by the presence of John Hoyt as Davis's best friend, publisher Stacy Grant. With the barbs and bon mots and the sister-confessor attitude, the role almost seemed to have been intended for Eve Arden, with not even a name change required. Hoyt's caustic allure was an oasis amid the interminably lugubrious dramatics, sporadically salvaging a script far beneath anything Webb was given. The most notable scene in the entire film was Stacy testily telling off a lunkhead sailor by revealing that, far from being a decadent slacker, he'd been a war hero. Yes, "they" served too, and they served damn well. Men younger than Hoyt and Tobin also ventured into this territory. Mel Ferrer, often one of the dullest presences in fifties cinema, was gayer than usual (in all senses) in Nicholas Ray's *Born to Be Bad* (1950). As the only person in San Francisco who sees through schemer Joan Fontaine, Ferrer served drily as a play-by-play chorus, commenting on Fontaine's machinations and mentioning that part of his job as a portrait painter was to convince husbands that their wives were safe with him.

David Wayne's celebrated comic turn as Kip in George Cukor's feminist comedy *Adam's Rib* (1949) also falls into this younger-Webb vein. Kip is, and there's no getting around it, a real bitch. A talented Cole Porterish songwriter and man about town, he's cute and dapper, brimming over with the sort of insincere wit that society women treasure and most men (straight and gay) find bratty.[13] Without resorting to fruit-colored mannerisms, Wayne makes Kip both convincing and, in the words of one critic, "almost more repulsive than necessary." He fawns over Katharine Hepburn's Amanda with fulsome compliments and opens like a flower to any opportunity to put down her husband, Adam

---

[13]His resemblance to Cole Porter may or may not have been deliberate. What is unquestionable is that the song Kip writes and performs, "Farewell, Amanda," was a genuine, and notably below-par, Porter creation.

(Spencer Tracy). In one memorable scene, he offers running commentary on their home movies, a fey outsider mocking marriage and all its accoutrements. Praising Amanda's crusade for female equality, Kip pipes up that her arguments have convinced him to go out and become a woman. "He wouldn't have far to go, either," Adam mutters. Yet the comment, which seems to nail Kip's sexuality so obviously, is said less in the spirit of gay-bashing than in relief that Kip finally has a chink in his armor that permits a riposte. The arch-insulter has finally gotten one hurled back at him, even though Amanda shushes Adam to make sure that Kip doesn't hear the remark. (What would he do if he heard it? Cringe and weep?) The character and performance work extremely well until the unconvincing climax dreamed up by writers Ruth Gordon and Garson Kanin to resolve the Tracy-Hepburn conflict and give Kip a hetero redemption. In jarring contrast to everything seen and heard up to this scene, Kip professes his love for Amanda, attempts to break up her marriage, and makes a clumsy pass. His actions set it up for the Tracy character to break in, threaten to shoot them, and force the terrified Amanda to rescind her earlier argument that a woman has the right to defend her marriage by packing a gun. The cumulative effect diminishes Kip even more than it does Amanda, since his supposedly ardent lovemaking is completely out of character; this guy would only pitch such vigorous woo (to either a woman or man) as a nasty practical joke. Such an abrupt shift might seem a Production Code gambit to make sure Kip wouldn't rate the Breen "pansy" label, yet the scene is present in all the early drafts of the script. More in character, at least, is Kip's plea to Amanda to kiss him, just like the legendary stage pair: "You be Lunt," he says, "and I'll be Fontanne!" Like Algie the Miner so many years ago, a character can be gay so long as there's a straight mask to wear at fadeout time.

For the decade's most feverish melodrama, the darker side of the Webb-derived character served with nasty proficiency. *Gilda* (1946) is a *Call Her Savage* for a post-Code age, missing no opportunity to cloak a sensational woman star in layer after layer of obsessive eroticism. So intense is *Gilda's* iconic insinuation that Rita Hayworth's hair is far more a germane issue than the nefarious plot intrigues involving gambling and cartels. Like some other first-rate guilty pleasures, *Gilda* is less a cohesive narrative film than a compulsively watchable collage of individual scenes and set pieces. An action scene here, a dance there, love scenes every ten minutes, mild Breen-sanctioned double entendres to give seasoning. And, leading off the whole package, quite startling insinuations of a gay relationship between Glenn Ford, as Hayworth's old lover, and George Macready, as her icy consort. As Ballan Mundsen, Macready is the Clifton Webb aesthetic taken to the extreme: wit without humor, romance without love, sex without humanity. His demeanor is one of total control, with a phallic cane as his talisman and a facial scar the only crack in the façade. Yet Ford is able to tell him, "I was born last night when I met you," and the relationship seems as close personally as it is professionally. When Hayworth arrives on the scene Johnny (Ford) ruefully returns the housekey Ballan had given him; his reason for giving back the key, "Tact," is as provocatively vague as anything else in the movie. That is the charm of *Gilda:* apart from Hayworth's all-out display of high-wire star quality, neither its plot nor its emotions nor even its sexuality can be fully pinned down. The romantic tension between Hayworth and Ford is constantly heightened not through love scenes but through discussions and demonstrations of the interchangeability of love and hate. Into such a masochistically ambiguous terrain, a relationship between the two men fits with ease.

There is, however, a conundrum regarding just what may originally have been intended. Director Charles Vidor reportedly protested that he knew nothing of the relationship between Ballan and Johnny, while Glenn Ford, for his part, admitted in an interview that yes, the characters were lovers. Nowhere in the script is the relationship explicitly spelled out, and the Production Code folk were so busy fretting about adultery and stripteases that they made no mention of it. Certainly it's difficult to envision that a sophisticated émigré like Vidor would not have made some projection about the affair; perhaps it was easier just to disclaim any knowledge and move on. (Vidor died in 1959, well before the permissive age in movies, so we are denied his retrospective.) Perhaps, if Vidor's claim is true, it was producer-writer Virginia Van Upp who engineered the whole thing, the better to provide (as Irving Thalberg had done with *Queen Christina*) some heightening in an already heated erotic atmosphere. In a postwar environment still governed by the Production Code, such enhancement would have to be done with as much tact as that which caused Johnny to return Ballan's key. Once again, it is a relationship that would speak only to those attentive to it, and less loudly than to the cult that embraced *The Uninvited*. But *Gilda* without homoeroticism is hard to conceive; in its fevered escapism it works hard to cover every sensual base.[14]

A totally incomprehensible plot is even less of a deterrent in *The Big Sleep* than in *Gilda*. With Humphrey Bogart as Philip Marlowe and a perfect noir-sleaze atmosphere, the parts vastly outstrip the incoherent whole. As in *Gilda*, sex is always on the fringe, with porno-blackmail as a main plot point and Bogart landing almost every woman in sight. There was also homosexuality in

---

[14]Subjects for further research department: the Technicolor melodrama *Desert Fury* (1948) is as overheated as *Gilda*, if not as audacious or as compulsively warped. One of its central relationships is one of unwonted closeness between bad guys John Hodiak and Wendell Corey, and though this one seems less overt than that of Ford and Macready, it becomes increasingly difficult, as the years go on, not to read them as boyfriends.

Raymond Chandler's original book: the murder of Geiger, the blackmailer, is avenged by his lover, Lundgren. That relationship went unmentioned in the final film, although in early script drafts Marlowe referred to Lundgren by the sometimes-code-word *punk*. What did turn up onscreen was an amusing Bogart stunt. To track down some information, Marlowe goes to Geiger's bookstore posing as a fussy gay man. We see the physical transformation in progress: the hat brim is flipped up at an odd Bowery Boy angle, a pair of dark glasses comes on, and the hands assume an attitude of nervous prayer. The voice changes too, with a slight lisp (naturally!) perched atop Bogart's normal one. "You *do* thell bookth, hmmmmm?" he asks the testy clerk, looking over the glasses in snappish emphasis. And when he pronounces "ceramics," it comes out as the name of some strange patent medicine: "Thera-Mix." Why is it funny and not merely offensive? Possibly because, as with so many things in *The Big Sleep*, it's totally unexpected, another of the quirky things waiting around a corner in this movie. In Bogart's hands, the act seems like parodistic fun, not condescending cartoon. At any rate, the guise drops in short order when Marlowe unfolds the hat brim and trots over to another bookshop where a pretty clerk (Dorothy Malone) engages him in banter and, clearly enough conveyed, quickie sex.

By 1948 the names of Richard Loeb and Nathan Leopold had become negative shorthand for gayness, and for a particularly nasty brand of evil. More than twenty years after their ultrasensational thrill killing, the dom-sub gay couple still represented, for millions of people, the personification of nasty urges and flaunted amorality. (That their trial was conducted amid a frenzy of homophobia and anti-Semitism was less well remembered.) Patrick Hamilton usually protested that his play *Rope*, which opened in London in 1929, had nothing to do with the case—but few believed him.[15] Alfred Hitchcock likely did not, either when saw the play onstage or on its pioneer BBC telecast in 1939. When he embarked on independent production in 1946, with Warner Bros. as his distributor, he took on *Rope* as his first project. The play, in Hitchcock's estimation, could be used to work out some of his own ideas about cinema, just as its protagonists murdered to verify their theories of Nietzschean superiority. His concept was of a completely seamless film run in real time without cuts—theatrical, yet mirroring the continuity of life. How well the Hitchcock film version of *Rope* mirrored life is eminently debatable; less arguably, it marked a turning point in the cinema's depiction of gayness. With *Rope*, the candid allusions of *Dorian Gray* and *The Uninvited* shot up as close to the surface as they possibly could in a buttoned-up time, and again the critics and discerning spectators were able to look past the coding to the gay actuality.

---

[15]When the play came to American shores, it was retitled *Rope's End*.

Ostensibly, Hitchcock was drawn less to the drama of *Rope* than to the technical considerations involved in making a nonedited film of a play. He reveled in the mechanics and the control involved: choreographing the camera movements, designing the sets and furniture to accommodate these movements, and ensuring that the actors had the control to play a whole eight- to nine-minute scene without stopping.[16] This is not to say that his fascination with the sensational and the gruesome did not come into play. There were too many macabre opportunities for the director to be completely disengaged, and it was one of the few opportunities he had had up to that time to put his fascination with homosexuality onto film. For Hitchcock, gay men in particular were intriguingly exotic, and he viewed them with neither disapproval nor longing. They were, for him, yet another of the odd facets of humanity that he found interesting, and perhaps worth exploring on the screen; *Murder*, back in 1930, had featured a memorable transvestite killer. Upon submitting the original playscript to the Breen Office in September 1946, he was told that the play was acceptable under the Code so long as "compensating moral values" were stressed and the murderers properly discredited. He decided to do this by putting back into *Rope* some of what Hamilton had removed: the sensational nature of the Loeb-Leopold case and some meticulously implied gayness. As would become standard with producers trying to get "objectionable" material past the Breenites, he waited till late in the game to submit his screenplay. The murder had been made more graphic, and so had the relationship between the killers, Brandon and Philip. Breen's associates put a magnifying glass to the script, objecting to lines that had such gay tinges as the use of the word *lovely*. Few changes were necessary: as had been done with Mrs. Danvers, the implications were skillfully engineered without being made verbal, through direction and characterization and staging, through art direction and nuance and the tolerant presence of a genial mother-hen housekeeper. Then, in the manner of a true provocateur, Hitchcock cast gay actors. John Dall was the domineering sadist Brandon, and masochistic Philip was played by Farley Granger.[17] The gay vibes, for some spectators, would be off the charts. "It was just a thing that was assumed," Farley Granger said much later. "Either you got it or you didn't."

---

[16]Eight or nine minutes being the length of one reel of film. At the reel changes, the camera would move to a shadowy place and the next reel's setup would start in the same location. Yes, it's a fascinating gimmick, and an exhaustingly mannered one.

[17]Granger took the role after, yes, Montgomery Clift turned it down. Apparently Hitchcock also cast a gay actor (Dick Hogan) as the murder victim. While Granger has generally been tight-lipped about his personal life, he was involved at the time with Arthur Laurents, who wrote most of *Rope*'s screenplay. Dall's gayness was well known; as with Clifton Webb, it was his ostentatious devotion to his mother, not his homosexuality per se, that educed jokes in the film community.

After some final protestations to the Breen Office that no, there wasn't going to be any depiction of homosexuality, and no, it wasn't about Loeb and Leopold, Hitchcock shot *Rope* over twenty-one nerve-wracking days in January 1948. The format—the longest of long takes—meant that one small fluff would be cause for the whole scene to be repeated, and some of the actors' resulting anguish is visible in the finished film. A few weeks after shooting was done, studio head Jack Warner got wind of something fishy. A fellow mogul (Barney Balaban of Paramount) wrote to him asking why on earth the studio had made a film about Loeb and Leopold. Before Warner replied, he checked with Hitchcock about it, and the master showman lied and lied.

> Hitchcock . . . emphatically told me that it has nothing whatsoever to do with the Loeb-Leopold case. . . . It is strictly an impersonal melodrama and I have the assurance of Hitchcock and the others . . . that no direct reference to the Loeb-Leopold case will be made in the advertising; also, that there is no reference to the case in the picture.
>
> Very confidentially, Barney, had you or someone else called my attention to the resemblance between the case and this picture before the picture was made, Warner Bros. would not have made any deal to release the picture. However, it is now completed and . . . it is not our property and that we have only a small financial interest in it. . . .
>
> I am sure you know that we would not release any picture where a finger could be pointed at our people [Jews] or give someone a bad name.

The ads for *Rope* bore the curious tag line "Nothing ever held you like its false love!" and, wouldn't you know it, one review after another mentioned Loeb and Leopold—one went so far as to say that viewing *Rope* was like rereading the newspaper accounts of the trial. Some of the critics were also compelled to come up with a few euphemisms to describe Brandon and Philip. The traditional "aesthetes" was used, and the more lustrous (and who knew it was a noun?) "exquisites." The public outcry began soon afterward, and the objections had nothing to do with sexuality. With a strangulation in its very first seconds, staged in excrutiating Technicolor closeup, and with endless talk about the finer points of committing the perfect murder, *Rope* was seen by many as a how-to primer. Even *Variety* felt that it was in dubious taste, and a number of viewers took the trouble to let Warners know their feelings. "Your picture *Rope*," one postcard ran, "is about the most disgusting and disgraceful picture I have ever seen." The strangulation scene was cut in Pennsylvania, Ohio, and Maryland, while Italy, India, and the Netherlands banned the film in toto. The next step was financial flop, and not even the top-billed presence of Jimmy Stewart (as the boys' headmaster) could fend off the flood of red ink. There was also the peculiar fate, in later years, of cinematic oblivion: for decades *Rope* was

Farley Granger (submissively uncertain) and John Dall (dominantly triumphant) are Loeb and Leopold in all but name, and in leather gloves, in *Rope*. The body of their freshly-killed victim is in the trunk. *Photofest*

completely out of circulation, more difficult to see than any of Hitchcock's other American films.

Intriguing technique and strong gay implications do not a great film make. *Rope* is ice-cold without being spellbinding, nasty without being truly engrossing, fraught without being tingling. The gay relationship is the most believable thing in it—the smooth Dahl does seem to dominate the edgy Granger—yet the pair is made so wrong, with their misplaced sense of superiority, that they're not even villains you want to root for. Three years later, in *Strangers on a Train*, Hitchcock would create a portrait of gay psychosis far more entertaining and appealing than the "normal" heroes. In *Rope* no one carries any particular appeal; a gay spectator can find the two lovers physically attractive, certainly, and even be drawn to Brandon's snooty argument of "superiority." But their actions, especially when depicted as blatantly and unpleasantly as here, rule out any chance of identification. One reacts to the gay lovers of *Rope* as one does to the movie as a whole: with detached interest, with some appreciation of the effrontery of it, and with precious little affection.

Unfortunately, in the years following *Rope* the concept of gays as villains would not diminish. On the contrary—as the frankness of the portrayals quietly increased, so did a stronger negative element underlying them. It had already been clear, by the end of the war, that the warmth of a Pangborn was giving way to the archness, sometimes malevolence, of a Webb or a Hatfield. The gay threat that DeMille tried to evoke with Ancaria in *The Sign of the Cross* was becoming further realized as the forties ended: this is the time when the true demonization of gays by film has its roots. As gays started to be more visible on the screen, there was a high price to pay: corruption, weakness, in some cases genuine evil. No wonder, in the witch-hunts coming up presently, the gays would be purged along with the alleged commies. In films like *The Uninvited* and *House of Horrors* and *Rope*, gay ceases to be good.

TEN

Tempests and Teapots

ry to think of a time and place more contradictory than America in the 1950s. Here was the decade as oxymoron, filled with jangling coexistences that had no business trying to get along. In a time of postwar prosperity, and with a benignant grandfather in charge, the country acted like everything was jim-dandy. Never mind that there were witch-hunts afoot, treating many with the grace and generosity of the Reign of Terror. Never mind that a race was moving past untold injustices only by overcoming the greatest imaginable number of obstacles. Never mind the bloody doings in Korea that the guys in charge wouldn't call a war. Never mind, too, that a few women and men in a few cities like Los Angeles, New York, and San Francisco were beginning to talk about oppression and the need for equality for those who loved within their own sex. With new suburbias filled with television screens, with bumper crops of kids to be harvested as never before, who could worry about those tiresome little nicks on the American picture window?

Certainly not the movies. As the decade opened, most of the studio big shots were pretending that it was still business as usual. Their ability to deny the truth sometimes reached the levels of self-deceit that ran through all that phony Eisenhower optimism, for the profit sheets were showing a different story. The studios had been divested of their theater chains—the result of an antitrust suit—the old production formulas were beginning to seem less foolproof, and a surge of movies from overseas often made the American product look wan and artificial. Then there was television to cause all the worry in the world. The studios were stymied for a time, and as they groped to survive, they kept the assembly line busy with the production of clichéd movies having no relevance and less value. As the losses mounted, they attempted to take the competitor by its rabbit ears and outdo it with things not available on the home screen. Costume spectacles were one way, wide-screen and 3-D movies another, and a third was, very occasionally, maintaining the mid-1940s move toward more adult fare. This was sometimes manifested in films with a social conscience, and more often with a heightened frankness achieved through whatever means the omnipresent Production Code would sanction.

As the decade began, it was clear that the whole economy of movies—the making and the viewing—was never again going to unreel effortlessly. The studios could no longer take their audiences for granted, and the public had to make a greater effort to move past the TV set to get out and go see them. Some of the most conspicuous films of 1950 demonstrated how the American movie industry would respond to the changing times and trends. On one hand, there were big-budget blowouts like *Samson and Delilah* and *King Solomon's Mines* and *Annie Get Your Gun*, lush fare that TV screens could not contain. On the other, there were films more incisive or candid than anything on the home screen: *Sunset Boulevard*, *The Asphalt Jungle*, *All About Eve*. Beyond these, there were millions of miles of the same schlock, dinosaur movies more obsolete than anyone knew, fitting escapist symbols for the colossal denial of the era. Not for them would there be any hint of honesty or integrity, but in some of the standard fare of 1950, as well as some of the big titles, there were intermittent reaches toward something more authentic. In their stumbling fashion, a number of movies released in 1950 dealt a little with what it meant to be gay; indeed, it could be said that lesbians were more prominent onscreen in that year than they had possibly ever been in American film up to that time.

After *The Uninvited*, with its unwitting appeal to a sapphic cult, woman-love was in virtually no evidence for the rest of the 1940s, just as—with *Rope* excepted—the last years of that decade had seen little in the way of overt male gayness. That the change came immediately as the numbers flipped over for the new decade says something interesting, perhaps even mystical. Women had not had their equivalent of a Clifton Webb figure, unless one cares to consider Eve Arden's work in a certain, perhaps slanted, light. Arden's persona was too crisp to be spinsterish, too sharply breezy to seem repressed or androgynous. In many films—above all *Mildred Pierce*—she was the heroine's friend and sibyl, most often neither requiring nor desiring undue male attention. As such, with her innate intelligence and nifty capacity for spiky repartee, she could be considered a cryptolesbian. But that side is far less evident in Arden than in the women of *The Uninvited* or *Rebecca* or *The Seventh Victim*. As knowing as she was, she lacked Webb's insider relish, nor would she have had his inherent flair for giving gay inflection to straight roles. Yet in her wisecracks and delivery, which ever served as adrenaline to one lousy script after another, there were on rare occasions traces of something more private. In *Tea for Two*, a dinosaur movie if ever there was one (and one of the biggest hits of 1950), Arden is present in accustomed mode, a wise and serpent-tongued chorus. At one point, she

BUGS BUNNY

Born Burbank, Calif., Spring 1939

The magnificent androgyne, the chameleon survivor of cinema, the distillation of profound self-awareness—call him what you will, and Bugs will transcend it. Neither pen nor paper can hold him, this auteur and star, who by 1950 had assumed his full, indeed all-enveloping powers. Not even his best directors (Chuck Jones, Bob Clampett) can totally encompass him; only Mel Blanc, who gave him voice for millions of years, could truly know him. Sexuality is only one of Bugs's many parts, but it is a prominent one. Julian Eltinge? Forget about him: here is the screen's premier male actress. With an inexhaustible wardrobe awaiting him just offscreen, as well as wigs and makeup and accessories (supplied, most likely, by the Acme Corp.), Bugs is ever willing to don drag in the service of art and survival. With less than a wave of a hand (or paw), he becomes a voluptuous Daisy Mae in *Hillbilly Hare*, a geisha vamp in *Bugs Bunny Nips the Nips*, the epitome of Empire esprit in *Napoleon Bunny-part*, and a busty ballerina in *A Corny Concerto*. His Tasmanian She-Devil in *Bedeviled Rabbit* puts the exoticism of Maria Montez to shame, and his Brunnhilde in Jones's *What's Opera, Doc?* defines Wagnerian glamour more vividly than a dozen *Ring* cycles. Invariably, an ear or tail will pop out from beneath a skirt or hat, clueing Elmer Fudd that the temptress is a sham. Yet the disguise has served, and we never fail to marvel at the achievements of Bugs and Blanc and all the artists who made these Warner Bros. shorts. Female impersonation can get no richer than to encompass the whole of womanhood while yet retaining one's own masculine personality. Yet on a few occasions Bugs went further, projecting sexual ambiguity without external trappings. He finishes *What's Cookin', Doc?* (1943) in a double role as himself (briefly wearing a Carmen Miranda fruit medley) and a booby-prize Oscar that strikes a glamour-girl pose. (In profoundly justifiable narcissism, one Bugs kisses the other.) And in two mad scientist epics, *Hair Raising Hare* (1946), and *Water, Water Every Hare* (1949), he finds the most resourceful way to handle a huge fuzzy orange monster with tennis shoes. He poses as a prattling, fawning beautician out of *The Women:* "My stars! Such an *iinnn*-teresting monster!" In the first film, the creature ends up with a mousetrap manicure; the second subjects him to a permanent that is literally dynamite. And in all of this, Bugs goes about his frilly business sans benefit of drag. Not even a pink uniform—this is Bugs unadorned. Is Bugs-as-manicurist supposed to be male? Female? Straight? Gay? Most likely, all of the above. Bugs is Bugs, a drag queen hero and a tough guy heroine, a rabbity satyr and a chased saint, a truly self-actualized screen presence . . . an eternally, infinitely, unceasingly *iinnn*-teresting role-player.

"She's a cute trick." Lee Patrick aims a fond eye offscreen at Eleanor Parker in
Caged, while Hope Emerson offers a convincing imitation of a large mean-tempered
tree. *Photofest*

adds a double-edged sword to her arsenal when she and roomie Doris Day are
preparing to retire for the night:

> DAY: Put out the light.
> ARDEN: Why does a *girl* always say that to me?

Not much, but in a dauntingly sterile musical, one so self-deluded that it casts
Billy De Wolfe as a lady-killing lothario, it's manna.

Apart from such ephemera, several films in 1950 were surprisingly forward with their intimations of lesbianism. Only one ran into trouble with the
Breen Office, not always the juggernaut of old and now choosing its battles
more carefully. Some scripts, in fact, seem to have been deliberately passed
over. The most surprising of these, and one of the year's frankest films on any
level, was Warner Bros.' *Caged.* As with *White Heat* the previous year, *Caged*
was designed to refract the studio's crime-and-punishment tales of the thirties

through postwar toughness. Whether through design or simple fate, it was the definitive women's prison movie, at once honest and overwrought, candid and campy, brutal and sentimental. Even its creation smacked of high melodrama: screenwriter Virginia Kellogg, deciding to go for authenticity, pulled some strings and greased some palms to acquire a false identity and get herself incarcerated for a few weeks. She watched and listened and scribbled notes, and after getting sprung assembled a log of her experiences titled *Women without Men*. It was not a script, simply a compendium of observations and a glossary of terms. She wrote of the innocents tossed in alongside the vets, the matrons on the take, the overcrowding and underfunding. Sex was conspicuous in her research, too, with accounts of the punishment given inmates caught in the act, and a list of such terms as lez, bulldiker, and (more obscurely) bundle. Kellogg's notes were configured into a screenplay by Bernard Schoenfield, with a victimized-underdog plot and slice-of-life supporting characters. For Marie Allen (Eleanor Parker), prison is a tour through the Book of Job: her husband is killed during a bungled robbery, she is jailed as an accessory, her baby is taken away, her parole is denied, and she is tormented by the colossal and evil matron Evelyn Harper (Hope Emerson). By the time her term ends, she has skidded downhill into the thrall of a silky vice queen, Elvira Powell (Lee Patrick), and an only-at-Warners ending augurs a dark future. "Keep her file open," warden Agnes Moorehead sadly observes. "She'll be back."

Despite the script's minefield of censorable elements, the Production Code administrators offered only minor resistance to some of the details in *Caged*. References to drug addiction and abortion were taken out, along with the implication that Powell's main racket was prostitution.[1] The only objection to lesbianism came in the warden's warning words as Marie started her sentence:

> . . . First offenders like you, Marie, are our greatest concern. Unfortunately, they have to be crowded in with three-time losers and lifers simply because we haven't more space. You'll be with such women. Watch out for them. Many things go on here that are unhealthy. All of us have to

---

[1]There had already been a few drug references in postwar American film, but Breen tried to keep a lid on it whenever possible. Likewise with abortion. While MGM's *Doctor and the Girl* featured Gloria DeHaven dying of a botched abortion, Warners' *Beyond the Forest* had recently been recut to remove any notion that Bette Davis was seeking one. For *Caged*, the vice queen's chief income-earner was changed from hooking to shoplifting, although one inmate (Jan Sterling) was referred to as "C.P.— Common Prostitute" and could boast about having a pair of shoes for each night of the week.

have some outlet for affection. I don't mind girls making friends, but keep it wholesome. Do you understand what I mean?
(*Marie nods, embarrassed.*)

After a consultation with Joe Breen and company, the screenwriters softened the line to:

You find all kinds of women in here, just as you would outside. . . . First offenders like you, Marie, are our greatest concern. Unfortunately they have to be crowded in with more experienced women simply because we haven't more space. And you'll be with such women. Of course I want you to have friends, all of us need an outlet for affection . . . but no prison is a normal place.

One of the censors' leading concerns gives an interesting insight into the priorities of the era. There was much fretting over allowing Eleanor Parker to show Marie's pregnancy, and just as with the costume stills that the MPAA required to assess for exposure, Warners had to submit photos of Parker in her prison maternity dress. The wonder of it was that the script, for one of the first times in American cinema, was allowed to retain the word *pregnant*.

When *Caged* hit theaters in the spring of 1950, the critical reaction was notably harsh. The objections were less to the melodrama or the card-stacking than to the idea that prisons really were this awful—a notion which Virginia Kellogg could have set aright. *Commonweal* made one of the very critical allusions to its sexuality: "A good cast of women illustrat[es] too realistically the statement made by the superintendent: 'No prison is a normal place.'" Neither the critics nor the Breens paid undue attention to the fact that *Caged* had gotten away with a substantial amount of adult content. As in *White Heat* there was some unsettling violence, and, courtesy of Kellogg's notes, some tough dialogue—most famously, the inmates' call to look over the fresh meat: "Pipe the new fish." More artfully, the "no prison is a normal place" message had come through in a number of covert signals and, less expectedly, in some startlingly forward scenes. The more subliminal moments involved the most blatant character—6'2" Hope Emerson as the most corrupt official in penal history. Evelyn Harper is a fascinating amalgam of the crudely feminine—reading romance magazines, using that gnarly whine of a voice to coquettishly suck up to a highly placed plutocrat—and the monstrously nasty. The sadomasochistic dynamics of her relationship with Marie are worked out with a sort of delicate bluntness—Harper forcing the pregnant girl to scrub floors with lye, slapping her for imagined slights, taking a pair of clippers to Marie's hair with grim glee. While Marie is especially vulnerable to Harper's cruelty, the script makes it clear that Harper's greatest thrill is seeing all her charges hurt or humiliated, as in the scene in which she regales them with the details of an upcoming hot date for the sole pleasure of watching them squirm in frustration. One prisoner anticipates Harper's delight when the prisoners' illegal lipsticks are confiscated: "That bloated buzzard! She'll drool when she sees the super comin' to take 'em away from us!" While Hope Emerson may have looked like the most nightmarish bull dyke caricature imaginable, the script covers its tracks somewhat, carefully having Harper discuss her boyfriend on the outside. In the early scripts she had a devoted pet inmate named Elaine, who lovingly manicures Harper's nails. The manicure was eliminated and the role reduced to a fast bit in the completed film. Perhaps, too, it may be that Harper seems just too monstrous, in all ways, to claim *any* sexuality.[2]

If there was some hedging in the role of Harper, the vice queens of *Caged* are drawn unequivocally. Kitty Starke (Betty Garde), the tough small-timer who eventually kills Harper, is butch from the word go, with a more feminine girlfriend who follows her everywhere. Her upscale rival, Powell, has her eye on Marie from her first scene onward. Ostensibly, it's to join her stable of shoplifters, but obviously there's a personal interest as well. "She's a cute trick," Lee Patrick says, with gleam in her eye somewhere between roguish and obscene. Then, for Christmas, Powell makes sure that Marie has a special gift: a garish heart-shaped compact with lipstick attached. The gesture is vulgar and also just a shade touching—this sleek middle-aged woman is offering the young tyro her heart, all metallic and rhinestone-studded. Marie, refusing the gift, sneers that rhinestones are phony. Nothing could be more pointed than Powell's reply, spoken by Patrick with creamy insinuation: "You can have real ones, any time you change your type!" The scene was in the film from the first draft onward, and it can only be wondered what Breen and his cohorts thought it meant, or what "your type" referred to—Marie's brand of lipstick? If it weren't obvious enough, the line recurred in the voice-over montage that runs when Marie is put in solitary, although it was taken out of the final cut. Clearly, Powell is meant to embody the seductiveness of a life of crime, and at the end, when Marie takes back the compact, her efforts have been successful.

The popular success of *Caged* was the kind that would spawn a horde of copycats, even unto four decades later in the R-rated bullpens of *Caged Heat*

---

[2]One of the great moments in Hollywood history—OK, an overstatement, but great nonetheless—occurred at the *Caged* premiere. The fact that Harper's onscreen murder had been met with wild cheering did not prepare Hope Emerson for the reception she would get afterward. As she began to exit the theater, pushing her aged mother in a wheelchair, she was surrounded by a deafening wall of boos and hisses. The Oscar nomination a few months later was at least a more civil way to praise her work.

and the like. Its closest imitator would not be its wan remake, *House of Women* (1962), but a much smaller movie that followed *Caged* by only a few weeks. *So Young, So Bad* seems in most ways a blatant clone of *Caged*, with many of the same incidents—pregnant inmate, hair-clipping, suicide, Emerson-like matron, and so on—and was treated as an inferior retread by critics who had not liked *Caged* to begin with. In the *New York Times* Bosley Crowther spewed forth without mercy: "The apparent intention was to ape all the women's prison films that have ever been made, most particularly the Warners' recent lalapaloooza, *Caged*. . . . *Caged* was pretty awful, but this film is so much worse—so clumsily made and acted—that it is downright embarrassing to watch."

It wasn't that bad, although its box-office performance was at best indifferent. Its similarity to *Caged* is even more startling given their production circumstances. They were filmed at exactly the same time, summer 1949, at opposite ends of the country, and it's more likely that the *Caged* script was leaked out at some point than that their resemblance is totally coincidental. Shot at the former Paramount studio in Astoria, Queens, under the title *Runaway*, *So Young, So Bad* was one of the first of a group of low-budget independent films, released by United Artists, designed to bring film production back to New York City. Its coproducer, Paul Henreid, starred as a crusading do-gooder (essentially, the Agnes Moorehead role) in charge of a state reform school for girls, fighting against a corrupt staff and a large evil matron (Grace Coppin). Instead of one "pure" inmate at its center, there were four, three of them played by august performers embarking on long careers. Anne Francis had already made two films, but for Rita (still called Rosita) Moreno and Anne Jackson, this was the debut. Francis and Moreno were cast as vagrants, Jackson and Enid Pulver played Jackie and Jane, a pair of teenaged thieves.

The Breen Office, which had given a free pass to the older women in *Caged*, exploded heavy flak on Jackie and Jane's relationship and gave Paul Henreid due warning:

> There must be nothing suggestive of a Lesbian in the characterization of Jackie. There should be no peculiar shadings in her relationship to the other girls, nor should her boyish bob haircut or general appearance be suggestive of an abnormal girl, in any manner, shape or form.
>
> In this same connection, her line on page 58, "You make me sick. All you think about is guys!" will have to be deleted if it is intended to convey any abnormal aversion to men on her part.

In January 1950, when the completed film came up for review under the title *Escape If You Can*, it was summarily rejected by the MPAA. The problem was, again, Jackie and Jane, who traveled and worked together and were clearly

So Young, So Bad, and so much in love: Scruffy delinquents Enid Pulver and Anne Jackson engage the sympathies of psychologist Paul Henreid. *Photofest*

more than just sisters in crime; Jackie's jealousy when Jane is with other people was considered particularly troublesome. The usual course of events ensued: the producers professed to deny any homoerotic intention, then Breen and company prevailed. It took two rounds of recutting to get a Code seal, and the cuts were evident and sometimes glaring.

An in-house memo at the MPAA noted that the result was at best a draw. It was felt—albeit not too enthusiastically—that the remaining scenes between Jackie and Jane would come through without any suggestion of sex perversion, but merely indicating a very strong friendship between the two girls. Deleted footage included Jackie's glowering reaction to Jane's visit from her father, Henreid and a social worker discussing Jackie's behavior, and an especially big gouge at the end to eliminate "Jackie's very questionable reaction to being parted from Jane." In spite of the cuts, the bonding was sufficiently strong for the pair's butch-fem closeness to remain evident. So was Anne Jackson's acting skill; looking absurdly young, she managed to make Jackie as appealing and sympathetic as she was tough. *Caged* had gotten a free ride, *So Young, So Bad* had not, and in both cases, even with censorship, the public would see at least some aspects of an honest woman-woman relationship. The cultists who had flocked to *The Uninvited* here had something more forceful to see. In some ways, it was also more positive.

Aside from the ghettos of women's prisons, 1950 was an eventful time for women on film to love their own sex. Another film shot in that busy summer of 1949 was Warners' *Young Man with a Horn*, with Kirk Douglas as a Bix Beiderbecke-type bent on self-destruction. Along with nonstop drinking, his most counterproductive act is a dead-end marriage to a lacerating sophisticate, played to the manner born by Lauren Bacall. With dour poise, Bacall glowers at Douglas, spouts reams of fatalistic self-loathing dialogue, smashes her husband's prized record collection, and leaves him for another woman. "I met a girl the other day, an artist. Maybe we'll go to Paris together." Soon enough, we see Bacall with her new friend, Miss Carson (Katherine Kurasch), who lights up when she discusses her sketches with Bacall and becomes immediately nervous when she sees Douglas. Not surprisingly, such behavior must be editorialized, with Douglas informing Bacall that she's "a sick girl." Yes, she is . . . and would be so regardless of her sexuality. What is most germane is how obvious this affair is, and how blithely it was passed over by the Production Code folk and the state censorship boards. There had been considerable censorial concern about excessive drinking—and not one word about Amy. Her sexuality is subtle, yes, but to the adult audiences for whom this film was geared it was readily evident. Critics spoke of the Bacall character in suitably ambiguous terms: "confused [and] mentally sick," "a neurotic socialite who marries him as something of an experiment," "even more confused about life than he is." Overall, *Young Man with a Horn* was judged a disappointment, but for its compromises and hedges it still has some impact, not least as a small step forward in gay visibility.

The precincts of film noir were still very much open in the fifties, with forties expressionism gradually giving way, as the new decade moved on, to a pessimism notably and laudably out of sync with the purported national mood. *Johnny One-Eye* (shot 1949, released 1950) was an independently produced and uneasily effected combination of film noir and Damon Runyon schmaltz. The sentimentality was supplied by a little girl and by the title character, a dog; in a less warm-fuzzy vein were the portrayals of a stool pigeon and his lover. Ambrose (Lawrence Cregar) wears nifty clothes and comports himself in the best unctuous-Webb fashion; Freddy (Harry Bronson), works in the district attorney's office and presumably supplies his partner with some profit-making pillow talk. The two men were shown conversing in so intimate a fashion that their relationship was plainly obvious, and Joe Breen tried to have the scene deleted. Nothing doing—the sequence remained, culminating in an ugly outburst in which Pat O'Brien, the film's hero, goads Freddy into shooting Ambrose.

In noir and out of it director Nicholas Ray was especially absorbed with depicting offbeat relationships, and occasionally with portrayals of tough, tough women and ambiguously sensitive men. If they were not necessarily gay prototypes, they certainly were characters who sent messages. Ray's *In a Lonely Place* (1950) was pessimism printed on film, with Humphrey Bogart dangerous and disenchanted as a neurotic screenwriter involved with murder and with Gloria Grahame. Apart from its forward sex-may-equal death portrait of the Bogart-Grahame affair, *In a Lonely Place* placed a large and strong woman in the mix of Ray's Hollywood. This is the character discussed enigmatically in *The Celluloid Closet*: "Everyone except the screenwriter remembers a lesbian masseuse. Perhaps there should have been a lesbian masseuse." Guess again. Whether or not the script designated one, Ray certainly placed one in a scene, a hushed-voice blonde named Martha (Ruth Gillette). "Come on, angel, relax," she murmurs to the naked Grahame in insinuating tones. Calling herself Grahame's only friend, Martha dispenses advice with the rubdowns, asserting that Bogart is trouble. As with *Rope*, as with *Romance on the High Seas* and even *The Reluctant Dragon*, the gayness lies less in what is in the script than in the staging and acting. By directing Ruth Gillette to speak her lines with such purring intimacy, by lining up the shots to stress the woman-on-woman physicality, Nicholas Ray was clearly choosing to stress the sexual resonance. He did so again two years later, in the *The Lusty Men*, which featured a supporting character who was heterosexual on paper and less so on film. As a sinewy rodeo rider, Maria Hart talks about her affair with Robert Mitchum, but seems more than solicitous to rodeo wife Susan Hayward.[3] In Ray's most legendary minefield of political and sexual subtext, *Johnny Guitar* (1954), the toughness of women is ratcheted up several notches as Joan Crawford and Mercedes McCambridge duke it out while the men are reduced to being milksops and boytoys. Crawford, perhaps in an unwitting attempt at Method acting, nursed a hatred of McCambridge offscreen as well, and the butch versus butch sight of these two going at each other is enough to make the celluloid melt.

Half a century and more after she connived her way into our hearts and minds, do we really know all about Eve? It might seem so; the film is far from a lost or undiscovered gem. Reams and books have been written about *All about Eve*; it has been repeatedly stolen from—most notoriously in *Showgirls*—and it maintains a status as, essentially, a gay holy relic. Is there anything more to tell about the film and its title character? Factually, perhaps not; nevertheless, this prime work of American art (perhaps the faintly derogatory qualifier "popular"

---

[3]Hart normally appeared in westerns, to equally leathery effect. In *The Fighting Stallion* (1950) she portrayed a character known only as Dude, and in the gender-bending *Outlaw Women* (1951) she was the meanest of a protofeminist band terrorizing a western town.

can be grounded for the moment) is constantly opening itself up, much in the manner of that artichoke Bette Davis mentions so memorably at one point. As with *Citizen Kane*, the passing years and steady dumbing-down of pop film only make it seem more alert and intelligent and clever. More golden, in fact. Yet it has acquired, inextricably, the damning praise of that C word, as witness one writer's mixed-signal comment from some years back. "It is certainly a masterpiece of a kind. . . . But it is also the campiest major production Hollywood ever produced."

Some kinds of brilliance, apparently, need qualification. A movie that creates a self-contained theatrical universe, that regales the listener with dialogue beyond cleverness, that matches its words to some of the sharpest acting ever imaged on film—all things labeled "camp" should attain such dignity. For some, that bothersome word would be applicable if only for the presence, and at full strength, of Bette Davis. Yet if *camp* in one of its most powerful senses refers to the unwittingly amusing divergence between intent and result, *All About Eve* immediately disqualifies. Perhaps, however, if we substitute the word *gay* for *campy*, *Eve*'s appeal becomes more explicable. Like *The Women* or *Our Betters* or *Auntie Mame*, its screenplay could easily be reconfigured with an entirely male cast.[4] And, for a 1950 movie, it projects a notably gay-friendly environment, recalling the early-thirties musicals and comedies that laid out a theatrical world inherently hospitable to gay men and women. There's even a gay throwaway line in an early scene. When Bette Davis/Margo finds that her lover and director Bill is rattling on about his upcoming Hollywood job under Darryl F. Zanuck, she mock-lashes out at him: "Zanuck, Zanuck, Zanuck—what are you two, lovers?" "Only in some ways" is the calm reply, and nary a murmur was heard from the Breen Office. In this case, it helped that Zanuck ran one of the town's more notorious heterosexual casting couches.

Unlike *The Women* and the others, *All About Eve* emanated entirely from a heterosexual sensibility, that of its writer and director and auteur. Joseph L. Mankiewicz's understanding of matters female had been burnished by extremely close contact with some of the world's most flamboyant and high-profile women. "I don't know of any woman at all who wasn't in love with him," Joan Crawford would remember. She was in good company: both Judy Garland and Linda Darnell regarded him, ever after, as their greatest love, and in addition to Crawford there were such as Loretta Young and Gene Tierney. Part of his magnetism, evidently, was a comprehension of women's minds that verged

---

[4]Marilyn Monroe's Miss Caswell, for example, is most certainly conceivable as a flavor-du-jour hunk with dreamy abs and constricted mental skills. Surely Betty Comden and Adolph Green understood this interchangeability when, in transforming *All About Eve* into the Broadway musical *Applause*, they turned Thelma Ritter's maid-companion into a gay man.

on the empathic, and indeed his work on *Eve* shows an acute mindfulness of that tense plane on which ego, glamour, and neediness intersect.

Yet if Mankiewicz understood straight women because they loved him, and straight men because he was one, what of his comprehension of lesbians and gay men? Yes, they are present in *All About Eve*, and in somewhat tortured incarnations. The archest of arch columnists Addison DeWitt is the ultimate Clifton Webb character, and indeed Webb was one of the actors considered for the role before it went to Dorian Gray's mentor, George Sanders. DeWitt is spoken of as though he were a gay man—"that venomous fishwife"—and expresses himself in the hyperliterate fashion of a Wildean aesthete. But his gayness is more a matter of subtext and conjecture, in part a product of the film's implicitly gay-insider atmosphere. He is, in fact, a magnet for ambitious women, as Mankiewicz was, and the writer-director admitted later that there was a lot of Mankiewicz in DeWitt. Addison's self-loathing—he speaks of his "inability to love and be loved"—fits the 1950s psychiatric definition of the purported illness of homosexuality, and indeed Mankiewicz was a true believer in psychoanalysis. Certainly in Addison's liaison with Eve there is nothing of love or even lust, nothing except a certain kind of "killer to killer" fascination. It is assuredly, as Addison notes, an affair predicated on "the height of improbability." He is, then, somewhat of an uptown brother to that rodeo princess in *The Lusty Men*, with words and actions that indicate one thing, and an affect that indicates something else entirely.

Eve Harrington's duplicity is more intentional, for surely she is the greatest insincere character in all of film. While Addison exposes her lies and some of her past, her sexuality remains unmentioned, if not undepicted. Eve is gay, and not only as a matter of hindsight conjecture. Mankiewicz knew it, Anne Baxter knew it, and it informed their collaboration.[5] In the subtle you'll-know-if-it's-there fashion of *Rope*, there are indications in Eve's somewhat androgynous look and dress and her loving solicitousness to Margo. There was also a nervy line in an early script, later deleted, when Addison commented on Eve's lack of opening-night jitters: "Eisenhower isn't half the man you are." Eve's carefully manufactured persona outs her as well, for it functions precisely as a closet; the only time she is ever seen out of that closet and away from the people she is duping, she is with women companions. In the movie's nastiest scene, she smiles—frighteningly—as she puts her arm around the boardinghouse girlfriend she's enlisted to lie for her. Then, in the final scene, she accepts the attention of a

---

[5]Mankiewicz was always reticent about talking of Eve's sexuality. As with the film itself, one has to look for hints and clues here and there. But in 1986, when he spoke at Anne Baxter's memorial service, he talked, in careful tones, about how he explained that part of Eve's nature to Baxter and how she grasped it completely.

young admirer with Eve-like designs on her who intends to sleep over. Like Lauren Bacall's Amy in *Young Man with a Horn*, her lesbianism is superficially irrelevant to her cruelties, for she's not a rat and a user simply because she enjoys sex with women. Ultimately, though, it feels calculated to give her a negative cast, her sexual being as an integral part of her poisonous nature. Just as Tennessee Williams wrote of men whose gayness leads them to destroy themselves, Eve's lesbianism is part of her dishonesty. When she tries to seduce men to get ahead, she's being as deceptive as when she spins her lies about her poignant past. Perhaps Mankiewicz's Freudian inclinations tripped him up, although this part of Eve is one of her more intriguing secrets. In 1950 it was laid bare only to sophisticated viewers, and seemed more palatable than it does today. *All About Eve* is eternal, but perceptions change.

The Tennessee Williams variety of gay torment was in fact causing a sizable amount of trouble at the same time *Eve* was being shot and edited. *A Streetcar Named Desire* had been an immediate sensation when it opened on Broadway late in 1947, but unlike most such hot properties it was not immediately snapped up by the movies. Blanche and Stanley and company were not remotely the types to be smiled upon in such precincts as the Breen Office and the Legion of Decency. In fact, the play's very title became so synonymous with steam that, shades of *These Three*, Joe Breen expressed doubt that it could be used.[6] It was well known in the industry that the MPAA would be watching this one closely, and so there were few inquiries about the film rights. In 1949, when director William Wyler expressed interest in filming it (reportedly with Bette Davis), Breen and his cohorts laid out the three fundamental problems, all of them considered integral to the play and unacceptable under the Code:

1. Blanche's prostitution.
2. Blanche's rape by Stanley.
3. Blanche's recollection of her husband's suicide after she finds him with another man.

With the major studios unwilling to work through such restrictions, the challenge was assumed by independent producer Charles K. Feldman. He arranged to distribute *Streetcar* through Warner Bros. and in early 1950 began the thankless task of ironing out the censorship problems. Under Feldman and

---

[6]Williams's later troubles with the Code over *Baby Doll* and *Suddenly, Last Summer* only intensified his eternal reputation in the American heartland as the Country's Dirtiest Playwright. In the late 1960s, when the meek 1950 film of *The Glass Menagerie* was scheduled to run on television for the first time, at least one mother told an adolescent son, "No child of mine is going to be watching something by Tennessee Williams!"

director Elia Kazan, a somewhat unwilling Tennessee Williams labored to produce an acceptable screenplay. The husband's sexuality was the first of the elements to get worked out after Breen repeatedly insisted to Feldman and Jack L.
Warner upon changes "*affirmatively* establishing that the boy's problem is
something *other* than homosexuality." The solution was found in a vague general "weakness" of character, along with possible impotence. When Breen
expressed concern that some of the original flavor might be sneaked back in,
Kazan mollified him with a toadying letter:

> I wouldn't put the homosexuality back in the picture, if the Code had been revised
> last night and it was now permissible. I don't want it. I prefer the delicately sug-
> gested impotence theme; I prefer debility and weakness over any kind of sugges-
> tion of perversion. [However,] I never hope to get any shock in the movie compara-
> ble to her walking into a room and finding her husband with another man.

As it appears in the finished film, Blanche's speech about her husband's suicide
seems less veiled than it does oddly truncated. Just as Blanche sets up her
cheap lampshades to avoid the harsh glare of reality, so is the existence of her
husband made to seem incomplete to those not familiar with the play. It seems
clear that the scene was offered up as a sacrifice so that Stanley would still be
permitted to get away with raping Blanche. This latter plot point had prompted
a testy letter from Tennessee Williams to Joe Breen: "We will use every legiti-
mate means that any of us has at his or her disposal to protect the things in this
film which we think cannot be sacrificed." Even those things ran into trouble
eventually, for after *Streetcar* received its MPAA seal of approval the Legion
of Decency threatened it with a Condemned rating. As was common, when the
Legion threatened, the Code complied, and several cuts were made. These were
reinstated over forty years later, but there could be no salvaging Blanche's sad,
mysterious husband.

The attention being given to *Streetcar* was possibly a boon to Alfred
Hitchcock, who was also at Warners at that time working on his best film in
some years. With its rigorously worked-out concept of parallel lives and the
transference of guilt, *Strangers on a Train* could have been one of Hitchcock's
less involving works, a schematic exercise on the order of *Rope*. That it is,
instead, riveting and nastily funny is a tribute to Hitchcock's skill and his
inspired collaboration with Robert Walker, unforgettably cast as the charming
wastrel Bruno Antony. Witty, natty, and bright, Bruno could almost be a gay role
model for the early fifties. He's not a stereotype, certainly, and he's more clever,
funny, and likable than anyone else in the movie. Unfortunately, he's also a psy-
chopathic killer. "Dear, degenerate Bruno," Pauline Kael once called him, and
as directed by Hitchcock, Walker had the role of a lifetime. A short lifetime,

alas: he died (mainly of alcoholism) just a few months after *Strangers* was released. The dissipation that makes Walker look notably older than his thirty-two years is, in fact, integral to his performance—he's no longer the nice soldier-boy-next-door of such films as *Since You Went Away* and *The Clock*. The air of genial debauchery is authentic, as it was in the later performances of Errol Flynn, and Hitchcock was clearly spellbound by both the role and the actor. Bruno chats up tennis star Guy Haines (Farley Granger) after they meet in a time-honored gay fashion: Guy sits down in a smoking car and as he crosses his legs he accidentally bumps into Bruno. Bruno, with his easy charm and slight lisp, all but seduces Guy into talking about his life, and wangles the loose assurance that they can "swap" the murders of Guy's unfaithful wife and Bruno's monolithic father. Granger doesn't take it seriously, and of course Walker does.

One of the subversive delights of *Strangers on a Train* is that Hitchcock clearly prefers the bad guys to the heroes. Farley Granger and Ruth Roman (as his chilly fiancée) are forced to fend for themselves, while the director makes Walker and his murder victim Laura Elliott (as the nasty wife) so riveting that we almost root for them. As a sort of more-butch Rex O'Malley type, Walker even maintains his appeal when he tells Guy, post-murder, that "I've had a *strenuous* evening!" His charisma functions as his closet, hiding less his sexuality than his insanity. It's been said that making Bruno gay was Walker's idea, yet it seems sufficiently implicit in the screenplay as well as in Patricia Highsmith's original novel. Bruno dotes on his deranged mom (Marion Lorne, doing an Aunt Clara years before *Bewitched*), hates his father and, in an intimate tone of voice tells Guy (Granger) such gay-code things as "We do talk the same language, don't we?" *Strangers* is as gleefully insidious about Bruno's homosexuality as Bruno himself is about, well, everything. In *Rope*, Hitchcock and his actors had trod a narrow line to avoid the censure of Breen and the Catholic Church, but here the implications were made more deftly and with the protective coloration of a strong plot. The MPAA was concerned about the murder scene and the wife's pregnancy and even expressed some concern that Bruno's relationship with his mother might seem incestuous; but his sexuality was never mentioned . . . at least until the reviews came out. "Similar to *Rope* in its pathology," was one critic's euphemistic assessment, and Manny Farber, writing in *The Nation*, used some homophobic insinuations to criticize Hitchcock's methodology at the same time that he praised Walker:

> Because chases and homicides and Pearl White escapes clutter his pictures, no one notices the general emasculation Hitchcock has perpetrated on the thriller. Brittle soft-cheeked, petulant pretty boys ([such as Farley] Granger) are projected into high melodrama. These characters seem to disappear like clothes dummies

within their tweedy carefully unpressed Brooks Brothers jackets and slacks. . . . The movie by the way is built around the travestied homosexuality of the murderer. Robert Walker provides the role with a meatier, more introverted, unhealthier savor than the stars usually give a Hollywood production.

The implications were even clearer outside the United States. In overseas prints of *Strangers on a Train* Hitchcock allowed Bruno about a minute more to intimate himself with Guy. The major difference lay in the deletion, in the American cut, of Bruno offhandedly discussing Guy's wife's promiscuity. Also, a scene of him ordering dinner on the train and inviting Guy to join him seems just a shade, almost subliminally, more seductive. The deletion of these moments don't make that much difference in the final analysis, though it's good that home video has made them available. What matters the most, besides a corking suspense movie, is that an actor and director collaborated to create a compellingly rounded prime early-fifties portrait of a fascinating gay man. The portrait was, ultimately, a negative one, given Bruno's murderous bent, but in light of how most gays were portrayed on film some twenty years later it seems less objectionable.[7]

Out in the "real" world of early the 1950s, there had begun the first stirrings of the Mattachine Society and the Daughters of Bilitis, as well as the McCarthy purges of gays in government offices. The film industry was rooted in a different kind of reality, for (*A Streetcar Named Desire* excepted) the main censorship battles of the early 1950s had little concern with homosexuality. It was an odd collection of movies causing all the trouble: Otto Preminger's wispy sex comedy *The Moon Is Blue*, with its timid innuendo and talk of professional virginity; the Italian *The Miracle*, which the Legion of Decency felt to be sacrilegious as well as carnal; and the Jane Russell musical *The French Line*, in which producer Howard Hughes's fetish for large breasts was enhanced by 3-D photography.[8] In contrast to these were the subtle or sneaky insertions of gayness into a few Hollywood movies. The 1952 filming of Carson McCuller's novel and play *The Member of the Wedding* was gay without being specifically so. Its yearning tomboy (Julie Harris) and happy sissy-boy (Brandon de Wilde)

---

[7]Immediately after *Strangers on a Train*, Walker played the title role in Leo McCarey's ghastly Red Scare melodrama *My Son John*. He brought a good deal of his gay-Bruno baggage with him, and so John's communism was, clearly enough, not his only "subversive" trait. Walker died while *John* was still in production, and pieces of his *Strangers* death scene were inserted to give the McCarey film something of a conclusion.

[8]*The French Line* did raise some concern at the MPAA over a subsidiary male character—the film was set in a never-never land of haute-couture—being too pansyish. The character was rewritten; Hughes had another battlefield (all right, two of them) upon which he preferred to fight.

spurred likely oceans of identification from audience members who in an anonymous era were engaged, like Harris's Frankie, in the search for "the we of me." Less poignantly, the plight of one unseen little boy, Freddie Gubenheffer, was an isolated spikey moment in the humdrum 1952 comedy *Love Is Better than Ever*, which featured Elizabeth Taylor as a small-town dance teacher in pursuit of Broadway wolf Larry Parks. (Latter-day snips have been known to dub it *Liz Is Bigger than Ever.*) When Taylor's behavior (in the film) causes tongues to wag, the parents of her students forge excuses to take their kids out of her school. For Freddie, the reason is one of the prototypical fears of parents whose boys want to dance (cf. *Billy Elliott*). But it's a sham, as Liz learns from a helpful snitch: "Freddie Gubenheffer isn't becoming too effeminate. He's taking ballet!"

Poor, or lucky, Freddie. As susceptible as he may have been to the corrupting influence of dance, he likely would have been equally scathed had he gone, one year later, to see one of the most insidiously oddball of all fifties films. Some films have cultishness thrust upon them, but the musical fantasy *The 5,000 Fingers of Dr. T.* is an automatic candidate. Dr. Seuss wrote the screenplay for this tale of a little boy who imagines his hated piano teacher, Dr. Terwilliker, as an evil genius who forces 500 captive boys to play on the world's largest piano.[9] Terwilliker's castle is naturally laden with Seussian creatures and touches, which when writ on a large Technicolor canvas move from the eccentric to the bizarrely Freudian. Produced by Stanley Kramer for Columbia, *Dr. T.* was made with a combination of factors guaranteed to spell failure: a sizable budget, no major stars, wildly off-center subject matter, and comparatively little capitulation to conventional cinema. "[Its] box-office chances [are] as unpredictable as its wild expressions of fantasy," *Variety* said, but its huge flop was really no surprise. Seuss was not yet the Green Eggs–Cat in the Hat icon he would be presently, and even after five decades *Dr. T.* seems pretty out there in some ways, far darker and more adventurous than the gimmicky live-action film of *The Grinch*. Not the least of *Dr. T.*'s outré charms are to be found in some singularly gay moments—which, as placed in essentially an escapist film for young boys, make the whole enterprise even more subversive. One is a strange all-male ballet involving green torsos and musical instruments, choreographed by Eugene Loring upon that odd stage that intersects baroque and beefcake. Then there is Dr. Terwilliker, played by Hans Conreid as a cross between the Grinch and

---

[9]While Seuss shared script credit with Allan Scott, most of the work is clearly his—no one else ever came up with such ideas. In his real-life identity as Ted Geisel, he had had a curious brush with Hollywood some years earlier: in 1947 he had done a screenplay treatment, for Warner Bros., of the nonfiction study *Rebel without a Cause*. By the time *Rebel* reached the screen eight years later, no trace survived of either the original book or Dr. Seuss's adaptation.

It doesn't take 5,000 fingers to fasten a garter, but Dr. T. (Hans Conreid) prepares for his day of triumph with the help of some attentive retainers. *Photofest*

Mommie Dearest—high-strung, fey, egocentric, and malevolent. Terwilliker speaks nonsensically evil commands with Shakespearean precision, and his most gleeful moment comes in his salute to the dawn of the great day when 500 little prisoners will play his concerto. In the most peculiar of the movie's Seuss-penned songs (music by Frederick Hollander), Dr. T. commands his minions to outfit him for the grand occasion. "Come on and dress me, dress me, dress me," he chimes, and goes through a staggeringly Seussian absurdist/queer list of outfits and accessories: undulating undies with marabou frills, purple nylon girdle with orange blossom buds, peekaboo blouse lined with Chesapeake mouse, cutie booties with leopard skin bows, pink brocaded bodice with fluffy ruffs, organdy snood, chiffon Mother Hubbard lined with Hudson Bay rat. The damned song is about drag, it's *in* drag, really, and Seuss underscores the point by a prominent mention of "lavender spats." For its climactic peroration, Seuss replaced his original lyric "So come and dress me in the blossoms of a hundred million trees" with the more pointed "blossoms of a million pink trees." As Terwilliker finishes the song, his retainers make like handmaidens in a DeMille movie, strewing the outlandishly dressed Conreid (sans snood) with those same pink buds. Seldom is

JACK COLE

Real name: John Ewing Richter. Born New Brunswick, N.J., April 27, 1911; died Hollywood, Calif., February 17, 1974

"Very important movie stars, they adored me and trusted me and I became the brother/mother, trying to make them look good without much talent."

Cole was fierce—in his talent, in his physical and emotional demands on coworkers, in his sexuality. He was almost a caricature of a driven, temperamental choreographer, one less affable than Randy, the dance director he played in Vincente Minnelli's *Designing Woman* (1957). Jazz dance, that crucial intersection of modern and theatrical choreography, exists because of Cole, though because he never had one defining hit show (*Kismet* came closest), he still awaits posterity's deserved salute. His work on such films as *Down to Earth* (1947) and *The Merry Widow* (1952) shows a flair and concentration rare in musicals at that time; he had complete control over the design and photography of most of his sequences and devised little recurring signature motifs. He himself was very aware of his special gift for making nondancers (Monroe, Russell, Dietrich) look good, and decent dancers (Hayworth and Grable) look more special. (*Gilda*'s "Put the Blame on Mame" was his.) He also had an unfailing knack for highlighting the homoerotic aspects of his steamy aesthetic: Cole's appreciation of the male form shows in much of his work. (At a 1994 Cole retrospective, Jane Russell chuckled as she recalled his fondness for male pornography.) Few other dance directors used as many underdressed men as Cole did—his bent toward tropical or Caribbean themes ensured that this occurred often. To grasp Cole's ethos, contrast the musclemen in *Gentlemen Prefer Blondes* with a similar number, the Gene Kelly–Stanley Donen "Baby, You Knock Me Out" sequence in *It's Always Fair Weather* (1955). With Kelly and Donen, the athletes noncommittally celebrate Cyd Charisse. With Cole, they nonchalantly ignore Jane Russell and celebrate each other. Unlike his equally hard-edged contemporaries Jerome Robbins and Bob Fosse, he has not been given a "Here's Cole" Broadway compendium. But watch musicals like *Meet Me after the Show* and *Golden Girl*—films of devastating mediocrity until the music starts and the dancers appear. Intricately engineered movement, offhanded genius, and moments of ripe gay sensuality: that's Cole.

that fey delicate pivot between whimsy and camp trod upon with more galumphing giddiness. Dr. T. is a Bruno Antony for Saturday matinees, scaring and maybe delighting all those little Freddies with excess on all fronts.

The year 1953 was special for music-minded gayness. In recent years, the Doris Day musical *Calamity Jane* has become a proud dyke icon: Day's rugged sunniness and bonding with pal/rival Allyn McLerie seem in retrospect joy-ously celebratory. The women are what propel *Calamity Jane*'s plot; the men stand by and react and serve as objects. They also wear drag: a plot device com-pels Howard Keel to dress as a Native American mother (with baby), and song-and-dance man Dick Wessel to go way over the top when he shimmies in span-gles to a song called "I've Got a Hive Full of Honey." ("He can be timid and shy, but for obvious reasons should not be excessively effeminate," Joe Breen coun-seled Jack L. Warner.) The constant subversion of standard roles and the cross-dressing, plus the hit song "Secret Love," make *Calamity Jane* a virtual theme park of secret things made manifest. In 1953 there was naturally far less con-sciousness of the implications, except, possibly, in the Warner Bros. publicity department. Some of the print ads for *Jane* were available in two different ver-sions: one featured a figure of Doris Day dressed as in the movie, in buckskin pants; another had an identical likeness, but dressed in short shorts that aren't in the film but may have been more comforting to certain viewers.[10]

Gentlemen Prefer Blondes, also from 1953, has become legendary for more reasons than anyone can count: Marilyn Monroe's defining moment, Jane Russell's finest hour, "Diamonds Are a Girl's Best Friend" as launchpad of Marilyn-to-Madonna culture-camp. Its director, Howard Hawks, was responsi-ble, consciously so, for the homoerotic overtones in a number of his most cele-brated films. Besides Bogart's gay masquerade in *The Big Sleep*, and Cary Grant's all-of-a-sudden gayness in *Bringing Up Baby*, such films as *Ceiling Zero, Only Angels Have Wings, Red River*, and *The Big Sky* all have elements of male bonding that seem to approach and sometimes cross the line into gay-related intent. The inveterately hetero Hawks gleefully embraced the notion of "a love story between two men," with the wide spectrum of connotation so implied, and enjoyed mentioning it when discussing his films.[11] Yet the most extreme homoeroticism in any of his films was not of his doing. It occurred in *Gentleman Prefer Blondes*, not within the extra-close friendship of Russell and Monroe, but in a nearly extraneous production number with Russell and a troupe of Olympic athletes to whom she pleads, "Ain't There Anyone Here for Love?" The whole point of it is that the exercise-minded athletes are completely

---

[10]*Calamity Jane* has always seemed one of Day's defining roles, one she takes to with more vigor and ease than in her later coy-kitty sex comedies. It's inevitable, then, that the exhaustively myopic Bosley Crowther offered, in his *Times* review, the opinion that she was "a bit terrify-ing . . . tomboyishness is not the lady's forte."

[11]Nor was Hawks alone in celebrating the thin line between bonding and romance. Another tough director, Henry Hathaway, effected something similar in *Lives of a Bengal Lancer* (1935) and proudly talked about it many years later: "That was the first time we had a love story between two men instead of a man and a woman. Because there is no woman in that picture." (There *was* a woman, but Gary Cooper and Richard Cromwell did seem more interested in each other.)

oblivious to Russell and far more interested in each other's company. Moreover, in their skin-colored trunks, the muscled hunks look naked, and in one extraordinary moment they seem to moon Russell while she waves tennis rackets at them. The number was the work of the audacious choreographer Jack Cole, who with his assistant Gwen Verdon worked independently from Hawks. The Breen-related paranoia that lay heavily over the set of *Gentlemen Prefer Blondes* did not concern itself with Cole's muscle boys. Every costume worn by Monroe and Russell was inspected for the minutest hint of bounce or cleavage, and the initial concept and costume for "Diamonds Are a Girl's Best Friend" were scrapped over worries about what Monroe would wear and how she would move.[12] With such distractions afoot, "Ain't There Anyone Here for Love?" was given a pass; watchdogs in the United Kingdom saw and felt differently and took the number out of all the prints exhibited there. How ironic, in this definitive Technicolor celebration of 1950s sensuality, that the most explicitly sexual moment is not only gay but, thanks to Cole, extremely gay.

A few other musicals of the time also rate mention. Vincente Minnelli's *An American in Paris* (1951) is less overwhelmingly gay in conception than his forties work—it lacks the swanked-up overdrive of *Yolanda and the Thief;* nor does Gene Kelly get all hot and sexy the way he did for Minnelli in *The Pirate* (save for that one moment in the ballet when he impersonates the Toulouse-Lautrec jockey: one of the great butt-watching moments in American cinema). Nevertheless, for quick eyes there's a revealing moment. At the Artists' Ball just prior to the ballet, Minnelli and his designers engineered an all-black-and-white effect as a palate-cleanser before the immense color splash to follow. He shot far more footage of the ball than he used, and as a result it seems hectically haphazard, lacking the cannibalistic sophistication of the party sequences that run as a motif through his films. The ball ran into trouble in Spain, Indonesia, and Ireland, where censors deleted a shot of a woman making a drunken leap off a balcony into strong arms below. What the censors (and Breen) missed was a quick shot of a pair of revelers: a hunky, bare-chested guy in a tutu strolls through the crowd hand in hand with an equally hot boyfriend. The following year, *Singin' in the Rain* ran afoul of Breen for one innocuous innuendo: Donald O'Connor demonstrates voice-dubbing to Gene Kelly by moving his lips to Debbie Reynold's voice. Kelly responded, "What are you doing later?" At least

---

[12]Several other numbers were filmed and then cut, less for content than for dead weight. The most enticing deletion was "Down Boy," a duet for MM and that chubby old horned-toad Charles Coburn. Although Monroe was not present in the too-gay Jane Russell number, she did have a close encounter with onscreen gayness two years later in the archetypal fifties sex comedy *The Seven Year Itch.* Mentioned, but never seen, is a gay couple living in the same brownstone as MM and Tom Ewell. The tip-off: they're interior decorators.

he did until the line was ordered dropped from the script. There were no gay innuendoes cut from the script of George Cukor's *A Star Is Born,* and the most overt content was a brief appearance by Cukor's friend Grady Sutton as a gossip columnist. But, once again, Cukor produced a film that seems gay not in its characters but in its attitudes, technique, design, and in Judy Garland's emergence as the most high-voltage of gay icons. When Esther (Garland) is preparing nervously for her screen test, her mentor (James Mason) soothes her by telling her to ignore the camera and crew, to just focus on singing as if she were doing one of her standard numbers at an after-hours club. "It's the Downbeat Club at three o'clock in the morning, and you're singing for yourself and for the boys in the band." From Moss Hart's pen, through James Mason's mouth, to Mart Crowley's ear: just sometimes, there are tiny moments in history, bridges from past to future, when we can see torches being passed.

As "respectable" cinema groped uncertainly through the early fifties with the concept of more adult content, the exploitation people plied their own trade with scuzzy diligence. One hallmark of this part of the business was the idea of release-in-perpetuity: "adult" films could be run and rerun indefinitely, sometimes under changing titles and with footage added or removed. This was as porno as most people could get: going anonymously into pesthole theaters in big cities for some dingy moments of lust and a hint of skin. That egregious gay pioneer *Children of Loneliness* was part of this hallowed tradition too, and it was in the early 1950s that it made its last recorded stand: a few big-city engagements, including one in the Times Square area, before it vanished into stag-film oblivion. The new face of exploitation filmmaking in the early 1950s belonged to Ed Wood (Edward D. Wood, Jr., as billed), who in his first creative paroxysm managed to touch on gay themes with the same skill and taste he brought to all areas of his work. *Glen or Glenda* (1953; a.k.a. *I Changed My Sex,* a.k.a. *I Led Two Lives*) really does deserve any reputation accruing to it: as heartfelt plea for the transvestite community, as intrepid pioneer for concerns of the transgendered and angora fetishists, and, truly, as one of the funniest and worst movies ever made.[13] At no time before or since has there been quite so arresting a marriage of sincere intent (one of many things that Tim Burton's *Ed Wood* movie got right) with colossal . . . well, *incompetence* is a nice word for it. Buried within this trove of demented cinema, jangled psychology, bad drag, and Bela Lugosi pronouncements is an interesting take on fifties gay courtship. To demonstrate

---

[13]Well, watchable worst movies, anyway, as opposed to the likes of *Myra Breckinridge. Glen or Glenda* repays its viewers with endless good cheer; *Myra* gives them yawns and really, really bad headaches.

In addition to at least four alternate titles (common currency among exploitation fare), *Glen or Glenda* was sometimes billed punctuated by a question mark. If ever a movie deserved one, here it is.

how transvestites are assuredly not homosexual, Wood gives us two short vignettes set on what is presumably a street corner—which in this auteur's expressionistic economy is a plain black background. There a willowy young man stands, wearing the coded outfit for bohemians: a turtleneck. A somewhat older man approaches him, chats him up and takes out a cigarette to get a light.[14] As Turtleneck strikes the match, the older man touches his hand caressingly and gets an immediate rebuff, although not a punch or a putdown. Turtleneck moves on to the next vignette, in which he comes on to the lissome Glen/Glenda him/herself, played pseudonymously by Ed Wood. That Wood does not an attractive woman make is one of the key fascinations of this movie, of course, and it is unstated whether the character was approached because Turtleneck knew he was a man in drag or if he was blind enough to think this could be a real woman. In 1953 the Hollywood mainstream would never have permitted anything like the cigarette-lighting come-on; it was possible in *Glen or Glenda* because exploitation films operated outside the MPAA (as, years later, porn movies would get automatic X ratings). Even so, the scene was cut in some areas and is missing from some of the copies of this chef d'oeuvre that are available today.

By the decade's midpoint change was manifesting itself in many areas. Race relations, certainly, were entering a different phase, and if the sexual revolution (straight and gay) was not yet completely active, it was effecting an enormous split in society and culture. Youth, sexually driven, was the motivator here, asserting itself for the first time in music, film, and other public forums. The change was almost immediately felt in film: MGM's *The Blackboard Jungle* was a sincere attempt to portray urban deliquency, with "Rock around the Clock" jangling on the soundtrack under the credits. And Warner Bros., after nearly two decades of social irrelevance (*Caged* being a rare exception), was taking the lead in portraying teen disaffection on the screen. Even if it had not starred James Dean, and even if Dean had still been alive at the time of its release, *Rebel without a Cause* would have been a hit, and the conscious definition of its era. The hostility of teens, the estrangement from parents, the need to act out and fight unnamed battles against the older generations, the drag races and violence, the exploding hormones—the timing was too perfect. Dean's own sexuality made his Jim a magnet for young men and women alike, in the film and in the huge fan cult that started before he died, and afterward was fanned with the intense flames of "Live fast, die young." For some young viewers, however, a more intense identification came with Plato, the ill-adjusted teenager

---

[14]We don't hear the conversation; as this is a documentary, we get a greasy narrator (Timothy Farrell) instead. And in this narration is an early use of the word *homosexual*—possibly the first time it was spoken aloud in a commercial American film.

with a palpable crush on Jim—and once again the actor's sexuality filled in the gaps that the script could not make explicit. Sal Mineo's loving gazes at James Dean made his feelings plain, aided by such telling details as the pin-up picture of Alan Ladd in his locker and Plato's ever-absent parents and coddling surrogate mother/housekeeper.[15] The feelings were plain enough in the script that the new voice of the Breen Office, Geoffrey Shurlock, cautioned Warners about it. The strictures of an organization such as the MPAA seem miserably anachronistic juxtaposed with intelligent filmmaking striving for honesty; such was Hollywood in the mid-1950s onward, and such was the Eisenhower age. "It is of course vital that there be no inference of a questionable or homosexual relationship between Plato and Jim," Shurlock cautioned, warning against the use of that oddly double-edged word *punk*. Yet Plato's yearnings were clear enough as portrayed by Mineo: one critic's labeling of Plato as "an eccentric and lonely child" might apply to the actor as well as the role. In a time when the American family was being undermined by unspoken resentments, the surrogate family set up in *Rebel* by Dean, Mineo, and Natalie Wood carried immense resonance beyond the movie's flashier and more immediate attractions.

A more explicit bonding—indeed, a full-fledged male-male marriage—was one of the many fascinations of a 1955 film noir, *The Big Combo*. As with its scabrous contemporaries *The Big Heat* and *Kiss Me Deadly*, a number of years passed before its value became evident: often it takes a half century's perspective to change a throwaway B film into a work claiming great esteem. In this tale of an obsessed cop (Cornel Wilde) who squares off against a vice czar (Richard Conte), violence is the main commodity, despair the leading component. The shadowy suggestions of evil in forties noir are here brought into the light by director Joseph Lewis with unsettling brutality: one scene in particular, in which a hearing aid is used as a torture device, is more disquieting than a thousand explosions or car chases. Conte conducts his icy evil with an air of cool urbanity, leaving the dirty work to his henchmen Fante (Lee Van Cleef) and Mingo (Earl Holliman). For the first half of *The Big Combo*, these two are invariably shown together, carrying out Conte's plots and plans. At about midway, it becomes clear that their personal attachment is not just of a dirty-business nature. They speak familiarly, they touch occasionally, and finally, when Conte calls them late at night to give orders, we see that they live and sleep together. As with any married couple in fifties film or television, they sleep in twin beds, just like Lucy and Ricky Ricardo; the sexual tinge becomes clearer when it's

---

[15]The choice for Plato's movie-star adoration was interesting as well. Evidently Burt Lancaster had been the first choice for screenwriter Stewart Stern, but Warners overruled him in favor of Ladd, then under contract to the studio. Nevertheless, was it mere coincidence that Mineo/Plato would choose the one major male star as short as he himself?

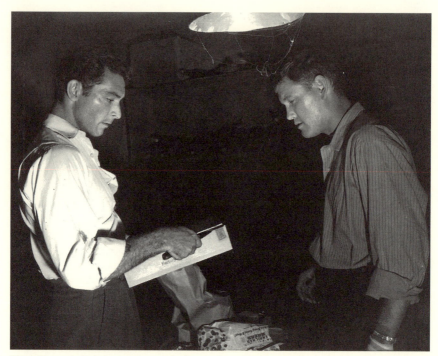

With film noir lighting and a symbolic spider web, boyfriends Lee Van Cleef and Earl Holliman participate in yet another nefarious scheme in *The Big Combo. Photofest*

shown that Van Cleef (the dom to Holliman's sub) sleeps without a shirt. They seem amoral, as opposed to Conte's total evil, and too unsophisticated to have the Nietszchean aspirations of the couple in *Rope*. In some ways the relationship is a more explicit inverse of the bonded couples in Howard Hawks's films, almost a gay Bonnie and Clyde without the folk-hero overlay. "Lee Van Cleef and Earl Holliman [steal] much of the film's footage," one trade critic approved, and their romance comes to a suitably operatic end when Conte double-crosses them with a well-placed bomb. Van Cleef dies immediately, but Holliman survives long enough to have a Pietà moment: "Don't leave me, Fante," he sobs. "I played square with him [Conte], he shouldn't have hurt Fante!" His grief over his lover's corpse enables Wilde to crack the case and break Conte. "Low moral tone" was the assessment of the Legion of Decency, who gave *The Big Combo* a B rating, but this relationship seems less low than most of the evil that surrounds it in this nasty and compulsively watchable movie.

In 1956 much of the news in onscreen morality was being made by *Baby Doll*, Tennessee William's wry look at white-trash heterosexuality and, in retrospect, almost as mild a "shocker" as *The Moon Is Blue*. At about the same time, two vastly dissimilar films, neither of them an apparent flashpoint, charted a conspicuous turning point in the battle to portray homosexuality onscreen. While both were ultimately cop-outs, one looked to the past and another portended the future. *Serenade* was an improbable candidate for any kind of cinematic veneration, yet its genesis had been long and complicated. As a 1937 novel by James M. Cain, it was a deliberate shocker, more so than Cain's more famous books—*The Postman Always Rings Twice*, *Double Indemnity*, *Mildred Pierce*. Rarely, in popular fiction, had gayness and bisexuality been represented so openly as in this garish farrago: the hero, Johnny, is a young opera singer whose career is being sponsored by his conductor-socialite lover, Winston Hawes. When Hawes's high-octane attention becomes too much for him, Johnny loses his voice and flees to Mexico. With a major assist from a fiery prostitute named Juana, he recovers both his voice and his heterosexuality. Back in the States with Juana at his side, he prevails on Winston to stage his smash Carnegie Hall comeback. When the male ex learns about his female successor, he attempts to have her deported. As a further humiliation he invites the pair to a drag party and goads Juana into demonstrating her bullfighting skills for the guests. As she does so she ends Winston's taunting, his conducting career, and his life with a well-aimed sword blow to the crotch. Singer and hooker lam it back to Mexico, where divos and whores can ply their trades without such nasty intrusions and where passionate women such as Juana can die unhappily without pressure from immigration authorities.

A more comprehensive catalogue of Code-unfriendly material can scarcely be imagined. When the book came out, it was somewhat of a joke that this had to be one of the least filmable novels ever written. Yet, with proper laundering, *Double Indemnity* and *Mildred Pierce* and *Postman* all made smash-hit films, and just as Warner Bros. was concluding its production of *Mildred Pierce*, it bought the rights to *Serenade*. Over the next ten years, various Warner screenwriters grappled with this hard-scrabble blend of gay sex, opera, prostitution, Mexican culture, and castration. Always, when treatments were submitted, the MPAA's reply came back the same: "It will have to be affirmatively established that there is no homosexuality," and Cain himself made the suggestion at one point that the character of Winston could be transformed into a woman. The need to produce an acceptable script became more urgent when Warners signed up a bona fide opera-singing movie star, Mario Lanza. As with *The Lost Weekend* and *Crossfire*, the story was ultimately given a massive dose of heteroization, and Winston was ultimately split into two characters: as a love interest, he became Kendall, played by a lacquered Joan Fontaine, and as a professional mentor he was (with some gay undertones) Vincent Price's Charles Winthrop. Juana, meanwhile, was changed into a redemptive madonna (Sarita Montiel) with a bent for bullfighting only—no commercial sex or genital mutilation. For

Serenade's target audience, which consisted entirely of Lanza fans, such alterations were of no import. "The Thrill of His Voice! The Thrill of a Great Story!" the ads blared, accurate by no more than half. With "the homosexual angle" out of the picture, *Variety* noted, all that remained was "a basic love tussle between two girls over a man." Verdi and Puccini emerged the winners, at least for those who could countenance Lanza's pressurized *tenorismo*, and Cain and homosexuality were relegated to the status of supernumeraries.

Milestones, in film, can be extraordinarily deceptive. The major events of history or art generally present themselves in a torrent of importance, their resonance apparent even as their repercussions are still activating. In movies, though, the breakthroughs, the seminal events or big firsts, can be misleading, even egregious. *Lights of New York* is the template here: a 1928 sort-of gangster movie shot on an infinitesimal budget by toilsome menials. And yet it's of vast historical importance as the first all-talking movie; it is the film more responsible (in some ways) than *The Jazz Singer* for bringing home the talkie revolution. Major event. But all the reverberations in the cosmos could not make it a work of any intrinsic worth whatever, of any value beyond its effect. It owes history an apology for causing so much with so little class. There are a few other such cases scattered through film history, unassuming pieces of vast effect and little worth: who would think, today, that tripe like *Bwana Devil* or *The Moon Is Blue* or *I Am Curious (Yellow)* could have produced their various sensations? One of these odd milestones punctuates the thirty-years-plus struggle between filmmakers and moral police to put gay images and characters on film. Earlier, *The Sign of the Cross* was one of the weightiest causes of the newly rigorous Production Code, and after the Code was working its censorious effects, there was an implausibly heated struggle over the gossamer likes of *Turnabout*. Then, from 1953 to 1956, a war of primal impact raged over a hit Broadway play that many said should never be filmed. A boldly pioneering look at gay relationships in a postwar world? Or even a Tennessee Williams–grotesque look at closeted self-loathing? Not a chance. It was a work of unutterable gentility, a self-consciously "daring" piece with all the guts of a panty raid. Its meekly gracious title, seen at the time to belie its hot content, now seems quaintly appropriate. This, then, is *Tea and Sympathy*, on the stage and on the screen.

Robert Anderson's play, when it opened on Broadway in the fall of 1953, was an improbable sensation. At a time when Tennessee Williams and Arthur Miller were creating their best work, *Tea and Sympathy* would appear to neither break dramatic ground nor push moral envelopes to excess. Yet, at the time, it was judged to be a work of perception and skill—a feel-good shocker, even. Deborah Kerr, making her Broadway debut under the direction of Elia Kazan, enhanced the aura of class that Anderson (and audiences) so fervently thought his play evoked. Its plot was in some ways a puny indictment of McCarthyism:

Tom, a misfit teenage boy at a boarding school, is mercilessly taunted by his classmates for being gay, even though he's just "sensitive" and has no gay feelings. The wife of the martinet headmaster (who is himself a likely closet case) sets things aright by taking the kid to bed. As uttered in Deborah Kerr's tremulous cultured tones, Laura's curtain line became an immediate classic: "Years from now," she says, as she unbuttons her blouse, "when you talk about this, and you will, be kind." How inversely fitting, then, that the passage of time has been so unkind to *Tea and Sympathy*. As with so many "daring" works, the whole thing was essentially a sham. If the boy knew he wasn't homosexual, and in fact was relatively secure in that knowledge, what was the point of his seduction? It wasn't even a "rescue" mission from the perils of being a homo, although that was the connotation that accrued to it. It was, in truth, more of a wish fulfillment for non-macho men: a "tribute" paid to sensitive nonconformists by reassuring them that they don't have to be football stars to score big. Ultimately, *Tea and Sympathy* was a glorified medicine show, pandering to upper-middle-class spectators who fancied themselves "permissive" in an Eisenhower age. For a work that purported to be in large part "about" homosexuality, it said nothing insightful (let alone favorable) about the subject. On the contrary, it vied with *The Children's Hour* as a work of negative reinforcement; in this world, fifty years ago, an allegation of gayness really was the worst thing you could say about someone, a notion no less present and no less obnoxious today.

A sexy Broadway hit is its own justification, however, and Kerr's blouse had not been unbuttoned more than a few times when Hollywood began to pounce. All the major studios—MGM, Paramount, Fox, Warners, Columbia, Goldwyn—immediately began investigating its film possibilities. For Joe Breen, fading but still game for a big skirmish, such enquiries were somewhat inspiriting, a way of reasserting his and the Code's hold over the filmmakers. He judged that the play hinged completely on two points inadmissible under the Code, adultery and the inference of homosexuality. Never mind that adultery had been frequently portrayed in film and that actual homosexuality flowed through censors' sieves regularly. This play, like *A Streetcar Named Desire*, would be a test case to show that film would remain cleaner than the stage. And, curiously, the MPAA remained harder-nosed in its insistence than it had on the more blatant and infinitely superior *Streetcar*. Even Elia Kazan played into Breen's hands by avowing that *Tea and Sympathy* should not be made into a film and that he would not try. Robert Anderson, for his part, stated that neither of those two major points could be tampered with or removed. Such conflicting insistences are usually a nightmare to a producer, but MGM chief Dore Schary, a self-styled deliverer of "message" films, decided to take on the cause. He wanted to film *Tea and Sympathy*, and he argued to an unconvinced contingent from the MPAA that the play had nothing to do with being queer, that changing the charges to "cowardice and lack of manliness" would have the same effect. He was in some ways correct, since those things did, in Anderson's murky dramaturgy, connote being gay. But no one wanted to know; to a wide public, *Tea and Sympathy* was a play about being saved from being a fag. Geoffrey Shurlock, whose power in the Breen Office was steadily growing, showed Schary the chapter and verse of the Production Code stating that "the inference of sex perversion" is forbidden. Undeterred, Schary proceeded to pay an enormous $400,000 for the film rights and hired Anderson to produce an adaptation acceptable under the Code.

For Joe Breen, the arguments about *Tea and Sympathy* were part of that same holy crusade he had waged with studios for the previous twenty years. They were also among his final skirmishes before retiring in the fall of 1954. A few months earlier, he had received a special Academy Award for "his conscientious, open-minded and dignified management of the Production Code Administration," and the valedictory tone of that tribute was enhanced by the death of Will Hays that same year. As Breen's successor, Geoffrey Shurlock was capable of much of the open-mindedness the Academy had erroneously attributed to Breen, and he would find Code enforcement in a changing world to be an increasingly tough proposition. For *Tea and Sympathy*, one of his first test cases, Shurlock held firm to the Breen tradition. In a letter to Dore Schary on March 25, 1955, he rejected Anderson's extensively laundered rewrite.

> . . . In spite of the work that has been done, in an effort to remove the Code objections, the present version . . . still appears to be in violation of the Code.
>
> It seems to us that in spite of the writing the problem of the boy is still his fear that he may be a homo-sexual. And the wife's giving herself to him in adultery still appears to us to violate the Code. . . .

For the first time since *Turnabout*, and far more drastically, "the homosexual angle" (so termed by Deborah Kerr) was at the heart of the matter. Unlike *Rope* and *Streetcar* and other films where homosexuality was essentially a subsidiary concern, the gay accusations in *Tea and Sympathy* were as central to the matter as the adultery, perhaps even more so. The equation of "unmanliness" (whatever that may be) with homosexuality was at the heart of Anderson's thesis, setting up new reinforcements of old prejudicial stereotypes. The logical extension of this argument is that if Tom really were gay, he would have earned his classmates' scorn—but he has actually had no such doubts, none of the fear that Shurlock cited. He may have felt less a man than his taunting classmates, so sexually inept that he contemplates suicide, but he knew his own heterosexuality. So pervasive, however, was the mystique of this play that even intelligent observers thought that it was about Tom's gay panic. When Dore Schary tried to

Bless the imaginative artist in MGM's publicity department who took the title *Tea and Sympathy* as literally as possible. Here, then, is a Liptonish rendering of Deborah and John Kerr's big moment. *Photofest*

counter the PCA's arguments by insisting that Tom feared impotence, not queerness, no one was convinced. Thus stymied, MGM resorted to the extreme measure of filing an appeal to the MPAA Board of Directors. The Board, not too surprisingly, ruled in favor of Code-mandated cleanliness.

With the shooting of *Tea and Sympathy* delayed until after Deborah Kerr completed work on *The King and I*, there was ample time to craft a diluted version acceptable to all concerned.[16] The key to dealing with the gay-related issues was the Milquetoast term *sister-boy* which in the completed film is bandied about to exhausting effect. Presumably the word *sister*, as opposed to *sissy*, was of sufficient euphemistic value to split the difference between the quirkily non-macho and the possibly queer. The implications, however pejorative, would still be transmitted between those altered lines to an understanding audience by an empathetic director, Vincente Minnelli—whose Tom-like "sensitive aesthete" image in real life was a façade for someone who really was gay. The issue of adultery fared less well, and so Laura/Kerr, in the tradition of great

---

[16]For Kerr the script changes were a bitter pill, for she considered *Tea and Sympathy* "a play about persecution of the individual, and compassion and pity and love of one human being for another in a crisis." In a letter to the director of the film version of *Tea*, Vincente Minnelli, she fumed about the prudery of the PCA: "Adultery is o.k.—impotence is o.k.—but perversion is their bete noir!"

Production Code sinners, was made to pay for taking her boy to bed. In a few script drafts she was even killed off, but in the end the entire story was set into a flashback frame, in which the grown Tom (now married, naturally) reads a letter in which Laura natters on about "the wrong we did" and how she ruined her husband's life. "There are always consequences," Kerr says in voice-over—a truth more applicable to the Production Code than to *Tea and Sympathy.*

As with *Streetcar* and others, not even the extensive laundering softened the ire of the Legion of Decency, which pressured MGM to strengthen the final letter scene even further. Ultimately, *Tea and Sympathy* was released in September 1956 with a Code seal, a B rating from the Legion, and an ad campaign that tried to stress hot sex and good taste at the same time: "Even the Most Daring Story can be brought to the screen when done with Courage, Honesty, and Good Taste. MGM presents Such A Story . . ." In the coming-attractions trailer, the offscreen narrator was moved to effuse, "It brings together the sensitive school boy and the housemaster's wife who knows he is more the man than any of those who call him 'Sister-Boy.'" In spite of all the compromises, the simultaneously listless and overwrought tone, and John Kerr's unappealing performance as Tom, the critics were sufficiently prompted by the delicate packaging to follow Laura's directive, "Be kind." For daring to shepherd the material past the PCA, MGM received a major goodwill/sympathy vote; never before had the Code seemed so anachronistic. In the *Times,* Bosley Crowther was moved to write a feature piece called "Loosening the Code" in which he erroneously stated that the script's depiction of adultery had caused more trouble for MGM than the gay allegations. He did predict, however, that the film portended a more liberal future: "The fact that *Tea and Sympathy* could be put upon the screen for all the mature values in it is fair token of the broadening of the Code." While *Variety* mentioned the "clearly implied homosexuality" and "stirring presentation of 'sissy-boy' theme," *Time* was notably less stirred when it noted that "obviously the American public isn't old enough to know that there is such a thing as homosexuality." At any rate, in a moviegoing season that also saw *The Ten Commandments, Around the World in 80 Days,* and *Giant, Tea and Sympathy* fared indifferently, posting a slight loss despite its nominal cost. Its greater importance lay ahead, as more studios and artists would strive to buck the Code and attempt, just attempt, to be somewhat more honest about sexuality.

In its self-important "sensitivity," in the completely laudable intentions that framed its bleeding-heart hypocrisy, *Tea and Sympathy* was the film that mid-fifties America deserved. Denial can seldom run deeper than in its double-negative approach to "the homosexual angle": something not true, in the play, was transformed in the film into something that didn't exist. Yet all the battles attending its genesis were justified by one epic paradox: this mawkish piece ultimately did an enormous amount of good. Not the good of showing nerdy boys that they could land the right understanding dream woman, but by opening up and exposing the issue of homosexuality, and contemplating how film might depict it. On various positive and negative planes, films of more consequence than *Tea and Sympathy* would deal with that issue quite promptly. There would not be positive reinforcement, not for a long time—but soon enough there would be increasing awareness and visibility and, on the rare occasion, candor. A precedent for all this was needed, and how strange it is that the impetus came from the mild and compromised climes of *Tea and Sympathy*. As it was overseeing these bemusing events, it's quite likely that history recognized the ironic humor of it all and allowed itself, just a bit, to have a good chuckle.

ELEVEN

Something Evil

W ith its old-Hollywood pedigree and timid defiance of Production Code guidelines, *Tea and Sympathy* was a breakthrough in the stealthiest sense of that word. It induced change through the most conventional of means, indicating new possibilities at the same time that similarly quiet, if braver, battles were gearing up in the so-called real world. Nascent groups of gays and lesbians were preparing, in that same closed-door fashion, to stand up for their identities and their preferences. The quietude of such movements as the Mattachine Society and the Daughters of Bilitis was a studied contrast to other alterations besetting the social and artistic terrain. The civil rights movement was beginning to be anything but quiet, and so was the explosion of rock 'n' roll that was beginning to reconfigure the entertainment industry. America, like it or not, was being compelled to address its diversity, and popular culture would have to be part of that process.

It would be some time before the film industry ratified the racial and sexual revolutions, but by 1955 it was prepared, in its own skewed fashion, to address the newly emergent fact that young people had different tastes, a different culture, in fact. They required their own music, wanted their own movies, and soon would be asserting their desire for their own societies and sexualities. Duly, and with churlish dispatch, Hollywood attempted to cater to them in ways previously unheard of in the movie business. There arose, in the mid-1950s, a whole youth film industry that ostensibly marketed rebellion and nonconformity along with the rock music and youthful protagonists. Under the hip façade it was just as before, an avidly recycling of the same old movie tropes of horror, melodrama, musicals, and love stories. The home plate for this pseudo-relevant exploitation was the new independent studio American International Pictures, founded in

1955.[1] With the minimalist auteur Roger Corman as its guiding guru, AIP turned out microscopically budgeted schlock that spoke directly, if not intelligently, to teen minds, hearts, and wallets. AIP movies seemed projectable only on drive-in movie screens, teasing their teen viewers with an expert aura of simulated cool while actually stressing the most regressive of fifties values. (Anyone doubting the conservative nature of these teen movies should spend a few days communing with the complete cinematic oeuvre of Elvis Presley.) Such cinema was not disposed to buck the Code as *Baby Doll* and *Tea and Sympathy* were doing, yet some of its early output managed to stir gay sex into the mix. In the years before the studio found its ultimate bearings with a mixture of Edgar Allan Poe and *Beach Blanket Bingo*, it occasionally spoke to its young audiences through subsidiary characters having notably gay tendencies. With black-and-white fifties morality piled atop one-dimensional AIP writing, these characters were, needless to say, mostly villainous. Just as the mainstream Hollywood studios had been doing since the mid-1940s, AIP was using homosexuality to connote evil.

AIP's *Girls in Prison* (1956) was, like a number of the studio's early efforts, not even a teen flick. A third-hand epic with an adult cast, it traced its lineage back to *Caged* via Columbia Pictures' scruffy *Women's Prison* (1955). Like *Caged* (and unlike *Women's Prison*, which didn't really try), it sidestepped the Production Code with sufficient brio to be relatively forward in portraying lesbianism behind bars. Code administrator Geoffrey Shurlock had indeed warned producer Alex Gordon about the script—"We must caution you most urgently that you eliminate any suggestion of Lesbianism, either in mannerisms or physical appearance of the woman involved"—after which the lines and scenes in question were mostly retained. Code vigilance was growing more lax, especially in productions at the other end of the prestige spectrum from *Tea and Sympathy*. In the release print of *Girls in Prison*, there was no questioning the proclivities of Melanee (Helen Gilbert), a steel magnolia inmate who uses her julep accent and coquettish manner to put the make on heroine Anne Carson (Joan Taylor). When Anne rebuffs her, their hard-bitten cellmate (Adele Jergens) observes the rejected pass and comments, "Who was it said something about a woman scorned?" Quite promptly, Melanee turns nasty and villainous and comes to a bad end, but what's surprising is how she's portrayed; no Hope Emerson type here. Helen Gilbert had been an ingenue at MGM in the late 1930s, and by

---

[1]Not the least of AIP's sleazy charms was that its name, like its product, could be considered an oxymoron. When one AIP epic ran on the mock-movies-with-running-critique TV show *Mystery Science Theater 3000*, the studio name was manna for one of the show's smart-mouthed commentators, who complained, "How can a movie be both American *and* International?"

1956 her blond prettiness, while intact, had grown a shade frayed around the edges. If such a look may have been predictable for a genteel woman's prison villainess, it was surprising and maybe even refreshing for a Hollywood portrayal of a lesbian. Lesbians onscreen, rare as they were, would less and less be associated with the tweedy old Mannish-Woman stereotypes, and for all her nastiness Melanee marked a small step forward.[2]

By the following year AIP was assuming a more youthful mien, and *Reform School Girl* was its juvenile (delinquent) answer to *Girls in Prison*. With an innocent lamb (Gloria Castillo) amid the wolves at a correctional facility, it was certainly true to its ideals, such as they were, and reasonably indicative of the studio ethos. The nastiest and butchest of Castillo's adversaries was played by a young blonde named Sally Kellerman, making an improbable start to an interestingly uneven film career. "My first film was also my worst," she would remember years later. "I played the school dyke and carried a tool case. When I came on the screen, everybody in the theater laughed. I didn't work for three years after that."

AIP's troubled teens also turned up in horror films, such as the 1957 double bill of *I was a Teenage Frankenstein* and *Blood of Dracula*. The former had homoerotic overtones in its creation of a muscular monster (Gary Conway); the latter was AIP's take on *Maedchen in Uniform*. Nancy (Sandra Harrison), an innocent at a girl's school, falls under the spell of her science teacher, Miss Branding (Louise Lewis), with disastrous results. The girl rapidly loses interest in her boyfriend, and not even a pajama-party rendition of the song "Puppy Love" (not Paul Anka's version) can set things aright. The evil Branding's control of Nancy turns the girl into a hairy Ms. Hyde-esque bloodsucker, and amidst a welter of hand-me-down Freudianisms *Blood of Dracula* trundled to an unhappy conclusion. Nor was it a coincidence that the school's headmistress is named Mrs. Thornedyke. Branding, for her part, was an updated and AIP-ified version of *The Uninvited*'s Miss Holloway, and *Blood of Dracula* was a clear entry in the genre of coded lesbian horror. Similar mind control came into play in the unabashedly self-referential *How to Make a Monster* (1958), which used the catchy ad line "It will scare the living yell out of you!" This one, set on the lot of a Hollywood studio eerily resembling AIP, recalled *House of Horrors* in its tale of a deranged gay man who nurses a grudge against the world and

---

[2]In the Odd Coincidence and Gossip Dept., two items on *Girls in Prison:* Perhaps Helen Gilbert (whose last film this was) looked a tad unraveled because in the late 1940s she had weathered a brief marriage to the mob-connected gigolo Johnny Stompanato—who, two years after this movie, was stabbed to death by Lana Turner's daughter, Cheryl. And one of the *Girls in Prison* guards was, of all people, Luana Walters, who more than two decades earlier had been the unwilling recipient of lesbian advances in that pioneer gay shlockfest *Children of Loneliness*.

eventually strikes out. Here the artist is a makeup man (Robert H. Harris) famous for his horrific creations. When he is discharged from the studio, he produce a corps of murderous brutes by drugging the makeup of a hunky bevy of young horror-film actors. Through it all, his lover/assistant (Paul Brinegar) gives him both aid and comfort, and the pair's relationship is portrayed clearly and pejoratively, as is the careful attention they direct to their muscle-bound charges. As in *Girls in Prison*, a character's gayness is given added dimension through the comments of an observer. Here a cop leeringly questions the artist about his accomplice: "Sure he's your assistant . . . how far does his assistance go?"

The American International brand of sci-fi and horror translated to other studios as well, often without the hep-teen overlay. *Voodoo Island* (1957), produced independently and released by United Artists, was typical, one of many low-budget vehicles testifying to the fact that poor Boris Karloff would seldom resist the urge to take the money and run. Here, in an anomalous burst of casting imagination, he played a *non*-mad scientist hired to disprove the presence of supernatural doings on a tropical island scheduled for resort development. Insofar as voodoo and zombies don't tend to attract wealthy vacationers, Karloff flies down to investigate. His party also includes his assistant Sarah Adams (Beverly Tyler) and, among others, Clair Winter (Jean Engstrom), the hotel's interior designer. In an atmosphere of man-eating plants, pin-impaled dolls, and a shrinking cast list, Karloff eventually discovers that voodoo exists in sufficient measure to make for a truly depressing vacation. On the surface, this type of Saturday-matinee dreck would seem to embrace nothing of any interest, which is probably why *Voodoo Island* remained immune from Production Code–related meddling and more recent historical gaydar. But there's no need for "creative interpretation" here. In both writing and performance Clair Winter is the most forward portrayal of any lesbian character since Joyzelle danced "The Naked Moon."

As the wintry Clair, Engstrom is sleek and fortyish, given to tailored white outfits and a long Webb-like cigarette holder. Interior decorators have been maligned in film since the days of *Syncopation*, and Clair is no exception. With her tightly drawn blond hair and brittle air, she's a late and bad remnant from the Eve Arden school of spinster chic. Yet, in a movie with no other sense of characterization whatever, she's drawn in a way that at least approaches humanity, and her attraction to and pursuit of Sarah is made startlingly clear. *Variety* noted that "[she] likes Miss Tyler more than the men on the trip," and indeed Clair begins her attempted conquest even before the plane takes off. "You wouldn't teach her any bad habits, would you?" leers one of her colleagues. Certainly not for lack of trying. When the party reaches the island, her designs are less about the hotel than about Sarah. "I could do a lot for you if you'd let

Even as the carnivorous plants of *Voodoo Island* encroach, the charms of skipper Rhodes Reason hold no interest for Clair Winter (Jean Engstrom). *Photofest*

me," she purrs. "I could make you become alive, dear." To make the point doubly clear, Clair rebuffs the advances of a local hunk in unambiguous terms: "You stay out of my world," Engstrom snarls, "and I'll stay out of yours." Most interestingly, her actions are not particularly condemned by either the filmmakers or the characters. Sarah, although not interested in her romantically, remains friendly with her and grieves when she is strangled by nasty flora. This fate seems less a punishment for her sexuality than part of the requisite body count, and is staged to be both sympathetic and titillating. Clair discovers a lake and a waterfall, goes for a skinny-dip, and, as the camera plays aquatic peekaboo, runs afoul of the voodooey vegetation. ("Carnivoroutth plannth!" Karloff marvels when he sees her body.) The Production Code Administration, which examined the *Voodoo Island* script eight months after it had taken issue with the lesbianism-behind-bars of *Girls in Prison*, had made no comment about Clair, nor did it have any objection to the completed film. Once again the PCA was starting to choose its battles; in a woman's prison melodrama, lesbianism would be expected far more than in a tropical horror movie, and neither would rate a minute fraction of the attention given to a *Baby Doll*. The oversight obviously did not come through excessive subtlety on the filmmakers' part, for Clair was singled out in several of the film's few reviews. "Miss Engstrom [plays] a crisp sophisticate whose character has surprising implications for a picture of this type," *The Hollywood Reporter* murmured. "This type," in this case, meant a low-grade double feature aimed squarely at adolescent boys hoping for a good scare. Clair wouldn't have frightened them, but she may well have mystified them. Demographics aren't really possible here, but Clair Winter was quite likely some young people's first exposure to open homosexuality.[3]

The low-budget product of American International and its imitators was one indicator that movie audiences of the mid-fifties were changing quickly and profoundly. On a more elevated plane, acting styles were undergoing equal upheaval. The key word was Method, and the prime deity was Marlon Brando. Method actors began turning up in film after film—even, sometimes, at AIP— and the tortured candor of their performance style made for a different kind of drama, often a more honest onscreen sexuality. Columbia's *The Strange One* (1957) paid due obeisance to Methodology with a cast of intense New York actors making their film debuts. Adapted from Calder Willingham's novel and subsequent play *End as a Man*, this was the un–*Tea and Sympathy*—an insidiously jagged look at life in a southern military academy, and a far darker coming-of-age story than Willingham's best-known credit, as cowriter of *The Graduate*. The portrayal of the cadets' ritualized life and the youthful virility under wraps would have in itself made for a homoerotic subtext, but Willingham went much further with his antihero, a cool Mephistopheles with an unforgettably porno-style name. Jocko de Paris is a despotic jerk with endless charisma, bending the other cadets to his will without breaking a sweat while taunting his adoring one-man fan club, a nerdy misfit called Cockroach. Appointing himself Jocko's Boswell, Cockroach follows his idol constantly and places him at the center of a homoerotic novel à clef, *Nightboy*. When all Jocko's victims finally turn on him in a burst of vigilante justice, only Cockroach mourns. The play, featuring Ben Gazzara as Jocko, attracted considerable attention on Broadway in 1955, but it was nowhere near a hit. Nevertheless, at this time the Method was selling, and Gazzara would be pitched implicitly as the latest Brando or Dean. The producer of *The Strange One*, Sam Spiegel, had recently triumphed with *On the Waterfront*, so the

---

[3]Saturday-matinee sci-fi lesbianism turned up more covertly the following year in the deathless Zsa Zsa Gabor classic *Queen of Outer Space*, which predictably populated the planet Venus entirely with women, some of whom (but not Zsa Zsa) are virulently anti-male. With a CinemaScope screen filled with slit skirts, Springolator pumps, and chauvinist dialogue, *Queen* was less an evocation of alternative sexuality than an interplanetary Wigstock. "I hate her," Zsa Zsa seethes in her paprika English, "I hate that qveen!"

As *The Strange One*, Ben Gazzara has fun in the shower with the put-upon and adoring Cockroach (Paul E. Richards). *Photofest*

Brando connection was plausible. Clearly, the cachet of an Actor's Studio cast was far more bankable than the subject matter.

In this age of the Johnston Office, it was sometimes possible to handle things in a fashion that would have made Joe Breen livid. Sam Spiegel, who preferred to operate outside the studio mainstream, saw to it that *The Strange One* proceeded to the screen in a fashion bearing no resemblance to the three-year enduro that attended *Tea and Sympathy*. He submitted the script just prior to shooting the entire picture on location in Georgia, and all Shurlock could do was mention that a Code seal would be issued only after approval of the finished film. When reviewed in early March 1957, the film was subjected to three minutes of cuts, all of them concerned with Jocko's relationship with the overtly gay Cockroach. In past years those cuts would have been the final word, but Breen was gone and the world was changing. Protesting the deletions, Spiegel petitioned for their reinstatement, and, just prior to the New York opening, nearly half of the censored material was put back into the movie—the job done so hastily and clumsily that the splices are visible and audible to this day. Much of the protest revolved around a long scene between Jocko and Cockroach (Paul E.

Richards) in which the adoring undergrad reads aloud from *Nightboy* and twice touches Jocko's hand suggestively. The *Nightboy* passages were largely deleted, but what remained now seems the most forward aspect of the scene: Jocko's reaction makes it clear that this is not merely unrequited hero worship, that he is neither repelled by nor indifferent to Cockroach's attentions. "I had no idea you were so talented," Gazzara murmurs, as the latent feelings lying beneath Jocko's control and sadism begin to surface and he holds his head in his hands in awareness. His affection here seems more genuine than in his scenes with a blond floozy (future cabaret star Julie Wilson), which were obviously built up for box-office reasons. In a later scene, when Jocko is taking her out, Cockroach runs over and pesters him, "Leave that girl and come with me." The scene was cut, then reinstated when director Jack Garfein agreed to have a car horn blare over the words "come with me." Lip-readers had no trouble, and the basic nature of the relationship was preserved. The cuts were retained in the scene of Cockroach's anguish at Jocko's comeuppance, but the essence was still clear. An earlier sequence which survived without any tampering came just prior to a shower scene with a fair amount of male flesh. As he heads toward the shower, Jocko snaps his towel at Cockroach and taunts, "You're a three-dollar bill, aren't you?" The words "as queer as" did not need to be spoken to make the meaning clear. While critics noted that the play and novel had been toned down, the final result still emerged as far less compromised than *Tea and Sympathy*. More compelling, too, certainly more sexually adventurous and implicitly less condemnatory. *Variety,* practical as always, fretted over the commercial prospects: "Stories involving military schools haven't been too popular with filmgoers nor do homosexual themes figure to be either." This assessment was not inaccurate, for *The Strange One* was not a popular film, despite the attention given the film debuts of Gazzara, Wilson, and George Peppard. It did, however, signify both a change and an advance.

Crime in the Streets (1956) also carried Method overtones as well as a distinct aura of sleeping-with-the-enemy. Like an increasing number of feature films it was adapted from a television play, with John Cassavetes—not his first film, although advertised as such—repeating his small-screen role as a disaffected teen gang leader. James Whitmore played a social worker who tries to reform him and Sal Mineo a sweet punk who follows him, and with self-conscious dialogue and studio sets all its roots were plainly in view. On a big screen Cassavetes was clearly too old to try to make like James Dean, and the schematic working-out of the Reginald Rose screenplay militated against the tough atmosphere created by director Don Siegel. Another repeater from the televised version was Mark Rydell as Cassavetes's sidekick Lou. While the script gave no indication of Lou's sexuality, the actor obviously had his own ideas, and through body language and expression and mannerism created a bona fide teenaged gay hood. While he is quite capable of violence, Lou smiles coyly a great deal of the time, undulates when he walks, and has an easy familiarity with both Cassavetes and Mineo.[4] It was another performance that would go under the radar of many observers, although one critic in particular saw lavender as well as red and complained about "the countenancing of a clear suggestion of homosexuality in the actions of one of the principal youth-gang characters. This subject is flatly taboo in any form in the film Production Code." Radar, after all, does not always broadcast only on friendly wavelengths.

Tea and Sympathy, that most radar-prone of dramas, had not been an especially personal project for its director, Vincente Minnelli, despite the parallels with his own life. His next film, *Designing Woman*, offered him more possibilities and, ultimately, more autobiography as well. Supposedly based on a story outline by MGM costumier Helen Rose, it was actually a smart fifties updating of the studio's 1942 hit *Woman of the Year*, with Lauren Bacall and Gregory Peck in the Hepburn-Tracy roles.[5] In the earlier film the battle of the sexes had played out in the marriage of a serious journalist to a sportswriter; in 1957 the gap was widened by turning the journalist into a costume designer. In both films the man's virility scores points by its juxtaposition with an effete male from the woman's world. Dan Tobin, the Clifton Webb knockoff from *The Velvet Touch*, appeared in 1942 as Hepburn's Milquetoast assistant Gerald, and the Tracy character did indeed score some points by asserting Gerald's lack in the manliness department. Fifteen years later the juxtaposition skyrocketed with Peck's antipathy toward Bacall's world, as floridly personified by a theatrical choreographer named Randy Owens. With Central Casting no longer maintaining a stable of Bobby Watson types, it apparently was Minnelli who decided to forgo a standard character actor in the role and cast from life. Jack Cole had appeared onstage and on film as a dancer but had never acted before, a fact which, while not deterring Minnelli, would be obvious in the final film. Randy is not a swish, in the manner of thirties dance masters (cf. Barnett Parker in *The King Steps Out*); visually he's a cousin of Kip in *Adam's Rib* and completely wrapped up in pink gels, dry ice, and pliés. Cole's woodenness as an actor actually helps to convey Randy's immersion in a world where nothing is more important than a costume that lets you move. The central sequence in *Designing Woman*, obviously geared to put *!MISMATCH!* on the marquee of this marriage, has Peck and his cigar-chomping cronies in a game of poker at the same time that Bacall,

---

[4]Mineo's role is underdeveloped, especially in contrast to his Plato in *Rebel without a Cause*. At any rate, since so many of this actor's roles touch on his own gay sexuality, it's possible to view Mineo and Rydell as the teen version of Fante and Mingo in *The Big Combo*.

[5]The similarity between the two stories became even clearer many years later, when *Woman of the Year* was reconfigured as a Broadway musical vehicle for . . . Lauren Bacall.

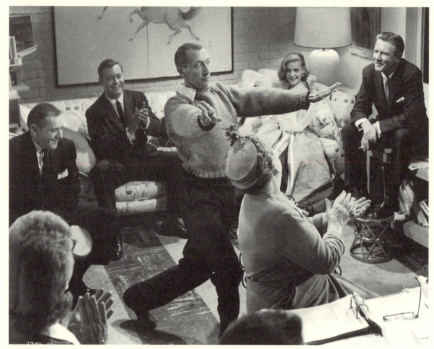

Jack Cole's seahorse imitation gets the nod of approval from Lauren Bacall and her colleagues (Tom Helmore on the right) in *Designing Woman. Photofest*

Cole, and attendants plan an upcoming show. Minnelli may have intended otherwise, but it appears that the audience is obviously meant to share Peck's irritation as Randy babbles on about a new ballet while real men are drinking and
playing poker. The ballet aesthetic Cole/Randy envisions is, however, quintessential Minnelli:

> RANDY: Behind closed doors anything can happen. It's the basis of all my
> work. The entrance of the unexpected—a closed door—when it's open,
> anything can come through. . . . Seahorses!

And to a jazzed-up bongo beat, he starts to writhe with hip ostentation, evoking
those seahorses as they canter through a glitz-studded ocean. Peck and his
poker buddies are dumbstruck, even more so when Randy knocks over the card
table and ruins the game. Later, when Randy overhears Peck casting aspersions
on his manhood, he has a ready defense. Reaching inside his wallet, he pulls
out a snapshot of a wife and three boys, the oldest of them a football player.
Then he proposes to beat up Peck. In an otherwise airy farce this scene is an

odd throwback to *Tea and Sympathy*, and as a Minnelli scholar once observed, the director had his own snapshots of wives and kids to pull out on cue. Even the most rococo confection, it seems, must be underpinned by virility of one kind or another. Be it Randy's seahorses or any number of Minnelli's ornate arabesques, it must have the stamp of a "real man" who, in a closeted age, might father children as one way to show his stuff. Another way to show it comes in a later scene, when Randy uses his agility to literally fly to Peck's defense against some mob types. With a few well-placed Cole kicks, Randy saves the day and the marriage. Seahorse ballets are obviously more palatable when they're staged by heroes.

The harmless farce of *Designing Woman* created no problems with the Johnston Office, but a series of films over the next three years would provide major Code-bursting headaches for creative artists and moral guardians alike. Times were changing faster than movies were, and the strain showed when films attempted to traffic in candor and honesty. Between 1958 and 1960 several significant battles were waged over gay male content; lesbian portrayals were, by contrast, mostly brief and far less troublesome, and all were in films released in 1958. In *Touch of Evil*, Orson Welles's mesmerizing plunge into bordertown corruption (among many other things), one of the most insidious jolts came with the brief, nasty bit by Mercedes McCambridge as a butch biker wanting to watch Janet Leigh get gang-banged. The role and the line "I wanta watch" stayed in the script despite repeated pleas from the Code office to remove it. McCambridge, onscreen in her unbilled bit for only a few moments, managed to embody not a touch but an entire universe of evil. In a vastly different part of the forest, there was *Auntie Mame*, which as book and play and film fired up hordes of gay cultists. Mame was a drag artiste's dream woman, the mentoring force that every sissy boy wanted. Her nephew Patrick did not necessarily fall into that category, but neither was he harmed by early exposure to homosexuality. As he enters Mame's apartment for the first time during one of her marathon parties, the first thing he sees is a gay couple, an aging pair of tweedy women. Patrick's future life may not be a well of loneliness, but in Mame's world it clearly takes all kinds. In the Method-driven *The Goddess*, Elizabeth Wilson brought back the repressed spinster type as the dowdy aide excessively devoted to her charge, the Marilyn-like star Kim Stanley. And in the insistently seamy murder mystery *Screaming Mimi*, handsome reporter Phil Carey has a surprise in store when he pays an off-hours visit to Gypsy Rose Lee, proprietor of the strip club El Madhouse. Chatting with her, he slowly becomes aware of a young woman glowering at him from a corner. He gets his bearings and makes a speedy retreat:

CAREY: Sorry, girls, I didn't realize it was "Tea for Two."
GYPSY: Don't call us, we'll call you!

While the censorship furor over *Baby Doll* in 1956 did not remotely lessen Hollywood's fascination with Tennessee Williams's work, it did serve to put the filming of his plays under especially intense scrutiny. When *Cat on a Hot Tin Roof* opened on Broadway in 1955 (with *Strange One* actors Ben Gazzara and Pat Hingle as Brick and his brother Gooper), the situation was precisely as it had been with *A Streetcar Named Desire* and, for that matter, *Tea and Sympathy*: a number of studios found their initial interest banked with threats of Production Code interference. Discussing one studio inquiry, Geoffrey Shurlock noted, "I made it plain that it would be necessary to remove every inference or implication of sex perversion and to substitute some other problem for the young husband." Once again a major plot point hinged on gayness—not unfounded allegations as in *Tea*, or in the feelings of an offstage character like *Streetcar*, but a hero who won't sleep with his wife because he's tormented about his feelings for a friend whose homosexuality led him to suicide. As he had with *Streetcar*, Williams made his own gay neurosis part of the plot structure, a questionable patina of fifties psychology overlying the more solid drama beneath. His plays are far too good not to be revived, yet their brilliance is sometimes tempered by his incessant torment and self-loathing. As we get a time-capsule sense of how a talented gay man saw himself in the 1950s, we are struck by the chasm separating the timeless writing from attitudes that now seem woefully regressive. It was these attitudes, of course, that caused the film versions of these plays to be so utterly compromised in the first place.

For *Cat*, MGM once again stepped in where others feared the Code. Dore Schary proposed that the story could be altered to fit a different Freudian frame: Brick's memories of Skipper are colored less by love than by hero worship, which causes the resentment of his father, Big Daddy. Screenwriter James Poe went so far as to construct an elaborate set of flashbacks featuring Brick, Skipper, and Brick's wife Maggie. These were ultimately scrapped, and Brick's problem was transformed into a case of vaguely arrested development with some vagrant gay overtones. Taking some of the emphasis off Brick's relationship with Skipper may in some ways have made the play's thesis more palatable, but it made for a hole at the center of the film. Some of the problem was camouflaged by the general excellence of the film and its actors, but critics continued the phenomenon that began with *Tea and Sympathy*: one after another they decried the compromises imposed on the film by the Production Code. Even Bosley Crowther noted the gaps: "The ways in which these problems are solved do not represent supreme achievements of ingenuity or logic in dramatic art. . . . No wonder, the baffled father, in trying to find out what gives, roars with indignation: 'Something's missing here!'"

Enough remained, nevertheless, to earn the film six Oscar nominations and an enormous amount of money. Clearly, Elizabeth Taylor begging Paul Newman

to take her to bed was sufficient lure for most viewers, regardless of the mud-
died nature of the underlying psychology. The more positive and oblique gay
references in *Cat*—Williams's sly digs at breeders who produce litters of "no-
neck monsters"—had fortunately remained intact, perhaps even making the
work seem more gay-friendly than intended. That positive balance would, alas,
be redressed the following year, when Williams and Taylor would reteam and
move from Delta Gothic to Southern-fried apocalypse.

In the so-called popular view of the time, male homosexuality was still
associated primarily with two forces: Oscar Wilde, the decadent artist, and the
Loeb-Leopold case, in which sexuality and psychosis were inextricably
entwined. The late fifties saw both concepts addressed cinematically—Wilde
with two biographical films from Britain (Peter Finch in one, Robert Morley the
other) that ran in some American art houses despite censorship difficulties, and
Loeb-Leopold with a second fictionalized story, *Compulsion*. In 1948 Alfred
Hitchcock professed to deny that *Rope* was tied in any way to the thrill killers;
despite ten years of change, Twentieth Century-Fox was impelled to make the

It's Loeb and Leopold redux as Dean Stockwell (as Steiner) and Bradford Dillman (as
Strauss) await their verdict in *Compulsion*. Behind them is Wilton Graff as Steiner's father.

same denial when it filmed *Compulsion*, which was adapted from Meyer Levin's novel and play. Yet Artie Straus and Judd Steiner were Richard Loeb and Nathan Leopold in all but name, and in all but a fully drawn picture of their sexual relationship. "It will be essential that there be nothing suggestive of Homo-sexuality in the casting and portrayal of your two leads," Geoffrey Shurlock warned Fox . . . and it could be wondered whether, in that mention of "casting," there was any cloudy remembrance that the leads in *Rope* had both been played by gay actors. With Bradford Dillman as the brashly dominant Artie and Dean Stockwell as the quietly submissive Judd, *Compulsion* was far more about the killing and the trial than it was about the killers' relationship. The overwhelming presence (and person) of Orson Welles as the Clarence Darrow figure ensured that a great deal of attention was diverted from the young men, and there was also some especially unconvincing "normal" love interest tossed in for balance. Even so, the origins of the story were clear enough to withstand all of Fox's denials, and the retelling was bolstered by portrayals by Dillman and Stockwell that at least alluded to aspects of the truth.[6] Most critics tended to refer to the story's homosexuality as a given despite the caution involved, one of the first instances of that type of offhanded visibility. Unfortunately, there was an ugly high price to pay for that visibility in the steadily increasing tendency to link homosexuality with aberrant, even ghastly, behavior. The awful peak of this trend would be reached in short order.

"*Suddenly, Last Summer*," the ads gasped, "Cathy knew she was being used for Something Evil!" That Something was, of course, gay sex, of the rougher-trade variety. The user was Catherine's cousin Sebastian, a "sensitive" New Orleans poet with an eye for young boys' bodies and a colossal disregard for their humanity. Even by Tennessee Williams standards, this one was a shocker: in a village on the Spanish coast, Sebastian uses Catherine as bait to lure boys, who finally and literally get fed up. They hunt him down, tear him to pieces, and devour him. Back in N'Awlins, the poet-vampire's imperious Jocasta of a mother, who had served the same come-on function prior to Catherine, attempts to silence her niece's memories with a lobotomy. Catherine's memories of Sebastian's death finally rip through her mental blocks, and as she finds release her aunt retreats into madness. As a one-act play, *Suddenly, Last Summer* was an effective if grotesque horror story and a comparatively minor work in the Williams canon. Apart from the charismatic repugnance of the subject matter, it

---

[6]True enough, in any case, for Nathan Leopold to initiate a suit against Twentieth Century–Fox for $1.5 million. It would be another thirty-four years until the case made it back to the screen, this time under the rightful names and with all the trial's prejudices amply displayed. Tom Kalin's *Swoon* (1992) was one of the earliest entries in the new gay and lesbian independent cinema of the 1990s, and one of the best.

was most notable as a therapeutic exercise, Williams's attempt to cope with the lobotomy given his sister, Rose. In making the journey to its cinematic incarnation, the play rapidly lost whatever allusiveness or quirky delicacy it possessed. As a two-hour feature with Big Stars, a Famous Director, and Lots of Horror, it became a Code-baiting freak show—a high baroque buffet of sexual frenzy. Another of the ad lines ran "These are powers and passions without precedent in motion pictures," and for once there was truth in advertising.

Whatever credit and blame attaches to *Suddenly, Last Summer* must begin and end with its producer, Sam Spiegel, just then coming into his own as the Sam Goldwyn of the Cold War Era. Spiegel pushed hard, took chances, and got such results as *The African Queen* and *On the Waterfront* and *The Bridge on the River Kwai.* With the daring and uncommercial *The Strange One*, he developed a unique and successful strategy for dealing with the Production Code. It had two parts. While appearing to play by the rules, avoid whenever possible submitting a script in advance, and shoot your films away from Hollywood to avoid interference. Later, if the Production Code Administration insists on cuts, contest them. *Suddenly, Last Summer*, if produced by a major studio, would have been as diluted as *Tea and Sympathy* or *Cat on a Hot Tin Roof*, if not more so. The cannibalism and the gay sex would both have been completely removed somehow, or else made so veiled as to be inexplicable, and the battles over the script would have delayed filming indefinitely. Yet Spiegel's outsider clout made for a vastly altered contest. He hired major names before and behind the camera—Elizabeth Taylor, Katharine Hepburn, Montgomery Clift, Joseph L. Mankiewicz, Gore Vidal—and planned to shoot the interiors in London and the flashback exteriors in Spain. When he submitted his script to the PCA several weeks before filming, he was not asking for permission so much as he was announcing what he would be doing. All that the helpless Geoffrey Shurlock could do was to catalog his objections to, essentially, everything. Spiegel quickly countered with such spurious arguments as "The cannibalism can be removed with the deletion of one line," and "The story admittedly deals with an homosexual, but one who pays for his sin with his life." It was agreed to let him make the film and take the consequences, then file an appeal if necessary.

It is no secret that a number of movies have backstories as interesting as anything on the screen. Naturally there are the classics with significant or compelling evolutions—*The Wizard of Oz, Citizen Kane, The Godfather.* Occasionally, too, the timeless follies or duds—*Cleopatra* and *Heaven's Gate* and the like—offer sharp object lessons in artistry, hubris, or stupidity. *Suddenly, Last Summer*, poised midway between the extremes of gem and turkey, offers a comparable amount of drama-in-process riches. With such a conglomeration of high-pressure personalities atop such high-intensity material, fireworks were a given. Mankiewicz, who started the decade with the triumphant *All About Eve*, had more recently borne the

artistic disaster of *The Quiet American* and the personal tragedy of his wife's suicide. Williams and Vidal, brilliant gay men in a buttoned-up time, were working
on a screenplay that was at once uniquely gay and horrifically homophobic.
Taylor, who married Eddie Fisher just as filming began, was at one of the most
controversial and lurid junctures of her life—no small feat, that. Clift was himself
a gay character out of a Williams tragedy, a tormented mass of physical and emotional scar tissue barely pasted together with a variety of substances.[7] Hepburn,
normally the farthest thing from a Method actor, here echoed all too precisely the
stifling denials of her character: the woman who had played Sylvia Scarlett and
starred for George Cukor on eight occasions was known to heatedly dispute the
very existence of homosexuality. She bore the filming unhappily, and when it was
all over, she fired off a parting shot to Mankiewicz by spitting in his face.
Purportedly it was over his treatment of Clift, and likely for a myriad of other real
and imagined infractions as well.

All these *monstres sacrés* were put at the service of Tennessee Williams's
most luxuriantly self-hating fancies, as augmented and made more literal by
Mankiewicz and Vidal. The one-set play was opened up extensively, numerous
asylum sequences being tossed in to add to the *Snake Pit*–Grand Guignol flavor.
Most crucially, Catherine's climactic recollection of her cousin's death was
made visual, with the overheated Williams text serving as a voice-over for the
images of Cabeza de Lobo and Sebastian and his boys. At once cinematic and
stagy, the sequence epitomized the tone of the entire movie—hysterical yet controlled, poetic yet gross, stylized yet realistic, simultaneously adventurous and
regressive. Just like Jesus in the concurrent *Ben-Hur*, Sebastian was made a
real presence and person, yet without a seeable face . . . something so evil, in
this case, that it seemed to defy visualization.[8]

When filming and editing were finally completed, *Suddenly, Last Summer*
was submitted for a Production Code seal—and summarily rejected. Despite
the cannibalism and hinted incest and blasphemy, the specific grounds were
those of sexual perversion. "In view of the fact that the dead man, Sebastian,
is definitely indicated to have been a homo-sexual, we are unable to issue the
Association's Certificate of Approval." Knowing that his film would get scant

---

[7]Mercedes McCambridge, who played Taylor's Tobacco Road mother, was witness to some of Clift's
self-inflicted wounds on mornings when she rode with him to the studio. As they passed the
Wormwood Scrubs Prison, Clift would order the limo driver to stop. Transfixed by the sight of the
jail, he would utter curses and laugh horribly about how the real criminals were those such as he—
not the ones not behind bars.

[8]The unbilled actor playing Sebastian even rated a rave notice in *The Nation*: "Whoever portrays
him beautifully demonstrates by gesture and attitude the epicene young tyrant his mother's infatuated monologue has earlier suggested."

distribution without a Code seal, Spiegel filed an appeal, which ruled in favor of the Code. Required to make alterations to conform to Code standards, Spiegel and his editors saw to it that the deletions were as slight as possible, doing very little to alter the dramatic tone or the nature of Sebastian's life and death. The seal was duly granted in late November 1959, the entire process of rejection, appeal, and ultimate approval being notably smooth and without Breen-style rancor. The true anger would fall upon the heads of the Code administrators after the film opened.

Philip K. Scheur, of the *Los Angeles Times*, said:

> I have talked with people, intelligent people, who don't understand what *Suddenly, Last Summer* is all about. I think I know what most of it is about. But in one sense the situation is ironic in its reflection on the reasoning of moviemakers. They boast of their new-found hard-earned freedom to be "adult." Actually, this picture contains (as do others) as many evasions, obscurities and furtive hints as the movie of a dozen years ago did when it "boldly" tried to suggest an illicit but at least normal sex relationship.

Time was even more direct:

> *Suddenly, Last Summer* . . . may not be the greatest movie ever made, but one thing can definitely be said of it: it is the only movie that has ever offered the paying public, for a single admission, a practicing homosexual, a psychotic heroine, a procuress-mother, a cannibalistic orgy and a sadistic nun. Showman Spiegel, who to Hollywood's amazement won a seal of approval for *Suddenly, Last Summer* from both the Production Code Admin. And the Legion of Decency . . . has shrewdly presented the whole morbid mess as "an adult horror picture" about a woman "who is suddenly too old to procure boys for her son." Says Spiegel: "Why, it's a theme the masses can identify themselves with."
>
> To wonder about this story is to realize that it is nothing more than a psychiatric nursery drama, a homosexual fantasy of guilty pleasure and pleasurable punishment. . . .

Echoing his producer's dubious denials, Mankiewicz professed that such a fantasy was completely delusional. "I never thought about homosexuality or cannibalism while I was directing it," he claimed, evidently with a straight face, "only its basic humanity." *Variety*, endearingly crass as always, had no difficulty in making a far more candid assessment. It ran its review of *Suddenly, Last Summer* under a blurb that announced: "Homo whose procurer is his mama. A weirdo by any standard." Following promptly on the heels of such notices was a sizable amount of protest from several quarters, mostly conservative. John Wayne was one of the highest of the profiles to denounce *Suddenly,*

Vacation spot: Sebastian Venable literally runs afoul of a group of prospective tricks. It could only be *Suddenly, Last Summer. Photofest*

Last Summer as garbage, despite the fact that he hadn't actually seen it. In Washington, a House Subcommittee compelled MPAA chief Eric Johnston to defend *Suddenly, Last Summer*'s Code seal. "You can read homosexuality into it or you can read incest if you wish," he stated, continuing the Spiegel line. "But I don't think there is anything like that in the picture. It is a story of deep motherly affection. . . ."

Maternal devotion was not responsible for the ultimate financial success of *Suddenly, Last Summer*, and neither was shock value. Nor were the contributions of Hepburn, Vidal, Clift, Mankiewicz, or even Williams. It was Elizabeth Taylor's supremely bankable combination of beauty and notoriety that would, in late 1959, have made a hit film out of a page-by page transcription of *Pilgrim's Progress*. Ironically, given Taylor's status as one of the most gay-friendly of performers, her star voltage brought heightened attention to a malignant carnival of masochistic gay-bashing. Unlike *Voodoo Island* or *Blood of Dracula*, this was no irrelevant sideshow. Its creators and cast gave it prestige and credence, and the unfortunate result was to make gayness worse than merely immaterial or undesirable. With Williams's fanciest poetry put to the service of the most regressive sub-Freudian nonsense, homosexuality was made to seem truly evil, as rare and exotic and unpleasant as the Venus flytraps raised by Mrs. Venable. As embodied by Sebastian, gayness was placed on a par with all things offensive to God, family, and country. No wonder that some gay men who saw the film in its initial release later reported that it made them feel frightened and ashamed. While raising the profile of gays on film, *Suddenly, Last Summer* gave that profile the most sickening mien possible. Here, as in succeeding years, visibility did as much harm as good. Possibly more.

A less fraught entertainment from 1959, Alfred Hitchcock's *North by Northwest*, offered a gay evil somewhat less insidious and encompassing than Sebastian Venable. As Leonard, right-hand henchman to kingpin James Mason, Martin Landau was as cold as his ice-blue eyes, a dapper malevolent force without humor or humanity who meets a deserved end on Mount Rushmore. Here again was the old implied-gay-villain gambit of the previous decade, Leonard's sexuality being chiefly a matter of read-into-it-what-thou-wilt. It had not originally been intended so, but unlike Sam Spiegel Hitchcock worked within the studio system and was subject to cautions from the Production Code Administration: "If there is any inference whatever in your completed picture that this man is an homosexual, we will be unable to approve it." This warning, issued nine months before the submission of the *Suddenly, Last Summer* script, seems both anachronistic and daft. Leonard was indeed toned down, and his relationship to Mason's character made for one of the less dynamic mysteries that abounded in *North by Northwest*.

While Hitchcock declined to challenge the Code over *North by Northwest*, he would stand firm for *Psycho* one year later. Writer-director Billy Wilder, however, was gleefully prepared to do battle with the prudes on a comic terrain teeming with sexual confusion. *Some Like It Hot* is the inverse correlative to *Suddenly, Last Summer:* nearly as audacious in its themes, preoccupied with sex, replacing Williams's gay = bad equation with jokes and affection. In *Suddenly, Last Summer* truth is horror and sex is destruction. For the bunch in *Some Like It Hot*, constantly disguising their realities, truth and sex are the prizes at the very bottom of the Cracker Jack box. In 1959 and now, *Some Like It Hot* is more than one of the greatest of all comedies; it is also an antic carnival of sexual liberation and self-discovery. It is as if all the female impersonations of earlier films—from Julian Eltinge to Bugs Bunny—were a warm-up for Wilder's tale of Joe and Jerry, a.k.a. Josephine and Daphne, for whom drag is a literal lifesaver. Nor, except for documentaries such as *The Queen* and *Paris Is Burning*, have subsequent drag movies so much as touched the hems of Curtis's and Lemmon's gowns. The mere mention of *Some Like It Hot* obliterates the paltry likes of *Mrs. Doubtfire*, *Flawless*, or *Big Momma's House*; only *Tootsie* and *The Crying Game*, in their vastly dissimilar spheres, can begin to approach this sybaritic throne. "Hilariously innocent," Pauline Kael called *Some Like It Hot*, "though always on the brink of really disastrous double entendre." That brink is in fact the stage upon which Wilder's people strut and fret, and it is the precipice carved out by those slender lines dividing gender inversion from drag from androgyny from homosexuality. All of these lines have forever been a part of gayness on film, and *Some Like It Hot* traverses them with innocence, as Kael said, and also with supreme awareness. Marilyn Monroe's onscreen innocence is unquestioned, yet it occurs even as she wears the most body-baring gowns yet seen on a major star. There is a kind of skewed innocence too in the honest desperation—fear of mob extermination— that forces Jack Lemmon and Tony Curtis to put on dresses and makeup. As the world of *Some Like It Hot* evolves, genders and sexualities and innocence are made to be bent. Lemmon's character in particular finds a delirious freedom in crossing sexual lines that didn't even seem to be there, and that assuredly had not existed so openly in movie comedy up to that time. While in drag, he snuggles with Monroe in an upper berth and comes across like the most unholy inmate in *Caged*—a post–Radcliffe Hall nightmare of a man trapped in a woman's persona. And when his Daphne quickly catches the eye of the roué moneybags Joe E. Brown, he's not so much repelled as mystified, since he's not even pretty.[9] Yet he endures, and eventually enjoys, a date with Brown, including the most epochal cinematic tango since Rudolph Valentino strode onscreen in *The Four Horseman of the Apocalypse.* Most marvelously, the premise is completely followed through in such a way as to leave no wig unflipped. Curtis stirs up lesbian hysteria when he (as Josephine) plants a big kiss on Monroe, and soon afterward there is that legendary final shot. Brown's "Nobody's perfect" line to Lemmon on discovering he's a man is the best payoff imaginable: audacious, suggestive, generous, and hysterically funny, a wonderful ending implying a wild new beginning.

To his credit, Geoffrey Shurlock of the Production Code Administration recognized the merit of *Some Like It Hot* from the very beginning. There was little or no tampering with the script or the final print, although Monroe's see-through/plunging wardrobe was cause for some discomfort.[10] In a far cry from the Breen years, works

---

[9]Lemmon/Daphne's line to Joe E. Brown at their first meeting pretty much destroys any argument about the script's double entendres being either innocent or unwitting. Attempting a fresh conquest, Brown tells Lemmon that he has come to Florida for the deep-sea fishing. Daphne's retort, courtesy of Wilder and cowriter I. A. L. Diamond: "Pull in your reel, Mr. Fielding—you're barking up the wrong fish!"

[10]Even today Monroe's gowns startle, which was her intention—the better to deflect interest from her bedragged costars. That was also seen to in the screen credits, which said merely "Miss Monroe's Gowns by Orry-Kelly," though Kelly had also dressed Lemmon and Curtis. Presumably Kelly's Oscar (the only one *Hot* received) compensated for the incomplete attribution. Other gay presences on the set received no screen credit at all. Jack Cole helped Monroe with the moves for her songs, and several female impersonators came in from time to time to help Lemmon and Curtis with their own moves.

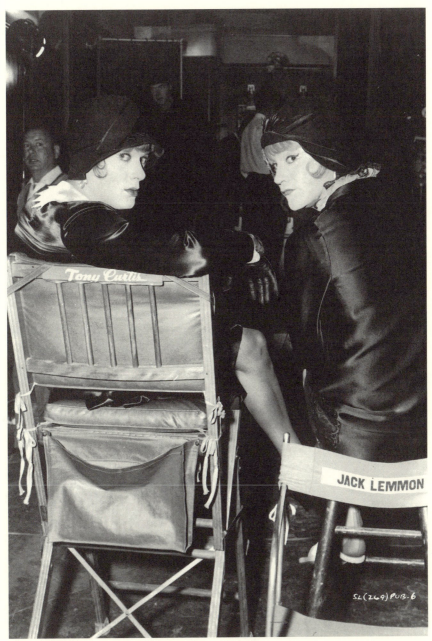

The coaching from those drag queens obviously helped. Jack Lemmon and Tony Curtis stay in character between takes on the set of *Some Like It Hot. Photofest*

of discernible quality were beginning to receive less stringent treatment under the Code. Less leniently, if predictably, the Legion of Decency issued a B rating and a pointed complaint to Shurlock and the PCA. Even with all the other raciness, the gay implications were at the heart of the objections:

> This film, though it purports to be a comedy, contains screen material elements that are judged to be seriously offensive to Christian and traditional standards of morality and decency. Furthermore, its treatment dwells almost without relief on gross suggestiveness in costuming, dialogue and situations.
>
> Since the initiation of the triple A method of classifying films in December 1957, this film has given the Legion the greatest cause for concern in its evaluation of Code Seal pictures. As you can well imagine, it bordered on condemnation. The subject matter of "transvestism" naturally leads to complications; in this film there seemed to us to be clear inferences of homosexuality and lesbianism. The dialogue was not only "double entendre" but outright smut.

Shurlock defended the Code seal by (perhaps disingenuously) citing *As You Like It, Twelfth Night,* and *Charley's Aunt,* which did little to steady the now-tenuous alliance between the PCA and the Legion. Nor was it helped by the smashing reviews and box-office response.[11] Along with *Suddenly, Last Summer* and Otto Preminger's *Anatomy of a Murder, Some Like It Hot* was one of three highly successful American films released in 1959 to portend a new decade of more permissive filmmaking. All three were black-and-white productions in an age of spectacle and color, all were from major directors and dealt frankly with sex—two of them with gay sex. All this, less than four years after the saga of *Tea and Sympathy.*

In 1959 cutting-edge black-and-white filmmaking made headlines, competed with European product, and seemed to echo the times more accurately than the usual candy-box Hollywood schlock. Nevertheless, at that time the movie capital was still a fiefdom of moguls and big studios that were making truckloads of costly whimsy designed to lure people away from their TVs. Artistically it was all beginning to seem out of touch, financially it was increasingly precarious, but even as the big-studio system crumbled, no one knew how to do anything else. And no one made a bigger effort than MGM, which by the end of the decade was in a state of financial disarray. Its answer to home entertainment and red ink was an immense blowout of a remake of *Ben-Hur.* Ancient-world spectacles, those lurid and sanctimonious staples of earlier times,

---

[11]The reviews were nearly unparalleled for a movie comedy; the box-office response was on a par with two other smash comedies that year, *Operation Petticoat* and *Pillow Talk. Some Like It Hot* was a one-time-only smash, but *Pillow Talk,* which opened yet another comedic can of partly gay worms, spawned a whole school of imitators. More on those movies, and those worms, in the next chapter.

had gone on hiatus soon after *The Sign of the Cross.* DeMille engineered their comeback in 1949 with *Samson and Delilah,* and the field soon opened up to encompass *David and Bathsheba, Quo Vadis, Salome, The Robe,* and others, culminating with DeMille's last will and testament, *The Ten Commandments.* The costs of these sandaled shindigs were lofty, and when spent luridly and well enough the grosses spiked through the roof. MGM had had one success in this realm, *Quo Vadis,* and one disaster, *The Prodigal.* Its third would be in size the biggest of them all, and in intent the most lofty. *Ben-Hur* had been the studio's first big production in the mid-1920s, a catalogue of miscalculations and reshoots and ultimately a major success. Even in the 1950s it was still legendary, especially for the chariot race, and so MGM went for broke with $15 million, a presold title, and DeMille's own Moses, Charlton Heston. (Rock Hudson, the first choice, was unavailable for the role originally played by Ramon Novarro.) This was designed as the un-DeMille epic, the Thinking Man's Spectacle: a prestige director (William Wyler), dialogue that attempted to keep away from the "Behold thou my wrath!" school of Bible talk, and little or no glitzy sex.

The moon that hung over this *Ben-Hur* was, therefore, emphatically nonnaked. But did it still shine upon gay sex? Was there a conspiracy behind Heston's back to make Judah Ben-Hur half of a male-male romance? Gore Vidal has claimed so, most conspicuously and amusingly in the book and film *The Celluloid Closet.* Vidal, one of many writers working on the script, says that he proposed to Wyler that Judah's backstory friendship with Messala (Stephen Boyd) might have been a passionate romance out of a Mary Renault novel, and that when Messala returns to Jerusalem after many years, he intends to resume it. When Wyler blanched, Vidal pressed the issue, claiming that this subtext would give the relationship, and Boyd's performance, more resonance. Accordingly, Vidal talked it over with Boyd, and the scenes between the men were played with that undertone and without Heston's knowledge. Boyd would thus give Messala's hostility toward Judah the fire of a spurned lover, not merely the ire of a disappointed friend. Heston purportedly only discovered this after the publication of *The Celluloid Closet,* after which his denials that such a thing could occur heated up incrementally with his increased predilection toward right-wing politics and the right to bear arms. The more angry and superior Heston became in denying that his Oscar-winning role had a gay aspect, the more wryly amused Vidal would be in recalling how Wyler would warn him, "Don't tell Chuck!"

With Wyler and Boyd both dead, the "He said/He said" aspects of this Gay *Ben-Hur* Controversy seem to rest upon who one prefers to believe and what one prefers to see on the screen. Look closer, then, at this disagreement: it's about more than just a big-budget movie and its subtext, or an Oscar-winning actor, or an estimably witty writer. Heston's denial that there were gay things in *Ben-Hur* is a symbol, as proud and visible and self-righteous as the man himself. It attempts to eliminate possibilities and potentially even to rewrite history: that "gay exception" mentioned earlier, that tendency to deny and bury the homosexual past, becomes more proud in the hands of someone like Heston. "No, no, *that* wasn't gay . . . we wouldn't have thought that way back then!" Such negative affirmations resound through gay history in the twentieth century, repudiating the presence of gays on film just as they do the presence of gays on the street. Charlton Heston himself seems an unfortunately apt embodiment of this type of oppression. Sometime in the mid-to-late 1960s, Heston's politics took a rightward turn and grew steadily more conservative as the century drew to a close. Finally, as his political renown equaled and often undermined the fame he had achieved as Ben-Hur and Moses and El Cid and the guy in *Planet of the Apes*, he worked tirelessly to bring histrionic weight to pronouncements decrying gun control and espousing distrust of all things liberal (and Vidalian). Such qualities would not seem, to put it mildly, to reside in a person willing to acknowledge covert gay struggles, and indeed he began to evince belligerence and condescension about the issue to publications such as *The Advocate*. Vidal, for his part, has remained ever the calm and superior gadfly, continuing ceaselessly to mock and criticize the Hestons of the world. With no desire to be a spokesman for any cause other than his own craft, he has maintained a measured distance from gay struggles and causes. The *Ben-Hur* dispute could hardly have been divided between more opposite camps and personalities—which only adds to its fascination and fun.

Heston has said that Vidal's contributions to *Ben-Hur* were perfunctory at best and had nothing to do with any prior relationship between Ben-Hur and Messala. After the release of the *Celluloid Closet* documentary, he responded with a letter sent to various high-profile publications (among them *Time* and the *Los Angeles Times*):

> Vidal [is] irrationally determined to pass himself off as a screenwriter, particularly of the script for *Ben-Hur*. . . . His ludicrous claim that he somehow slipped in a scene implying a homosexual relationship between the two characters insults Willy Wyler and, I have to say, irritates the hell out of me. A gay friend of mine, reading this letter said, "Oh, Vidal's turned into an old queen; just the kind of thing that gives homosexuality a bad name."

Vidal was quick to refute Heston's remarks, and in tones less wry than sober he cited dates, diary entries, and specific incidents to back up his assertions. It is true that Vidal's name is not prominent in the surviving mountains of script fragments that were patched together for this herculean project. There was never any final "shooting script" per se, and Vidal was in fact part of a large coterie of notable writers (including Christopher Fry and Maxwell Anderson) who worked

SCENES FROM THE "GAY *BEN-HUR*"

1. Lines remaining in the final cut:

   MESSALA: I said I'd come back.
   BEN-HUR: And I never thought you would . . . I'm glad. I'm so glad.

   MESSALA (*referring to their javelin throws*): After all these years, still close.
   BEN-HUR: In every way.

2. An exchange between Messala and Ben-Hur in their first scene, filmed and later cut:

   MESSALA: When we were younger I was taller. Remember?
   BEN-HUR: Yes, I remember. Everything.

3. In a preliminary, unused script, Ben-Hur goes to temple to pray. Originally, he was to have prayed the kaddish; this was then changed to a prayer to the God "who has created the bond that united David and Jonathan." He then hears a nearby man reading the Bible passage "And Jonathan made David swear again because he loved him; for he loved him as he loved his own soul."

4. Messala's line to Ben-Hur was originally: Is there anything so sad as unreciprocated love? In the final version (and in the film) "unreciprocated" was changed to "unrequited."

5. After Ben-Hur gives Messala a horse, Messala says, "Judah, you are good, and it's going to be like old times. I know it!" The script originally continued the scene by having (in what it called "a warm moment") Messala embrace Ben-Hur.

6. An unused exchange between Messala and the servant Amrah:

   AMRAH: Has the young master taken himself a wife?
   MESSALA: No, Amrah. I'm not yet willing to give up the prolonged pleasure of choosing.

7. A cut line for Messala just before he leaves Ben-Hur's house in a rage: "Remember, I begged you."

on *Ben-Hur* without credit.[12] In some of those script pieces, in fact, there are indeed sprinkled some hints here and there that quietly indicate a gay subtext may have been intended, and not only by Gore Vidal. Some of these slight, allusive passages were shot and then cut, others exist only in preliminary scripts, and a few are in the completed film (see box). Just as entire queer worlds could

---

[12]It was the decision of the Screen Writers Guild to credit the *Ben-Hur* script solely to Karl Tunberg, which caused director Wyler to protest the omission of Fry in particular. It was thought that the controversy may have cost Tunberg an Oscar; Heston, in his own Oscar acceptance speech, made it a point to mention Fry's contribution.

be constructed around secondary characters in thirties films, so do these lines hint at the "other," non-Heston *Ben-Hur*. It is this film that a waggish critic praised for the "homoerotic subtext [that] is the film's most obvious draw." And as if to highlight the presence of a virile gay sexuality that remains covert, *Ben-Hur* also gives the audience a decadently queeny Pontius Pilate, played with sullen relish by the Australian actor Frank Thring.[13]

As its filmmakers surely intended, *Ben-Hur* was an ending, not a beginning. If it did not quite signal the finale of the big-studio blockbuster (those ended with some flop musicals about ten years later), it did mark the end of a style and an attitude. That it was shot in Italy did not matter: this was High Hollywood, conservative in every way save budget. The following year, its direct successor, *Spartacus*, was less beholden to the old movie trends and traditions. On the surface it was even more conventional than *Ben-Hur*, with its made-in-California trappings (including the ludicrous use of W. R. Hearst's estate to simulate a Roman villa) and glossy anachronisms. It was also a product of the industry's most crass assembly line, Universal. Yet it looked away from the DeMille–*Ben-Hur* school more than it honored it. As written by the formerly blacklisted Dalton Trumbo and directed by the emergent maverick Stanley Kubrick, *Spartacus* was a blockbuster with a liberal soul. Its ideas and themes—politics, war, freedom, sex, and love—were the standard ones, yet given franker and more adult spins. Most frank was the portrayal of the charismatic Roman villain Crassus (Laurence Olivier) as an unapologetic bisexual in pursuit of a slave girl (Jean Simmons) and a slave boy (Tony Curtis). Most famously, Curtis's Antoninus was compelled to bathe Crassus while being, in effect, sexually harassed; Crassus makes his tastes clear with a savory euphemism, noting that his tastes embrace both "snails and oysters." This revelation plunges Antoninus into such a frenzy of gay panic that he escapes Crassus to join Spartacus (Kirk Douglas) and his slave army. (In an early script draft, the panic had been even more drastic: Antoninus killed himself.)

The snails-and-oysters scene, or its equivalent, had not appeared in the original novel by Howard Fast; it was the creation of Trumbo alone and was present in the *Spartacus* script from the beginning. In 1958, after reading the preliminary screenplay, Geoffrey Shurlock warned Universal about characterizing Crassus as "very probably a sex pervert." With each script submission the warnings continued, yet the scene was never deleted. In the Sam Spiegel tradition, *Spartacus* was shot and assembled with its objectionable scenes intact, then presented for a Code seal. In May 1960 Shurlock and his staff screened

---

[13]Thring and his haughty moue were at it again two years later in equally biblical surroundings. As Herod Antipas in Nicholas Ray's *King of Kings*, he seemed less interested in Salome than in John the Baptist.

Spartacus and once more objected to "snails and oysters," along with Jean Simmons's nudity in two scenes and an unprecedentedly gory shot of a soldier's arm being lopped off.[14] In the Breen days these would all have been summarily rejected, in the unlikely event that they'd been shot in the first place. In 1960 the Code had become a more negotiable force, and for the price of Simmons's exposure and the severed arm Crassus was allowed to come on to Antoninus. Older-school cinematic homosexuality was present as well, and passed without comment: *Rope*'s John Dall as a lily-souled Roman patrician, and John Hoyt (the Webb-like Stacy in *Winter Meeting*) as Peter Ustinov's swishy servant Caius.[15]

The Code seal was granted and *Spartacus* was readied for release . . . and then the Legion of Decency weighed in. The Production Code Administration was somewhat malleable, but the Church was less disposed toward compromise. *Spartacus* had been screened for critics and premiered with its ambisexual shellfish intact. The review in the Catholic magazine *America* served, possibly, as an omen:

> [*Spartacus* was] apparently made by men who do not believe in Chrstianity and who [attempted] to affirm human dignity and the brotherhood of man by creating, as it were, a substitute Christ who is purely human. . . . The producers . . . have included some blatantly spelled-out sex, an almost intolerable amount of graphic brutality and even some coyly oblique inferences of homosexuality in a film which, at the same time, they are actively promoting as a valuable historical document for all school levels.

The Legion, in taking on *Spartacus*, promptly made one thing clear: until "snails and oysters" was deleted, *Spartacus* would not get an approved rating, which meant that millions of Catholic filmgoers would be ordered to stay away. Universal complied, and from the premiered final cut to the approved version *Spartacus* lost seven minutes. In the prints seen for the next thirty years Antoninus turned up at Spartacus's camp for no evident reason. Nevertheless,

---

[14]It's been alleged that the ever-helpful Shurlock even proposed at one point that "snails and oysters" be changed to "truffles and artichokes"—an amusing thought that does not appear in the PCA papers. The actor on the receiving end of the arm severing (and the deletion) was real-life amputee Bill Raisch, who gained cult recognition as the suspicious "One-Armed Man" in the sixties TV drama *The Fugitive*.

[15]Caius was a throwback to that old "eunuch = sissy" school in operation since Griffith's *Judith of Bethulia*. In 1963 there would be a latecomer to the ranks in in Joseph Mankiewicz's *Cleopatra*. Pothinus, as played with mascaraed prissiness by Gregoire Aslan, is clearly the snake in this excessively fertilized garden of hetero lust, and possibly even a pedophile. As with Mankiewicz's Sebastian, he is indicated to the audience as a Bad Lot Utterly Deserving His Dire Fate.

enough people had seen the sequence prior to its deletion, or heard about it, for it to be somewhat of a cause-célèbre, a testimony to the power of the censors to continue their repression of homosexuality on film.[16] On the screen Crassus was a victor; in movie history he was something of a martyr.

In 1991 Crassus and his creators were finally vindicated with the release of a new *Spartacus*. New, in the sense that there was a gleaming new print with its deleted gore and gay seduction restored. Such were the vagaries of film preservation—or the power of the Legion of Decency—that the sound track of the Olivier-Curtis scene had been lost and required reconstruction. Curtis respoke his lines, Anthony Hopkins substituted (expertly) for the now-dead Olivier, and the reviews seldom failed to mention the scene and its enrichment of the film. Nearly a decade later the reviews of an even more successful epic, *Gladiator*, frequently cited the subtleties and strengths of this "complete" *Spartacus*. After forty years the earlier blockbuster seemed, to most observers, the superior work. In *Spartacus* homoeroticism is placed at the service of plot and character, while in *Gladiator* it exists solely to serve up a large portion of beefcake.

Most audiences in 1960 were not permitted to witness the gay content in *Spartacus*, just as they had been shielded from such things in *Tea and Sympathy* and *Cat on a Hot Tin Roof* and in cuts made in *The Strange One*. In *Suddenly, Last Summer* they were permitted more contact, so long as gayness was tantamount to godlessness. It served a similar function in a film concurrent with *Spartacus*. In Otto Preminger's *Exodus* unwanted homosexual advances incited a rebel to action, as they had with Antoninus: Sal Mineo's Israeli freedom fighter Dov is impelled, at least in part, by memories of his abuse by his captors at Dachau. In an emotional scene so effective that it won Mineo an Oscar nomination and became part of the ad campaign, Dov weeps uncontrollably as he remembers, "They used me . . . like a woman!" *Exodus* confined gay references to the realm of allusion, whereas *Spartacus* presented its gayness outright and paid a high price for doing so. Even so, few observers felt that such attempts at frankness would end with Crassus and Antoninus. Slowly, and notwithstanding the Legion of Decency, some barriers were coming down. The joyous *Some Like It Hot* implicitly celebrated this victory, and *Suddenly, Last Summer* offered its own morbid celebration as well. In their wake would come, very shortly, a battery of comedies and dramas eager to include homosexuality in one form or another. Over the next few years gayness would be more present on film than ever before, and in ways that were both funny and horrible, often at the same time.

---

[16]The Legion continued its crusade in 1967 when *Spartacus* was reissued in a version shortened by some twenty minutes. For the final scene of Simmons with the crucified Spartacus, all of Kirk Douglas's close-ups were removed, evidently for reasons of both gore and (alleged) sacrilege.

TWELVE

That Touch of Mink

SEX AND THE SIXTIES

In terms of artistry and laughs *Some Like It Hot* was the most success-ful film comedy of its time. In financial profitability and in immediate influence, it was outshone by another 1959 film that played sex for laughs. *Pillow Talk* would be the film that set the tone for the new decade, the matrix for how most American comedies would greet their audiences—urban-set, purportedly sophisticated and adult, crammed with jokes about virginity and adultery and sexuality. Eventually, *Pillow Talk* and its progeny would encapsulate an entire Kennedyesque pre-Vietnam era: a time of big hair and sniggering seduction and synthetic entertainment. Heterosexuality in these movies was a wink-wink thing of leers and smirks. Gay sex was present as well: artificial, cartoonish, and snide. The romantic farces of the early 1960s are perhaps the least timeless movies ever made. They are rooted, to an alarming extent, in a time and place and attitude so pronounced and defining that they might as well be stamped on the edge of the film stock. You can almost smell the hairspray when watching these movies, with their overlit sets and overdressed stars and eternal puerile teasing. The movies had ever treated sex as a joke, and they had done their bit to laugh with (or at) gayness as well—but these movies took all this to farther and coarser climes. In the minds of their creators they were sleek and sharp updatings of the screwball classics; in reality they were less evocative of their era than indicative of its prob-lems. As the age of the big-studio system staggered to its close, these final prod-ucts were a sorry summation of the art of commercial American film, circa 1961. Their artifice was stultifying and total: they were phony films about phony people, telling lies about sex, both straight and gay. Their efforts would be suitably rewarded with laughs that were equally phony.

The sex in sixties comedy was disingenuous from the word go, gay sexuality most of all. Lesbians did not exist in this world, and male gayness served most conspicuously to highlight the redbloodedness of the straight heroes out for a conquest. Sometimes homosexuality would serve as a cheap disguise assumed by the hero, while at other times it was given over to supporting characters, expendable weaklings unworthy of penetrating the heroine's enameled façade. The proposition became even more Byzantine, of course, with the fact that many—most, even—of these movies starred the era's foremost closeted actor. Rock Hudson's gayness, normally an aesthetically irrelevant factor in his career, suddenly becomes germane here in the most tortuous existential ways: a gay man pretending to be a straight man was enacting a straight man pretending to be a gay man, all for the most sniggering laughs. This weird, *bal masqué* impersonation was even more layered than the faux-chic Jean Louis gowns worn by Hudson's costar.

Poor Doris Day. For a decade she had been one of the most straightforward of stars: direct, honest, unaffected by the trappings of bogus sexuality or fabricated glamour. Even with her singing talent, she seemed like a uniquely plausible luminary, as if a particularly talented friend had somehow wangled a movie deal and was getting up there and learning the ropes as she went along. None of the Technicolor, the spangles and paint and manufactured hooey, could disguise her genuineness. Her films were seldom as direct and unambiguous as Day herself, and gay subterfuge was a surprisingly frequent part of their gambit. The very first of them, *Romance on the High Seas*, had featured the gay triumvirate of Franklin Pangborn, Grady Sutton, and Eric Blore, with a surprising quota of gay snickers from Sutton. *Tea for Two* had further incursions, courtesy of Eve Arden and Billy DeWolfe, and *Calamity Jane* made of itself a brassy carnival of gender inversion. Day's contact with gay matters subsided once she moved away from musicals in the mid-fifties, but a bad marital comedy from 1958, *Tunnel of Love*, indicated a new direction for her: the scrubbed good sense and take-charge energy would be filtered through banked sexual fires.

With *Pillow Talk*, Doris Day became the most popular star in American film. In its wake, and under the guidance of her producer-husband Martin Melcher, her stardom changed, her appearance changed, and her movies changed most of all. With devastating ease and dispatch, she became the symbol of an era, and soon enough an American joke. Wholesomeness became antiseptic pseudovirginity, with foggily diffused close-ups barely revealing the made-up face beneath the glazed slabs of bleached hair. The girl next door had morphed into the gauzy embodiment of everyone in America who found sex a cause for simpering, giggling, and mock distress. In the sixties comedies that began with *Pillow Talk* and continued into the Lyndon Johnson years, female sexuality became a prize for the most devious bidder, male heterosexuality was the stuff of Rat Pack barnyard boasting, and homosexuality was an infantile charade. All these were set off by the lacquered commercialism present in every frame of film. Sterile furnishings were placed in unreal and overilluminated sets, then populated by mannequins wearing beyond-ultra costumes and a surfeit of accessories; *Time* magazine went so far as to maintain that Day and Hudson seemed less like actors than like 1960 Cadillacs parked side by side.[1] These faux-luxe accoutrements, plus the sex, were the coin of these movies, both of them exceeding what television could supply.

In contrast to the comparatively lowdown black-and-white *Some Like It Hot*, *Pillow Talk* was all pastel gloss, a pretend-posh tiptoe around the true nature of relationships and sex. Its producer, Ross Hunter, had established a standardized line of slick products, supervising a series of laminated comedies and soap operas in which his own intensively closeted gay sexuality seemed to be expressed through an exhaustive obsession with tactile glamour. In *Pillow Talk*, the plain-spoken Day and the amiable lug Hudson were cast jarringly against type—she as Manhattan's foremost interior decorator, he as a Casanova songwriter. The hinge of the plot was their shared party-line telephone—dated technology by 1959, as well as lazy comedy—and the courtship, mistaken identity, and laughs were all predictable. The newer, or at least relatively novel, elements were the packaging, the star teaming, and the promise to be "daring." Day would be "sexy" for, purportedly, the first time on film, and Hudson would conquer women with the mere sound of his voice. She would sing "Possess Me" while contemplating seduction, and he would grab her attention by pretending to be gay. In the guise of a Texas mother's boy called Rex Stetson, Hudson offered an updated version of Wally in *The Dude Wrangler*, suggesting a condescending gayness through a bad drawl and aw-shucks coyness. Not that Rex—a fake character enacted by a fake character—was really gay; he just emitted telltale gay signals in order to nail Day's sympathy and to nail Day. In the original script the gay allusions in the Rex masquerade were fairly explicit until the Production Code Administration cautioned Universal against going into this "prohibited area," an admonition which makes gayness sound a bit like a nuclear test site. In the film as released, Rex's assumed sexuality was alluded to coyly. First, Rock-as-wolf baits the trap over the phone by warning Doris against men who are "very devoted to their mothers, . . . collect cooking recipes, exchange bits of gossip. . . . You better make sure!" Then Rock-as-Rex starts prattling about how nice it is that interior decorators get to fiddle with "all them colors and fabrics." The point was made with timorous clarity, aided by codes and signals more transparent than any since the pansy craze. Day naturally takes it upon herself to ensure that Rex is a "real man," and so on and so on through all the tropes: unmasking, revenge by bad decorating, fade-out embrace. Between the sexual promise, the star power, and all the embellishments, *Pillow Talk* lulled audiences into massive submission. It even won an Academy Award for that leer of a script

---

[1] The consumerism of these movies is so shrill that they are undistinguishable from television commercials. In one of the least successful of them, *Paris When It Sizzles* (1964), even Audrey Hepburn's perfume rates a screen credit.

and fixed the shimmer-filtered face of early-sixties escapism: a world of poses and faux farce, a place where homosexuality would be safe for all to ridicule.

It would be nearly two years before the trend was set. In the meantime Rock Hudson moved back to interchangeable action dramas and Doris Day had a final contact with more "normal" comedy. In *Please Don't Eat the Daisies* (1960) she played a Manhattan wife and mother with a yen for suburban life—that sensible fresh-air quality reasserting itself after the hermetic *Pillow Talk*. Again she brushed up against some stereotypical gay portrayals: a snotty Macy's salesman who tries to sell her a fabric that will look divine with an alabaster bowl, and a butch small-town veterinarian who one of her kids mistakes for a man. The rematch with Hudson arrived early in 1962 with *Lover Come Back*, an even bigger hit than *Pillow Talk*. Once again there was disguise, a thwarted seduction, and various glossy digressions, this time done with a shade more wit. Rock's masquerade in this outing involved his posing as a shy and sheltered scientist—not so much gay as virginal—and Day's profession shifted from décor to Madison Avenue. (Another odd choice for this no-nonsense personality, who once seemed wholly alien to pandering and devious hype.) In an early scene, Day confers with Leonard (Chet Stratton), an art director, on ads for a new floor wax. The layout looks good, except:

> DAY: What color is that floor?
> LEONARD (*proudly*): Lilac.
> DAY (*double take*): Lilac? Leonard, who has a lilac floor in their kitchen?
> LEONARD (*wounded, if still proud*): *I* have.
> DAY (*pauses a beat to realize what's what*): Oh. (*Pause to regain diplomatic composure*) Well, Leonard, not everyone is as artistic as you are. (*He beams proudly while she gives a secret "Oh, brother!" look.*) We have to sell this wax to average, ordinary, everyday people.
> LEONARD (*with a nauseous look*): Ewwwww, *them . . . !*

Like the scene in *Stage Mother* so many years before, this little exchange is a near-complete lexicon of cues and attitudes. But unlike Mr. Sterling, Leonard must be a target for the kind of condescension that would become increasingly frequent in the cinema of the 1960s. It's necessary for Day to coddle him, coax him, and downright lie to him to get him to work. He's so caught up in a realm of lilac fantasy that he has no concept of, and even less respect for, "normal" people who don't live in his princess-precious ghetto. He's Randy in *Designing Woman* without the redeeming talent. Design must equal femininity, which must in men be gay, and therefore the opposite of rock-solid Rock Hudson masculinity. Nor does Day show any genuine respect for Leonard; through her sideways looks and double takes she telegraphs that this "artistic" non-man is utterly expendable—someone as far removed as possible from the devious, yet ultimately "average, ordinary, everyday" Rock Hudson–type playboy. And lilac, of course, is as close to lavender as a screenwriter could get without eliciting the wrath of the Production Code Administration.

For a film as attentively pre-fab as *Lover Come Back*, smashing success was as preordained as eye shadow at a drag show, and Day duly continued her comedic "renaissance" by moving on to another celebrated partner, Cary Grant. (Hudson had already tried out another comedic costar, the monolith/diva Gina Lollobrigida, in *Come September*.) *That Touch of Mink*, Day's costarring vehicle with Grant, consolidated her success as America's *über*-movie-star and nurtured the seeds of her decline. Here is the movie that gave birth to the "oldest living virgin" label that disfigured Day's image and blurred her already notable achievements. In its star glitter, in its attitudes toward sex, women, and homosexuality, and in its treatment by the moral guardians, *That Touch of Mink* was the sateen-lined epitome of the sixties sex farce. The ads promised "daring" and "adult," a spicy battle of the sexes enacted by two deities of film, and compounded its appeal to star-watchers by adding appearances by Mickey Mantle, Roger Maris, and Yogi Berra—the baseball equivalent of top-flight movie stars. The consumerist quotient was further raised with an extraneous fashion show, complete with ooh-aah reaction shots of Day, barely visible behind the gauze and nearly in tears over the sheer magnificence of these Gowns. The plot, naturally, took fourth place to the materialism, the star display, and the sex. Again Day strained credulity, this time as a computer operator pounding the unemployment line in Jackie-esque outfits and shellacked hair. Grant suffered no such financial constraints, playing a zillionaire who meets Day when his limo splashes mud on her. Everything came down to one point: would confident he get spunky her into bed before they got married? No one, in 1962, would have supplied the wrong answer, and it was partly as a result of this foregone conclusion that Grant ambled through the proceedings on a take-the-millions-and-run autopilot.

Like others of its kind, *That Touch of Mink* is most notable for the sexual dread underlying its peepshow promises. Day's roommate (Audrey Meadows) spends most of her time weeping at the idea of her friend's lost virtue, and even a visit to the unemployment office involves negotiating an obstacle course of lust: the man (John Astin) who gives Day her weekly check is a scummy sexual harasser. On Grant's part, his phallic self-possession is counterbalanced by a love-hate relationship with his assistant, a self-loathing dipsomaniac intellectual named Roger, played by the perpetual also-ran Gig Young.[2] Roger's sexual-

---

[2]Another assistant is far less prominent, in an unintentional *hommage* to the gayness in *Lover Come Back*. Day's high-fashion makeover is administered by one Leonard, a Bergdorf Goodman coordinator. Less snippy than the lilac-floor Leonard, this one is played by William Lanteau, who essayed a similarly fey turn (as Sylvester) two years later in the sub-Day-Hudson farce *Sex and the Single Girl*.

ity is never specified in the film, yet he is so obsessed with his employer that he spends much of his time in psychoanalysis discussing Grant's sexual and financial acumen. The movies' respect for psychiatry had declined steadily since the forties, and by this time the headshrinking charlatan had become a comedy cliché. Dr. Gruber (Alan Hewitt), Roger's analyst, is a typical hack-fraud, taking Roger's money while remaining uninterested in helping him. His only concern, in fact, is to procure the stock tips that Roger sometimes mentions in his stream-of-consciousness musings. Roger, for his part, is so fascinated by Day's unwillingness to succumb to Grant that he begins telling his doctor about the affair in detail. Gruber, however, has left the room to call his stockbroker and so misses the setup to the story of a wealthy man in pursuit of a feisty young woman, which is recounted in the first person. When the doctor walks in, he hears Roger going on about the man who bought "me" a mink coat, took "me" to Bermuda, and so forth, and reaches the obvious conclusion: Roger has come out and has a rich man chasing after him. The scene goes on for some minutes, far longer than a similar mistaken-identity bit in *Pillow Talk* that had Rock Hudson inadvertently making an appointment to see an obstetrician. The sequence ends with a nasty capper: the doctor calls his stockbroker again and cancels the order because of the "instability" of his source. Then, in several later scenes, Roger calls Gruber to report on the progress of the affair. When he mentions that the topic of marriage has come up, the doctor numbly decides to return to Vienna for a "refresher course." Finally, there is an epilogue with Day and Grant, now married, walking through Central Park with a baby carriage and Roger in tow. They leave briefly, and while Roger is minding the baby Dr. Gruber enters, newly returned from Vienna. Roger happily reports that all has gone well. There has been a wedding, he says, then proudly shows off the blessed event. Fade out on the doctor's astonishment.

The misunderstanding between the lush and his quack shrink is in itself neither daring nor extraordinary, neither offensive nor particularly amusing. So little in these comedies had any real bite that the doctor's presumption that Roger is gay and eventually bears a child is as innocuous as the running gags about Day surrendering her treasured maidenhead. By 1962, after *Some Like It Hot* and *Suddenly, Last Summer*, timid gay jokes were certainly turning up in films, and (as the next chapter will detail) the Production Code Administration was loosening some of its bans on "serious" gay content in films such as *The Children's Hour* and *Walk on the Wild Side*. But the gay subplot in *That Touch of Mink* caused enormous tension between Universal and the Motion Picture Association of America. As with *Tea and Sympathy*, it was the Milquetoast conventional movie, not the forward envelope-pusher, which incited the gravest controversy. When the script treatment for *That Touch of Mink* was first submitted to the Production Code office in December

Gig Young and Alan Hewitt as neurotic patient and mercenary, misunderstanding shrink in *That Touch of Mink*. *Photofest*

1960, it was found to be unacceptable under Code strictures. This was due in part to the Grant character's presumed immorality and the possible "mistress" situation with Day. Firmer objections, however, came with the psychiatrist subplot. Geoffrey Shurlock cited his objection to "the running homosexual comedy routine [which] is in complete violation of the Code." As script negotiations continued over the subsequent months, the Code people made the suggestion that perhaps the doctor might view his patient's "problem" as having a male-female dual personality, not an attack of homosexuality. Nevertheless, the producers fought to retain the scenes as written, despite Shurlock's heated objection to that last scene, in which the doctor thinks that Roger has had his lover's baby. "Upon submission of the finished picture," Universal was warned on July 6, 1961, "if this sequence proves unacceptable, it is our understanding that this part of the picture will be shot in such a way that these scenes could be eliminated."

The war over Roger and his doctor continued over the subsequent months as the film was shot and previewed. The PCA was still saying no, and to prevent a threatened ban, Universal was required to produce evidence that the scenes would not unduly shock or offend viewers. Its proof came in the form of numerous comments culled from cards filled out by preview audiences, which did indeed seem to bear out that the gay-tinged scenes in *That Touch of Mink* were less than a public menace. The reactions of these viewers, as sent from Universal to the PCA, survive as a window on mainstream audiences in 1962 meekly beginning their approach to lightly queer movies:

> "When Gig Young showed the baby to the psychiatrist, it was funny" (female viewer)

> "I found the scenes involving the situation with the psychiatrist to be particularly humerous [sic]" (male viewer)

> "The scenes with Gig Young in the psychiatrist's office added a minor theme which made the main theme less cloying" (male viewer)

> "Sorry to see the homosexual angle injected" (male viewer)

> "The *sick* humor with the psychiatrist was too much!" (male viewer)

Overall, the objections to the doctor scenes were less vehement than the PCA might have expected or perhaps hoped for; predictably, more of the protest came from male spectators. That *Touch of Mink* was granted a Code seal with the scenes retained, albeit with added insurance in the form of a little-seen compromise. For squeamish exhibitors Universal supplied an alternate version which wrapped up the plot with Day and Grant on their honeymoon and then faded to the end title—completely eliminating the baby and the final scene. After it became clear that most audiences were sufficiently grown-up to cope with the raw gutsiness of those final fifty-five seconds, the alternate version promptly disappeared. The unedited version drew the graphic displeasure of the Legion of Decency, who gave it a B rating and complained of "the false glamour with which it surrounds illicit sex. In addition, a sub-plot which uses perversion as a vehicle for humor is highly offensive and unacceptable in a mass medium of entertainment."

The war over *That Touch of Mink*, which recalled the controversy over *Turnabout*, was waged at the precise time when film was attempting more candor about gayness in such films as *Victim* and *Advise and Consent*. Why on earth, then, would something so innocuous be treated with so much gravitas? So much trouble, even a different version, over a few little jokes? Clearly, the double standards were now in place: homosexuality was a Serious Subject in 1962, one not to be joked about. At least yet. For all the seduction humor in *That Touch of Mink*, it was this buffoonish misunderstanding that was singled out for offense. In the days when the Production Code strictures were being loosened, such reactionary conduct is positively bemusing—a throwback to the frets over

Mischa Auer in *Lady in the Dark*. Possibly some of the upset came with the fact that Roger was not only being mistaken for a gay man, but for a sexually active one. Not a Sebastian Venable, perhaps, but one with desires that are acted upon. Even this was not so extraordinary by 1962—it had turned up in films as various as *Voodoo Island* and *The Strange One*—but with a big budget and major stars and gloss, it raised hackles. Nevertheless, the Doris Day comedies were concerned more than anything else with making money, and *That Touch of Mink* was an eminent success in that area. It played holdover engagements throughout America and overseas, and Day retreated ever deeper into a niche she would occupy for the rest of her career.

Films as successful as *Pillow Talk* and *Lover Come Back* and *That Touch of Mink* do not exist in vacuums. As unoriginal as they were in most particulars, they were the standard-bearers for many more glossed-up comedies that waged battles of the sexes with innuendoes and an air of feigned chic. The titles of some of these movies say a great deal about their nature and their era: *The Honeymoon Machine, Sex and the Single Girl, If a Man Answers, Who's Been Sleeping in My Bed?* Some of these were original screenplays, and others were plays or books reconfigured to fit the same mold—the seductions, the settings, the disguise or mistaken identity, the psychiatric and gay jokes. The dramatis personae were consistent as well. Day and Hudson were the trailblazers, and others followed: James Garner, Natalie Wood, Dean Martin, Jane Fonda, Tony Curtis, Jack Lemmon, even Marilyn Monroe in her last, unfinished movie.[3] The interchangeability of the plots was equaled by the sets and costumes, and even the photography, which bathed the sets and the few exteriors in an unvarying glare. At Universal, where these comedies were born, a penchant for fiscal dispatch ensured that sets and furniture would be reused in endless permutations, just like the jokes, all faintly redolent of drying paint and nail polish. As if in homage, that same look was unremittingly replicated at other studios as well. MGM's *The Wheeler Dealers* was a typical example, an attempt at satire that seemed less clever than protracted. James Garner starred as a "real" Rex Stetson type—a Texas longhorn loosed in Manhattan and determined to bluff and deal his way into a stock-market fortune. Lee Remick took the Day role, as an ambitious stock trader, and there were the predictable skirmishes and lunges for laughs. The mood was less leering than tiring, for *The Wheeler Dealers*, with its endless chatter about stock options and unconcerned direction by Arthur Hiller, was just a talky, arduous bore.

---

[3]When Monroe's aborted *Something's Got to Give* finally made it to the screen, it was, fittingly enough, with Doris Day. Sporting notably Marilynesque hair, Day was directed in the retitled *Move Over, Darling* by *Pillow Talk* auteur Michael Gordon.

While the emphasis frequently seemed more on high finance than sex, there was time-out for the standard stupid gay jokes, collected once again into a miniretrospective of established fag shtick. Remick's haughty boyfriend, played by Elliott Reid, is named (once again!) Leonard, an art critic as supercilious as those in *House of Horrors*. In a central sequence, he holds forth at a nightmarish gallery opening filled with fawning matrons and silly fruits. One of them (Bernie Kopell, years before *The Love Boat*) runs around seeking his oracle, Leonard, screaming "Nardo! Nardo!" As in *No Time for Love*, it takes genuine machismo to show up this band of effete twits; here it's Garner the audience is supposed to identify with as he looks askance at the abstracts and drawls to Remick, "Personally, I like horse paintin's!" Kandinskys are for fairies; real men go for Remingtons.

Goodbye, Charlie (1964) was exceptional in this group of films in that it substituted for the usual cheesy gay jokes cheesy lesbian jokes. It was also one of the rare sex comedies with a director of distinction—Vincente Minnelli, at the lowest point of his career to date. (He would follow *Goodbye, Charlie* with even worse dreck, an Elizabeth Taylor–Richard Burton debauch called *The Sandpiper.*) *Charlie* was a sniggering replay of the *Turnabout* gambit, with a Hollywood satyr murdered by a vengeful husband and reincarnated as Debbie Reynolds. Seeing Reynolds enacting a horny Malibu hustler plunked down in a petite female body is a quease-making experience, something akin to sitting in the front row at a staged Brownie reading of *Portnoy's Complaint*. Posing as Charlie's supposed widow, Reynolds leers ceaselessly at other women, grunting with weird bravado as she whacks them on their posteriors. On Broadway George Axelrod's seamy farce had at least had the benefit of Lauren Bacall's baritoney panache; Twentieth Century–Fox originally bought the property for Marilyn Monroe, who might also have given it some intriguing edges. Instead, there was a heavy-breathing Reynolds and a stymied Minnelli, who managed—by attempting to handle Axelrod's smarmy and cynical allusions with antiseptic élan—to make the proceedings even more unpleasant.

Given the influence of the Doris Day–Rock Hudson films, it's easy to forget that the team was paired only three times. Their final outing, *Send Me No Flowers* (1964), differed from the others in significant ways. It was based on a play, featured them as a married couple, and was more concerned with hypochondria than seduction, with less time out for sexual misunderstandings and with suburbia standing in for the usual urban gloss. Because of these differences, and perhaps because of changing times, the grosses and reviews fell off noticeably. Day and Hudson made no more films together; in fact, they made no joint appearances to speak of until the 1985 press conference that made it clear there was something terribly wrong with Rock Hudson. Yet the gay overtones in *Send Me No Flowers* were not totally negligible, nor were they completely intentional. They came, not through gay disguise or allusion, but through an actor who would gaily imprint film and television over the ensuing decade and a half, as surely as Franklin Pangborn had done in the thirties and forties. Paul Lynde had made his first mark on Broadway and was slowly becoming a film presence in such things as *Bye, Bye Birdie*, where he sweated bullets as a harassed dad. But Paul Lynde as a father? No, no, no . . . His affect was too gay, even when covert, to pretend such things. *Send Me No Flowers* was one of the movies that set him aright. In a role lasting just a few minutes, that of a preternaturally cheerful funeral director eagerly hawking his product, he strolled off with all honors and laid waste to Hudson's attempts at comedic timing. Here was a genuine clown—a gay clown at that—and more and more through the decade he would keep on stealing movies and TV shows from more famous names. In *The Glass-Bottom Boat* (1966), as a federal agent in disguise, he offered the funniest drag routine since Jack Lemmon's Daphne. Soon enough he would be one of the cornerstones of television's queerest sitcom, *Bewitched*, and in the 1970s he brought authentically camp sarcasm into millions of American homes at the center of *The Hollywood Squares*. Lynde's gayness was total, and brinksmanship was his gambit: he traded on every last allusion and connotation of gay humor while maintaining the sheerest translucent membrane of straight conventionality. From *Send Me No Flowers* onward, as a bridge from pre- to post-Stonewall, Paul Lynde was the gay man America wanted—closeted yet out, unthreatening and, often enough, breathtakingly funny.[4]

Rock Hudson, on the other hand, was the gay man who needed to hide. Unlike Paul Lynde, and unlike the Grady Suttons of an earlier age, his gayness was kept entirely separate from his work, except when that work needed to comfort Americans with doses of gay ridicule. Nothing else can account for the comedy he made the year after *Send Me No Flowers*. After a Lollobrigida rematch called *Strange Bedfellows*, the corporate wisdom of Universal Studios returned him to *Pillow Talk* territory in *A Very Special Favor*. It probably seemed like a sure thing—casting him as Paul Chadwick, a Manhattan playboy so devastating that women line up in the morning to cook his breakfast and do his laundry, and then having him match wills and libidos with stern yet pliant (after all, she's French) psychologist Leslie Caron. The tussles and tropes were essentially the same as

---

[4]Paul Rudnick, whose writing often reflected the spirit of queens past, paid interesting tribute to Lynde in his one-act play *On the Fence* (2001). In Rudnick's conceit, the martyred Matthew Shepard was attended, at the moment of death, by two iconically queer angels: Eleanor Roosevelt, all common sense and compassion, and the bitchy, Bloody Mary–swilling Lynde. The playwright's intentions were a bit wobbly, but it was good to see Lynde given something like his cultural due.

ROCK HUDSON

Real name: Roy Harold Scherer, Jr. Born Winnetka, Ill., November 17, 1925; died Beverly Hills, Calif., October 2, 1985

It's unlikely that Rock ever intended to be a symbol of anything. By all accounts he was a nice guy as well as a busy and hardworking movie star, one of the very last to be made by the old studio system. These things, for him, would have made a decent epitaph. How odd, then, that after his death his work was virtually obliterated by the revelations of his gayness and death from AIDS. He was not the first prominent person to die from AIDS, and hardly the last—but he was the breakthrough, the catalyst that brought the horror home and inspired people like his friend and former costar, Elizabeth Taylor, to AIDS activism. Many of us knew, long before his death, that he was gay. Yet the careful construction of the Hollywood closet was never more obvious than here. From himbo starlet to big-time leading man and TV star, Rock maintained a careful façade: a pleasant nature, one short-lived beard-style marriage to his (gay) agent's secretary, and otherwise a private life carefully kept well under fan radar. In a prolific career laden with mediocre ephemera, he did give good performances on a few occasions, as in *Giant* and *Seconds*. Most often, neither his roles nor his films were so much exceptional as commercially viable, with his acting technique, such as it was, consisting of an amiable blandness, a modest macho bravado. Tucked in with all the action pictures and nondescript dramas were his sex comedies with Doris Day and others, which were among the most profitable of his career. How did he feel about the gay jokes in these movies? How on earth did he handle the layers of disguise he was compelled to effect? We likely won't ever know the full story, and it may be that Rock himself never communed totally with the irony of these movies, certainly not in the incisive fashion of Mark Rapoport's memorable *Rock Hudson's Home Movies*. In the course of being a professional movie star, he knew all too well how to play the straight card. But playing straight playing gay, as he did in those comedies—that was another, odder story, and like the rest of Hudson's life it was far more interesting than most of his movies.

before, which was not surprising, considering the return presences of director Michael Gordon and of cowriter Stanley Shapiro, who had won an Oscar for *Pillow Talk* and a nomination for *That Touch of Mink*. The presence of Caron and Charles Boyer was obviously intended to add ooh-la-la to the proceedings, as the ads asserted that "Only a French father would ask for such *A Very Special Favor*!" And within the first few minutes of screen time, with Hudson standing before grainy process shots of Paris, it was clear that the meager genre of the sixties sex comedy had more than exhausted its potential. The winks were replaced by yawns, and the tired TV-style musical score could have easily been replaced with the sound of a mimeograph machine cranking out script pages. It was perhaps fitting, therefore, that in this sour and sorry excuse for entertainment the gay jokes of these movies would reach their pathetic climax.

From its very first frames *A Very Special Favor* promised effervescence—the opening credits featured a glass filled to the rim with the finest champagne—and, it was soon clear, was only prepared to deliver flatulence. Within a few minutes, the essential premise was in place: good old Yankee machismo, as embodied by Hudson, will win out every single time. French suavity, as elegantly embodied by Boyer, prevails on American seduction (Hudson) to free Caron (as Boyer's daughter) from her prissy mama's boy fiancé (Dick Shawn). This is the favor of the title, as set into a context so familiar that it amounted to a retrospective: masquerade, as in *Pillow Talk* and *Lover Come Back;* skirmishes and shrink jokes à la *That Touch of Mink*, he-man versus effete jokes out of *The Wheeler Dealers*, the same bogus married-with-children fade-out as *Lover* and *Mink*, and even more gay insinuations than with Roger and Dr. Gruber. Hudson, looking baggy-eyed and uninterested, went through the same old motions amid Universal's ghastly evocations of New York and Paris—all-metal accessories, modernist paintings, and a curious assortment of blood-red walls illuminated by those harsh lights that made every scene, indoors and out, seem like high noon. After Hudson's salary, the highest item on the budget must have been for bulbs and electricity. As a cringing specimen named Arnold (why not Leonard?), Dick Shawn was particularly ill-treated in all this, eternally kowtowing to Caron and to his domineering mom. Moreover, the central subterfuges were notably unpleasant. Hudson/Chadwick first poses as a helpless sexual compulsive in order to trap Caron; realizing what he's up to, she then parries by inventing an affair with a Spanish superman, spinning such sizzling tales that he becomes, apparently, impotent. It goes without saying that these maneuvers were depicted at extreme length and without any detectable humor. Even Hudson, in a later interview, complained about the unpleasantness of it all: "The things I had to do to Leslie Caron were cruel. They weren't funny [and] her revenge, that was also too cruel; it completely castrated me and it didn't work. It was just too strong."

It was the final payoff of *A Very Special Favor*, however, that saves it from the deserved oblivion of most nonmovies. Hudson's ultimate gambit (with Boyer's help) to steal Caron from Shawn, which occupies the last reel of the movie, is an inexorably nightmarish procession of smirks and shtick. Broken and defeated by her talk of hot Spanish sex, Rock is revived only when Boyer inspires him to go one step further. The ploy unfolds, in a series of short scenes, like a deranged rehash of *Tea and Sympathy:*

A TRAGIC MISTAKE:

A Very Special Favor, Reel 11

SCENE: Paul Chadwick's Office *Chadwick [Hudson] and Michel [Boyer] discuss what to do next:*

MICHEL: What if you went off with another woman?

CHADWICK: She'd never believe it. At this point she's convinced I'm afraid to touch them. Another woman wouldn't work.

MICHEL: Unfortunately, you don't have much choice. You can't run off with a man.

CHADWICK: Heh . . . why not? . . . She's a psychologist—according to her predictions that's what could happen. After what she did to me, *that* she might believe!

SCENE: Lobby of Chadwick's Building (a residence hotel) *Chadwick speaks to Mickey the switchboard operator [Nita Talbot] about going away with him for the weekend*

CHADWICK: First I want you to cut your hair. . . . We'll go to Brooks Brothers and get you a nice conservative business suit.

MICKEY: A man's suit? . . . Where are we going for the weekend, the YMCA?

SCENE: Chadwick's Bedroom *Mickey has short hair and is dressing up in a man's suit and tie.*

CHADWICK: You know why I have to do this, don't you?

MICKEY: You have to be seen leaving with a man . . . so she'll follow you. . . . I always wanted to be part of a triangle, but I never thought I'd end up as the other man!

SCENE: Lobby of Chadwick's Building *Arnold [Shawn] helps his mother [Norma Varden] to check out*

MOTHER: I'd feel much better if you went back to West Palm Beach with me. New York's a wicked place, son. The women are not to be trusted.

ARNOLD: I know Lauren was a disappointment, Mother, but I'm moving into this men's club tomorrow. I'll be safe there.

The elevator door opens and Chadwick and Mickey (dressed as a man) scamper out.

CHADWICK *(takes Mickey's hand):* Mickey, you're an angel. I'll never forget what you're doing. *(Kisses her hand.)*

MOTHER *(outraged):* You *are* coming home. In this city, you're not even safe in a men's club!

SCENE: Exterior of Chadwick's Building *Chadwick and Mickey run toward a cab*

CHADWICK *(to the doorman):* If anyone asks, I'll be at the Stardust Motel on Long Island for the weekend. *(Tips doorman, gets in cab with Mickey, and drives off)*

SCENE: A Car. *Etienne [Walter Slezak] drives Lauren [Caron] and Michel to Chadwick's building.*
MICHEL: I thought you'd be overjoyed.
LAUREN: I broke his spirit . . . I pushed him too far!

SCENE: Exterior of Chadwick's building *Etienne's car pulls up.*
MICHEL: Did you see Mr. Chadwick go out?
DOORMAN: Yes sir, he said he'd be at the Stardust Motel on Long Island.
LAUREN: Was he alone?
DOORMAN: No, he was with a man . . . strange-looking little fellow! *(Lauren puts her hand up to her face in distress.)*

SCENE: A motel room *Chadwick sees Lauren approaching and makes Mickey exit through a window. A distraught Lauren rushes in.*
LAUREN: Where is your . . . your companion?
CHADWICK: Mickey? Left to get groceries. *(Lauren locks the door.)* What are you doing?
LAUREN: Trying to keep you from making a tragic mistake. *(Drops the key down her dress.)*
CHADWICK *(in mock-feminine shock.):* Don't do this to me!
LAUREN: But I'm on your side. I want to help. You want the key? *(She removes her coat.)* Take it. *(She continues to make advances while he registers prissy dismay.)*
CHADWICK *(tries to break down the door):* It's too late for therapy. *(He starts to climb through the window)*
LAUREN: It's not too late. You must fight. . . . You were once a magnificent man. Women pleaded for your favors! *(She continues to encourage him, and finally he unzips her dress and carries her to the bedroom.)*
CHADWICK: It's all coming back!
LAUREN: You won't forget a thing!

SCENE: A maternity ward. *A nurse shows a baby to Chadwick and Michel.*
MICHEL: A granddaughter. There is only one joy more infinite.
CHADWICK: No more favors.
MICHEL: What am I asking for? A grandson . . . I beg you, Paul—a grandson. One last favor?
CHADWICK: Okay, okay. . . . but this is absolutely the last time. Come on, let's go see Mommy! *(He and Michel escort five little girls to Lauren's room.)*
END TITLE

1955-57

Amidst the elegant appointments of a quickie Long Island motel, Leslie Caron endeavors to save Rock Hudson from homosexuality in *A Very Special Favor*. *Photofest*

Give it this: it is endlessly fascinating, in the manner of a particularly awful train wreck. In its own tacky way, the whole sequence seems to sum up everything wrong with mid-sixties entertainment. More than anything else it lacks guts, even the courage of its shabby convictions. The timorousness of the approach is as glaring as the lighting, and it is not surprising that some of this was dictated by the fading, if still righteous, Production Code Administration. The first script submitted to the MPAA was rejected outright: "The story is preoccupied totally with the sex act—in this case, illicit sex. . . . the dialogue and action deals exclusively with either attempting, plotting, lying about, or being interrupted in, seduction. To further complicate this matter the suspicion of homosexuality is introduced into the plot." Some of the sex was duly toned down, and the emasculation (as it were) of the whole ruse made it even more smarmy. That tone underscored the fake psychology (and bad comedy) underlying the idea that heterosexual failure and impotence naturally lead to homosexuality, and the whole idea of employing a woman to dress as a man seems senseless. Ultimately, this movie goes further than perhaps any other comedy in its assertion that (supposed) true love can only come about through deception.

Serving as the cornerstone of this whole enterprise is the willing presence of (possibly) the biggest gay star in film history. Since *Pillow Talk* and *Lover Come Back*, Hudson's comic technique had become as bleary as his appearance. When he was required to register male weakness, he simpers and whines like a stereotyped Hollywood coed. A close look at his face during these "gay" scenes reveals no trace of self-recognition; by 1964 he had long since perfected the supreme compartmentalization of a gay man living a publicly straight life. (Note also that in his later comments about the movie, he made no mention of the gay angle.) However, his face betrays nothing else, either—not the awareness that he's been playing these stupid roles much too often, or that appearing in such crap was ultimately a vile way to earn a well-paid living. As he shepherds a woman in male drag to a seedy Long Island motel, he seems to be encompassing all of America's lies about sexuality, indeed about human feeling. Small wonder that films such as this one hastened the end of the big-studio system. The other companies were being bought out and merged, and in short order Universal would transfer much of its conveyer-belt movie operation to television, where Hudson would obtain much of his later employment. The response to *A Very Special Favor* certainly hastened such changes. *Time*'s label of "Desperately tasteless" summed up the critical reaction, and *Newsweek*, calling it "a Hudson-formula movie," complained about the *Tea and Sympathy* ploy and perceptively noted that Hudson and Caron's marriage at the fade-out was "the ultimate mutual revenge"—a stern fate indeed for a supposed breezy romance.

Changing times and tastes, and the increasingly base quality of the films themselves, would soon spell an end to the likes of *A Very Special Favor*. One of its few successors was *Any Wednesday* (1966), one of the farces Jane Fonda appeared in before she became, in effect, Jane Fonda. Here, as the mistress of tycoon Jason Robards, she has a close encounter with a hummingbird of an interior decorator named Felix (Jack Fletcher), who behaves as if caught in an *Our Betters* time warp. "Oh my dear," he sputters, "you're so wrong for this room—so stark wrong!" And since the sixties were beginning to be more frank, he is obliged, before he sweeps out, to allude to his own promiscuity: "My *dear,* the rumpled beds I've seen in my lifetime . . . not to mention the beds I personally have rumpled!" That's an interesting line, since gays onscreen were usually kept separate from sex, but it's still old wine in new bottles: more frank than earlier years, yet possibly even less enlightened.

Struggles to retain virginity, feigned gayness as a tool of seduction, revenge and deceit beyond reckoning—such was the state of escapism in an America on the verge of Vietnam and the sexual revolution. The pillow-talk comedies of the sixties sold themselves to viewers as offering more lowdown on sex than ever before. In so doing, they deceived themselves even more than they did the millions who paid to see them. Marketing lies has always been a prime part of the movie mechanism, but these deluded specimens took that premise further than usual, and in the wrong direction. The glazed frenzy of these movies became increasingly off-kilter with reality, even the reality, such as it was, of movies. No wonder that America's sexualities, and its filmmaking, began taking such a sharp left turn. Even as these comedies were being made, America's more "serious" films were beginning to deal openly with gayness. Not necessarily with skill, and certainly not with total honesty or compassion, but alongside *A Very Special Favor* they did seem like an advance. The next chapter will chart that slow move forward, which occurred even as the gay movement was torturously gaining momentum. Meanwhile, we can consign the bouffant glories of *That Touch of Mink* to the landfills operating in all our minds.

THIRTEEN

The Wild Side

"Mature" treatment of prostitution and girl-meets-girl situations . . .
—Heading of *Variety* review of *Walk on the Wild Side*

I had a miserable time at the picture and I am disposed to remark, as the late Heywood Broun once did, "The Lesbian said about it the better."
—Philip K. Scheur, *Los Angeles Times* review of *The Children's Hour*

Blinded as they were by their own tawdry glow, the sixties sex comedies were almost poignantly unaware that they were being made in an age whose most salient feature was constant, drastic change. Cinema of denial may in fact have been the only way for commercial Hollywood to operate in a decade whose ending was so completely out of sync with its beginning. There was little sense of continuity in a time that moved from Nixon losing to Nixon winning, from the Rat Pack to flower children, from a tense cold war to an outright hot war, from "High Hopes" to "Proud Mary," and all the time enclosing the struggles of race, gender, and sexuality that revealed America's supposed homogeneity for the sham it was. As each year brought more change and crisis, the house continued to divide against itself while it somehow remained standing. For those who chose not to go the denial route, the movies, very slowly, were lowering their guard, at times even approaching relevance.

The epochal moments of the sixties are well known past the point of cliché: from the elections to the assassinations and riots, from Selma to Saigon to Stonewall, the profound transformations in the way we thought, looked, and interacted. A less draconian milestone concerned the movies' capacity to mirror these realities. With the Production Code becoming more of an anachronism

every year, more producers were willing, in the early sixties, to defy it and operate outside its strictures and risk the denial of a seal of approval. The major battles of the 1950s had weakened the Code in many areas, and the next bastion to
crumble would be the official ban against homosexuality. Beginning in 1960 and
culminating more than a year later, a series of events, mainly nonrelated, led to
changes in the Production Code that would officially allow the movies to look at
homosexuality. Those queer things previously sneaked in could now, under the
proper circumstances, be allowed. In the films of 1962 the visibility and specificity shot up markedly, making the old codes and signals no longer necessary.

As lame a step as the Code alteration now seems, more than seven years
before the Stonewall riots it was somewhat of a liberal victory. It also had a
depressingly familiar downside, for its blessings were at best spectacularly
mixed. "Proper circumstances" was the key, a rude caveat entailing not only
seriousness but also some sort of condemnation. As allusive permissiveness
gave way to specificity, there would be, more than ever, sanctioned condemnation and ridicule, the sense of the pejorative spiking from the judgmental to the
demonizing. Yet for thousands, even millions of men and women, the morass of
negativity was transcended by the new visibility being purveyed. The plain fact
was that some of these people would now see parts of themselves onscreen in
clearer relief, and a few of them could even find ways, in that unsung gay year
of 1962, to escape the feeling that they were being told they were bad.

Perhaps it was fitting that Tennessee Williams, his artistry ever tempered
by distressed psychology, was in attendance as this change was in progress. In
this case it was the film of his only novella, *The Roman Spring of Mrs. Stone.*
Here was shocking autobiography of a sort, another of the through-a-shot-glass-
darkly psychodramas in which Williams projected his manifold neuroses onto a
compellingly sad heroine. Karen Stone is a glamorous, aging hack of a stage star
at the end of a luxurious tether. Her husband dead and her career in shreds, she
finds herself in the Eternal City blessed only with money and time. She is, in
short, an easy mark for a luscious opportunist, and his name is Paolo. When
her insecurity and his venal ambivalence combine to kill the affair, an angel of
death hovers expectantly. Karen was a kind of Blanche with a touch of Scarletty
grit, so quite naturally she was portrayed by Vivien Leigh, nearing the end of
her own fraying rope. Warren Beatty, struggling with the accent in his second
film but visually quite the picture, was Paolo.

Ostensibly, *The Roman Spring of Mrs. Stone* is about Karen's crush-and-
burn affair with Paolo, its script peppered with brutal lines about aging and
aimlessness and death. "Four more years and a slit throat would be a conve-
nience," Leigh declares in her driest tones. So it's not specifically about gay
sex. Or is it? Even more than in other Williams stories, the subtexts dominate,
and this is another of those *Our Betters*–type films that now seem completely

gay: the writer, the scenarist (Gavin Lambert), the director (José Quintero, a Williams specialist directing his only film), and a cast of queer icons (Leigh, Lotte Lenya, Ernest Thesiger, even Cleo Laine singing in one scene). The gayness sprang less from the specifics than from mood and allusion and detail, starting immediately after the prologue and credits. One of the first shots charts the terrain without blinking: Quintero's camera immediately spots a cute young Italian boy hooking up with an aging businessman on the Spanish Steps, after which we get ogling views of young boys (one in a bottoms-up pose) waiting for their pickups. Soon enough, several scenes make it clear that Paolo's pimp (Lenya) connects her studs with johns of both sexes.

As the nasty procuress, Lenya delivers the epigraph that nails the whole show unerringly, even more harshly than Karen's exhortation to a slit throat. More cruel yet, it is intended that Karen should overhear herself being discussed with such sour delight:

> CONTESSA [Lenya]: Recently, I've heard her described as a chicken hawk. . . . A chicken hawk is a bird of prey with a sharp beak, long claws, and a terrible appetite. (*Cackles*) She feeds exclusively on the flesh of tender young chickens. Oddly enough, the species is American!

The comments make their mark, and the final rift between Karen and Paolo comes a few minutes later. As she takes her leave, Lenya surveys the ruins with a sarcastic "Wunderbar," the one bellowed word carrying the weight of an especially baleful Brecht/Weill ballad. But . . . when has a woman ever, *ever* been referred to as a chicken hawk? The term was strictly one of gay slang, and the coded displacement can only be seen as deliberate. More visibly than usual, the gay intentions behind so much of Williams's heterosexual characters welled all the way up to the surface.[1] *Mrs. Stone*'s terrors appeared muted after the lacerations of *Suddenly, Last Summer*, and it was a notable box-office failure. The mixed reviews were echoed by its subsequent reputation in gay and straight quarters alike; even opinions of Leigh's brittle, delicately sardonic performance vary wildly. In a brash and unsettled year it made for an oddly wistful oasis, one of Williams's most interesting works and a genuine and notably unsung gay cult movie.

Wistfulness of another sort came around that same time in, of all things, a Tony Curtis movie about a war hero, produced by Universal. Offbeat for Curtis and downbeat for early-sixties Hollywood, *The Outsider* was the relatively

---

[1]Not enough onto the surface, nevertheless, for the Production Code people, who were deep into the "there are none so blind" mode. At the same time they were going nuts over *That Touch of Mink*, they offered only two cautions for *Mrs. Stone*'s script, cautioning against a too-graphic sex scene and wincing at Leigh's use of the word *pimp*.

unvarnished biography of Ira Hayes, the Native American soldier who was one of the six marines to raise the flag on Iwo Jima. This was less a morale-rouser than a study of one man's losing battle with prejudice, fame, and alcohol, and Curtis was so sturdy in the role that even his makeup and wig were convincing. Also convincing was Hayes's strong bond with a fellow marine named Jim Sorenson (James Franciscus), a blond WASP whose death after Iwo Jima precipitates Hayes's decline and early death. *The Outsider* was one of the last of the allusive "read into it what you want to" Hollywood movies, the relationship between Hayes and Sorenson obvious for some and just pals for others. Nevertheless, the signals came through quite strongly, especially in a sheepish morning-after scene and with the use of the old Gertrude Niesen ballad "Where Are You?" which obviously becomes "their song." After Sorenson is killed, it becomes the dirge that accompanies Hayes's trips to the bottle. At the very end of his life he goes out under the stars and cries out, "Where are you?" With no ingenue in the wings, the implication is clear, perhaps more so than if Hayes had not been an ethnic type. While white heroes require whitewashing, Hayes's outsider status permitted somewhat more candor than the Production Code normally allowed.

Exactly what the Code would allow was becoming a matter of noisy dispute. In 1960, when the Legion of Decency overruled Geoffrey Shurlock and his Production Code associates over the snails and oysters of *Spartacus*, its position was bolstered by the constraints of the Code itself. Shurlock and company, in trying to look forward, had been hindered not only by the Roman Catholic Church but also by the sheer regressiveness of the document they were charged to uphold. It was obvious that such battles would continue to occur, only to abate if the Code were changed. In short order, several projects were in the works that seemed specifically designed to challenge the Code's ban on homosexual content. While these were not operating in any deliberate concord, obviously some currents of inevitability were determined to run in a certain direction. William Wyler's "authentic" remake of *The Children's Hour* is usually given the most credit for the eventual Code amendment, and Otto Preminger's *Advise and Consent*, with its gay blackmail subplot, is known to have bolstered the argument as well. Nevertheless, don't expect history to offer too many shortcuts or clear-cuts. The move to change the Code stemmed from pressures emanating from a number of different quarters, beginning before the *Spartacus* contretemps. Nothing is new under the sun, and so it was that many of the forces effecting that ultimate change have already been encountered in earlier incarnations: Wyler, *The Children's Hour*, Preminger, and producer Charles K. Feldman. Plus, wouldn't you know it, those older-than-the-hills standbys of decadent sexuality, Sodom and Gomorrah.

In the early autumn of 1960 Feldman submitted a troublesome script for Code approval. Ostensibly it was based on Nelson Algren's novel *A Walk on the*

Wild Side, the tough and seamy tale of a randy Texas boy who finds himself out-matched in a world of New Orleans vice. The novel lost the first word of its title, and just about everything else as well—this had as much to do with its source material as had the recent film of *The Sound and the Fury*. In the course of a tumultuous evolution the project passed through the hands of any number of screenwriters, including novelist John Fante, Clifford Odets, Ben Hecht, and Wendell Hayes, and ended up a messy retread of lost-love clichés with overlays of prostitution, civic corruption, Mexican food, and lesbianism. Feldman had dual intentions for *Walk on the Wild Side*. It was to cement the stardom of his mistress, Capucine, and it was to be a Code-confronting envelope-pusher in the tradition of another filmed Algren novel, *The Man with the Golden Arm*. While the brothel setting had been part of the novel, it was Hayes who later took the credit for putting it under the domination of a madam having an affair with the Capucine character. Geoffrey Shurlock's response to the submitted script could not have been a surprise to Feldman. There were, he said, "two definite Code problems . . . the lesbian relationship between your two leading characters [and] an unacceptably detailed portrayal of brothel activities." A few weeks later, Code officials met with *Wild Side* director Edward Dmytryk, and an altered Production Code was proposed. That idea was promptly rejected, and Feldman and his staff were urged to tone down the script.

The comparative bravado that enabled Feldman to confront the Code was the stock in trade of Hollywood's highest-profile bluenose-tweaker, Otto Preminger. From *The Moon Is Blue* to *The Man with the Golden Arm* to *Anatomy of a Murder*, he took special pleasure in breaking down Code limitations, risking the denial of a Code seal, and glorying in the resulting controversy, publicity, and profit. (Think of him, with a little stretch, as a bald, male, Teutonic Madonna.) With sex, drugs, and rape already under his belt (filmically speaking), he decided, after completing *Exodus* in 1960, to take on politics and homosexuality. *Advise and Consent*, Allen Drury's 1959 novel of D.C. skullduggery (adapted for Broadway the following year), could not have been filmed with any fidelity before the 1960s. Its take on political chicanery as the capital's prime currency would, in a McCarthyish time, have been branded instant Commie. Added to this was the fact that one of its leading characters, Senator Brig Anderson, is being black-mailed about his gay past—a fact, not an allegation. Canny provocateur that he was, Preminger knew that, in a time after both Eisenhower and *Suddenly, Last Summer*, this could work on the screen. And, despite his protestations to the contrary—made to mollify Code administrators—he planned to highlight, not obscure, the gay subplot.

At this same time another high-profile director was planning to mount his own take on Washington. Gore Vidal's play *The Best Man* (1960) had taken a pre-dictably mordant and droll look at the phenomenon of the political convention, with a good/liberal candidate (allegedly based on JFK and Adlai Stevenson) vying with a bad/conservative one (think: Nixon) for the presidential nomination. Behold, gay blackmail surfaces once again, this time with charges against the creep that the good guy declines to use. While the play had not had a long run, it seemed, in one director's opinion, like the right movie stuff for the Kennedy age. This director had made one of the few good movies about American politics, and more than twenty years after *Mr. Smith Goes to Washington* Frank Capra decided to give his own spin to Vidal's Washington merry-go-round. It was soon clear, unfortunately, that this spin emanated from someone deep into an artistic decline. Determining that Vidal's Democratic wryness had un-American overtones, the Republican Capra began transforming the play into a gee-whiz look at how a great guy can overcome the obstacles and be a winner. An early script drew, from one United Artists executive, what might be termed an unenthusiastic response: "No one could take that many [clichés], back to back, without vomiting." Nevertheless, Capra's name was still attached to *The Best Man* in the spring of 1961, when UA officials took notice that, with this project and *Advise and Consent* both on the company schedule, the studio would be challenging the Production Code with two films dealing with gay accusations.

Make that three films. Ostensibly refreshed after the grueling Roman holiday of *Ben-Hur*, William Wyler was planning a return to filmmaking that would be both a regression and an advance. *These Three* had been his breakthrough into the top echelons a quarter of a century earlier, and he felt that now was the time to call a spade a spade . . . or, rather, call it *The Children's Hour* and do it again, this time with genuine lesbianism. When the play was revived on Broadway in 1952, directed by Lillian Hellman herself and with Kim Hunter and Patricia Neal in the leads, it seemed unusually pertinent, a prescient reflection of McCarthyist character assassination. Nine years later Wyler—now one of the most prestige-encrusted of directors—looked at it again. His interest stoked by a combination of a changed climate and a certain nostalgia, he contacted Hellman to do the screenplay once again. Following the death of Hellman's companion, Dashiell Hammett, the job passed to John Michael Hayes, who had collaborated successfully with Hitchcock on *North by Northwest*. In 1936 the title *The Children's Hour* was too notorious to be used; in 1961 it was initially thought too meek. Certainly the new title given the project jibed quite well with the playwright's take on lesbianism: Wyler and Hayes called it *Infamous!* and submitted it for Production Code approval. Geoffrey Shurlock's response, dated May 3, 1961, was interestingly ambiguous:

> Inasmuch as this story deals with a false charge of homosexuality between your two female leads, we could not approve it under the present Code regulations, which read: "Sex perversion or any inference of it is forbidden."

As I further indicated, the Code problem stems from the subject matter itself. We found nothing in the treatment of this subject in the script itself that would seem to be offensive.

Even without creative interpretation, Shurlock's drift is clear. He knew that the Code ban on homosexuality was even more outdated than the Code itself, was likely to change, and seems to have been giving that change a tacit welcome. Accordingly, MPAA president Eric Johnston received a letter several days later from United Artists CEO Arthur C. Krim.[2] Krim noted that his company had three films on its upcoming slate—*Advise and Consent, The Best Man,* and *Infamous!*—dealing with homosexuality. He mentioned that in none of the trio would there be *actual* sexuality; the first two titles dealt with charges of past behavior, and *Infamous! / The Children's Hour* dealt with allegations. (He also fudged a bit by saying that those charges were totally false, when the play ultimately revealed that Martha did indeed have concealed longings.) The letter ended with a request, brief and to the point: "We are most anxious to distribute these three pictures with a Code seal, and I am hopeful that you will initiate the steps necessary for consideration of an amendment to the Code which will permit this." The appeal had been officially made.

As Krim pushed for a Code change, some other queer matters were also occupying the MPAA. Two months before the Krim petition, an independent company called Transcontinental Films had submitted a script for a film version of Arthur Miller's play (originally a one-acter, later revised and enlarged) *A View from the Bridge.* Again, the script largely centered on that pesky recurring concept of alleged gayness, in this case false and stemming from the semi-incestuous longings of a loudmouthed longshoreman for his niece. (He bashes, and eventually and contemptuously kisses, the niece's willowy fiancé.) The planned film was not particularly beholden to the U.S. studio system, with European financing, an international cast, and interiors shot in Paris. For this reason, the producers reacted with notable outrage when Shurlock quoted them Code chapter and verse about gay matters. Noting that shooting had already started, Transcontinental's Paul Graetz proceeded to lay into the Code:

> After I read your letter, the first thing I did was to check the date to make sure that it really had been written in 1961, and one of the first questions that comes to my mind is whether or not the Code Administration is at all conscious of the fact that we are all obliged to march towards new horizons. . . . The comments

---

[2]Then, as always, United Artists functioned less as a movie studio than as a releasing organization. Krim was not a mogul producer on the order of Darryl Zanuck or (in a later time) Harvey Weinstein; he had éclat but not true blockbuster *clout.* He was also the husband of Dr. Mathilde Krim, in later decades one of the most estimable pioneers in AIDS research.

contained in your letter of March 15th make it apparent to me that you certainly have not seen the play and did not read the screen play. There is as much homosexuality in this picture as you or I are Chinese dancers. . . . If pictures like "Suddenly Last Summer" are being distributed throughout the world with the benediction of your Code Administration, how is it humanly possible that your office can write me a letter refusing to give your Production Code Seal to A VIEW FROM THE BRIDGE on account of its homosexual inferences.

Who would have talked to Joe Breen that way? Obviously Transcontinental was prepared to let the Code go hang, if necessary, and release *A View from the Bridge* without a seal.

A cacophony of Code-induced alarms was being sounded at this time by yet another international coproduction. Never mind that the cities of the plain were destroyed for a multitude of sins; in the popular imagination, Sodom and Gomorrah were most associated with one particular attribute. And certainly sodomy, or other displays of homosexuality, would be more photogenically lurid than the inhospitality cited by the book of Genesis as the chief cause of God's displeasure. The film *Sodom and Gomorrah* would be, at any rate, a true conglomeration, a virtual United Nations of a pseudobiblical epic. With imposingly assured cluelessness, producer Joseph E. Levine managed to encompass both the American blockbusterism of *Ben-Hur* and the toga-party Italian penny-wisdom of his biggest hit, *Hercules.* The cast mingled fifties Hollywood actors (Stewart Granger and Pier Angeli) with the more cosmopolitan Stanley Baker and Anouk Aimée, plus a mostly Italian cast of trillions and the oddly chosen American director Robert Aldrich.[3] The assistant director actually did as much of the work—Sergio Leone, soon-to-be father of the Clint Eastwood spaghetti western. The title was as much of a hodgepodge as the script, being given in some places as *The Last Days of Sodom and Gomorrah* and onscreen as SODOM AND GOMORRAH with a tiny "The Last Days of" meekly superimposed over it. What mattered most to the Production Code people was the amount and the nature of Sodom's sins. Sure enough, Levine was getting ready to howl. It was *The Sign of the Cross* all over again, with teased hair and blue eye shadow tossed in: sin had to be shown in order to be condemned, and incidentally in the most erotic fashion possible. It was judged that male homosexuality would be far less appealing than lesbianism, and so the Scriptures came in for a rewrite. Sodom's King Bera was given a tidy sex-reassignment, and in the chic jet-setty person of Aimée the Queen was shown dallying with playmates past (Angeli,

---

[3]Talk about offbeat career paths. Aldrich was hitting Sodom some years after the noir nihilism of *Kiss Me Deadly* and just prior to the fag-hag Guignol of *What Ever Happened to Baby Jane?* The ascetic sensationalism of *The Killing of Sister George* lay a few years in the future.

later Lot's salinized wife) and present (a Bond-girl-type Asian honey).[4] Besides lesbianism, Sodom's chief sin was here depicted as a thirst for particularly nasty types of spectator torture, including a giant human rotisserie and a trick dungeon with movable crushing walls. The hapless Shurlock could only, in reply to this script, sputter helplessly before proceeding with an exhaustive list of thou-shalt-nots:

> It would seem to be difficult to tell a story of Sodom and Gomorrah that does not contain an inference of sex perversion, inasmuch as this is generally accepted as the reason the cities were destroyed.
> It would seem therefore, to meet the Code requirement, that it would be necessary to tell a different story, particularly as regards the relationship between the Queen and Ildith [Angeli]; and to specifically give some other reason for the catastrophe.

Given that *Sodom and Gomorrah* was European-based in both its funding and its production, Shurlock's objections mattered little. A film such as this would be released in several different versions and languages, its explicitness tailored to the requirements of each country. Cinema was more international than ever, and with the likes of *La Dolce Vita* (which featured some incidental gay couples) leading the way, the Code seemed daft and obsolete.

In Great Britain, certainly, Code prohibitions were not a factor in two films made as the American controversies churned. By way of extreme contrast, the homosexuality in these English dramas was less an evil than a fact of life. In *A Taste of Honey*, directed by Tony Richardson from Shelagh Delaney's play, an unmarried pregnant girl (Rita Tushingham) is comforted by an effeminate gay man (Murray Melvin)—the first person to neither abuse nor desert her. The British press took this friendship in stride, especially given Richardson's skillful juxtaposition of sentimental drama with kitchen-sink realism. In *Victim* the gayness was more central, even confrontational, particularly as enacted by Dirk Bogarde, Britain's leading heartthrob. In the annals of gay film, *Victim* occupies a special Olympian niche, an example of true guts in a business rarely noted for courageous endeavor. For the American public it served as the most powerful and positive import in the field since *Maedchen in Uniform*, and for the British something far greater: a genuine public service, railing against and eventually helping to overturn Britain's archaic laws against male homosexuality. The diffident

---

[4]Aimée, who was responsible for most of the amusement this film proffered, was given one immortal line by the screenwriters. At one point in the murkily convoluted plot, Lot's tribe teams up with the soldiers of Sodom to rout a mutual enemy. When they return in triumph to the walls of the city, Aimée's Queen Bera lauds them with hostessy graciousness: "Hebrews and Sodomites," she beams, "greetings!"

"courage" of *Tea and Sympathy* was nowhere to be found here. Nor were the misshapen falsehoods of *Suddenly, Last Summer*. Shrewd as well as forward-looking, *Victim* expertly set its social agenda into the frame of a well-crafted commercial thriller. Nothing, in 1961, could be more germane to a film about being gay in Britain than the subject of blackmail, a threat far more real and widespread than the melodramatic variety dramatized in *Advise and Consent*. Making the project both more viable and more risky were the unflinching treatment and the star at its center. When he took the role of Melville Farr, the divorced barrister blackmailed for an unconsummated gay affair, Dirk Bogarde was simultaneously solidifying and endangering his status as the country's most popular leading man. Until that time, most of his roles had been romantic gloss, to the point where he later labeled himself "the male Loretta Young." While a more mature and substantial role in an adult drama would certainly be a venturesome step, Bogarde had a Melville Farr secret of his own. The obliging British press deigned to leave his personal life alone, but the carefully unstated truth was that Bogarde had a longtime male companion.[5] Carefully maintaining that invisible iron curtain between the private and the professional, Bogarde was the driving force behind *Victim*. He shouldered much of the responsibility for keeping the production on track despite a great deal of resistance, and he contributed to the script. This was a film about homosexuality, not simply an entertainment with a gay theme, and it took notable care to show that gayness came in many different forms. Inevitably, its somber and prudent tone was not totally free from a "let them live their miserable lives in peace" type of condescension. "I can't help the way I am," mutters an older gay man at one point. But give the British credit: this movie manages to cover nearly all the bases without losing its footing, and reserves as much venom for anti-gay prejudice as for blackmail. There would be nothing like this in American entertainment until *That Certain Summer*, a TV movie, and no close big-screen equivalent until more than thirty years later when, in the less intrepid climes of *Philadelphia*, a major star would spearhead a gay-oriented entertainment intended as both cinema and public service. Bogarde's gamble paid off: the British press gave *Victim* excellent reviews, with raves coming from some of the Roman Catholic publications. With this and the enthusiastic public response, Bogarde's career status moved from pop-dreamboat to respected actor.

For the Production Code Administration the summer of 1961 was possibly the busiest time since its fateful inception thirty-seven summers previous. And

---

[5]At the height of his career as a romantic lead, Bogarde was called "the British Rock Hudson." The title was repeated, with a touch of bemused irony, in the pieces that appeared after his death in 1999, in which his forty-year relationship with Tony Forwood could finally be discussed. The career choices made by these two heartthrobs say volumes about how they felt they could deal with gayness on a professional level: Bogarde did *Victim* and *Death in Venice*, while with Hudson we had *Pillow Talk* and *A Very Special Favor*.

as the advance ads for *It Ain't No Sin* had announced during that earlier fraught age, "Coming events cast their shadows before." Just as *Victim* was opening in London, more high-pressure challenges beset the regulation of sexual content in American films. In addition to *The Children's Hour*, *Advise and Consent*, and others, Geoffrey Shurlock and his associates were attempting to cope with a film embodying the ultimate taboos: *Lolita*. No matter how carefully and safely Stanley Kubrick would adapt Nabokov's tale of quasi-incestuous pedophilia, this film would offer the Code a challenge far beyond the imaginings of Joe Breen. Shurlock, who respected the Code at the same time that he understood its flaws and limitations, recognized that a controversy over *Lolita* (and just think of the fights with the Legion of Decency over this one!) might crack the Code completely.[6] He had clearly not been unsympathetic to the pleas from Arthur Krim about liberalizing the Code to embrace homosexuality, and there were the cases of *Walk on the Wild Side* and *Sodom and Gomorrah* and *A View from the Bridge* to deal with as well. There had also been, just a few months prior, that ridiculous battle over *That Touch of Mink*. As *Lolita* cast its own shadow before, Shurlock and his team worked with the MPAA's board to devise a new amendment that would retain the Code's basic tenets while allowing for the Kubrick film and all those gay stories. Dated October 3, 1961, the amendment was both specific and vague: "In keeping with the culture, the mores and values of our time, homosexuality and other sexual aberrations may now be treated with care, discretion and restraint." These words immediately drew fire and accusations of "Cave-in!" from such conservative quarters as the *Motion Picture Herald*, but Shurlock knew that with this document he was buying time for the Code.

Otto Preminger, working in his relentless self-promoter vein, had already announced days in advance that the Code had been changed and that he, in pushing to make *Advise and Consent* more honest and hard-hitting, was responsible. Indeed, most of the pertinent films had already been shot. Having been chided, in time-honored chapter-and-verse fashion, about all the Code-unfriendly elements, the filmmakers essentially disregarded the warnings and kept the questionable material, knowing that they might run the risk of being denied a Code seal. Of all of them, only the producers of *A View from the Bridge* would have likely risked releasing a film without a seal. Perhaps Wyler and Preminger and the others had inside knowledge that they could get by with these projects, or it may be that they were simply aware that times were changing. There was no single film or specific force or even person that deserves full credit

---

[6]When *Lolita* was finally released in 1962, its producers made full use of this fact, and even implied the struggles attending its filming. "How," the ads persistently demanded, "did they *ever* make a movie of *Lolita*?" For some of the more hostile critics, who complained about the toning-down of the material, the answer to this question was just too self-evident: "They didn't!"

for the amendment. History, and multitudinous societal forces, had caused that Hollywood pendulum to start swinging, and it was now time to yield before the force that had gathered. For years gayness on film had worn a cunning cloak; now, with this addition to the Production Code, it would be more evident, at least under properly unhappy circumstances.

In spite of a revamped Code, the most important and affirmative of the films would not be sanctioned. On November 13, 1961, *Victim* was denied a Code seal for its American release. There were two relevant problems, as Geoffrey Shurlock explained in his ruling:

> The film contains a number of scenes in which the psychology of homosexuality is discussed candidly and in such detail as to verge on the clinical.
>
> Underlying the story there is an overtly expressed plea for an acceptance of homosexuality, almost to the point of suggesting that it be made socially tolerable. We feel that in these two major respects, the film does not conform to what the Board of Directors intended should be approved by the Production Code Administration regulation.

There it was. With its sympathetic tone and persuasive arguments, *Victim* had dared too much to (literally) speak the name "homosexual" and, what is more, to accept it. The American distributor, Pathé-American, appealed the ruling without success. In the end, *Victim* went out on the same type of release given many non-Code foreign films—the art-house circuit, where lots of spectators wore black turtlenecks, sipped complimentary coffee, and made sure they said "film" instead of "movies." Under these circumstances, *Victim* did reasonably well and garnered generally fine notices, a number of them mentioning its travails with the Production Code Administration; *Newsweek* bemoaned the "sublime illogic" of its nonapproved Code status. Other critics found its arguments surprisingly convincing despite their own stated prejudices. "Anyone expecting the many homosexuals portrayed in this movie to simper and swish in the usual theatrical manner will be disappointed," was the observation of one perhaps-rueful critic. Nevertheless, and this many years after *Maedchen in Uniform*, it remained a fringe movie, its merits denied to many mainstream filmgoers, especially in smaller communities. In contrast to its British release, *Victim* in its United States run preached mainly to an eager audience of the converted.[7]

---

[7] *A Taste of Honey*, which otherwise won praise along with a Code seal, did engender some puzzlement and even hostility from American critics for its sympathetic portrayal of nellie gayness. Pauline Kael, who was not especially homophobic, was not precisely the fount of acceptance where gay characters in films were concerned. Calling the character in *A Taste of Honey* "a sad-eyed queen," she felt that he was not so much a dramatic creation as an easy device to elicit pity from do-gooding liberal audiences.

The tone taken by *The Children's Hour* was far more in line with Code directives, so perhaps it was poetic justice that caused it to be the first of the newer-franker-gayer Code-sealed films to reach the mainstream movie public, and under its old title. (There were Oscar-nomination showings late in 1961, then a wider release starting a couple of months later.) After the flurry of press about the newly liberalized Code, this film would represent the face of New Adult Hollywood, in some ways a test case for the viability of gay (or anti-gay) material in movies. The whole of the Production Code saga seemed in fact to be encompassed by the two film versions of Hellman's play, and perhaps in a cinematically just world closing the circle would have produced an ecstatic fulfillment. The components of triumph seemed to be in place. Audrey Hepburn was coming straight from an enormous personal success in *Breakfast at Tiffany's*, Shirley MacLaine had recently scored her second Academy nomination for *The Apartment*, and Wyler was William *"Ben-Hur"* Wyler. Additional interest came from stunt casting: in the interest of historical continuity Miriam Hopkins, Martha (MacLaine's new role) in *These Three*, now appeared as Martha's insufferably self-dramatizing aunt, Lily Mortar, and Wyler cast an unknown child actor, Karen Balkin, as the horrific moppet whose lie triggers all the trouble. The ad campaign cleverly invoked both literate decorum and sensationalistic whoopee: a "classic" play directed for the second, franker time by a lauded director, with two of Hollywood's biggest playing characters suspected of being "that way." The poster art featured a drawing of the two women standing close together, all attention focused on MacLaine's hand placed firmly on Hepburn's arm. Next to them, in large letters, was the one word slogan "Different . . ."

The result, after all the battles and publicity and Wylerian craftsmanship, was about a hair short of disastrous. The dire commercial performance and large financial loss were surprising enough; the real kicker came with the reviews. Not for the first time, the critics were ahead of the filmmakers. Wyler's overwrought devotion to Hellman's archaic thesis drew both jeers and some startling editorializing. As the collected reviews of *The Children's Hour* make clear, homophobia was not to be taken as a given by many of the widest read film critics in 1962. Over and over, their reviews asked why so many people would have believed the lie in the first place (particularly as shrieked in Karen Balkin's annoying tones) and—most arrestingly—what all the trouble was about anyway. Many of them were evidently prepared to accept lesbianism as a fact not requiring the garnish of undue hostility.

Its premises, psychological, sociological, legal and even economic, fail to hold water.

Moira Walsh, *America*

Perhaps the whole thing should have been left back in the 1930s. . . . Would two supposedly intelligent school teachers, who probably had Psych I and II and several education courses in college, be so naïve about their situation and so thrown by adversity? Would the doctor-fiancé of one of the women believe the lie and walk out on her? Would the other teacher, suddenly realizing her love for this woman, believe that this is the end of the world for her?

Philip T. Hartung, Commonweal

What has begun and grown as a drama of classic Rumor, engaging our sympathy for the victims' innocence and our anger at people's eagerness to believe ill, switches suddenly to pronounce the thesis that smoke means fire. Shirley MacLaine, who is in the film, said in an interview: "It's a story about the fact that in every lie there's an ounce of truth." In other words, you are guilty if accused, and God sits in Heaven flanked by Torquemada and Joe McCarthy.

Stanley Kauffman, The New Republic

What was considered too daring for 1936 is almost too tame for 1962. Indeed, although set in the present, the entire film seems curiously dated, as if all the characters had been strangely insulated against any knowledge of modern psychology.

Arthur Knight, The Saturday Review

From the way Mr. Wyler carries on, you might suppose that he had only just learned about the existence of such [lesbian] relationships and was feeling distinctly let down by human nature. Grown men and women whisper fearful home truths that we in the audience aren't allowed to hear, eyes roll, bodies totter, and I wound up every bit as angry at Mr. Wyler as I was at the nasty little brat who started all the trouble. . . . The poor child who plays the brat appears to have learned acting by sitting through thirty-five consecutive screenings of "Psycho."

Brendan Gill, The New Yorker

Much of the critical antipathy stemmed from a central scene in which the teachers and Karen's fiancé (James Garner) confront the girl and her grandmother (Fay Bainter). The overwrought tone is as attributable (and perhaps more so) to Wyler as to Hellman, and the director's choices, in the blocking and delivery of lines and everything else, seems to editorialize the situation horribly. Just as Brendan Gill implied in *The New Yorker*, the scene views lesbianism as a thing far more distasteful than promiscuous character assassination.[8] Adding to the general air of stridency was the deletion of

---

[8]Interestingly, the parallels with McCarthy-style tactics were seldom addressed in the reviews (*The New Republic* was an exception), perhaps because it was still too early in the day for the mainstream press to denounce the witch-hunts. With the comparison left so unmade, *The Children's Hour* came across as even more of a meekly face-lifted antique.

Demon child Karen Balkin assures James Garner that yes, those horrible things she said are really true. Fay Bainter, Shirley MacLaine, and Audrey Hepburn look suitably disheartened, as were audiences watching *The Children's Hour.*

some other material, including a scene of the women at their unsuccessful slander trial, that had added some warmer subtleties to MacLaine's performance. Even so, she, along with Bainter, captured the best reviews.[9] Her work was of sufficient depth, in fact, to give credence to the critics who maintained that Martha's suicide was dated psychologically and false dramatically. This did not prevent MacLaine's anguish in her big confession scene from being sadly convincing, with her anthem—"I feel so damn sick and dirty I can't stand it anymore!"—ringing true as a cry of men and women who have been told (often by films such as this) that self-loathing is their

[9]Bainter came out of retirement to play the icily bigoted dowager and was rewarded with the film's only Oscar nomination. Another outstanding performance, and less heralded, came from Veronica Cartwright, as the cowed liar in cahoots with Balkin's Mary. From *The Children's Hour* she moved on to a second outing as the victim of a screeching terror. A whole flock of them, actually—Hitchcock's *The Birds.*

only option.[10] In later years, to her credit, MacLaine readily assumed some of the responsibility for the opinions expressed in *The Children's Hour*. "We were unaware," she mused. "The profundity of this subject was not in the lexicon of our rehearsal period, even. Audrey and I never talked about this. Isn't that amazing? Truly amazing . . ." And in some ways, as that title had suggested, infamous.

With its stars and director and source material, *The Children's Hour* attempted to don a mantle of eminence and class. *Walk on the Wild Side*, released at exactly the same time, tried for something a bit more base. Its main ad line proudly bragged, "A side of life you never thought you'd see on the screen!" and said side was evidently twofold: an allegedly no-holds-barred look at prostitution, and a candid portrayal of a lesbian relationship. During a contentious shooting period Charles K. Feldman and his team left Algren's work far behind in their quest for some tony exploitation. The result was fairly entertaining and by most artistic standards quite putrid. Much of the blame fell, properly so, on the heads of the two leads. Laurence Harvey, whom everyone wanted to kill at one point or another during the filming, was a dim, ludicrously miscast hero, and Capucine, Feldman's inamorata, made an inanimate (if intriguingly bisexual) heroine. Interest shifted, then, to one hot plot thread and two costars, tyro and veteran. As a hoyden-turned–French Quarter hooker, Jane Fonda gave an exciting, if undisciplined, taste of things to come. In the role of her employer, Barbara Stanwyck offered an arresting combination of historical resonance and shock value, for she was the first major American star to play a role clearly defined as gay or lesbian. Jo Courtney is not only the madam of the Doll House brothel, she is intensely in love with Hallie (Capucine), her choicest girl. To flavor it with a Freudian sauce (and to indicate the screenwriters' subtlety), she is also married to a legless man who trundles around in a little cart. Stanwyck was likely cast more for her trademarked toughness than anything else—Jo is not (to put it meekly) a sympathetic character. While her performance was not especially well reviewed (one critic said that Stanwyck seemed made of chrome), she managed to impart more dimension than may have been intended. Jo is a tough one, all right, but she shows a great deal of tenderness toward Hallie and turns nasty only when fighting to hold on to her, or when chewing out her husband for presuming to think that any man knows anything about love. Not that the script gave her any help at all. At one point Hallie rebels against her gilded-cage life and tells Jo that she's going to go downstairs into the salon and sit and drink with a man. "You're being perverse," Stanwyck glowers. In a more palatable film, it might

---

[10]It had been noted, when the script was originally submitted to the Code office, that there was a bit too much swearing. However, MacLaine's "damn" here was likely considered forgivable under the circumstances; in the world view of *The Children's Hour*, how the hell else *could* you feel?

Barbara Stanwyck could glare and scowl with the best of them, and *Walk on the Wild Side* gave her ample opportunity. *Photofest*

have all meant something; as it was, only Fonda escaped unscathed, along with Saul Bass's black-cat-on-the-prowl title sequence. With no critical respect and negligible financial success, the first overt lesbian relationship in American film went very nearly for naught.[11]

[11]Over and apart from its role in gay film history, and in addition to its much-liked credit sequence, *Walk on the Wild Side* is best known not as a film or novel but as a near-legendary Lou Reed song. And, surprise, they're not unrelated. As Reed once reported, the song came from a failed attempt to make a musical of the Algren book. When the project was called off, he changed the song's characters from figures in the book to people he'd known at Andy Warhol's Factory—and came up with his biggest hit.

BARBARA STANWYCK

Real name: Ruby Stevens. Born Brooklyn, N.Y., July 16, 1907; died Santa Monica, Calif., January 20, 1990

She was not the most popular of film stars, nor the most talented or glamorous. Such things took a backseat to the qualities she had in excelsis: versatility, guts, and awe-inspiring durability. Professionalism seldom comes in a more complete package than in the woman who said, in her Hollywood/Brooklyn snarl, "I want to go on working until they shoot me." It was a fitting credo for someone starring in films since 1929, after a decent Broadway career. In the course of all that work, there was a fair amount of gold: for starters, *Stella Dallas, Remember the Night, The Lady Eve, Double Indemnity,* and *Sorry, Wrong Number.* Into her fifties, almost alone among her peers, she worked and worked, and when movie parts dried up, she moved to television. The role of Jo Courtney in *Walk on the Wild Side* was something of a comeback, and under the right circumstances it would have been a sensation. Approaching the challenge wryly, she quipped, "Chalk up another first for Stanwyck." Her immersion in her work was such that she likely wasn't aware that it was the most provocative career choice imaginable. It was, after all, widely rumored that her twelve-year marriage to Robert Taylor was the film community's leading example of lavender P.R. In the event, her sexuality (like Taylor's) has never been convincingly confirmed, possibly because it was too complicated for labels. What happened onscreen mattered far more to Stanwyck than such personal matters as rumors about her sex life or, more verifiably, an abusive nonrelationship with her adopted son. Playing a lesbian in *Walk on the Wild Side,* and giving more art and conviction to the role than it deserved, would always be more important to her than being a real or rumored lesbian off the screen.

That same ratio of high attention and low grosses continued as gay-themed releases proceeded in 1962. *A View from the Bridge* also opened during that busy spring, and director Sidney Lumet's handling of the climactic kissing scene between Raf Vallone and Jean Sorel received special praise. Unlike *Victim,* there were also the rewards of a Code seal and a commendation from Shurlock for exceptional artistry. None of the praise prevented it from being as much of a succèse d'estime as *Victim,* seen mainly by art-house audiences intelligent enough to grasp that one of Miller's main premises was the equation of gay-baiting with witch-hunts. Another would-be provocative theatrical adaptation fared less well a few months later, and to even fewer audiences, when a small American company called Zenith International produced a mediocre version of *No Exit.* Sartre's one-act view of hell as unending existentialist frustration was expanded with flashbacks that charted, to little effect, the course of its unhappy central trio (coward Morgan Sterne, nymphomaniac Rita Gam, lesbian Viveca Lindfors). "Miss Lindfors plays the lesbo with earnest conviction," *Variety* editorialized, "never trying to justify her abnormality." It was a worthy attempt at forward-looking independent filmmaking, and ultimately it played out as dated in its attitudes as *The Children's Hour*.

John Frankenheimer's *All Fall Down*, which opened in April, was at once up-to-date and a throwback. A penetrating family drama with fine performances and impeccable credentials (screenplay by William Inge from a novel by James Leo Herlihy), it offered Warren Beatty as yet another corrupt dreamboat, here an abusive charmer named Berry-Berry. He is idolized by his younger brother Clinton (Brandon de Wilde), and as the title implies, the fall is all the greater when the pedestal is high. Clinton's journey to discovery begins in the Florida Keys, where his brother is in jail for beating up a hooker. She still loves him, she tells Clinton, when he goes to see her at a seedy strip club. The more popular view of Berry-Berry is espoused by the bar's bouncer-bartender, tough and

Neither Madame Spivy nor her lobster tattoo is impressed by Brandon de Wilde in *All Fall Down*. Between them, and cutting him a bit more slack, is the winsomely redundant Evans Evans. *Photofest*

burly and abundantly tattooed, who kicks Clinton out upon discovering whose
brother he is. The bouncer is a woman, and is played by Madame Spivy, who
sang dirty songs in New York cabarets in the forties and fifties and appeared in
a few movies. Making the bouncer a beyond-butch dyke was forward-looking in
its frankness even as it recalled the spicy cameos of the early thirties; she is
essentially a more explicit cousin to the cigar-and-tie women in such films as
One-Way Passage. Simultaneously stereotypical and chillingly fresh, Spivy's bit
in *All Fall Down* is indelible as it is brief, in some ways the precise clue needed
to tell the boy what he needs to know about his brother.[12]

Otto Preminger's spin on gayness came at the end of May, by which time
Advise and Consent had passed from United Artists to Columbia. Drury's acidic
Washington panorama made for an entertaining if unreal experience as a potent
cast of veteran actors acted out the slash-and-burn games of senatorial chess,
with the talking point as much sexual as political. No matter that the main
drama hinged on whether Henry Fonda's past dabbling in Communism made
him unacceptable as the new secretary of state, or that the main senatorial players included Walter Pidgeon, Charles Laughton, Peter Lawford, and George
Grizzard, with Franchot Tone and Lew Ayres as the president and vice president. It was the gay episode that attracted as much attention as anything else,
for several reasons, including the casting. Brigham Anderson, the Utah conservative with a gay indiscretion in his wartime past, was played by Don Murray, a
Kennedy-style hunk with a sex appeal owned by few senators then or now; small
wonder that Preminger had him take off his shirt. Then the director expanded
and heightened the entire subplot to include Brig's trip to meet his black-
mailing ex in a busy Manhattan gay bar—the first such excursion since *Call
Her Savage.* Throughout the whole sequence the word *homosexual* is not spoken
(as it had been in *Victim*), which would have been superfluous anyway. This is
homo hell in a way not dreamed of in *No Exit*, with blackmailers to make those
in *Victim* look like altruists. The bar itself (Club 602) seems on the surface to be
authentic, but look closer. As a Frank Sinatra record plays a lonely exhortation
to one-night stands—"Come to me and be what I need you to be"—Preminger
gives a quick and devastating tour of the Life. The main room of the bar is at the
end of a long dingy hall, with roving spotlights that expose and then conceal the
men who talk and drink and cruise. To make it more furtive and faux festive, a
revolving color wheel adds an aluminum-Christmas-tree aura. Some of the leering faces appear to be wearing makeup, and a couple of the older men have the
haughtiest affect since the heyday of Bobby Watson. Interestingly, there is at

---

[12]Frankenheimer was at the peak of his powers in 1962, and he used Spivy in his next project as
well, in somewhat more "womanly" mode. In *The Manchurian Candidate*, she was the most sinis-
ter of the garden club ladies in the soldier-prisoners' drugged hallucinations.

least one African-American man; in 1962, movies were still portraying segrega-
tion in public places, but Preminger's nightmare land is an equal-opportunity
place for losers. The milieu is intended as one of total repellency, a clear invitation for the audience to empathize with the revulsion that propels Anderson out
of this hellhole posthaste.[13] His duplicitous former lover Ray (John Granger)
spots him and follows him outside, and in another editorial gesture is pushed
down into a puddle-filled gutter. There is nothing left but for the young senator
to go back to Washington and slash his throat.

Preminger's movies had already become frequent targets of critical scorn,
a trend that would reach a deserved climax several years later with *Hurry
Sundown* and *Skidoo*. Here the material and cast commanded a certain degree
of respect, with criticism reserved for the treatment of the gay plot:

> Good scenes keep giving way bewilderingly to bad ones. . . . Explicitly I would
> quarrel with director Otto Preminger for including a Cook's tour of New York's
> homosexual haunts.
>
> Moira Walsh, *America*

> In an extraordinary scene never shown in a movie before but made as repulsive as
> possible, [Senator Anderson] finds his former companion in a hangout for homo-
> sexuals. . . . While one can understand the despair felt by the young senator as his
> standards, his family and his whole future are threatened, one cannot understand
> that he would use suicide as a way out.
>
> Philip T. Hartung, *Commonweal*

> By turns highhanded and condescending. . . . And when it comes to dramatizing
> the homosexual charge against Senator Anderson, Preminger throws subtlety to the
> winds. Anderson's pursuit of his blackmailer takes him to the rooms of a fat, unctu-
> ous male pimp, then to a bar where most of the men wear make-up. . . . At a time
> when Hollywood is often unjustly criticized for sensationalism, Preminger has
> turned out one of the most reprehensibly sensational movies in years.
>
> *Newsweek*

> There is always a feeling of calculation about the picture—as if Preminger had
> said, "We need a little sex here, and let's hit the homosexuality there. If we throw in
> a scene of a pansy bar, it's bound to start talk. . . .
>
> As a consequence, for all the surface realism, the scenes have an artificial ring
> to them. Preminger, expert that he is, pulls the strings, but what jumps are puppets
> instead of people.
>
> Hollis Alpert, *Saturday Review*

---

[13]One person's hell is another's oasis. A number of gay male viewers of a certain age still recall that
scene as an early, and not at all bad, contact with a shared gay experience. In spite of Preminger's
better efforts, his gay underworld was as inviting for some people as that Sinatra ballad.

One of the most widely read reviews used the bar sequence as its centerpiece. "The scene is highly compelling," *Life* said, "but it throws the movie off-kilter. By giving so much emphasis to the hounded homosexual, Preminger has turned *Advise and Consent* into mere melodrama." The magazine then proceeded to echo this lopsided treatment by running a photo of the bar scene alongside the review. With his sensationalistic approach Preminger had turned a potentially compelling political mosaic into a reincarnation of Sebastian's trip to Cabeza de Lobo. Scandal does not equal success, and the box-office returns for *Advise and Consent* were extremely disappointing.

Gayness was also a factor, a notably slippery one, in the biggest film of 1962—the only film to have both gay themes and financial success. In an earlier age *Lawrence of Arabia* would have been painstakingly heterosexualized, with T. E. Lawrence's tortured homo-psyche obscured in the mists of a bogus straight romance. David Lean and screenwriter Robert Bolt did not take that route, although in 1962 (and 2002, for that matter), a blockbuster-hero's sexuality would not be reproduced with homoerotic candor. There were instead some vagrant hints, as in Lawrence's close friendship with a pair of Arab boys, for those in the know. The vagueness was perhaps deliberate, and in the tide of rapturous reviews greeting *Lawrence of Arabia*, many observed the hollowness at the center of the massive epic: even as made physical by Peter O'Toole, Lawrence remained totally unknowable, most of all in his sexuality. One critic stated the flat truth: "The few hints that Lawrence may have been homosexual are as ambiguous as the rest of him." There was a more prominent gayness in *Lawrence* as well, and it wore an evil face. Jose Ferrer, one of the era's more prominent hams, emoted in his usual icy-feverish style as a Turkish bey who abuses the imprisoned Lawrence. The implications were clear enough, certainly less cryptic than in the release print of *Spartacus*, yet were sufficiently allusive to draw no comment from the Production Code office. The effect, ultimately, was to demonize homosexuality without being up-front about Lawrence himself—an eat-your-cake-and-have-it-too approach that recalled DeMille's demonization-through-demonstration. It also showed how the liberalization of the Code would proceed: making gayness clearer in order to make its condemnation more fearful. The ad line for an Alfred Hitchcock movie a few years previous best expressed what was happening. A little knowledge, it said, can be a dangerous thing.

The increasing prevalence of a negative tone was one fact that had become clear in 1962. Another was that films with gay or lesbian themes did not fare well with the mainstream moviegoing public. Whether overt (*The Children's Hour*) or subsidiary (*Advise and Consent*), the subject matter had not made for big financial returns. Audrey Hepburn and Shirley MacLaine had not made it play, nor had the "Here's Sin!" marketing of *Walk on the Wild Side*, nor even the blockbuster-debauch lure of *Sodom and Gomorrah*. Had all or any of these films been a success there likely would have been more of them, with ultimately greater and perhaps more sympathetic attention paid to the subject matter years before Stonewall. It's a big and intriguing what-if?, and in the land of the bottom-line balance sheet it was not to be. Over the subsequent four decades, the pattern begun in 1962 would continue: every few years several producers would try out major or mainstream films with a gay theme. The larger viewing public is disinterested and the idea dies until the cycle recurs. The truly large exceptions, such as *Victor/Victoria* or *Philadelphia* or *The Bird Cage*, are conspicuous for their scarcity. For anyone wondering why there haven't been more mainstream films dealing with homosexuality, here is a main answer. Not bigotry, nor uncertain attitudes, nor the stars' fear of guilt by association. It's the money.

Why don't the films perform better? The reasons are both obvious and baffling. One main constituent is the way in which the larger (i.e., straight) public views gayness. Even as far back as *That Touch of Mink*, it isn't necessarily homophobia or overt hostility, although they can be present. It's more a matter of how the ticket-buying public looks at movies; the audiences that bring in the big grosses view movies as escapist diversions—that is, distractions. Even when an intelligent film will provoke thought and discussion, it does not always do so in a directly confrontational way. The makers of *Victim*, for example, knew to place their polemic within the appealing context of a nail-chewing thriller.[14] With most films that use homosexuality as a leading subject matter, this is not the case. Rightly or wrongly, these are seen as "gay films," and the simple truth is that a large percentage of the audience sees this as too "real" to accept it as part of its escapism. Nor is the gay viewing public large enough to put such efforts into the credit column: the gay public is diverse and sometimes unpredictable, as witness its general failure in forming a cohesive political movement. A number of the movies in later years certainly deserved their financial failure—*Staircase* and *Partners* and *A Different Story*, and possibly *Personal Best*, should only be drawing flies. For some of the others, interested gay men and women and liberal or sympathetic straights did not form a sufficient percentage of the audience to bring in profits. The other people in the audience, most of the time, simply didn't want to know.

Because of these steady financial failures, it was television that eventually proved a more hospitable place, as did, eventually, the burgeoning world of independent cinema. In venues where the financial stakes were not as high and artistry might occasionally be more germane, there were more opportunities for candor and success. Put that in the present tense: despite the so-called

---

[14]Even *Victim*, despite its acclaim and positive response in the United Kingdom, spawned few follow-ups. Save for some forward-looking subsidiary gay characters in films like *The L-Shaped Room* and *The Leather Boys*, few British films of the 1960s cared to look much in that direction.

mainstreaming of gay life in the twenty-first century, such parameters remain basically unchanged, and commercial Hollywood movies deal very little with homosexuality.[15] The failures of those films in 1962 would be the beginning of a major, long-lived trend in American cinema. Instead of using the liberalizing of the Production Code as a positive force, the film industry made the greater public's acceptance of gayness an even slower process. It could have been a new beginning, this newfound freedom. The increased gay visibility in films of the later 1960s and 1970s might have made homosexuality something more than either a demon or a sideshow. Instead, through fear and ignorance and a penny-mongering philosophy, the movie people made gayness to seem more irrelevant and unappealing than ever. Next to these movies the forgotten films of the pre-Code era were a love feast, a virtual carnival of acceptance. For gay and lesbian spectators, going to the movies in 1962 and afterward would be like playing a game of dodgeball. They would strive to glean whatever good they could from the projected images, while attempting to avoid the negativity being hurled at them.

---

[15]They still seem, in fact, to work overtime at keeping it out of sight. The much-lauded and ostensibly biographical *A Beautiful Mind* (2001) pulled a *Night and Day* and deleted any mention of its hero's bisexuality, just as *Midnight in the Garden of Good and Evil* (1997) added a fake romance (with its director's daughter!) to straighten up its protagonist. Lots of other examples, too—*Fried Green Tomatoes*, *The Man without a Face*, and on and on. Years ago, during their reign as the country's hottest comedy team, Mike Nichols and Elaine May turned a blowtorch to this tradition in a wicked sketch featuring May as a dim-bulb sexpot plugging her latest movie. It's a big Technicolor musical called *Two Gals in Paris*, in which the dumdum diva stars as, who else, Gertrude Stein. Heading the supporting cast: "Sal Mineo, as my lover Ernest Hemingway."

FOURTEEN

"I'm No Queer," He Lied

t was not the best of times, and it did not produce the best of movies. The old and the new were attempting a stormy coexistence in the mid-1960s, with all the seams showing and near the bursting point. They would split in Watts, in Hanoi and Gaza, and in Greenwich Village just east of Seventh Avenue. Everything seemed inevitable even as nothing made sense, and truisms seemed to change daily in the movie business, as everywhere else. With every new film hit a hopeful new trend would attempt to catch the notoriously intractable brass ring of public imagination. Spy films, historical blockbusters, bloated musicals—they were still the coin of the realm, and the king was dying. In those twilight times of crumbling studios and a cracking Code, the movies pretended to reflect the times even as they strove mightily to believe that it was still 1946.

The epic denial that had been the reigning aesthetic of those pillow-talky sex comedies translated over in varying ways to the rest of the American commercial product as well. To look at most of the mainstream Hollywood movies of the mid-sixties, it would be hard to guess that the civil rights movement was reaching a head, or that an unpopular war was escalating, or that gays and lesbians were striving for identity. Or that, sometimes, they even existed. Even in a business that professed to manufacture dreams, these were really la-la stuff; even TV sitcoms owned as much authenticity as most American films of this time, if not more. Many of them weren't, essentially, *about* anything. A few directors and actors and writers seemed to have some concept of the situation, and began to change and to try new things. In most places it was, for the time being, old business. And after the gay and lesbian cinematic bust of 1962, Hollywood seemed less interested in that side of life than at any time since the dank heyday of Joe Breen.

Only two serious American films released in 1963 dealt with gay (specifically lesbian) themes in any way, and it must be said that both were at least more interesting than that awful *Wheeler Dealers*-type mainstream. One of them was a hopeful piece of art house esoterica portending the newer-more-adult wave of independent films, and the other was an up-to-date commercial thriller more literate than most. With valiant and self-conscious zeal, *The Balcony* attempted to put Jean Genet's world-as-a-brothel microcosm onto film, with actors like Shelley Winters and Peter Falk tottering somewhere between the worlds of *The Story of O* and *Playhouse 90*. Producer-director Joseph Strick portrayed the ritualized fetishism with an abashed literalness that sat oddly upon the film's one imaginative conceit, making the bordello into an obvious soundstage movie set. While most of the eroticism seemed less sardonic than simply uneasy, the lesbian relationship between the madam (Winters) and her secretary (Lee Grant) was given fairly adroit treatment. Winters and Grant shared one of the first woman-woman screen kisses since the days of *Queen Christina*, and the general effect was less crass than the *Variety* critic's description of their romance as "a lesbian lech."[1]

For *The Balcony* the Production Code was essentially a nonissue, but for more commercial projects Code strictures were still in play. Even as homosexuality was being sanctioned for certain films, other scripts were being tagged for lacking compensatory "seriousness" or, more to the point, condemnation. One such was *The Haunting*, a stylish and quite scary ghost story with a modish psychological overlay—a clear return, with sharper jolts, to the days of *The Uninvited* and *The Seventh Victim*. Like them, it was notably more intelligent than most movies that go "Boo," and a striking digression for director Robert Wise from the blockbuster musical climes of *West Side Story* and *The Sound of Music*.[2] Also like them, lesbianism was one of its more striking components. Julie Harris and Claire Bloom starred as psychics who bring interesting baggage when they are called in to chart the poltergeistic doings in Boston's creepiest haunted house. Harris is a repressive, terminally neurotic virgin, Bloom an unapologetic Greenwich Village lesbian named Theodora—Theo for short. A successful businesswoman as well as a gifted clairvoyant, Theo develops an interest in Eleanor (Harris) despite both her own long-term relationship and her ability to read Eleanor's tortured mind. As with the coded characters in films

---

[1]Three years after *The Balcony*, one of its costars, Leonard Nimoy, appeared in another adaptation of a Genet play with gay elements. Almost no one saw *Deathwatch*, adapted from Genet's *Haute Surveillance*, which featured two soon-to-be-famous comers: the future Mr. Spock and, as a gay prisoner, budding film director Paul Mazursky.

[2]*The Haunting* was in some ways Wise's *hommage* to the oeuvre of Val Lewton, who had given Wise his start as a director. Besides *The Seventh Victim*, *The Haunting* bore traces of Wise's own films for Lewton, *Curse of the Cat People* and *The Body Snatcher*—although here the scare quotient was raised markedly.

Running a successful bordello may be hard work, but Lee Grant and Shelley Winters are able to find warm respite in *The Balcony*.

like *Bride of Frankenstein* and *House of Horrors*, Theo is an outsider . . . but then so is Eleanor. The ESP that sets them apart from others also gives them a secret and charged bond.

Apart from its jolts, *The Haunting* was the unique American film of its era (albeit produced in England) to keep its homosexuality both evident and reasonably positive. This was due both to the script and to Bloom, who tendered one of the most smartly rounded gay characterizations in film up to that time. Theo's feelings for Eleanor do not make her cruel like Jo Courtney (*Walk on the Wild Side*) or tortured/sick in the manner of Martha Dobie (*The Children's Hour*). She is chic and wittily sarcastic, speaking her mind and making her feelings plain, brushing off unwanted male advances and touching Eleanor (she calls her "Nell") frequently. Her attempts at closeness are hindered mainly by Eleanor's own neuroses and by a series of warnings from the Production Code Administration. "We think it would be a drastic mistake to portray *any* physical intimacies, even of the most fragile sort, between these two," Geoffrey Shurlock cautioned, railing against the physical contact stipulated in the script. The most sensational of these points of contact was a scene of Theo painting Eleanor's toenails—a sensualist rite that had just been used to heated effect in *Lolita*. Harris ended up having to do her own nails, and some of the touching was toned down. As a result, some of the effect of Bloom's characterization was muted; nevertheless, the austere swank of her performance was an anomaly in a time when, more and more, negative portrayals would be the rule.[3]

The subversion of *The Haunting*, so out of sync with its *Children's Hour* age, becomes most vivid when Theo taunts Eleanor for her crush on the doctor (Richard Johnson) supervising the psychic experiment. The acid spews violently:

> THEO: You poor stupid innocent.
> ELEANOR: I'd rather be innocent than like you.
> THEO: Meaning what?
> ELEANOR: Now who's being stupid and innocent? You know perfectly well what I mean.
> THEO: Is this another of your crazy hallucinations?
> ELEANOR: I'm not crazy.
> THEO: Crazy as a loon. You really expect me to believe that you're sane and the rest of the world is mad.
> ELEANOR: Well, why not? The world is filled with inconsistencies. Unnatural things . . . nature's mistakes, they're called. You, for instance! (*Theo gasps and flinches.*)

But what things really are unnatural? *The Haunting* seems intent on conveying that Theo is not among them. At least one critic saw and stated the obvious: "Miss Bloom is elegant and amusing as one accused by Miss Harris of being 'unnatural,' when it is actually Miss Harris who is wholly unnatural in a different way altogether." Theo is not punished for her thoughts and deeds; it is Eleanor, the stifled hysteric, who is viewed as the troubled soul, and the one eventually destroyed by the forces at play in Hill House. Theo survives and presumably goes back to the Village, where a career and partner wait for her. Neither gays nor lesbians would have it so good again in such an important film for a long time.

The next few years were mainly a time of shreds and cartoons and vamp-until-ready. As the Production Code tottered to its grave, the comparatively few queer images in American film made for an odd mixture. Few of them carried

---

[3]The previous year, in George Cukor's *Chapman Report*, Bloom had skirted another stereotype in equally striking fashion. As a nymphomaniac, she offered tragic dignity where most actors would have played with feverish panting. Such fever finally beset *The Haunting* at the time of its unnecessary 1999 remake. Special effects and noise replaced the genuine chills of the original, and Catherine Zeta-Jones's Theo was permitted little of Bloom's intense subtlety.

In one of the less spooky moments of *The Haunting*, Claire Bloom helps Julie Harris get into a relaxed pajama-party mood. *Photofest*

much weight, fewer were positive in tone, and a choice two or three were hopeless. After Bloom's stylish Theo, the lesbian portrayals in particular seemed desperately regressive, unsubtle in a way that earlier portrayals had not been. It's possible, in surveying this time, to look back with wistful nostalgia to the forward-looking likes of *Voodoo Island*. With the sudden smash of the James Bond movies there arrived two comic-strip characters—Lotte Lenya's nasty Rosa Klebb in *From Russia with Love* and Honor Blackman's porno-prototype Pussy Galore in *Goldfinger*, dispensing judo and hating men until the irresistible Bond sets her aright. There was also, nearly forty years after *The Crystal Cup*, the return (sans cigar) of the Mannish Repressed Spinster. These would be less demonized than offered as objects for pity—a "There but for the grace of God go I" attitude that seems less progressive than the smart butch novelist in *The Office Wife* back in 1930. John Ford's final film was *7 Women* (1966), a box-office catastrophe and an indefensible debacle to all except hardened cultists. Its merits are certainly contestable; less open to dispute are the banked lesbian fires smoldering beneath the missionary zeal of one of its leading characters, Agatha Andrews. As played by Margaret Leighton in the finest clenched-constrained style, Agatha runs her Mongolian mission outpost with the same rigidity that ensures her unawareness of her own sexuality.[4] The urges almost surface in her contact with her young underling, Emma Clark, played by Sue Lyon—Kubrick's Lolita a few years later, and still an object of temptation. In one scene Agatha goes into Emma's room, begins to reach out to her longingly, and draws back. One critic later noted (not entirely fairly) that Ford directed the scene "as if someone had explained to him what a lesbian was five minutes before shooting and he hadn't had time to recover from the shock."

Agatha's better-latent-than-never sexuality was also the lot of another tightly wound middle-aged woman who—through coincidence and the MGM casting department—also lusts unknowingly after a nymph played by Sue Lyon. It was through a nasty spot of inevitability that this one came from Tennessee Williams, whose wit, daring, and self-hatred were once again doing as much harm as good. On Broadway in 1961 and in John Huston's film in 1964, *The Night of the Iguana* was a highly enjoyable Williams entertainment that showed the master declining into repetition and self-caricature.[5] The repression was even more acrid this time, as presented in the person of Judith Fellowes (Grayson Hall), a spinster schoolteacher from Texas tensely in charge of a hellish bus tour of Mexico. In her guise of chaperone, Fellowes nurses a crush on her young charge Charlotte (Lyon) and goes ballistic when the girl sets her sights on defrocked-minister-turned-tour-guide Richard Burton. Fellowes's feelings—the role was built up from the play—are clear to all observers save her, and in a climactic moment she almost finds out the truth. As she starts laying in to Burton one more time, she is stopped short by Ava Gardner's earthy hotel proprietor Maxine:

> MAXINE: What subject do you teach back in that college of yours, honey?
> FELLOWES: Voice, if that's got anything to do with it.
> MAXINE: Well, geography is my speciality. Did you know that if it wasn't for the dikes, the plains of Texas would be engulfed by the gulf—
> SHANNON [Burton]: Maxine!
> MAXINE: Let's level for a while, Butch old gal. You know what you're sore about, what you're really sore about is that that little quail of yours has a natural preference for men instead of—

---

[4]Ford's original choice for Agatha was his old friend (and flame) Katharine Hepburn, who certainly might have been striking in the role. Given her well-documented opinions regarding homosexuality, it's fair to assume that Agatha's longings were a large part of the reason she turned down the role.

[5]Not the least of *Iguana*'s initial interest (and gay appeal) came from its Broadway cast. A few years before Agatha Andrews, Margaret Leighton essayed another (and hetero) spinster, while the bawdy Maxine was played first by Bette Davis and then (no less blatantly, to be sure) by Shelley Winters.

SHANNON: Maxine!

FELLOWES: What is she talking about?

SHANNON: You'd better go now, Miss Fellowes. The party's over . . . (*Fellowes runs off.*)

MAXINE: What'd you shut me up for? It's time someone told that old dame off.

SHANNON: Miss Fellowes is a highly moral person. If she ever recognized the truth about herself, it would destroy her.

Maxine, that potty-mouthed earth mother, is obviously speaking with Williams's voice. So, unfortunately, is Shannon—"moral" people must repress their gay tendencies or else kill themselves. Or get devoured. As with the other Williams films, the juiciness and sheer actability of the dialogue conceals, on first view, the self-reflexive homophobia. Ava Gardner spits out her double-edged dike/dyke line with breaded-and-deep-fried Carolina relish, some of her savor likely coming from the relaxed Code strictures that enabled the character's frankness. As for Fellowes, Grayson Hall conveyed the woman's strident longings with such force that she was nominated for an Oscar. It was, in fact, the first explicitly gay/lesbian performance to earn that distinction, setting aside the clear-if-unlabeled likes of *Caged* and *All about Eve*.[6]

In the title role of *Lilith* (1964), Jean Seberg at least presented a refreshing and uncaricatured outward appearance. Unfortunately, Lilith is an inmate in an asylum, and her bisexuality is meant to encompass both her instability and her destructiveness. Warren Beatty, that unwitting participant in proto-queer cinema, played an asylum worker who falls under Lilith's spell and is incensed to discover her relationship with Mrs. Meaghan (Anne Meacham). *Lilith* was one of those failed mid-decade attempts at an American "art cinema," with an air of dour quirkiness that did not redeem the negativity underlining the tone of its lesbian relationship. The romance between Lilith and Mrs. Meaghan lacked even the resonance of the Hallie-Jo liaison in *Walk on the Wild Side*; Mrs. Meaghan was more a symbol than a character, and once the Beatty character asserted his "rights" over Lilith she promptly disappeared.

For homosexuality, male division, the situation was similarly bleak. One exception was Gore Vidal's *Best Man*, which finally reached theaters in 1964 without either the participation of Frank Capra or his cloyingly upbeat alterations. Unlike *Advise and Consent*, the gay accusations were handled without seamy digressions and without a great deal of judgment. Joe Cantwell (Cliff

---

[6]For Hall, whose bray of "Se-dooooo-cer!!" will resound through movie eternity, *Iguana* was the highlight of a brief film career otherwise mired in such ephemera as *Qui-êtes vous, Polly Magoo* (1966). Later she won another cult audience as the sympathetic vampire doctor in television's first (deliberate) horror soap opera, *Dark Shadows*.

Robertson), the opportunistic conservative running for the presidential nomination, is enmeshed in a situation similar to that of *Advise*'s Brig Anderson, being threatened with the exposure of a same-sex wartime affair. Unlike Anderson, Cantwell reacts by fighting back—no residual anguish for this Nixon redux. Even before his opponent, Bill Russell (Henry Fonda), learns about his gay past, Cantwell has been circulating his own smears about Russell's stint in a mental ward. Ultimately Russell opts to bow out of the race and not spread the story on Cantwell—bearing out Vidal's moral, and the film's ad slogan, "Does the best man always get to the White House?" In the discussion of Cantwell's past, the discreet euphemism "degenerate" was employed. Later, though, in a heated confrontation between Cantwell and Russell, the H word does indeed come up—probably for the first time in an American feature since *Glen or Glenda*. Cantwell accuses Russell of trying "to smear me as a homosexual, which I'm not." Maybe he's not, which doesn't mean the affair didn't happen. Either way, it's beside the point of *The Best Man*. Cantwell is not a louse because he's gay or had a fling, but because he's a liar and user and total creep, an Eve Harrington of the D.C. stage. That, Vidal avers, is sufficient reason to keep him out of the White House. Personal lives don't need to factor into political maneuvers, a worthy truth increasingly forgotten in politics over the ensuing forty years.

Gays and lesbians were hardly the only minority being excluded from, then timorously included in, sixties film. Just as it had been discovered that films with gay themes did not make for box-office success, it was also clear that, barring an occasional exception like *The Defiant Ones*, neither did films about race relations. In the early sixties there began the occasional worthy effort like *A Raisin in the Sun* and *Nothing but a Man*, although the situation would not get better, in mainstream film, for many, many years.[7] One attempt at racially responsible filmmaking was as embarrassing as it was well intended. *Black Like Me* (1964), adapted from the book by the white journalist John Howard Griffin, was real-life dynamite. Griffin, in order to get the inside story on the state of the races circa 1961, had changed his skin color convincingly enough to fool everyone and cross the color line. He saw it all and wrote about it unblinkingly—the open and concealed bigotry, the slurs and violence, the hate-filled looks, the harassment and the leering sexual comments. It could have made quite a movie. Unfortunately, it fell into the hands of a group of independent filmmakers who were neither competent nor inventive, and the result leaned uncomfortably and

---

[7]As with gays in film, it could be wondered if it has ever gotten much better. There are some interesting parallels to draw between the two "minorities on film," though of course for people of color there was no equivalent of that time-honored "safe zone," the professional closet established for and by gays in Hollywood.

inappropriately toward exploitation. Moreover, one central problem was never addressed satisfactorily: anyone wondering how Griffin could pass convincingly for black would not find out here. As the transformed Griffin (called Horton in the film), James Whitmore looked exactly like what he was, and somewhat like the negative-film version of Godfrey Cambridge in *Watermelon Man*. The suspension of disbelief was made tougher yet by seeing Whitmore alongside a number of talented actors of color, doing good work even as they were trapped in an unworthy botch.

Most of the embarrassment of *Black Like Me* came through sheer ineptitude, the sorry sight of a worthy message told, in essence, by idiots. A more textured incompetence came in one atrocious scene that rudely filtered a plea for equality though homophobia. In a southern restaurant, Horton is chatted up by Charles Maynard (Andrew Bergmann), a youngish white man working on a Ph.D. on "The Urbanization of Rural Populations." "I bet there's a lot I can learn from you," Maynard smiles, and invites Horton to his motel room for a drink and more talk. Before long, the motel-room chat turns—as many conversations do in this

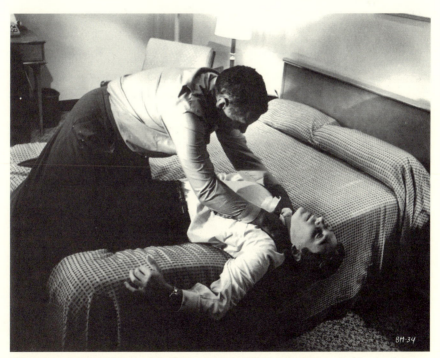

When research projects go horribly wrong: in *Black Like Me*, a darkly dyed James Whitmore takes exception with Andrew Bergmann's genitally-oriented questioning. *Photofest*

movie—to sexual matters. Maynard, the ostensibly liberal intellectual, presents his case for the sexual difference between the races, with guilt-ridden whites and hedonistic blacks. As Horton gets angrier, Maynard makes his points more personal with a reference to the "scientific fact that the Negro's organs are larger." Absolute nonsense, retorts Horton in a close-up that makes Whitmore look more unconvincing than ever. Maynard reacts by going further. "Prove it to me," he presses. "We're about the same age." The proof he gets is Horton yelling, "You filthy drunk," and trying to strangle him; when Horton finally lets go of his throat Maynard murmurs sorrowfully, "I'm no queer . . . Honest, I'm no queer." Cut from a shot of the mortified Horton walking out of the motel to a close-up of a crucified Jesus: Horton goes straight to a priest for confession. He tried to kill a man, he says, although he had provocation. Racial slurs must be suffered, but a mild sexual pass—from a northern intellectual who closets both his gayness and his prejudice—warrants attempted murder. By reducing its racial dialogue to this burlesque level, *Black Like Me* manages to demean everyone and everything; even bigots deserve a more balanced portrayal. Bosley Crowther in the *Times* was being a shade less dense than usual when he found the Maynard sequence to be "a deliberate sensation-seeking trick, and one wonders how purposely the picture has been angled to this intent." *Variety*, noticing how much of the stress was on sex, did not need to wonder. *Black Like Me*, it intimated, would find its most enthusiastic audiences "via sexploitation houses and drive-ins."

At the far opposite end of the social-consciousness spectrum, Sidney Lumet's *Pawnbroker* stirred up one of the biggest censorship controversies in years. Given the predilections of the Production Code and the Legion of Decency, it follows naturally that the trouble came not through *The Pawnbroker*'s arrestingly bleak look at guilt and survival, but through a flash of bare breasts. When the dust settled, there was a Code seal and a Condemned rating from the Legion, both of which appeared more immaterial than ever. In an otherwise praiseworthy effort, there was also some gay negativity in the person of Rodriguez (Brock Peters), a slick and brutal Harlem vice czar. Like Elvira Powell in *Caged*, he has a stable of underlings and an affinity for same-sex relationships, with a blond Caucasian "secretary" usually in attendance. The boyfriend is intended, obviously, as a silent reminder of Rodriguez's essential corruption—a type of bitter shorthand that would become increasingly familiar.

Inside Daisy Clover (1966) was less judgmental and more compromised. Adapted from a novel by Gavin Lambert, *Daisy* starred Natalie Wood as a tough gamine who becomes a thirties Garland-like luminary and quickly finds the dung under the tinsel. As it turned out, the more penetrating story would have been "The Inside on *Daisy* . . . or All about Choices and Capitulations." Wood was not quite up to the challenge, let alone the singing, and a production bent on being darkly hip was instead styleless and barren. No flavor, no authenticity, almost no feeling. The two saving graces were Ruth Gordon as Daisy's sweet loon of a mother and Robert Redford as Wade Lewis, an evanescent dreamboat who romances the girl and abandons her on their wedding night. Exactly what was going on inside Wade is a matter of some debate. In the novel he was gay and the marriage an arranged union out of the Hollywood memory books. The original script was consistent with this, and Lambert intended to show a boyfriend hovering in the background in one scene. Director Robert Mulligan then apparently decided that the character should be reconfigured as a pansexual narcissist, which is how it was played. According to Redford, when he saw the final cut, he was startled to discover that postproduction tampering had made Wade gay again, with the revelation punched up for shock value.

> I then confronted [producer Alan] Pakula and Mulligan [and] said, "Hey, it wasn't too cool. You could have told me, and done me the courtesy, so I was at least prepared for the fact that you turned my character into something I didn't play." But because I liked them, and I was pretty young, I chose not to make a big deal out of it. . . .

All the decisions to "transform" Wade one way or another were made totally within the walls of Warner Bros., and were in no way mandated by the Production Code office. The final cut, which seems to imply his gayness, was effected by excising any prior mention of his sexuality and having Daisy learn the truth after her aborted honeymoon. The studio chief's dipsomaniac wife (Katherine Bard), in love with Wade herself, drunkenly rants about him to Daisy and finally blurts out, in a post-synched line, "Your husband never could resist a charming boy!" There are two short reaction shots and then an abrupt cut to a distraught Wood running out of the room. Like everything else in *Daisy*, the scene is not enough; a potentially biting episode is so trimmed of excess that it ends up meaning nothing. Yet Redford may be shortchanging his own performance. However the character's sexuality plays out, Wade still comes across as the essence of showbiz egotism: an embodiment of physical beauty so self-contained that sex in any form is just a type of homage, like a good review or a seven-figure contract. With an effortless charm that can come only from deep and conflicted self-adoration, Wade needs to attract everyone. That's why he lives, and why men like Wade and Cary Grant and Tyrone Power and [*Insert name of your favorite star of ambiguous sexuality here*] need to become famous. It was true in 1965, it's true today, and at neither time would it be the kind of role that many up-and-coming proto-stars would be willing to accept. Despite the subsequent alteration, and the disappointment of *Daisy* in general, it remains one of Redford's most layered and brave and interesting performances.

A coeval and more knowingly disreputable jab at Hollywood, *The Loved One* (1965), was not exactly bent on subtlety. Evelyn Waugh's nastily contained satire of the movieland death culture was blown up to both amusing and destructive extremes by the anarchic Terry Southern, directed by Tony Richardson with ramshackle élan, and enacted with egalitarian zest by a huge cast whose names ran the gamut from Berle to Gielgud. One would not turn to such a project for measured glimpses of gayness, or anything else; the ad campaign proudly and hopefully used this as the basis to lure in audiences by billing it as "The Motion Picture With Something to Offend Everyone." Most audiences cared little one way or the other; the small groups of viewers who did go found wonderment and some laughter at Rod Steiger's portrayal of Joyboy, the faggy undertaker fawning over his epically eating-disordered mom. There were also cameos by Hollywood's ultimate gay-in-a-gilded-closet, Liberace, doing perhaps the best work of his career as an effortlessly smooth casket salesman, and by John Gielgud, trying hard to be droll as a washed-up and obviously gay art director who commits suicide. To show that it still had some clout, the Production Code Administration issued warnings about "unacceptable" items, such as the scripts use of the word *dikey*, which was eliminated, and the presentation of a studio commissary as a gay bar, which was trimmed and soft-pedaled. Comedy was also at least the purported genre of a failed object called *The Last of the Secret Agents? A Very Special Favor* seemed like Molière next to this junk, a vehicle for the seventh-rate team of Marty Allen (the fuzzy-haired one) and Steve Rossi (the Dean Martin knockoff). Spy films were the big wave in mid-decade, spy spoofs were popular, and this one, which involved a search for the Venus de Milo's arms, was the worst. With nothing amusing or original to say, it was not surprising that Allen and Rossi revived the old gag of "practicing lovemaking on your friend and having someone overhear it and think you're queer," earlier seen in *Reaching for the Moon, Up in Arms*, and many others. It was done here without candor or dexterity, its only distinction being that this late in the game, October 1965, Geoffrey Shurlock was still cautioning producers against the use of "an unacceptable homosexual joke." In its fading days, the Code was still a force in lesser-grade productions such as this one, where the stakes were as low as the quality.

There were also, on a comparable level of artistic prowess, various strata of exploitation films that used gayness in one way or another. *Who Killed Teddy Bear?* (1965) was a New York–shot curiosity that tottered on a wobbly plane between adults-only trash and B-grade film noir, and so palpably unpleasant that a viewer would want to take a bath as soon as the end title came up. It made an odd showcase for the cultish talents of Sal Mineo, whose stature and sensitivity, more than his gayness, made him hard to cast in adult roles. As an obsessive stalker trailing nightclub dancer Juliet Prowse, he appeared in several wildly homoerotic scenes in which he lay in bed lost in fantasies while writhing in tightey-whitey briefs. While Prowse's dance sequences were tame by comparison, there was an ugly scene in which she kicks her employer out of her apartment after accusing the woman of making a pass at her. Out on the street, the employer promptly gets herself killed by the stalker. The role was given more stature than it merited by the efforts of once-and-future Broadway diva Elaine Stritch, although the scene was handled with sufficient imprecision that it was unclear whether she really was making a pass. Prowse's homo panic was all too clear, however, and in a movie like *Who Killed Teddy Bear?* that could be sufficient reason to get oneself murdered. On a still-lower rung, *Promises! Promises!* (1963) and *Three Nuts in Search of a Bolt* (1964) were sad fulfillments of a bombshell truism valid from the early-sixties onward: when all else fails, take it off. The stripping ex-goddesses in this seedy pair were Jayne Mansfield and Mamie Van Doren, and the overripe amusement supplied by their presence was bolstered by the more intentionally louche efforts of female impersonator T. C. Jones. How strange, and weirdly apropos, that the trenchcoat audiences going to see these for one reason only (make that two reasons) were confronted with the laugh-getting efforts of a talented, wildly gay entertainer.[8]

In 1966, as more and more major productions were offering deliberate challenges to the Production Code, the Motion Picture Association of America appointed a new president to oversee the struggles over film content. While the aging Shurlock maintained his leadership of the Code, Jack Valenti, special assistant to President Johnson, became the industry spokesperson. A slicker Will Hays for a new film age, he had his mettle tested at once by Warner Bros.' *Who's Afraid of Virginia Woolf?* Edward Albee's famously coded bitch-slap had been made even more gay-friendly on film with the addition of Elizabeth Taylor, and the industry shook from the repercussions of its scabrous dialogue. A less daunting challenge came from Sidney Lumet's film version of the Mary McCarthy's novel *The Group*, which was a major disappointment on every level. As Lakey, the Vassar coed who comes back from the Continent with a baroness lover in tow, Candice Bergen made a visually striking but dramatically wan debut; the character had been so pared in both writing and editing that only a

---

[8]Similar cleavage-and-queer delights greeted the nudie enthusiast in *SinDerella and the Golden Bra* (1964), which featured a large number of large breasts plus a big fat queen of a Fairy Godfather (Sid Lassick). Lest anyone doubt the integrity of the filmmakers, the damned thing was, uh, padded with a number of Disneyesque songs and dances—although, somehow, the extended sequence of village maidens trying on the title garment seemed more germane.

While T. C. Jones's brief movie career was devoted mostly to trashy adults-only fare, his last film was a couple of rungs higher. In a demented melodrama called *The Name of the Game Is Kill* (1968) he was pretty memorable as a trouble-plagued Arizona mom who is actually a more trouble-beset dad.

few moments had much impact. One of them was especially boorish: an alcoholic louse (Larry Hagman) asking her if she was "A Sapphic . . . a Lesbo." A great deal of publicity had come from the casting of this child of Hollywood in such a "daring" role, and *The Group* ran in some places as an adults-only attraction, promising but not giving its audience something in the way of maturity or titillation. For all its seaminess, *Walk on the Wild Side* at least had a hint of substance behind its promise. With billing and publicity far larger than her role, Bergen was another in the procession of gays on the cutting-room floor, continuing a tradition that continues up to the present day. Her role was conspicuously editorialized as well: with her tailored outfit and even more tailored companion, Lakey is clearly marked as the group's outsider, fulfilled on her own terms but unable to act as part of a larger community.

More from reputation than content, *The Group* received a Code seal only after lobbying and pressure, which energies seemed by mid-decade patently absurd. The Code was tailored to, and thrived in, a particular industrial context. By the middle of the 1960s the circumstances had changed radically, and so had the audiences. Between coffins arriving from Vietnam and race riots and Haight-Ashbury and *Virginia Woolf* and all the rest of it, the kind of enforceable decorum offered by a Production Code had little to do with current realities. As long as this sort of censorship existed, more and more filmmakers would be willing to challenge or ignore it. In an effort to keep the peace, Valenti unveiled a new Code in the autumn of 1966. In place of the old prohibitions, there were provisos advising caution on such areas as violence, nudity, and sexual content, and Shurlock and the Code office were entrusted to label certain films with a somewhat gracious advisory informing viewers that said movie was "Suggested for Mature Audiences." The new Code was as controversial as the old one. "A glittering diadem of hypocrisy" was how *Newsweek* put it, and its effects were immediately noticeable. Here is where the violence and exposure and coarse language started getting revved up, to some good and many bad artistic ends. Another increase, equally visible, was in the number of gay and lesbian portrayals. Almost all of them were negative.

The filmmaking period starting in 1967 and moving into the 1980s—following the initial change in the Production Code, and the subsequent rating system—was the primary focus of the book *The Celluloid Closet*. It was also the main and justifiable cause for much of the book's irate tone. The liberalization of the Code was not a license for either acceptance or honesty. Instead, it made even the early fifties seem by comparison like a sanctuary of tolerance. The comparatively allusive nature of *Strangers on a Train* or even *So Young, So Bad* seems infinitely preferable to what was produced once the sensationalists stepped in and began to tread rudely. An early example came from the production line at Universal, which reflected cinema's new permissiveness by turning out theatrical films that were completely interchangeable with its made-for-TV product, save for the addition of a little flesh, a few swear words, or . . . how about a dollop of institutionalized stereotyped homophobia? *P.J.*, shot early in 1967 and shelved for a year, was a puny rematch between George Peppard and director John Guillermin, who had successfully refurbished World War I airborne heroics in *The Blue Max*. With a singular lack of presence and self-mocking wit, Peppard played a rundown bum of a private eye whose charm peaks when he's being nasty to faggots. They, of course, deserve P.J.'s scorn, particularly one homo-unctuous creep with the drawly lispy name Shelton Kwell (Severn Darden), to whom Peppard tosses a purported witticism about being at the bottom of the garden. Later, his case takes P.J. to a bar called (nudge, nudge) the Gay Caballero, where he beats up twenty or so patrons. Except for scratches on his face from a few flighty twits, he does his gay-bashing without breaking a sweat. *Walk on the Wild Side* is beginning to seem like nirvana.

Another actor trying to go the Bogart route was that paragon of ring-a-ding, Frank Sinatra, whose mid-sixties film career was mired in total junk. After some Rat Pack droppings and failed action dramas, he decided to be a hard-boiled dick, with wisecracks and terse dialogue and shapely women and scummy bad guys. In *Tony Rome* (1967) and its sequel *Lady in Cement* (1968) he was a private eye in Miami, and in *The Detective* (1968) he was a New York cop—and only in *Lady in Cement* was the screen not spattered with snide and condescending bitterness towards homosexuals. *Tony Rome* was less a cohesive narrative than a "Miami Uncensored" shockumentary, filled with neon and hoods and blackmailers—and a trip to something called the Flora Dora Club, the hangout for a lesbian stripper named Georgia (Deanna Lund) and Vic Rood, a gay drug pusher (Lloyd Bochner). Rood has an apartment decorated in precious taste, while Georgia lives in a mobile home with a drooling oversized partner, Irma (Elizabeth Fraser). While Rome watches this trailer-trash pair with leering superiority, Georgia and Irma bicker, come to blows, and kiss and make up. "You want the lights on or off?" Sinatra smirks on his way out.

Even *Advise and Consent* looked good next to *The Detective*, which looms high as one of the most homophobic movies ever made. Sinatra cast himself as a "liberal" police officer named Joe Leland, whose virtue is contrasted with that of a fellow cop (Robert Duvall) who goes on about the joys of queer-bashing. Leland, the supposed paragon, shows his enlightenment by making illegal arrests in gay bars and roughing up gay suspects. The whole ghastly thing hinges on the false conviction and execution of an unstable gay man (Tony Musante) for the murder of his "roommate" (James Inman). As it turns out, the killer was a nasty closet case (William Windom) who later kills himself less for being a murderer than for being gay. It plays out like a loathsome warmup for *Cruising*, without the potentially camp joy of seeing Sinatra dancing in a leather

In *The Detective*, James Inman discovers that bringing William Windom home wasn't a good idea. *Photofest*

bar.[9] Purportedly, this is the tale of Leland's redemption, although such qualities were lost in the torrent of ugly images and in Sinatra's sneering condescension to the gay characters, which seemed part of both the character and the star. "It exploits its lurid subject matter in a show-offy, heavy-handed way designed as much to tease as to teach compassion," commented Vincent Canby in the *New York Times*. If someone organized a scavenger hunt to find the compassion in *The Detective*, there would be no winners. The only good coming out of this scabby mess was that its comparative financial success did not lead Sinatra or anyone else to more of the same. At least yet.

A far more "respectable" entertainment than the Sinatra films, *Reflections in a Golden Eye* (1967) at least attempted to be true to its source and play it fair with the gayness. Except for *The Member of the Wedding* and *The Heart Is a*

---

[9]It might be worth noting that the gay supporting characters and extras in *The Detective* were not portrayed or costumed with a striking amount of verisimilitude. Indeed, they seemed bent on establishing that lost link between Frederick's of Hollywood and Tom of Finland. Let one British critic have a word: "[They] all look as if they had strayed onto the set from the chorus of *West Side Story.*"

Putting on a show: Zorro David's talents are obviously more suited to Julie Harris's taste than to Brian Keith's in *Reflections in a Golden Eye*. *Photofest*

Lonely Hunter, one doesn't go to Carson McCullers for gentle nuance. *Reflections*, accordingly, had a striking cast of oddballs, dolts, and nutcases. Elizabeth Taylor and Brian Keith were the doltish, comparatively normal straights, Julie Harris, as Keith's wife, was the loony, and Marlon Brando was an epic misfit— one of the screen's great portrayals of the perils of a closeted existence. As Weldon Penderton, an army major at a Georgia outpost, Brando spared himself and the audience nothing in revealing the priss beneath the martinet, the gay man trapped in a marriage to a luscious dingbat (Taylor) and nursing a crush on a hunky private (Robert Forster). Whether it was courage or outré glee, Brando went the distance in presenting the man as disjointed, unappealing, and ridiculous, as in one scene where he tries on makeup and seems more Pagliacci than drag queen. Don't ask, don't tell, indeed—Penderton's army discipline forms the walls of his closet, which finally explodes in a burst of tragedy and gunfire.[10] In

---

[10]For real-life freakiness, consider that Elizabeth Taylor had originally requested that her old friend and costar Montgomery Clift be cast as Penderton. Clift's disastrous physical and mental state militated against his insurability, and then he died. Had he been cast, it's easy to imagine that the pressures on one unstable closeted man playing another would have been horrendous and possibly lethal.

extreme contrast, there is Anacleto, Harris's houseboy. As played by a New York hairdresser named Zorro David, Anacleto has long since moved past conventional effeminacy. He offers, instead, an alternative universe, populated by only himself and Harris's deranged Alison. He spins fantasies for her and they play games and do arts and crafts, and director John Huston is oddly respectful, discreet enough not to editorialize. For many straight and gay viewers, Anacleto would be beyond ultra, an *Our Betters* Ernest for the Vietnam era. Others might find the portrayal, and the relationship between Anacleto and Alison, a warm reminder of some familiar (if odd) things—the need for some fey grace amid oppressive surroundings, the ability to be yourself, and the quest for soulmates in a wretched world. Unfortunately, the general response to *Reflections* was wretched as well. The Legion of Decency's "Condemned" still carried clout in many areas, there was a large sheaf of bad reviews, and the presence of Taylor and Brando, both beginning a bad career patch, added to the aura of flop sweat. Essentially, there never was a chance for this to be anything other than a failure.[11] McCullers's quirky grotesquerie is difficult to capture on film, and Huston's success in that area has always been debatable. Certainly he made a genuine attempt to find the author's weird poignancy and make it comprehensible. Not everyone will or should respond favorably, but in a time when Frank Sinatra was doing his hipster bashing, it was not a shameful achievement.

Let it not be said, either, that the "Suggested for Mature Audiences" year of 1967 did not end in a blaze of queer glory. *Bonnie and Clyde?* No. Warren Beatty saw to it that Clyde Barrow's real-life homosexuality was not a part of that script. *The Incident?* No. Despite its conspicuous and negative portrayal of a gay loser (Robert Fields) menaced by subway thugs, it was a minor film seen by few, a moldy continuation of the *Advise and Consent* line of condemnation-through-supposed-tolerance. No, the palm must go to one of the year's biggest box-office successes and a beloved gay cult film for lo, many a year. In its progress from the all-thumbs typewriter of Jacqueline Susann, through the glitzy and imbecilic production maw of Twentieth Century–Fox, *Valley of the Dolls* is a resplendent achievement. Nothing, save for a couple of vagrant and almost unintentionally good moments, is remotely authentic, sincere, or human. The shrillness, the phony tinsel, the hairdos—it's all here, along with some of the first show-biz references to gay men since *Myrt and Marge*. Alongside *Valley of the Dolls*, *Myrt*, with its well-integrated gay Clarence, resembles either

---

[11]The initial theater engagements drew a hostile response less for the film itself (although there was that) than for the way it looked. Huston had decided to take the title literally and have the prints bathed in a gold-sepia wash, which drained out most of the color. Later prints, and the version available today, had a more conventional Technicolor look; as with the movie itself, the success of Huston's gimmick is certainly a topic for discussion.

Proust or cinéma-verité. The screenwriters eliminated a major lesbian plot in the book and confined the actual gayness, ludicrously enough, to one unnamed choreographer who gives Neely O'Hara (Patty Duke) a great nightclub act and an addiction to uppers. The majority of the homosexuality in this Susann valley is in fact bogus: the rumors swirling around master couturier Ted Casablanca (Alex Davion). "Ted Casablanca is not a fag," Patty Duke says, in a delivery that tries amusingly to approximate a snarl, "and I'm the dame that can prove it." Apparently she is, and when Ted's manhood flags later on, he finds various young women to prop it up. With *The Incident*, *Valley of the Dolls* marks one of the very first uses of the F word ("fag," that is), on several occasions. With all the vocal color in her micronic arsenal, Sharon Tate sums up the popular view of Ted Casablanca: "You know how bitchy fags can be." It's tremendously indicative of the era that even here, in a camp-trashy showbiz world created by a gay-friendly writer, gayness is a nasty rumor and a foul accusation. Ted is not gay (nor apparently was *Valley*'s own costume designer, William Travilla), and in this showbiz fantasy of virile studs and beautiful broads gayness must be avoided, or at least denigrated, at all costs. In one early script, Ted reveals his true self to Neely by unexpectedly deep-kissing her and saying, when he sees her astonishment, "I know. Everyone thinks I'm a fag." That scene was not used, but the climactic powder-room bout between Neely and harridan-diva Helen Lawson (Susan Hayward), which originally stayed away from gay matters, was punched up with an added exchange:

HELEN: Now you get outta my way 'cause I gotta man waiting for me!
NEELY: That's a switch from the fags you're usually stuck with.
HELEN: At least I never married one.
NEELY: You take that back, you . . . (*Mayhem ensues. Neely snatches off Helen's wig and attempts to flush it down the toilet.*)

Valley of the Dolls is twice blessed, both for its lovably atrocious intrinsic self (including the wig flushing) and the fact that Judy Garland was fired after a couple of days' shooting. Posterity was thus blissfully spared the spectacle of the dilapidated Garland, with her hordes of gay husbands and fans, spitting out Helen's line about marrying a fag. Too, it is fortunate that *Valley*'s picturesque gay attitudes are set in the context of an epic hoot, whereas the horrors of *The Detective* could not be laughed at by anyone save the most desiccated postmodern ironist.

Lest *Valley of the Dolls* lead anyone to think that gays and showbiz were mutually exclusive, the balance was redressed a few months later with the advent of *The Producers*. The film, not the deliriously successful Broadway musical that followed more than three decades later. The gays in *The Producers* are like everything and everyone else in the cast, from Zero Mostel on down—cartoons, and proud and joyful to be so. Their names are lushly indicative—Roger DeBris (Christopher Hewitt), the talent-bereft theatre director, and Carmen Giya (Andreas Voutsinas), Roger's hairdresser-boyfriend. Roger is first beheld in ill-suited drag, preparing to go to a ball dressed as Anastasia. The fact that Hewitt plays him as a bombastic fool rather then a simpy queen makes the whole thing even funnier, and Voutsinas—with his eye shadow and weird curled-up beard—does the queeny thing well enough for both of them. As Roger hears Max Bialystock (Mostel) talk about *Springtime for Hitler*, his eyes radiate with the vision that can come only from inspired incompetence. He glows as he begins to think about the S.S. chorus line in black leather . . . "S/M," he asides to Carmen Giya. "Love it!" is the fervently whispered response, in a real gay-insider moment. Later, when we see the opening production number, we cannot question that Roger does indeed function as the master of his useless domain. He's like Ed Wood: absence of talent, when this monumental, can be infinitely more inspiring than run-of-the-mill competence. In writing and directing these flamers, is Mel Brooks demeaning gays? Not on your life. On Brooks's Broadway, nothing is sacred: not Nazis or Jews, not gays or horny old ladies. It's all part of the carnival of bad taste and good cheer.[12]

Like its inverse *The Detective*, *The Producers* opened in the spring of 1968 in the midst of the new "Suggested for Mature Audiences" age. Films were being labeled for adult content in a nation that, since 1962, had matured the hard way. A war, a civil rights movement, and an assassination (with two more anon) had all added lines to the national complexion, and the concept of being gay was beginning to change as well. More publications and organizations, new people less willing to hide or defer, more doctors and psychiatrists dealing with it as a condition instead of a disease, and with a simmering distaff sibling called feminism: a movement was in the making, and it would find its definition in the hot summer of 1969. The Stonewall riots were no more the start of Gay Liberation than the Montgomery bus boycott initiated the civil rights movement, but they would imply and clarify and point the way. In both movements, popular culture was simultaneously salve and salt, adding visibility while propagating stereotypes.

As the movie portrayals heated up, television was beginning to do its share as well: a 1967 CBS documentary called, simply, *The Homosexuals* was filled

---

[12]It became an even greater part of the carnival for that smash stage incarnation. The L.S.D. character of the film, played by Dick Shawn, was eliminated, and the role of Hitler in the show-within-a-show is taken, in a *42nd Street*-understudy twist, by the terrified, yet ultimately game, Roger DeBris. By the twenty-first century, druggy hippies had obviously run their course as comic material, while silly queens remain fresh.

with quietly smug sensationalism and tearoom busts at the same time that it allowed a few people to speak feelingly from the shadows about having to hide and feel apart. For those who counted any publicity as a plus, *The Homosexuals* was at least more of an affirmation than *The Detective* or *P.J.*, in fact more than what many recent films had been giving. In short time, homosexuality would become an incendiary plot point in such televised dramas as *Medical Center* and *The Bold Ones*. On Broadway, too, the terrain was altered almost instantaneously with the opening of Mart Crowley's *Boys in the Band*. Unlike earlier plays, even Frank Marcus's *Killing of Sister George*, it seemed definitive, even all-encompassing. It was, for many, the Gay Play. All of this seemed to be implying something different. It might be possible for the movies to reflect this implication. Or would they prefer to keep nurturing those lurid hordes of closeted killers and repressed dykes?

FIFTEEN

Open Season

HOMO 'N' LESBO FILMS AT PEAK
Deviate Films Now 'Boxoffice'

—*Variety* headline, January 15, 1969

I t had been so different in 1934, when the Production Code was born. All those odd swirls and eddies of history had been intersecting and feeding each other to create a time and a circumstance when film and morality would be as one. By 1968 it was time for a legal separation. The mutually reflective relationship of the movies and morality had become a tense stand-off; too much had been said and done to ever think that one could possibly control the other. In film and in life, that phony old innocence was long gone, and so was the desire to allude to or conceal. Even if the liberalization of the Production Code had been continued and extended, history had already seen to it that the Code was useless and moribund. It lacked teeth and it lacked tact, and it was as dead as Joe Breen. That "Suggested for Mature Audiences" warning was inviting, not discouraging, tides of permissiveness that no set of guidelines could squelch. Unlike 1934, there were no waves of reform in 1968 to cause anything like a Code to seem remotely viable. Even the Catholic Church stopped caring very much. Other wars being fought seemed far more necessary than this one.

As the old hands in the Production Code office fought to hold on to their mandate, the final knell was sounded by no less than the U.S. Supreme Court. Two cases in the spring of 1968 would change the way the country could police the sale or exhibition of adult material; one involved selling an adult magazine to a minor, the other disputed the ability of a local censorship board to ban young people from a movie.[1] The outcome effectively curbed censorship, and so questions were fired right and left about how to regulate film. For months the MPAA's Jack Valenti had been advocating a rating system, and the industry was finally compelled to accept his proposal. It was an extension of the "Mature" tag then in effect, which at some points also operated as a "Restricted" rating that allowed people under the age of sixteen to see the film only with a parent or guardian. It was not perfect, and many found it abhorrent, but there were few alternatives. The formal end came on November 1, 1968, when the Motion Picture Association of America announced the new system of ratings that would govern film content. The ratings were similar to those used in Great Britain, with that same X to denote the most extreme no-nos. The G was the realm of Disney and the like, and the M (later GP and then PG) and R were the area in which most films would find themselves. The face of filmgoing in American was decisively and almost instantaneously altered.

The old studio system had been dying an even more lingering death than the Code. The decay had started in the late 1940s when the film companies lost their chains of movie theaters and the nation's leisure time began to find itself directed to a far smaller screen. By the sixties most of the remaining studios were more successful in their television production than in making features, which in some ways accelerated the drive toward more adult fare. More and more, films would be made by production companies, not studios in the traditional sense, and the director would become an increasingly powerful figure. Here the era of the auteur truly begins. Making movies became different, and going to them changed as well. The old urban movie palaces were giving way to the suburban multiplex theaters that, by the late 1970s, would be the preferred locus of filmgoing. And with the unlamented departure of the Code there was another shift in the process: there would be no one to officially scan the content of a film script for perceived unsuitability. A film, to obtain its rating, would be judged on the basis of its final cut. Going to the cinema had become a different proposition, in some ways truly a more adult one. At the very beginning of the ratings era, it would be more gay as well.

Beginning in 1968 a series of high-profile movies, mostly from major studios, would revel in film's newfound freedom to depict homosexuality openly. It was the second wave of the trend that first surfaced in 1962 in reaction to the liberalization of the Code. This new one came with its demise, and lasted roughly two years. It most intimately embraced seven feature films of varying

---

[1]The city in the dispute was Dallas, and the film was Louis Malle's comedy *Viva Maria!* One clear parallel with 1934: the movie was not particularly racy, but its star was synonymous, in the heartland, with untrammeled cinematic sex. Like Mae West back in the Depression, Brigitte Bardot was an easy and curvaceous target upon which to (barely) drape a great deal of sexual dread.

importance, quality, and consequence. They were obviously intended to exploit the anything-goes new spirit of American cinema, to expand on the gay images present in the previous year—more films like *The Detective*, perhaps?—and to compete with independent product and foreign imports. The independents included Andy Warhol movies like *Flesh* and *Trash*, which viewed all sexuality with addled hipness; at that level of nonchalance there was no room to be judgmental. There was also the start, with such foreign films as *Therese and Isabelle*, of the lesbianism-is-such-a-turn-on school of filmmaking that would soon enrapture leering hordes of heterosexual male spectators. (It is also around this time that the hard-core porn industry has its above-ground beginnings.) The more conventional American product, which did not pander quite so overtly, indicated how mainstream film would take on the subject and how audiences would respond. Widening the historical lens a little: perhaps it is a coincidence that these movies precisely frame the Stonewall riots. Still, we can wonder again about those pushy and insistent currents that seem to shove so many unrelated events together, and by these juxtapositions make us understand how history works. What is certain is that these seven films ultimately carried more weight and repercussion than the group from 1962. In some ways they were the movies' own equivalent of Stonewall, a new beginning and perhaps a dead end.

The Fox, a U.S. and Canadian coproduction, opened in February of 1968. Like *Virginia Woolf?*, *In Cold Blood*, and some others, it was one of the pre-rating "Restricted" films, proudly brandishing the name of D. H. Lawrence as it gamely strove to make film a temple of solemn eroticism. Eight years earlier, a British-French adaptation of *Lady Chatterley's Lover* had instigated court battles and censorious wrath. By the time of *The Fox*, censors were becoming unemployed, and Lawrence could use some neon heightening. What had been implied and allusive in print became, in the movie, clearly queer, for as with *Reflections in a Golden Eye*, it pointed up and specified the story's sexuality. Specters of films past—*Serenade* and *The Lost Weekend* and the rest—trembled in truncated righteousness as *The Fox* made the closely bonded rural women of Lawrence's novella, who were perhaps lovers, into the indubitably real thing.[2] With Sandy Dennis as Jill and Anne Heywood as the more "masculine" Ellen, *The Fox* featured woman-woman love scenes, a great deal of touching, and a garish scene of Heywood masturbating—all in the name, perhaps, of art, and all calculated for maximum pow. Keir Dullea was the foxy outsider who came between the women and eventually won Heywood, and the

---

[2] Another past film also weighed in on *The Fox*, which was the first feature directed by Mark Rydell. A dozen years earlier Rydell had vividly portrayed a gay street punk in *Crime in the Streets* by employing the same technique he would bring to *The Fox:* he amplified the writer's intent in order to make the gayness more visible.

whole thing made a very 1968 kind of splash as it courted controversy and notoriety with gustatory glee. The blaring ad campaign made sure everyone knew: "Even a year ago, *The Fox* could not have been made. . . . Not THIS way!" Certainly not with an Oscar-winner (Dennis) as a lesbian who gets killed by the Freudian force of a falling tree. The formula proceeded like clockwork, with the critics arguing about the treatment and the lines forming at the theaters. Some found the made-in-Canada austerity and glum pacing and sterile sensationalism to be art; others saw it as resembling an Ingmar Bergman production of *Walk on the Wild Side*. Renata Adler, writing in the *Times*, was so torn that she bemoaned the excesses as ludicrous while at the same time praising the guts it took to create them. Six years after *The Children's Hour*, less than two after the Code-fearing caution of *The Group*, lesbianism was now being handled with more flash than care, and with the preaching and condemnation more insidiously subtle. There was in fact a very DeMille quality to *The Fox*. The women's lives were shown in detail in order to justify an ultimate end: Heywood needed a man, and so Dennis could be killed off to bring about True Love. In the book the Dullea character had engineered Jill's death; in the movie it seems essentially self-willed. The liberal surface of films such as *The Fox* would serve as a trendy veneer for further confused messages of acceptance, condescension, and damnation.

Two of the oddest holiday attractions of all time delivered these messages near the end of 1968. *The Sergeant* was absolutely hell-bent on being the Breakthrough Gay Movie, proudly sporting one of the new R ratings and outfitted with Oscary prestige. With vast praise for *The Pawnbroker* and a new gold statuette for *In the Heat of the Night*, Rod Steiger was the film community's new actor's actor, a non-glamour-puss who took chances and stretched in any number of directions. He had already gone the gay-allusive route twice, with *The Loved One* and *No Way to Treat a Lady*, in which a swish turn was one of several guises assumed by his psycho (and possibly latently gay) serial killer, and he embraced the role of Sgt. Albert Callan with characteristic gusto. Both the script and the original novel were written by Dennis Murphy, who culled and heightened some of his own war experiences to form the story of a bullishly repressed master sergeant in postwar France who develops a case on a cute Pfc. When both Callan and the private discover what's going on, the sergeant blows his own brains out. There were obvious echoes of *Reflections in a Golden Eye*, and without the McCullers Gothic overlay the psychology seemed dim and reactionary. This did not stop the filmmakers from considering themselves bold and possibly forward-looking, especially for 1968, and with casting that would make it viable. Having just done a dreamboy stint as the angel in *Barbarella*, John Phillip Law made a drably viable object of affection, the actor's dullness serving as an indicator of the private's inability to comprehend a queer gaze.[3] The much-touted payoff of *The Sergeant* was Steiger drunkenly kissing an appalled Law, which was intended as a shocking moment à la *A View from the Bridge*. Steiger was reportedly gleeful that he was going to be the first man—at least the first man playing a sort-of gay man—to do this on the screen.

When it opened in December 1968, *The Sergeant* proved to be the axis of a bemusing paradox. It was sufficiently frank to have not been filmable earlier, yet it seemed unhip, in fact, old-fashioned. The kill-yourself-when you-discover-you're-gay school, as led by Tennessee Williams, had run its course in the minds of many, and here, more than in *The Fox*, the bipolar disorder of tolerance vs. morality cast a heavy pall. It lacked the intriguing baroque sheen of *Reflections in a Golden Eye*, and its Big Secret was all too obvious. Scarcely fifteen minutes had elapsed when it was clear to the audience who Callan was and where it was all headed, and the ninety minutes remaining until the climactic kiss were filled with !All Steiger, All the Time! Method shtick—every nuance emblazoned in wide-screen Technicolor. Many critics who thought the film otherwise unconvincing did indeed buy into the promise of the ad slogan "Rod Steiger STUNS as *The Sergeant*"; in 1968 there was the advantage of not having been been subjected to more than thirty years of dire overplaying by this prodigiously gifted and peerlessly hammy actor. Vincent Canby in the *New York Times* was not among those applauding either the actor or his vehicle, expressing annoyance with director John Flynn's heavily phallic mise-en-scène and zeroing in on star excess: "Although Steiger is too good an actor to camp it up, he comes on with all the subtlety of a drag queen." Not even the more enthusiastic reviews could offset the general public apathy, and Steiger failed to win the Oscar nomination the filmmakers hoped for.[4]

The disappointment surrounding *The Sergeant* enforced the truism, already made clear in 1962, about homosexuality's weak attraction for a mainstream audience. Lesbians in *The Fox* might do it, but Rod Steiger laying a big wet one on John Philip Law (or possibly any living creature) was not box-office bait. Since everyone knew in advance what this movie was about, ultimately it all seemed something like a one-joke premise without the joke. For gay audiences

---

[3]The producer had favored either Ryan O'Neal or Jon Voight (immediately pre–*Midnight Cowboy*) as Private Swanson. The less inspiring Law came in with Steiger as, essentially, part of a William Morris Agency package deal. With the death of the studio system, agents were finding more power, and casting was becoming a new form of corporate art.

[4]It was in fact a lightweight year for lead actor performances, and the ultimate winner—Cliff Robertson in *Charly*—was not precisely one for the thespian ages; Steiger's omission must have thus been somewhat galling.

there was not much more: you knew that this one wouldn't be giving you any sort of validation—going to see it would be a form of guilt-stoking masochism. It was Mae West, of all people, who zeroed in, however unwittingly, on what was wrong with *The Sergeant*. Not for her any analysis of the movie's outdated and false psychology, bogus liberalist piety, or questionable dramatics. When the producers asked for her reaction after an invitational screening, she cut to the chase. "Poor sonovabitch of a sergeant," she drawled. "If only that kid had given in to him, he wouldn't have had t'kill himself!"

The starkness and negativity of *The Sergeant* were of a kind that would make gay viewers hope for some kind of antidote, and for some of them a soothing balm was only a few days away. Perhaps 1968, with its war and riots and assassins and ratings system, needed odd movies for its holiday season; at very least, the end-of-the-year Oscar bait seemed more outré than usual. Robert Aldrich was a director who seemed to thrive on offbeat provocation, in which package he sometimes included lesbianism. Following his sojourn in Sodom and Gomorrah, and a gargoyles-in-drag doubleheader with Bette Davis, he returned briefly to more conventionally rough-edged heroics with *The Flight of the Phoenix* and *The Dirty Dozen*. His tinselly self-indulgence then led him to *The Legend of Lylah Clare*, a Hollywood fable so dissipated that no one, including Aldrich, could figure out whether it was serious or a put-on. As in *Sodom and Gomorrah*, he managed to cite lesbianism as one of the chief debauches of a sinful town, with a drug-addled "dialogue coach" (Rosella Falk) precipitating crises without end when she seduces Kim Novak's Lylah. *Lylah* proved to be a bomb of multidimensional proportions, and Aldrich moved on to the reasonably conventional climes of a straightforward theatrical adaptation. The play, however, was *The Killing of Sister George*, and Aldrich was not a man given to understatement.

Onstage, Frank Marcus's tragicomedy had owed its modest success less to the novelty of its portrayal of London lesbians than to some strong dialogue and powerhouse acting, especially by Beryl Reid. As June Buckridge, the butch dyke who plays "Sister George" on a BBC soap opera, Reid was funny, horrifying, lacerating and finally poignant. The "killing" referred to the character being written out of the show—and also alluded to June/George herself. Stuffed into tight tweeds, smoking cigars and drinking too much, making boisterously off-color jokes, conducting rituals of punishment with her lover Alice (Susannah York), George is a walking, creaking anachronism as an actor and as a gay woman. She's not uproarious and obnoxious because she's a lesbian, or a drunk, or even an actor; she's being herself, too undisciplined and honest to fit in anywhere. Lacking the guile to play the suck-up game at work, she loses at home as well when Alice goes off with a sleek network executive (Coral Browne). When it's all done, George is dead in all but body, reduced to doing the voice of a cartoon cow. "Moo," she lows. The end.

The film adaptation of *Sister George* generated all the controversy that *The Sergeant* had attempted to raise. Aldrich, whose acquaintance with subtlety was usually tenuous, attempted to make Marcus's small tale a veritable epic of sapphic love, covering all bases in the most conspicuous fashion possible. The adaptation (by Aldrich's traditional collaborator Lucas Heller, writer of *Baby Jane* among others) opened up the play to uneven effect, retaining some tedious stagey passages while adding new sequences both funny and "exotic." The scenes of George running amok at the studio are among the best in the film, as is a bawdy skit involving her drunkenly terrorizing a pair of nuns. In those moments, Beryl Reid is magnificent—funny without being calculating, sad without grabbing for sympathy. The scenes adhering closer to the play script turned out less well, reminding the audience all too well that Reid had done this role *so* many times onstage. The decibel level rises alarmingly and subtlety takes a walk.

It was Aldrich's quest for the exotic and erotic that stirred up most of the fuss. His intentions were praiseworthy, for he completely eschewed any sort of *Advise and Consent* "This is the face of evil" quality and tried, as much as he was capable, to create a small and sadly funny tragedy. Nevertheless, he was seldom capable of directing anything without heavy-handed emphasis— remember, this is the director who had Bette Davis serve Joan Crawford a broiled rat. It was unfortunately predictable that he would come up with such things as underlining Alice's femme role in the relationship—she's nicknamed Childie—by having her prance out in a pink baby-doll nightie. He shot one

Two views of the *Killing of Sister George* ad logo. On the left, the standard double-entendre model. Next to it, the breast-reduced and hair-extensioned model created by more squeamish publications.

central sequence on location at London's Gateways Club, a busy and purportedly notorious lesbian bar. Reid, York, and Browne mingled with real-life bar patrons while a rock band played and the camera fixed its intent and leering gaze upon every woman with clipped hair.[5] Despite Reid and York's amusing Laurel and Hardy routine, the scene goes on and on and on. Another addition, in fact the climax (literally) of the movie, was more crucial in sealing its fate as a sensation piece: the executive's smooth seduction of Alice, culminating in Susannah York's noisy simulation of an orgasm. In trying so hard to be scorching and erotic, it comes off as merely obtrusive and calculated. Renata Adler of the *Times* was again a withering observer: "It is the longest, most unerotic, cash-conscious scene between a person and a breast there has ever been on screen, and outside a surgeon's office." Browne, in particular, is so tense that she's about ready to shatter; she seems to be wishing she were back in *Auntie Mame*. While it's debatable whether or not the scene was totally responsible for *George*'s subsequent X rating, it was what everyone talked about.

Without the love scene and X, *George* might have been accepted on its own terms. With them, for all but a knowing coterie of spectators, it was a lurid carnival, a fact simultaneously averred and denied by faux-dignified ads with the (inaccurate) slogan, "The story of three consenting adults in the privacy of their own home." One unenlightened critic after another ran on tediously about the despair of the lesbian world—assuming that there is such a thing. Most conspicuous among these was Richard Schickel in *Life*, who continued what was becoming his standard tack of snide condescension toward homosexuality: "Tacky, tawdry, repellent—and true," he droned. "There is nothing soft or graceful about it; the emphasis is on people using each other, not loving each other." This was, dear reader, a favorable review. Such notices would not necessarily cause an audience to stampede, and the X rating, one of the very first given to a major film release, ultimately did act as a deterrent. Not just for *The Killing of Sister George*, but for gay and especially lesbian-themed films in general. Perhaps it had just been a case of too much (138 minutes), too loud (that onstage-type screeching), too blatant (the sex scene), and too soon. There would be no more Lesbian Mainstream films in pop American cinema until the brazen male-stoking likes of *Basic Instinct*. For all Robert Aldrich's good intentions, he had created a work in which the merits and dross were too jumbled to be sorted out. It was fascinating, and ultimately it was a blind alley.

---

[5]The gaze was explicit enough to cost at least one patron her job. Aldrich reported that the woman, employed as a receptionist, was fired when a picture of the Gateways scene was published in a London newspaper. That this happened is doubly shameful because the scene is far from documentary or honest in effect. With its Aldrichian excess, it might just as well have been shot in a studio.

This fact was not yet clear when the *Variety* article ran some weeks after *Sister George* opened. With both *George* and *The Sergeant* still in theaters, and numerous projects on the way, it did indeed seem like queer cinema was a hot new trend, regardless of the prospect that the sheer presence of "homosexual content" might be grounds for an X rating. For gay and lesbian spectators, the upcoming *Midnight Cowboy*, *Staircase*, and *The Boys in the Band* seemed to portend some fertile possibilities. The optimists envisioned greater visibility, possibly some degree of affirmation, a way to educate and entertain. The pessimists thought of demonization, of Rod Steiger shooting himself, and of a world depicted as "tacky, tawdry, repellent—and true." For the realists, a look back to 1962 would be most instructive. History would not alter its design any time soon.

There was, however, a wild card in history's deck. The world did not stop turning when, in June 1969, a ragged assortment of barflies and drag queens and street kids decided they would no longer accept police harassment. The popular press gave but cursory attention to the matter and on the surface that seemed to be that. Then it slowly became clear that Stonewall had, as they say in the business, legs. Groups started forming, discussions opened up, and existences were rethought. A revolution that began so noisily would proceed, in fact, could proceed, only inches at a time. Millimeters, in some places. Certainly the motion picture business would not profess to derive any sort of impact any time soon, which gives the two films that framed the Stonewall riots a particularly recherché kind of resonance. *Midnight Cowboy* opened a few weeks before Stonewall, *Staircase* premiered a short time after. One was a shocker and a hit, the other a dodo flop. One prided itself on its gritty shot-on-New-York-streets realism, the other was so phony that it was set in London but shot on a Paris soundstage. One looked askance at homosexuality, and the other offered derision and pity. On the surface they seemed to be from different worlds, one from the unlamented old studio days and the other from the edgy time of now. Yet both were at heart conventional movies, old wine in new bottles.

Like *The Killing of Sister George*, *Midnight Cowboy* was the rare "big" movie with an X rating and some queer subject matter. Unlike *George*, it was a substantial hit commercially and critically, to the extent that it won the Academy Award as best film of 1969—an event most important for certifying the death of the old studio/Production Code era.[6] On the surface, with subject matter timed just right to tap into post-Code daring, it all seemed as hot and new as a movie could, the ideal capper for a decade in which shocking change had been a weekly occurrence. James Leo Herlihy's novel about a would-be stud from Texas finding disillusion and tricks on the streets of Manhattan

---

[6]Two years later the X rating was rescinded and changed to an R without any cuts being made. The same thing happened, eventually, to *The Killing of Sister George*.

seemed, by 1969, to encapsulate the nation's feelings. You set your sights high, you go out there and try hard, and it all ends up in the toilet. Instead of servicing Park Avenue's choicest matrons, Joe Buck finds that most of his clients are losers and self-haters, male variety. Only in his bonding with a tubercular creep named Ratso is there redemption, a scuzzy Damon and Pythias to counterpoint a city filled with users and sex fiends. It worked on the screen through one of those happy combinations of skill and timing and plain luck. For Dustin Hoffman, the newest face of stardom after *The Graduate*, Ratso was an arresting about-face. Jon Voight was an even newer face, intense and innocently sexy, and director John Schlesinger, who had already summed up the emptiness of the swinging sixties with *Darling*, brought a mordant British objectivity to bear on Joe's odyssey. Instead of glossy New York vistas, there were grainy images that seemed to mock the falseness of the old studio days, while on the sound track Harry Nilsson plaintively sang, "Everybody's talkin' at me."

Midnight Cowboy worked hard to wear its honesty on Joe Buck's buckskin-fringed sleeve. Many bought it, and even those disagreeing with its philosophy could not help but be captivated. The underground film movement seemed here to be breaking into the mainstream—the best of both worlds combining to make the movies more real. Only a small group of observers could perceive that under all the skill and grit there was still a sort of fake romanticism and—more crucially—that same lousy view of gays as despairing and degraded. Joe's male tricks are not really worse than his contacts with women, but his reactions to them, and the reactions the audience is led to have, are far uglier. A furtive grope with a geek student in a movie house, a bizarre encounter with a religious fanatic, and—most horribly—a violent run-in with a nice, meek, self-hating older man (Barnard Hughes) whom Joe beats and robs. The poor old guy says he deserves it, and Joe runs out and gets on a bus to Florida with Ratso, who can die where the air is clear and friendships are more pure. Under all that hipness, there were old messages. Queers were degenerates and users, and whenever they were victims they deserved it. If Joe has latent gay feelings, they are best sublimated into friendship, and Ratso gets to put down "fags," despite whatever sexual inclinations he may nurse. Perhaps it's inevitable that John Schlesinger was at this time a closeted gay man . . . unwittingly continuing a Cukoresque tradition of self-inflicted gay putdowns.

In *Staircase* the putdowns came from the outside. This British-American coproduction from Twentieth Century–Fox is a splendid argument in favor of the death of the old studio system. At a time when overblown spectacles were starting to tank and little films were going through the roof, here was a small-scale project that traversed the corporate-commercial gauntlet and came out a big-budget eyesore. Worse, this monstrosity can be viewed as a film that did more than any other to kill off the idea of a gay-themed movie achieving mainstream success. You watch *Staircase* and see it self-destruct from the first frame onward, every choice a bad one. A bunch of emphatically, overtly straight artists, led by the director Stanley Donen and Richard Burton and Rex Harrison, decided to go on a camping expedition, not the kind with tents. This is what they came up with. For shame.

Charles Dyer's play *Staircase* was essentially a duet, with autobiographical overtones, for aging lovers. Charlie and Harry are a pair of low-rent London barbers not unlike George and Martha in *Virginia Woolf.* They snipe at each other unmercifully, Harry frets incessantly about losing his hair as he takes care of a senile crone mother, and Charlie assumes superiority because he had once been married and fathered a child. There are some moments of warmth and humor, but the overall effect—far more than in *The Killing of Sister George*—is that Dyer wants us to think that Charlie and Harry are Everyfags, their story that of gay men everywhere. Frank Marcus, and then Robert Aldrich, had taken pains to differentiate between lesbians in general and June Buckridge in particular; while she may have symbolized certain things, she was not a prototype. *Staircase*, as filtered through its playwright's evident self-pity, means to be a documentary, an intimate epic on how being an outsider and a loser and a fairy are all the same thing. Pity them, it tells you. On stage in 1966, under the auspices of the Royal Shakespeare Company, its dubious thesis seemed less patent as directed by Peter Hall and enacted by Paul Scofield and Patrick Magee. The public and the press applauded and professed to be touched. On Broadway, early in 1968, it seemed less absorbing, lasting only two months despite the efforts of stars Milo O'Shea and Eli Wallach. Paul Scofield's prestige and personal success in the London production led Stanley Donen to persuade Fox to buy the play . . . after which Scofield promptly turned down the film. Left with a dicey property without stars, Donen suggested to the studio heads, not entirely seriously, that the lovers could be played by the illustriously non-queer Burton and Harrison. Fox bought the idea, and despite his misgivings Donen went through with it. For a near-record $1.25 million each, Burton and Harrison, previously the Antony and Caesar of Fox's bloated *Cleopatra*, would play bitching boyfriends.

First the casting. Then the location. Burton's tax situation made an English shoot unfeasible, and he would not be separated from Elizabeth Taylor, then preparing to shoot another waterlogged corpse for Fox called *The Only Game in Town.* So the Brixton neighborhood of *Staircase* and the Las Vegas casinos of *Game* were put up on soundstages in, where else, Paris. The smell of disaster was in the air, and it continued so as Burton and Harrison both realized what they had gotten themselves into. The idea of a famously heterosexual actor doing a flaming gay turn might be fun in theory for said actor, and perhaps a dramatic challenge, but doing it successfully is another matter. Burton's confidence was not uplifted when, at a press conference, his wife responded to a reporter's comment:

> REPORTER: Mr. Burton says that you are a very nice girl.
> ELIZABETH TAYLOR: I'm glad that he decided that. Considering the part he's playing now in *Staircase*, he's a very nice girl too.

So Burton drank and forgot his lines. Harrison, who remembered his lines, was so demoralized by them that he walked off the set and fled to Italy, returning only when threatened with legal action. After the shooting stopped, Fox was compelled to find ways to market an expensive and trendy product that seemed to be entirely without merit. With the gay theme of *Staircase* present on every Panavision-Color by DeLuxe frame, it was decided to jettison all caution. The publicity department took pains to sell the thing as a pageant of pity and loathing:

> *Staircase* deals with the human condition, with loneliness and the dependence of us all on one another as its basic theme. [It] neither promotes nor deplores the condition of this unusual couple. With a rare and disturbing comprehension, it chronicles their pathetic life, revealing it in all its sad reality.

The slogans—the come-ons designed to attract customers—continued the message:

> What makes a man live with another man? What makes them claw at each other . . . humiliate each other . . . yet never leave each other?
>
> The story of a marriage made in hell.
>
> Charlie and Harry are going home for their nightly game of show and tell.
>
> Can this marriage last?

Another tag line was perhaps inevitable:

> Richard Burton & Rex Harrison play *what?*

The logo for *Staircase* harked far, far back in gay film history, back to a time when Bobby Watson and Tyrell Davis and Barnett Parker and Clarence roamed the earth. They, however, would have looked askance at the picture of Harrison and Burton holding hands, each kicking a leg up, and above them emblazoned the one-word pansy craze legend. Below the title, four words summed it all up. (See photo.)

The unyielding good taste of *Staircase*'s ad campaign.

The reviews, it almost goes without saying, were far sadder. *No one* liked this movie. Some confined their comments to aesthetic matters, and others exercised their homophobia. In most cities it ran for a week or less, only to be remembered months later when critics assembled their lists of the worst films of the year. The loss to Fox was high and to gays it was higher. At a time when it might have been possible to start portraying homosexuality on film in an intelligent and balanced fashion, here comes this stupid charade making it all a detestable joke. The failure is so multilayered, in fact, that it can't help but be fascinating.[7] The blame cannot be placed entirely on the casting, as inappropriate as that is. Harrison thinks he's playing Henry Higgins, Burton purses his lips and tries to be pitiful, and they never, ever stop telegraphing their superiority to the script and the characters. Harrison, barely visible beneath a badger-like mod wig, is especially guilty. Dyer's script mixes failed bon mots (say it in American, not with a French pronunciation; these dogs deserve no better) and constant thudding metaphors about staircases—the one from the barber shop to the home upstairs, and from a life of wretched faggotry to something divine. The ultimate blame must fall with Stanley Donen, who apparently lost interest the minute that Paul Scofield bailed out. The breakdown starts right after the Twentieth Century–Fox drums finish with a huge close-up of feathers, then a cut to a pair of unappealing drag queens singing an insipid title song, by Dudley Moore yet. After the credits, we are treated to ten reels of back-and-forth insults garnished with some insidious and false "they really love each other" poignancy. Bull. There's no love, there's no physical affection, there's nothing except codependence and self-pity for not being hetero. As in *Sister George*, the vitriol is completely unmodulated, directed toward a hard-of-hearing stage audience, with constant feminine-gender pronouns and insults molded out of the sourest reheated bar-chat: "Bloody hell, I hope your nipples drop off!" "Ramshackle old queen . . . you'll be sorry when I'm dead!" "Oh, you cruel sot! All you do is snap and snarl . . . and cut your toenails in bed!" "Look at you— hen is too delicate a term. *Pelican.* You're a pregnant pelican, mate!" They seem to be doing a serious version of that "You know how bitchy fags can be" nonsense that *The Producers* had already obliterated. The devastation is nearly total, with a few atoms of truth only at the very core of it to indicate why these two are together, and what kind of drama might have been created with disciplined actors, an attentive director, and a script less focused on gaudy bathos. But who wants to be portrayed this way? It's one for the time capsule, this

---

[7]As with a number of late-swinging-sixties fiascoes, *Staircase* almost never turns up. Only a couple of showings on cable television have kept it from archival obscurity, which is really too bad: something this misguided generates its own type of allure.

Staircase, and the horrifying thing is that all these years later there are still people out there who would like to think that it's accurate.

When sights are set far lower, the crash is less drastic. The entire budget for *The Gay Deceivers*, also from mid-1969, was less than the salary of one of the stars of *Staircase*, an unsurprising fact given that it was made by a shifty outfit called Fanfare Film Productions. In intent and execution, this was a tacky, R-rated romp, the kind made for drive-ins as soon as it was okay to show breasts and say a few dirty words. It was also okay to deal with gays, and it was a time when guys would do anything to get out of being shipped to Vietnam, so voilà. Danny (Kevin Coughlin) and Elliot (Larry Casey) are straight buddies whose aversion to the draft has less to do with conscientious objection than to California-dude indolence. Danny has a girlfriend and Elliot is a lifeguard stud. So they check the box on the draft form that says they've had sex with men, and the whole sitcom premise is set up. As the ads said, "They had to keep their hands off girls in order to keep the Army's hands off them!" Finding out that the army will investigate their claims, they pose as lovers and move to a quaintly all-gay L.A. apartment complex. Their Ethel Mertz–like landlord is Malcolm (Michael Greer), a swishy charmer who enthusiastically welcomes them to fey married life. The expected things just keep happening—parents and a girl-friend that don't believe it's a fake, a quickie for the stud that almost gives it all away, a masquerade party to introduce the boys to gay society—until finally there's something of a surprise ending. They've played the game so successfully that no one believes they're not gay. Ostracized, they go their separate ways to start over. The army colonel who has been tailing them sees them split and breathes a satisfied sigh—to his sergeant boyfriend. The army, he chuckles, is a better place without these two fakers.

You don't dig for diamonds in a salt mine, and you don't expect class or insight with something like *The Gay Deceivers*. Neither, curiously enough, do you get an exclusively disapproving or even patronizing attitude toward gays. Instead, this movie scans all over the map, mocking and ridiculing and stereo-typing at the same time that it throws out crumbs of praise and asks for tolerance. (Lesbians are, naturally, a nonissue.) It laughs at and with homosexuality at the same time, sometimes in the same shot. Along with the straight-type yucks, there's a lot of gay humor, vintage '69, and Larry Casey displays a trim and naked rear end on several occasions. Taken all together, it raises the question: Who was the target audience for this movie? The gay-friendly humor makes it insuffi-cient for straight audiences, and things like the fake lisps and the pink French Provincial décor in the boys' bedroom make it too skewed in the wrong way for most gays. There seems, in the filmmaking process, to have been some sort of derailment. The science of throwing together a cheap exploitation film is not exact, and evidently the original fast-buck hetero intentions became more and

MICHAEL GREER

Born Galesburg, Ill., April 20, 1943

For someone whose film career has consisted of a handful of credits, he's quite a pioneer. Just a few weeks after Stonewall, here was an openly gay entertainer playing an openly gay man on the screen in *The Gay Deceivers*, rewriting most of his dialogue and laying waste to whatever homophobic ideas the filmmakers may have nurtured. He then costarred in an LSD-era epic called *The Magic Garden of Stanley Sweetheart*, and in 1971 made another strong impression in grim surroundings—as Queenie in *Fortune and Men's Eyes*. After those there was only fleeting film work (including a bit in Bette Midler's *The Rose*), so his subsequent career has been mostly on the stage as an actor, impressionist, and later director. His Tallulah was sufficiently sharp that he recorded an all-Bankhead album, and he could imitate Bette Davis so uncannily that, when the real Bette was unavailable, he was called in to loop some of her dialogue for a TV movie. Undoubtedly he was just too out there for his time—gay showbiz was mainly a shadowy Castro-Village thing when Greer started. Yet with *The Gay Deceivers*—especially after this nearly lost film resurfaced—we can see him writing a small, real, and endearingly flamboyant piece of gay history. All in bright big letters, of course, and swirling flourishes. For some men, the word *queen* can be a true compliment.

more diluted. It occurred here in part because of the ragged nature of the material and partly because of the bracing presence of Michael Greer in the film and on the set. Instead of being a silly caricature—even in the hip Roger DeBris style—Malcolm becomes the engaging center of the action. There is warmth in this flamer, humor and style and competence as well as the old swish mechanisms and hissy fits. There is also, by the way, a successful long-term relationship with a tolerant fellow named Craig (Sebastian Brook). The authenticity of Greer's presence makes a sham of the simpering farce and subverts much of the ridicule. Malcolm is the one we remember, not Danny and Elliot and their predicament. With his rewrites and ad-libs, Greer tosses small and telling reminders of what it was like to be out and gay in the late sixties. "Don't forget your heart pill," he advises one geriatric cruiser, at once bitchy and caring. Even when Malcolm is made ridiculous, Greer is the victor, just as Franklin Pangborn always seemed far sturdier than the dyspeptic floorwalkers and hotel clerks that were his lot. It was clear that here, amid the draft board jokes and mistaken-identity farce, was a genuine gay man having fun onscreen, making this shabby movie better with his every appearance. His success was echoed by the reviews ("Marvelous," *Variety* called him) and some of the advertising. This is the kind of

True love: Michael Greer and Sebastian Brook in *The Gay Deceivers*. The makeup was not for everyday wear; they're at a costume party. *Photofest*

movie that runs more in regional areas than in urban centers—remember, it's a Fanfare Film. Exhibitors were not given much promotional material to work with, and when it was clear that Greer was stealing the movie, some theater owners made makeshift new ads spotlighting Malcolm instead of the putative leads. The result was holdover runs in some cities; *Staircase* would have been lucky to get a fraction of the profits earned by *The Gay Deceivers*. With something like this there could be no follow-up, and no other fly-by-night producers thought of putting gay humor (much less lesbian humor) into a quick-buck exploitation flick. Nevertheless, there was something good here for some people. Impressionable adolescent boys remembered this movie, and into middle age recalled it with affection. In all its cartoon-queen caricature and dollhouse accoutrements, there was the indication that maybe there would be a place where two men could live together and share a real, not a mock, relationship. Quite a load of effect for producers who were just thinking they could take in some bucks by making fun of fruits.

The last of the seven "out" movies is the one everyone remembers. Many still think of it as the first film to deal with homosexuality on any level. Hardly so—which doesn't stop *The Boys in the Band* from being a milestone. In some ways it was a bang-up start and in others it was a nail in the coffin, setting precedents and opening windows while making follow-ups unfeasible. Here are collected all the imposing paradoxes history can offer. By being unnervingly real at the same time that it is rackingly phony, *The Boys in the Band* makes of itself both a rapturous high and a dirty shame. It exalts with its affection and intimate truths and stunning insights, and crashes and burns with pessimism and blame and falsehoods. Where homosexuals and homosexuality on film is concerned, this is *The Birth of a Nation.* As with D. W. Griffith's epic, it innovates and codifies with immense skill, meriting vast praise and admiration. At the same time, it is steeped in many conventions of its time that shove it into historical brackets and compel its audiences to deal with inappropriate stereotypes and defunct concepts. In some ways it became dated more suddenly than its creators could have divined. A defining incident—the Stonewall riots—followed the play *The Boys in the Band* by about a year and preceded the film's release by nine months. This procession of events forces the play and the film and the audience into a sort of microwave time warp, pelting us with old and new images and concepts that don't really belong together. It asks for sympathy and tolerance without raising the ante to a post-Stonewall type of acceptance. It contains some of the spirit that caused Stonewall to happen, as well as some of the angst that Stonewall worked to erase. Here it all is: a title in homage to the greatest Old Gay icon, Judy Garland, a love-is-torture, gay-is-pain attitude out of the closeted Tennessee Williams era, a nellie flamer to embarrass Barnett Parker, and a truckload of that famous herpes-like recurring ill, self-loathing. Here also is sense and affection and some people striving to look forward and build lives and relationships. *The Boys in the Band*, especially in its film version, made the whole shebang visible and accessible. For some, it was already passé; others needed to see it, needed the identification and whatever positive vibes were to be had from it. Is it the way we were? Not really. Maybe it's the way we *thought* we were.

On Broadway, in 1968, it seemed for some the last word in honesty. For thousands of gays, for some lesbians too, it was Our Play. It defined. With an enormous amount of courage and audacity Mart Crowley put all his thoughts and selves into writing the story of Michael and Harold and the birthday party that gets far too serious. It required further guts for the producers and the cast to make it real. Instantaneously it was a smash. *The Killing of Sister George*, for all its power, didn't come from the inside the way this one did. Liberal straights liked it because they thought it made them understand and be more tolerant. Privileged closeted gays—including the Leonard Bernsteins and Stephen Sondheims of the world—applauded loudly, even wept, because they felt that they were being signified. The moralists shook their heads, but then didn't worry too much: this was a New York phenomenon, and people like these could not exist outside a few blocks of New York and San Francisco. What was most arresting was the feeling of verisimilitude. In spite of Crowley's ponderous dramatic mechanisms, the characters he gathered to bare their lives seemed to have aspects of distinct authenticity. They weren't grotesques like Sebastian Venable or that dreadful murderer in *The Detective*, nor were they tortured to the point of suicide like Senator Brig Anderson or Blanche DuBois's husband.[8] They functioned, they shot off their smart clever mouths, they said things that appeared for all the world to be clinical truths. Some treated it as an exotic panorama, others as a documentary. Few were bored.

If it seems somewhat surprising that the film version of *The Boys in the Band* was ever made, it was actually inevitable. Plays this successful were at the time always made into films, period. Had the Production Code still been in effect, there would probably have been a small-scale version released without an MPAA certificate. With the death of the Code, the material was now doable, perhaps even desirable and commercial. The year happened to be a favorable time for adult-oriented films to stretch toward hotter topics; several years later it would not have happened, and many years later such a property would have gone straight to cable television. Somehow this one came at just the right moment to make it into commercial movie houses. It was, obviously, meant to be. The debate will ever go on about how successfully it was done, or if it even should have happened.

Two crucial factors shaped the film of *The Boys in the Band*. Much of the defining aura came from its director, William Friedkin, who made it just prior to the one-two punch of *The French Connection* and *The Exorcist*, which made him an Oscar-winner and a household name, respectively. *The Boys in the Band* brought him early attention and intense scrutiny, to which he responded by playing the compassionate/heterosexist card. It wasn't a film about homosexuality, he would say, at the same time that his direction was mocking his words. He didn't film Crowley's play in a low-key fashion to better undercut the flamboyance and hysterics. He treated it exactly as its reputation would have everyone believe: it was THE GAY PLAY, in neon. Charles Dyer's quest for the queer microcosm in *Staircase* was as nothing alongside Friedkin's inflation of what had already been set in bold letters. The use under the credits of the Harper's Bizarre recording of "Anything Goes" is an early indicator. Crowley's screenplay had already been shaded and punched up; the schematic devices that could pass muster on the stage looked florid and mannered on a large projected

---

[8]Sebastian did rate a mention in the script, however, which also included in its catalogue of camp iconography Maria Montez ("Maria was a good woman"), Billy DeWolfe, and much else from Garland on down.

surface. Friedkin then treated the script as if it had been carved on stone tablets. Pauline Kael was one of a number of critics to point up the formulaic nature of the slice-of-life dramatis personae, each character a symbol more than a personality. Kael likened it to *The Women*, as enacted by the bomber crew of a forties epic, and that is how it seemed. Each of these symbol-laden representatives of the Life gets his time in the sun and the spotlight, every big moment lit and framed as if the actors were marble busts in a museum display.[9] The effect, monumental and emblematic, shades the tone toward the negative and pathetic. The play's most famous line, and the one that has sealed its fate as a period piece of the bad old days, is Michael's "You show me a happy homosexual and I'll show you a gay corpse." In the play it's said almost casually, clearly not meant to be an Ultimate Truth. With Friedkin directing, it becomes the slogan the movie wears as a badge on its neatly pressed lapel.

The cast of the stage play repeated their roles in toto. It happens in the movies: an actor is given the opportunity to record a great performance for posterity, and a couple of things may go wrong. Either the actor does not adjust to the different ambience and scale of cinema, or else he has done the role too many times and become mechanical.[10] All the actors in *The Boys in the Band* were competent, and some (Leonard Frey in particular) were notably gifted. In front of the movie camera, several of them began to overscale alarmingly, the most extreme characters predictably becoming the most overplayed. While the producers were understandably low-key about the fact that most of the cast actually was gay, it was a kind of stunt casting to put Cliff Gorman as Emory, the swirling lisp of a poodle-toting interior decorator. Emory is so immersed in queen-high subculture that he could not recognize a masculine pronoun if it rolled over him, and Gorman diligently played the role all-out on the stage and in the movie while making sure he gave as many interviews as possible to tell the world how straight he was. In the performance, too, he seems to be telegraphing his own heterosexuality and implicit superiority. We all know Emorys, and their like has come down the ages through such incarnations as Jack on *Will and Grace* and Emmett (an homage to Emery?) on *Queer as Folk*. This one is just too much, ultimately too fake. For those who object to the gay

---

[9]The technique was particularly noticeable because of Friedkin's habit of parking the camera on the person speaking, with only sparse, italicized reaction shots. As a result, this movie sometimes resembles an early talkie, with Drew Demarest hovering in the wings. Again, Kael was spot on, and evoking a gay icon to boot. Referring to the big nuance-heavy close-ups, she snapped, "It's all so solemn—like Joan Crawford when she's thinking."

[10]Any aficionado of filmed theater can give you a list of choices. For some, a crowning example is Rex Harrison in *My Fair Lady*—a controversial choice, admittedly, for those who like the film version would rip your tongue out for alleging such a thing. (Kindly note that this observation was made shortly after an anguished viewing of *Staircase*.)

actors doing the Uncle Tom routine and playing stereotypes, as in the thirties, behold—it can get more odious when an outsider takes over. Contrast Gorman's Emory with Michael Greer's Malcolm in *The Gay Deceivers*. The voice and affectations and "Marys" are all as rudely applied trim on a garment that has already been accessorized to death.

The self-loathing Catholic center of the play is ultimately the character Michael, and in Kenneth Nelson's performance the time spent onstage is clearly a deterrent. One of Michael's flaws is his lack of spontaneity, his need to calculate and manipulate; couple this with an actor who's planned out every syllable and there's no freshness to be had. When Michael is in a lighter mood early on, Nelson's line readings are overstressed and deliberate, stylized beyond necessity. Later, Michael's drunken initiation of the nasty telephone game of truth—Crowley's most transparent dramatic device—is played as a cross between a B movie Nazi and Cruella DeVil. Nelson glowers and seethes, and when his comeuppance comes, he collapses like Camille. Fresher and at a distance it could work; in big fat Friedkin close-ups, it offends. Even a drama queen needs his space.

So there are these overdone performances and direction that totters on the verge of disdain. There are levels of offensiveness for us now, as there were for enlightened and liberated viewers in 1970. Why did this movie grab so many people, then? Why did it matter? After all these years, why does it still matter? Some of it, naturally, is historical, and not just the history of a reasonably faithful adaptation of a groundbreaking work. Here is a distillation of what it might be like to be mostly white and mostly well off on the eve of Gay Liberation. You had your friends and your tricks (that buzzword comes up prominently in the script); you had your gay and straight existences neatly segregated. You cruised and drank and smoked grass when it was doable, you worshiped at the temples of Marlene and Judy and Bette, you thought about having a lover and sometimes succeeded, and even if you had no belief system, you wondered why God made you this way. This was how Mart Crowley saw a large part of his own reality in the mid-sixties, and he did not flinch from putting it on paper and on the boards and on film. The fact is that many people can still watch *The Boys in the Band* and feel an active sense of identification with much of what the characters say and do. Crowley knew himself and his sector of gay life well enough to capture it with some truth, and truth often luxuriates in its own permanence. There are people today who wonder still why they are gay or lesbian, unable to get past the guilt imposed by parents or institutions and all too willing to listen to pronouncements of damnation from the narrow and bigoted. While the advances continue, there are still the hordes of the uncomprehending, like Michael's friend Alan. People like Bernard remain too, surviving as well as possible under the strain of being part of a sexual minority as well as a racial one.

On screen and in print, the *Boys in the Band* film wore two hats. One was the austere "serious theatre" look shown in the cast picture at the top. Left to right, top to bottom, Laurence Luckinbill, Keith Prentice, Kenneth Nelson, Leonard Frey, Frederick Combs, Robert La Tourneaux, Reuben Greene, Cliff Gorman, Peter White. The other was the crass "queens on parade" look exemplified by this opening-credits shot of Gorman, poodle and all. *Photofest*

By the time the *Boys* film had come out, Stonewall had already begun to make an impact. Those at the hip and angry forefront of the battles in New York and Los Angeles and San Francisco saw in Crowley's work the face of the obsolete and the unwelcome. It was time, instead, to embrace oneself and move ahead. For millions of others, this movie was a beacon. People in the South and Midwest, the Bible Belt and Plains, wept and glowed. They were seeing themselves apparently defined as never before. Not with the absurdity of *Staircase* or the nudge-wink of *The Gay Deceivers*, to name the most recent. Nor with quite the garish expressionism of *The Killing of Sister George*. It was as if all those little privileged moments from thirties and forties and fifties films—those short scenes in which gay men or women would be momentarily conspicuous on the screen—had been spliced together to make a long documentary called *That's Validation!* If you were gay or lesbian and lived in a place where Gay Liberation meetings were already happening, you likely wouldn't feel much warmth toward *The Boys in the Band.* If you lived in a small town and were trying gamely and quietly to have some sort of gay life, you were either appalled by how brazen these men were or enchanted by their openness. Maybe both. If you were young and questioning, you might have to go to the movie theater in secret, even be sneaky about buying the copy of *Look* magazine containing a feature article on the movie with portraits of the cast. In the face of identification, the passages of despair and self-hatred could be filtered out. It was as if Dorothy were making it back to Kansas or staying in a shiny Technicolor Oz. With these placarded gay men and their sad and silly birthday party, with the wisecracks and queer-pop references and thudding revelations and mind games, you somehow might feel that you belonged.

A work does not have to be of great artistic import to carry immense historical weight (cf. *Uncle Tom's Cabin*). Few would claim that *The Boys in the Band* is any kind of art, especially as it turned out in its movie version. Yet this does not hinder its ability to embrace the entire history of gays on film. Emory takes us back to the days of the pansy craze, when the Clarences got by on their wits and found their own compatible levels. Michael recalls—and would not be unhappy to do so—the time of both Tennessee Williams and Dracula's daughter, when you could hate yourself if you did it with sufficient style. In the insouciant wisecracking carryings-on, there are echoes of *Lady in the Dark* and *Our Betters* and even *The Reluctant Dragon*—those secret pockets of inside-humor aimed squarely at those in the know. In Hank and Larry, the pair of lovers who really do try to make it work, we see the strangely poignant past figures who did attempt to reach out in love: Elvira Powell in *Caged*, the runaways of *So Young, So Bad*, the silent adoration of Sal Mineo in *Rebel without a Cause*. In the drive to seize onto the warm and affirming moments and slough off those that are pitying or contemptuous, there is a century of gay and lesbian spectatorship, a constant search for affirmative things in the face of hostility and pain. The nine actors that make up the cast supply resonances as well. With Cliff Gorman there is that perennial discomfort of seeing someone work too hard to play gay. With many of the other actors, we must recall the Pangborns and Suttons and Webbs and Cunninghams of the earlier years, all gay and closeted, all playing gay (to a greater or lesser extent) on the screen, all exposing inner truths while maintaining a false outer shell. Another historical resonance with the actors is far more stark: six of the nine men would eventually die of AIDS, as would the play's original director, Robert Moore.

The reviews of *The Boys in the Band* were somewhat mixed, if excellent overall. New York critics knew that the play had been diminished and inflated on the screen, and to no one's surprise there were a number of comments of the "their pathetic life" variety, tut-tutting about these poor creatures making wisecracks through their misery. To sell it, the producers devised that famous ad campaign with a group shot of the cast all dressed in black and the legend "*The Boys in the Band* is not a musical." A gaudier ad was declined by most newpapers: side-by-side shots of Leonard Frey and Robert La Tourneaux (as the hustler Cowboy), with the caption "Today is Harold's birthday. This is his present." While the talk and the titillation and the novelty all stirred up interest, the bottom line was as before, reaffirming that pattern established eight years earlier. Once again, the lack of financial success with a larger audience joined with inherent prejudices to doom the possibility of successors. The truism was borne out further over the following two years with *Some of My Best Friends Are . . .* and *Fortune and Men's Eyes*, which did even less well. The hoped-for messianic harbinger of a new gay openness in film, *The Boys in the Band*, was actually a culmination. For the time being, things would be the same as they had been, only less so. American cinema went back into the closet for a number of years, the silence broken occasionally by a queer villain or expendable buffoon. Lesbians and gay men became far more visible in the outside world than on movie screens until eventually the tide and the country changed. That is another story and another history. In 1970 queer movies were breaking, after their strangely extravagant seven-decade odyssey, for something of an intermission.

An Epiloque

It had seemed that there was so much promise. A movement was underway, the movies seemed primed to be a part of it, there were good intentions, and enlightenment seemed to be slowly approaching. So—how great a role do any of these play in the film industry's bottom line? The answer was clear after the disappointing financial performance of *The Boys in the Band*. It became clearer still over the next few years. Where lesbians and gays were concerned, the film experience essentially came down to seeing themselves in big movies as bit players or evil or invisible. There were a few nuggets in indie films and imports, and there was porn. Otherwise the heightened awareness and visibility, the sense of identity that came with the rise of the Gay Liberation movement, were in no way reflected on the screen in the 1970s. The disconnect seemed nearly total.

The traversal of the desert of that decade is well known and well documented, as is the outcry in 1980 over *Cruising*—directed, please note, by William Friedkind. In the early 1980s there was a brief renaissance, in part a reflection of the sensational stateside hit of the French farce *La Cage aux Folles*. *Victor/ Victoria*, *Making Love*, *Partners*, and the simultaneously lesbophile/lesbophobic *Personal Best* all tried for either more positive or more overt commercial gayness. The interest subsided after, once more, a mostly uninspiring public response. Through the 1980s, with a gay-unfriendly administration and a health crisis of devastating gravity, the emphasis continued to shift to independent films and television, where the economic factors more favorable to creativity. *My Beautiful Laundrette* and *Taxi zum Klo* indicated potential from abroad, as did the small-scale domestic *Desert Hearts* and *Parting Glances* and the cable sitcom *Brothers*. Occasionally there would arise the attention-getting or prestige-stoked mainstream effort: crassly controversial, like *Basic Instinct*, or intrepidly genteel, as with *Maurice*, or idiosyncratic, such as *Torch Song Trilogy*. *Longtime Companion* and then *Philadelphia* finally told stories about AIDS, the longtime elephant in

Middle America's living room. Increasingly, the slack was picked up with an occasional made-for-TV film and the isolated series episode. This too began to accelerate when such major productions as *Serving in Silence* and *And the Band Played On* brought the prestige and authority of big-time cinema to the home screen. These were films that should have been playing in movie houses; the dynamics and demographics and economics put them on television instead.

By the late 1990s the various playing areas had formed. Independent cinema was the most intrepid, with its *Go Fish* and *Swoon* and *Poison* opening up new expressive realms. Network television had the successes of Ellen DeGeneres and *Will and Grace*, while cable pushed harder with *Queer as Folk* and *Oz*. The central axis of Hollywood cinema was the least productive. Every few years there would be a freak hit like *The Bird Cage*—a smash despite its marked inferiority to the original *La Cage aux Folles*—and the occasional *My Best Friend's Wedding* and *Chasing Amy* and *The Opposite of Sex*. Movies began to have more supporting characters and—with glaring exceptions—fewer antigay jokes. Now and then, there would be a moderate success on the order of *In and Out* and *The Object of My Affection*, plus a near-breakthrough such as *Gods and Monsters*, which in its embellished tale of James Whale's last days neatly tied together gay cinema's past and present. If the doors to the local multiplexes remained largely closed, such films would finally present the odd opportunity to pry them ajar.

The heightened visibility that came with the loosening and then demise of the Production Code would have had achieved better ends only if the audiences had been large. For nearly seventy years American cinema had played with homosexuality in a secret way, as a members-only club for the participants and audiences in the know. Only in times of the greatest duress, in the early Depression, was it accessible to all, and then the watchdogs stopped it. When it was possible to make it more evident, it became more of a problem—an evil, a thing of ridicule and marginalization. The movies began to function as sort of a walking rebuke to the advances that Stonewall symbolized. Like the federal government or the Supreme Court, Hollywood's actions seemed to say, "You think you've come far? You're learning who you are and think that you have rights. Well, you're bad and you're wrong." As far as Hollywood was concerned, gayness after 1970 would mainly be a trifling sort of toy, a gimmicky surprise or something to be shunted over onto the side or ridiculed or disproved.

By the early years of the twenty-first century, the gay experience had encompassed a great deal: plagues and murders, court cases and evil legislation, conversion therapy and Don't ask, don't tell. It had also seen unmistakable advances, some slow and others startling and ongoing. Visibility has been heightened, laws have been put on the books, there are discussions and hopes about greater equality. Some of the hopes will find actuality, and others will remain hopes. As the progress creeps along, popular art and culture will continue to pay increasing heed to where homosexuality has been as well as where it's going. For those willing to go that route, the mainstreaming of a formerly outlaw (or concealed) way of life continues. As it does so, it should be remembered that all of these advances and processes found much of their early life in movie theaters. From the days of flitting decorators and cigar-smoking women, on to Gothic spinsters and sardonic men-about-town, through all the years of guilt-ridden or cheerily subversive characters, thousands of tiny pieces of film have given identification and meaning to those who otherwise felt disenfranchised. In the 1930s and 1940s, a movie projector was as a lighthouse for gay men and women, and a movie with even the briefest queer moments could be a solace. In later times, when the guilt and admonitions came, some accepted them and others ignored and fought back. Whether it validated or condemned, film was forthright enough to take the first step: it acknowledged. It has not always served either its creators or its viewers honorably, but it has been faithful in its fashion.

History is seldom so cooperative as to give us a smooth path or an easy transition, yet the queer movie past does project itself indelibly onto its present. Dorothy Mackaill in *The Crystal Cup* gives way to Sister George; Bobby Watson in *Manhattan Parade* is the opening act for Rupert Everett in *My Best Friend's Wedding*. Joyzelle hitting on the Christians becomes Sharon Stone shocking the cops. As long as the dots stay connected, no one is alone. There were forebears who paved the subversive way, and their successors will find more and new ways of expression. Despite the setbacks and the opaque corporate minds, gays and lesbians will continue to find their way into the movies, on and behind the screen. In the controversy over homosexuality, differences will matter less and less as more and more people see it in the movies and in their lives. As Franklin Pangborn dithers and seethes from some heavenly seat, all of us may find our existences gradually shifting and intensifying with a heightened sense of identity. Meanwhile, in darkened cinemas, we are ever reflected under the naked moon of a projected image.

Notes on Sources

After the films themselves, the files of the Production Code Administration (PCA) form a large portion of the research for this book. Unless indicated otherwise, all correspondence quoted in the book (including in-house memos) is from the PCA Files at the Margaret Herrick Library, Academy of Motion Picture Arts and Sciences.

Abbreviations used here are as follows:

MH   Margaret Herrick Library
MH/OH   Oral History Collection, Margaret Herrick Library
MH/PCA   Production Code Administration files, Margaret Herrick Library
MH/Par   Paramount Script Collection, Margaret Herrick Library
USC/Fox   Fox and Twentieth Century–Fox Collection, University of
            Southern California
USC/MGM   Metro-Goldwyn-Mayer Collection, University of Southern
            California
USC/Univ   Universal Collection, University of Southern California
USC/WB   Warner Bros. Collection, University of Southern California

Chapter 1: Silent Existences

The Clever Mrs. Carfax—"It is marred . . .": *Motion Picture News*, November 17, 1917.
A Florida Enchantment—"The most silly 'comedy' . . .": *Variety*, August 14, 1914.
Salome—"The heroic figures . . ." *Variety*, January 5, 1923.
Irene—". . . nothing fresh . . ." *Variety*, March 3, 1926.
Gilbert Clark: "more temperamental . . .": Howard Greer, quoted in David Chierichetti,
    Hollywood Costume Design (New York: Harmony Books, 1976).
My Lady of Whims—"the motives . . .": *Film Daily*, January 17, 1926.
The Crystal Cup—"Had it been . . .": *Motion Picture News*, November 25, 1927.

Chapter 2: Speaking Plainly

Syncopation—"a nance . . .": *Variety,* April 10, 1929.
Chasing Rainbows—preliminary scripts: USC/MGM
Ramon Novarro—"Frankly, Ramon . . .": *Picturegoer,* quoted in David Shipman,
   The Great Movie Stars: The Golden Years (New York: Crown, 1970). "Ramon has
   never . . .": *Motion Picture,* August 1933.

Chapter 3: Codes of Behavior

The Love Parade—letter-writing campaigns: MH/PCA
Just Imagine—MH/PCA.
The Old Dark House and James Whale: Mark Gatiss, *James Whale: A Biography*
   (London: Cassell, 1995).
Pathé newsreel: "Broadway cokies . . .": *Variety,* November 10, 1931. See also *Variety,*
   November 17, 1931; November 24, 1931; December 29, 1931.
Hell's Highway—MH/PCA.
The Sport Parade—Ronald Eric Gregg, *The Representation and Censorship of Male
   Homosexuality in Hollywood Film, 1930–1935* (Ph.D. Dissertation, University of
   Oregon Press, 1996). "High camp . . .": William Gargan, *Why Me?: An Autobiography*
   (Garden City, N.Y.: Doubleday, 1969).
Call Her Savage—USC/Fox. Also, MH/PCA.

Chapter 4: The Naked Moon

The Sign of the Cross—MH/PCA. "DeMille's bang-'em-on-the-head . . .": Pauline Kael,
   5001 Nights at the Movies: A Guide from A to Z (New York: Holt, Rinehart and
   Winston, 1982). First draft screenplay: MH/Par. "The sets are . . .": Arch Reeve,
   interviewed in *Motion Picture Herald,* December 3, 1932. "Cecil said . . .": Agnes
   deMille, interview in *The Story of Cecil B. DeMille* (BBC documentary, 1981).
   "A representation . . .": *Harrison's Reports,* December 17, 1932. "It has a . . .":
   Variety, December 6, 1932. "Nauseating . . .": *Commonweal,* December 21, 1932.
   "We are required . . .": *Motion Picture Herald,* December 3, 1932. "Damnable
   hypocrisy . . .": *America,* December 17, 1932.

Chapter 5: Pansies and Lesbos of 1933

So This Is Africa—MH/PCA. Also, Edward Watz, *Wheeler and Woolsey: The Vaudeville
   Comic Duo and Their Films, 1929–1937* (Jefferson, N.C.: McFarland & Company,
   1994).
Cavalcade—MH/PCA. Earl Luick: Earl Luick Oral History, MH/OH.

Our Betters—MH/PCA. "A dark little man . . .": W. Somerset Maugham, *Our Betters*, in *English Drama in Transition, 1880–1920*, ed. Henry F. Salerno (New York: Pegasus, 1968). "At the finish . . .": *Variety*, February 28, 1933. "The only false note . . .": quoted in letter from Maurine McKenzie [Will Hays's assistant] to James Wingate, February 25, 1933.

The Warrior's Husband—"the panze scenes . . .": *Variety*, May 16, 1933.

Sailor's Luck—USC/Fox

Ladies They Talk About—MH/PCA.

42nd Street—See Rocco Fumenti, Introduction to *42nd Street* screenplay (Madison: University of Wisconsin Press, 1980). Also, USC/WB.

Stage Mother—USC/MGM, which file includes a transcript of the Ropes novel.

Myrt and Marge—"When I was a kid . . .": Peter Conway, quoted in John Loughery, *The Other Side of Silence: Men's Lives and Gay Identities: A Twentieth-Century History* (New York: Henry Holt, 1998).

Son of a Sailor—MH/PCA.

Design for Living—MH/PCA. Also, MH/Par. "Literary heresy . . .": *Variety*, November 28, 1933.

International House—MH/PCA. "Popularity as a comedian . . .": *Motion Picture Herald*, September 2, 1933.

Franklin Pangborn—"It is not faintly . . .": Boyd MacDonald, *Cruising the Movies: A Sexual Guide to "Oldies" on TV* (New York: Gay Presses of New York, 1985). "Call [him] a sissy . . .": promotional material for *Professional Sweetheart*, quoted in MacDonald.

Only Yesterday—MH/PCA.

Blood Money—USC/Fox, also MH/PCA.

Queen Christina—MH/PCA. All script drafts: USC/MGM. "I imagined myself . . ." and "Christina's affection . . .": quoted in Mark A. Vieira, *Sin in Soft Focus: Pre-Code Hollywood* (New York: Harry N. Abrams, 1999).

"Over 80% . . .": *Variety*, June 13, 1933.

Chapter 6: Legions and Decency

Wonder Bar—USC/WB, also MH/PCA.

John McCain—"I don't understand . . .": and "I'd love to be . . .": quoted in *Entertainment Weekly*, October 20, 2000.

"We believed we were dealing . . ."—quoted in Thomas Doherty, *Pre-Code Hollywood: Sex, Immorality, and Insurrection in American Cinema, 1930–1934* (New York: Columbia University Press, 1999).

Belle of the Nineties [*It Ain't No Sin*]—MH/PCA.

Joseph Breen—". . . are simply a rotten bunch . . .": quoted in Gregory D. Black, *Hollywood Censored: Morality Codes, Catholics, and the Movies* (Cambridge: Cambridge University Press, 1994). "The mainspring . . .": Jack Vizzard, *See No Evil: Life Inside a Hollywood Censor* (New York: Simon & Schuster, 1970).

"All of Hollywood . . ."—*Motion Picture*, September 1934.
"With the western world . . ."—quoted in Doherty, *Pre-Code Hollywood*.

Chapter 7: Turnabout: Life in a Coded World

George White's Scandals (1934 and 1935)—MH/PCA.
Sylvia Scarlett—MH/PCA. "Tended to put lace . . .": quoted in A. Scott Berg, *Goldwyn: A Biography* (New York: Knopf, 1989).
Bride of Frankenstein—MH/PCA. Also: Gatiss, *James Whale*.
Dracula's Daughter—MH/PCA.
These Three—MH/PCA. Also: William Wyler Collection, MH; Berg, *Goldwyn;* William Wright, *Lillian Hellman: The Image, the Woman* (New York: Simon & Schuster, 1986).
The King Steps Out—MH/PCA.
The Big Noise—I am indebted to David Lugowski for his research on this obscure film.
Bringing Up Baby—MH/PCA. "It seems likely . . .": George Chauncey, *Gay New York: Gender, Urban Culture, and the Making of the Gay Male World, 1890–1940* (New York: Basic Books, 1994). Kael on Grant: *The New Yorker*, July 14, 1975.
Mitchell Leisen and *Midnight*—"Leisen spent more time . . .": quoted in Maurice Zolotow, *Billy Wilder in Hollywood* (New York: G. P. Putnam's Sons, 1977). "He was a tall . . .": Zolotow, *Billy Wilder*. "I made Rex play . . .": quoted in David Chierichetti, *Mitchell Leisen: Hollywood Director* (Los Angeles: Photoventures Press, 1995).
Children of Loneliness—MH/PCA. Also: *Motion Picture Daily*, November 15, 1937; *Variety*, January 12, 1934. "Your reporter inferred . . .": *Motion Picture Herald*, November 20, 1937.
Live, Love and Learn—MH/PCA.
Allyn Joslyn and *Café Society*—Richard Lamparski, *Whatever Became Of . . . ?*, Fourth Series (New York: Crown Books, 1973).
Turnabout—MH/PCA.

Chapter 8: Reluctant Flamboyance: Forties Escapism

"It was kind of 'in' . . ."—Rita Maxwell, quoted in Gerald Clarke, *Get Happy: The Life of Judy Garland* (New York: Random House, 2000).
The Reluctant Dragon—MH/PCA. "A pleasant old girl" and "The fabulous amusement": *Variety*, June 11, 1941.
Star Spangled Rhythm—MH/PCA.
No Time for Love—MH/PCA. Also, MH/Par.
Lady in the Dark—MH/PCA. "Mischa Auer carries . . .": *Hollywood Reporter*, February 10, 1944.
This Is the Army—MH/PCA.
Night and Day—USC/WB. Also: William McBrien, *Cole Porter: A Biography* (New York: Knopf, 1998).

Up in Arms—MH/PCA.

Romance on the High Seas—USC/WB. Also: MH/PCA.

Chapter 9: Dark Passages: Forties Drama

Louella Parsons on Sigmund Freud—George Eels, *Hedda and Louella: A Dual Biography of Hedda Hopper and Louella Parsons* (New York: G. P. Putnam's Sons, 1972).

Rebecca—MH/PCA.

The Maltese Falcon—USC/WB. Also: MH/PCA. "Peter Lorre brings . . .": *Brooklyn Eagle*, October 4, 1941.

The Seventh Victim—MH/PCA.

The Uninvited—MH/PCA.

The Picture of Dorian Gray—MH/PCA, USC/MGM. "The film didn't . . .": quoted in Doug McClelland, *Forties Film Talk: Oral Histories of Hollywood, with 120 Lobby Posters* (Jefferson, N.C.: McFarland & Company, 1992). "In the adaptation . . .": *Variety*, March 7, 1945. "Mr. Lewin has . . .": *Hollywood Reporter*, February 26, 1945. "Those familiar with . . .": [Daily] *Variety*, February 26, 1945. "A fine, artistically . . .": *Motion Picture Herald*, March 3, 1945. Nearly $3 million: Howard Strickling Collection, MH.

House of Horrors—USC/Univ. Also, MH/PCA. Martin Kosleck: Charles Higham, *Marlene: The Life of Marlene Dietrich* (New York: W. W. Norton, 1977).

Clifton Webb: "My dear boy . . .": quoted in interview with Richard Sale in McClelland, *Forties Film Talk*.

The Razor's Edge—USC/Fox. Also, MH/PCA. "Effete characterization": *Variety*, November 20, 1946.

The Velvet Touch—MH/PCA. "One only wonders . . ." *New York Times*, August 26, 1948.

Adam's Rib—USC/MGM. Also, MH/PCA. "Almost more repulsive . . .": *New Republic*, January 9, 1950.

Gilda—MH/PCA. Also, Vito Russo, *The Celluloid Closet*, rev. ed. (New York: Harper & Row, 1987), and James Robert Parish, *Gays and Lesbians in Mainstream Cinema: Plots, Critiques, Casts and Credits for 272 Theatrical and Made-for-Television Hollywood Releases* (Jefferson, N.C.: McFarland & Company, 1993).

The Big Sleep—MH/PCA.

Rope—USC/WB. Also, MH/PCA; Donald Spoto, *The Dark Side of Genius: The Life of Alfred Hitchcock* (Boston: Little, Brown, 1983); Arthur Laurents, *Original Story By: A Memoir of Broadway and Hollywood* (New York: Knopf, 2000). "It was just a thing . . .": in McClelland, *Forties Film Talk*. "Your picture *Rope* . . .": J. A. Walker (Staten Island, N.Y.), in USC/WB.

Chapter 10: Tempests and Teapots

Caged—WB/USC. Also, MH/PCA. Hope Emerson at the premiere: Charles Higham, *Warner Brothers* (New York: Charles Scribner's Sons, 1975).

So Young, So Bad—MH/PCA. "The apparent intention . . .": *New York Times*, July 24, 1950.

Young Man with a Horn—MH/PCA. "Confused . . .": *New York Times*, February 10, 1950. "A neurotic socialite . . .": *Motion Picture Daily*, February 8, 1950. "Even more confused . . .": *Commonweal*, February 17, 1950.

Johnny One-Eye—MH/PCA.

All About Eve—Sam Staggs, *All About All About Eve: The Complete Behind-the-Scenes Story of the Bitchiest Film Ever Made* (New York: St. Martin's Press, 2000). Also: Kenneth L. Geist, *Pictures Will Talk: The Life and Films of Joseph L. Mankeiwicz* (New York: Charles Scribner's Sons, 1978); MH/PCA.

A Streetcar Named Desire—MH/PCA.

Strangers on a Train—USC/WB. Also, MH/PCA. "Dear, degenerate Bruno": Kael, *5001 Nights at the Movies.* "Similar to *Rope* . . .": *New Yorker*, July 14, 1951. "Because chases . . .": *The Nation*, July 16, 1951.

Love Is Better than Ever—USC/MGM. Also, MH/PCA.

The 5,000 Fingers of Dr. T.—MH/PCA.

Calamity Jane—USC/WB. Also, MH/PCA. "A bit terrifying . . .": *New York Times*, November 5, 1953.

Gentlemen Prefer Blondes—MH/PCA. "A love story . . .": quoted in Todd McCarthy, *Howard Hawks: The Grey Fox of Hollywood* (New York: Grove Press, 1997). "That was the first time . . .": quoted in John Kobal, *People Will Talk* (New York: Alfred A. Knopf, 1985).

Jack Cole—"Very important movie stars . . .": quoted in Kobal, *People Will Talk.*

An American in Paris—MH/PCA.

Singin' in the Rain—MH/PCA.

Rebel without a Cause—USC/WB. Also, MH/PCA. "An eccentric . . .": *Motion Picture Daily*, October 20, 1955.

The Big Combo—MH/PCA. "Lee Van Cleef . . .": *Motion Picture Daily*, February 10, 1955.

Serenade—USC/WB. Also, MH/PCA. "The homosexual angle . . .": [Daily] *Variety*, March 13, 1956.

Tea and Sympathy—USC/MGM; MH/PCA. "A play about persecution . . .": Deborah Kerr letter in Vincente Minnelli Collection, MH. "Loosening the Code": *New York Times*, October 7, 1956. "Clearly implied homosexuality . . .": *Variety*, September 26, 1956. "Obviously the American public . . .": *Time*, October 8, 1956.

Chapter 11: Something Evil

Girls in Prison—MH/PCA.

Blood of Dracula and *How to Make a Monster*—There are particularly astute analyses of these films in Harry M. Benshoff, *Monsters in the Closet: Homosexuality and the Horror Film* (Manchester, England: Manchester University Press, 1997). Also, MH/PCA.

Voodoo Island—MH/PCA. "[She] likes . . .": *Variety*, February 13, 1957. "Miss Engstrom . . .": *Hollywood Reporter*, February 7, 1957.

The Strange One—MH/PCA. "Stories involving military schools . . .": *Variety*, April 2, 1957.

Crime in the Streets—MH/PCA. "The countenancing . . .": [Los Angeles] *Mirror-News*, July 31, 1956.

Designing Woman—USC/MGM. Also, MH/PCA.

Touch of Evil—MH/PCA.

Cat on a Hot Tin Roof—USC/MGM; MH/PCA. "The ways in which . . .": *New York Times*, September 19, 1958.

Compulsion—MH/PCA. Also, USC/Fox.

Suddenly, Last Summer—MH/PCA. Also, Geist, *Pictures Will Talk*. "Whoever portrays him . . .": *The Nation*, January 16, 1960. "I have talked . . .": *Los Angeles Times*, December 20, 1959. "*Suddenly, Last Summer* . . . may not be . . .": *Time*, January 11, 1960. "I never thought . . .": *Los Angeles Times*, undated article. "Homo whose procurer . . .": *Variety*, December 16, 1959.

North by Northwest—MH/PCA.

Some Like it Hot—MH/PCA. "Hilariously innocent . . .": Kael, in *5001 Nights at the Movies*.

Ben-Hur—Script files, MH. Also, William Wyler Collection, MH; MH/PCA. There is an extensive account (including Heston's open letter) of the Vidal-Heston argument in the booklet accompanying the DVD of the documentary film *The Celluloid Closet*.

Spartacus—MH/PCA. Also, USC/Univ; information in the *Spartacus* Criterion laser disc. ". . . apparently made by men . . .": *America*, November 12, 1960.

Chapter 12: That Touch of Mink: Sex and the Sixties

Pillow Talk—MH/PCA. Also, USC/Univ. Ross Hunter: William Mann, *Behind the Screen: How Gays and Lesbians Shaped Hollywood, 1910–1969* (New York: Viking, 2001).

Lover Come Back—MH/PCA.

That Touch of Mink—MH/PCA [including the preview comments]. Also, USC/Univ.

A Very Special Favor—MH/PCA. Also, USC/Univ. "The things I had to do . . .": quoted in James Robert Parish and Don E. Stanke, *The All-Americans* (New Rochelle, N.Y.: Arlington House, 1977). "Desperately tasteless": *Time*, September 10, 1965. "A Hudson-formula movie": *Newsweek*, September 13, 1965.

Chapter 13: The Wild Side

" 'Mature treatment' . . ."—*Variety*, January 31, 1962.

"I had a miserable time . . ."—*Los Angeles Times*, December 20, 1962.

The Roman Spring of Mrs. Stone—MH/PCA.

Walk on the Wild Side—MH/PCA.

The Best Man—MH/PCA. "No one could take . . .": quoted in Joseph McBride, *Frank Capra: The Catastrophe of Success.* (New York: Simon & Schuster, 1992).

A View from the Bridge—MH/PCA.

Sodom and Gomorrah—MH/PCA.

Victim—MH/PCA. Bogarde obituary: *New York Times*, May 9, 1999.

A Taste of Honey—"Sad-eyed queen": Pauline Kael, *I Lost It at the Movies* (Boston: Little, Brown, 1965).

The Children's Hour—MH/PCA. Also, William Wyler Collection, MH; Wright, *Lillian Hellman.* "Its premises . . .": *America*, June 2, 1962. "Perhaps the whole . . .": *Commonweal*, March 2, 1962. "What has begun . . .": *New Republic*, April 16, 1962. "What was considered . . .": *Saturday Review*, February 24, 1962. "From the way . . .": *New Yorker*, March 17, 1962. "We were unaware . . .": Shirley MacLaine, interview in the *Celluloid Closet* documentary.

No Exit—"Miss Lindfors . . .": *Variety*, July 11, 1962.

Advise and Consent—MH/PCA. Also: Otto Preminger, *Preminger: An Autobiography* (New York: Doubleday, 1977); Russo, *The Celluloid Closet.* "Good scenes . . .": *America*, June 30, 1962. "In an extraordinary scene . . .": *Commonweal*, June 8, 1962. "By turns highhanded . . .": *Newsweek*, June 11, 1962. "There is always . . .": *Saturday Review*, June 2, 1962.

Lawrence of Arabia: MH/PCA. "The few hints . . .": *Los Angeles Times*, December 1, 1962.

Chapter 14: "I'm No Queer," He Lied

The Balcony—"Lesbian lech": *Variety*, March 20, 1963.

The Haunting—MH/PCA. "Miss Bloom . . .": *Hollywood Reporter*, August 21, 1963.

7 Women—"As if someone . . .": Robin Wood, quoted in Joseph McBride, *Searching for John Ford: A Life* (New York: St. Martin's Press, 2001).

Black Like Me—"A deliberate sensation-seeking trick . . .": *New York Times*, May 21, 1964. "Via sexploitation houses . . .": *Variety*, May 20, 1964.

Inside Daisy Clover—MH/PCA. "I then confronted . . .": Robert Redford, quoted in Suzanne Finstad, *Natasha: The Biography of Natalie Wood* (New York: Harmony Books, 2001).

The Loved One—MH/PCA.

The Last of the Secret Agents?—MH/PCA.

The Detective—"It exploits . . .": *New York Times*, May 29, 1968. "[They] all look . . .": Jan Dawson, quoted in Parish, *Gays and Lesbians.*

Valley of the Dolls—USC/Fox.

Chapter 15: Open Season

The Fox—Renata Adler: *New York Times*, February 8, 1968.

The Sergeant—Richard Goldstone Oral History, MH [including Mae West quote]. "Although Steiger . . .": *New York Times*, December 26, 1968.

The Killing of Sister George—"Tacky, tawdry . . .": *Life*, November 1, 1968.

Staircase—Stephen M. Silverman, *Dancing on the Ceiling: Stanley Donen and His Movies* (New York: Knopf, 1996). "Mr. Burton says . . .": quoted in Dick Sheppard, *Elizabeth: The Life and Career of Elizabeth Taylor* (Garden City, N.Y.: Doubleday, 1974). "*Staircase* deals with . . .": *Staircase* promotional manual.

The Gay Deceivers—"Marvelous": *Variety*, June 11, 1969.

The Boys in the Band—Charles Kaiser, *The Gay Metropolis: 1940–1996* (New York: Houghton Mifflin, 1997). "It's all so solemn . . .": Pauline Kael, *Deeper into Movies* (Little, Brown, 1973).

Selected Bibliography

A. Books on Film

Balio, Tino, ed. *The American Film Industry.* Madison: University of Wisconsin Press, 1976.

Balio, Tino. *Grand Design: Hollywood as a Modern Business Enterprise, 1930–1939.* Berkeley: University of California Press, 1993.

Benshoff, Harry M. *Monsters in the Closet: Homosexuality and the Horror Film.* Manchester, England: Manchester University Press, 1997.

Black, Gregory D. *Hollywood Censored: Morality Codes, Catholics and the Movies.* Cambridge: Cambridge University Press, 1994.

Bryant, Wayne M. *Bisexual Characters in Film: From Anaïs to Zee.* Binghamton, N.Y.: Harrington Park Press, 1997.

Crafton, Donald. *The Talkies: American Cinema's Transition to Sound, 1926–1931.* Berkeley: University of California Press, 1997.

Davis, Ronald L. *The Glamour Factory: Inside Hollywood's Big Studio System.* Dallas: Southern Methodist University Press, 1993.

Doherty, Thomas. *Pre-Code Hollywood: Sex, Immorality, and Insurrection in American Cinema, 1930–1934.* New York: Columbia University Press, 1999.

Dyer, Richard. *Only Entertainment.* London: Routledge, 1992.

Ehrenstein, David. *Open Secret: Gay Hollywood, 1928–1998.* New York: William Morrow, 1998.

Forman, Henry James. *Our Movie-Made Children.* New York: Macmillan, 1933.

Higham, Charles. *Warner Brothers.* New York: Scribner's, 1975.

Kael, Pauline. *5001 Nights at the Movies: A Guide from A to Z.* New York: Holt, Rinehart and Winston, 1982.

Kobal, John. *People Will Talk.* New York: Knopf, 1985.

Leff, Leonard J., and Jerold L. Simmons. *The Dame in the Kimono: Hollywood, Censorship and the Production Code from the 1920s to the 1960s.* London: Weidenfeld and Nicolson, 1990.

Mann, William J. *Behind the Screen: How Gays and Lesbians Shaped Hollywood, 1910–1969.* New York: Viking, 2001.

Mast, Gerald, ed. *The Movies in Our Midst: Documents in the Cultural History of Film in America.* Chicago: University of Chicago Press, 1982.

McCarthy, Todd. *Howard Hawks: The Grey Fox of Hollywood.* New York: Grove Press, 1997.

McClelland, Doug. *Forties Film Talk: Oral Histories of Hollywood, with 120 Lobby Posters.* Jefferson, N.C.: McFarland & Company, 1992.

McDonald, Boyd. *Cruising the Movies: A Sexual Guide to "Oldies" on TV.* New York: Gay Presses of New York, 1985.

Mordden, Ethan. *Medium Cool: The Movies of the 1960s.* New York: Knopf, 1990.

———. *The Hollywood Studios: House Style in the Golden Age of the Movies.* New York: Knopf, 1988.

Parish, James Robert. *Gays and Lesbians in Mainstream Cinema: Plots, Critiques, Casts and Credits for 272 Theatrical and Made-for-Television Hollywood Releases.* Jefferson, N.C.: McFarland & Company, 1993.

———, and Don E. Stanke. *The All-Americans.* New Rochelle: Arlington House, 1977.

Russo, Vito. *The Celluloid Closet: Homosexuality in the Movies,* rev. ed. New York: Harper & Row, 1987.

Schatz, Thomas. *The Genius of the System: Hollywood Filmmaking in the Studio Era.* New York: Henry Holt, 1996.

Staggs, Sam. *All about All about Eve: The Complete Behind-the-Scenes Story of the Bitchiest Film Ever Made.* New York: St. Martin's Press, 2000.

Tyler, Parker. *Screening the Sexes: Homosexuality in the Movies.* New York: Da Capo Press, 1993.

Vieira, Mark A. *Sin in Soft Focus: Pre-Code Hollywood.* New York: Harry N. Abrams, 1999.

Vizzard, Jack. *See No Evil: Life Inside a Hollywood Censor.* New York: Simon & Schuster, 1970.

Walsh, Frank. *Sin and Censorship: The Catholic Church and the Motion Picture Industry.* New Haven: Yale University Press, 1996.

Weiss, Andrea. *Vampires and Violets: Lesbians in Film.* New York: Penguin Books, 1993.

B. Biography and Autobiography

Bach, Steven. *Marlene Dietrich: Life and Legend.* New York: William Morrow, 1992.

Callow, Simon. *Charles Laughton: A Difficult Actor.* London: Methuen, 1987.

Chierichetti, David. *Mitchell Leisen: Hollywood Director.* Los Angeles: Photoventures Press, 1995.

Clarke, Gerald. *Get Happy: The Life of Judy Garland.* New York: Random House, 2000.

DeMille, Cecil B. *The Autobiography of Cecil B. DeMille.* Edited by Donald Hayne. Englewood Cliffs, N.J.: Prentice-Hall, 1959.

Gatiss, Mark. *James Whale: A Biography.* London: Cassell, 1995.

Geist, Kenneth L. *Pictures Will Talk: The Life and Films of Joseph L. Mankiewicz.* New York: Scribner's, 1978.

Finstad, Suzanne. *Natasha: The Biography of Natalie Wood* (New York: Harmony Books, 2001).

Harvey, Stephen. *Directed by Vincente Minnelli.* New York: Museum of Modern Art, 1989.

Higham, Charles. *Marlene: The Life of Marlene Dietrich.* New York: Norton, 1977.

Kaplan, Fred. *Gore Vidal.* New York: Doubleday, 2000.

Lambert, Gavin. *On Cukor.* London: W. H. Allen, 1973.

Levy, Emmanuel. *George Cukor: Master of Elegance.* New York: William Morrow, 1994.

Loney, Glenn. *Unsung Genius: The Passion of Dancer-Choreographer Jack Cole.* New York: Franklin Watts, 1984.

Madsen, Axel. *Stanwyck.* New York: HarperCollins, 1994.

Mann, William J. *Wisecracker: The Life and Times of William Haines, Hollywood's First Openly Gay Star.* New York: Viking, 1998.

Mayne, Judith. *Directed by Dorothy Arzner.* Bloomington: Indiana University Press, 1994.

McBride, Joseph. *Frank Capra: The Catastrophe of Success.* New York: Simon & Schuster, 1992.

McBrien, William. *Cole Porter: A Biography.* New York: Knopf, 1998.

McGilligan, Patrick. *George Cukor: A Double Life: A Biography of the Gentleman Director.* New York: St. Martin's, 1991.

Paris, Barry. *Garbo: A Biography.* New York: Knopf, 1995.

Preminger, Otto. *Preminger: An Autobiography.* New York: Doubleday, 1977.

Schwartz, Charles. *Cole Porter: A Biography.* New York: Da Capo Press, 1979.

Seaman, Barbara. *Lovely Me: The Life of Jacqueline Susann.* New York: William Morrow, 1987.

Silverman, Stephen M. *Dancing on the Ceiling: Stanley Donen and His Movies.* New York: Knopf, 1996.

Zolotow, Maurice. *Billy Wilder in Hollywood.* New York: Putnam's, 1977.

C. Other Books

Bergman, David, ed. *Camp Grounds: Style and Homosexuality.* Amherst: University of Massachusetts Press, 1993.

Berubé, Allan. *Coming Out under Fire: The History of Gay Men and Women in World War II.* New York: Penguin, 1990.

Bronski, Michael. *Culture Clash: The Making of Gay Sensibility.* Boston: South End Press, 1984.

Chauncey, George. *Gay New York: Gender, Urban Culture, and the Making of the Gay Male World, 1890–1940.* New York: BasicBooks, 1994.

Duberman, Martin. *Left Out: The Politics of Exclusion.* New York: BasicBooks, 1999.
———. *Stonewall.* New York: Dutton, 1993.

Kaiser, Charles. *The Gay Metropolis: 1940–1996.* New York: Houghton Mifflin, 1997.

Katz, Jonathan Ned. *Gay/Lesbian Almanac: A New Documentary.* New York: Harper & Row, 1983.

————. *The Invention of Heterosexuality.* New York: Plume, 1996.

Loughery, John. *The Other Side of Silence: Men's Lives and Gay Identities: A Twentieth-Century History.* New York: Henry Holt, 1998.

Newton, Esther. *Mother Camp: Female Impersonators in America.* Chicago: University of Chicago Press, 1979.

Sedgwick, Eve Kosofsky. *Epistemology of the Closet.* Berkeley: University of California Press, 1992.

Slide, Anthony. *The Great Pretenders: A History of Female and Male Impersonation in the Performing Arts.* Lombard, Ill.: Wallace Homestead, 1986.

Van Leer, David. *The Queening of America: Gay Culture in Straight Society.* New York: Routledge, 1995.

D. Periodicals

The Advocate	*Motion Picture Daily*
America	*Motion Picture Herald*
Billboard	*The Nation*
Cinema Journal	*The New Republic*
Commonweal	*New York Herald-Tribune*
Exhibitors Herald-World	*The New York Times*
Film Daily	*The New Yorker*
Harrison's Reports	*Newsweek*
Hollywood Reporter	*Photoplay*
Life	*Saturday Review*
Look	*Time*
Los Angeles Times	*Vanity Fair*
Motion Picture	*Variety*

E. Other Sources

The Celluloid Closet. Documentary. Special Edition DVD, Sony Pictures Classics, 2001.

Gay! Gay! Hollywood. Documentary. Wavelength Video, 1994.

Gregg, Ronald Eric. *The Representation and Censorship of Male Homosexuality in Hollywood Film, 1930–1935.* Ph.D. dissertation, University of Oregon, 1996.

Homo Promo. Documentary. Wolfe Video, 1991.

The Lavender Lens: 100 Years of Celluloid Queers! Documentary. Sister Boy Productions, 1995.

Lugowski, David M. *Queering the (New) Deal: Lesbian, Gay and Queer Representation in U.S. Cinema of the Great Depression, 1929–1941.* Ph.D. dissertation, New York University, 1999.

Index

Characters in italics indicate a photograph. Characters in boldface indicate a biographical sketch. Numbers following the letter "n" indicate the footnote on the page number preceding the "n."

Abbott, Bud, and Costello, Lou 201
Abbott, George 43
Academy Awards ["Oscars"] 37, 112n10, 196, 202, 204, 219n2, 242, 266n10, 269, 271n12, 274, 277, 286, 305, 307n9, 323, 342, 343, 347, 357
Adam's Rib (1949) 205–6, 255
Adler, Renata 342
Adrian, [Gilbert] 28
Advise and Consent 282, 296, 297, 298, 299, 302, 303, 312–4, 323, 324, 331, 334, 345
Advocate, The 270
African Queen, The 261
Aherne, Brian 149
Aimée, Anouk 300, 301n4
"Ain't There Anyone Here For Love?" 233–4
Albee, Edward 329
Aldrich, Robert 300, 344–5, 346
Alexis, Demetrius *124*
Algie, the Miner 17–*18*, *24*, *31*
Algren, Nelson 296, 297, 308
Alice in Wonderland (1933) 139
All About Eve *43*, *194*, *204*, *214*, 223–6, *261*, *323*
All Fall Down 311–2
All Over Town 115
Allen, Marty, and Rossi, Steve 328
Allen, Gracie 116

Allister, Claud 170
Alpert, Hollis 313
Alton, Robert 168
America [magazine] 57, 273, 305, 313
American in Paris, An 234
American-International Pictures 247–9, 252
"Anatole of Paris" 178, 181
Anatomy of a Murder 268, 297
Anchors Aweigh 178
And the Band Played On 364
Anders an die Anderen *22*
Anderson, Judith 118, 119, 186, *203*
Anderson, Maxwell 270
Anderson, Robert 240, 241–2
Andrews, Dana 178
Angeli, Pier 300, 301
Anger, Kenneth 12
Animal Crackers 83n3, 140
Anka, Paul 249
Annie Get Your Gun 214
Any Rags? 110
Any Wednesday 291–2
"Anything Goes" 357
Apartment, The 305
Applause [play] 224n4
Arbuckle, Roscoe "Fatty" 19, 22
Arden, Eve 205, 214, 216, 250, 276
Arizona to Broadway 104–5
Arlen, Richard 36

Armetta, Henry 98
Armstrong, Robert 71
Around the World in 80 Days 244
Arrow Pictures 32
Arrowsmith 140
Arthur, George K. 27–8, 43
Arthur, Jean 161
Arthur, Johnny 25–6, **26**, *27*, 31, 36,
    40–1, 43, 67, 143, 174, 196
Arzner, Dorothy 49–50, 156
As Thousands Cheer *202*
Aslan, Gregoire 273n15
Asphalt Jungle, The 214
Astaire,Fred 202
Astin, John 279
Astor, Mary 157, 158
Atherton, Gertrude Franklin 34
Atkinson, Frank 105
Auer, Mischa 78, 173–5, *174*, 181, 201,
    283
Auntie Mame [film] 224, 257, 346
Awful Truth, The (1937) 155
Axelrod, George 284
Ayres, Lew 312

Baby Doll 226n6, 238, 248, 251, 258
Baby Face 58, 83, 138
Bacall, Lauren 184n1, 222, 226, 255, *256*,
    284
Bainter, Fay 306, *307*
Baker, Stanley 300
Balaban, Barney 210
Balcony, The 318, *319*
Baldwin, Faith 61, 62
Balkin, Karen 305, 306, *307*
Bancroft, George 118, 119n14
Bank Dick, The 115, 163, 166, 179
Bankhead, Tallulah 354
Banky, Vilma 46
Bara, Theda 16
Barbarella 342
Barbarian, The *49*
Bard, Ben *189*
Bard, Katherine 327
Bardot, Brigitte 340n1
Barrett, Wilson 82, 85
Barrymore, John 47, 157
Barrymore, Lionel 47
Barthelmess, Richard 46
Basic Instinct *11*, *159*, *346*, *363*
Basquette, Lina 51–3, *52*

Bass, Saul 309
Baxter, Anne 225
Baxter, Warner 107
BBB Cellar Revue 102, 103
Beach Blanket Bingo 248
Beardsley, Aubrey 23, 24, 194
Beaton, Betsey 98n2
Beatty, Warren 294, 295, 311, 323, 334
Beautiful Mind, A 316n15
Bed of Roses 71
Bedeviled Rabbit 215
Bedlam 190n6
Beery, Wallace 19, 46
Behind the Screen [book] 7
Behind the Screen [film] 19
Beiderbecke, Bix 222
Belle of the Nineties [a.k.a. *It Ain't No
    Sin*] 136, 139, 303
Belle of the Yukon 173n5
Belmore, Lionel *30*
Benchley, Robert 78n8, 169
Bendix, William 175
Ben–Hur (1926) 48, 84n4, 193, 269
Ben–Hur (1959) 48n8, 262, 268–72, 298,
    300, 305
Ben–Hur [play] 115
Bennett, Barbara 42
Bennett, Constance 61, 94, 99
Beranger, André de [a.k.a. André
    Berenger] 29, 154
Bergen, Candice 329–30
Bergmann, Andrew *325*
Berkeley, Busby 69, 107
Berkeley Square 139
Berle, Milton 328
Berlin, Irving 66, 175
Bernstein, Leonard 356
Berra, Yogi 279
Best Man, The 297–8, *299*, 323–4
Betty Boop 110
Betty Boop for President 110
Betty Boop's Penthouse 110
Bewitched [TV series] 228, 285
Bey, Turhan 187
Beyond the Forest 217n1
Big Combo, The 237–8, 255
Big Heat, The 237
Big Momma's House 265
Big Noise, The (1936) 154
Big Sky, The 233
Big Sleep, The (1946) 207–8, 233

"Bige" 42,
Billy Elliott 230
Bird Cage, The 315, 364
Birds, The 307n9
Birth of a Nation, The 21n4, 356
Bitter Sweet 113
Black Like Me 324–6, *325*
Blackboard Jungle, The 236
Blackman, Honor 321
Blanc, Mel 215
Blonde Venus 64, 80
Blood Money 118–9
Blood of Dracula 249, 264
Bloom, Claire 318, 319, 320, *321*
Bloomer, Amelia 135
Blore, Eric 147, 179, 276
Blue Max, The 331
Blue Skies 176
Blumer, Herbert 119
Bochner, Lloyd 331
Body Snatcher, The 318n2
Bogarde, Dirk 301, 302
Bogart, Humphrey 184n1, 207–8, 223, 233
Bois, Curt 154, 171, 174, 187
Bold Ones, The 337
Bolt, Robert 314
Bonnell, Bonny 109
Bonnie and Clyde 334
Borden, Olive 29
Born to Be Bad (1950) 205
Born to be Kissed. See *The Girl from Missouri*.
Born to Dance 67, 153
Bow, Clara 27, 31–2, 33, 34, 36, 46, 49–50, 78–9, 90, 106n8, 134
"Boy Friends, The" 179
Boyd, Stephen 269
Boyer, Charles 286, 287
Boys in the Band, The [film] 5, 53, 347, 355–63, *360*
Boys in the Band, The [play] 172, 337, 356–7, 358, 359, 362
Brackett, Charles 158
Brady, Alice 74, 108
Brando, Marlon 252, 333, 334
Breakfast at Tiffany's 305
Breen, Joseph I. 57, 94, 97, 101, 114, 121, 122n15, 123, 132, 133–4, 136–8, *137*, 139–40, 140–1, 148, 152, 160, 164–5, 168, 172, 173–4, 178, 186, 187, 190, 197, 198, 201, 204, 206, 218, 221, 226, 227, 233, 234, 241, 242, 253, 266, 273, 317, 339
Breen Office. *See* Hays Office; Production Code Administration; Motion Picture Association of America.
Brendel, El 44, 62
Brent, Evelyn *189*
Brick Foxhole, The 185
Bride of Frankenstein 64, 150, 319
Brideless Groom 178n8
Bridge on the River Kwai, The 82, 261
Bright Eyes *10*
Bright, Susie 186
Brinegar, Paul 250
Bringing Up Baby 154–5, 233
Broadway Melody, The 37–40, *39*, *42*, *43*, *46*, *106*, *154*
Broadway Rhythm 175–6
Bronson, Harry 222
Brook, Sebastian 354, *355*
Brooks, Jean 188, *189*
Brooks, Mel 336
Brooks, Richard 185
Brothers 363
Broun, Heywood 293
Brown, Joe E. 74, *75*, 112, 154, 266
Brown, Tom 75, *76*
Browne, Bothwell 20
Browne, Coral 344, 346
Bruggeman, Georges 84–5
Brute Man, The 199n12
Bryant, Charles 23, 24
Buchanan, Patrick 189
Buchman, Sidney 88n6
Bugs Bunny **215**, 265
Bugs Bunny Nips the Nips 215
Burns, David 153
Burns, George *116*
Burton, Martin 74
Burton, Richard 284, 322, 349–50, *351*, 352
Burton, Tim 235
Bushman, Francis X. 51
Buzzell, Eddie 41
Bwana Devil 240
By Jupiter 102n5
Bye, Bye Birdie 285

Café Society 160–1
Cage aux Folles, La *12*, *363*, *364*
Caged 11, *216*–20, 221, 236, 266, 323, 326, 361

Caged Heat 219
Cagney, James 61, 74, 107, 112n10, 129,
Cain and Mabel 148n1
Cain, James M. 239
Calamity Jane 232–3, 276
Call Her Savage *5, 78–80, 104, 118, 134,
206, 312*
Call of the Flesh *48*
Callahans and the Murphys, The *56, 125,
131, 133*
Cambridge, Godfrey 325
Camille (1936) 157
Canby, Vincent 332, 343
Canterville Ghost, The 192
Cantor, Eddie 45, 69, 70, 161, 177
Capra, Frank 29, 30, 97, 298, 323
Captive, The 127
Capucine 297, 308
Carey, Phil [Philip] 257
Carmen, Jean 159
Caron, Leslie 285, 286, 287, *290*, 291
Carson, Jack 179–80
Cartwright, Veronica 307n9
Casablanca 167
Casey, Larry [Lawrence] 353
Cassavetes, John 254, 255
Castillo, Gloria 249
Cat and the Fiddle, The 140
Cat on a Hot Tin Roof [film] 11, 258–9,
261, 274
Cat on a Hot Tin Roof [play] 258
Catered Affair, The 205
Cavalcade 83n3, 95, 98–9, 104, 113,
139, 140, 147
Cavanaugh, Hobart 72
Ceiling Zero 233
Celluloid Closet, The [book] 4–6, 11, 12,
117, 123, 162, 222, 269, 330
Celluloid Closet, The [documentary] 16,
25, 186
Chandler, Chick 119
Chandler, Raymond 208
Chaney, Lon 25, 27, 46
Chaplin, Charles 18, 19, 22, 45, 47
Chapman, Edythe *35*
Chapman Report, The 320
Charisse, Cyd 232
Charly 343n4
Chasing Amy 364
Chasing Rainbows *43*
Chatterton, Ruth 112

Chauncey, George 65n4, 154
Cheaper by the Dozen 204
Chevalier, Maurice 56
Child Bride 159
Children of Loneliness 158–60, 235,
249n2
Children's Hour, The [film] 153, 280,
293, 296, 298, 299, 303, 305–8, *307*,
311, 314, 319, 320, 342
Children's Hour, The [play] 151–3, 241,
298
Citizen Kane 135, 224, 261
Claire, Ina 73
Clair, René 171
Clampett, Robert 215
Clark, Gilbert 28
Clarke, Mae *68*, 141
Cleopatra (1934) 89
Cleopatra (1963) 261, 273n15, 349
Clever Mrs. Carfax, The *19, 20*
Clift, Montgomery 211n17, 261, 262, 264,
333n10
Clinging Vine, The *33, 34, 62*
Clock, The 228
Cobb, Lee J. 187
Coburn, Charles 324n12
Cockeyed World, The 56
Cohn, Harry 97, 98
Cohn, Roy 11
Colbert, Claudette 82, 84, 89, 157, 172
Cole, Jack **232**, 234, 255–7, *256*, 266n10
Coleman, Charles 73
Collier, William, Jr. 1
Colman, Ronald 46, 175
Columbia Pictures Corporation 1, 29,
97–8, 112, 122, 153, 230, 241, 248,
252, 312
Combs, Frederick *360*
Comden, Betty, and Green, Adolph 224n4
Come September 279
Commonweal 92, 218, 306, 313
Compulsion 6, 259–60
Conrad, Joseph 192n9
Conreid, Hans 230, *231*
Conte, Richard 237, 238
Convention City 96, 118, 141n9
Conway, Gary 249
Cook, Donald 112
Cook, Elisha, Jr. 187
Cooper, Gary 62, 63, 113, 114, 163,
233n11

Cooper, Violet Kemble 99, *100*
Coppin, Grace 220
Corey, Wendell 207n14
Corman, Roger 248
Corny Concerto, A 215
Costello, Dolores 33
Coughlan, Charles E., Fr. 133
Coughlin, Kevin 353
Countess Charming, The *19*
Cowan, Jerome 192n9
Coward, Noël 98, 113, 114
Craig, James 169n2
Crane, Cheryl 249n2
Crawford, Joan 61, 188, 223, 224, 345, 358n9
Cregar, Lawrence 222
Crime in the Streets 254–5, 341n2
Crisp, Quentin 18, 24, 169
Cromwell, Richard 75, *76*, 233n11
Crooner 71
Crosby, Bing 70, 176
Crossfire 185, 239
Crowley, Mart 235, 337, 356, 357, 359, 361
Crowther, Bosley 196, 205, 233n10, 244, 258, 326
Cruising 331, 363
Crying Game, The 265
Crystal Cup, The *33–4*, 35, *61*, *321*, *365*
Cukor, George 6, 99, 100, 101, 148–50, 157, 160, 168, 188, 198, 203, 205, 235, 262, 320n3, 348
Cunningham, Cecil 64, 106, 147, **155**, *156*, 362
Curse of the Cat People, The 318n2
Curtis, Tony 266, *267*, 272, 274, 283, 295–6
Curtiz, Michael 180, 181n9

D'Albrook, Sidney *30*
Dall, John 209, *211*, 273
Damerel, Donna 109
Dance Charlie Dance 154
Dancing Lady 71, 104, 105n7
Daniels, Bebe 66
Daniels, Billy 157n7
Darden, Severn 331
Dark Corner, The 202
Dark Passage 184n1
Dark Shadows 323
Dark Victory 184n2

Darling 348
Darnell, Linda 224
Daughters of Bilitis 229, 247
David and Bathsheba 269
David, Zorro *333*, 334
Davies Marion 148n1
Davion, Alex 335
Davis, Bette 140, 176, 177n7, 184n2, 205, 217n1, 224, 226, 322n5, 344, 345, 354, 359
Davis, Tyrell [a.k.a.Tyrrell] 99–101, *100*, 350
Day, Doris 176, 178–9, 180, 181n9, 216, 232–3, 276–9, 280, 281, 283, 284, 286
de Wilde, Brandon 229, *311*
de Wolfe, Billy 176, 205, 216, 276, 357n7
Dean, James 236–7, 252, 254
Death in Venice 302n5
Death Kiss, The 71
Deathwatch 318n1
Dee, Frances 118
Dee, Sandra 176
Defiant Ones, The 324
DeFore, Don 179
DeGeneres, Ellen 13, 48n9, 364
DeHaven, Gloria 217n1
Del Rio, Dolores 139, 144
Delaney, Shelagh 301
Delehanty, Thornton 101
Demarest, Drew (a.k.a. Demorest) 38, *39*, 43, 45–6, 174, 185, 358n9
deMille, Agnes 89
DeMille, Cecil B. 6, 23, 28, 51, 57, 80, 81–6, 88n6, 89, 91, 93–4, 122, 130, 141–2, 146, 157, 212, 231, 268, 272, 314, 342
Dennis, Sandy 341, 342
Desert Fury 207n14
Desert Hearts 363
Desert Song, The (1929) 26, 40–1, 42, 44
Design for Living 113–4, 117, 118, 140
Designing Woman 232, 255–7, *256*, 278
DeSylva, B. G. "Buddy" 172n4
Detective, The (1968) 331–2, 335, 336, 337, 341, 357
Devil May Care *48*
Diamond, I.A.L. 266n9
"Diamonds are a Girl's Best Friend" 233, 234
Dietrich, Marlene 7, 62–4, *63*, 89, 119, 149, 162, 171, 232, 359

Different Story, A 315
Dillman, Bradford *259*, 260
Dinner at Eight 95
Dirty Dozen, The 344
Dishonored 64
Disney, Walt 110, 169, 171n3
Divine 21, 169
Dizzy Red Riding Hood 110
Dmytryk, Edward 297
Doctor and the Girl, The 217n1
Dolce Vita, La 301
Donen, Stanley 232, 349, 352
Donne, John 188
Double Indemnity 239, 310
Dougherty, Dennis Cardinal 132, 133n6
Doughnuts and Society 163
Douglas, Kirk 222, 272, 274n16
Douglas, Melvyn 65, 161–2
Down to Earth (1947) 232
Dracula (1931) 65n5, 150
Dracula's Daughter 65n5, 150–1
Drag, The 135
Drake, Tom 177
Dream Lady, The *22*
Dream's End 163
Dressler, Marie 46
Drew, Sidney 21
Drury, Allen 297, 312
Dude Wrangler, The *50–53*, 52, *70*, *103*, 277
Dudes are Pretty People 180
Dudgeon, Elspeth (a.k.a. John) 65
Duke, Patty 335
Dullea, Keir 341, *342*
Dumbo 169
Dunn, James 105
Dunne, Irene 155
Durante, Jimmy 73, 111
Duryea, George [Tom Keene] 51–3, *52*
Duvall, Robert 331
Dyer, Charles 349, 352, 357

Eagels, Jeanne 140
"Easter Parade" 202
Eastwood, Clint 300, 316n15
Eaton, Jay 108, 205
Eaton, Shirley 190n6
Ed Wood 235
Eddy, Nelson 148n2
Edens, Roger 168
Edison, Thomas 16

Edwards, Blake 20
Egyptian Melodies 110
Eight Bells 148
Eilers, Sally 105
Eisenhower, Dwight D. 11, 59, 126, 213, 241
Eliot, T. S. 126
Elliott, Laura [a.k.a. Kasey Rogers] 228
Eltinge, Julian 19–20, 50, 63, 215, 265
Emerson, Hope *216*, 217, 218–9, 220, 248
Emerson, Kathleen 21
End as a Man 252
Engstrom, Jean 250, *251*, 252
Enlighten Thy Daughter 159
Erickson, Knute 27
Erwin, Stuart 154
Evans, Evans *311*
Everett, Rupert 365
Ewell, Tom 234n12
Exhibitors Herald [a.k.a. *Exhibitors Herald–World*] 57
Exit Smiling *29*, *36*, *114*
Exodus 274, 297
Exorcist, The 357

Fairbanks, Douglas 20, 46, 65–6
Fairbanks, Douglas, Jr. 61
Falk, Peter 318
Falk, Rosella 344
Family Research Council 129n2
Fanfare Film Productions 353, 355
Fantasia 169
Fante, John 297
Farber, Manny 228–9
"Farewell, Amanda" 205n13
Farewell to Arms, A (1932) [film] 140
Farewell to Arms, A [play] 102n3
Farrell, Glenda 154
Farrell, Timothy 236n14
Fassbinder, Rainer Werner 12
Fast, Howard 272
Fast Workers 71
Faulkner, William 96
Faylen, Frank 185n3
Fazenda, Louise 41
Feldman, Charles K. 226–7, 296–7, 308
Female 112
Ferdinand the Bull 169
Ferrer, José 314
Ferrer, Mel 205
Fetchit, Stepin 9, 101

Fields, Robert 334
Fields, W. C. 72, 114, 115, 163, 179
Fierstein, Harvey 25
Fifty Million Frenchmen 71
Fig Leaves *28–9*
Fighting Stallion, The 223
Finch, Peter 259
Fine, Sylvia 178
Fisher, Eddie 262
Fitzgerald, Barry 202
5,000 Fingers of Dr. T, The 230–2, *231*
Flame of New Orleans, The 171
Flawless 265
Fleming, Victor 161
Flesh (1968) 341
Flesh and the Devil *27n5*
Fletcher, Jack 291
Flight of the Phoenix, The 344
Florida Enchantment, A *20–22, 163*
Flying Down to Rio *10, 144*
Flynn, Errol 228
Flynn, John 343
Fonda, Henry 312, 324
Fonda, Jane 283, 291, 308, 309
Fontaine, Joan 186, 205, 239
Fontanne, Lynn 113, 206
Footlight Parade 107
Ford, Corey 77–8
Ford, Glenn 206, 207
Ford, John 146, 321, 322
Forman, Henry James 130
Forster, Robert 333
Fortune and Men's Eyes 354, 362
42nd Street 95, 107
Forwood, Tony 302n5
Fosse, Bob 232
Four Horsemen of the Apocalypse, The
    (1921) 266
Fox, The 341–2, 343
Fox Film Corporation (*later* Twentieth
    Century–Fox) 58, 62, 70, 98, 102, 104,
    111, 118, 139, 145, 147–8
Foy, Eddie, Jr. 124n1
"Fractured Fairy Tales" 143
Francis, Anne 220
Franciscus, James 296
Frankenheimer, John 311, 312n12
Frankenstein (1931) 64
Fraser, Elizabeth 331
Freddie the Freshman 110
Frederici, Blanche 61–2

Freed, Arthur 168
Freeman, Howard 199, 201
French Connection, The 357
French Line, The 198, 229
Freud, Sigmund 146, 184
Frey, Leonard 358, *360*, 362
Fried Green Tomatoes 316n15
Friedkind, William 5, 357–8, 363
From Russia With Love 321
Fry, Christopher 270, 271n12
Fung, Willie 74
Funny Lady *43*

Gable, Clark 80, 161
Gabor, Zsa Zsa 252n3
Gam, Rita 311
Gang's All Here, The 143, 167
Garbo, Greta 27n5, 28, 33, 46, 48, 71,
    119–22, *121*, 140, 157
Garde, Betty 219
Gardner, Ava 322, 323
Garfein, Jack 254
Gargan, William 76–8, *77*
Garland, Judy 161, 224, 235, 335, 356,
    357n8, 359
Garner, James 283, 284, 306, *307*
Gay Bride, The 141
Gay Deceivers, The 353–5, 359, 361
Gay Divorce 142
Gay Divorcée, The 142–4
Gay New York 65n4 154–5
Gazzara, Ben 252, *253*, 254, 258
Genet, Jean 318
Gentle Annie 169n2
Gentlemen Prefer Blondes 232, 233–4
George White's Scandals 142, 147–8
George White's 1935 Scandals 147–8
Geraghty, Carmelita 31–2
Gershwin, Ira 173
Getting Gertie's Garter *36*
Ghost Ship, The 190n6
Giant 82, 244, 286
Gielgud, John 328
Gilbert, Helen 248–9
Gilbert, John 27n5, 47, 120, 121
Gilda 206–7, 232
Gill, Brendan 306
Gillette, Ruth 223
Gilmore, Lowell 194
Girl from Missouri, The (a.k.a. *Born to
    be Kissed*) 139

Girl Without a Room 90, 105n7
Girls in Prison 248–9, 250, 251
Gish, Lillian 33, 46
Gladiator 274
Glass Menagerie, The 226n6
Glass–Bottom Boat, The 285
Glen or Glenda (a.k.a. *I Changed My Sex*; *I Led Two Lives*) 235–6, 324
Gless, Sharon 166n10
Glorifying the American Girl *43–4*
Go Fish *364*
Go Into Your Dance 90
Goddess, The 257
Godfather, The 261
Godless Girl, The *51*
Gods and Monsters 64, 364
Goebbels, Joseph 199
Going Hollywood 71, 107
Going My Way 202
Gold Diggers of 1933 95, 107
Gold Diggers of Broadway *43*
Golden Girl 232
Goldfinger 190n6, 321
Goldwyn, Samuel 69n6, 149, 151, 177–8, 241
Gone with the Wind 161, 186
Good Earth, The 193
Goodbye, Charlie *20, 284*
Gordon, Alex 248
Gordon, C. Henry 72
Gordon, Michael 283, 286
Gordon, Ruth 206, 327
Gorman, Cliff 358–9, *360*, 362
Gottschalk, Ferdinand 71, 85, *86*, 103
Goulding, Edmund 203
Grable, Betty 69, *144*, 232
Graduate, The 252
Graetz, Paul 299–300
Graff, Wilton *259*
Grahame, Gloria 223
Grahame, Kenneth 169
Grand Hotel 71, 80, 85, 105
Grand Slam 105
Granger, Farley 209, *211*, 228
Granger, John 313
Granger, Stewart 300
Grant, Cary 136, 154–6, 177, 233, 279–80, 282, 327
Grant, Lee 318, *319*
Granville, Bonita *152*

Great Ziegfeld, The 153
Green Bay Tree, The 127
Greene, Reuben 360
Greenwich Village 175
Greer, Howard 28
Greer, Michael 353, **354**, *355*, 359
Gregory, Paul 45
Grey, Nan 151
Grey, Virginia 199
Griffin, John Howard 324, 325
Griffith, Corinne 46
Griffith, D.W. 20, 36, 67, 135, 273n15, 356
Grizzard, George 312
Group, The 329–30, 342
Guillerman, John 331
Guy–Blaché, Alice 17, 18

Hagman, Larry 330
Haines, William 47–8, 161
Hair Raising Hare 215
Half–Naked Truth, The 114
Hall, Grayson 322, 323
Hall, Jon 174
Hall, Peter 349
Hall, Radclyffe 1, 16, 147, 158
Hamilton, Patrick 208, 209
Hammett, Dashiell 187, 298
Hard Hombre *53n11*
Harding, Warren G. 22
Hardwicke, Sir Cedric 192n9
Hardy, Oliver 18, 45, 46, 111–2. 163, 346
Harlow, Jean 74, 80, 94, 122, 139
Harper's Bizarre 357
Harris, Julie 229, 230, 318, 320, *321*, *333*, 334
Harris, Robert H. 250
Harrison, Rex 349, 350, *351*, 352, 358n10
Harrison, Sandra 249
Harrison's Reports 89–90
Hart, Lorenz 102n3, 177
Hart, Maria 223
Hart, Moss 235
Hart, William S. 34n7
Hartung, Philip T. 306, 313
Harvey, Laurence 308
Harwood, H. M. 120
Hasso, Signe 192n8
Hatfield, Hurd 194–6, *195*
Hathaway, Henry 233n11
Hatton, Rondo 199, *200*

Haunting, The (1963) 318–20, *321*
Haunting, The (1999) 320n3
Haute Surveillance 318n1
Hawks, Howard 29, 233
Haydn, Richard 172
Hayes, Ira 296
Hayes, John Michael 298
Hayes, Wendell 297
Hays, Will H. 22–3, 57, 93, 97, 125, 130,
    133, 139, 142, 143, 151, 152, 190, 192,
    198, 242, 329
Hays Office 13, 23, 56, 57, 71, 73, 76, 77,
    88n6, 93, 97–8, 101, 103, 106, 113,
    114, 116, 118, 120, 133, 146
Hayward, Susan 223, 335
Hayworth, Rita 206, 207, 232
He Was Her Man 139
Head, Edith 157
Hearst, William Randolph 272
Heart is a Lonely Hunter, The 332
Heart of New York, The 138
Heaven's Gate 261
Hecht, Ben 113, 297
Hedda Gabler 204
Hedge, Ray 109, 110
Hell's Highway 72, 75
Heller, Lucas 345
Hellman, Lillian 151–3, 298, 305
Helmore, Tom *256*
Henie, Sonja 176
Henreid, Paul 220, *221*
Hepburn, Audrey 21, 277n1, 305, *307*,
    308, 314
Hepburn, Katharine 102, *149*–50, 154,
    205, 206, 255, 261, 262, 264, 322n4
Hercules (1959) 300
Here Comes the Navy 112n10
Hergesheimer, Joseph 112
Herlihy, James Leo 311, 347
Herrick, Robert 172
Heston, Charlton 269–70, 272
Hewitt, Alan 280, *281*
Hewitt, Christopher 336
Heywood, Anne 341
High Hat 163
High Wall 184
Highsmith, Patricia 228
Hillbilly Hare 215
Hiller, Arthur 283
Hingle, Pat 258

Hips Hips Hooray 72, 107, 139
His Day Out *18*
Hitchcock, Alfred 186, 208–11, 227–9,
    259, 265, 307n9, 314
Hitler, Adolf 53n11, 67
Hitler Gang, The 67
Hodiak, John 207n14
Hoffman, Dustin 348
Hogan, Dick 211n17
Holden, Gloria 151
Hollander, Frederick 231
Holliman, Earl 237, *238*
Hollywood Hotel 154, 171
Hollywood Party 111
Hollywood Reporter, [*The*] 174, 183,
    196–7, 252
Hollywood Squares, The 285
Holt, Jack 112
Homosexuals, The 336–7
Honeymoon Machine, The 283
Hope, Bob 172n4
Hopkins, Anthony 274
Hopkins, Miriam 113, 114, *152*, 605
Hopper, Hedda 157n7
Horne, Lena 175
Horton, Edward Everett 24, 25, 66, 67,
    113, 118, *143*, *144*, 147,
Hot Saturday 179
House of Horrors 65n5, 198–201, *200*,
    212, 249, 284, 319
House of Women 220
House on 92nd Street, The 192n8
Housewife 72
How to Make a Monster 249–50
Howard, Leslie 147
Hoyt, John 205, 273
Hubbard, John *164*, 165–6
Hubbard, (Dr.?) S. Dana, 158
Huddle 49
Hudson, Rock 7–8, 168, 269, 276–9, 280,
    283, 284–7, **286**, *290*, 291, 302n5
Hughes, Barnard 348
Hughes, Howard 229
Hunt, John, Msgr. 132
Hunter, Kim 188
Hunter, Ross 277
Hunter, Tab 168
Hurry Sundown 313
Huston, John 187, 322, 334
Hutton, Betty 172n4, 176, 178

"I Am a Gay Gaballero" 148
I Am Curious (Yellow) 240
I Am Suzanne! 111
I Love Lucy 173n5, 237
I Love That Man 104, 105n7
I Was a Teenage Frankenstein 249
I'm No Angel 72, 96, 135, 136
If a Man Answers 283
In a Lonely Place 223
In and Out 364
In Caliente 143
In Cold Blood 341
In Gay Madrid *48*
In the Heat of the Night 342
Incident, The 334, 335
Ingagi 93n9
Inge, William 311
Inman, James 331, *332*
Inside Daisy Clover 326–7
International House 72, 114, *116*
Invisible Man, The 64
Irene (1926) 27–8
Irene (1940) 28n6
It 27
It Ain't No Sin. See *Belle of the Nineties*
It's Always Fair Weather 232
It's Love I'm After 147
Ivanhoe *(1952) 53*
Iwerks, Ub 110, 148

Jackson, Anne 220, *221*
Jaffe, Sam 187
Jailhouse Rock *53*
James, Walter *27*
Jannings, Emil 46
Jazz Singer, The (1927) 37, 135, 240
Jergens, Adele 248
Jessel, George 51n10
Jewel Productions 158, 159
Jewell, Isabel *189*
Jimmy the Gent 139
Johnny Guitar 223
Johnny One-Eye 222
Johnson, Lyndon B. 276, 329
Johnson, Richard 320
Johnston Office. *See* Motion Picture
    Association of America, Production
    Code Administration.
Johnston, Eric A. 198, 264, 299,
Jolson, Al 90, 123, *124*, 144

Jones, Charles M. [Chuck] 215
Jones, T. C. 329
Jordan, Dorothy 48
Joslyn, Allyn 160
Joy, Jason, Col. 91
Joy, Leatrice 18, 23, 33
Joyzelle [Joyner] 44, 85, 86, 87–9, **90**, 94,
    250, 365
Judith of Bethulia *20, 273n15*
Jungle Captive 199n12
Just Imagine *44, 60, 62, 69, 78n8, 90,
    104*

Kael, Pauline 82–3, 156n5, 227, 265–6,
    304n7, 358
Kaley, Charles 46
Kalin, Tom 260n6
Kanin, Garson 206
Karloff, Boris 65, 150, 250, 251
Kauffman, Stanley 306
Kaufman, George S. 171–2
Kaye, Danny 173, 177–8
Kazan, Elia 187, 227, 240, 241
Keaton, Buster 20n2, 46
Keel, Howard 233
Keeler, Ruby 107
Keene, Tom. *see* Duryea, George
Keith, Brian *333*
Keith, Donald 32, *32*
Kellerman, Sally 249
Kellogg, Virginia 217, 218
Kelly, Gene 67, 232, 234
Kelly, Patsy 147
Kennedy, John F. 275, 298, 312
Kennedy, King 171
Kern, Jerome 177
Kerr, Deborah 240, 241, 242, *243*, 244
Kerr, John *243*, 244
Kibbee, Guy 154
Killing of Sister George, The [film]
    300n3, 344–7, *345*, 349, 352, 361, 365
Killing of Sister George, The [play] 337,
    344–5, 349, 356
King and I, The [film] 243
King, Charles 43
King Klunk 101
King Kong (1933) 83, 95, 101, 140
King of Gamblers 155
King of Kings, The (1927) 81, 82
King of Kings (1961) 272n13

King Solomon's Mines (1950) 214
King Steps Out, The 153, 160, 255
Kismet [musical play] 232
Kiss Before the Mirror, The 140
Kiss Me Again (1930) 44–5, 107
Kiss Me Deadly 237, 300n3
Knight, Arthur 306
Kopell, Bernie 284
Kosleck, Martin 187, 198, 199–*200*
Krafft–Ebbing, Richard von 8, 84
Kramer, Stanley 230
Kramer vs. Kramer 141
Krim, Arthur C. 299, 303
Krim, Dr. Mathilde 299n2
Kubrick, Stanley 272, 303, 322
Kurasch, Katherine 222

La Guardia, Fiorello 116
La Tourneaux, Robert *360*, 362
Ladd, Alan 237
"Ladies of the Chorus" 175
Ladies of the Mob 106n8
Ladies They Talk About 106
Lady Eve, The 310
Lady for a Day 72
Lady in Cement 331
Lady in the Dark [film] 7, 24, 172–5,
   174, 201, 283, 361
Lady in the Dark [play] 173, 178
Lady Lies, The *56*
Lady of the Pavements *36, 114*
Lady Scarface 186n3
Lahr, Bert 161
Laine, Cleo 295
Lake, Veronica 176, 178
Lambert, Gavin 295, 326, 327
Lancaster, Burt 237n15
Lanchester, Elsa 150
Landau, Martin 265
Landi, Elissa 85, *86*, 87, 94, 102
Landis, Carole *164*, 165–6
Lang, Fritz 146
Langdon, Harry 46
Lanoe, J. Jiquel 20
Lanteau, William 279n2
Lanza, Mario 239–40
Lassick, Sid 329n8
*Last Days of Sodom and Gomorrah,
   The. See Sodom and Gomorrah*
Last of the Secret Agents?, The 328

Laughing Boy *49*
Laughton, Charles 6, 65, 82, 84–5, 92, 312
Laura 201–2, *203*, 205
Laurel, Stan 24, 45, 46, 111–2, 163, 346
Laurents, Arthur 211n17
Law, John Phillip 342–3
Lawford, Peter 312
Lawrence, D. H. 341
Lawrence,T. E. 314
Lawrence of Arabia 314
Lawyer Man 72
Lean, David 314
Leather Boys, The 315n14
Lederer, Francis 157
Lee, Gypsy Rose 257
Legend of Lylah Clare, The 344
Legion of Decency, Roman Catholic 10, 11,
   55, 91, 124–5, 132–3, 136, 138, 165–6,
   190–2, 196–8, 226, 227, 229, 244, 268,
   273–4, 282, 296, 303, 326,334
Leigh, Janet 257
Leigh, Vivien 294, 295
Leighton, Margaret 321–2
Leisen, Mitchell 7, 28, 155, 156, 157–8,
   168, 172–3
Lemmon, Jack 266, *267*, 283, 285
Lenya, Lotte 295, 321
Leone, Sergio 300
Letter, The (1929 and 1940) 140
Levant, Oscar 180, 181n9
Levin, Meyer 260
Levine, Joseph E. 300
Lewin, Albert 192–4, 196–7, 198
Lewis, Joseph H. 237
Lewis, Louise 249
Lewton, Val 188–9, 190n6, 318n2
Liberace 328
Liberty [comedy short] 45
Life 203, 314, 346
Life of the Party, The (1930) 72
Lightner, Winnie 43, 66, 72
Lights of New York 240
Lilith 323
Lillie, Beatrice 29
Lindfors, Viveca 311
Linow, Ivan 44, 62, 78n8
Little Caesar 60, 61
Little Giant (1933) 72, 119n14
Little Women (1933) 101n4, 139
Live, Love, and Learn 160

Lives of a Bengal Lancer 233n11
Lloyd, Ethel 21
Lloyd, Harold 46
Loeb, Richard and Leopold, Nathan 6, 10,
  92, 208, 209, 210, 211, 259–60
Lolita (1962) 303, 320, 322
Lollobrigida, Gina 279, 285
Longtime Companion *11, 363*
Look 361
Loper, Don 173n5
Lord Byron of Broadway *46, 47n6*
Lord, Daniel, Fr.57
Lorentz, Pare 95, 96, 118, 119
Loring, Eugene 230
Lorne, Marion 228
Lorre, Peter 187, 199
Los Angeles Times 263, 270, 293
Lost Weekend, The 185, 239, 341
Louis, Jean 276
Louise, Anita 99
Love Boat, The 284
Love Happy 181n9
Love is Better than Ever 230
Love Life of a Gorilla 159
Love Me Tonight 83n3, 140
Love of Women 150
Love on Toast 115, 163
Love Parade, The *56*
Love, Bessie 29–*30*, 43
Loved One, The 328, 342
Lover Come Back (1962) 278–9, 283,
  287, 291
Lowery, Robert 199
Loy, Myrna 49, 126
L–Shaped Room, The 315n14
Lubitsch, Ernst 56, 113, 114
Luckinbill, Laurence *360*
Lugosi, Bela 235
Luick, Earl 98n2
Lumet, Sidney 310, 326, 329
Lund, Deanna 331
Lunt, Alfred 114, 206
Lusty Men, The 223, 225
Lynde, Paul 285
Lyon, Sue 322
Lysistrata 102

MGM 28, 46, 47–8, 81, 104, 111, 114,
  118, 119, 120, 122, 131, 135, 139–40,
  153, 160, 163, 168, 193, 198, 217n1,

  236, 241, 243, 244, 248, 255, 258, 268,
  283, 322
McCain, John, Sen. 128–9, 130
McCambridge, Mercedes 223, 257, 262n7
McCarey, Leo 229n7
McCarthy, Joseph R., Sen. 11, 59, 240,
  297, 298, 306
McCarthy, Mary 329
McClafferty, John T., Msgr. 197–8
McCrea, Joel 65n5, 76–8, 77, 152
McCullers, Carson 229, 333, 334, 342
McDaniel, Hattie 115
MacDonald, Boyd 115
MacDonald, Jeanette 56, 73, 104n6, 140,
  148n2
MacDowell, Roddy 43
Mackaill, Dorothy 34, *35*, 61, 365
McGrath, Paul 172
McHugh, Frank 44–5, 105, 107, 112
MacLaine, Shirley 305, 306, *307*–8, 314
McLerie, Allyn [Ann] 233
MacMurray, Fred 161–2, 171, 172
MacPherson, Aimee Semple 131
Macready, George 206
Madam Satan 81
Madame DuBarry 139
Madame, Behave *19*
Madison, Guy 168
Madonna 135, 233, 297
Maedchen in Uniform (1931) 12, 92, 96,
  119–20, 121, 249, 301, 304
Magee, Patrick 349
Magic Garden of Stanley Sweetheart,
  The 354
Maid to Order *50*
"Make–Believe Ladies Man, A" 44–5
Making Love 363
Malin, Jean 51, 102, 104–5
Malle, Louis 340n1
Malone, Dorothy 208
Maltese Falcon, The 187, 199
Mamoulian, Rouben 122n15
Man Who Came to Dinner, The 177n7
Man with the Golden Arm, The 297
Man Without a Face, The 316n15
Manchurian Candidate, The 312n12
Manhattan Parade *6, 66*–*8, 69, 70, 154,*
  365
Mankiewicz, Joseph L. 224–5, 226, 261–2,
  263, 264, 273n15

Mann, William 7
Mansfield, Jayne 329
Manslaughter *23, 84*
Mantle, Mickey 279
Mapplethorpe, Robert 134
March, Fredric 49, 84, 85, *86,* 89, 113
Marcus, Frank 337, 344, 345, 349
Marie Antoinette (1938) 179
Maris, Roger 279
Marlowe, John *124*
Marsh, Marian 76, 77, 78
Martin, Dean 283, 328
Martinez, A. 105
Marx, Groucho 181n9
Mary's Little Lamb 148
Mask of Fu Manchu, The 65n5
Mason, James 235, 265
Masquerade in Mexico 158
Mata Hari *48, 83, 140*
Matinee Idol, The *29–31,* 30, *60, 69*
Mattachine Society 188, 229, 247
Maugham, W(illiam) Somerset 6, 99, 140,
   161, 193, 202, 203
Maurice 363
Mayer, Louis B. 46, 160
Maynard, Kermit "Tex" 31
Mazursky, Paul 318n1
Meachem, Anne 323
Meadows, Audrey 279
Medical Center 337
Meet Me After the Show 232
Meet the Baron 135
Melcher, Martin 276
Melvin, Murray 301
Member of the Wedding, The 229–30,
   332
Menu 114
Merkel, Una 1, 74, 114
Merry Widow, The (1934) 139–40
Merry Widow, The (1952) 232
Metro–Goldwyn–Mayer. See MGM
Michigan Catholic 132
Midler, Bette 354
Midnight *(1939) 157–8*
Midnight Cowboy 343n3, 347–8
*Midnight in the Garden of Good and
   Evil* 316n15
Mildred Pierce 214, 239
Milland, Ray 28n6, 171, 173, 185n3
Miller, Arthur 240, 299, 310

Mineo, Sal 237, 254, 255, 274, 316n15,
   328–9, 361
Minjir, Harold 71
Minnelli, Vincente 168, 176n6, 234, 243,
   255–7, 284,
Mir, David 29–*30*
Miracle, The (1948) 198, 229
Miranda, Carmen 175, 215
Miss Tatlock's Millions 205
Mr. Deeds Goes to Town 163
Mister Scoutmaster 202
Mr. Smith Goes to Washington 88n6,
   298
Mr. Wrong 48n9
Mrs. Doubtfire 265
Mitchum, Robert 223
Moffitt, Jack 177
Monroe, Marilyn 224n4, 232, 233, 234,
   257, 266, 283, 284
Monster, The *25–6,* 27, *31*
Montez, Maria 167. 215, 357n8
Montgomery, Robert 160
Montiel, Sarita 239
Moon and Sixpence, The 193
Moon is Blue, The 229, 238, 240, 297
Moonlight and Pretzels 73, 107
Moore, Colleen 33, 46
Moore, Dickie 141
Moore, Dudley 352
Moore, Eva 65
Moore, Robert 362
Moorehead, Agnes 184n1, 217, 220
Moran, Polly 47
Moreno, Rita [a.k.a. Rosita] 220
Morley, Robert 259
Morocco 60, 62–4, *63,* 162
Most Dangerous Game, The 65n5
Mostel, Zero 336
Motion Picture Association of America
   198, 217, 218, 220–1, 226, 227, 228,
   229n8, 236, 237, 239, 241–2, 243, 253,
   257, 262–3, 264, 291, 298, 303, 329,
   339–41, 357, rating systems 330, 334.
   336, 339–41, 346, 347, 353, *Motion
   Picture Herald,* [*The*] 92–3, 116, 159,
   160, 197
Motion Picture News *20, 34*
Motion Picture Producers and Distributors
   of America, Inc. See Hays Office,
   Production Code Administration.

Motion Picture Research Council, The 129–30
Move Over, Darling 283
Movie Crazy 73, 179
Movies and Conduct 119
Mulligan, Robert 327
Mundelein, George Cardinal 131
Murder 209
Murder at the Vanities 133n6
Murphy, Dean 175–6
Murphy, Dennis 342
Murphy, Dudley 78
Murray, Don 312
Murray, Mae 46
Musante, Tony 331
My Beautiful Laundrette 363
My Best Friend's Wedding 364, 365
My Fair Lady 358n10
My Favorite Wife 156n5
My Friend from India *36*
My Lady of Whims *31–3*, 32, *49–50*
My Man Godfrey (1936) 163
My Son John 229n7
Myra Breckinridge *20*, *235n13*
Myrt and Marge 109–10, 118, 147, 153, 334
Mystery Science Theater 3000 248n1

Naish, J. Carroll
Name of the Game is Kill, The 329n8
Napier, Alan 198
Napoleon Bunny–part 215
Nash, Florence 161
Nation, The *228–9*
National Board of Review 97
Naughty Marietta 148n2
Nazimova, Alla 23, 24
Nazty Nuisance, The *[a.k.a.* That Nazty Nuisance*] 26, 67*
Neagle, Anna 28n6
Negri, Pola 46
Nelson, Kenneth 359, *360*
New Republic, The 306
New York Evening Post 101
New York Herald–Tribune 142
New York Times, [*The*] 196, 205, 233n10, 244, 326, 332, 342, 343
New Yorker, [*The*] 83, 156n5, 306
Newman, Paul 258
Newsweek 291, 304, 313
Newton, Mary 188, *189*

Nichols, Mike, and May, Elaine 316n15
Niesen, Gertrude 296
Night after Night 73
Night and Day 176–7, 316n15
Night Life of the Gods, The 163
Night Must Fall *(1937)* 53
Night of the Iguana, The [film] 322–3
Night of the Iguana, The [play] 322
Night Out, A 18
Night World 73
Nilsson, Harry 348
Nimoy, Leonard 318n1
Nixon, Richard M. 293, 298, 324
No Exit 310–1, 312
No Time for Love 172, 284
No Way to Treat a Lady 342
Noon, Paisley 73
Norman, Karyl 51
North by Northwest 265
Norton, Barry 73, 117
Nothing but a Man 324
Novak, Kim 344
Novarro, Ramon 7, 47–9, 140, 260

O'Brien, Pat 222
O'Connor, Donald 67, 234
O'Hara, Shirley 50
O'Malley, Rex 147, 156–7, 160, 169, 171, 176, 177, 204, 228
O'Neal, Ryan 343n3
O'Shea, Milo 349
O'Sullivan, Maureen 108
O'Toole, Peter 314
Oberon, Merle *152*
Object of My Affection, The 364
Odets, Clifford 297
Of Human Bondage (1934) 133n6
Office Wife, The 60, 61–2, 69, 321
Oh, For a Man! 73, 104n6
Old Dark House, The 64–5
Old Maid in the Drawing Room, The *19*
Olivier, Laurence 186, 272, 274
Olmstead, Gertrude 25
Olsen, Ole, and Johnson, Chic 71
On the Fence 285
On the Waterfront 252, 261
On Trial (1928) 36
One Hour With You 73
One–Way Passage 73, 312
Only Angels Have Wings 233
Only Game in Town, The 349

Only Yesterday 73, 115, 117–18
Operation Petticoat 268n11
Opposite of Sex, The 364
Organ Grinder, The 110
Orry–Kelly, [George] 266n10
Other Half, The *22*
Our Betters [film] 6, 24, 99–102, *100*,
    105, 141, 149, 161, 172, 188, 222, 292,
    294, 334, 361
Our Betters *[play]* 99n3, *100*
Our Daily Bread *53n11*
Our Gang [film series] 26, 163
Our Movie–Made Children 130, 131,
    132, 150
Outlaw, The 198
Outlaw Women 223
Outsider, The 295–6
Overman, Lynne 171
Oz 364

P.J. 331, 337
PRC (Producers Releasing Corporation)
    199n12
Pagan, The *48*
Paige, Janis 179
Pakula, Alan J. 327
Palm Beach Story, The 115
Palmy Days 69, 70, 117
Pangborn, Franklin 5, 7, 10, 13, 24, 25,
    26, 29, 36, 67, 71, 72, 73, 113–4, **115**,
    116, 117–18, 141, 143, 147, 148, 156,
    162–6, 171, 176, 179, 204, 211, 276,
    285, 354, 362, 365
"Pansy Craze" 51–2, 96, 102, 104, 107,
    114, 116, 123, 127
Paramount Pictures 28, 70, 81, 82, 90, 94,
    96, 98, 104, 105n7, 113, 114, 136, 140,
    157, 160, 168, 172, 173, 190, 192, 210,
    220, 241,
Pardon My Gun *50*
Paris is Burning 265
Paris When it Sizzles 277n1
Parker, Barnett 147, 153, 160, 169–71,
    170, 185, 255, 350, 356
Parker, Eleanor 216, 217, 218
Parks, Larry 230
Parsons, Louella O. 184n2
Parsons, Wilfred, Fr. 137
Parting Glances 363
Partners 315, 363
Pathé newsreel 70, 80

Pathé–American 304
Patrick, Lee *216*, 217, 219
Pawnbroker, The 326, 342
Payne Fund 129, 130
Pearl of Death, The 199n12
Peck, Gregory 255
Peppard, George 254, 331
Personal Best 159, 315, 363
Personality *26*
Peters, Brock 326
Phantom President, The 73
Philadelphia *11*, *302*, *315*, *363*
Photoplay 85
Pickford, Mary 22, 46
Picture of Dorian Gray, The (1945) 183,
    192–8, *195*, 208
Picturegoer *48*
Pidgeon, Walter 312
Pillow Talk 268n11, 275, 276–8, 280,
    283, 285, 287, 291, 302n5
Pinocchio 169, 171n3
Pirate, The 234
Pitts, ZaSu 1–2, *3*, 70, 158
Plan Nine From Outer Space 53n11
Planet of the Apes (1968) 270
Please Don't Eat the Daisies 278
Poe, James 258
Poison 364
Porcasi, Paul *63*
Porter, Cole 142, 176–7, 205
Postman Always Rings Twice, The
    (1946) 239
Powell, Dick 107
Powell, William 46, 72
Power, Tyrone 327
Preminger, Otto 201, 229, 268, 274, 296,
    297, 303, 312, 313, 314
Prentice, Keith *360*
Presley, Elvis 248
Price, Vincent *203*, 239
Prinz, LeRoy 88
Prodigal, The (1955) 269
Producers, The 108n9, 335–6, 352
Production Code Administration (a.k.a.
    Breen Office, Johnston Office) 103, 134,
    138, 139, 140, 142, 146, 148, 150–1,
    153, 165, 166, 175, 179, 187, 196, 197,
    209, 216, 242, 243–4, 251, 257, 261,
    265, 268, 272–3, 280–2, 291, 299–300,
    302–4, 308n10, 314, 319, 327, 328,
    339–40

Production Code, Motion Picture 10, 13, 55, 60–1, 62, 64, 75, 83, 89, 90, 91, 94, 96, 101, 112, 121–22, 125, 136, 146, 147, 150, 158, 163, 165, 168, 178, 185, 196, 198, 206, 207, 226n6, 241, 242, 244, 247, 248, 254, 258, 262, 293–4, 305, 310, 317, 318, 320, 326, 328, 329, 340, 357, creation of 56–9, 60, 80, 131, 339, strengthening of 124–6, 128, 133–4, 139, 141–2, alteration of 296–7, 298–9, 300, 302–4, 314, 316, 323, 330, 340, dismantling of 339–41, 347, 364
Professional Sweetheart 117
Prohibition 22, 126–28
Promises! Promises! 329
Prowse, Juliet 328, 329
Psycho 188, 265, 306
Public Enemy, The 61, 66, 140
Pullman, Bill 48n9
Pulver, Enid 220, *221*
Purviance, Edna 19

Queen, The 265
Queen Christina 118, 119–22, *121*, 132, 134, 318
Queen of Outer Space 252n3
Queer as Folk [U.S.] 13, 166n10, 358, 364
Quiet American, The 261
Qui–êtes vous, Polly Magoo 323n6
Quigley, Martin 57, 58, 94, 97, 132, 133, 139–40
Quintero, José 295
Quirk, Billy 17, *17*
Quo Vadis (1951) 269

RKO–Radio [a.k.a. Radio Pictures] 41, 75, 77, 97, 98, 101, 114, 117, 142
Raisch, Bill 273n14
Raisin in the Sun, A 324
Ralph, Jessie 160
Ralston, Jobyna 36
Rambeau, Marjorie 102, *103*
Rambova, Natacha 23, 24
Ramsaye, Terry 92–3
Rapoport, Mark 286
Ray, Nicholas 205, 223, 272n13
Razor's Edge, The 202–4
Reaching for the Moon 65–6, 69, 112, 328
Reagan, Ronald 11, 115, 126, 175
Reason, Rhodes *251*

Rebecca 186, 214
Rebecca of Sunnybrook Farm (1938) 115
Rebel Without a Cause 230n9, 236–7, 255n4, 361
Rebound 73
Red Dust 74
Red Headed Woman 74, 127
Red River 233
Redford, Robert 327
Reed, Donna 194
Reed, Philip 112
Reed, Lou 309n11
Reefer Madness [a.k.a. *Tell Your Children; The Burning Question*] 159
Reflections in a Golden Eye 332–4, *323*, 341, 342, 343
Reform School Girl 249
Reid, Beryl 344, 345, 346
Reid, Elliott 284
Reid, Wallace 22
Reisner, Christian F., Rev. Dr. 90
Reluctant Dragon, The 169–71, 223, 361
Remember the Night 310
Remick, Lee 283, 284
Reynolds, Debbie 234, 284
Richards, Paul E. *253*, 254
Richardson, Tony 301, 328
Rime of the Ancient Mariner, The *31*
Rimsky–Korsakov, Nikolay 176
Rio Rita (1929) 45
Ritter, Thelma 43
Roach, Hal 163–6, 180
Robards, Jason (Jr.) 291
Robbins, Jerome 232
Robe, The 269
Robertson, Cliff 323–4, 343n4
Robinson, Edward G. 61, 72, 119n14
Robson, May 72, 154
Rock Hudson's Home Movies *286*
Rocky and Bullwinkle [a.k.a. The Adventures of Rocky and Bullwinkle] [TV series] 143
Rodgers, Richard 102n3, 176, 177
Rogers, Al 31
Rogers, Charles "Buddy" 36
Rogers, Ginger *frontispiece*, 173
Roland, Gilbert 79, 99
Roman Spring of Mrs. Stone, The 294–5
Roman, Ruth 228

Romance on the High Seas 178–81, 223, 276
Rooney, Mickey 177
Roosevelt, Eleanor 136, 175, 285n4
Roosevelt, Franklin D. 95, 127, 128, 142, 175
Rope 208–12, *211*, 214, 223, 225, 227, 228, 242, 259, 260, 273
Rope [play; a.k.a. *Rope's End*] 208, 209
Ropes, Bradford 107–8, 109
Rose, Helen 255
Rose, Reginald 254
Rose, The 354
Rosing, Bodil 73
Roth, Lillian 106
Rudnick, Paul 285n4
Ruggles, Charles 73
Ruggles of Red Gap (1925) 25
Runyon, Damon 222
Russell, Gail *191*
Russell, Jane 198, 229, 232, 233–4
Russell, Rosalind 33, 161, 204
Russo, Vito 4–6, 11, 25, 117, 162n8
Rydell, Mark 254–5, 341n2

Safe in Hell *34n7, 155*
Sagan, Leontine 92, 119
Sailor's Luck *43, 105*
Salome (1922) 23–4
Salome (1953) 269
St. Denis, Ruth 44
Samson and Delilah 214, 260
Sanctuary 96
Sanders, George 186, 194 *195*, 225
Sandpiper, The 284
Saroni, Gilbert 19
Sartre, Jean–Paul 310
Saturday Review, The 306, 313
Scarface *(1932) 58, 83, 127*
Schaefer, Natalie 158
Schary, Dore 241–2, 258
Scheur, Philip K. 263, 293
Schickel, Richard 346
Schilling, Gus 171
Schlesinger, John 348
Schlesinger, Dr. Laura 18
Schoenfield, Bernard 217
Schrembs, Joseph, Bishop 93
Schumann, Robert 177
Scofield, Paul 349, 352
Scott, Allan 230n9

Scott, Randolph 115
Screaming Mimi 257
Scruples 203
Seagal, Steven 176
Searchers, The 82
Seberg, Jean 323
Seconds 286
Secret Life of Walter Mitty, The 178
"Secret Love" 233
Secret Witness, The *1–2, 70*
Seinfeld, Jerry 19
Selznick, David O. 161, 168, 186
Send Me No Flowers 284–5
Sennett, Mack 20, 114
Serenade 239–40, 341
Sergeant, The 342–4, 345, 346
Serving in Silence 364
Seuss, Dr. [a.k.a. Theodor S. Geisel] 230–1
Seven Chances *20n2*
Seven Days Leave (1942) 171
Seven Sinners (1940) 162
7 Women 321–2
Seven Year Itch, The 234n12
Seventh Commandment, The 74
Seventh Victim, The 188–90, *187*, 214, 318
Sex and the Single Girl 279n2
Shapiro, Stanley 286
Sharaff, Irene 168
Shawn, Dick 287, 336n12
Shawn, Ted 44
She Couldn't Say No (1930) 43
She Done Him Wrong 58, 74, 94, 95–6, 131, 135, 136, 140, 142
She Had to Eat 163
Shearer, Norma 46
Sheehan, Winfield 98n2
Shepard, Matthew 40, 285n4
Sheik, The 27
Short, Howard 272
Short, William H., Rev. 129, 130, 131
Show of Shows, The *26*
Showgirls 159, 223
Shurlock, Geoffrey M. 198, 237, 242, 248, 253, 258, 260, 261, 266, 268, 272–3, 296, 297, 298–9, 301, 303, 304, 310, 319, 328
Siegel, Don 254
Sign of the Cross, The [film] 6, 81–94, *86*, 95, 96, 97, 98, 102n3, 118, 125, 127, 131, 134, 136, 140–1, 142, 159, 212, 240, 269, 300

Sign of the Cross, The [play] 82, 85
Sills, Milton 46
Silverman, Sime 21
Simmons, Jean 272, 273
Simms, Ginny 175
Sinatra, Frank 312, 313n13, 331–2, 334
Since You Went Away 228
SinDerella and the Golden Bra 329n8
Singin' in the Rain 46, 67, 234–5
Sitting Pretty (1948) 202, 204
Skidoo 313
Skinner, Cornelia Otis 190, *191*
Skinner, Richard Dana 92
Slezak, Walter 289
Slippery Silks 148
Smith, C. Aubrey *121*
Smith, Jack 12
Smith, Thorne 163, 166
Snake Pit, The 184, 262
Snow White and the Seven Dwarfs 169
So This is Africa 97–8, *121*, 134, 139
So Young, So Bad 220–2, *221*, 330, 361
Soda Squirt, The 110, *111*
Sodom and Gomorrah [a.k.a. *The Last Days of Sodom and Gomorrah*]
    300–1, 303, 314, 344
Soilers, The *24*
Some Like It Hot 265–8, *267*, 274, *275*, 280
Some of My Best Friends Are… 362
Something's Got to Give 283
Son of a Sailor 112
Son–Daughter, The *49*
Sondheim, Stephen 356
Sono–Art Productions [a.k.a. Sono–Art–World Wide] 50, 51, *52*
Sorel, Jean 310
Sorry, Wrong Number 310
Sound and the Fury, The 297
Sound of Music, The 318
Sousa, John Philip 204
Southern, Terry 328
Spartacus 272–4, 296, 314
Spellbound 184
Spellman, Francis Cardinal 133
Spider Woman Strikes Back, The 199n12
Spiegel, Sam 252–3, 261, 263, 265, 272
Spivy, Madame *311*, 312
Sport Parade, The 76–8, *77*, 113

Springtime for Henry 143
Stage Door 179
Stage Door Canteen 115
Stage Mother 107–8, 109, 117, 172
Staircase *[film]* 53, *315*, 347, *348–53*, 351, *355, 357, 358n10, 361*
Staircase *[play] 349*
Stanley, Kim 257
Stanwyck, Barbara 7, 96, 106, 308–**10**, 309
Star is Born, A (1937) 50, 163
Star is Born, A (1954) 235
Star Wars 135
Starrett, Charles 65n5
Stars and Stripes Forever 204
Star–Spangled Rhythm 171–2, 175
State Fair (1933) 95
Steiger, Rod 328, 342–3, 347
Stein, Gertrude 108n9, 316n15
"Stella by Starlight" 190
Stella Dallas (1937) 310
Sterling, Jan 217n1
Stern, Stewart 237n15
Sternberg, Josef von 62, 63n3, 64
Sterne, Morgan 311
Stevenson, Adlai 298
Stewart, James 175, 210
Stockwell, Dean *259*, 260
Stompanato, Johnny 249n2
Stone, George E. 61, 107
Stone, Lewis 61, 62, 139n7
Stone, Sharon 365
Stonewall riots 12, 293, 294, 315, 317, 336, 341, 347, 356, 361, 364
Storey, Edith 21
Story of Temple Drake, The 58, 96, 113
Stradling, Harry 196
Strange Bedfellows 285
Strange One, The 252–4, *253*, 258, 261, 274, 283
Strangers on a Train 211, 227–9, 330
Stratton, Chet 278
Stray Lamb, The 163
Streetcar Named Desire, A [film] 198, 226–7, 229, 242, 244
Streetcar Named Desire, A [play] 226–7, 258
Strick, Joseph 318
Stritch, Elaine 329
Stroheim, Erich von 193

Struss, Karl 88
Stuart, Gloria 65
Studio Relations Committee. *See* Hays
 Office
Sturges, Preston 115, 157, 163, 166
Suddenly, Last Summer [film] 11,
 260–5, *264*, 268, 274, 280, 295, 302,
 314, 357
Suddenly, Last Summer [play] 260–1
Sul–te–wan, Madame 106
Sunday, Billy 131
Sunset Boulevard 214
Susan Lennox: Her Fall and Rise 155
Susann, Jacqueline 334, 335
Suspicion 186n3
Sutton, Grady 73, 147, 171, 176, **179**–81,
 180, 204, 276, 362
Swanson, Gloria 46
Sweedie [film series] 19
Sweet and Low *51n10*
Swing High, Swing Low 155
Switch *20*
Swoon 260n6, 364
Sylvia Scarlett 149–*50*, *262*
Symphony of Six Million, The 138
Syncopation (1929) 41–2, 43, 66, 67, 250

Talbot, Nita 288
Talent Scout 153–4
Talmadge, Norma 33, 46
Tampico 112
Tarzan, the Ape Man (1932) 44n5
Taste of Honey, A 301, 304n7
Tate, Sharon 335
Taxi zum Klo 363
Taylor, Elizabeth 230, 258–9, 261, 262,
 264, 284, 286, 329, 333, 334, 349, 350
Taylor, Joan 248
Taylor, Robert 157, 310
Taylor, William Desmond 22
"Tchaikovsky" 174
Tea and Sympathy [film] 11, 240–5, *243*,
 247, 248, 254, 255, 261, 268, 274, 280,
 287, 291, 302
Tea and Sympathy [play] 240–1, 242,
 244, 258
Tea for Two 176, 214, 216, 276
Technicolor 29, 38, 44, 67–8, 90, 114,
 173, 174, 193, 210, 230, 234, 343
Temple, Shirley 10, 115, 145, 161

Ten Commandments, The (1923) 23
Ten Commandments, The (1956) 244,
 269
Tenderfoot, The 74, 75, 154,
Terry, Ethelind 46
Thalberg, Irving G. 119–20, 121, 139–40,
 193
That Certain Summer 302
That Royle Girl 67
That Touch of Mink 279–83, 286, 287,
 292, 295, 303, 315
Thayer, Tiffany 78
Their First Mistake 111–2
Therese and Isabelle **341**
These Three 151–3, *152*, 298
Thesiger, Ernest 65, 150, 295
Thin Man, The 133n6
This Day and Age 138
This Is the Army 175
This Side of Heaven 68, 141
Thompson, Julian 102
Thompson, Kay 168
Thorpe, Richard 53
Three Coins in the Fountain 202
Three Nuts in Search of a Bolt 329
Three Stooges, The 109, 148, 178n8
Thring, Frank 272
Thurber, James 178
Tierney, Gene *203*, 224
Time 244, 263, 270, 277, 291
Times, The [London] 85
Titanic (1952) 204
To Mary—With Love 126
Tobin, Dan 204–5, 255
Todd, Thelma 79
Toler, Sidney 73
Tom Brown of Culver 75–6
Tomorrow's Youth 141
Tone, Franchot 171, 312
Tony Rome 331
Too Many Husbands 161–2
Tootsie 265
Topper 163, 166n10
Torch Song Trilogy *11*, *363*
Torres, Raquel 112
Touch of Evil 257
Tracy, Spencer 206, 255
Transcontinental Films 299, 300
Trash 341
Travilla, William 335

Treen, Mary 154
Trevor, Claire
Tristan und Isolde 190n7
Truex, Ernest 102, *103*
Trumbo, Dalton 272
Tugboat Annie 95
Tunberg, Karl 271n12
Tunnel of Love 276
Turnabout *[book]* 163, *164*
Turnabout [film] 20, 163–6, *164*, 167,
    240, 242, 284
Turner, Lana 249n2
Tushingham, Rita 301
Twentieth Century–Fox (*formerly* Fox
    Film Corporation) 145, 175, 202, 203,
    259–60, 334, 348, 349, 350, 352
Two Black Crows (a.k.a. Moran and Mack)
    43n4
Two–Faced Woman 198
Tyler, Beverly 250

UCLA Film and Television Archive 83
Uninvited, The 6, 190–2, *191*, 197, 198,
    207, 208, 212, 214, 222, 249, 318
United Artists 220, 298, 299, 312
Universal Pictures (a.k.a.
    Universal–International) 65, 75, 150,
    166, 198, 199, 272, 273, 277, 280, 283,
    285, 287, 295, 330–1
Unknown Purple, The *25*
Up in Arms 178, 328
Ustinov, Peter 273

Vail, Myrtle 109
Vajda, Ernest 120
Valenti, Jack 329, 330, 340
Valentino, Rudolph 23, 27, 46, 48, 49, 266
Valley of the Dolls 334–5
Vallone, Raf 310
Van Cleef, Lee 237, *238*
Van Doren, Mamie 329
Van Upp, Virginia 206
Vanity Fair [magazine] 95, 96
Varden, Norma 288
Variety *[newspaper]* 10, 21, 24, 42,
    69–70, 80, 91, 98, 99, 100–1, 102,
    105, 114, 122, 170, 196, 197, 203,
    210, 240, 244, 250, 254, 263, 293,
    311, 318, 326, 339, 347, 354
Veidt, Conrad 187, 188

Velez, Lupe 36
Velvet Touch, The 204–5
Verdon, Gwen 234
Very Special Favor, A 285–91, *290, 292,*
    302n5, 328
Victim *12, 282, 301–2, 303, 304, 312,*
    315
Victor/Victoria 315, 363
Victory (1940) 192n9
Vidal, Gore 261, 262, 264, 269–71, 297–8,
    323, 324
Vidor, Charles 206
Vidor, King 22, 53n11
Viertel, Salka 119, 120
View From the Bridge, A 299–300, 303,
    310
Viva Maria! 340n1
Vizzard, Jack 138
Voight, Jon 343n3, 348
Voodoo Island *6, 250–2, 251, 264, 283,*
    321
Voutsinas, Andreas 336

Walk on the Wild Side *7, 280, 293,*
    296–7, 303, 308–10, 309, 314, 319,
    323, 330, 331
Walker, Johnny *30*
Walker, Robert 227–9
Wallach, Eli 349
Wallis, Hal B. 177, 187
Walsh, Moira 305, 313
Walsh, Raoul 105
Walters, Charles 168
Walters, Luana 159, 249n2
Walton, Douglas 194
Wanderer of the West *31, 51*
Wanger, Walter 120
Ward, Mackenzie 42
Warhol, Andy 309n11, 341
Warner Bros. Pictures, Inc. 26, 36, 44, 60,
    61, 66, 96, 118, 123, 145, 153, 154,
    175, 176–7, 178, 184n1, 208, 216, 217,
    220, 222, 226, 227, 230n9, 236,
    237n15, 239, 241, 327, 329
Warner, Jack L. 145, 187, 210, 227, 233
Warner, Sam 51
Warrior's Husband, The [film] 5, 102–4,
    103, 118, 122
Warrior's Husband, The *[play] 102, 141*
Water, Water, Every Hare *215*

Watermelon Man 325

Watson, Bobby 42, 66–8, **67**, *68*, 72, 73, 74, 77, 96, 103, 107, 108, 141, 147, 153, 174, 199, 205, 255, 312, 350, 365

Watts, Richard, Jr. 142

Waugh, Evelyn 328

Way Out West (1930) 47–8

Wayne, David 205–6

Wayne, John 115, 263

Webb, Clifton 7, 201–4, **202**, *203*, 205, 206, 211n17, 212, 214, 225, 250, 255, 273, 362

Webb, Mabelle 202, 211n17

Weber, Lois 22

Weill, Kurt 173, 295

Weinstein, Harvey 299n2

Weissmuller, Johnny 44, 115

Well of Loneliness, The 1–2, 3, 8, 16, 33, 92, 147, 158,

Welles, Orson 257, 260

Wellman, William A. 35

Wessel, Dick 233

West Side Story 318, 332n9

West, Billy 18

West, Claudine 120

West, Mae 72, 73, 74, 94, 96, 105, 122, 125, 131, 135–6, 139, 142, 169, 340n1, 344

Whale, James 64–5, 140, 150, 155, 170, 364

What Ever Happened to Baby Jane? 300n3, 345

What's Cookin', Doc? 215

What's Opera, Doc? 215

Wheeler Dealers, The 283–4, 287, 318

Wheeler, Bert, and Woolsey, Robert 45, 97, 98, 107, 139

When Ladies Meet (1933) 74

"Where are You?" 296

Whistlin' Dan 90

White Heat 216, 218

White, George 148

White, Peter 360

Whitmore, James 254, *325*, 326

Who Killed Teddy Bear? 328–9

Who's Afraid of Virginia Woolf? 329, 330, 341

Who's Been Sleeping in My Bed? 283

Whoopee! *45*

Why Bring that Up 43

Wild Party, The *(1929) 49–50, 78*

Wild People 90

Wilde, Cornel 237

Wilde, Oscar 8, 10, 16, 23, 24, 85, 159, 192–4, 259

Wilder, Billy 157, 265, 266

Wildmon, Donald, Rev. 129n2

Will and Grace *13, 358, 364*

William, Warren 105

Williams, Kathlyn 119

Williams, Robert 73

Williams, Rose 261

Williams, Tennessee 226–7, 238, 240, 258–9, 260–1, 262, 263, 294–5, 322–3, 343, 356

Willingham, Calder 252

Wills, Brember 65

Willson, Henry 168

Wilson, Elizabeth 257

Wilson, John V. 62

Wilson, Julie 254

Windom, William 331, *332*

Wine, Women, and Song 74, 107

Wingate, James, Dr. 91, 97, 101, 113, 114

Wings 34–6, 49

Winner Take All 74

Winter Meeting 205, 273

Winters, Shelley 318, *319*, 322n5

Wise, Robert 318

Wives Under Suspicion 140, 155

Wizard of Oz, The (1939) 53n11, 67, 161, 193, 261

Woman I Stole, The 112–3, 122

Woman of the Year 255

Woman of Affairs, A 27n5

Woman of the Year 255

Woman's Face, A 188

Women, The 101, 160, 215, 222, 358

Women Without Men 217

Women's Prison 248

Wonder Bar 123–4, 138, 147

Wood, Edward D., Jr. [Ed; a.k.a. Daniel Davis] 53n11, 235–6, 336

Wood, Natalie 237, 283, 326

Woolley, Monty 177n7

Words and Music (1948) 177

Wray, Fay 112

Wyler, William 152, 153, 226, 268–9, 271n12, 296, 298, 303, 305, 306

Yankee Doodle in Berlin *20*
Yates, Herbert J. 145
Yellow Book, The 194
Yolanda and the Thief 24, 176n6, 234
York, Susannah 344, 346
Young as You Feel 74
Young, Gig 279–80, *281*, 282
Young Man with a Horn 222, 226

Young, Elizabeth 120
Young, Loretta 105, 224, 302

Zanuck, Darryl F. 104, 118, 145, 202, 222, 299n2
Zenith International 310
Zeta–Jones, Catherine 320n3
Zolotow, Maurice 157